David E. Lilienthal

David E. Lilienthal

Full Text of the Official Report

ATOMIC ENERGY
FOR MILITARY PURPOSES

By HENRY D. SMYTH

A General Account of the
Scientific Research and Technical
Development That Went into the
Making of Atomic Bombs

The Journey of an American Liberal

Steven M. Neuse

The University of Tennessee Press • Knoxville

The paper in this book meets the minimum requirements of the
American National Standard for Permanence of Paper for Printed
Library Materials. The binding materials have been chosen
for strength and durability.

♻   Printed on recycled paper.

Library of Congress Cataloging-in-Publication Data

Neuse, Steven M., 1941–
    David E. Lilenthal: the journey of an American liberal /
    Steven M. Neuse.—1st ed.
    p.   cm.
    Contents: The formative years—Depauw College, Harvard Law School, and Helen—A young
professional makes his mark—The Wisconsin Public Service Commission: crucible for a reformer—
TVA: the tumultuous years—TVA: vindication and consolidation—Crafting vision—TVA: wartime
administration and expansion—The atomic trust: bright fires, bright hopes—The atomic trust: reality—Mid-century passage: transformation and transition—Lilenthal and the world—Life at a "high
trot": unfinished business—Assessment.
    ISBN 0-87049-940-8 (cloth : alk. paper)
    1. Lilenthal, David Eli, 1899–1981. 2. Statesmen—United States—Biography.
    3. Tennessee Valley Authority—History. 4. Energy policy—United States—
History—20th century. 5. U.S. Atomic Energy Commission—History.
    6. Nuclear energy—Government policy—United States—History.
    7. Development and Resources Corporation—History.
    8. Economic development projects—History—20th century.   I. Title.
E748.L7N48 1996
973.9'092—dc20
[B]   95-50237
                                                                       CIP

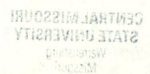

To my life companion and best friend, Jeanine Nowotny Neuse

Contents

Illustrations

Lilienthal and the Shah of Iran Tasting Sugar Cane in Khuzistan,
Late 1950s
Map of Khuzistan Project from Development and Resources
Corporation, 1959
Robert McNamara, President Johnson, Walter Rostow,
John McNaughton, and Lilienthal on Air Force One, March 1967

Following page 198:
Lilienthal Press Conference after First Trip to Vietnam, February 1967
Note from President Johnson to Lilienthal at Cabinet Meeting, December
1967
Lilienthal Reporting about Vietnam Trip to Johnson Cabinet, December
1967
Lilienthal in Conference with President Johnson before Trip to Vietnam,
April 1968
Gerald Levin, D&R Manager and Executive, 1968–71, CEO of Time
Warner-Turner, 1995
Andrea Pampanini, D&R Executive Vice-President, 1971–77
John Macy, D&R President, 1975–79
The Shah of Iran and His Generals, 1960s or 1970s
The Shah aboard USS Kitty Hawk, 1974
David and Helen Lilienthal, 1978
Lilienthal at Topside, July 4, 1975
Judge Robert Taylor, General Counsel Herb Sanger, Retired General
Counsel Robert Marquis, and Lilienthal at TVA Reunion, May 1979
Lilienthal Gravesite, Martha's Vineyard
Production of Radioactive Isotopes at Oak Ridge National Laboratories,
about 1946

Preface

Then a new king rose over Egypt, who had no knowledge of
Joseph

—Exodus 1:8

There is always a first step in any long-range project such as this study. I
unknowingly took mine in Mexico City in 1981 while doing research on
the influence of the Tennessee Valley Authority (TVA) on regional development in Latin America. During an interview, one of Mexico's most influential elder statesmen and longtime director of the Ministry of Water Resources, Adolfo Orive de Alba, stated rather proudly that he knew David
Lilienthal and that "he impressed me very, very much. He is a very great,
great man." At the time, the remark made little impression. I was involved
in the TVA research and in the process of moving from the University of
Tennessee to the University of Arkansas. In any case, David Lilienthal was
only a faint image from a past that had retreated into distant memory.

Orive de Alba's praise must have registered, however. Over the next few
years I kept asking myself, "What was it about Lilienthal that inspired such
a statement from a powerful confidant of presidents in his own land?" In
early 1984, S. David Freeman, then chair of the TVA Board, congratulated
me on a retrospective piece I had done on the occasion of the fiftieth anniversary of TVA, calling it the best thing on TVA since Lilienthal's *Democracy on the March*. (I took *that* compliment with a large block of salt since
I knew Freeman was a consummate politician and because I knew that
Democracy on the March was one of America's finest examples of political
rhetoric.)

Nevertheless, Freeman's gracious gesture was hook number two. I
quickly read the book with which he had compared my writing. I was fascinated by Lilienthal's infectious enthusiasm and his rhetorical sleight of
hand, which equated bureaucratic decision making with "grass roots"
democratic participation. By mid-1985 I had digested all seven volumes of
his published journals and later that year presented a paper on Lilienthal at
the Southern Political Science Association in Nashville. During discussion,
Erwin Hargrove, a distinguished political scientist at Vanderbilt and a

Lilienthal scholar in his own right, said that my paper was one of the most thoughtful studies on Lilienthal he had seen. Hook number three!

And I was in the race. For the next four years, mainly summers, I crossed the land in quest of this "Joseph" who seemed to have been forgotten by the legions of modern historians. I was encouraged in my quest and critiqued by friends in Tennessee including Hargrove, David Welborn at the University of Tennessee, Danny Schaffer (formerly of TVA), and others. Roy Talbert Jr., Arthur E. Morgan's biographer and historian at Coastal Carolina College, was also an encouraging critic. Meredith Morris-Babb, acquisitions editor at the University of Tennessee Press, was patient and encouraging through two years of polishing the manuscript. I also thank Meredith for choosing a "murderers' row" of reviewers who made my work much better. Since I know two of them and guessed a third, I can thank these people publicly—much gratitude to Bruce Wheeler of the University of Tennessee, Roy Talbert Jr., and Erwin Hargrove. I also gratefully acknowledge the efforts of Stan Ivester, managing editor at the University of Tennessee Press, and Alexa Selph, freelance copyeditor.

My research would not have been possible without generous support from the Franklin D. Roosevelt Foundation, the Harry S. Truman Presidential Library, the Herbert Hoover Presidential Library, the American Philosophical Society, the American Council of Learned Societies, and the National Endowment for the Humanities. I am also indebted to the Fulbright College of Arts and Sciences at the University of Arkansas for two research grants and two semesters of leave to finish the work.

My colleagues at the University of Arkansas never failed to encourage, and my two chairs, Don Kelley and Bob Savage, always covered for me when I traveled. I especially appreciate a bit of sage advice from colleague Diane Blair, who responded to one of my "I don't think I can write this thing" laments: she bluntly told me that writing a book was a lot like being pregnant, and I was too far gone to have much of a choice anymore—thanks Diane! Thanks too to my former secretary Sarah Nothdurft, who typed and edited countless drafts; to Linda Gardner, our present secretary for additional help; and to graduate assistants, especially Patrick McKeehan, Clay Price, Lance Heater, Curtis Barnett, Brian Swain, Ronda King, and Missy Lockaby, who were of invaluable assistance in library research.

I must also acknowledge my sources. The archives and libraries I visited were marvelously cooperative. Nancy Bressler and Jean Holliday, curators of Lilienthal's papers at the Princeton's Seeley G. Mudd Library, gave me a home away from home for three summers. And Princeton's Special Conferences staff, Cindy Horr and Eric Hamblin, were gracious in finding me living quarters. Archivists at the four presidential libraries I visited went out of their way to locate every last scrap of paper relating to Lilienthal. The same was true at the Iowa Historical Society in Iowa City, the TVA Technical Library at Knoxville, and the University of Memphis Archives. Marty Jilensky, librarian at the Wisconsin Public Service Commission, helped me at long distance to piece together information from 1930 to 1933, the period of Lilienthal's life for which I had the least information. Even the secretive forces at the Department of Energy History Division in Germantown, Maryland, and the large impersonal systems at the National Archives and Library of Congress Manuscript Collection provided excellent services. I especially appreciate the efforts of Patricia Bernard Ezzell at TVA and Marie Hallion at the Department of Energy History Division for providing many public-domain photographs. And a final thanks to all the people at Mullins Library on my campus—especially in the Interlibrary Loan, Reference, and Audio-Visual Departments—who were helpful beyond the call of duty.

Mrs. Helen L. Lilienthal was a gracious host at her home in Hightstown, New Jersey, and the summer homestead on Martha's Vineyard. I cherish the hours of conversation about her beloved "Dave" and their life together. My wife, Jeanine, and I will always remember the days we spent with her in the summer of 1988. I am also grateful to David Lilienthal Jr., who as executor of his father's estate gave me carte blanche access to his father's papers, and to Lilienthal's daughter Nancy for her help. And to the others I interviewed, I offer much appreciation for sharing what they knew about Lilienthal and for their own experience as men and women who lived and labored through the exciting days of both the New Deal and the Fair Deal and through the exhilarating times after 1955 when Lilienthal tried to forge new paths to international development. I owe special thanks to Rodman C. Rockefeller and Andrea Pampanini, who worked with Lilienthal and his Development and Resources Corporation; access to their corporate and personal papers provided an invaluable perspective on Lilienthal's later years.

I thank my family most of all. Jonathan and Micah tolerated an absentee father several summers—but most of all they contributed by being low-maintenance young men, excelling in their college studies and becoming adult friends to their parents. Jeanine cheerfully endured summer widowhood and put up with endless hours of emotional swings as I wrestled (much like Jacob) with my own version of destiny, struggling with the story of David E. Lilienthal.

In sum, I owe a great deal to many people and institutions. This should not obscure my ultimate responsibility: any error in fact or interpretation is mine alone.

Introduction

The Journals of David E. Lilienthal tell their own story—a story that deals with important events of the recent past. It is a personal and often an emotional narrative rather than history; it is the stuff of which history is written.

—Henry Steele Commager,
in Introduction to volume 1 of
The Journals of David E. Lilienthal

This is the story of a distinguished American, David E. Lilienthal. In the fourth and fifth decades of the twentieth century he spent nineteen uninterrupted years in the upper echelons of public administration, as public service commissioner for the state of Wisconsin, as one of three founding directors of the Tennessee Valley Authority (TVA), and as first chairman of the Atomic Energy Commission (AEC). In 1950 Lilienthal resigned the latter post and embarked on a thirty-year career in the private sector. He worked first with André Meyer at the renowned Lazard Frères investment firm in New York City and served briefly, but with great financial success, as chief executive officer of the struggling Minerals and Separations Corporation. In 1955, Lilienthal and Gordon Clapp, his successor at TVA, created Development and Resources (D&R) Corporation, a firm dedicated to economic and social development in the far corners of the globe until its tragic fall in 1979.

In both his public and private careers, between his 1923 graduation from Harvard Law School and his death on January 14, 1981, Lilienthal was an inveterate communicator. His seven published volumes of journals provide thoughtful witness to the trials and travails of his times. Next to Helen, Lilienthal's journal was his most constant companion. Until he became serious about publishing this record, it was, much like Helen, a wellspring of strength and a sanctuary. His first entry was recorded the same spring he met Helen; his last, a jubilant notation celebrating successful cataract surgery a few days before his death in January 1981. The published journal was enormous, spanning seven volumes and more than four thousand pages.

His motivation for keeping a journal was complex, and no doubt changed over time. His first entry in May 1917 told that "a young lawyer . . . noticed how seriously I was looking at life . . . and suggested as a remedy for this and a source of amusement and self-cultivation the keeping of a diary." His passion for recording all manner of concerns was strongly reflected in his letters. In one, he told Helen about his first meeting with Professor Felix Frankfurter "partly because you are interested, and partly because I want to get my reactions down while they are warm." In "A Diarist's Note" to the first journal volume in 1964, he revealed that he had persisted because of a love of writing, to gain perspective, for emotional release, and to help think through the ideas and issues he faced. A year earlier in a 1963 entry, he confided that his journal writing was an important part of closing the circle—"the experiences through which I have gone *would not be complete* until I have somehow recorded my feeling about those experiences."[1]

When evaluating any autobiographical writing, it is important to ask about intent. The task is especially crucial since Lilienthal's journals purport to be an objective chronicle and scores of scholars have relied on his accounts with nary a critical eye. Much of the credibility hinges on whether or not Lilienthal intended to make the work public. The record seems clear that he thought little until the late 1950s of doing anything with his secrets. In 1954, in response to the revelations of Harold Ickes's petty personality in Ickes's just-published diaries, Lilienthal thought that such writings could be "too darned revealing actually, if later they are exposed to public view." Nevertheless, in the introduction to the first volume he wrote that "I must, from time to time, have had the notion that some day such a record would be useful to me or to others." But that notion rarely surfaced until he was nearly sixty. In 1943, William I. Nichols, editor of *This Week* magazine, told Lilienthal there was "something worth publishing there." At the time, however, Lilienthal was consumed with finishing up *TVA: Democracy on the March* and there was no record of a response.[2]

Indeed, the person responsible for spurring Lilienthal's interest was his son-in-law Sylvain Bromberger. In the spring of 1957, Bromberger, a Princeton University instructor, arranged a meeting with historians Robert Lively and William Ward, and university librarian William Dix regarding the use of the journals and Lilienthal's papers. Nothing much happened until two years later when Bromberger prompted his father-in-law to think about publishing the journals. Soon after, Lilienthal wrote Cass Canfield at Harper & Row and proposed a "memoir or autobiography" in which the journal entries would be accompanied by a thematic narrative. After considerable discussion with son David, a writer himself, and Harper, Lilienthal decided to publish the journals much as they were, with minimal connecting material. The first two volumes, primarily covering TVA and Atomic Energy Commission years, were published in 1964 to generally positive reviews in publications as diverse as the *New York Times, The Economist, Time,* and the *Journal of Politics*.[3]

Soon after Bromberger sparked Lilienthal's interest in making the journals public, however, the relationship between the author and his writings changed dramatically. For the first forty years the private musings provided a soothing and therapeutic respite, a place the author could reflect, pontificate, or indulge himself without fear of discovery. In later years, the journal was often a cruel and demanding mistress. His 1939–58 typescript entries filled, on the average, less than one and a third loose-leaf binders a year. Between 1959 and 1977, his entries filled nearly *five* binders a year. As early as 1958 he fretted about the impending breach of privacy, noting that "unless I want a stranger reading through these sometimes introspective personal passages (which I certainly don't), somehow these journals have to be read and divided up." Shortly before the first volumes were published, he worried that "the sense of privacy, of 'writing as I please' . . . is now pretty well shot."[4]

In a thoughtful memorandum in 1961 to his father, David Jr. raised another concern when he emphasized that "DEL does not seek experiences in order to be able to make Journal entries (*although this is probably not an inconsiderable factor*) [emphasis mine], but for the sake of the experiences themselves." The danger exists, when one knows private writings will become public, of tailoring those writings to future audiences or, worse, letting the writings control the life of the journalist. Lilienthal was concerned about the problem and he never resolved it satisfactorily. In 1962 he asked if the knowledge that his entries would be printed "pretty much as written . . . [affects] the way in which the journals continue to be written?" In 1966 Lilienthal wrote about a conversation with former Roosevelt advisor Lauchlin Currie, who said, "Sometimes . . . a journal takes over a man, becomes his reason for doing things so he can write about them. Has that happened to you?" Hal Frederiksen, a former Development & Resources vice-president whose relationship with Lilienthal ended acrimoniously in the mid-1970s, thought the journal sometimes took charge of his boss. On trips to Brazil in the early 1970s, Frederiksen recalled that at times Lilienthal declined to participate in events that he anticipated would not turn out well for fear he would have to admit failure in the journal. Other times, Frederiksen charged that Lilienthal recorded conclusions about this or that event or person and then became angry when others demonstrated problems or flaws in the conclusions, which were by then set in stone in journal entries.[5]

In spite of the warning of one journal reviewer that "instinctively one distrusts a dialogue with the self which is designed to be overheard," the journals must be taken seriously. The first four volumes, covering his life through July 1959, are probably as devoid of calculation as any public diary, and certainly more so than most autobiographies. With few exceptions and editing for clarity, grammar, and spelling, the original entries are published word for word. However, the status of the last three volumes is more problematic, considering that Lilienthal knew those entries would probably see the light of day. Nevertheless, the journal was a constant companion most of his adult life. Sometimes faithful, sometimes treacherous; often a refuge, often bothersome; it was always present, and always an intimate partner. The story of David Lilienthal, the facts and the deeper reality, cannot be told without it.[6]

His most famous book, *TVA: Democracy on the March,* is arguably the finest example of political rhetoric in the century. Add to that a legacy of five other books, scores of articles in scholarly and popular forums, and countless public speeches, and one sees the evolution of a deep and abiding concern regarding the capacity of democratic institutions to control large government bureaucracies and of the ability of popular will to maintain control over the mandates of technology and science. At TVA, he popularized the concept of "grass roots" democracy, and as a staunch internationalist he was vitally concerned with nuclear proliferation, disarmament, and the role of the multinational corporation (a term he coined).

Lilienthal was an immensely public person in another sense. While he loved and cherished his private life with his wife Helen, family, and friends—especially at the beloved "Topside" cottage on Martha's Vineyard—his enormous sense of self-importance led him to save and ultimately make public all his private papers, except for a few that might threaten the safety of people he had worked with in Iran. His effusive and gloriously romantic letters to Helen before marriage were carefully preserved—at his request. His unpublished journal reveals all—the paradox of an unquenchable ego and an agonizing sense of self-doubt, the constant fear of fiscal insufficiency, a tortured soul racked by psychic and physical pain and insomnia in his later years, and a devastating family split over Vietnam. At first a chronicle of events and sometimes therapeutic device, the journal took on a life of its own in the last twenty-five years, and no subject was spared in the frenetic writing, which consumed more than twice the volume of the published journals. In releasing his papers at Princeton, he allowed public access to his most private thoughts, the most revealing insights of a remarkable life lived, as Harcourt A. Morgan, his mentor at TVA, used to say, at a "high trot."

In his public career, Lilienthal was brilliant with his sense of political timing and in the use of a rhetoric that often masked reality. He was no less the master of the ability to marshal support for himself, for the causes he championed, and his agencies. In a word, he was a consummate bureaucratic politician. Possessed of virtually boundless (some would say compulsive) energies, he stretched the horizons of public purpose. With the Public Service Commission in Wisconsin, he brought a sense of urgency and innovative thinking to public utility regulation, emphasizing the need for executive leadership and a meritocratic elite to meet the challenge of the power trust. In the Tennessee Valley, he took advantage of an unknown quantity, the TVA, to consummate his journey from progressivism to the positivism of state capitalism. He knew little more than anyone else what President Roosevelt had intended for TVA, but he was first among equals with the other two founding directors, H. A. Morgan and Arthur E. Morgan (no relation), in forging one of the most successful programs of the New Deal.

While never really comfortable at the AEC, Lilienthal nevertheless entered the uncharted realm of the atom and invested prodigious energies. His tumultuous four-year tenure shaped debate on questions relating to government secrecy, civilian versus military control of the atom, and the wisdom of committing vast public resources to the hydrogen bomb project. Moreover, the idealistic 1946 Acheson-Lilienthal report, which recommended the internationalization of the atom, stands as a farsighted recommendation to a world not yet free from atomic terrors. Lilienthal's entire public tenure was marked by political controversy, commitment to open government, and enormous popular support.

His private years were no less dramatic. After five years in big business, he became restless and again yearned for public-seeking opportunities. To this end, with Lazard's financial backing, he organized D&R, a company dedicated to meshing international capital and national will in pursuit of integrated development. He helped inspire the well-known Cauca Valley project in Colombia and many other smaller development initiatives throughout the world. His greatest objective, however, was the transformation of the vast Iranian Khuzistan region into a Persian TVA. He labored toward that end for nearly a quarter-century. In his international endeavors he reveled in relationships with presidents and cabinet officials of the nations he advised and was especially proud of his ties to the Shah of Iran.

By the early 1970s, however, time was beginning to run out. His vision was still lively, but his institutional access and personal energy had waned. His last hurrah with an American president, directing the planning for a postwar Vietnam economic-development project for Lyndon Johnson, was laced with disappointment and bitterness as he became temporarily alienated from his children and grandchildren, Richard Nixon became president, and American forces left Vietnam. Because of the financial vagaries of working in the third world, his corporation always struggled to keep afloat, finally coming under the hegemony of the Rockefeller family, which promised, but failed to provide, badly needed capital. And the events in Iran, the revolution and the fall of the Shah, conspired to negate what influence he had in that, his favorite of distant lands—and his corporation came tumbling down. In his time he ran a glorious race, but as always, time won out.

In so many respects, the story of David Lilienthal has its roots in the Old Testament tale of another David and his encounter with Goliath. But that metaphor goes only so far. Lilienthal was a *real* David at TVA and to a lesser extent with the AEC. He was very much a mover and a fighter in the transformation, sometimes against great odds, of American life from an emphasis on private virtue and initiative to a belief in the primacy of public values and the positive state. But, like his namesake, his own reputation was always shadowed by charges of opportunism and a compulsive ego that never seemed to find personal satisfaction.

Nevertheless, Joseph C. Harsch was correct in his late 1949 assessment:

The resignation of David Lilienthal from the Atomic Energy Commission . . . is in itself only a footnote to history. But it is one of those footnotes which somehow encompasses a whole span of history and reminds us . . . how great has been the change in our way of living and our way of thinking over a period of

time as brief as 20 years. . . . The ideas which Mr. Lilienthal executed have
come to be such an established part of our national existence that most Americans today no longer realize that only a generation ago the idea of government
in business seemed . . . either absurd or vicious.

Lilienthal fought the power interests and won in Wisconsin and the Tennessee Valley. With his fellow board members at TVA he made government
enterprise work. He struggled successfully to keep atomic energy out of the
hands of the military. And all along he wrote and spoke of the grave responsibilities of public man as well as bureaucratic responsiveness and accountability.[7]

After leaving the AEC in early 1950, he was never as successful as he
had been as a public executive in imposing his will in the situations he
faced: as hard as he tried, his stone would never again bring down a giant.
In part he was stymied by the cautious demeanor of institutions such as the
World Bank, the Agency for International Development, and traditional
bureaucracies in countries such as Iran and Brazil, which had their own
reservations about D&R and its small band of corporate visionaries. However, Lilienthal also failed because of his own personal limitations. In spite
of his claim to great management skills, Lilienthal was more entrepreneur
than manager. When Clapp died in 1963, D&R lost its institutional compass. Others who tried to take day-to-day charge of the corporation were
never able to overcome the centrifugal force of Lilienthal's great energy and
mercurial moods.

Unlike his uncanny sensitivity to bureaucratic politics in his own land,
he never really understood the nuances of politics abroad. His development
philosophy often seemed a tired litany of the TVA story: what Lilienthal
failed to realize in Iran, for example, was that Iran was not the Tennessee
Valley, and his patron, the Shah, was not Franklin Roosevelt, and that no
matter how successful his vast Khuzistan project might be, grass roots democracy could never take hold in that country. In many respects, Lilienthal
was a metaphor for America's vision as a world leader. He believed in big
technical solutions and good will. He was an undaunted optimist who tolerated no obvious abuse of human rights in the countries he served. But
when the Shah's house of cards tumbled, Lilienthal was struck with a crushing sense of despair.

The unifying thread in this story is Lilienthal's odyssey as an American
liberal. Without a doubt he epitomized the prevailing winds of that pervasive and uniquely American perspective at each stage of his life: his actions
were always guided by optimism, inventiveness, and pragmatic drive as he
sought to enlarge and empower the public realm at the expense of narrow
private interests. As a young Progressive with Brandeisian reservations
about large impersonal public or private institutions, he strove to use the
law and the skill of lawyers to achieve the public good. In the cauldron of
Wisconsin regulatory politics, Lilienthal quickly learned that the only way

to achieve public ends was through powerful government institutions with substantial resources. At TVA and AEC he became an unabashed proponent of the notion that government should extend itself more than it ever had in pursuing massive intervention on behalf of the citizens of the realm. His practical skills at TVA won out over the ideological visions of his tenacious foe A. E. Morgan and were largely responsible for a powerful institution that under other circumstances might have evolved into a much less formidable agency. The AEC experience was clear witness to his unquenchable optimism. In 1946, he cochaired the committee that boldly called for the internationalization of nuclear technology. Throughout his tenure, he fought against unnecessary secrecy in the belief that the American people had a right to know and participate in atomic decisions. Finally, in 1949, in his fight against development of thermonuclear weapons, he was optimistic that the genies of massive destruction could somehow be slowed, if not stilled, and the world could step back from the abyss.

Lilienthal continued his liberal journey as a private citizen. As an enthusiastic convert to American free enterprise, he became an unapologetic booster of the notion that American know-how and ingenuity could bring the country and ultimately the world to new levels of progress and prosperity. As an internationalist, Lilienthal exhibited all the characteristics of American liberalism abroad. He was well intentioned and decent in his overseas affairs. He and Clapp stood up to a dictator in Colombia and refused to participate in projects where bribes were expected. Lilienthal truly believed that TVA-like programs across the globe would greatly benefit the ordinary people in the countries where he preached and practiced his ideas.

And yet, he was curiously innocent. Although he did not particularly support the Vietnam war, nor did he approve of the despotic tendencies of the Shah's regime (he hardly recognized these tendencies until nearly the end of his quarter-century in Iran), he allowed himself to become caught up in two of the greatest failures of American foreign policy of the century, Vietnam and Iran. Lilienthal was driven by two forces, both inspired by American liberalism: optimism and the almost compelling drive, as Louis Hartz noted, "either to withdraw from 'alien' things or to transform them." All too often, Lilienthal's can-do spirit and his successes at home blinded him to the prospects for success abroad. In the case of Vietnam, for example, he genuinely thought that the implacable differences between North and South could be overcome by the sheer appeal and promise of his postwar development plan. On the other hand, this son of the heartland had long ago rejected isolationism as a national option. He was an internationalist—but he was incredibly naive, believing that American political and economic values and technologies could easily be exported. Lilienthal was little different from most other post–World War II administration or foreign policy experts of either party. James A. Bill's remarkable recitation of American elites who supported the Shah bears witness to this reality.[8]

In sum, Lilienthal was one of the century's most noteworthy public figures. His life and accomplishments mirror those of this country during his time of public eminence. Both reflect the yoking of great optimism and ego in pursuit of national goals that had never before been achieved, or even imagined. And both reflect the uncertain results that occur when such optimism and ego fail to heed the reality of a world with many dark corners and relentless opposing forces.

CHAPTER I

The Formative Years

Everyone must, at some time or another, in one form or another, ask this question: "Why am I as I am?"

—Helen Lilienthal,
unpublished *Family Chronicle*

Those Who Came Before

David Eli Lilienthal was born July 8, 1899, in the quarters at the rear of his parents' first grocery store and haberdashery in Morton, Illinois. He was named for his great-grandfather, who had raised a family of ten not far from Bratislava, in what is now the Slovak Republic. The Lilienthal men and women were impractical dreamers in the Old World, and for the most part impious Jews. One great-uncle was a bookbinder, another a merchant, and his uncle Max was an inventor and an actor. According to Lilienthal's aunt Hermine Lilienthal Szold, they were all "educated fools . . . [but] fascinating. . . . Today you would call them shiftless, or maybe geniuses." His grandfather Adolph was described by Hermine as "the great chess champion of Vienna" and a linguist who knew both Hebrew and Chinese.[1]

Like the Lilienthals, the Rosenaks and Szolds, David's matrilineage, were nurtured in the Bratislava environs, but north of the Danube in the foothills of the Little Carpathian Mountains. They, however, were more practical and attentive to their Jewish roots. Over the centuries they had been victims of anti-Semitic persecution in the area. Several of Lilienthal's great-uncles were rabbis, and according to his uncle Max Rosenak, "All of them . . . functioned as cantors in their community synagogues."

Several years before Lilienthal's mother and father met, the families, Lilienthal, Rosenak, and Szold had begun to merge. Lilienthal's aunt Hermine married Jacob Szold, the nephew of Bertha Szold. Another of Leo's sisters, Bertha, married Minna's older brother Adolph. By the early 1890s, many of the Rosenaks and Szolds had migrated to the United States and had become successful merchants in the Peoria, Illinois, area, and in northern Indiana.[2]

Leo Lilienthal, David's father, was born in 1868 in central Hungary and worked from a young age in stores and at manual labor. He served for several years in the Hungarian army, then moved to Vienna for a short time in 1892 before migrating to Illinois in 1893, where he found employment with the older Jacob Szold, his sister Hermine's uncle by marriage. Minna Rosenak, David's mother, was born in 1874 and lived with her family in Szomolany, Hungary, until she left for America at the age of seventeen. Like most girls of the time, her life was close to the hearth. She helped bake bread at her father's inn and, with other Jewish children, shared a private tutor. In 1891 she moved to Peoria to live with her mother's brother, Jacob Szold. Speaking halting English, she worked as a clerk in stores in Peoria and Chicago until she and Leo married.[3]

Minna and Leo's courtship was traditional and, according to Helen Lilienthal, an arranged affair. The union, solemnized on September 19, 1897, was not easy at first. According to daughter-in-law Helen, her husband, their son, remembered "many stormy scenes between them, . . . the cause of which he never knew." One difference was religion. Like the rest of his family, Leo was not religious. While identifying as a Jew, he neither attended services nor observed religious holidays—and he allowed his eldest sons, David and Ted, to take only the most superficial religious training. While he relented somewhat with youngest son Allen, Leo was always steadfast in his convictions. As he lay dying in 1951, Minna had to remind her son when he asked if a rabbi ought to visit, "Dad never cared for any of that, you know." Minna, however, was steeped in her faith. But once married, she followed Leo's lead and did not worship on a regular basis—a grievous error, according to Helen, since "she felt at home really only in a Jewish community." Tragically for Minna, there were few opportunities in the small midwestern towns where they raised their family.[4]

They were also very different in temperament. According to Helen, Leo was "kind and forebearing, gentle and generous." He was forced by circumstance most of his life "into business, for which he had little aptitude, or interest." His real interest, as with his father and uncles before, "was in intellectual activities." On the other hand, Minna was mercurial, "emotional and non-intellectual . . . and felt the need for . . . a love and sympathy she did not get from her husband." Moreover, there was a self-centeredness such that "she had little capacity, or even interest, in understanding another's viewpoint."[5]

Their marriage was also plagued by the tension of unsuccessful vocation. Leo struggled all his life in the dry goods business, always as a very junior partner in the Szold-Rosenak clan. Both Helen and Minna felt that Leo "had been given the less lucrative stores, . . . and for many years had not been able to establish himself independently." He stayed only a short while at his first dry goods store in Morton before moving through a succession of disappointments in Valparaiso, Michigan City, and Winamac, Indiana; Springfield, Missouri; and later Daytona Beach, Florida. It did not help that Minna worked in the stores and that, as Helen, paraphrasing her husband, observed, "perhaps she was a better business woman than he was a business man." These sharp edges were tempered by the fact that Leo "never lost his optimism, and never so far as I could see, seemed to hold a grudge against his relatives." Leo finally found success with his own store, the Lilly Hat & Dress Shop in Michigan City.[6]

However great the turmoil of the early years and the personality differences that remained, the marriage was strong and endured more than five decades, until Leo's death. They began their family life with the birth of their first son in 1899, a child named for a David Eli of a different generation in the Old World, but a child destined to mark his era in a new world.

Growing Up

David Lilienthal's first home, Morton, Illinois, was a small village settled by Swiss and South Germans and with a population of nearly a thousand citizens. It is likely that the Lilienthals were the only Jewish family in town. Their isolation was accentuated because the interurban line had not yet come, necessitating a hard buggy ride to Peoria, a dozen miles away. David's brother Theodore was born in Morton in May 1902. The Lilienthals spoke German at home until David was about six, about the time Leo and Minna moved to Valparaiso, Indiana, in March 1905. Except for a period of a few months, Indiana was home for young David Lilienthal until he left for Harvard Law School in 1923.[7]

The family lived in Valparaiso until the summer of 1913. Their life was normal, disturbed at times by the stormy parental relationship and Leo's tribulations as he moved from store to store in search of success. Valparaiso, a town of just over seven thousand at the time, could, as Lilienthal's childhood friend Fred Arvin wrote, "hardly have been more typical, even more standard, than it was, as a small Middle Western Community early in the century." While only an hour from Chicago by rail, and much closer to the United States Steel company town of Gary, it remained a farming center and county seat untouched by the complexities of urban and industrial life. To Fred, Valparaiso was "still essentially a small 'middle border' town of the age of Garfield and McKinley." Its most notable landmark at the time was Valparaiso University, where the father of the Tennessee Valley Authority, George Norris, earned his law degree in 1882 before moving on to Nebraska.[8]

Valparaiso was tolerant, homogeneous, and strongly Republican. Fred Arvin noted there "was certainly not, in the industrial sense, a proletariat . . . [but only] families of a vaguely working-class sort." Most citizens were garden-variety Christians, and the majority Protestant and minority Catholic communities lived in harmony. The Episcopal parish was small, the number of Jewish families could easily be counted on two hands, and there were no Unitarians. Arvin remembered "one Negro woman" who happened to attend his Episcopal church. Neither Arvin nor Lilienthal remembered any anti-Semitism. Lilienthal could "recall . . . no single instance of exclusion or hindrance because of my being a Jew. . . . [A]nd I don't suppose I realized my Jewishness a dozen times in all the years I lived in Valparaiso." In fact, he remembered no untoward events, even through his years at DePauw College.[9]

Lilienthal's callow years were typical of the times. He collected cigar bands and stamps, worked as "an unwilling helper in his father's store," and had a paper route. He schemed to make his fortune, first cornering the local market on an alleged rare variety of the 1912 Lincoln-head penny and then with a shoe-shine stand outside his father's store. Unfortunately, the first scheme came to an end when the bank complained to his dad after David kept coming in with dollars to exchange for pennies. His second venture, a partnership with "Dee Muster, my hard-boiled friend," made only enough to cover "the cost of polish—and probably little else." He was also a "club man." In the barn behind their house on Indiana Street, David used wooden packing boxes to set up an exclusive fraternity that Fred described as "a combination of a men's club and a museum, with even a touch of the political headquarters thrown in for good measure."[10]

The real mark on Lilienthal during those years was Fred Newton Arvin, later distinguished literary critic, Smith College professor, and National Book Award–winning biographer of Herman Melville. Arvin (always Fred to Lilienthal, but Newton to the rest of the world) was from Valparaiso and a year younger than his friend. Fred was out of place in his time, considered a sissy by his father and peers, and given to withdraw "in dismay from all attempts to mingle with other coevals of my own sex." David was Fred's protector, his leader, and his one friend. He provided David with a steady source of adulation and loyalty—which young Lilienthal's ego must have found exhilarating.[11]

They were so different, David and Fred, one coming of age with a sense of presence in the world, the other shy and diffident, having to struggle with the pain of sexual ambiguity. But in those differences they found commonalities that would bind them for life. Fred first remembered his friend's kindness when one day in the winter of 1907–8 "another small boy noticing that I had no mittens . . . took off his own mittens and gave them to me." That boy was David Lilienthal—a "bright-eyed, dark-haired, rather chubby and round faced boy, with an engaging smile." For the next five years, they were inseparable, sometimes in "the ordinary childish activities of barefoot explorations in the summer and sliding down Main Street hill in the winter." They often shared in serious intellectual exploration: "Much of our reading was done in common, and we constantly shared our untutored opinions about what we read." David was enriched by Fred's "extraordinary mind, from whom I could and did learn so much about literature, words, history." Lilienthal recalled that Fred "had read everything; . . . knew the great names and places and battles and kings, all the things I, in my slower plodding way, didn't know, but thirsted to know." The friendship, forged in their young years and strengthened later by frequent visits and hundreds of letters, lasted more than half a century, until Fred's death from pancreatic cancer in 1963.[12]

For the most part, their intellectual adventure was heavy on history and literature and light on social and political issues. Lilienthal's understanding of the contemporary world did not fully blossom until after he left Valparaiso—but even then, there were beginnings. He later recalled that as a boy of seven or eight he heard William Jennings Bryan at a rally at Winoa Lake, Indiana. The only thing he could remember, however, was that the great orator had stepped on his bare foot "so that I was barely able to resist howling aloud." Much later he remembered the 1912 presidential campaign and "my father's enthusiasm for Teddy and the Bull Moose Party." He also recalled his "first lessons in politics listening to the 'old man' in Massey's barbershop, in the basement of my father's store, in Valpo."[13]

Fred remembered the influence on David of James H. McGill, a local factory owner who was also a "strongly-marked original—a radical of some sort" with a "leaning toward Henry George and the Single Tax." Locals in Valparaiso still recall visits early in the century to McGill's home of such notable progressives and radicals as Eugene Debs, Clarence Darrow, and the senior Robert A. La Follette. Fred wrote that McGill "was particularly generous to my friend David Lilienthal, whom he rightly spotted at an early age as the promising small boy he was, and whom he befriended in one way or another." Many years later, in 1942, Lilienthal told presidential aide Jonathan Daniels that McGill, "his second father," had given him a copy of George's *Progress and Poverty,* which inspired him along the path he eventually took.[14]

Much to Fred's dismay, the Lilienthals moved away in 1913. Leo's kind heart was no match for the vicissitudes of commerce and the seeming insensitivities of Minna's family. Between 1905 and 1909, he worked his way up from a small five-and-dime store to a partnership with Louis Szold in a large multifloor establishment in the heart of town. In February 1913, however, the two cousins by marriage closed the Lilienthal-Szold Department Store and went their separate ways. By summer, Leo's new establishment, a shoe store, facing competition from two other dry goods stores, shut down, and the family was forced to leave Valparaiso. After an unsuccessful attempt to establish a store in Springfield, Missouri, the Lilienthals, now five in number with the birth of Allen in 1911, moved back to Indiana, this time to Michigan City, where Leo worked in a store owned by his brothers-in-law.[15]

The move to the south shore of Lake Michigan was of great significance for young David. He stayed for a while in 1913–14 with Aunt Hermine and Uncle Jacob and completed the tenth grade at Gary High School. While living with the Szolds, he became close to their daughter Bernadine, one of his life's "most important influences." Bernadine, or Dee, was a rebellious young woman, five years Lilienthal's senior. Already married, a bohemian and aspiring newspaper reporter, Dee was instrumental in introducing her young cousin to the Progressive movement in Chicago. Sometime in the winter of 1914 Dee's husband, Albert Carver, took the fourteen-year-old boy to a Chicago labor meeting where he heard Emma Goldman and Ben Reitman. Lilienthal was impressed by what they said, but was most taken by the power of their presence and speech. To the young man, Reitman's "voice was that of a bull—no tone quality, no variation, but tremendous bass power." Of Goldman he remembered "the almost aristocratic and surely intellectual set of the head" and a voice "deep and strong, with a quick turn and a lash to it which was more of the type possessed by some sharp-witted man." Soon after, Dee and Albert became involved in a messy divorce. Lilienthal sealed his friendship with his cousin by filching some damaging letters of hers from Albert which "were not inclined to help her fight."[16]

In 1914 Lilienthal moved back with his parents and finished at Isaac C. Elston High School in Michigan City. His grades were good but undistinguished, except in stenography, which served him well all his life. But young Dave had an agenda other than academic rigor. As a recent Elston High librarian noted, "David must have hit this school like a whirlwind." In his junior year he starred in the class play and was the first Elstonian ever to win the gold medal in the Northern Indiana Oratorical Contest. As the report of that victory was recorded, "little Davy had the honor of being almost knocked to pieces while carried about on the shoulders of his schoolmates." A few months before his death, he remembered that event and "a tall rawboned teacher . . . who prepared me to face an audience without my shaking knees . . . , the first big audience. . . . The title? 'The Predatory Rich.' I knew even then what stirred me."[17]

While his rhetorical skills blossomed in his junior year, his will to lead matured when he was a senior. He was the editor of the yearbook and a cofounder of both the Boys' Oratorical Association and the Latin Society. He took the lead in the first annual Cicero play and also starred in the senior play, about which a reviewer noted that his role "could not have been done any better." In the yearbook, he took, as he often did later, the moral high ground with an essay entitled "A Protest." In it he lamented that "the average American youth is becoming lax—lax in his morals, his conduct, his speech, his habits of work and play." He railed against the sins of "rampant discourtesy," and the vices of tobacco and alcohol. In conclusion, he hoped that his words might "cause some young man to think upon this subject . . . and do as his own better sense tells him." There was no ambivalence in the quotation next to his class picture in the *Elstonian:* "Always true to his word, his work, and his friends."[18]

The young man's activities were not limited to school doings. He also worked from time to time at Uncle Adolph's store and once got into trouble for "lifting coins from the cash drawer" to buy a present for a high school sweetheart. He had a part-time job reporting for the local paper, an interest he pursued in college. He was listed in the 1916 city directory as "David Lilienthal, 820 Buffalo St., Reporter, THE EVENING DISPATCH." And he kept up a lively correspondence with Fred: they took turns quizzing each other about facts of history, literature, and the classics, each trying to stump the other.[19]

The Marks of Youth

The connections between past and present are never easy to establish, and so it is in Lilienthal's case. His intellect, curiosity, and restless spirit were mirrored in the disposition of many of the men on his father's side. Like his grandfather and great-uncles, David Lilienthal was full of ideas and energized by them. Lilienthal excelled in the practical arts of life and was blessed with a strong entrepreneurial drive that sustained him in both public and private endeavors. From his high school years on, David Lilienthal was always moving and calculating his next step with deliberation.[20]

There is no doubt of the parental influence. Helen wrote that she understood her husband much better after knowing Minna for several years: "He had, I felt inherited much of his mother's temperament. He needed affection and love, he was emotional and liked gaiety." Alluding to Leo's influence, she continued that "he had in addition an intellectual capacity that [his mother] never had, a critical mind, an imagination, an interest in intellectual things." On the eve of his mother's eightieth birthday, Lilienthal reflected that "she must have contributed a great deal to my temperament, drive, for she has great energy, even now, and restlessness. Her abruptness . . . may be partly the response of a strong and forceful person who did not intend to be pushed around." Brother Allen noted that David inherited a temper and impatience from their mother, a combination that allowed neither to suffer fools with much grace.[21]

Both Helen and Allen Lilienthal noted that Leo gave his son intellectual drive and curiosity. Lilienthal later acknowledged his father's legacy as "a love of books and reading." The son followed his father's lead in matters of faith, never becoming a devoutly religious Jew. And Leo's work ethic, persevering again and again in the face of failure, could not have failed to impress the eldest son. Perhaps most important, however, may be the fact that the deep and abiding love between father and son, reflected throughout the journals and David's early letters to Helen, gave the young man a sense of compassion and a stable foundation that sustained him through the many crises in his public life.[22]

What about the influence of the times? In all likelihood, David was little touched by partisan politics. While Henry Steele Commager was correct in observing that "young David was old enough to have read the First Inaugural Address [of Woodrow Wilson] with interest," there is no evidence that he did so. He was probably unaware of two landmark interpretations of the American Commonwealth published during his youth, Herbert Croly's *The Promise of American Life* (1909) and Charles A. Beard's *Economic Interpretation of the Constitution of the United States* (1913). More than likely, he had little sense at the time of the difference between "New Nationalism" and "New Freedom." Bit by bit, however, his critical faculties matured and his awareness of the world grew. In Valparaiso, Fred stimulated his intellectual appetite, and Jim McGill imparted a sense of the wonder and excitement of progressive thought. Certainly, Dee's influence was seminal—so important that the concerns of labor remained central throughout college and law school and into his first professional years.[23]

He was also influenced by his midwestern roots. In 1970, he mused, "I regard myself as a Hoosier. . . . I bear the mark of a boyhood and young manhood in Indiana and the middle west more than any other place I have lived or worked." Over the years, he and Helen probably contributed as much to their Indiana alma mater, DePauw University, as they did to any other institution or charity. Yet, for all his worldliness and international dealings, Lilienthal always reflected an almost childlike understanding of the rest of the world, so much like the deep currents of isolationism that prevailed in his Indiana heartland.[24]

There was one final sense in which youth seemed to mark him. In his last year of life, he recalled that he had experienced little poverty in his life. However, it was also true that Leo's chronic economic woes must have made the whole family uneasy about having to live on the edge of, if not poverty, at least a precarious middle-class existence. Through his life, Lilienthal was always anxious about money. Many of his journal entries reflected this obsessive concern, even after he "made his million" in the early 1950s. A few months before his death, he wrote that "money became a preoccupation of mine long, long ago." He was a generous father and husband, and he frequently supported ailing friends and family members on a regular basis. But still, the David of adulthood could never let the memory of those uncertain boyhood times go.[25]

All in all, the youthful years were good to David Lilienthal. Leo and Minna, whatever their personal difficulties, provided fertile soil for their sons to develop to productive manhood. Contemporaries, especially Fred and Dee, and mentors such as Jim McGill and the "big raw-boned teacher" whetted his intellectual and social appetites and opened his eyes to the larger world. Perhaps most important, Lilienthal took every opportunity and challenge to achieve a maturity far beyond his seventeen years. The stage was set for the next step—DePauw, Helen, Harvard Law School, and the beginning of his journey. In September 1916, as they waited for the train to take him to DePauw College "at the old ramshackle Monon station in Michigan City," David and his parents could hardly have anticipated the changes that would come over the next seven years.[26]

Lilienthal & Company, site of Leo Lilienthal's grocery store and haberdashery and Lilienthal birthplace in Morton, Illinois, about 1900. Courtesy of Morton, Illinois, Public Library.

Lilienthal birthplace in 1961. Courtesy of Tazewell Publishing Company and Illinois State Historical Library.

Lilienthal boyhood home, 55 Erie, Valparaiso, Indiana, in late 1980s. Courtesy of George E. Neeley.

Lilienthal boyhood home, 605 Indiana, Valparaiso, Indiana, in late 1980s. Courtesy of George E. Neeley.

Frederick Newton Arvin, high school
senior picture, 1917. Courtesy of
Genealogical Department, Valparaiso
Indiana, Public Library.

James H. McGill, Valparaiso, Indiana,
industrialist and Lilienthal mentor.
Courtesy of J. McGill.

Lilienthal's high school in Michigan City, Indiana, in the *Elstonian*, 1915.
Courtesy of the Michigan City Area Schools.

DAVID LILIENTHAL

"Always true to his word, his work, and his friends."

Editor-in-Chief of the Elstonian
Gold Medal, Oratorical Contest N. I. O. and A. L. '15
Special Mention State Fire Prevention Essay Contest
Junior Play
Senior Play
B. O. A. Charter Member
Consul, Cavici Societas
Debating Team
Business Manager, Senior Play
Secretary of Finance Committee of B. A. A. '15-'16
Glee Club '15-'16
Latin Play

Lilienthal's high school senior picture in the *Elstonian*, 1915. Courtesy of the Michigan City Area Schools.

Helen Lamb, senior picture in the *Mirage*, 1919. Courtesy of the DePauw University Archives and Special Collections.

Lilienthal at DePauw University, in front of Delta Upsilon fraternity house, around 1918. Courtesy of the Lilienthal family.

Delta Sigma Rho

David Lilienthal,
Albert T. Freeman,   Robert E. O'Brien,
Simeon Leland.
"AN INDIAN, A JEW, AN IRISHMAN AND A MUGWUMP"

Delta Sigma Rho is an honorary oratorical fraternity, founded at Chicago University in 1906 with 37 active chapters. The Chapter at DePauw was founded in 1913.

Only winners of oratorical contests and two years debate men are elected to this organization.

Its purpose is to promote an interest in oratorical contests and intercollegiate debates.

Lilienthal and fellow Delta Sigma Rho members in the *Mirage*, 1918. Courtesy of the DePauw University Archives and Special Collections.

The DePauw Daily

FAIR AND WARMER.   FRIDAY, APRIL 4, 1919.   VOL. 13.   NO. 51.

STUDENTS MUST DECIDE AS TO R.O.T.C. WORK

DR. BLANCHARD SAYS THAT UNIT WILL BE MAINTAINED UNLESS MEN OBJECT

SCHOOL AWAITING OUTCOME

Complaints of Men Must Be Organized Before Faculty Will Abolish Drill.

Co-incident to the announcement of the Daily last evening stating that a straw vote on the R. O. T. C. would be taken on the popularity of the movement came the authoritative statement that the university was not bound in any way to continue the unit here.

If the students of DePauw are opposed to the continuance of the R. O. T. C. here next year, it will probably be discontinued, according to a statement made by Doctor Blanchard this morning. There has been considerable complaint about the R. O. T. C., but it has not been strong enough to have any influence with the faculty, and they have voted to continue the training next year. The drill, instruction and physical training periods will take place at 11:30 a. m. as far as possible.

Doctor Blanchard stated that it would please the faculty if the men of the university would call a mass meeting for the purpose of openly discussing the R. O. T. C. If it seems to be a good thing, the faculty will give it their loyal support, but if the men decide, for good reasons, that they would rather not have the training next year, the probability is that the faculty will discontinue it after this year. It is up to all the men of the university to show what their wishes are in the matter. The Daily is now conducting a straw vote among the men who are compelled to take R. O. T. C. training in an endeavor to find out its standing in their estimation.

Co-eds Will Issue Daily On May Day

At the meeting of the W. S. G. A. last night at 7 o'clock in Alverd Hall, Bowman gymnasium, it was decided to publish the annual co-ed edition of the DePauw Daily on May Day.

Previously the co-ed edition has been issued on Old Gold Day, but this year because of the S. A. T. C. and the fact that the Daily had not been started, the publication had to be delayed. May Day is really the co-eds' day at DePauw and so the S. G. A. is planning to have the co-ed issue of the Daily published annually on May Day, it was stated. The editorial staff elected at the meeting last night comprised:

Editor-in-Chief—Berthe Tucker.
Business Manager—Frances Cavanah.

(Continued on page two)

April Showers

HONOR SYSTEM SEEMS SHELVED

STUDENT COUNCIL PRESIDENT STATES NO ACTION TAKEN ON MATTER HERE

NO REASON IS GIVEN

Action upon the "honor" system at DePauw has been postponed by the student council for the present, and will not be taken up until better working conditions are at hand, it was authoritatively announced today. John Rabb Emison, president of the student council, when asked just what had been done in regard to the proposed measure, said: "No definite action has been decided upon, and I feel safe in saying that the matter will be dropped for the present and that the student council has no statement to make as outcome of action upon the matter."

Emison was also asked what was the opinion of the representative council of the student body as individuals in regard to the system. He said this could not be ascertained because there had been few definite opinions expressed before the council.

No reason was given for the shelving of the proposed plan by the council at this time.

Dr. and Mrs. W. W. Tucker have received word from their son, Dr. Cassell Tucker, saying that he expected to start for home soon. Dr. Tucker is now in London, where he was decorated by the king and will go to France immediately, where he will receive his discharge.

NEW ENGLAND ALUMNI OF DEPAUW TO GIVE BANQUET

The New England Alumni Association of DePauw will hold annual banquet and reunion in Boston April 29. Invitations have been sent all DePauw men and women throughout New England and a large attendance is promised. According to an announcement received here Bishop McConnell, President Murlin and Bishop Hughes and others will be speakers. W. W. Krider is secretary of the association.

PROF. SWEET MAY RESIGN

PRESIDENCY OF KANSAS WESLEYAN OFFERED TO HIM

Matter Undecided Yet

Dr. W. W. Sweet of DePauw University has been tendered the presidency of the Kansas Wesleyan University, at Lindsborg, Kas. Dr. Sweet has the matter of acceptance under advisement and is undecided as to whether he will accept the place or not, a dispatch in the Salina, Kas. Journal has the following:

LINDSBORG, Kans. March 29—The board of trustees of Kansas Wesleyan university late yesterday afternoon tendered the presidency of Kansas Wesleyan to Prof. W. W. Sweet of the chair of history in DePauw University, Greencastle, Ind.

Prof. Sweet met with the board for a brief conference and said he would return to Indiana and give the invitation most careful consideration. He hopes to return an answer in a few weeks.

Prof. Sweet is a son of the late Dr. W. H. Sweet, veteran minister, for some time a professor at the Wesleyan pastor of churches at Salina and other places. The young man is es-

(Continued on page two)

BASEBALL GAME IS POSTPONED

TIGERS FAIL TO GET INTO ACTION IN FIRST FRAY OF YEAR

TO MEET NORMAL MONDAY

DePauw baseball men failed to get into action today in the first scheduled game of the year carded with State Normal when the weather man called the engagement off. The game will be played Monday according to present plans.

With the eligibility ruling still holding up several of the Old Gold nine, the postponement is considered an advantage with the chances fifty-fifty that some of those under the weather may come to by Monday. Coach Conklin will put his squad through the last workout tomorrow afternoon and is making a strong effort to get all his material in line at this time to build up a dependable infield.

E. C. Buss, athletic director, issued a call late this afternoon, when it appeared that the present Tiger infield would be badly shot because of the eligibility rules to all men in the university to come out for practice if they were able to play ball to any extent whatever. As it appears now, Captain Julien will work on the mound Monday with Miller behind the bat, Isenbarger, Tuhey, Cartwright and Bastian are being depended upon to take care of the infield with Davis, B. Guild, M. Guild and Donner in line for duty in the outfield.

Wabash will be met in the second game of the year at Crawfordsville next Friday. This will be the first of a our-game series. Practice tomorrow will start at 2:30.

TO BRIDGE GAP BETWEEN PROFS AND STUDENTS

PROPOSAL MADE BY D. E. LILIENTHAL LAST NIGHT

DEFINITE ACTION LACKING

Attempt to Eliminate Present Lack of Harmony Between Student Body and Faculty.

A plan by which the misunderstanding which has admittedly arisen between the faculty and student body of DePauw as the result of the recent "cribbing" scandal may be cleared away was proposed at a meeting of representative DePauw men held last night.

D. E. Lilienthal was the author of the proposal which if adopted, it is averred, would bring student opinion of the sanest sort direct to the faculty and bridge the gulf which now separates that body from the students. The plan was discussed by the caucus of delegates.

Lilienthal recommended the formation of what he termed a students' administrative council, to be made up of duly elected representative of any duly elected representative of each fraternity and each sorority, together with elected representatives of the unorganized men and women. This board, he suggested, was to meet and determine upon fundamental matters which are now only in a vague form. The board would then elect from its membership an executive committee of five which would prepare and publish the findings of the board, and confer with the president and faculty representatives on constructive plans.

In concluding his remarks on the plan Lilienthal said: "If the faculty and administration will meet the students half way, the state of mutual distrust, suspicion and dissatisfaction between faculty and students, and the growing state of jealousy and factionalism between students will soon be changed, and we can feel that we are building toward something which will be of permanent benefit."

It was urged that all fraternities and sororities and non-Greeks proceed at once to the election of representative who will be qualified to act for them. The date of the next meeting was not set, being dependent upon later developments.

Following discussion, the men decided to report back to their organizations, determine the exact state of affairs at present, find out what things are needed from the student point of view, and then take more definite action later, in case the situation warranted it.

SURPLUS OF LABOR IN TEN INDIANA CITIES

Eight of ten Indiana cities show a surplus of workers over the opportunities available for their employment, in the reports to the United States employment office for the past week. Indianapolis continues to lead, as before, in the total of unemployment, although the showing of the state capital is an improvement over that for the preceding week.

The Student Voice

GREENCASTLE, INDIANA.   EDITED BY PAUL W. NEFF   SATURDAY MAY 15, 1920

Since the faculty of DePauw University ha sconfiscated Friday's issue of students of the University regard Student paper of DePauw University, because of articles in said issue of the Daily setting forth the opinions of students of the University regard ing the control of the Daily and put ing the control of the Daily and put ting it entirely in the hands of the dir ector of the course in Journalism, we, the undersigned student organ izations of De Pauw University, hereby subscribe funds to publish these articles as student opinion under the name of the STUDENT VOICE

PHI KAPPA PSI	KAPPA ALPHA THETA	ALPHA PHI	KAPPA KAPPA GAMMA
BETA THETA PI	DELTA TAU DELTA	SIGMA CHI	DELTA UPSILON
ALPHA CHI OMEGA	DELTA ZETA	DELTA SIGMA PSI	LAMBDA CHI ALPHA
SIGMA NU	PHI DELTA THETA	DELTA KAPPA EPSILON	ALPHA OMICRON PI
SIGMA DELTA CHI	PHI GAMMA DELTA	DELTA DELTA DELTA	MORTAR BOARD

The following stories are lifted from Friday's DePauw Daily.

THE WILL OF DE PAUW
By the Editor

Faculty members who voted Wednesday to place the control of the Daily in the hands of the instructor of journalism are given an opportunity by reading today's issue of learning the student sentiment on the matter.

L. E. Mitchell instructor in journalearning the campus reaction to his assertion that that DePauw needs is a weekly or bi-weekly paper.

Who will say that the Daily this year has been "entirely unsatisfactory" to DePauw's student body after these expressions of individuals and organizations?

Who will contend that a weekly or favor of departmental paper, nor a weekly. The Daily should be run by the students.

Dave Lilienthal, former president of the student body — The Daily should not become a laboratory for classes in journalism any more than the campus should be a laboratory for the Physics class.

Richard McGinnis— Reducing the DePauw Daily to a weekly is destroying one of the institutions of school which has been perpetuated for 13 years. While we step forward in athletics , shall DePauw lag in Journalism, and fall back into a class with Earlham, Franklin, Butler and Wabash?

dents of this institution to have such an organ at their disposal. I don t believe the paper can be the same when conducted as a "laboratory" for the course in Journalism. Is the staff of the Daily to be restricted to the students of some one department? Some people may call that democracy but I have another name for it. It each student supposed to muster up all of his loyalty and pay a laboratory fee for a publication that is avowedly intended to give students something to experiment with?

The Daily has been of real service to DePauw. It has passed the experiment stage. It has proven itself to be a real-for-sure grownup newspaper. It ought to be continued on the same lines.

At any rate I believe that the students appreciate the hard work and

they believed in it, and because they wished to maintain the record which it now has—one of the few college dailies which did not suspend or alter publication during the war.

If three students and no professors could publish a Daily two years ago, then an entire department and all the students in it ought to publish two editions a day, six days a week instead of talking about reducing the number of issues.

"The Daily is to be a laboratory for the students taking Journalism". The weekly "News Bulletin" which was started as a laboratory for embryo journalists is a shining example of what will happen to the once famous DePauw Daily when its prestige is taken away and it becomes a plaything for beginners.

If DePauw is too small for a daily

Lilienthal's protest over faculty action turning the student newspaper over to journalism faculty, in ad hoc "underground newspaper," 1920. Courtesy of the DePauw University Archives and Special Collections.

Lilienthal, senior picture in the *Mirage,* 1920. Courtesy of the DePauw University Archives and Special Collections.

LAW SCHOOL OF HARVARD UNIVERSITY
CAMBRIDGE, MASS. 02138

Office of the Registrar   617-495-4612   Griswold Hall

RECORD OF _____ David Eli Lilienthal

Attended from
September 20, 1920	to	June 23, 1921	
September 21, 1921	to	June 22, 1922	
September 23, 1922	to	June 21, 1923	

Lilienthal, David Eli

DATE OF LAW DEGREE
LL.B.--June 21, 1923   (over)

FIRST YEAR	Date	Mark	Folio	SECOND YEAR	Date	Mark	Folio	THIRD YEAR	Date	Mark	Folio
Civil Procedure	⁶/₂₁	70		Agency	¹/₂₃	72		Conf. of Laws	¹/₂₄	76	
Contracts	"	57		Bills & Notes				Constitutional Law	¹/₂₃	78	
Criminal Law	"	39		Equity	²/₁₂	74		Corporations	⁶/₂₃	70	
Liability DEALE	"	36		Evidence	"	72		Equity	"	74	
Property	⁶/₂₁	73		Insurance				Partnership			
Torts	"	65		Property II.	⁴/₁₂	66		Property III.			
				Public Utilities		75		Suretyship & Mortgage			
				Sales	¹/₁₂	67		Admiralty			
				Trusts	"	68		Bankruptcy			
				Damages				Federal Jur. & Pro.			
				Persons				Municipal Corporations			
								Quasi-Contracts			
Average, 1st Year	340	68						Restraint of Trade	⁴/₁₃	40	
								Administrative Law			
								International Law			
								Jurisprudence			
								Roman Law			
General Average	1210	71						Labor Law	¹/₂₃	38	
Class Standing				Average	422	70		Average	448	75	

Red marks indicate 3rd yr. work   ✦Extra   Library Bureau 042802

KEY TO GRADES

Full Course		Half Course
75 and up	— A —	37.5 and up
70-74	— B —	35-37
66-69	— C+ —	33-34.5
62-65	— C —	31-32.5
55-61	— D —	27.5-30.5
Below 55	— F —	Below 27.5

Half marks are given for courses of two or three hours credit, but all grades in the second and third years and in graduate work are weighted in accordance with the number of hours in the course.

Dated ___ 1989 OCT 2 6 ___   (Signed) _Charlotte M. Robinson_

Charlotte M. Robinson, Registrar

Lilienthal's Harvard Law School final transcript, 1923. Courtesy of the Lilienthal family.

Lilienthal's first boss, Donald R. Richberg, probably 1920s. Courtesy of the Chicago Historical Society.

of which, including the entire Arbitration article, I drafted will apparently be enacted this session. The Supreme Court reversed Judge Wilkerson in the Robertson case, adopting the line of reasoning (and even the material) in the brief which I prepared in large part: this was a great satisfaction.

January 3, 1926

My interest in the practice of law seems to continue to thrive. Most of my work is on some labor law problem (proposed legislation, consultation on legal rights, or the like) or some other phase of public law, including the valuation problem. I feel at times that it would be better for me if I did more general practice (commercial litigation, drafting of agreements, probate etc), so that I would be rounded out a bit more. Of course these days one must simply realize first as last that he can't know well the whole field of practice, as the small town practitioner is expected to. Fortunately perhaps, there are enough matters of general practice arising to make me keep my hand in, in some fields of law at least. Last year, for example I did research on the admissability of a deceased insured's statements tending to show fraud in her insurance application, in a suit for cancellation for fraud; and a brief on the nature and effect of a joint enterprise agreement.

One of the finest and the most stimulating part of my working experience is my association with Mr. Richberg. I am constantly amazed at the fertility of his mind. He is not simply a brilliant lawyer, but a social philosophy runs through everything he does. In some ways our temperaments are similar, and this has helped our friendship and professional association as well. For example, he has a distaste for commercial law, except when it presents some intellectual problem of some sort. Our labor sympathies spring from similar sources. Our interest in writing (what Mal Sharp yesterday called "a journalistic bent") is helpful. He is one man for whom I have come to have almost daily more and more re-

Excerpt from Lilienthal's private journal, January 1926. Courtesy of the Public Policy Papers, Seeley G. Mudd Manuscript Library, Department of Rare Books and Special Collections, Princeton University Libraries.

Philip La Follette at desk in executive
office, 1932. Courtesy of the State
Historical Society of Wisconsin
(negative no. WHi [X3] 18342).

Lilienthal as
Wisconsin Public
Utility Commissioner,
1933. Courtesy of
Public Utilities
Reports,
Incorporated.

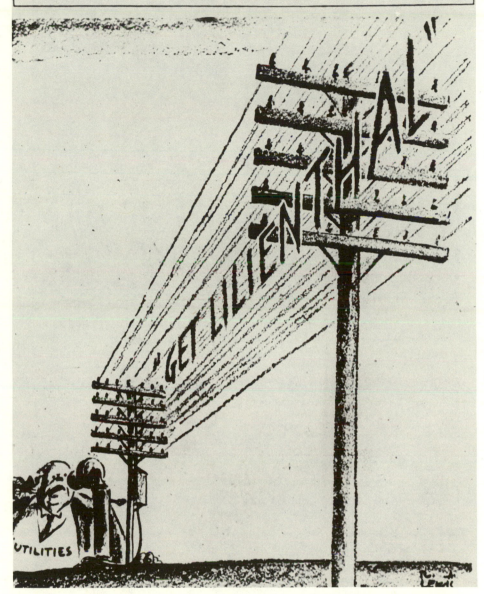

Editorial cartoon, *Milwaukee Journal*, May 1933. Courtesy of the *Milwaukee Journal*.

Original TVA Board, H. A. Morgan, A. E. Morgan, and Lilienthal, 1933.
Courtesy of the Tennessee Valley Authority.

President Roosevelt, Eleanor Roosevelt, and A. E. Morgan at Norris
Dam, November 1934. Courtesy of the Tennessee Valley Authority.

CHAPTER 2

DePauw College, Harvard Law School, and Helen

Your unwavering, steady belief that I will do the right thing
sharpens my judgement—sets all my senses on edge, so that
often I can do things which my abilities do not warrant, being
lent added powers by this thrilling sense of Faith.
                              —Letter, David to Helen, 1919

Miss Lamb

However shopworn the adage regarding a successful man and the
woman in his life, it says much about David Lilienthal and Helen Lamb's
relationship, which began in cautious friendship in the spring of 1917 and
stretched into a sixty-five-year love affair. Without a doubt, Helen Lamb
Lilienthal was the center of her husband's private realm. She nurtured, listened, encouraged, and above all else tolerated. She was his best friend, and
forceful alter ego. Without her steadying influence, it is easy to imagine that
Lilienthal might never have achieved as much as he did.

Helen was born to William and Alma McCluer Lamb on April 3, 1896,
in McAlester, Oklahoma. William Lamb was a Federal Circuit Court clerk
who later established a successful property and title search abstract company. Alma Lamb was a homemaker. The family lived in Oklahoma, most
of the time in Perry, until the end of Helen's sophomore year in high school.
In 1913 the family moved to her mother's hometown of Crawfordsville,
Indiana, where her father recuperated from a heart ailment. After her parents returned to Perry in early 1914, Helen stayed with her grandparents and
finished high school in Crawfordsville. During Helen's senior year, in October
1914, her father died, and Alma Lamb moved back to Crawfordsville.

Although conservative, her parents felt that "in politics . . . everyone
should be on an equal basis, and that individual merit should be the sole
criterion." Helen learned social responsibility from her maternal grandmother, who served, through the local Methodist church as "the informal
director of all charity work in Crawfordsville." Her intellectual capacity

was strengthened by inveterate reading, including all the neighbors' books, those in the small town library, and her family's collection, which included Emerson, Twain, Shakespeare, and Dickens. In Crawfordsville, she reveled in the larger Carnegie Library and introduced herself at age twelve to her Uncle Gayle's collection of Balzac and Hugo. As she grew, she wrote and expressed a firm "ambition to become an author." By college, she was a poet, and in her early married days often sold poems for pin money or to pay for treats for special occasions such as David's birthday.[1]

Her last two years of high school in Crawfordsville were bittersweet. Her grandparents, along with "plenty of dates, dances, and my first (unhappy) love affair" were all sources of joy. Her father's death and her mother's grief, "so intensive that mine in his death was shadowed," followed closely by her grandmother McCluer's death, cast a pall over the years. In fall 1915, Helen matriculated at the University of Illinois in Champaign. After an unhappy semester, she returned to Crawfordsville to be with her still-grieving mother, and next fall enrolled at nearby DePauw College.[2]

Lilienthal's first recollection of Helen was as a young woman in his English literature class. She infuriated the men because she could always answer the professor's questions, no matter how difficult. Some time later the same semester, an older fraternity brother ordered a socially deficient Lilienthal to ask a Miss Lamb of Alpha Chi Omega out. Helen recalled that they "met and glowered at each other for a short time," but soon found they had much in common. Although they agreed to maintain only a "platonic friendship," their affection soon became much more. In December 1917, Lilienthal made his first journal note of the blue-eyed woman with the long dark braids: "It has never been my good fortune to know even as a bare acquaintance anyone, male or otherwise, who combined intellectuality, delightful social charm and with a deep, womanly, yet universal, sympathy as does this girl." Until Helen's graduation in 1919, a year ahead of David, they were inseparable. During her senior year they admitted "that what we had was a love affair." Later that year David reminded her that "platonic friendship is the gun you didn't know was loaded."[3]

Helen wrote of DePauw that "more stress [was] put on student activities than on scholarship." She majored in English literature and continued her interest in poetry. While conventional in most respects, Miss Lamb was out of place in others. She was president of her senior class, an honor rarely bestowed on women. That she was a unique individual was evidenced by the quotations next to her photographs in the 1918 and 1919 DePauw College yearbooks: as a junior the editors noted, "A lawyer she aspires to be." Her senior picture was accompanied by a pithy description, "A miniature General." In summer 1918, she returned to Perry "to decide whether I wanted to take over my father's partnership." Although she "enjoyed the work . . . and . . . being . . . . among my friends," that and every other prospect fell by the wayside when she and David decided to plan a future together.[4]

The evolution of their relationship was captured in a set of David's letters that began in 1918 and ceased in 1922, when Helen entered graduate school at Radcliffe. The several hundred letters covered Helen's time in Perry in the summer of 1918, her teaching years there between 1919 and 1921, and her year as a teacher in Crawfordsville. They provide keen insight into the maturation of a young man and his perspectives. They are also telling witness to Helen's lifelong role in relation to David.

Through the written word, she quickly became the font of his driving ambition. She insisted on the force of his personality by "claiming for [him] the power of 'influencing people's lives' by touching them." He recognized this role in telling her that "having *you* to write to makes everything so much more vital and near," and again two years later, in 1921, when he confessed that "in you I find my chiefest hope for an inspiration and a fortification which, unsupported, my heart and limbs lack." Her shoulder was there even as a "platonic friend" early in 1918 when he lost an important oratorical contest. She was there in 1919, when he came in second in the Rhodes scholarship competition, an honor he coveted deeply. But she was his critic also—she scolded him on his tendency to overwork and become prostrate with exhaustion, a common failing throughout his life. She also insisted that he do as much as possible in his "hyper-criticality" to "ward against losing the human touch" in his relations with "other men" and "toward human things in general."[5]

It was clear from that first journal reference that Lilienthal was smitten by the young woman three years his elder. His letters to her, especially after 1920, were rife with sweet prose and left no doubt of his commitment to her—"Just as 'our star' shines yet with the steadfastness of the night we first viewed it together, and as it shall continue faithfully to shine, when we look up at it through eternity—so is my love for You—Elena, my dearest." Another letter stresses that their "life will be three-fold in its phases." They must be "spiritual pals," their life "must be Human," and it should be informed always by "an intellectual consanguinity."[6]

Like her mother before, Helen stayed home and kept the hearth. Many years later a frail but alert nonagenarian confided without regret that her "life had been lived vicariously through him." In a late journal entry, Lilienthal recorded his reaction to a conversation with his wife about that commitment. He confessed that as a young man he hadn't wanted "his wife to have a *separate* career," an attitude that now seemed "so 'square' . . . even to the old man." His wife of more than fifty-six years pointedly reminded him after he explained "how he had made the old lady financially completely independent" that "I have had a very interesting life, a happy life. But it was because I was *your* wife, not because of what I did." For all of those years, Helen Lilienthal was the rock and foundation for her partner. Under other circumstances, she would have flourished on her own. Without her, David Lilienthal might never have been able to pursue his ambitions as far as he did.[7]

DePauw College

Tiny DePauw, a sensible heartland college in Greencastle, Indiana, hardly seemed the place for the son of Austro-Hungarian Jewish immigrants. Nevertheless, the small Methodist college was nearby and its tuition was within Leo Lilienthal's means. Moreover, the school provided a humane atmosphere for development—a place where teachers taught and Lilienthal's religious background was noted only because of its uniqueness. Founded in 1837, DePauw was not without distinction. By the time young Lilienthal matriculated, the school boasted among its alumni five United States senators, two Indiana governors, and a U.S. Supreme Court justice. David Graham Phillips, an early feminist writer, was an alumnus, and the distinguished historians Charles and Mary Beard graduated in the late 1890s. Margaret Mead, in an otherwise uncomplimentary chronicle of her year at DePauw in 1919–20, reported that she "thoroughly enjoyed the magnificent teaching" at the college. She wrote that "the training in writing given me by Professor Pence was never equaled by anyone else," and that her courses in religion provided a sturdy foundation in ethics.[8]

Lilienthal's academic record at DePauw was good but not exceptional. He completed more courses in public speaking than in any other subject, but concentrated on economics, political science, and modern history his last two years "to bring to bear upon the great public questions which will confront the men and women of my generation, a mind competent to cope successfully with these problems."[9]

He excelled in every other activity. He served as president of the local forensic society, Delta Sigma Rho; Duzer Du, the campus dramatic club; and his social fraternity, Delta Upsilon. In the spring of 1919 he was elected student body president, beating his "Progressive" opponent by a two-to-one margin. Interestingly, the budding liberal ran on the Conservative party ticket, a party "established with the idea of eliminating graft in DePauw activities and of giving DePauw cleaner politics." His platform called for more scholarships, credit for work in dramatics and on the school paper, and "promotion of an honorable 'honor system.'" In the fall of 1919 the college nominated him for a Rhodes Fellowship, an honor that failed to materialize.[10]

While more indifferent to athletics than other endeavors, he was also active in that realm. He dawdled in varsity football two years, but was known for his pugilistic skills, conducting boxing classes and organizing tournaments as a senior. Boxing was a reflection of his combative personality and demonstrated "competence at defending yourself as a means of preserving your personal independence."[11]

Lilienthal participated in oratorical competitions as a freshman and sophomore, the latter year narrowly missing an interstate title. He also kept up his theatrical interests as a frequent leading man and producer in Duzer Du. In June 1920 his first publication appeared in *Theatre Magazine*. It was vintage Lilienthal—strident and rhetorical. In no uncertain terms the young thespian proclaimed "the downward tendency of the theatre . . . [because] of those who have driven art from the theatre for the sake of gold." He argued for decent facilities at DePauw and concluded that the nation's youth "are demanding the custody of the dramatic art of the nation, that they may effect its rejuvenation and rehabilitation!"[12]

Until Armistice Day in November 1918 Lilienthal was fascinated, like most young men, with the Great War. At first suspicious of claims of "brutalities committed by Germans on their prisoners or non-combatants," he eventually became outraged by eyewitness accounts and mused that his anger was interesting "for one who was but a short time ago a pacifist and almost a non-resistant." He wrote Helen about possibly signing up as a Jewish relief volunteer. In the summer of 1918 he applied to the Jewish Welfare Board as a welfare worker to Jewish soldiers but was rejected because of his age. He also tried to enlist in the army, but was denied then because of "the condition of my arches." His case of war fever was satisfied eventually by joining the short-lived DePauw Student Army Training Corps in the fall of 1918.[13]

Distinguished by virtue of his achievements, Lilienthal was also distinctive by virtue of his religion. A 1918 yearbook feature on oratory recognized him as a Jew, and the caption beneath one group photograph that included Lilienthal identified those in the picture as "an Indian, a Jew, an Irishman and a Mugwump." Margaret Mead wrote about "five of us at DePauw who were religious rejects—myself [an Episcopalian], one Roman Catholic, one Greek Orthodox, one Lutheran, and one Jew. The Jew was David Lilienthal." Once, when Lilienthal spoke to a Methodist Sunday school class on Judaism, he wrote Helen, asking, "Can you, by a severe wrench of all your imaginative powers, picture me, your David E. Lilienthal, speaking for 30 minutes to a Sunday School class of 60 girls—Freshmen and Sophomores?" Young Lilienthal was already learning how to turn a potential handicap into a favorable advantage.

Except for one summer of school, college life was interrupted by summers filled with a range of experiences and extended family visits. Lilienthal worked on farms, in a railroad car assembly plant, on a Lake Michigan ore boat, and as a reporter. His longest-lived job was at the *Gary Tribune,* where he worked the summer of 1918. After graduation he caught a train west but ran out of money in Omaha. The highlight of his return was the thrill of riding on the same train with Wobbly William "Big Bill" Haywood, leader of the International Workers of the World.[14]

Lilienthal remained close to his parents. The family moved to Winamac, Indiana, in the spring of 1918, where Leo managed another Rosenak and Szold store. According to Helen, Leo "spent the happiest years he had there." Nevertheless, he struggled to support David and to anticipate middle son Ted's college expenses, which were to begin in 1920. It is clear that the elder Lilienthal never wavered in doing what he could for his son at DePauw and Harvard Law School.[15]

Lilienthal fretted all through college about his family's financial straits.

He wrote Helen that his father's situation made "getting friend Cecil R's scholarship more imperative." Other letters demonstrated a deep concern for Leo's well-being as he struggled "to provide for all of us." He also worried about a chronically strained relationship between Leo and Ted, who was somewhat irresponsible. David sternly judged his brother for the grief he caused their father and for his lack of direction. In contrast to his own deliberative style, he told Helen that Ted's "chief trouble is that he has no solid, legitimate, worthy *interest* to which he can attach himself." He frequently mediated disputes between Leo and Ted, and the equally stormy relationship between Aunt Bernadine and Uncle Jacob Szold and daughter Bernadine. Needless to say, Lilienthal was moved by his father's sturdy character and constant support when he wrote Helen in 1919, "I pray when I get where he is (he was 51 a few days since) I can *try* to do the square thing as honestly as he does." In exchange for the herculean efforts of his parents, especially in providing law school support, Lilienthal promised to help brother Allen through college when his turn came.[16]

Realizing the objections that might arise to their marriage plans, Helen and David held off telling their parents until he was a senior. When they broke the news, neither Helen's mother nor Leo raised much question. Minna Lilienthal was more reluctant: once in a while she would lament, as David reported, that her son was "not going to marry a Jewess." In general, she was supportive and worked diligently to accept and love her prospective daughter-in-law. As Helen Lilienthal observed, however, perhaps the parents "were more reconciled because there was no immediate prospect of marriage"—David still had to finish law school. Perhaps the parents felt time and distance would dim their ardor. If it did not, then the match might be worth making.[17]

In his years at DePauw, Lilienthal began to experience wide mood swings and compulsive tendencies, which disturbed Helen and would increasingly haunt him later in life. The early neuroses were noted in his early self-assessment that he was "a victim of the 'extremes'" and "rarely moderate in any of my activities, be they social, personal or what not." Helen made every effort from afar to slow him down, but in the spring of his senior year he wrote about seeing an osteopath because of his "nervous condition" and "rather unfortunate spells of exhaustion." Her advice to him to guard his energies, to drop some of his activities, helped as little then as it did in the next sixty-odd years. Through his sometimes frenetic activities, however, or perhaps in spite of them, Lilienthal began to formulate a coherent notion of his ideas, both sacred and secular, and of the mark he wanted to make in the world.[18]

A Point of View

As with students of every age, college life afforded Lilienthal the freedom to think critically about issues he had only dimly sensed earlier. By the end of his years at DePauw and Harvard Law School, he had worked out sophisticated and liberal frameworks of religious and civic understanding, both of which helped him formulate an expansive commitment to public life.

His early journal entries, letters, orations, and occasional jottings reflected a young man who recognized his Jewish roots, but who chafed at the constrictions of creed. His letters to Helen revealed the belief that all organized religion denied essential individuality. On one hand he rejected the orthodoxy of his mother's family as "narrow and dimly lighted as far as independent action and thought is concerned." It was important to "see things as a PERSON, not as a Lilienthal, or a Jew, or anything but an Individual." To protect his individuality, he was willing to risk being seen by family as a "temporarily deranged young Jew, who hasn't had the Jewish clan ideal pounded sufficiently into his instinctive being." Another time, he wrote of a confrontation with a fellow student, a "future 'pillar of the WCTU-Ladies' Aid-Sunday School' type," where he argued that he did not believe people "so lacking in individuality as to immediately be poured into some set mould of religion, as provided by the Baptists, the Methodists, the Jews, the Nazarenes, etc."[19]

His most revealing testimony was his sophomore oration. A half-year in the making, "The Mission of the Jew" was a tour de force, winning local, state, and regional competitions, suffering narrow defeat only after a tardy judge interrupted his oration in the Western Interstate contest. He gave the speech all over Indiana in assemblies and churches of every denomination. The first time around, critics called the speech "a trifle long," but said that it showed "thorough preparation and deep thinking." The five faculty members judging delivery gave him a unanimous first place over his two rivals. After his state victory, the school paper reported, with typical college enthusiasm, he "delivered his oration with the combined art of the actor and the orator. . . . His voice was perfect, his gestures were natural, and radiated the free spirit of the speaker who has his subject at heart, and is thoroughly familiar with his audience." It was, as the DePauw yearbook reported, "the first time . . . one orator was awarded first by every judge, both on manuscript and delivery."[20]

At one level the address was a means to an end—the successful execution of the "oratorical tricks of the kind fashionable at that time." He was attentive to effects, of the "deathlike silences when I became passionate, the thrill which went through the audience when I had finished." At another level, perhaps quite unexpectedly, it was an epiphany for a young man raised without the traditional trappings of faith. A few hours after the first delivery on December 19, 1917, he wrote that what had started merely as a contest ended "with an emotion and a passion I hardly believed I was capable of. My voice spoke truly the quiverings, the pleading, the tears, of my heart."[21]

The speech began with a passionate reprise of the plight of the Jew, "a people without a country, doomed to play the role of a despised wanderer, a perpetual 'world tragedy'." Nevertheless, faith endured, and so too the hope for the Jew and the whole world. In spite of persecution, in spite of the plight of nations pitting Jew against Jew, "this night shall end" in the "real-

ization of the mightiest of themes—THE UNITY OF GOD and THE UNITY OF MAN!"
For the young orator, monotheism and the brotherhood of man were the
indivisible components of all religion. Jews everywhere must transform "social clannishness [and a] vision of the Unity of God . . . into a compelling
concept of the Unity of Man!" He emphasized that world unity could come
only through peaceful transformation and love. The speech reflected a
strong reform spirit, rejecting the particularism of orthodoxy and celebrating the universality and oneness of God and man. Faith was important for
what it brought to the table of life—but once at the table, once put into
action, religion, at least creedal religion, was irrelevant.[22]

After this series of speeches, for the rest of his life, Lilienthal rarely
mentioned religion. Even when he did, it had no denominational reference.
As Helen Lilienthal noted, her husband "believed in God, but not God
confined to four walls." Lilienthal expressed faith in terms of publicness—
openness and unity rather than exclusiveness and division. All his life he
struggled to translate the worldly implications of that faith into a secular
doctrine of action.[23]

Lilienthal's political views also took shape at DePauw: he demonstrated
a keen sense of the depth of injustice in industrial America without suc-
cumbing to either cynical apathy or radicalism. College offered a chance to
exploit "an early interest in the study of history and politics, augmented by
considerable independent reading and observation." He suggested books
to Helen and was an avid reader of the *New Republic*. In his last two years
he concentrated on the social sciences, declaring, this was "the first time I
have had the opportunity of studying society and social forces in anything
resembling an organized fashion." During Christmas break of his senior
year, DePauw paid his way to the annual meeting of the American Economic Association and Sociology Society in Chicago. In addition to attend-
ing the conference, he interviewed "Big Bill" Haywood, leader of the International Workers of the World, for a school paper. In it, he concluded, "It
will be our wish that the country assume a changed front towards the problem of its radicals, substituting for the superficial and dangerous course of
concern one of intelleigent [sic] and tolerant understanding."[24]

While formal college training was crucial to the development of his
social views, his frequent visits to Chicago and the industrial suburbs also
contributed. He worked as a laborer the summer after his freshman year
and was struck by the dehumanizing nature of such work. He tried hard not
"to yield to the natural (for me) temptation to speak about socialism . . . , but
it seems evident and latent that all *is not* well—and something should be
changed to right an inhuman practice."[25]

His experience the next summer with the *Gary Tribune* moved him
even more. He was impressed by the violence of "a bloody fight between
black men, armed with razors" that he covered. A month into the job he
wrote Helen in a pitiable letter that "I am becoming less sure of my convictions, formed in the altruism and filmy idealism of secluded Greencastle."
Everything was tentative now, "my faith in the common man—in a true

democracy, in the end of wars—in the golden rule—in honesty." Two weeks later his confidence returned as he wrote her that "the 'boss' of this town, the Steel Corporation 'czar,' and I are now complete enemies."[26]

He kept in touch with cousin Bernadine (Dee) in Chicago during his DePauw days, writing often and visiting when he could. Both Dee and her second husband, Hi Simons, education director of the Workers Institute, an organization pledged "For the Education of the Workers by the Workers," tried to talk Lilienthal into joining the movement. In 1919, Simons urged him to "find your place in . . . the international proletarian revolution." Shortly before Lilienthal's graduation, Simons, this time writing as secretary of a prisoner amnesty group, the American Freedom Foundation, offered him a stenographer's job. Hi reminded Lilienthal that "you are radically, or at least liberally inclined . . . . [but] . . . you are about to decide upon a conservative career." Dee also wrote and urged him to take the job. She accused her cousin of "losing your virility—your aliveness—you seem to be out of harmony with the big pendulum of moving things," and pleaded with him "to get in it before you get to where you'll be past it for always."[27]

By this time Lilienthal had decided that the radical path was not for him. He concluded at the end of 1919 that he was interested in the question of labor, but that "for the present, I want to be a *student* of the problem," not a member of "any group aiming at an improvement or overthrowal of existing economic conditions." A year later he reviewed his own journey from early anarchism inspired by Emma Goldman and Alexander Berkman "to the strange debris which now clutters my mind." He adamantly rejected the "terrific quantity of cant and . . . large chunks of sticky, syruplike sentimentalism in the present radical revolutionary movement," and concluded that "too much passion is being lavished on dreaming of the revolution—too little thought expended on how it will be made a sane happy orderly revolution."[28]

In 1920, in recognition of its progressive reputation, Lilienthal tried to support the Republican ticket. He concluded, however, that the Harding camp had "so completely put to route the progressive element that I feel very skeptical." That summer, he attended the Farmer-Labor Party Convention in Chicago and came away with a new loyalty. He was thrilled to be "in touch with the *reality* of the labor movement and [to have his] academic conclusions and viewpoints drawn nearer the truth." In November 1920 he cast his first presidential ballot for the Farmer Labor candidate P. P. Christensen of Utah. Little could he realize that the ticket he first supported was the forerunner of the party of the La Follettes and that barely ten years later he would be a vital part of a Progressive administration in Wisconsin.[29]

Coming of Age—Ambition, Leadership, and Vocation

Lilienthal's early journal entries and letters revealed a young man obsessed with ambition—every action and activity was calculated for the future. His attraction to football was not camaraderie, but "the demand it makes of the fighting spirit." In his sophomore year one of his professors challenged, "I can take any student . . . . of only average ability, and . . . make a great man or women of him or her." Without hesitation, Lilienthal "stopped after class and challenged him to try it on me." He was not hesitant in using his prize-winning oration to extend his influence. In January 1918, he boldly asked an Indianapolis rabbi for help in "increas[ing] my audience either orally or thru the printing of the manuscript." He even offered to change the speech "to suit a Jewish audience better than [the present speech] which is intended for a Gentile one."[30]

By the end of 1918, he felt good about being able "to know men better than ever before, and to *demand* more, rather than timidly ask." In August 1919 he confessed to Helen that "my old ambitions—the adolescent dreams of greatness and fame and power—have been coming back over me like an irresistable [sic] flood." He continued that "I honestly crave a chance to use my powers for the sake of something bigger than myself, bigger than any individual." A month earlier, he signed another letter to Helen, "Son of Jessee [sic]"—a signature any Jew, secular or not, would recognize as an allusion to the Messiah.[31]

At DePauw, Lilienthal took every opportunity to prepare for the future. He was ecstatic about being able to delegate responsibility, telling Helen that "the training in letting others take care of details and saving your strength has been bigger than anything I've ever had before." He recognized the power of his "spirit of initiative" and his skill in mediating disputes "between members of the Freshman and Sophomore classes, [and] the 'Daily' staff and the Administration." As a junior, he was instrumental in ending a clash between students and faculty over a cheating scandal. The faculty wanted students to report cheating but the students wanted an honor system. Always the reconciler, Lilienthal asked the two groups to meet halfway. If they did, "the growing state of jealousy and factionalism between students will soon be changed." The *DePauw Daily* praised his proposal, which would "bring student opinion of the sanest sort directly to the faculty and bridge the gulf which now separates that body from the students." For several months, until the students finally prevailed, the student newspaper kept close track of every move of this energetic student leader.[32]

In his last spring, Lilienthal became involved in several controversies that piqued the faculty. In February, he protested the use of ineligible athletes. In May, after the faculty voted to take over the *DePauw Daily*, Lilienthal once again took to his charismatic pen. He called the decision to place the paper "in the hands of a department-dictator . . . a grave mistake," and charged, "It seems very clear that high-school methods are being applied, by high-school–minded people, to college men and women, living in a college atmosphere." In a hastily published underground paper, Lilienthal asserted that "the Daily should not become a laboratory for classes in journalism any more than the electrict [sic] lighting system on the campus should be a laboratory for the Physics class." According to a somewhat shaken young man, only the intervention of faculty mentors kept him from discipline that might have delayed his graduation. In retrospect, these controversies provided good seasoning for future battles with much higher stakes and more serious consequences.[33]

Rhetoric was another carefully cultivated skill. Lilienthal was a keen student of the spoken word, sometimes more interested in the delivery of a speech than in its content. He evaluated "Mission of the Jew" more in terms of "the expanding influence of the training . . . [and] . . . getting up before every sort of audience" than in terms of its impact on religious understanding. In reacting to a labor speech in December 1919, he was less concerned with substance than the clinical observation that "*big* men, really great men, can say radical things which a smaller one would be deported for, and get downright conservatives to applaud them." While covering a Progressive candidate for Congress for the Matoon, Illinois, *Daily Journal Gazette* in the summer of 1920, he was impressed that the candidate "made folks believe it, because he spoke their language." The same summer at the Farmer-Labor Convention, he reported that he learned "something of the tricks and devices of convincing speakers and its effect on a most unusual and critical audience." While he reflected some on substance, most of his commentary on the convention focused on speechmaking and the psychological dimensions of the gathering.[34]

But what kind of vocation could satisfy such ambition? Early on, the young dreamer thought of "social service." As a junior, he told the state Rhodes Scholarship committee that he was going "to prepare for the public service, through an apprenticeship in the study and practice of law." Inspired by the roll of lawyers at the 1920 Farm-Labor Convention, Lilienthal concluded that the legal profession was the highest calling. Occasionally, as a senior, his lawyerly resolve wavered. He was concerned about his father's ability to finance him, and worried that "the average of young lawyer's fees make the traditionally pinched college professor look like a malefactor of great wealth." Another time he became anxious about Harvard Law School standards and asked Fred Arvin, then a Harvard undergraduate, to investigate. His friend wrote back that no doubt, "Harvard Law School is a dam [*sic*] tough proposition and . . . means three years of a pretty stiff grind." Nevertheless, he assured his friend that all the "grind" did was "clear out the incompetents, and leave the men who really show promise." Fred pulled out all the stops in convincing David that he was a "promising" prospect.[35]

He talked about working awhile at manual labor to understand those "who have not enjoyed the sheltered, protected life which has been mine." Granting the nobility of his sentiments, it is likely that this option, like Hi and Dee Simons's offer, was not serious. Lilienthal was in a hurry. He turned down the job Simons had offered him because he thought it would place him further behind in making his mark. So would a year in a factory. Moreover, he craved the security of a "definite profession" while pursing "social construction work." Being a realist, Lilienthal understood that the key to power lay in lawyering and not laboring. After the 1920 convention, he recalled the "distrust of lawyers expressed by most of the speakers in the . . . convention." Nevertheless, "when something had to be done, they got lawyers to do it." Most of the leaders were lawyers, the greatest speeches were made by lawyers, and all the nominees for president, except Eugene Debs, were lawyers. He concluded, "It seems to me that political control inevitably devolves into the hand of the student of the law—the lawyer—almost whether he wills it or not." If there had been lingering doubts, this revelation probably did them in. Law school it was —and nothing less than Harvard Law School would do.[36]

Harvard Law School

First among equals, the Cambridge school had been *the* law school ever since Dean Christopher Columbus Langdell left his mark in the late nineteenth century. His legacy of a tough professional curriculum guided by the Socratic case method was precisely the challenge to appeal to someone of ambition. Lilienthal was attracted to Harvard because of its reputation "as the best law school in the country," and also for the chance to sample the cosmopolitan landscape of New England. He was drawn most of all, however, by its reputation for emphasizing the economic and political issues of the times. Roscoe Pound, who assumed the deanship after the death of Ezra Ripley Thayer in 1915, initiated what Arthur E. Sutherland called the era of "social and governmental trends." Along with Pound, who believed that law must relate to the everyday social and economic realties, the faculty included Zechariah Chafee and Felix Frankfurter, both considered by many alumni to be "obnoxious radicals."[37]

Fred Arvin was on target in advising David that "considering the 'advertiser' element in your make-up, it seems to me the chances would be strong for your being very enthusiastic about the place." In his first semester, he thrilled at the adversarial challenges, "feeling much as a fencer does when he has just crossed swords with a master." By his second year the amateur was reveling in his ability to match the master. In October 1921 he told Helen he had held his own in a debate with Professor Calvert Magruder over "the use of the injunction in labor disputes." (Lilienthal was against it.) He reported that their set-to, which ended amicably, was "as wild a polemical discourse as you ever see," and was immensely pleased at the "wholesome and healthful self-confidence" it gave him.[38]

His first-year average was 68, a solid C+. He did best in Criminal Law and Property, missing a B average only because of D work in Contracts. He was not above embellishing his record a bit, even to Helen: when he received his grades he told her he had a B+ average. He also informed lawyer Frank Walsh that his first-year average "puts me well up in my class." As a junior, his average rose to 70. He performed best under Frankfurter in Public Utilities class and in Equity under his sparring partner Magruder, recently returned from a clerkship with Justice Brandeis. Buoyed by Helen's presence at nearby Radcliffe his last year, he had an A average with high marks in Constitutional Law, Restraint of Trade, and Labor Law. He earned a faculty scholarship his senior year and was asked by Dean Pound to supervise a first-year club.[39]

But Lilienthal's Harvard years (at least until Helen moved east) were not without their low spots. He continued fretting over his father's financial reverses, first a $5,000 business loss and a further setback when Ted dropped out of DePauw after his dad had invested a considerable sum. He complained on a regular basis of sickly spells and in June 1921 was afflicted by the first of his many lifetime bouts with insomnia.

In a comedy of misunderstanding with his father in January 1922, Lilienthal momentarily felt "much inclined to pitch up the whole business, and go into the labor movement the way I'd like to [as a labor organizer]." Leo, already concerned about David's labor law ambitions, saw a pamphlet on John Reed which James McGill had sent his son. Since David had talked about going to Europe the next summer, Leo inexplicably panicked and warned his son that radical forces were "working to send you in to Russia to openly connect you with the movement and likely make a goat of you and kill your chances for ever." He pleaded with his son not "to throw your life away before you start it, on something visionary, something that will take hundreds of years to hammer in to the world." After David's strong letter of denial and reassurance, Leo sheepishly replied that he had overreacted to the parallels between Reed and his son (both Harvard men, both "labor men," both with interests in Europe) and lovingly reiterated his wholehearted support.[40]

Whatever Lilienthal's momentary hesitations, they were easily stilled by his drive and uncanny sense of calculation. He wrote Helen during his second year "—but God!—I am ambitious. . . . I don't often admit it, even to myself—this inordinate desire for leadership, but that I have it, I never can honestly deny." He continued, noting "I want power because I want to breathe the breath of life into ideas—great rugged ideas which have stalked for centuries, as ghosts in the hearts of slaves and persecuted."[41]

He knew for sure the end of his first semester that "corporation work" was not for him. The lawyers who did "the sort of thing I hope to do" included "Mr. Justice Brandeis, with his great . . . briefs; Mr. Clarence Darrow in the many labor leader trials he has fought in; Frankfurter and Chafee, who have opposed repression during the war . . . ; and Mr. Frank P. Walsh, former Chairman of the Industrial Relations Commission." In his second year, he observed that because of "the establishment of boards of skilled men, such as the Inter-state Commerce Commission, the state utilities commissions, the Labor Board, . . . the field of work for men trained in legal and quasi-legal methods has widened, not narrowed." Already he was looking toward the opportunity that might propel him to some yet undefined prominence.[42]

And he began thinking about getting "such a man as Brandeis or Walsh interested in me and my ambitions." At Helen's suggestion he wrote Walsh in 1921. Perhaps to his later (but only temporary) regret, Walsh promptly replied. That was all the encouragement the aggressive student needed. For the next year and a half he plied Walsh with letters, each graciously answered, about everything under the sun—law school chatter, Lilienthal's ideas about labor, reading habits, and even summer activities. He traveled to New York City twice to see his hero and was crushed both times when Walsh was unavailable. Finally, on his way from Indiana to Cambridge in September 1922, he met the legendary attorney. While there seems little doubt that Lilienthal made a pest of himself with his relentless petitions, he ultimately made the favorable impression he wanted: In November 1922, Walsh offered to help him look for a job after graduation.[43]

Lilienthal approached Frankfurter with similar enthusiasm. At their first meeting in May 1921, he told the professor "there is no one in the country better qualified than you" to advise about a career in labor law. Later that month he wrote Helen that Frankfurter had taken to him and affirmed that labor law afforded "a grand opportunity" for any young man. He told the freshman that to succeed, one needed to be proficient in *all* of the law—"to know as much about corporation law as the so-called corporation lawyer, and as much about the laws of persons as the divorce lawyer." Frankfurter inveighed against "radical lawyers" because they lacked broad training and suggested the only "reason the unions pick them up . . . was because they . . . couldn't trust the others." Near the close of the letter Lilienthal revealed his long-range plan for Frankfurter: After three years, "I should be well acquainted with him. Then I ought to be ready to bear the fruits of such an acquaintanceship, if not by that time, friendship. I am very optimistic of the results." Once again, the student from Indiana had good reason for optimism. Whichever way he might turn, he was building a sturdy network for the years to come.[44]

Intellectual Seasoning

While at Harvard, Lilienthal sampled widely from opinions about American labor. Less influenced now by Dee and the Chicago crowd because of distance, he still listened to the radical alternative. He attended meetings where W. Z. Foster, head of the Communist-dominated Trade Union Education League, railed against the "selfishness and corruption on the part of the old-line leadership" and called for a new militancy in American labor. But those exhortations, like the earlier ones by Dee and Hi, had little effect, especially when weighed against the influence of professors like Frankfurter who, although called radical, were extremely critical of truly radical options.[45]

Lilienthal became a hard realist for whom "life is very complex, and no such simple solution [as revolution] is available." In 1921 he wrote Helen that an impending railroad strike was "an example of what the private ownership and exploitation of a purely public function leads to. . . . To allow private citizens to own and exploit [the railroads] for private purposes naturally leads to disorder." Nevertheless, he was skeptical of the chances for success because present law and injunctive powers gave private interests the upper hand. He reiterated that "one strike won't end this dispute, and it is better for labor to lose now, than to win what can only be a temporary victory—a truce—under present fighting conditions."[46]

In May 1923, Lilienthal, with Fred Arvin's help, published his first article in the *New Republic*. He was pleased that it "created a good deal of comment among my colleagues and teachers." The article, entitled "Labor and the Courts," reflected his finely honed position—pro-labor, anti-revolutionary, with a heavy dose of sociological jurisprudence. The near-graduate observed, "Labor has a thoroughgoing distrust and suspicion of the courts" and warned that "the presence of a court, enjoying the confidence of people generally is really all that lies between social adjustment and social disorder." For Lilienthal, legislative reform was only part of the solution. In the main, reform would happen only when a new breed of judges took over. Invoking Brandeisian logic, he called for "great judges—men who can discern the *social* principles involved in the legal problem before them," who can cast off "the exaggerated importance of property, and a disregard of industrial and economic facts in face of preconceived legal doctrines." In concluding, he invoked "Holmes, Brandeis, Baker, Alschuler, George W. Anderson and Cardozo" in support of his prediction that "within a generation the bench will be at least strongly flavored with the type of socially-minded, creative judge I have spoken of."[47]

The article was a fitting valedictory for seven years of intellectual development and preparation for vocation. It reflected a keen mind, with critical yet optimistic inclinations, and a sure sense of commitment to the labor struggles of the 1920s. It was an apt bridge between the intellectual life of a student and a professional beginning under one of the most distinguished labor attorneys of the times, Donald R. Richberg.

CHAPTER 3

A Young Professional Makes His Mark

By far the most exhaustive and authoritative study that has
yet appeared on [the holding company] is that by Mr. David
E. Lilienthal.
 —James C. Bonbright and Gardiner C. Means,
 *The Holding Company: Its Public Significance
 and Its Regulation,* 1932

A Fast Start: Job, Marriage, and Family

In November 1922, Lilienthal wrote Frank Walsh that he did not
want to work in a small city that might disfavor someone who "took an
active interest in the problems of the working people" or one with a large
firm with "little chance of contact with the older and more experienced
lawyers." Walsh advised his young charge to forget about the South because it "is about where we were twenty five years ago." He recommended
Chicago, Kansas City, or Cleveland, and advised, "I would pick [Donald
Richberg] . . . of all the lawyers that I know, if I were in your position."[1]

Walsh could not have suggested a better mentor. A native of Chicago,
Richberg graduated from the University of Chicago in 1901 and Harvard
Law School in 1904 and started practice in his father's Chicago firm. At
first, law for Richberg was only a tedious vocation serving a critical muck-
raking pen and a love of local reform politics. He quickly became allied
with leaders of the movement, including Jane Addams, Charles E. Merriam,
and Harold Ickes Sr., his law partner between 1913 and 1923, and in 1912,
he worked hard to certify Progressive candidates for the Illinois ballot.

In his early years he was best known for his work on behalf of the city
of Chicago against Samuel Insull's Peoples Gas Corporation. In 1920, "in a
curiously indirect way," Richberg entered the fray on labor's side. Glen
Plumb, Richberg's gas case associate, was a well-known labor attorney and
author of "The Plumb Plan," which proposed returning the nationalized
American railway system to a tripartite council of owners, government,

and labor representatives. He also offered to help Senator Robert A. La Follette Sr. develop a comprehensive valuation of American railway properties. By 1920, Plumb was overwhelmed by his responsibilities, and Richberg took over the valuation task. In May 1923 Richberg became general counsel of the National Conference on Valuation of Railroads. Plumb's untimely death in 1922 further thrust Richberg in the midst of American railway labor activities.[2]

Lilienthal quickly responded to Walsh's advice with a letter to Richberg. Although he explored other options and received several offers, Richberg was the constant target of his affections: "The more I heard of Mr. Richberg, the more eager I became to make that connection." For the next eight months, Lilienthal plied Richberg with letter after fawning letter. In December he vowed not to take any position until "you have definitely rejected my application." In the same letter he commended Richberg for a recent *Yale Law Review* article, telling him that Frankfurter liked the study and that "I was deeply impressed with the skill which you applied present day economic doctrines and economic facts to a legal problem." In other winter and spring letters and a visit during spring break, Lilienthal constantly emphasized his desire to work for Richberg.[3]

In spite of Walsh's and Frankfurter's strong recommendations, the job with Richberg proved elusive. In November, he told Lilienthal he could not promise a job since he was severing ties with his father's firm to practice alone. In December he advised the student not to come to Chicago since "such a trip would not bring about any satisfactory results at the present time." In March 1923 Richberg wrote, "I do not see a reasonable possibility of offering you a place in the near future." By May, however, pressed by several labor cases, his new role as general counsel for the National Conference on Valuation of Railroads, and pressure from Frankfurter, Richberg hinted that something might open up in June. After a long summer wait and an August visit with Richberg, the anxious young attorney finally recorded, "He decided to take me on immediately [and] I began work on the 20th."[4]

Two weeks later, on September 4, Helen and David were married in Crawfordsville by Dr. George Gross, president of DePauw. According to Lilienthal, the joy of the wedding day followed six weeks of family debate over "the prospect of my marrying a 'shicksa.'" Led by Aunt Bertha and Uncle Adolph Rosenak, all the relatives exerted pressure to cancel the wedding. At one point Bertha complained to Leo, "but he told her, after what must have been a stormy session, that this was none of her business." Unbeknownst to Helen until afterwards, the protestations had no effect on either strong-willed David or his faithful parents.[5]

Immediately after the wedding David and Helen moved to a Southside Chicago hotel and then to a one-room apartment facing Jackson Park on East Sixty-seventh Street. Helen taught part-time at the Starrett School for Girls for $125 a month, $25 more than David's initial salary. Their first year together ended with Helen spending a month in a local osteopathic hospital gravely ill with typhoid fever. Lilienthal was deeply shaken, confessing that he was never "more desolate than during the first ten days of Helen's illness." At year's end, he summed up its momentous events; marriage, graduation from Harvard, his job, and a budding "hoped for 'literary' career," and asked, "Will I *ever* have more things happen to me in one little year?"[6]

A Decade of Trial: The Struggle for Labor Justice

Lilienthal could not have picked a more inauspicious time to begin his career. The twenties was a seductive era, characterized by glitter without and decline within. On one hand, it was a hopeful time, and prosperity seemed within reach of the ordinary citizen. In the aggregate, incomes rose and even outpaced inflation. Business thrived and technical advances promised a cornucopia of never-imagined consumer wonders. But the glitter sparkled for only a relative few. High unemployment figures persisted, ranging from 10 to 13 percent over the decade. At one point in the 1920s, one-third of all American families made less than $2,000 a year, the minimum for a decent life style. Wage earners had few fringe benefits, old age pensions were nonexistent, and personal savings minimal.

Organized labor seemed helpless in the face of this unsettling reality. Between 1920 and 1923, AFL membership fell 25 percent and unions did little organizing outside the traditional sectors. In part, the problem lay in the vast rural and southern black migration, spurred by the disastrous collapse of agricultural prices. This new mass defied traditional organizing strategies and provided a willing labor pool to keep those with jobs in line. Other forces vitiating the influence of organized labor included a pervasive positive business image, the threat of new technology to old jobs, company unions, and the deceptive patina of prosperity.

Institutional stagnation posed the main threat to American labor. By the 1920s, organized labor had chosen accommodation as the surest road to success. Samuel Gompers, the only leader the American Federation of Labor (AFL) ever had, became increasingly conservative and business oriented, and his virulent anticommunism shut the door to European influences. His opposition to social and minimum wage legislation, unemployment and health insurance, and old age pensions further stifled innovative concepts and ideas. Moreover, in standing firm for craft unionism in an era in which industrywide organization seemed more appropriate, Gompers and his cohorts failed to capitalize on a large unorganized mass. Ultimately however, mainstream labor leaders may merely have been realists. As Bernstein noted, "With business supreme, the AFL sought to sell itself as a necessary auxiliary of business."[7]

The redefinition of public purpose in Washington was almost as devastating. As Wilson became first warrior, and then invalid, his progressive vision retreated into memory. Moreover, increasing official assaults on the left, symbolized by the Sedition Act of 1918 and Attorney General A.

Mitchell Palmer's infamous raids on political agitators in 1920 further discouraged those who hoped that reform would continue. The election of Warren Harding in 1920 was the crowning blow to the notion that government should have an active and positive role in the life of the nation. Not many months passed before the commissions and boards established to regulate business and special interests became apologists and protectors for those same interests.

Worst of all, the courts took dead aim at unions. Inspired by Chief Justice William Howard Taft, who warned in 1922 that labor was "that faction we have to hit every little while," judges were merciless in their handling of antitrust suits and injunctions. Between 1919 and 1929, unions or members were defendants in more Sherman Anti-Trust cases than in the previous thirty years, and the restraining order was used with a vengeance to stifle labor protest. Of nearly two thousand injunctions ordered by state and federal courts between 1880 and 1930, more than nine hundred were issued in the 1920s. For Richberg, the most damaging was "an outrageous restraining order by Judge [James] Wilkerson in Chicago against railway shopmen in the railroad strike of 1922." The order, instigated by U.S. Attorney General Harry S. Daugherty, handcuffed everyone on labor's side, even attorneys, and charged striking workers with seventeen thousand crimes. It was no wonder, as Lilienthal observed in his 1923 *New Republic* article, that "labor has a thoroughgoing distrust and suspicion of the courts."[8]

Richberg and Lilienthal

Nevertheless, labor could count on a small, dedicated coterie of lawyers like Donald R. Richberg, who fought passionately for the working man. Lilienthal's three-year tenure with Richberg provided a strong lesson about the strength of private privilege in America—and the power of law in fighting that privilege. Richberg was quick to praise, not afraid of delegating responsibility, and gentle in criticism. Lilienthal responded with a zeal that often left him physically and mentally drained. Their bond was strong because of similarities and because the student learned easily from the master. In 1923, Richberg wrote Lilienthal and another associate, Leo J. Hassenauer, that part of his job was "to help in the self-development of younger men who will carry the same sort of work on to better service than I shall be able to perform," and he was pleased with "the way you both go at your work." Lilienthal answered that his first months had "been the happiest of my life. You have been so much more than an able lawyer, from whom I could learn . . . : for that ineffable something . . . I am deeply and humbly grateful." Two years later he wrote in his journal that "our temperaments are similar. . . . Our labor sympathies spring from similar sources. Our interest in writing is helpful. . . . A conference with him is the greatest imaginable mental stimulus and I sometimes have enough from a couple hours talk . . . to keep me at a pitch of enthusiasm for weeks."[9]

Both had a strong need for acceptance, fierce pride of ambition, and a sometimes annoying self-righteousness. Each had rejected formal religion and shared a strong literary bent. While neither man was particularly original, they both demonstrated, as Richberg's biographer, Thomas E. Vadney, noted of his subject, an "ability to articulate and synthesize much of what people . . . were thinking." In calling Richberg "a skilled popularizer and propagandist," Vadney could not have described Richberg's young colleague any better.[10]

Thoroughgoing progressives, they had similar views of society and the role of law. Both rejected radicalism and sought fair treatment and equity for labor, not revolutionary ends. In a similar fashion their views on public utility reform stressed fair consumer rates, not socialization. Both men believed in the crucial role of law and lawyers. Just as Lilienthal was impressed by lawyers at the 1920 Farmer-Labor Convention and by the power of "legal procedure" in the service of reform, Richberg's early indifference to the law had given way to a strong belief in its key role in politics. If law and the courts could act as handmaidens for vested interests, Richberg reasoned, they could also serve labor's interests. Vadney's description of Richberg as a technician "in the service of reform," as a "man with the know-how to protect the public interest," fit Lilienthal as well. Thoroughness in work was always one of Lilienthal's strong points. By the end of the decade he was well schooled in utility law and ready to apply that knowledge to new challenges in public life.[11]

Lilienthal's years with Richberg provided a grand opportunity for professional maturation. With their boss in Washington much of the time working for the Valuation Conference or on new railroad legislation, Lilienthal and Hassenauer were left with broad discretion. While worrying on occasion about overspecializing in labor law, Lilienthal did insurance fraud and contract case work, and was introduced to public utility law working with Richberg for the City of Chicago in a series of suits against Samuel Insull's Peoples Gas Corporation. His most dramatic moment came when he served as junior counsel to Clarence Darrow and Arthur Garfield Hays in the Ossian Sweet case in Detroit in 1925. After Sweet, a black medical doctor, escaped conviction for firing into a mob about to storm his house, Lilienthal concluded in The Nation that the "trial was probably the fairest ever accorded a Negro in this country" and represented great progress for "the black man."[12]

In 1924 he got his first touch of party politics, helping Richberg get Progressive Robert La Follette Sr.'s name on all forty-eight state presidential ballots. His feelings about the campaign reflected an ambiguity about the process. He was not much taken by the day-to-day grind, confiding to Fred Arvin, "I've lost the fine enthusiasm that we had when Teddy was fighting for Armageddon et al in 1912—I don't care much about trying to convert people as I did then." Right before the election he bragged to Fred that he and Helen had worked in their ward, but Helen later confessed they had worked "in the wrong precinct, over the line from the precinct we were supposed to be in."[13]

On the other hand, he delighted in the rhetorical game. Assigned to dig up dirt on Coolidge's running mate, Charles Dawes, Lilienthal wrote a raucous exposé in *The Nation* two weeks before the election. He pulled no punches, charging the self-described law-and-order candidate with being "personally involved in a shady piece of financial shystery, evasion of law and deception of public officials." He accused Dawes of illegally loaning a friend's bank $1,250,000 to keep a bank examiner from denying a state charter. He then ridiculed Dawes for praising the Daugherty railroad injunction "as the beginning of a new era of law and order" and for claiming "that the Constitution makes it *mandatory* upon our judges to issue injunctions against the workers whenever they strike [or] threaten to strike." Lilienthal concluded by juxtaposing "the private 'constitution'. . . designed to safeguard Mr. Dawes and his companions . . . [with] the Constitution of the United States, . . . which purports first of all to protect human rights and human liberties."[14]

Lilienthal's proudest work was squarely in labor law: he was largely responsible for preparing two U.S. Supreme Court briefs, a portion of a brief Richberg used in arguing an ICC railroad valuation case, and a major section of the 1926 Railroad Labor Act. Lilienthal's first assignment was "a considerable part of the brief to the U.S. Supreme Court" in *Michaelson v. U.S.*, a case involving railroad workers accused of criminal contempt for violating the 1922 railroad strike injunction. The defendants asked for a jury trial, claiming that Section 20 of the Clayton Act permitted juries when the act of contempt constituted a crime. The federal judge held the provision unconstitutional and convicted the men himself. After the first appeal lost, Richberg took over because "organized labor could not afford to have a federal law providing for jury trial held unconstitutional by any tribunal short of the Supreme Court."[15]

Richberg and Lilienthal argued that the circuit court decision erred in ruling that, by striking, the men voided the condition of employment and were no longer employees; in concluding that the defendants forfeited employee status, as the Boston Police had in 1919, because they participated in an illegal strike against a government agency, the Federal Labor Board; and finally, in declaring the jury provision of the Clayton Act unconstitutional. The brief addressed the first error, arguing that the defendants' status during the strike constituted "a *changed* but not a *terminated* relationship of employment." The brief challenged the second error, pointing out that the strike was against the companies, not the Federal Labor Board, which had little power to compel settlement. Finally, Richberg and Lilienthal's reply distinguished between civil and criminal contempt and argued that in the Anglo-American tradition, jury trials in *criminal* contempt cases constituted the norm. It concluded, in any case, that constitutional provisions in Article Three and the Sixth Amendment mandated jury trials in all criminal cases, including contempt.[16]

In what Richberg described as a "landmark decision," the court overturned the lower court in October 1924, holding that criminal contempt jury trials were constitutional. The court also ruled that the "Labor Board was not an employer, but an arbitrator, whose determination, moreover, had only the force of moral suasion." Lilienthal was thrilled over the part he had played and for the $100 bonus he received after the decision was handed down.[17]

His efforts were not so uncritically received by friends. Law school classmate Rudolf Berle, called the brief "convincing" but criticized the argument "that a strike does not terminate the *relation* of employer and employee." Berle felt that calling a striker an employee was awkward reasoning: Lilienthal, his friend noted, might better have argued that the Clayton Act used "the term 'employee' inartistically," and that Congress intended to extend the right of jury trial to all persons accused of criminal contempt regardless of employment status.[18]

Professor Frankfurter was blunter: "I was disappointed in your brief." He criticized Lilienthal for "trying to do too many things at the same time," and reminded him that he and Richberg "were trustees for some of the most vital issues in American constitutional law that have come before the Supreme Court." Frankfurter was particularly irked at the claim that a jury trial in criminal contempt cases was an absolute constitutional right. He told Lilienthal his argument "did not begin to scratch the surface and it resorted to arguments . . . that did not hold water because they have been conclusively rejected by the court." Lilienthal gamely admitted that "confining my energies has always been an extremely trying piece of discipline for me," and that the brief was written under an "extraordinary pressure of time." He persisted, however, in defending his argument, noting that Justice Holmes had said in another case that "trial by jury . . . has been thought not to extend to [criminal contempt cases] as a matter of constitutional right." Lilienthal justified his thin argument, pointing out that Holmes had said "*thought* not to extend to them" rather than "*does not* extend to them." Nevertheless, since the court ruled in favor of the defendants, neither of the purported lapses damaged the case.[19]

In 1924, Lilienthal became involved in "the most important piece of legal work on which I have been engaged so far." In June 1924, the Railroad Labor Board, believing a strike was imminent, subpoenaed 102 railroad employees to a Chicago hearing. Two respondents, J. B. Robertson of Cleveland and J. M. McGuire of Chicago, refused to testify, and the board asked Judge Wilkerson to issue a summons. Wilkerson did so, but they still refused. Richberg moved to dismiss Robertson's summons, claiming that Chicago courts had no jurisdiction over a Cleveland resident, and McGuire's because the actions violated Article 3 of the Constitution and the Fourth, Fifth, and Tenth Amendments. Wilkerson denied the motions, and the defense appealed.[20]

The Supreme Court accepted Robertson's appeal, and Lilienthal spent much of late 1924 on the case. The brief, which he prepared and Richberg revised, was more than 140 pages long and argued that Wilkerson overextended his authority in serving a process outside his district. Lilienthal recognized that the 1920 Transportation Act authorized the Labor Board to "invoke the aid of any United States District Court," but asserted that the courts and Congress had consistently interpreted "*any* court" to mean "any court of *competent* jurisdiction." He then asked the court to dismiss the order to testify because the Labor Board had no authority regarding legal rights and that citizens were compelled to testify only when such testimony was "sought for the purpose of determining legal rights and obligations." Therefore, mandatory testimony would deprive a defendant "of liberty and property without due process of law." In conclusion, Lilienthal ingeniously argued that in assisting a policy board such as the Railroad Labor Board, the court itself would become part of the policymaking process. Such action, he noted, would violate the "ancient policy" whereby "the determination of questions of public policy under our system of law . . . has always been refused by the courts."[21]

In June 1925 the Supreme Court reversed Wilkerson. Lilienthal was elated because they adopted "the line of reasoning (and even the material) in the brief which I prepared in large part." Justice Brandeis's opinion, however, based the court's reasoning only on the jurisdiction argument. He concluded that, whatever the wording of the Transportation Act, Congress had not intended to depart from a longstanding policy that restricted the jurisdiction of district courts "to the district of which the defendant is an inhabitant or in which he can be found."[22]

Always ready to capitalize, Lilienthal shaped his Robertson work into his first law review article in the April 1926 *Harvard Law Review*. He argued that courts had consistently allowed agencies such as the ICC and Federal Trade Commission to compel testimony in regulatory or rule-making cases, but not in fact-finding investigations. Lilienthal contended, however, that the courts had not denied Congress the power "to authorize the compulsion of testimony in purely fact-finding expeditions," but had struck down such attempts only because they never had legal authorization. He continued that Congress could constitutionally authorize any "testimonial duty, regardless of the character of the investigation." In conclusion, Lilienthal argued that national welfare "will some day depend upon the power of a public tribunal to secure full, complete and continuous access to the facts, . . . [and] the Supreme Court should give every possible weight to the judgment of Congress" should it extend the testimonial powers of government agencies. In doing so, Lilienthal reversed his earlier position that the Labor Board's summons was a breach of the Constitution. His new position was vindicated six years later when he crafted a tough public utility law in Wisconsin which authorized the Public Service Commission to conduct sweeping investigations on any matters related to public utilities.[23]

Lilienthal's other major responsibilities involved research on the *O'Fallon* railroad valuation case and helping prepare new national railroad legislation. In the *O'Fallon* case, Lilienthal's contribution was relatively minor, but his research gave him background on property rights which proved useful later in his efforts to challenge the private utilities' monopoly in the Tennessee Valley. *O'Fallon* was part of a debate about how utility properties should be valuated for rate and profit determination. Industry argued that valuation should be based on the current cost of reproducing the properties, and progressives countered that "reproduction cost" calculations almost always led to inflated appraisals and, hence, higher rates and profits. They called instead for a "Brandeisian" approach that combined original cost estimates plus relevant, or "prudent," company investments. Arguing the "prudent investment" theory, Richberg convinced the ICC to order the recapture of excess earnings by the St. Louis and O'Fallon Railway Company, which had appraised its properties on a "reproduction cost" basis. While the decision was ultimately reversed by the U.S. Supreme Court, it was a harbinger of a time when, as Richberg noted, "'prudent investment theory' . . . [would become] a part of the law of the land." In anticipation of O'Fallon's argument that recapture of earnings was unconstitutional property confiscation, Lilienthal's eighty-four-page essay stressed the limited sanctity of property rights. According to Lilienthal, the only limitation on legislatively mandated property confiscation was due process, which itself was "a *variable*, depending upon the time, the place, the balance between the public need and the private burden and upon the *mores* of the people of a particular community at a particular time."

In a 1927 article, Lilienthal argued that court-imposed remedies in cases like O'Fallon were often inferior to those of "expert administrators" such as the ICC. All too often, courts failed to consider economic or social factors. He concurred with ICC Commissioner Joseph Eastman's passionate defense of its *O'Fallon* decision, which relied extensively on economic factors: "But certainly we ought not to deprive the court of the help which it may gain from the special knowledge which it is our duty under the law to acquire."[24]

Lilienthal's longest-lived project for Richberg and the one for which he received the most public credit was his work on new railway legislation. The impetus for the act was the failure of the 1920 Transportation Act to establish a fair and stable bargaining process between railway workers and companies. Between 1921 and 1923, railroad disputes escalated and the Railroad Labor Board lost all effectiveness because of union mistrust. In June 1923, a "Special Legislative Committee Representing the Recognized Railroad Labor Organizations" asked Richberg to draft new legislation. When Lilienthal started in August 1923, Richberg, more and more involved in valuation matters and "busy . . . in the various investigations that exposed the utter rottenness of the Harding administration," put him to work on the legislation. According to Vadney, Lilienthal prepared sections of the bill on "arbitration, mediation, and conciliation; individual and collective employment contracts; and court precedents and statute law dealing with labor organization."[25]

After the bill was introduced in Congress in February 1924, Lilienthal became an ardent publicist. In March he circulated an impassioned paper defending the new bill as "a practical plan" drafted by "veteran railroaders . . . who know thoroughly the 'human side' of railroading." In April the

New Republic published his stinging rebuke of the 1920 Act: "Never before in the history of railroad labor legislation has a law so quickly and
overwhelmingly been proved a failure." He noted that all sides, including
the public, were disillusioned with the act, and called for new legislation to
provide fair representation and effective mediation, conciliation, and grievance procedures. In May he fired another salvo in the *Machinist's Monthly
Journal,* an influential labor publication. Lilienthal stressed there had "never
been a finer piece of practical industrial statesmanship" than the pending
bill. No longer would company unions take over or company power be
skewed by the so-called government-appointed "public representatives" in
bargaining. The new act would give labor the best opportunity for serving
the public's three greatest wishes, "continuity," "safety," and "efficiency."[26]

Even with Harding's and Coolidge's support and endorsements in the
three major 1924 platforms, the reform bill was stalled by the carriers until
the spring of 1926, when Congress overwhelmingly approved the bill and
Coolidge reluctantly signed it. The 1926 Railway Labor Act, according to
Bernstein, was "an artfully drawn composite of workable features of railroad labor laws going back to 1888 . . . and the only federal labor statute of
significance passed during the decade." He noted that the bill was drafted
by Richberg, "with the aid of his assistant, David E. Lilienthal." Richberg
gave Lilienthal credit for "infinitely valuable assistance" on the bill, attest-
ing that his contribution "laid the foundations for a great improvement in
arbitration technique and provided a model for many later enactments."
Bernstein contended that the arbitration provisions resulted in "remarkable surface success in resolving disputes over new contracts in the late
twenties." To be sure, conflicts were muted because the unions were weak
and wages were not strongly challenged, but nevertheless, the act was ac-
claimed as "a model labor law" for its time.[27]

In spite of thriving on the "Chief's" challenging intellect, by mid-1926
Lilienthal was looking for greener pastures. He enjoyed Richberg's frequent
absences because they gave him a chance to do things his way and pursue
his writing. Moreover, Richberg had encouraged him with frequent salary
increases. Lilienthal started at $100 a month and soon was raised to $125.
At Christmastime 1924, Richberg made both associates junior partners and
increased their salary to "a minimum of $250." In 1926, in his last months
with Richberg, he averaged nearly $340 a month.[28]

Still, Lilienthal worried about money. In the spring of 1926 he wrote
Fred that he was suffering "financial distress." Later in the summer he told
Helen that relatives were pressuring him to send money to his struggling
parents, and he was concerned about paying for Allen's education. Moreover, the birth of Nancy and David Jr. in 1925 and 1927, and his desire to
find a suburban home, fueled his anxieties even more. He was also inclined
to try his wings because by 1926, as Richberg observed, "Lilienthal was so
successful in attracting a personal clientele that I could not retain him in my
small office." Finally, his interests had begun to shift, ironically, to those
opposite from the interests of Richberg, from labor to public utility law. By

spring 1926, he recognized "a drifting away from my ten year interest in labor law," and was ready to "let the American labor movement stagger along as best it could." He also worried that continuing association with Richberg might stifle his growing public utility business.[29]

His public utility interest developed in part from his work on the Chicago gas case. It also developed from an acquaintance with Irving Rosenbaum, a fellow Harvard Law graduate. In early 1926 Rosenbaum asked Lilienthal to "join him in writing some articles on the regulation of motor vehicles." In July they coauthored their first work in the *Journal of Land & Public Utility Economics*. Soon after, William Kixmiller, owner of Commerce Clearing House (CCH), asked Lilienthal if he would be interested in preparing a legal service on motor carrier regulation. He jumped at the chance, telling Kixmiller yes but not for less "than I am now making, which I said was $7,000 last year." (According to income tax records, his 1925 income was $2,312.50) He also insisted that Rosenbaum be included as an equal partner. Two weeks later they signed a $10,000 contract for fifty weeks, plus expenses and future royalties, to complete a motor carrier regulation service. Gracious as ever, Richberg decided that Lilienthal could not do both jobs, but allowed his young friend to keep his office and to pay rent out of extra work that might come Richberg's way.[30]

On His Own

The next five years were much different from the first three. In November 1926, Lilienthal moved to new quarters, and by 1928, he had two young associates; his income jumped to $7,866 in 1927 and to $12,486 in 1930. The Lilienthals moved to Palos Park in 1927, where Richberg also lived. In 1930, in order to find good schools for Nancy, they bought, as Richberg noted, "a substantial North Shore home" in Wilmette.[31]

His interest in public utility law was even more focused than his labor work. He taught public utility law for two years at Northwestern University, becoming close to economists at the Institute for Research in Land Economics and Public Utilities, many of whom helped out later in Wisconsin and Tennessee. His writing became almost totally professional. While with Richberg he published only one law review article—the rest of his writings were short pieces in popular progressive journals and trade organs. In these later years, Lilienthal wrote a short article in praise of Clarence Darrow for *The Nation* and another in *Electrical World*. The remainder consisted of eight law review articles on public utility law with Irving Rosenbaum and three of his own. He also collaborated with Rosenbaum on two articles in the *Land & Public Utility Economics* journal and wrote one himself.[32]

The Rosenbaum association was both rewarding and frustrating. Between September 1926 and January 1929 Lilienthal realized more than $17,000 on the project. The service helped Lilienthal forge a new expertise and brought wide exposure in public utility circles, and their coauthored writings further enhanced his reputation. While six of the articles examined motor carrier regulation, the others ranged more widely. One piece surveyed state utility legislation, one analyzed judicial review of utility decisions in Ohio, and two others focused on public utility securities. None of the works were theoretical, but they demonstrated a solid technical expertise in a legal subfield just beginning to define itself.

The relationship between Lilienthal and Rosenbaum was complicated by other factors, including a long-distance partnership, with Lilienthal in Chicago and Rosenbaum in Cincinnati. Both men realized they had underestimated the demands of the job. By April 1927 the "half-time" project was taking all their time. In a letter to Rosenbaum that month, Lilienthal complained that he was forced to turn other business away, including a chance to work again with Richberg on the *O'Fallon* case, which had reached the federal courts. At first they double-checked each other's work. However, time and distance soon forced them to abandon the practice. Relations with Kixmiller and CCH also hurt the relationship. Being in Chicago where CCH was located, Lilienthal resented the extra responsibilities and also pressure "from the sales end (in which I'm being pushed more and more)." His most onerous duty was the annual renegotiation of terms with CCH. Although increasing the weekly payment in September 1927, Kixmiller refused to sign a new contract, and the two partners were left with a week-by-week arrangement. Rosenbaum chided his partner for not being more forceful, and Lilienthal sharply replied, "If anything further is done, I'm afraid you will have to . . . do it." In 1928, citing poor sales and increased publication costs, Kixmiller reduced their payments and told them there would be no royalties.[33]

In the end, however, personality and value differences broke the partnership. Lilienthal's bluntness only worsened the situation. He was short with Rosenbaum and well-meaning suggestions frequently sounded like peremptory commands. He could be unmercifully sarcastic, and his words sometimes cast a gloomy chill. Often, Lilienthal inundated Rosenbaum with self-pitying litanies about his own personal problems. Lilienthal once complained about the distasteful liaison with CCH, but grudgingly reassured Rosenbaum that he would not think of asking Irv to move to Chicago because of his "established family name, business connections, professional connections, etc., and the advantage of being with your folks." In one of their last letters in March 1929, Rosenbaum rejoiced over the end of these "years of complete frankness during which you spread your emotional, financial and intellectual self over reams of paper directed to me."[34]

The partnership began to erode when Lilienthal accused Rosenbaum of shoddy work. In December 1927 he returned some annotations because of poor writing. In 1928 Lilienthal's criticisms mounted and Rosenbaum promised to do better. In December he accused his partner of extreme carelessness in preparing citations on Tennessee and New Hampshire statutes. He also chastised Rosenbaum for sloppy and incomplete footnotes in one of Rosenbaum's *Yale Law Review* articles, footnotes that Lilienthal hoped to incorporate into the service. He ended with a crushing accusation, "Anyone makes slips now and then, but my God." Later that month he complained of errors in Michigan material and reminded Rosenbaum, "This hasn't been a very pleasant letter, but it has been much more pleasant than my thoughts."[35]

The relationship completely fell apart in January 1929. The previous fall Rosenbaum told Kixmiller and Lilienthal that he would terminate his relationship with CCH because he thought he would be appointed general counsel of the Ohio Public Service Commission. On or about December 15, 1928, according to Lilienthal and Kixmiller, Rosenbaum verbally resigned in their presence. Because of mounting financial problems at CCH, Rosenbaum's poor work, and the deteriorating relationship, Kixmiller accepted the resignation and told him his monthly payments would cease.

Almost immediately, spurred by disappointment in not getting the Ohio counsel position, Rosenbaum denied he had resigned and claimed that CCH owed him money for past and pending work. Lilienthal was caught in the middle. Rosenbaum accused him of being involved and held back material he had in Ohio. Lilienthal was enraged—"The only purpose that can possibly have is to embarrass and frustrate me." Rosenbaum shot back that his former friend was "affected very distinctly with a sense of self-pity," offering to "cooperate in finishing up as soon as Kix turns his attention . . . to our direction." Another volley was fired in March when Rosenbaum, still awaiting Kixmiller's reply, realized Lilienthal was continuing the service. Accusing him of stealing the service, Rosenbaum hoped that "the sense of decency and fairplay [will] again get hold of you." In a hot response, Lilienthal replied, "You have a quarrel with Kixmiller but you have none with me," and "Of one thing I am finally certain, and that is that we have done our last work together, of any kind." His words dripped with sarcasm as he said, "It is a source of consolation to me, when the complaints about the shoddy job on New York come in, . . . that even if your work was erratic and unlawyerlike it was at least constructive and idealistic." With that salvo, the relationship ended, and Lilienthal sighed, "I never had a personal relationship that gave me such distress and grief."[36]

In spite of the Rosenbaum distractions and the demands of the service, Lilienthal had time for other work. He was a lobbyist for the Illinois Osteopathic Association in 1926–27 and joined Richberg and Darrow in 1928 to thwart another Wilkerson injunction against Chicago musicians and theatrical workers. In October 1928, worrying again about money, he asked Frankfurter about future prospects. His mentor wrote back, "I am sorry that your association with Richberg should not be as profitable as it is happy," and reminded him that "the interests to which you are devoted are not on the side of the biggest money bags."[37]

But Lilienthal continued building his reputation. He wrote Fred that cutting loose from Rosenbaum meant "less 'cloistered solitude' and more activity and dealing with people." In 1929 he represented the Hot Springs Arkansas Electric Light and Power Company. He was a consultant for the Railway Express Agency, and the Haight, Adcock and Banning law firm. With the latter he served as technical consultant in their battle on behalf of

Chicago against Illinois Bell Telephone Company. His name became increasingly prominent in the utility industry as he continued as editor of *Public Utility Carrier Service*.[38]

He widened his legal research, moving from motor carrier regulation to groundbreaking work on holding companies. Since William Z. Ripley's influential 1926 essay in the *Atlantic Monthly*, "From Main Street to Wall Street," discussion had raged about shadowy corporations with vast networks of operating utilities sometimes two and three times removed from point of service. Lilienthal's 1929 essay, "The Regulation of Public Utility Holding Companies," was the first piece of legal scholarship to address problems the states faced in controlling absentee utility company owners. His second essay, also published in the *Columbia Law Review* in early 1931, built on the 1929 article and chronicled subsequent developments in the holding company controversy.

More than grist for the academic mill, the essays provided a basis of understanding for much of his reform effort in Wisconsin in the early 1930s. He argued in the 1929 essay that it was folly for states to institute direct control over holding companies. In the first place, holding companies were not in themselves public utilities, the only types of organizations public service commissions were allowed to regulate. Second, he cautioned that regulating distant and complex behemoths was too complicated for any state agency. Lastly, Lilienthal warned if the holding company became the focus of regulation, "the state's authority to regulate the local business of such a national, interstate institution might have been seriously curtailed."[39]

He argued instead that effective legislation entailed the "regulation of public utilities in their *relations* with holding companies." One aspect of such regulation, an important part of subsequent Wisconsin legislation, included monitoring contracts for services and commodities between local utilities and parent companies. Another involved careful scrutiny of securities relationships. In the 1931 article Lilienthal found that a stronger legal basis for such indirect controls had evolved. Both New York and Massachusetts had effectively strengthened state control over holding companies, thus establishing reform precedents for other states. Moreover, several recent court decisions had established the right of states to regulate such relations.[40]

Soon after the first essay, Adolf A. Berle Jr., then a Columbia University economist, complimented Lilienthal for "an excellent and scholarly piece of work." In a published comment following the second article, James Bonbright, a well-known public utility economist, called Lilienthal's analysis the "most authoritative study" in the area. In their influential work *The Holding Company: Its Public Significance and its Regulation*, Bonbright and Gardiner C. Means further acknowledged and praised Lilienthal's pioneering efforts.[41]

Lilienthal strengthened his reputation with a 1930 *Harvard Law Review* essay on federal court review of state public utility decisions. In a brave show he submitted his work to the one journal where conclusions contrary to those of his mentors might come to their attention while the manuscript was under review. He criticized Frankfurter and James Landis for being alarmed about the tendency of federal rather than state courts to handle appeals of state utility commission decisions. He countered their arguments that federal review was inappropriate because cases often involved local laws and contracts beyond the competence of federal judges with the finding that more than 80 percent of the federal utility cases since 1913 "did not involve an original interpretation of local law or franchise." Addressing Frankfurter's claim that the practice drained the time and energy of the federal judiciary, Lilienthal contended that since most cases ultimately involved constitutional issues, "it is more appropriate that these cases consume the time of the federal than of the state courts." Frankfurter saw the manuscript, but limited his criticism to Lilienthal's interpretation of two cases discussed in the article.[42]

Between 1923 and early 1931 Lilienthal authored or coauthored a total of more than thirty works, including a dozen law review articles, ten pieces in liberal journals such as *The Nation,* the *New Republic,* and *Outlook,* and three contributions to the influential *Journal of Land & Public Utility Economics.* His coeditorship of the Commerce Clearing House motor-carrier regulations, the two *Columbia Law Review* articles, and the 1930 *Harvard Law Review* essay brought national recognition and membership in a small but influential band of public utility reformers.[43]

Lilienthal was not shy about touting his successes or sharing his insights. In July 1930, he told the dean of the Northwestern University Law School that all public utility law courses should be interdisciplinary: "a single class attended by law students, economists and engineers." The letter reflected his argument in an earlier *Electrical World* article that the work of public utility lawyers and engineers needed to be better integrated. Later that year he proposed to William Ransom, then chairman of the Public Utility Section of the American Bar Association (ABA), that the section sponsor an extensive continuing education program on public utility law for state and local bar associations. He flooded the mails with copies of his work to former classmates, congressmen, federal judges, academicians, the *Wall Street Journal,* and the *New York World.* Many recipients responded positively and asked for advice. He was appointed to a special study commission of the ABA Section on Public Utility Law, and Richard Ely, progressive economist and director of the Land Economics Institute, asked for his counsel. By 1929 even Frankfurter was plying Lilienthal for advice. More than one of his letters in the late 1920s began with words such as "May I get some help from you?" And of course, Frankfurter knew just how to reciprocate—with heaps of praise. In one letter, Frankfurter told Lilienthal, "I thought your observations on utility regulation were admirable" and that he had shown them to "Mr. Justice Brandeis," who referred to them as "the very discerning comments of David Lilienthal."[44]

Enduring Foundations

The twenties was a period of intellectual growth and a time for setting foundations and patterns of behavior that influenced Lilienthal the rest of his life. His commitment to family was sure but conventional. After Nancy's birth, he and Helen agreed that her place was with the children—and David. She never returned to work. He spent time at home when he could, but work was always first. A loyal son, he sent nearly $1,000 to his father between 1929 and 1931 and covered Allen's college expenses. Never a man of leisure, he became an avid flower gardener, the one diversion he allowed himself. When they lived in Chicago, he spent many Sundays in Palos Park helping Florence Richberg garden and growing his own on a borrowed plot of land. When they moved to the park themselves, he could hardly contain his pride in a letter to Fred Arvin: "a background of graceful shrubs and an occasional Japanese fir or flaming sumac; a low border of gay calendulas, old-fashioned verbena, a haze of ageratum."[45]

His legal experience and incessant drive provided a foundation for future ambition that went beyond the confines of private practice. Not many young men in their twenties could savor the good fortune of toiling with Richberg and Darrow, or of benefiting from Frankfurter's advice or praise from Brandeis and Berle. Not many of any age could boast of briefs that influenced the highest court in the land, partial authorship of national legislation, and a multitude of publications in top progressive magazines and legal journals. Ultimately, as an eighty-year-old Lilienthal remembered, credit was due "the excessively ambitious young lawyer in his late twenties in Chicago." Lilienthal made it happen: he mastered the art of self-promotion and drove himself so hard that Frankfurter, Richberg, Fred Arvin, and sometimes Helen feared for his well-being. Most of all, Lilienthal took example from Richberg and became the quintessential technical expert. By the end of the decade, he may have been the best-schooled utility lawyer in the country, young or old.[46]

But ambition and ego had its dark side. He complained of nagging illnesses and work-related stress, and worried obsessively about money, even in his most prosperous years. At times friends and associates suffered from his driven personality, which seemed to have intensified since college days. Lilienthal's acrimonious relationship with Rosenbaum partly resulted from taking on more than he could effectively handle, a sign of bad judgment engendered by a "having to do it all" mentality. In late 1928, Fred criticized Lilienthal for being "more impatient with people, or even uninterested in them, than it is wholly wise for any of us to be." Lilienthal, who had not written Fred for months, apologized that work had affected his behavior toward others. Sometimes his ego provoked embarrassing moments. When his Sweet case article came back with one hundred words edited out, he petulantly accused the editor of *The Nation* of making the cuts because they "did not appeal to you." He defended the missing words, claiming "Mr. Darrow and some other friends . . . spoke kindly of them." The editor's response was restrained as she explained that editing was "for no other reason than to increase the value and effectiveness of the article." In any case Lilienthal made no protest and the article was published.[47]

Nevertheless, none of these flaws diminished Lilienthal's promise. Ambitious he might be, but it was ambition in search of larger service. Abusive of his own person and of others on occasion, he was committed to something bigger than his own petty concerns. Echoing earlier letters to Helen, he wrote Fred in 1927 about being driven by a "desire to 'put over' a 'Big Thing,'" but he did not "honestly think the prospect of big financial stakes enter[ed] into the picture much." Perhaps the best tribute to Lilienthal came from Richberg, writing nearly thirty years later. In spite of the fact that he had long abandoned the liberal creed Lilienthal still professed, in 1954 Richberg emphasized that "regardless of agreement or disagreement with his policies, I have never heard anyone suggest that Lilienthal was not a devoted public servant who gave the best years of his life to a tremendous straining effort to render the best of public service he could in three public positions of constantly increasing importance." He concluded with a thought about those faraway progressive days: "I may say that emotionally I have always been proud and happy to have been associated with so fine a character." For Lilienthal, private character and public purpose were about to merge.[48]

CHAPTER 4

The Wisconsin Public Service Commission: Crucible for a Reformer

You have lighted a fire and there will be no putting it out.
—Justice Louis Brandeis to Lilienthal, October 1932

Farewell to Private Life

By late 1930 Lilienthal was restless again. Helen recalled that "he was not happy in his work." He had been bruised by the conflict with Irving Rosenbaum, and his love of labor law had waned. He enjoyed growing prominence as a utility expert because of his editorship at the Commerce Clearing House (CCH), his publications, and his association with a Chicago telephone rate case. He realized, however, that to prosper in public utility law he would eventually have to throw in with the private utilities—and that prospect did not please him.[1]

The revitalization of the venerable Progressive movement in Wisconsin gave Lilienthal an opening. According to Forrest McDonald, Wisconsin progressivism was both "a state of mind, and . . . a number of tangible political-economic-social reforms." Crusading Mugwumps, Grangers, municipal reformers, and urban laborites emerged in a loose coalition in the late 1880s and were united by the idealism and political intuition of Robert M. La Follette Sr. in the mid-1890s. As a Progressive Republican governor at the turn of the century, he led the state to unprecedented reforms, including the first income tax law and direct primary, effective workers' compensation legislation, and a comprehensive labor code. In 1907, a year after La Follette's move to the U.S. Senate, the state shared honors with New York in authorizing the first public service commissions in the land.[2]

In spite of his Washington position, La Follette kept reform alive in Wisconsin the rest of his life. Although an occasional conservative Republican or Democrat won state office, the senator was, as Richard Hofstadter observed, "an extremely astute machine-master [with] . . . a militant and well-disciplined state organization." Even in his 1924 Progressive presidential campaign, he won his state, but no others. The next six years were difficult, however. The old senator died from pneumonia in 1925, and Progressivism languished across the nation. While Robert Jr. won his father's Senate seat, Progressive Republicans lost crucial gubernatorial primaries in 1926 and 1928. The economic collapse in October 1929 and young Philip La Follette's coming of age gave them another chance.[3]

The depression hit Wisconsin particularly hard as its economy contracted more rapidly than in surrounding states. Industrial income plummeted from $616 million in 1929 to $173 million in 1932; manufacturing employment fell from 309,397 to 179,365; and farm commodity prices declined 57 percent. The percentage of adults employed fell anywhere from 2.5 percent in Watertown to a whopping 50.6 percent in Waukesha, while Milwaukee, Madison, and Racine experienced declines of 30.1, 45, and 48 percent, respectively.[4]

Too young to take over his father's U.S. Senate seat in 1925, Philip La Follette bided his time and in 1930 took on Republican Governor Walter Kohler, a stalwart, unwavering party regular, beating him by 130,000 votes in the September primary and then defeating a weak Democratic candidate in November by an even greater margin. In a familiar echo from the old days, La Follette called for public works, a more progressive state income tax, limitations on chain stores and banks, and "a program of public utility regulation that will make it possible for Wisconsin to develop unhampered by restrictions of monopoly, and unretarded by exorbitant power and light rates."[5]

La Follette knew he had a good chance against the utilities. Wisconsin had a strong utility reform tradition and was a model for the rest of the nation. In 1907, the state mandated its new Railroad Commission to establish reasonable rates, adequate service standards, and standardized reporting requirements. In the 1920s, however, the utilities and the commission had faced unprecedented crises, which begged for new regulatory approaches. The companies were beset by labor shortages, an alarming rise in the cost of money, and increased operating costs. On top of that, their public image, never strong in Wisconsin, deteriorated even more as the holding company controversy grew, utility scandals in Pennsylvania and Illinois made the headlines, and the Public Ownership League of America mounted a challenge to private utilities everywhere.

On the other hand, the Wisconsin Commission faced its own crisis. Wisconsin residents depended on electricity more than ever: in 1930, 90 percent of the state's homes were electrified, compared to 25 percent in 1917, and the commission found it difficult to respond to the growing number of emergency rate increase requests from the beleaguered utilities. Regulation had become more difficult because distant holding companies had gained increasing control over local utilities. According to McDonald, in

1917, 312 companies provided electricity in the state. By 1930, 9 companies provided 90 percent of the power, and 8 of them were owned by three holding companies. In addition, courts at all levels were increasingly interfering with state regulatory decisions. As one scholar noted at the time, "The menace of an appeal to the federal courts has deterred many a commission from prosecuting issues and pressing rate cases." Finally, the once-powerful commissions were facing their own internal crises. The fluctuating value of the dollar in the 1920s made it extremely difficult to execute utility valuations and establish reasonable rates of return for the companies. Moreover, in spite of these increasingly complex challenges, state appropriations remained constant or actually declined. Many commissions resigned themselves to reacting to complaints instead of actively seeking out abuses in the utility industry.[6]

In addition to tradition, La Follette had momentum going for him with the Wisconsin League of Municipalities (WLM) and Milwaukee's socialist mayor, Daniel Hoan, both pushing hard for lower rates. La Follette thought he could turn the situation around—especially since he had two positions to fill on the commission. But he needed someone who could transform the commission into an aggressive advocate and rewrite the law to meet the power trust challenge. His choice for chairman was Theodore Kronshage, a Progressive WLM attorney. La Follette then "decided to pick the most outstanding man I could find anywhere in the United States." He asked Donald Richberg and James Landis of Harvard Law School, but they declined because, as Richberg noted, "private financial obligations demanded the making of an income far beyond the modest salaries available in Wisconsin." Richberg suggested Lilienthal but warned that he might also balk at the low salary. The Lilienthals had just purchased a home in Wilmette and David had leased an office through April 1934. His income had risen to over $12,000 in 1930. But when La Follette called, Lilienthal traveled to Madison to meet with him.[7]

La Follette explained that he could not appoint Lilienthal as chairman because of his youth and lack of Wisconsin roots. He emphasized, however, that he wanted Lilienthal to take the lead in drafting a comprehensive reform program. Lilienthal returned, according to Helen, "full of enthusiasm," but concerned about the $5,000 salary, another move, "the chance it involved, [and] the short tenure." Helen sensed his hesitancy and told him to take the job if he wanted it: "What is good for you is good for me and for us. As to the salary: we've lived on less . . . and we can do it again." That was all the encouragement he needed.[8]

On February 5, 1931, La Follette appointed him to a two-year term on the Railroad Commission and he was confirmed unanimously by the senate. Lilienthal settled up quickly in Chicago. He arranged a leave of absence from Commerce Clearing House and turned everything over to his associates Harry Booth and Joseph C. Swidler. Lilienthal arranged, with La Follette's approval, to receive a weekly check in payment for work already completed and office expenses incurred by Swidler and Booth in editing the

CCH service. This arrangement seemed innocent enough, but it proved to be a shoal upon which Lilienthal's Atomic Energy Commission nomination almost foundered sixteen years later, when the Chicago office manager, Meads Leitzell, testified that Lilienthal had received improper CCH payments after joining the commission.[9]

Little did David, Helen, or Donald Richberg and Felix Frankfurter realize at the time how significant the Wisconsin challenge would be. Lilienthal remembered much later, that until he went to Wisconsin he "was rather withdrawn." As Helen said later, "It was an exhilarating time to work in State Government." It was also the crucible for the public education of David E. Lilienthal, and he was a quick study.[10]

Fortuitous Circumstances

Lilienthal was sworn in on March 25. A week later he attended his first meeting and thought, "As I took my seat and looked out at the line-up of counsel . . . [I] thought being a judge wouldn't be so bad." Looking over this litigious battlefield, he could hardly fail to appreciate the fertile ground for reform that lay before him. Public utility reform was the heart and soul of the rejuvenated reform movement. The public power movement, led by organizations such as the National Popular Government League, provided a spark of conscience in an era of holding company abuses and congressional debates over public hydropower on the Colorado, Tennessee, and St. Lawrence Rivers. As a scholar noted at the time, "For twenty-five years [after the establishment of the first commissions in 1907], there were few noteworthy changes in regulatory methods until 1930–32."[11]

The market crash in October 1929 changed everything. Prices of commodities, services, and consumer products plummeted. So did personal and corporate incomes. Utilities remained strong, and steady rates and profits seemed obscenely high in the devastating times. The specter of distant holding companies manipulating the fortunes of local operating utilities further added to demands that the utilities be brought to heel.

In April 1930 the Academy of Political Science held a tumultuous conference in New York City on the utility crisis. The program committee, chaired by William L. Ransom, and including Frankfurter, James C. Bonbright, and Walter Lippmann, invited the true believers of private privilege and public power to speak. Martin Insull, Samuel Insull's younger brother and utility spokesman, and traditional regulatory officials, including William Prendergast and William Donovan of New York, argued against public ownership and insisted that present regulation was adequate. Progressive social scientists and economists such as William Mosher of Syracuse University, John Gray of American University, and Bonbright of Columbia University argued for radically new approaches, including active rather than passive regulation and stronger state laws to allow more control over holding companies. Moreover, they emphasized, the whole basis for rate making needed to be rethought.

For thirty years, since the landmark *Smyth v. Ames* U.S. Supreme Court decision, rate making had been guided, according to Mosher, by the "reproduction value" principle. Utilities were entitled to rates that would bring returns reflecting a proportion of the "fair value of the property." However, consensus was building that market value was irrelevant since utilities were "not bought and sold on the open market." In his 1930 Dodge Foundation lectures, Frankfurter noted that five estimates of the "reproduction value" of the New York Telephone Company in 1925 had ranged from $367 million to $615 million and that endless court battles to decide between widely varying estimates made the timely assignment of rates virtually impossible.[12]

The reproduction cost standard was more vexing because *Smyth v. Ames* was unclear about whether value should be defined as original cost or current value. Needless to say, since rates were tied to value determinations, utilities consistently argued for current value calculations, which usually resulted in the higher valuations. Reformers, on the other hand, supported original cost valuations, which meant smaller value estimates. By the early 1930s, because of real declines in commodity and labor costs, and in property values, reformers began to argue that rates should be cheaper since current value estimates were lower than in the past. The only solution was a new approach to rate making. Failing that, the last resort was public ownership, a prospect dreaded by the private companies.

Unfortunately for industry, the reform movement was not limited to academics or a few Progressives such as George W. Norris. The 1930 elections swept more than a dozen reformers into statehouses. Dan Turner of Iowa, Charles W. Bryan (brother to William Jennings Bryan) of Nebraska, and Floyd B. Olson of Minnesota were unabashed advocates of public ownership. La Follette, Julius Meier of Oregon, and Gifford Pinchot of Pennsylvania, had all run on reform platforms, and incumbent populists and Progressives including "Alfalfa" Bill Murray of Oklahoma and Franklin Roosevelt of New York were already in the midst of battle. Even before Lilienthal was sworn in, new utility laws had been proposed and rates slashed in more than a dozen states. The time was right in Wisconsin. Unlike other reform states—including New York, Pennsylvania, and California—the Wisconsin commission had unequivocal executive support and was united. La Follette gave Lilienthal free rein to prepare a new utility law and promised ample resources to enforce the law. In 1931 Wisconsin Railroad Commission expenditures increased to $490,000, more than $150,000 over 1930. The number of employees jumped from 89 to 126. Drawn by salaries of up to $8,500, progressive staffers came from across the nation to give Lilienthal the firepower he needed. It was crucial for Lilienthal that Kronshage, a much older man on the verge of retirement and in questionable health, had taken the chairmanship with the understanding that Lilienthal would shoulder the major responsibilities. Andrew McDonald, the third commissioner, a former locomotive engineer, had served since 1923 and was also satisfied in following Lilienthal's lead.[13]

Lilienthal was fortunate to have press support. Not only did the La Follette paper, *The Progressive,* and the liberal Madison *Capital Times* support reform, but so did the most influential paper in the state, the generally anti–La Follette *Milwaukee Journal*. The day after the Kronshage-Lilienthal appointments, the *Journal* grudgingly congratulated La Follette for setting a "standard of calling" with his appointments, and in the next two years, Lilienthal was praised in editorial after editorial.[14]

Learning the Trade

For the moment, it appeared that Lilienthal would indeed be a "gentleman regulator" of the type idealized by Ransom in a March testimonial dinner. Ransom praised his friend for his "courage, brains, character, and . . . fine idealism," and advised that "militancy must not be taken or mistaken for creative and constructive work." In a note of thanks, Lilienthal called Ransom's ideas worth "wide distribution" for exposing "die-hards on both sides." Shortly after, Frankfurter disabused Lilienthal of this view: "I hate him [Ransom] from the bottom of my heart," because, in Lilienthal's para-phrase of his former professor, "Ransom posed as a liberal whereas really he was not."[15]

Lilienthal soon found he had to move quickly because the opposition to reform was anything but "gentlemanly." The Wisconsin Security Holders Association condemned the reform package in January. Martin Insull testi-fied against La Follette's package, as did the state Association of Commerce, Wisconsin Telephone Company (WTC), Wisconsin Power and Light Com-pany (WP&L), and many of the "locally owned and operated telephone companies." Nevertheless, behind the unrelenting pressure of the militant WLM and Mayor Hoan, the legislature followed La Follette's lead. Within weeks the state assembly adopted two constitutional amendments strength-ening the authority of local governments to finance power projects and allowing the state to protect water power resources and develop a compre-hensive power coordination plan. It also passed two bills, one establishing a public power corporation to regulate public ownership and agreements with private utilities, and another authorizing cities with public utilities to expand their services outside corporate boundaries. Then, the legislature turned to a series of proposals that Lilienthal had drafted to strengthen the state regulatory agency.[16]

Introduced on April 10 by Socialist Senator Thomas Duncan, Lilienthal's recommendations echoed many of the points in his earlier *Co-lumbia Law Review* articles: the newly renamed Public Service Commis-sion (PSC) was authorized to control the relationships between local utili-ties and out-of-state holding companies, cancel common stock dividends in case of financial impairment, require all company directors to be Wisconsin residents, and control new construction and abandonment of services. The provisions were immediately attacked by the utilities for spelling "not regu-lation but state management."[17]

Two more provisions further strengthened the bill. One authorized the commission to charge the costs of utility investigations to the companies being investigated. The other gave the commission discretion to define the scope and breadth of its investigations and to decide when, where, and against whom action would be taken. No longer would it have to wait for petitions and complaints. This provision reflected Lilienthal's earlier position that government agencies should have the power to compel testimony and that the "Public Service Commission [should be] an aggressive fact-finding body."[18]

Criticism of the bill was fierce but surprisingly brief. Less than a week after the first hearings Lilienthal felt "a feeling of conscious satisfaction in realizing that [passage of the bill] is now almost fait accompli." The utilities backed off, since "adequate regulation [was] the only alternative to the spread of public ownership," a distinct possibility considering public power provisions in the rest of the package.[19]

Key compromises also helped assure quick approval. The resident directorship provision was dropped, and utilities were given more discretion in determining depreciation reserves and permitting new evidence to be admitted in reviews of commission decisions. The greatest objection was to the provision requiring utilities to pay the costs of investigation. Lilienthal found himself in a dilemma. While the practice was common in other states, he "had some fear for the program." He drafted a compromise stating "that the Comm. may exempt any utility from the duty of paying the costs of such investigations but only upon a finding that the public interest so requires." The revision proved acceptable, and the bill was approved by the assembly on May 28 and signed by La Follette on June 6. In July, the *New York Times* called Wisconsin "a leader in matters of public utility regulation and control," and in October the paper reported that the Wisconsin law was "the most far-reaching regulatory measure ever put into force in the country."[20]

Lilienthal passed his first test. He crafted a strong regulatory bill and the experience gave him his "first real insight into the workings of a Legislative body and democracy as she is practiced." Oddly enough, Kronshage, La Follette, and Duncan received most of the local public attention for the reforms. The national press, however, understood the young commissioner's role. Now, the *New York Times* editorialized, there was a means "to place under the strict eye of David Lilienthal . . . and of the other members of the railroad commission" all the doings of the "power trust" in Wisconsin.[21]

Brash and Brilliant

Within a week of La Follette's signature, the Public Service Commission launched an unprecedented assault. It made no difference whether the utility was large or small or whether its product was electricity, telephone services, or gas. The commission was relentless. On June 12, breaking from the traditional approach of investigating individual complaints one at a time, the commission ordered a comprehensive investigation of WP&L. Four days later, every public utility in the state was ordered to reveal all relationships with affiliated interests and holding companies. In late July, it took on the WTC in a case described as "the most difficult and ambitious ever undertaken by the regulatory body." Unlike WP&L, weakened by the imminent collapse of its Insull holding company, WTC was backed by the strong American Telephone and Telegraph Company (AT&T).[22]

And so it went. In a year-end report, Kronshage revealed the commission's breakneck pace: Before the new agency took over in April 1931, the old Railroad Commission had 149 pending cases. By year's end, the PSC had opened 452 informal and 401 formal cases, rendered 282 decisions, closed 370 cases, and conducted 335 hearings. Between 1925 and 1929 the Railroad Commission had initiated only 111 cases.[23]

Lilienthal was ebullient. Helen recalled that the reform atmosphere was "so stimulating that [David] worked most week-ends as well as long days." In December 1931, he reflected that he was pleased La Follette had not exerted improper political pressure on the commission, but he also understood that unless the commission made a big splash, it would "be . . . a dead weight on Phil in his [reelection] efforts." It was imperative "not only to deny the [WTC] increase but to order a decrease in existing rates." He proudly pointed out the commission's evenhanded resolve in one case in which it approved an unpopular rate increase, and another in which the commission ruled against a small municipal utility in a dispute with a larger company.[24]

His official pronouncements were imaginative. In one of his first opinions (called by *Public Utilities Fortnightly* "the most interesting feature of this decision"), Lilienthal ruled that municipal utility surpluses could not be transferred to city general funds because such diversions were unfair to rate payers. He also ordered that city utility boards be protected from partisan political wrangling. These policies became standard in Wisconsin and later part of every TVA agreement with local distribution agencies. He could also be off the mark. In November 1931, in an ironic observation, he questioned O. S. Loomis, a Progressive state senator, on "the practical soundness of your remarks about the importance of the natural resource of water power in Wisconsin." These early rulings left little doubt as to the source of energy and inspiration in Wisconsin. By October 1931 the *New York Times,* the *Milwaukee Journal,* and the *Public Utilities Fortnightly* had clearly identified this rising star of reform in Madison.[25]

Meanwhile, the utilities and conservative Republicans waited their turn. The first sign of the gathering storm came in November 1931, in a special legislative session to deal with a state court decision that ruled that allowing PSC to waive the cost of investigations was an improper delegation of legislative power. Lilienthal thought the objection could be met by merely eliminating the waiver power. The amendment passed in the house, but met a firestorm in the senate. Several senators called for an explanation for the high salaries of "outsiders" in state government. Lilienthal moaned that "we were chastised for paying high salaries, . . . going out of the state for so many of our new staff; we were accused [of] organizing a political machine, . . . and of course my name was brought into the debate." After strong resistance, only a tie-breaking vote by Lieutenant Governor Henry Huber on New Year's Eve kept the bill alive. Lilienthal was "more and more impressed with the importance of the so-called Third House: the lobbyists. . . and . . . [wondered] if we are tending in the direction of they [sic] syndicalistic notion of a legislature passing on economic subjects through economic or industrial representatives?" It was also an ominous portent as Lilienthal, the commission, and Philip La Follette faced an increasingly powerful opposition in anticipation of the 1932 election.[26]

The Pace Quickens

The new year started with more decisions. On January 6, two utilities and their holding companies were ordered before the commission and scolded by Lilienthal for having "no local officers" with management powers "and no resident directors." After conferring with company officials, he announced a solution, while at the same time indicating that he expected a substantial reduction in rates. In February, he asked Adolf Berle, whom he knew through Rudolf Berle and William Z. Ripley, to help draft tough securities regulation legislation. On February 15 he pressed his initiative on the radio by stressing that commissioners should do more than "merely sit[ting] back and listen[ing] to complaints." To be effective, modern commissions must be assertive and be supported by strong staffs with adequate financial resources.[27]

In mid-April, the commission faced a decision that made Lilienthal realize the gravity of his position. In January, he and Kronshage had met with the WP&L manager and Marshall Sampsell, one of Insull's lieutenants. The atmosphere was as gray and chilling as the mists outside the Capitol. Sampsell pleaded for permission to sell more WP&L securities to shore up the sinking Middle West Utilities holding company. Kronshage and Lilienthal refused and suggested that WP&L should cease common stock dividends altogether. According to Lilienthal, Sampsell was devastated: "the months of struggling to keep the ship afloat was evident upon his face."[28]

The decision was also critical for the commissioners. On one hand, dividends were hardly justified, considering the company's precarious situation. On the other, the suspension of dividends might push the holding company into receivership and threaten local utilities. Kronshage told Lilienthal that banker friends had told him that suspending dividends "would almost certainly result in a crash." The weight of the discussion hit Lilienthal hard: "That session will not be readily erased from my mind. Here was the ruthless businessman . . . asking for mercy from Kronshage, an old Progressive lawyer, friend, and associate of Old Bob La Follette— and a kid." Kronshage and Lilienthal held off for a while. On April 16, however, after the collapse of Middle West, Lilienthal ruled that the company's receiver could not drain assets from Wisconsin subsidiaries through dividends or fund transfers from local companies.[29]

In July the commission ordered seven more utilities to cease dividend payments on common stock owned by holding companies. The *New York Times* reported that the utilities had attacked the PSC for "exceed[ing] its authority in order to engage in a dramatized fishing expedition." Lilienthal fired back at the *Times* for publishing "the emotions of the utility men." He defended PSC actions, emphasizing that "there is no prejudice here against holding companies as such, but we do have a prejudice against unsound financial practices wherever they occur." Once more, it was clear who was in charge in Wisconsin.[30]

By mid-1932 the commission reported $2.35 million in rate reduction assessments. In September, on the eve of the state primary, the commission announced an additional $713,683 in reductions, bringing the total to over $3 million and affecting 564,383 customers. While half the total represented an order enjoined in federal court, it seemed clear that the commission had met its obligation to La Follette.[31]

Unfortunately, other factors tempered Lilienthal's triumphs. In April Irving Rosenbaum threatened to sue for breach of contract. A shaken commissioner wrote Frankfurter that a suit "would be a severe drain on my energies [and an] . . . opportunity . . . . for the unfriendly newspapers to use as ammunition." Frankfurter told Lilienthal not to "yield either to blackmail or to the blackmail of threatened undesirable publicity," and then asked an Ohio friend to get Rosenbaum to back down.[32]

Financial woes threatened that summer when CCH broke off with Lilienthal after he refused to confirm a verbal sale of the service allegedly made in 1930 by a now-deceased salesman to the Byllesby Engineering Corporation. Lilienthal told CCH that he could hardly pressure a company like Byllesby, which "had millions of dollars of property under control of our Commission." On August 20, William Kixmiller canceled Lilienthal's contract in part because "[Lilienthal] had declined to assist in selling a substantial order of the service." The affair reached its bitter conclusion when Lilienthal told Kixmiller the situation left him two choices: "a sacrifice of . . . principle" or suffering "a personal sacrifice of several thousand dollars."[33]

Another factor was fatigue. In its first year the commission tested the limits of regulation and human endurance. Kronshage hinted that the PSC had overextended itself when he told La Follette that the WP&L investigation had "been crippled by the heavy burdens of the telephone inquiry and budgetary limitations." The situation deteriorated in 1932 when Kronshage became ill and Lilienthal had to pick up the slack. In April he told Frankfurter that Kronshage's illness "has made things desperately hard for us. But the thing is still great fun." A week later he wrote that an important consideration of public administration "turns on the rather homely matter of the boundaries of human energies. . . . [John] Bickley, [Edward W.] Morehouse and myself are carrying loads which . . . no one can handle indefinitely." He continued that "it is the driving of others and yourself that seems to take the kink out of you, [and] . . . that the mediocrity of governmental administration . . . must be attributable to a considerable extent to nothing more . . . than just plain everyday weariness." He then admitted that "if this were a bright, cheery, warm spring day, and if I were not physically fatigued, and if I hadn't just learned that one of our ... men was dying of spinal meningitis, ... I suppose it could hardly be doubted that [today's] conference would begin and end differently than it is probably going to begin and end."[34]

To an extent, the fatigue was compounded by the tough encounter with WTC. That case cast Lilienthal as a brilliant and aggressive tactician who tried to win support for La Follette at the expense of a powerful and implacable foe. It turned out he won neither battle—La Follette was defeated and Lilienthal's legal arguments were denied time after time until the case was finally rejected many years later in 1939.

The Wisconsin Telephone Company Case: The Wisdom of Brandeis, the Tenacity of Frankfurter

While the PSC flooded the state with rate reductions, they had not yet landed their "big fish." In spite of substantial reductions, such as the $208,100 Wisconsin Gas and Electric order, the anticipated big catch, the WTC, was still under investigation. But even with twelve accountants on the case, progress was slow. Kronshage promised hearings in January 1932, but they were postponed. In December 1931 Lilienthal worried that a decision had to be made before the 1932 campaign, and a few weeks later he wondered "if there were not some way whereby rates could not be reduced on an emergency basis, ... before the final completion of the investigation."[35]

Lilienthal's solution was a creative rendering of Louis Brandeis's philosophy that social and economic facts should play an important role in legal decisions. Along with fellow commissioners and top staff members, he reasoned that the depression-induced imbalance between income and utility rates created unique regulatory challenges. First, if rates were too high, enough subscribers might cancel services to threaten the viability of the utility. Second, continuing high rates would impede economic recovery. Third, fairness dictated that the public should pay no more than the reasonable worth of the services. They concluded that if incomes fell and rates held, those rates would be "unreasonable" when compared with new income levels. This argument evolved last, but was the central thrust behind their controversial July 1932 decision. Lilienthal knew that if this argument prevailed, he would "be bitterly attacked from one end of the utility world to another."[36]

Nevertheless, he began plotting early in February. Utility expert James Bonbright assured him "that your proposal is [economically] sound" and if accepted, "it will spread throughout the country." The dialogue continued as Lilienthal, Bonbright, and chief PSC economist Ed Morehouse organized a distinguished panel of economists to testify. Bonbright suggested that their case could best be made by emphasizing "the existence of the emergency" rather than price imbalances. He felt WTC could effectively argue against rate decreases since rate and valuation increases had not kept up with rising prices and incomes in prosperous times. Moreover, they could claim that current services were more valuable now because of increased efficiencies. Lilienthal replied vehemently that while the "emergency" argument made sense, the telephone company had been "putting on the fat regularly and immoderately" for years through excessive returns, and it was time for the commission to expose past abuses to assure present equity. Moreover, a quick decision was imperative, not one which dallied "until the last T is crossed and the last I dotted a year from now." Lilienthal's combative stance belied the *Milwaukee Journal*'s assurance that "[Lilienthal] has an open mind on the matter."[37]

The hearings started April 1 with Lilienthal attempting to weaken WTC's credibility before introducing his controversial argument. Led by John H. Bickley and Special Examiner George C. Mathews, the PSC uncovered irregularities in the WTC-AT&T relationship. Tracing financial transactions to 1915, Bickley found that AT&T had earned over $33 million in WTC stock dividends and never missed a dividend payment. He also revealed that in 1930 WTC had assigned AT&T $12 million in stock which paid 8 percent dividends to pay off a loan charging 5.36 percent interest. The transaction netted AT&T an extra $250,000, all quite legal, but costly to the local utility. He also hinted that AT&T had overcharged WTC on a wide range of contracts.[38]

In late April the focus switched to the rate increase. Bickley and Mathews led the commission through a maze of data that showed questionable increases in maintenance costs, manipulation of depreciation reserves, and overbuilt facilities. At one point, Lilienthal asked Bickley sarcastically if testimony would "give an explanation of this extraordinary skyrocketing? Was there a tornado in Milwaukee in 1930?" The next day Mathews discredited WTC's claim of almost negligible earnings by showing that the company's profit margins were really 5.6 percent.[39]

Meanwhile, Lilienthal prepared the main assault. In March, he wrote in *Electrical World* that the PSC was obligated to "emphasize its administrative and inquisitorial powers" to achieve fair rates. A month later he told Marquis Childs of the *St. Louis Post-Dispatch* that "if we cannot control . . . the utility industry, then we have no Government in fact, merely a pathetic fiction of Government." Early in May he introduced the "reasonable worth" argument: not only are consumers paying more of their income on utilities but because current dollars have greater purchasing power, consumers "are now paying higher rates to utility services in terms of purchasing power than before their incomes and earning power were reduced." He wrote Bonbright "that by the time we are through . . . every important electric and gas utility in the state will have made a proposal for a voluntary rate reduction." The big fish was about to become an object lesson for every Wisconsin utility.[40]

Because of Kronshage's illness, Lilienthal led the assault with his panel of economists. Sparks flew as he and his distinguished entourage clashed with company attorneys who challenged every bit of testimony, calling it irrelevant to rate determination. Then, they claimed that the commission had loaded the deck and prejudged the case. At one point an exasperated WTC attorney asked why the newspapers but not they had advance copies of witness statements. Lilienthal brusquely denied every charge and challenge as he questioned venerable progressive scholars, including John R. Commons of the University of Wisconsin and Edwin Seligman of Columbia. Frank Fetter of Princeton, past president of the American Economic Association, Jacob Viner of the University of Chicago, and Bonbright added further weight to the new theory of rate determination.[41]

For three days, witnesses testified about the state of the economy. Then, Fetter, Viner, and Seligman hammered home the point that the economic crisis was partially a result of price and income disparities. It was logical to expect that lower utility rates, as Viner said, "would constitute a necessary part" of the cure. Bonbright concluded the hearings by summarizing his colleagues' arguments and adding two well-rehearsed conclusions. First, he warned, "we have a situation today where the whole economic organization is threatened, where a delay of even a few weeks, not to say a few months, or years, may be important." He contended that "none of the standardized theories of rate control" will meet the present emergency because "a return which . . . might be fair during prosperous times would now be grossly unfair to the consumers in view of the recent fall in incomes and in view of the increasing purchasing power of money."[42]

The circle was closed—the last volley had been fired. The April hearings raised doubts about the original rate request. The May hearings shifted the debate to another plane by suggesting that the crisis compelled a radically different rate-making rationale. In spite of denials, there is little doubt that Lilienthal anticipated a rate reduction long in advance. In June, Frankfurter told Lilienthal he was "troubled and rather startled that you should be contemplating" a speech revealing the commission's intentions while the case was pending. Lilienthal agreed not to say "that rates should go down," but insisted on stressing that the economic crisis "presents utility regulation with its most dire test." In spite of his mentor's advice, Lilienthal did, in the June 22 address, go beyond Frankfurter's cautions. One critic noted that it "clearly foreshadowed that this [rate reduction] was to be the policy of the Wisconsin commission." A week before the order, the *Milwaukee Journal* predicted within a fraction the exact amount of the decrease.[43]

On July 1 the commission announced a one-year 12.5 percent WTC rate cut and warned that more reductions were likely. In defense of the decision, the commissioners first argued that WTC rates were "unjust and unreasonable." Then, they claimed that economic crisis constituted an emergency that compelled the PSC to act. The commission finally justified the decision on a obscure clause in *Smyth v. Ames* which said that consumers should not be charged more by a utility "than the services rendered by it are reasonably worth." The commission reasoned that rate payers were forced to pay constant prices for utilities even though their incomes were greatly reduced. Moreover, the dollars left to rate payers were worth more than in the past. Assuming a "reasonable" relationship between services and past rates, they concluded that present charges were unreasonable: services had not improved, nor rates reduced. Nevertheless, the consumer was paying a larger portion of his income for utility services and what he was paying in dollars was worth more to the utility.[44]

Reaction was swift. The *Milwaukee Journal* said the decision promised "real relief" and urged the utilities to support it. The *New York Times* called it "a novel principle of rate-making. What the consumer should be asked to pay is put ahead of what the company may be entitled to earn." In response, WTC alleged nineteen "errors of fact and numerous erroneous conclusions," charging that the PSC acted peremptorily in denying the company a hearing before the decision and by a one-sided investigation. WTC disputed conclusions about profit margins, and said that the commission had not proven that the value of services was less than what consumers were paying. Denied a rehearing, WTC petitioned and was granted a temporary injunction on July 30, subject to a three-judge panel review.[45]

Meanwhile the debate raged. *Telephony* and *Nation's Business* said the decision was political and denied the right to make a profit. Responses in *Public Utility Fortnightly* were equally critical. William Prendergast, former chairman of the New York Public Service Commission, criticized the abandonment of the "universally-accepted theory of a reasonable return on the fair value of the property used and useful." *Fortnightly* editor Henry Spurr criticized the PSC for presuming to define value of service: "It is hard enough to ascertain the present value of a company's property for rate making, but this is child's play compared with the problem of determining the value of the service."[46]

In September 1932, another district panel enjoined the PSC on the grounds that it had not valuated company property. From there the dispute went to the U.S. Supreme Court, which remanded it back to the district court in March 1933, where it bounced back and forth between commission order and injunction for years. The case reached its end in a 1939 when the Wisconsin Supreme Court finally annulled the original reduction order. Later, in 1961, Bonbright concluded that "Lilienthal doubtless hoped to secure support from an early, cryptic dictum . . . in . . . *Smyth v. Ames*. But his gamble failed, for the import [of the reasonable worth standard] remains a mystery . . . [and] . . . the nature of the norm has gone undefined to this day."[47]

Throughout the rest of Lilienthal's days in Wisconsin, the battle raged. No sooner did WTC protest the 12.5 percent cut than the PSC threatened to reappraise WTC property values according to extremely low July 1932 prices, a move that might have resulted in a reproduction value so low that "the financial stability of the company [would have been] threatened." While the PSC did not follow through, the threat nevertheless was, according to a neutral observer, a counterproductive example of Lilienthal-inspired "regulation with a vengeance."[48]

Building a National Reputation

Lilienthal's extensive travel also contributed to his fatigue. In two years, he was out of state more than a dozen times, involving himself in several Progressive causes and frequently visiting with Frankfurter and Milo Maltbie, chairman of the New York Public Service Commission. These activities reflected the same energetic commitment, always calculated to maximize his reputation as a rising young Progressive star.

His first significant exposure was as a member of the Committee on Public Utilities, organized after the Washington Progressive Conference in March 1931. Called by U.S. Senators Robert M. La Follette Jr., George Norris, Burton Wheeler, and Bronson Cutting, the participants gathered to formulate a legislative agenda for 1932. After months of deliberation, the committee, created by Richberg, submitted a report to Conference Chairman Norris on October 8. Laced with calls for "public control of all public business," the report prompted strong reaction. On the right, Milton Harrison, president of the Security Owners' Association, called it "a step toward . . . complete socialization of American business." *Traffic World* said the report was another shopworn cry for government ownership. On the left, *The Nation* and the *New Republic* praised its "most practical and workable solution" for the utility crisis and a program to curb private interests that have "enriched themselves at public expense and have defied proper regulation."[49]

Lilienthal tried to moderate some of the language in the report. In August, he urged Richberg not to recommend stronger federal legislation. Anticipating his grass roots sentiments, he argued that federal agencies tended to be insensitive to local conditions and circumstances. His reaction was partly in response to lukewarm regulatory efforts by Republican administrations. It was also motivated by a concern that an expansion of federal controls might diminish state powers.[50]

In October, Lilienthal responded to Richberg's request for last comments. Criticizing Richberg's disdain for profits, he asked, "Must we not say [either] that the profit motive is inevitable and even desirable once properly controlled and limited, or that it is an unsound and anti-social basis for enterprise *in all fields.*" Lilienthal reminded Richberg that the latter conclusion implies that "we are no longer liberals . . . [but] socialists looking toward a totally and fundamentally different basis of production and distribution." Again, Lilienthal could not fail to realize that a massive conversion to public ownership would threaten his role as a regulator. In any case, his protest was not very loud, for he delayed mailing his objections until a day before Richberg had to submit his report.[51]

Lilienthal's first clash with the utilities outside Wisconsin was in Richmond, Virginia, at the annual meeting of the National Association of Railroad and Utilities Commissioners (NARUC) in October 1931. In comic opera fashion, the few Progressive delegates from New York, California, Pennsylvania, Oklahoma, and Wisconsin attempted to challenge the utility-dominated convention. Their goals were modest: banning utility representatives from the formal program; naming Washington, D.C., as the permanent site for future meetings; and withdrawing NARUC support from *Public Utilities Fortnightly* and *Public Utilities Reports, Annotated,* two publications with alleged utility ties. All three proposals were rejected by the convention.

Nevertheless, the protest got the utility crowd's attention. Soon after the conference, *Public Utilities Fortnightly* published an article about a left-wing insurgency: the trouble started when Milo Maltbie "from the state of Governor Franklin D. Roosevelt . . . strode deliberately down the aisle" to protest a rule referring all resolutions to the executive committee without debate. After Maltbie was declared out of order by NARUC President Harvey H. Hannah (according to Lilienthal, "a flannel-mouth Southern orator and windbag"), the article reported that "from the center of the assemblage rose the youthful figure of David E. Lilienthal . . . from the state of Governor La Follette—Wisconsin." Lilienthal asked for a ruling on Maltbie's request from the NARUC vice-president and chair of the executive committee, whereupon "the gavel of the presiding officer came down . . . with a bang." The minutes recorded Hannah's retort: "He will rule on it when they have the executive session and he is presiding. I am running the convention now. (Applause)". The article wondered ominously, "Were the government ownership elements beginning to 'bore within' the Association itself?"[52]

Lilienthal's reaction to the convention seemed at first only a prudish response. He wrote of "much drinking and boozing, and in the room next to Helen's and mine, . . . a 'distinguished Commissioner'. . . was engaged in a drinking bout with the chief lobbyist of the bus. assn and three young girls, one of whom passed out entirely." After the meeting, Lilienthal called a press conference in Wisconsin to expose NARUC and suggest that Wisconsin withdraw from the association.[53]

Lilienthal complained to Ransom about the "low-grade lobbying and entertaining," and how such abuse "could very easily destroy all the prestige which regulation has built up in some parts of the country." Ransom defended NARUC and warned him not to go public, since it was "rarely a necessary or effective weapon of real regulation." He reminded Lilienthal that Maltbie "never has to make a speech to let New York utilities know about conditions he wants ended."[54]

In spite of Ransom's advice, Lilienthal forged ahead. After writing Maltbie and others, he sent an open letter in January 1932 "respecting the conduct of the affairs of the Association" to all NARUC members, all governors, and the press. The letter was signed by the five California commissioners, Maltbie, Lilienthal and his colleagues. Several friendly commissioners declined to sign, partly because of its harsh tone.[55]

The letter was vintage Lilienthal. Although he thought it was "moderate and conciliatory," it was neither. It began by charging "that regulation in the several states is being seriously imperiled by the present conduct of the affairs of the National Association" and concluded: "When the Association imperils state regulation, as we are convinced it now does, either the association must change its course or we, as state members, now see no alternative but to withdraw." The letter accused the convention of suppressing debate, contended that "the junketing aspects of the Association Conventions has injured public confidence in regulation," and suggested that the only convention benefits were "those flowing from pleasant vacations at public expense."[56]

To some the threat to resign seemed rash, and the demand to permanently site the convention in Washington, D.C., while not without merit, was weak. NARUC President Thomas J. Murphy responded that convention location was an issue "upon which there is, to say the least, ground for honest difference of opinion," and that many states wanted the convention moved around "to equalize the advantage of nearness to the meeting places."

The demand that the utilities be excluded from the convention also seemed ill-advised. The move would do little to keep company representatives from lurking around. Furthermore, the 1931 meeting already limited the first two and a half days of the four-day program to members only. Murphy pointedly noted "that the disposition of the Executive Committee was to prepare a program for the 1932 convention which would fully respond to the" resolution to ban all utility participation.[57]

Murphy met the demand to dissolve relationships between NARUC and the two publications by arguing that the issue had not been discussed for years, and "was suddenly presented, without any preliminary investigation, or consideration." No doubt, on balance, the *Fortnightly* was conservative. However, it often published articles by reformers such as Bonbright, Emanuel Celler, Mosher, Pinchot, Seavey, and Lilienthal. Finally, Murphy noted that both publications, but especially *Public Utilities Reports, Annotated,* provided a much-needed service in disseminating state and national regulatory decisions.[58]

Murphy's defense of the issues was not nearly as devastating as his observation that none of the nine signatories except McDonald were regular NARUC participants—seven were at their first convention. He responded to their threat to resign, asking if "the fact that you have failed once to control the convention justifies that the Association . . . no longer is worthy of your support?" His concluding words were withering: "I doubt whether you intend to take the position that you should be permitted to dictate the action of the Association contrary to the judgment of the majority."[59]

In the end, Lilienthal's protest had little effect except to enhance his progressive credentials. Because of his rashness, however, he suffered one painful humiliation. In a bitter November 1932 letter, he told Frankfurter that he would not attend the convention that year because he would likely be censured for his post-Richmond remarks. The irony was all the greater as Theodore Kronshage guided a Lilienthal-inspired resolution calling for greater regulatory control over holding companies through the convention in Hot Springs, Arkansas.[60]

In early 1932, Lilienthal helped organize a utility regulation conference in New York City. He corresponded frequently with the chair, Morris L. Cooke, a former New York Power Authority member and dedicated public power advocate. The conference was an unqualified success for Lilienthal. The Wisconsin law was hailed as model legislation and the *New York Times* recognized Lilienthal as one of the prominent attendees. The conference also exposed him to prominent national figures including interstate commerce and federal power commissioners Joseph B. Eastman and Frank R. McNinch, and members of Roosevelt's circle of influence including Berle, Leland Olds, Cooke, and Maltbie.[61]

In the fall of 1932, Lilienthal spent a week in October consulting Frankfurter, Berle, Maltbie, and Brandeis about his future and addressing the American Bar Association meeting in Washington. After criticizing long-distance holding company management, he appealed to Brandeis's theory that large size and centralization detracted from institutional effectiveness. He argued that whatever economies holding companies might produce, "there is a social loss to the community . . . whenever we have long-distance management of matters which could be adequately handled by local managers." Lilienthal heard good words about the speech. Frankfurter told him of "high praise of your Washington speech." James Landis said that the speech "went down very well. I was surprised at such appreciation . . . for you certainly did not handle your subject with gloves."[62]

By early 1933, Lilienthal was a visible member of the public utility regulation fraternity. He was successful in Wisconsin and had become widely recognized outside the state. His high profile at the various conferences, his speeches, and friendships with other Progressives placed him in a favorable position for moving to the national stage, especially if the Democrats prevailed in the 1932 presidential election.[63]

Politics 1932: Defeat and Reassessment

While Lilienthal and his fellow commissioners did what they could, La Follette knew the 1932 race would be tough. The depression was enemy number one: just as it brought him to power, it now threatened to sweep him out of office. His utility and unemployment compensation programs were unquestionably popular and the tax reform package showed compassion. However, they could hardly stem a crisis of national proportions. La Follette recognized this when he told his brother in May that "economic conditions are getting rapidly worse. Unless something drastic is done, . . . I doubt if things will hold together."[64]

A second threat was a sea change in party alignment and support. In 1930, the Democratic gubernatorial primary attracted only 17,000 voters. In April 1932 more than 200,000 voted in the Wisconsin Democratic presidential primary. Given the conservative domination of the Republican presidential primary, La Follette sensed that Progressive Republicans would choose to vote in the Democratic state primary in September. Progressive Republicans were caught between two antagonistic forces. They had little chance in a Republican party increasingly dominated by stalwarts and former governor, now candidate, Kohler, who had a score to settle with La Follette. And, in spite of La Follette's friendly relations with Roosevelt, there was little place for them in a conservative state Democratic party, hungry for power on its own terms. Moreover, as good as he was, Philip La Follette was not his father. The younger son was often abrasive and impulsive—the "wild man of Madison," some said. Finally, a new Democratic progressivism threatened the identity and solidarity of Wisconsin's liberal Republicans and the La Follette mass base in the cities.[65]

Other factors were important. The relief tax bill weighed heavily on middle-class pocketbooks and the repeal of a dividend tax exemption alienated industrialists. The media campaign against La Follette was fierce. Most state papers were anti–La Follette and small-town stalwart newspaperman John B. Chapple's strident book, *La Follette Socialism,* accused the entire family of atheism and radicalism. Ironically, La Follette's success in 1930 had help spur the conservatives to "a much better financed and more professionally organized campaign" in 1932.[66]

Although La Follette sensed he would "be the first La Follette to go down to defeat in more than thirty years," he fought gamely. The stalwarts accused La Follette of "inflating bureaus and commissions [and] creating large increases in payrolls." The Democrats announced their opposition "to the present system of excessive regulation; administration by numerous boards which are ever seeking to increase their power." When La Follette took credit for the July 1932 WTC order, the *Milwaukee Journal* criticized him for "trying to make political capital out of" a nonpolitical decision. In late August, the stalwarts attacked him for taking credit for the WTC reduction that had just been enjoined in court.[67]

While neither stalwarts nor Democrats often attacked Lilienthal by name, he was not immune from criticism. In early July he addressed a group of campaign workers and accompanied La Follette to Sauk City for the kickoff campaign speech. For the first time the *Journal* criticized him, commenting that "Commissioner Lilienthal has a big enough job at his desk in Madison. There is where he should be—in the office and out of politics." [68]

In September, Kohler gave Lilienthal his first real public tongue-lashing. At a rally, he accused the young commissioner, who was present, of "prostitut[ing] public service" and "befoul[ing] his own nest." He savaged Lilienthal for being an outsider and bringing in "a hungry horde of expensive alleged experts when at the same time there were 100,000 Wisconsin residents out of work." While disturbed, Lilienthal was impressed by the speech for "how intensely personal it was." Helen Lilienthal wrote later that 1932 "was the first time that Dave was made an issue . . . , and he didn't like it."[69]

By mid-September, Lilienthal feared that middle-class support had eroded because "things are very much worse than they were two years ago. ... There is . . . a real chance . . . they will say, 'Let's try something else.'" He privately weighed "returning to private practice or staying on for another year or two in public service." The gloom was thick when Kohler routed La Follette in the Republican primary by almost 100,000 votes. Both the uncertainty of his personal situation and the fear of a new administration "wiping out . . . all the work I put in at such a cost of labor and worry" left the Lilienthals feeling low. The next day he wrote Frankfurter about "having to reconsider my own future course." Plaintively, he confessed he was "desperately anxious to talk over my personal problem with you."[70]

A few weeks later his spirits had risen. While uncertain of the outcome of the race between Kohler, who would not reappoint him, and Democrat A. G. Schmedeman, who might, Lilienthal was encouraged by pro-PSC editorials. While harboring no illusions about Republicans, he was pleased that their platform called for continuing "strict regulation." He was flattered that the Democrats had made "a plank out of me" and for commending "personnel of the public service commission . . . to be of the highest possible type obtainable," and was convinced that his reforms would be impossible to rescind whoever was in power.[71]

Nevertheless, Helen noted that their remaining time in Wisconsin was "an unhappy time for us both." Lilienthal pressed the WTC investigation, pushed through securities legislation in early 1933, and penned a strongly worded article for *Electrical World* reprising his earlier views on holding companies. Yet, his status remained uncertain. The victorious Schmedeman, a beneficiary of Roosevelt's coattails, had praised the commission in his campaign, and the *Milwaukee Journal* urged the new governor three times to reappoint Lilienthal. Even president-elect Roosevelt sent a letter of support on Lilienthal's behalf.[72]

But nothing happened. In early 1933 he suffered well-meaning but ignominious advice to step down to the PSC general counsel position. On February 6, Lilienthal's term expired and forced him to continue on an interim basis. His fear of financial loss added to his misery. In January he told Frankfurter he was really worried about how he and Helen were "going to work out our pecuniary obligations." He hated "to permit a few thousand dollars to interrupt work which gives me such pleasure, . . . but as you have said, the Lord doesn't provide."[73]

Schmedeman's signals were increasingly confusing. In late January he called for a $350,000 PSC budget cut. To compound the crisis, the legislature took off on witch-hunts and budget-slashing forays. Inspired by vindictive stalwarts and patronage-hungry Democrats, bills were introduced to cut administrative salaries by 40 percent and to strip civil servants of their rights if they had not been Wisconsin residents prior to employment. In addition, a special committee was created to investigate state agencies with an eye toward effecting economies, consolidation, and even elimination.[74]

And yet, rumors about reappointment persisted. In April one report announced that "whatever pressure was brought to get rid of Lilienthal evidently has failed." In early May the same source reported that "no amount of propaganda . . . will keep Gov. Schmedeman from reappointing David E. Lilienthal." Lilienthal knew, however, that "if I were able to continue in Wisconsin it would be only after a bitter, nasty, fight." Nevertheless, Richberg and Robert La Follette Jr. advised him to stay in Wisconsin no matter what. Frankfurter played a double game. While singing Lilienthal's virtues to Roosevelt, he counseled his protégé against a Washington appointment because "you're too damn young." Even in late April he advised Lilienthal, "Your place, for the present, is out there."[75]

Lilienthal's situation was ironic, however, because he was being forced out of a position he had long contemplated vacating. Helen wrote that he had taken the Wisconsin job because "we could get along all right, for the two years that he thought would be the time he'd want to stay." In December 1931, he concluded that his record would invite other offers "as I come closer to the end of my brief term."[76]

There was no doubt that Lilienthal was thinking about other options. Berle told him soon after La Follette's defeat that he would "make a bold attempt to get you some kind of a berth" should Roosevelt win. Maltbie said if Roosevelt won, Lilienthal would be a prime candidate for the Federal Power Commission (FPC) and Frankfurter told him "Roosevelt knows of your qualities and experience." Lilienthal told Berle in November, "I hope you are still keeping me in mind in connection with the federal activities." Trips east in October 1932, and several in early 1933, were filled visiting anyone who could help. He spent hours talking with a "Mr. X" about FPC reform. In late April he complained to Bonbright, "The pressure for jobs at Washington is so great" that without an organized campaign one hardly had a chance. Bonbright encouraged Lilienthal not to despair: letters had been sent "to Walsh, Cosgrove and Cooke of the New York Power Authority and to Moley, Berle and Tugwell in Washington bespeaking support for your appointment [to the Federal Power Commission]."[77]

Suddenly, Lilienthal began talking about *national* issues. Before La Follette's defeat, he had been little interested in national politics, except in his opposition to strong federal utility legislation. Now he was advocating strengthening the federal role in utility regulation. On November 5, he submitted a plan for a new Federal Utilities Commission to La Follette. The day after the election he sent his recommendations to Berle and Frankfurter. He continued to work on the federal power angle, but his hopes were dashed when "Mr. X" told him Roosevelt had appointed a southerner to the one available FPC slot and that national utility reform legislation was not on the president's immediate agenda. In mid-May he told Frankfurter he was not interested in the FPC in any capacity unless it was "thoroughly overhauled by legislation." But, by this time, the newspapers were linking him to a strange new agency called the Tennessee Valley Authority (TVA).[78]

A New Challenge

The first rumors of a TVA job came in a May 9 press notice. Lilienthal put little stock in the report since the bill was still in Congress and, as he told Frankfurter, he had little chance because "I am not a southerner and have no southern connections." Lilienthal was also skeptical because no one had approached him about the position. He knew his friends were shopping his name around, but he only knew about the FPC. Brandeis only told Lilienthal later that he had recommended him to Arthur E. Morgan, the new TVA chairman. Neither did he learn until early May that Roosevelt had said, "If we could get Lilienthal, it would be a ten-strike."[79]

The signs persisted. On May 13 *The Progressive* speculated about a Lilienthal appointment. On May 20, Forrest Allen of the *Memphis Press-Scimitar* wrote Lilienthal, "I am hoping that you are getting ready to be a member of the Tennessee Valley Authority." Allen told him his paper and other Scripps-Howard papers in Knoxville and Birmingham had "been pulling for you for several weeks." Lilienthal immediately asked Allen for "any word you can give me . . . as I am not at all well informed about this situation." He suggested the Scripps-Howard papers call several people about him, including Bonbright, Cooke, Norris, Frankfurter, Richberg, and *Nation* editor Ernest Gruening.[80]

In the meantime, Morgan, a former civil engineer and president of Antioch College in Ohio, looked first at Ezra Scattergood, of the Los Angeles Power Bureau, and Llewellyn Evans, director of the Tacoma municipal utility. He rejected both and turned to Brandeis's recommendation. Morgan dispatched an aide to Madison to evaluate Lilienthal. Algo Henderson came back with glowing reviews, but warned about some who "thought Lilienthal to be quickminded and vigorous but said that Lilienthal had overweening personal ambitions." In spite of the reports, Morgan arranged to meet Lilienthal in Chicago on May 30. He wired the White House that if the interview went well he would recommend Lilienthal for the board. Morgan reported that the young man was said to be "brilliant, thorough, accurate, aggressive, fair, loyal and committed to public interests." His only "shortcomings are . . . personal ambition and publicity."[81]

The meeting was a curious affair. Lilienthal presented himself well, prompting Morgan's biographer to speculate that Lilienthal had prepared for the interview. Other evidence suggests that the meeting was unexpected. Lilienthal rushed to Chicago after the White House tracked him down on a fishing trip in northern Wisconsin. Helen wrote that David knew little about TVA and that she "briefed him on all I'd read of this in the Congressional Record" while he "dressed and packed to go to Chicago."[82]

At the meeting, which Lilienthal remembered as running for five hours, he played coy and asked that the appointment not be announced until he could first work out "two or three" matters. He told Morgan he was negotiating with Joseph Eastman at the Interstate Commerce Commission about a position and asked if he might do that work while on the TVA board. Morgan was impressed with this "fresh, young, vigorous person," and indicated no problem with the Eastman deal. He remembered, however, that Lilienthal excused himself after "only a short time," and "wondered why, with so large a personal matter at stake, he could not find time for a longer interview." Nevertheless, Morgan wired his "hearty" approval to Washington, and Lilienthal was in.[83]

The nomination was announced on June 3, 1933. The Wisconsin press praised Lilienthal and criticized Schmedeman for letting him get away. The *Journal* said that Lilienthal's "efforts to make utility regulation work" justified the honor and charged that the appointment "makes [the Democrats'] fight against Lilienthal look pretty cheap." The *Capital Times* bemoaned the "gulf . . . between the liberal . . . Roosevelt administration . . . and the reactionary Schmedeman administration," and said "that Mr. Lilienthal's vision and ability will not be lost to the people of this country." The governor answered, somewhat disingenuously, that he had not appointed Lilienthal because he had known about the Washington decision for weeks. Frankfurter sent a note that included a reminder to his peripatetic friend: "Don't expect to ride any other horse than that for a long time. It will be more than enough to absorb you." Lilienthal responded with "heartfelt gratitude" and noted his "word of warning about trying to do anything else while carrying this load."[84]

On June 9, Lilienthal faced one last obstacle—Irving Rosenbaum. Senator La Follette called Lilienthal at 11 P.M., warning that Ohio Senator Bulkley might stall the confirmation vote because Rosenbaum's attorney protested the nomination. Lilienthal responded with a telegram early June 10. He also told La Follette of Frankfurter's previous involvement and how the law professor "expressed indignation at the scheme." Lilienthal telegraphed Frankfurter and asked him to "immediately wire Alfred Bettman [Frankfurter's Ohio confidant] to contact Bulkley before matter comes to vote and take such other steps you deem wise." While the wire was blunt, as telegrams are, it had none of the solicitous tone Lilienthal always used when communicating with Frankfurter. Perhaps the tone indicated just how much Lilienthal wanted this new opportunity on the national stage.[85]

Assessment

Although Lilienthal was in Wisconsin only two years, the experience taught him the importance of the executive's role in moving government beyond the "standpattism" of the 1920s. He learned to mobilize support and how to survive in a place where the phrase "Get Lilienthal" was more than an idle threat. His record reflected ambiguous character: ego, brilliance, and the paradox of a public spirit mixed with a streak of petty meanness.

During this time, he was transformed ideologically from progressivism to state capitalism. His eager assent to La Follette's actions reflected the progressive credo that public authority was best vested in a strong executive. So did his growing disenchantment with a legislative process sullied by patronage politics and lobbyists. He quickly moved from a classic Progressive emphasis on citizen mobilization and involvement to a commitment to beneficent statism. In his journal and letters he was skeptical of the will of the middle and working classes to defend their own interests. In many ways, he assumed the citizenry was unorganized, passive, and helpless in the face of private privilege. He was emphatic that public regulators should be "aggressive fact-find[ers]" instead of passive "judges" and that effective regulation meant making decisions *"regardless of public demand"* (emphasis added).[86]

Lilienthal's attitude toward regulation and administration also changed. By 1933, frustrated with the vast resources the utilities could marshal, Lilienthal realized that regulation as it had been practiced might not be enough. Now, government must become an aggressive and powerful meritocracy. In a speech in the spring of 1933, the embattled commissioner emphasized that regulation demanded more than "a mere bookkeeper who could only report to us that the items were actually expended and the books balanced." Good government required "an accountant experienced in public utility work [who] must be a real investigator [and] have a kind of sixth sense for detecting and ferreting out facts." Later in May, he stressed that to move beyond "rubber-stamping of the claims of the public utilities, . . . the commission must have experts who are able to match training with the well-paid representatives of the utilities." The key was "a considerable staff. . . well qualified . . . and rewarded with reasonably adequate salaries."[87]

Nevertheless, this personal transformation was not radical. In truth, it reflected the cautious centrism he had embraced since DePauw. In January 1932, he wrote Fred Arvin that the overthrow of the "existing economic order" is a long way off and that "it will be a long time after you have joined the John Reed Club before you will have the privilege of being shot on the barricade and buried under the American Kremlin." His criticism of Richberg's call for ending utility profits was a sign of his centrism. In Wisconsin, Lilienthal learned that the center moved, and that to remain there, one had to move with it. There is a certain irony in Lilienthal's cautious flexibility when compared with the fate of his mentors Richberg and La Follette. Both were to Lilienthal's left through the early 1930s. By the 1940s, however, both had moved substantially to the right. Lilienthal, however, adjusted to the center, first as a moderate progressive and then an ardent liberal statist during Roosevelt's New Deal and Truman's Fair Deal.[88]

Lilienthal's ability to mobilize support from different sides was extraordinary. Although an ardent proponent of regulation, he was the darling of the public ownership lobby. It was remarkable that he could remain in the favor of men such as Berle, Richberg, Frankfurter, and Brandeis, who fought so much among themselves. Brandeis, in his aversion to bigness, strongly opposed Richberg's early views. Moreover, not only did Berle and Frank-furter differ on that point, they had detested each other since Berle refused to bow to Professor Frankfurter's ego at Harvard Law School. Yet, all four remained steadfast Lilienthal supporters.[89]

While personal ambition moved Lilienthal mightily, he was also plagued by a restless spirit that led to precipitous action and overcommitment. Helen spoke of how David drove himself incessantly. Lilienthal's younger brother Allen, who lived with his brother in Madison, hinted at a darker drive when he observed, "In Wisconsin [David] worked three days on end without sleeping." Other signs, such as an oblique reference in 1932 that he had been ordered, one assumes by a physician, to take a vacation, indicated that a compulsive demon was laying an early claim to the young reformer's soul.[90]

All too often his lifelong habit of impatience turned from worthy virtue to ugly vice. It is clear, for example, that Lilienthal kept a heavy hand in his Chicago firm's affairs after leaving for Wisconsin. In letter after letter to Harry Booth, Joe Swidler, and Meads Leitzell, he was a petty tyrant, issuing brusque admonitions about workloads and telephone usage. There was little in this relationship to suggest his later concern for humane manage-ment.[91]

Others felt Lilienthal's manner may have been counterproductive in regulatory matters. Clemens contended that Lilienthal's "accomplishments must be offset to a degree by the friction and animosity he created in the relations between the utilities and the Commission." The depth of hostility toward Lilienthal in Wisconsin was perhaps best captured in the Wisconsin senate chamber on June 6, 1933, when eleven of twenty-nine senators voted against a harmless resolution commending Lilienthal for his record.[92]

Whatever his shortcomings, there is little doubt that Lilienthal had an impact on the Progressive movement in the early 1930s. He was young, brash, and charismatic; articulate, creative in thought, and ambitious. As a young man among older Progressives, Lilienthal energized the movement. He made a difference in Wisconsin where his fellow commissioners lacked the energy to do so. He provided inspiration and example at the national level through his energetic pursuit of Progressive goals. And he was much noticed by his elders who had long carried the reform banner.

Ambition was both a defect and a virtue for Lilienthal. There is little doubt that he took advantage of his formidable wits to promote himself and scheme for a position in a new national administration. In some re-spects, Wisconsin reform may have suffered because of his attention to a personal agenda. However, much more was at stake than personal ambi-tion. The new administration was a clarion call to the enlargement of the public realm and "rejection of the private values of the 1920s," and sig-naled a clear endorsement of the public good and of the role of positive government in achieving that good—it was right where Lilienthal wanted to be.[93]

When he returned to Madison after meeting Morgan, Lilienthal asked

La Follette for advice. The former governor recommended that he take Eastman's offer, because "the Tennessee matter is very likely to run onto the rocks and is wholly in the future." La Follette's law partner urged him to take the Tennessee job because "it was so challenging and because any kind of a success in it would stamp a man for life." That was what Lilienthal wanted to hear. Just as La Follette's offer had been right in 1931, the new offer was right in 1933. TVA offered a golden opportunity to work his will on a new agency with few preconceived objectives. Even better was the chance to work with a president who, much like Lilienthal, was flexible, opportunistic, and willing to commit the full faith and credit of the state to strengthening the public realm.[94]

Lilienthal at TVA Muscle Shoals chemical plant, about 1935. Courtesy of the Tennessee Valley Authority.

Lilienthal in Wilson Dam powerhouse, August 1933.
Courtesy of the Public Policy Papers, Seeley G. Mudd
Manuscript Library, Department of Rare Books and
Special Collections, Princeton University Libraries.

Senator George Norris at Norris Dam site. Lilienthal behind Norris, about 1934. Courtesy of the Tennessee Valley Authority.

Lilienthal at Wilson Dam, about 1935. Courtesy of the Tennessee Valley Authority.

Norris Dam under construction, about 1935. Courtesy of the Tennessee Valley Authority.

Julius A. (Cap) Krug, March 1939. Courtesy of the Tennessee Valley Authority.

Joseph C. Swidler, about 1939. Courtesy of the Tennessee Valley Authority.

The last gasp—Tennessee Electric Power Company making a final, futile protest over TVA's takeover of their services in Chattanooga, August 1939. Courtesy of the *Chattanooga Times*.

Gordon R. Clapp, 1940s. Courtesy
of the Tennessee Valley Authority.

Marguerite Owen, November
1962. Courtesy of the
Chattanooga Times.

Lilienthal's study in Norris, Tennessee, where he wrote most of *TVA: Democracy on the March,* December 1946. Reprinted by permission of *House Beautiful,* copyright © August 1947 The Hearst Corporation. All rights reserved. William Howland, photographer.

Wartime TVA Board, H. A. Morgan, Lilienthal, and James P. Pope. Gordon Clapp seated at Pope's left, 1940s. Courtesy of the Tennessee Valley Authority.

Lilienthal at Fontana Dam site (second from left). James P. Pope at Lilienthal's left, Gordon Clapp and H. A. Morgan, fifth and second from right respectively, August 1944. Courtesy of the Tennessee Valley Authority.

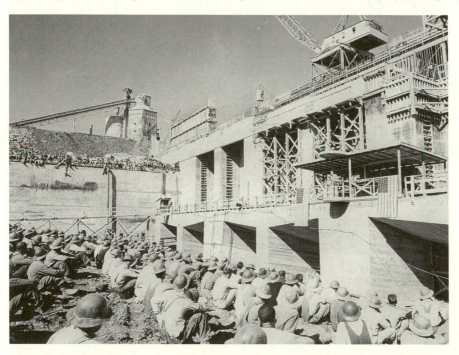

Lilienthal addressing workers at Douglas Dam site, October 1942. Courtesy of the Tennessee Valley Authority.

Lilienthal seated at his custom-made semi-circular desk, November 1945. Courtesy of the Tennessee Valley Authority.

Helen and David Lilienthal at home in Norris, December 1946. Reprinted by permission of *House Beautiful*, copyright © August 1947. The Hearst Corporation. All rights reserved. William Howland, photographer.

The Atomic Energy Act was signed by President Truman. Looking on were (left to right) U.S. Senators Tom Connally, Eugene D. Millikin, Edwin C. Johnson, Thomas C. Hart, Brien McMahon (whose name the bill carries), Warren R. Austin, and Richard B. Russell, August 1946. Courtesy of the History Division, U.S. Department of Energy.

The first Atomic Energy Commission. Robert F. Bacher, Sumner T. Pike, William W. Waymack, Lewis L. Strauss, and Lilienthal (left to right), probably 1946 or 1947. Courtesy of the History Division, U.S. Department of Energy.

Lilienthal at Oak Ridge with map of "far flung" Atomic Energy Commission empire map in background, April 1947. Courtesy of the History Division, U.S. Department of Energy.

General Leslie R. Groves and Lilienthal discussing Oak Ridge, October 1946. Courtesy of the History Division, U.S. Department of Energy.

CHAPTER 5

TVA: The Tumultuous Years

Never before in the Tennessee Country, and probably never
anywhere else in the world, had so great an enterprise gone so
rapidly into action. It seemed to be governed by a genius, zeal
and experience of a high order, and it also seemed to borrow
momentum from the enthusiastic upsurge of the first Roosevelt
administration.

—Donald Davidson, *The Tennessee:*
The New River, Civil War to TVA

An Uncertain Beginning

On March 5, 1933, a day after his inauguration, Franklin D.
Roosevelt set in motion a dramatic assault on the economic crisis that had
bedeviled the nation for more than three years. In special session for the
"Hundred Days," Congress authorized an unprecedented number of programs and policies designed to end the depression and raise the battered
morale of the American people. Within weeks the Emergency Banking Relief Act, the Economy Act, and the Civilian Conservation Corps Reforesta-
tion Relief Act were passed, giving hope that national leaders were finally
ready to do something about the economic crisis. In May and June, the rush
continued with the Agricultural Adjustment Act, the Federal Securities Act,
and other legislation designed to alleviate the terrible unemployment crisis
and to protect hundreds of thousands of homesteads through mortgage
refinancing. On June 16, the last day of the session, Congress capped the
amazing three months by passing the Glass-Steagall Banking Act, the Farm
Credit Act, the Emergency Railroad Transportation Act, and the National
Industrial Recovery Act. On April 10, Roosevelt sent a special message to
Congress asking them to "create a Tennessee Valley Authority—a corporation clothed with the power of government, but possessed of the flexibility
and initiative of a private enterprise." Five weeks later, on May 18, Congress approved his request, and the bold new regional experiment also became part of what William E. Leuchtenburg characterized as "the most
extraordinary series of reforms in the nation's history."[1]

In spite of the fact that TVA was very much a part of the great "Hundred Days," one could not help but wonder if David Lilienthal had second thoughts about his new job when he stepped off the train in Knoxville on July 6, 1933. There he was, his first time in the Tennessee Valley in the middle of a hot, southern summer—surroundings very different from temperate Wisconsin. He was alone. Helen was back in Madison, not planning to join him until August. Things were unsettled with TVA. Lilienthal had spent most of his time since confirmation back and forth between Wisconsin and Washington, tying up loose ends with the Public Service Commission and trying, as he told Forrest Allen, to "get the machinery of the corporation going." Anxieties were heightened by the scattered Authority quarters, a room in the Willard Hotel in Washington and a few offices in gloomy downtown Knoxville. As of June 30, none of the handful of TVA employees had even been paid. The only tangible realities were Roosevelt's June executive order authorizing the Cove Creek Dam north of Knoxville and the domineering presence of Chairman Arthur E. Morgan, already two months on the job.[2]

Already, it seemed that things at TVA would be as unsettled and controversial as they had been in Wisconsin. The first board meeting, a marathon eight-hour session in Washington on June 16, was frustrating for Lilienthal and his colleague Harcourt A. Morgan (no relation to A. E. Morgan). Chairman A. E. Morgan raced through a packed agenda in a peremptory and willy-nilly fashion, thoroughly alienating his colleagues. It was true that A. E. Morgan was the only full-time director at the time and that pressing decisions had to be made. Nevertheless, neither of the other two wanted to pass over issues that begged extensive discussion. H. A. Morgan, longtime president of the University of Tennessee, was disturbed that the chairman seemed more interested in details than in larger issues of direction and goals. Lilienthal was concerned about A. E. Morgan's conciliatory attitude toward the utilities. After forcing discussion on how to respond to Wendell Willkie, new president of the Commonwealth and Southern holding company (C&S), Lilienthal acknowledged differences with A. E. Morgan which he knew were going to "require a good deal of working out." During a short break, he and his partner had a "decisive conversation," which led to a pact to keep the chairman from dominating future board meetings.[3]

There were other factors that might have given Lilienthal pause for not having taken Phil La Follette's advice to reject the TVA job. Raymond Moley gave the authority eighteen months or less, and fellow brain-truster Rex Tugwell put TVA's survival odds at one in five. TVA was not just a new organization—it was the first of its kind anywhere. Its legacy was an idle government power and munitions complex at Muscle Shoals, Alabama, completed too late to contribute to the Great War. Through the 1920s the project had been the object of an incessant tug-of-war between Republican administrations that wanted to sell it off and a doughty band of Progressive senators, led by George Norris, who fought to keep it in the public domain. In 1933 the only national power program in the country was the Boulder Dam on the Colorado River. However, unlike Boulder, which could only sell power directly to the utilities, the new agency promised much more. The TVA Act sketched a broad vision of regional development, encompassing conservation, flood control, navigation, fertilizer, agriculture, power, and planning. Moreover, its structure was unique in that it had a national charter but regional autonomy.

The problem, however, was that no one knew exactly what the president wanted from TVA. The directors asked Tugwell in the fall of 1933 about Roosevelt's intentions, but even he dared not hazard a guess. To Norris, Roosevelt vaguely responded that "it's neither fish nor fowl, but, whatever it is, it will taste awfully good to the people of the Tennessee Valley." It was not the case, as Donald Davidson suggested, that the early TVA was bereft of a "grand scheme." There was a scheme, but it was largely rhetorical and symbolic. What the president failed to provide, in typical fashion, was a set of concrete directives. As such, the board was left largely to its own devices. That arrangement might have worked had the three directors been of one mind—but they were not, and they were all strong-willed.[4]

The lack of identity and disagreement within TVA was serious, but as internal issues they could temporarily be contained by the directors and staff. The greatest danger came from predators, including regional skeptics and the power trust. There were some who thought that Lilienthal, a Jew *and* a Yankee, might be too much for the South to swallow: the same doubts held for the chairman from Ohio, who was also an unorthodox and idealistic dreamer. Surprisingly, the regional factor proved to be of little importance. H. A. Morgan, a Canadian by birth, was widely respected in the region and provided the basis for almost immediate local acceptance.

The power interests were another story. C&S owned all the common stock in Tennessee Electric Power (TEPCO), Alabama Power, Georgia Power, and Mississippi Power, companies that were directly threatened by the new Authority. While critical of the TVA bill in spring 1933 congressional hearings, Willkie, a former Roosevelt supporter, recognized the inevitable and recommended that TVA be allowed to sell power only at the source. This way, the private companies could minimize the impact of the new agency, buying what they wanted and controlling the lucrative transmission and distribution components of their systems.

Although selling at the source of production might have been easier than the tough alternative of TVA going after its own markets and fighting the utilities, Lilienthal found Willkie's recommendation unacceptable. In the first place, the TVA Act mandated a preference for selling power to local public institutions over large private companies. Second, restriction to source-of-production sales would keep TVA from providing a yardstick comparison of the total cost of providing power, including production, transmission, and distribution. Also, the passive image of selling power only at the source did not sit well with Lilienthal, who wanted to compete on every front—besides, people wanted cheap power, and towns and rural districts throughout the region were clamoring for their own public systems. Having a say in transmission and distribution meant leverage over the companies who could never be quite sure when and where TVA and its allies would intervene next. Also, a broader role meant that TVA would wield considerably more influence in the Tennessee Valley than if it were restricted to selling electricity at the dam.[5]

There were certain strengths that played to TVA's advantage. First, there was ample evidence that the utilities had not provided adequate services. In 1928, in thirteen of the ninety-five Tennessee counties no towns had any electric service, and in nearly two-thirds of the counties fewer than three towns had service. In addition, sixteen counties were without any transmission lines and another eleven had only ten miles or less.[6]

Then, there was Roosevelt's unwavering support. TVA was, he told a reporter in 1936, "the apple of his eye." It was his creation and it embraced more of his concerns than any other federal agency, old or new. Perhaps the price the directors had to pay for vague executive direction was offset by the fact that Roosevelt thought that everything TVA was doing was important. In support of TVA, the president visited the Tennessee Valley more than once, and he always seemed available to the entreaties of both Lilienthal and A. E. Morgan and the concerns of TVA loyalists such as Norris, Morris Cooke, and Robert La Follette Jr.[7]

The most important advantage, perhaps, was the board. The directors were men of exceptional talents. Each brought unique skills and left permanent impressions. A. E. Morgan was a master engineer, dam builder, and social visionary. He had directed many water control projects across the land in the 1910s and 1920s. The cornerstone of his technical genius was the Miami River Conservancy project, which legitimated the idea of dry dams designed only to contain flood waters. The savior of Antioch College, A. E. Morgan used his academic pulpit to develop the co-op plan in which students combined work and study, to stimulate student industries, and to circulate his views on social transformation. A no-nonsense crusader, a disciple of Edward Bellamy's utopian vision, and an advocate of Frederick Taylor's scientific management theory, he had little sympathy for bureaucratic or political intrigue. A. E. Morgan believed that public works should be guided by spare efficiency, exacting competence, and enlightened labor policies. The string of dams along the Tennessee and one of the best personnel systems in the New Deal owed much to A. E. Morgan's farsighted vision and discipline.

If A. E. Morgan had a grand vision, H. A. Morgan provided legitimacy and a solid local basis of support so necessary while TVA was being rocked by other forces. A Tennessee Valley resident for half a century, he had been a popular field entomologist, dean of the University of Tennessee School of Agriculture, and tied to all manner of Tennessee Valley institutions through the State Extension Service and the University of Tennessee Agriculture Experiment Stations. Nor was H. A. Morgan without his own vision. For decades he lectured and wrote of "the Common Mooring," the indivisible unity of soil, air, water, and all life. Years later, Lilienthal credited this vision of unity as the basis for his theme of "grass roots" administration and democracy.[8]

Then there was Lilienthal. He liked to say, "I am the only [director] not named Morgan; I am the only one who is not a 'doctor,' and I am the only one who is not a college president." Where H. A. Morgan lent legitimacy, the youngest director provided the spark, extending TVA with his great energy and ability to inspire. Described by TVA associates as charismatic, a showman, a communicator, and a consummate politician, Lilienthal personalized TVA with his visibility and oratorical skills in a way neither Morgan could. H. A. was an inarticulate speaker, and the chairman, with his radical ideas and aversion to politics, was often unpopular when he spoke out in the Tennessee Valley and in Washington. Anathema to the power industry, Lilienthal played this opposition to the hilt, calling upon supporters such as Frankfurter, Cooke, La Follette, Frank Walsh, and Milo Maltbie to whisper in Roosevelt's ear whenever he or TVA was in a bind.[9]

Lilienthal drew great reserves of strength from his strong ego. Contemporaries described him as messianic, someone who liked to take credit, or "just a little bit too much concerned with Lilienthal." Another recalled that he was "purposely provocative" in order to draw attention to himself. And yet he was capable of generating strong allegiances. Many of his critics respected his ability to relate to all types of people, his brilliance, and even an ability, however grudging at times, to give credit to others. John Oliver, former TVA general manager and later vice-president with Lilienthal's Development and Resources Corporation, called him a "paragon" of the early TVA years. Harry Wiersema, first assistant director of TVA's Engineering Service Division and never a strong Lilienthal supporter, noted that "Lilienthal just ran the roost," and that he "was always very friendly to me."[10]

Lilienthal's other great strength was his ability to give total attention to an issue. Methodist bishop G. Bromley Oxnam called him "an administrator with a purpose." Transformed into a public power advocate by his frustrations in Wisconsin, he saw TVA as a righteous sword to revolutionize rate making and energy consumption practices throughout the nation. From 1933 to 1939 he pursued those ends with single-minded purpose, sometimes with ruthless abandon, but always prepared—both substantively and politically. Power engineer Roland Kampmeier, a longtime Lilienthal loyalist, described him as "sort of a schemer." Walter Kahoe, one of A. E. Morgan's right-hand men, recalled that "I never saw Dave miss a trick." In his ability to concentrate, he displayed yet another remarkable talent. Edward Falck, TVA's first chief rate engineer, recalled Lilienthal's capacity to transform other people's ideas into viable policies. In much that same manner, the philosophy of TVA power engineer Llewellyn Evans, that low rates would stimulate high enough consumption to pay for itself, became Lilienthal's evangelical message to the Tennessee Valley and a national example.[11]

Another advantage the early board enjoyed was the support within the normally isolated and suspicious Tennessee Valley and the almost immediate creation of a "TVA mystique." While all of the directors contributed to the aura of the new agency—A. E. Morgan with his unwavering commitment to technical excellence and austere sense of moral probity, H. A. Morgan with an exemplary record of service to the people of the South, and Lilienthal as a skillful orator and propagandist—there was another important factor, Franklin D. Roosevelt. For the first time in Tennessee Valley memory, the man in the White House and his federal legions were trying to do something for them, and on a grand scale at that. The Tennessee region was a national showcase, and towns lined up for TVA power. Neither did it hurt that the authority promised thousands of positions for a job-poor labor pool. TVA also gained quick acceptance because the top ranks were filled with hundreds of socially conscious managers, engineers, attorneys, and other professionals and technicians. These men, and a few women, were hungry for jobs, but they were also committed to good works and social justice.[12]

Lilienthal had an additional advantage—Helen. Supportive to a fault, she took charge of family affairs during his long days in Knoxville and frequent trips through the Tennessee Valley or to Washington. Because of her husband's politicking, Helen often played the role of unofficial TVA hostess, opening her house to countless guests and frequently filling in as a tour guide for visitors. She always accepted these tasks with good grace. She bragged how she helped her husband when they traveled together, asking questions "when his knowledge was a bit uncertain. . . . None of the experts expected me to know anything, and I didn't, so their explanation would enlighten Dave, while he could stand back and look indulgent." By her own account, Helen was happiest as his speech and literary critic, a role she filled their entire marriage. She was his sounding board and least indulgent critic, reminding him time and again that if she did not understand a point, others would not either. As she remembered, "When I would say that something wasn't clear, he'd groan and go back to work on it until I passed it." Perhaps most important, she gave refuge and strength. By her word, she was his only confidant.[13]

The First Months

By mid-1933 the three directors were on board, and in spite of initial uncertainties, TVA quickly took shape. To A. E. Morgan's credit, the Cove Creek project was on time, enlightened labor policies were in place, and TVA was known in Washington as a merit-driven agency. As early as June, Lilienthal checked with Frankfurter and Kenneth D. McKellar, the senior senator from Tennessee, about qualified southern lawyers for the legal staff. He asked Morris Cooke for help in hiring socially conscious engineers. Once in the Tennessee Valley, Lilienthal took the lead in selling TVA to all manner of civic and community groups. He moved quickly to establish power rates, develop a power policy he and A. E. Morgan could live with, firm up contracts with municipalities, and stabilize relationships between TVA and the private utilities. Lilienthal also worked hard to solidify his own position within the authority.[14]

Perhaps his most important early accomplishment was forging an enduring friendship with H. A. Morgan and keeping him on the board. Although thirty years apart in age, Lilienthal and "Doc Morgan" quickly took to each other. An alliance of convenience at first, they found they shared great deal more. Soon after Lilienthal's arrival, H. A. Morgan introduced Lilienthal around the Tennessee Valley. While A. E. Morgan thought the relationship a function of Lilienthal's manipulative skills, others saw it differently. Robert Sessions, who started work for H. A. Morgan in late 1933, found it difficult "to think of them [the two directors] separately because of the obvious rapport that had already been established." Much later, Lilienthal reflected that if H. A. Morgan "had not supported me, not alone on the policies, but for my way of going about these things, the conservative . . . leaders of the Tennessee Valley clearly would have rejected me."[15]

In July 1933, however, the question of survival concerned H. A. Morgan, not Lilienthal. Not yet comfortable in his new job nor sure how long he might remain a director—he took off only a year from the university— H. A. Morgan was bothered by the increasingly arbitrary chairman, who hired key personnel on his own and even accused his colleagues of delaying crucial appointments. A. E. Morgan's radical vision also clashed with that of the practical agriculturalist. Throughout the month of July, H. A. Morgan and his young colleague mulled over the situation. Lilienthal remembered a long North Carolina weekend where they discussed "how we were going to get this thing so it could work with Dr. Arthur Morgan going off in so many directions." At the end of July, they got their wake-up call.[16]

Still without offices, the board met on July 30 in the Farragut Hotel in Knoxville. A. E. Morgan held court for nine hours and tried to rush through a slew of proposals, many, according to H. A. Morgan, "of far-reaching and startling significance." The mass of detail was so great that A. E. Morgan slipped past a motion naming Cove Creek Dam after Senator Norris, a decision that irked a president adamantly opposed to naming public works for living persons. The most disturbing recommendations, particularly for H. A. Morgan, came from the chairman's twenty-two-point memorandum that appeared to codify his social experiments. Among his proposals were "the development of a general social and economic plan," programs fostering small industrial and agricultural communities and cooperative distribution systems, and a "commission to study the proper function of the real estate man in an organized society." Remembering the negative reaction to an earlier proposal by A. E. Morgan for a TVA employees' ethics code, the other directors feared that many of these "social engineering" projects would alienate conservative Tennessee Valley interests. To H. A. Morgan, the chairman's ideas were "impracticable and highly visionary or clearly outside the scope of our responsibility." Contrary to Lilienthal's desire to move cautiously in developing power resources, A. E. Morgan urged that

TVA proceed quickly on all the projects in an earlier Army Corps of Engineers report on the power potential of the Tennessee River.[17]

The next day H. A. Morgan told Lilienthal he would resign from the board if things did not change. They both worked on a memorandum that reached the chairman on August 3. The two directors complained about the lack of "a satisfactory or workable program, or procedure of administration." They called for a division of responsibilities among the directors with overall policy direction remaining with the board. A. E. Morgan's areas would include the integration of "various parts of the work into a unified program," Norris Dam and other engineering projects, navigation, and several "social experiments." H. A. Morgan was given all agriculture programs, while Lilienthal dealt with power and legal matters. At the time, A. E. Morgan took the challenge gracefully, defending himself by saying he was forced to make certain decisions and that "the apparent confusion" was due to the rapidity of events. Nevertheless, he did not criticize the new structure and even voted for it. He hoped, however, that this division would not interrupt certain activities that promised "revolutionary advancement."[18]

A. E. Morgan's acquiescence was only a facade. In 1938 he remembered the August 1933 action as a crass power grab, describing the August 5 atmosphere as "very hostile" and the action "aggressively resentful and dictatorial." In reality, no one liked the plan. J. Dudley Dawson, a former aide to A. E. Morgan, recalled that TVA personnel director Floyd Reeves called the decision "a terrible mistake" and had "disastrous consequences in the future." Lilienthal admitted later he thought it "unsound and so did Harcourt Morgan." For others, the policy violated the principle of administrative unity and blurred the line between policy making and administration. Moreover, dividing TVA into three fiefdoms only frustrated a much-needed sense of unity. Nevertheless, considering the strong personality differences and the fact that the directors had to be involved in many day-to-day decisions, the arrangement was probably best at the time.[19]

In spite of a surface calm, board relationships were tense the rest of 1933, perhaps a little less so the last two months. TVA managers remembered the confrontations at the first board meetings. Neil Bass recalled raucous shouting matches, and Earl Draper lamented that neither Lilienthal nor H. A. Morgan would give an inch to the chairman. In August, Floyd Reeves warned A. E. Morgan that Lilienthal was working against him. Next month, Arnold Kruckman of the Washington staff wrote the chairman that Lilienthal and Washington office director Marguerite Owen were undermining him. The chairman was also disturbed that private discussions about issues such as his TVA employee ethics code had been leaked and roundly ridiculed around the authority. He tried to deal with this "palace of intrigue" by complaining to Roosevelt about the new arrangements and Lilienthal's antics, but the president only listened. A. E. Morgan confronted Lilienthal, but the smooth-talking director assured him that the rumors were false. In spite of Lilienthal's denial, there is little reason to doubt that Lilienthal did actively undermine A. E. Morgan. As Jordan Schwarz observed, "Photographs of Lilienthal at TVA occasions often show him with a smirk suggesting contempt [toward A. E. Morgan]."[20]

Aside from internal battles, Lilienthal focused on the key ingredients for success—people and power. As always, he thrived before audiences. Roland Kampmeier remembered Lilienthal's successful speechifying as rooted "partly [in his] skillfulness with words [and] partly the charismatic nature of his personality." Joe Swidler called him "a pretty good actor" and an "excellent showman." Bishop Oxnam said "this administrator caused words to unbend." After his first tour with H. A. Morgan, Lilienthal redoubled his efforts, speaking to the issues people wanted to hear, selling himself, and having the people's "self-confidence confirmed and assured." One observer recalled a multitude of receptions and banquets with Lilienthal always waving a familiar white Panama hat. Lilienthal wrote of weeks of "four or five speeches a day . . . . in Alabama, Mississippi, Georgia, Kentucky." Soon, he bragged, he knew more important folks than H. A. Morgan in all of the Tennessee Valley except Tennessee. Helen remembered "countless impromptu [speeches] to small groups, . . . all the way down to a few farmers at a crossroads." And Lilienthal was savvy. Willson Whitman told of his being offered a home-cured Kentucky ham. At first he would not take it, explaining TVA's gift policy. Then the man who offered the ham retorted: "What's the matter with you TVA men? Fellow came through here a while back and I offered him a ham and he wouldn't take it either. Name of A. E. Morgan. I said then, a man that didn't have sense enough to take a Kentucky ham didn't have sense enough to build a dam." Needless to say, said Whitman, Lilienthal took the ham.[21]

In addition to the common folk, Lilienthal knew he had to win over a skeptical business community. To do so, he scheduled four summer and fall Rotary Club speeches in Knoxville, Chattanooga, Memphis, and Nashville, and another before the Atlanta Lawyers Club. The speeches were a masterful blend of persuasion and exhortation and constituted his first effort to articulate a TVA vision. The authority, he assured his audiences, was committed to cooperating with local institutions in a businesslike, nonpolitical manner to achieve economic development and raise the self-esteem and material well-being of everyone in the Tennessee Valley. TVA would not force itself upon the community—local initiative was crucial. At one moment he was conservative businessman, at another, prophet of the future. When he raised his voice in anger, it was always against outsiders—Yankee newspapers and distant utility companies lording it over southerners. And, at every chance, he talked about a wonderful new genie, electricity. While he mentioned agriculture, navigation, and conservation, it was clear that cheap and abundant power formed the foundation for his message of progress and prosperity.

While the speeches were identical in places, each reflected TVA's rapid progress. In Chattanooga, Lilienthal discussed the division of board authority and progress at Norris. He deftly announced that the long-awaited Chickamauga Dam near Chattanooga would be delayed because finishing the project then would increase TVA's power capacity beyond its market. You businessmen, he said, "would consider, as most unsound, any suggestion that you double the capacity of your plant . . . unless you were pretty sure that you would be able to develop a market for the increased product." In Memphis, he detailed the new rate structure and, in Nashville, announced that the new Tupelo contract would result in a 60 percent rate decrease for the Mississippi community.[22]

In each speech, power was increasingly emphasized. The November 25 Atlanta address was his most forceful. Noting that electricity consumption in the nation had fallen while power-generating capacities had increased, Lilienthal pledged "nothing less than the electrification of the homes and farms of the United States." Leading by example, TVA would stimulate a major increase in power use throughout the region. He promised that drastic rate reductions would lead to greatly increased consumption, and then suggested a joint government-industry appliance distribution program in which consumers could take even greater advantage of the new rates. Admittedly, he concluded, the job was not one for the "mere theorist," or "enthusiast who faints at the sight of a difficult business problem." The effort demanded everyone's attention, "the progressive leaders of the utility industry, of the electric manufacturing industry, and of government."[23]

By the end of November the public relations blitz had done its job. He sparked the imagination of the major regional interests and, as Swidler remembered, "showed an amazing capacity for acceptance by the people of the Tennessee Valley, considering that he was a Northerner, a child of Jewish parentage . . . [and] a Harvard Law School graduate, in an area where this was not a general recommendation." The pro-TVA *Knoxville News-Sentinel* applauded "his appreciation of the progressive works which have been done in the South." In Chattanooga, the friendly *News* commended his "power of words and personality." Even the anti-TVA *Times* called the address "spirited, optimistic and friendly," and observed that Lilienthal had "vitaliz[ed] every word with his own enthusiasm and a magnetic, confidence-winning personality." In the same issue, an editorial praised the young director for having "the good sense to oppose construction of Chickamauga dam . . . until there is a market for the kilowatts." A Nashville editorialist observed that Lilienthal had made "a splendid impression," and one in Memphis called his speech "as fair-minded as it was brilliant."[24]

While selling was important, everything hinged on sorting out certain policies. First, Lilienthal and A. E. Morgan had to work out their differences on power. Second, viable rate structures had to be developed. And third, TVA had to start securing municipal service contracts and agreements with the utilities to determine service boundaries and cooperative agreements. Although Lilienthal was not convinced that a definitive power statement was necessary, A. E. Morgan insisted on it. The other issues, however, were crucial. Without rates, there would be no basis for levying charges. Without an understanding with the utilities or power contracts, TVA would have no market.

Lilienthal's and A. E. Morgan's initial conflicts were sparked in part by disagreements over TVA's power mission and relationships with the utilities. A. E. Morgan had little experience with power—most of his work had been in water control. Moreover, his vision of TVA as a multidimensional social program had much less of a place for power. Finally, his vision was more in tune with the hopeful future of Edward Bellamy than the apocalyptic horror of Jack London—his world view emphasized cooperation among institutions rather than battles to the bloody end. He was willing to believe that the utilities' offer of cooperation had been made in good faith.

Not Lilienthal. While he had a vision, he was no visionary; while he was a liberal, he was always pragmatic. Unlike A. E. Morgan, Lilienthal knew power policy. As a scholarly attorney he had studied the regulatory struggles. As a public service commissioner he had been battered and seen his rulings thwarted by powerful companies with bottomless coffers and endless armies of lawyers. By mid-1933, he was little interested in cooperating with any utility. Moreover, he felt the pressure of mentors who had always loathed the power trust. He leaned heavily on Frankfurter for advice in the early months. In July, in response to a letter from Lilienthal about A. E. Morgan, Frankfurter said, "Of course you are right in your position. . . . The Chairman's proposal is fraught with every kind of danger. . . . Does he realize what a first-class row he is precipitating?" In a mid-August visit, Lilienthal regaled Frankfurter with more horror stories, and Frankfurter wrote Brandeis afterwards, "Arthur Morgan is incredibly naive—and defensive and worse." The rest of the year, Frankfurter and Brandeis persisted in reminding Lilienthal to watch out for the utilities.[25]

Morris Cooke was even more influential. He had known A. E. Morgan for years and, through earlier correspondence, Cooke knew that the chairman's attitudes toward the utilities were much more lenient than his own. By the summer of 1933, he was worried about what was going on in the Tennessee Valley. In July he wrote A. E. Morgan after hearing that a TVA official had said the authority would not compete with "existing power interests." A. E. Morgan answered immediately, calling the statement a misquote and avowing, "We shall certainly compete with private power if our plans do not fail or change." For the next month Cooke prodded Lilienthal to institute an aggressive power policy. Once, he warned his friend that TVA was "proceeding along lines which are dangerous." A week later, Cooke urged Lilienthal to "do Uncle Sam's job without promising any private interest anything" and not to allow "the private power interests to know your mind." In late August, he counseled Lilienthal to adopt "an aggressive policy and one sufficiently 'grandiose' to carry your public with you and weaken the morale of the enemy."[26]

In the meantime, tensions were building. Artfully wooed by Willkie, A. E. Morgan wanted a cooperative power policy with territorial division and a TVA pledge not to build duplicate power lines. Lilienthal, on the other hand, was little interested in tipping TVA's hand with a firm position, and was also opposed to any restrictive agreements. The battle was joined in mid-July when the two exchanged their first salvos on power. The tone of the letters only aggravated the conflict. A. E. Morgan's short, penciled note was a priggish lecture, punctuated seven times by haughty statements of principle prefaced by "I think" and "I believe." Preachy in tone, he cautioned against competition and told Lilienthal that TVA "should assume reasonableness, fair play and good will on the part of the utilities" and that negotiations should be "undertak[en] in good faith."[27]

Lilienthal's reply consisted of three single-spaced pages of tightly reasoned argument. Beginning with a barbed reference to A. E. Morgan's "pencil note," he lectured the chairman for being impractical and insisted it was too early to "formulate a policy which involves the making of far-reaching commitments the consequences of which we cannot foresee." More time was needed to understand "how the other interrelated objectives are going to work out," and to gather data about markets and rate bases before agreeing on anything. Moreover, he was skeptical about "genuine 'co-operation' with the private utilities," especially the notion that they would voluntarily give up territory. In a closing that must have irked A. E. Morgan, Lilienthal announced he was going to "sound out [Norris] on the matter," and that it might "be wise to confer with a few other time-tried men."[28]

On August 14 in Washington, A. E. Morgan handed Lilienthal another memorandum and told him he had arranged a board meeting with Roosevelt on August 16. Reiterating his "cooperative policy" in greater detail, he related that he had assured Willkie that TVA would "endeavor to work out some harmonious arrangement." Furthermore, he reminded his fellow directors that Roosevelt supported his position. When Lilienthal called Knoxville with the news, H. A. Morgan wired the chairman demanding he tell the president that power was Lilienthal's domain and that in not adopting territorial restrictions, the board had already spoken. A. E. Morgan then tried to cancel the meeting, but Roosevelt insisted on seeing him anyway. In the meantime, Lilienthal prepared a devastating response. Pointedly calling himself "Director in Charge of Power," he concluded that "no agreement should be entered into with private utilities." Lilienthal called A. E. Morgan's proposal "unscientific" and "impractical." Furthermore, he continued, it "serves no public interest" and "endangers the project." In the unkindest cut of all, he charged that "[A. E. Morgan's] proposal [is] opposed by time-tested public men." He then invoked the opinions of Norris, Cooke, La Follette, Frankfurter, Los Angeles Power Bureau chief E. F. Scattergood, and Federal Power Commission Chairman Frank McNinch, claiming they all felt it "a grave mistake for the Authority to try to negotiate a blanket agreement with private utilities."[29]

Realizing the serious nature of the conflict and also that something had to be done since the old power sale contract between Muscle Shoals and Alabama Power & Light was about to expire, Roosevelt called in Lilienthal and A. E. Morgan on August 19. Seeming to take A. E. Morgan's side, he told them to prepare a policy they could both live with. Later that day the two directors met to hammer out an agreement. On August 24, TVA announced an eleven-point policy. The agreement stressed the public nature of electric power but affirmed private producer rights as long as they did not violate the public interest. It pledged to avoid financially damaging the private companies and duplication of services, but hinted that under certain circumstances TVA might need to act against them. Two points inspired by Roosevelt addressed territorial restrictions. One stated that TVA would restrict its service area, but added that circumstances might warrant future expansion. The other suggested that TVA would eventually cover the entire Tennessee River basin and the rest of Tennessee. A final point emphasized that TVA would offer a valid "yardstick" to compare private costs and rates. The policy had two effects. First, because it was vague, the utilities were still unsure of the authority's next moves. Second, because A. E. Morgan was satisfied for the moment, Lilienthal could devote total attention to steering TVA into the power market.[30]

Setting rates was crucial. Lilienthal knew this, but he also knew that rate determination would be difficult. In 1933 there still was little consensus over how to establish fair rates for both the investor and the consumer. The root conflict involved rate basis—a complex calculation of operating costs and capital base value. The most vehement disagreements developed over the latter issue, valuation. Should a company calculate its value according to current reproduction costs, original investment, or prudent investment? The valuation problem was particularly vexing because TVA's entire capital base consisted of the Muscle Shoals properties, including Wilson Dam, which had been built haphazardly with construction often delayed for want of appropriations. As a result, project costs had been high. Had TVA been private, this would have been good news: a large capital base would translate into a high rate base, the ultimate justification for higher rates. However, TVA's goal was low rates. Hence, the authority could hardly afford to overestimate its rate base. An inflated base would necessitate higher wholesale rates and ultimately endanger a retail low-rate structure designed to encourage consumption. Lilienthal was also faced with an urgent public relations problem. In June and July, more than a dozen cities in the Muscle Shoals area, including some whose utility contracts had expired or were about to expire were clamoring for TVA power.[31]

In late July, the board authorized Lilienthal to begin community negotiations. Six days later, Llewellyn Evans submitted a preliminary report on costs and rates. Evans, former manager of the Tacoma, Washington, municipal power company, was, according to Joseph Swidler, a man who "moved by instinct and vision." Hired by Lilienthal, ironically at A. E. Morgan's suggestion, Evans was a perfect addition to the power team—he provided the ideas that Lilienthal translated into policy. Echoing his own experience, Evans argued that low rates would dramatically increase consumption and result in even lower costs. He recommended simple rate schedules, low rates for small users, and decreased rates for households opting for high-use home heating. From preliminary cost studies he assured Lilienthal that TVA could easily afford rates "as low as those of Tacoma or

Ontario [Hydro]," the legendary Canadian utility that had long inspired the American public power movement.[32]

On August 22, the board authorized Lilienthal to develop a rate plan "based on the principle that increased use of power . . . follows upon low rates." In the next three weeks, Evans, consulting engineer Walter Polakov, and their young boss tackled two questions: how much would TVA have to charge in wholesale rates to meet costs, and what level of retail rates would cover distribution costs and stimulate greater use? The first question rested on the sticky question of valuation. On September 8 and 9 Lilienthal and Evans went to Madison, Wisconsin, to consult with Lilienthal's former associates. Ed Morehouse remembered that they did not have "very many guidelines," and worked with the "best [data] we could get." As a result, much of the discussion was distinctly unscientific, with each participant expressing "what he thought were useful and reliable figures," and centered on designing a rate structure to meet "what the experiment of the TVA was designed to do." By the end of two eighteen-hour days, Evans's original figures and rate schedules were revised in light of Wisconsin's experience with municipal utilities. From Wisconsin, Lilienthal and Evans traveled to New York to confer with James C. Bonbright and Leland Olds of the New York Power Authority. Then, they returned to Knoxville to finalize their rate structure.[33]

Lilienthal carefully orchestrated the rate announcement. On September 13 he told the press that TVA would follow "sound business methods." He emphasized that TVA rates would provide a "yardstick" comparison for costs and rates throughout the industry and hinted of a home appliance purchase program to increase consumption and living standards. The next day he announced the good news. While private rates in the area ranged from 4.6 to 5.8 cents per kilowatt hour, TVA would charge three cents per kilowatt hour for the first fifty kilowatts, gradually decreasing to four mills for usage over four hundred kilowatts. He promised even lower rates in the future should consumption increase significantly. Despite the detailed retail rate schedules, other issues were broached with less candor. While Lilienthal's assurance that rates had been developed "after weeks of careful study of costs and market factors" was literally true, it avoided the awkward question as to whether even a few "weeks" were enough to do the job right. Second, the release virtually ignored thorny question of wholesale rates. That day, Lilienthal wanted the spotlight on what mattered most—how much consumers would have to pay.

Nevertheless, he didn't wait long. The next day another release covered wholesale rates. Lilienthal announced that the seven-mill wholesale figure was based on TVA's property value and cost factors including taxes, interest, repayment of capital to the treasury, depreciation, operation, and maintenance. Once again, he gave the rate figures more legitimacy than they deserved when he talked of "the best available data and weeks of close study and analysis, . . . subjected to the criticism of recognized rate experts." He might well have said that even expert advice was questionable without accurate and complete data.[34]

There is no doubt about Thomas McCraw's conclusion that the process was "highly speculative" and "an exercise in intuition." Thirty years later Lilienthal admitted as much when he wrote that the innovative rate schedule "was based on some kind of insight ('an idea') rather than an exhaustive rate analysis. . . . We created the supporting facts after the idea had been born and expressed." Nevertheless, the strategy worked. The assumption that low rates stimulated high consumption was validated throughout the region, especially in the rural areas where the utilities had always sworn that they could never make a profit. Moreover, for a restless Lilienthal, it was time to throw down the gauntlet and start making something of TVA. The announcements, particularly the one regarding wholesale rates, did just that. Next day the story made the front page of the *New York Times*. Almost as quickly, TVA rates became the talk of the editorial pages, with Scripps-Howard papers supportive, the *Times* skeptical, and the *Chicago Tribune* in vehement opposition. Wall Street recorded an immediate fall in utility stocks and bonds, and industry spokesmen accused Lilienthal of "putting municipal plants [distributors] in the South 'on the spot.' . . . Few of them will be able to survive."

Almost overnight the young director was labeled a radical. Yet, a close look at the initial decisions suggests that he was less a radical than a gambling innovator. Hurried as it was, the rate-making outcome was certainly not radical. In calculating rate basis, Lilienthal, Evans, and the consultants agreed to A. E. Morgan's conservative value estimate that raised the valuation of Wilson Dam from $19.5 to $24 million. Even the utilities acknowledged that the wholesale rate was not much different from their own. Moreover, everyone knew the rate structure had to be politically defensible and grounded in "cost of service" not a "social [good]" basis. As one of the Madison consultants, Hank Zinder, told Lilienthal, a "cost plan" is the best way of "avoiding criticism of the Authority by customers and utilities." On the retail side, Lilienthal's leadership reflected his uncanny ability to translate bold ideas into workable policies, and a willingness to gamble. For the plan to succeed, Leland Olds warned, monthly domestic consumption would have to double to one hundred kilowatt hours. No doubt this was a great risk, since the national domestic average was only fifty-five kilowatt hours per household.[35]

In spite of the outcry from the press and utilities, the remainder of the year passed relatively calmly. A. E. Morgan had his say on power policy and was busy with Norris dam and his pet project, the experimental town of Norris. Lilienthal was happy because the power program was his "baby" and A. E. Morgan no longer interfered. In fact, in a November speech in Boston to the National Academy of Science, the chairman praised his colleague for working out power policies "with vigor and dispatch, and I believe, in a masterful manner." Lilienthal was elated with the rapid progress. In November, his negotiators, led by Joe Swidler, signed up Tupelo, and later that month Knoxville voted overwhelmingly for TVA power. Some of his most rewarding moments toward the end of 1933 came, as he told Fred Arvin, in "horse-trading with the utilities" and the beginning of almost six years of negotiations with C&S President Wendell Willkie.[36]

They first met on October 4 in Washington. Lilienthal recalled that "we were two exceedingly cagey fellows." Willkie scared Lilienthal "pretty badly" when he predicted that public power support would wane, but the TVA director soon recovered his confidence. For the next two months, in a score of meetings and telephone conversations, the two men warily "walk[ed] around and around each other" looking for common ground. As the weeks passed, pressures mounted. Willkie knew TVA had authorized a transmission line from Wilson to Norris and that a growing number of cities were interested in TVA power. Lilienthal, on the other hand, needed a market other than Alabama Power. The Tupelo contract and Roosevelt's high-profile visit to the community in November provided the break he needed. Now he could challenge Willkie either to share his transmission lines or face the possibility of TVA building its own.

On December 12 and 13, the logjam began to break. At first, Willkie offered only to sell facilities at three towns near Wilson Dam. At a second meeting on the twelfth, Willkie came back looking "low and discouraged." He was caught both ways. The more facilities he sold, either to TVA or cities, the greater the justification for the TVA program. If he did not sell, however, TVA would build duplicate lines, and the cities, through Public Works Administration (PWA) loans, would duplicate private utility distribution systems and render his properties worthless. According to Lilienthal, Willkie threatened litigation and continuing resistance, but the next day he agreed to a five-year contract, or until six months after Norris came on line. Willkie's companies would sell certain properties in Mississippi, Tennessee, and Alabama, and both parties agreed not to compete with each other. Since the TVA market could not absorb all the Wilson power, the two agreed to selling most of the remainder to Alabama Power. They also pledged to develop a joint appliance promotion program. The agreement was signed on January 4, 1934. Momentarily, the prospects for peaceful coexistence seemed good.[37]

Power Is the Key

Between 1934 and early 1938 Lilienthal was involved in two struggles that tested every bit of his moral and political fiber. The continuing battle with A. E. Morgan and the relentless attack by the utilities brought out the best and the worst in him. He was a brilliant strategist and tactician with an uncanny sense of timing. He was constantly on the go—and on edge all the time. In April 1934, he admitted to Fred Arvin that because of the "ungodly pressure and poison of this job, on top of Wisconsin, I had a kind of nervous breakdown." In January and February he worked less than a week, took a two-week trip to Jamaica with Helen and another sixteen-day jaunt by himself to Florida. Still struggling, he wrote his doctor in July that "I am trying to reorganize my way of doing things to avoid another threatened smashup." In March 1936, a Knoxville doctor recorded that Lilienthal "never fully recovered" from his 1934 breakdown. Late that same year he spent six weeks in Florida fighting off another attack of exhaustion and despair.[38]

Lilienthal took the brunt of the massive assault by the utilities. H. A. Morgan was rarely challenged over the less controversial agriculture program, and A. E. Morgan seemed more often than not to be on the side of the utilities—once, he even asked the legal staff if the court could rule the power program unconstitutional and leave the rest of TVA intact. One of the interesting ironies that linked both conflicts was that A. E. Morgan had a higher regard for Wendell Willkie than he did for Lilienthal, a reality that made the latter only more resolute in their personal feud.[39]

Lilienthal was a consummate image maker. He gave forty major speeches between 1934 and 1937, sixteen of which focused almost entirely on power. In April 1934 he bragged to Frankfurter that his "campaign to change public opinion on public power has been successful beyond anything I could have asked for in 5 years, much less 5 months." What marked his efforts so much was his skill in giving the TVA power program a substantial image when in reality, it was no more than a Potemkin village. Three crucial elements in this campaign included TVA's "yardstick" mission, the Electric Home and Farm Authority (EHFA), and the crafting of a "partnership" with local governments and cooperatives in the Tennessee Valley. For Lilienthal, the yardstick was an apt symbol of his rate-reduction strategy, and EHFA provided evidence of TVA's commitment to raising living standards as a means for increasing the use of electricity. The partnership model reinforced both notions: the larger the service area the more accurate the yardstick and the greater the opportunity for stimulating consumption. It mattered little that Lilienthal's yardstick was vague and simplistic or that EHFA never really succeeded. Moreover, Lilienthal was so persuasive in touting TVA's partnership mission that few noticed in 1934 that less than 1 percent of TVA power was sold to municipalities—after a year the authority had only five public contracts with 6,500 customers. Indeed, by 1938 TVA had only nineteen municipal contractors, whose purchases constituted only 12 percent of all power revenues. What was important was that the power director was able, through rhetoric and skillful maneuvering, to craft an image of TVA that poorly matched its reality.[40]

The "yardstick" arose in the early 1900s in response to the inadequacy of public commission utility regulation. As much a reform slogan as anything, the concept evolved through three more or less distinct definitions. In its first incarnation as "institutional alternative," "yardstick" simply meant enabling local communities to buy and run their own utilities when traditional regulation no longer worked. This interpretation was reflected in the La Follette-Lilienthal reforms of 1931. The "cost comparison" yardstick arose later as public companies, notably Los Angeles, Tacoma, and Ontario Hydro in Canada, succeeded in combining good service and low rates. Public power advocates argued that these operations provided a benchmark for the entire industry. In the 1920s, with holding company scandals and an increasingly vocal public power movement as background, the yardstick took on coercive dimensions—that the institutional and comparative alternatives could be used to compel rate reductions or takeovers of private companies.[41]

Early on, Franklin Roosevelt touted the yardstick as a comparative standard for utilities and other industries. In the heat of the 1932 campaign, he introduced the "'birch rod' in the cupboard," a yardstick with the full force of government backing to compel fair rates. In Portland, Oregon, in 1932, Roosevelt emphasized that any community should be able to "create a yardstick of its own" by operating its own utility after being ill-served by a private company. In addition, he proposed four federal power projects on the St. Lawrence and Columbia Rivers, and at Muscle Shoals and Boulder Dam to anchor "a national yardstick to prevent extortion against the public and to encourage the wider use of . . . electricity." The problem, however, was that while the yardstick was a fetching campaign cry, Roosevelt never lent much substance to the concept.[42]

It was quite natural to see the same vagaries in congressional debate over TVA. While never mentioning the word *yardstick,* provisions in Section 14 of the TVA Act required the authority to measure costs of generation, transmission, and distribution, thus suggesting that Congress also intended for TVA rates to provide a comparative standard. It soon became obvious, however, that using TVA rates as a benchmark had serious problems. Comparability assumed that rate base factors such as construction, generation and distribution costs, methods of raising capital, operating procedures, and markets were similar. No matter how much the authority talked of strict accounting procedures to measure costs, TVA's unique position made any comparison highly suspect. For one thing, its hydroelectric base offered a poor comparison for the steam plant bases of most southern utilities.

Moreover, other factors tended to lower TVA rates, such as the imprecise practice of charging off capital costs to flood prevention and navigation, the efficiency inherent in a coordinated river system, and advantages unique to a government project, especially one that was "the apple of the president's eye." It was comforting to know that the agency could rely on regular appropriations and politically timely loans from agencies such as PWA. TVA was also unique in that, unlike most utilities, it was not a unified system. By leaving distribution to municipalities and rural cooperatives, TVA was not comparable to most companies, which combined production, transmission, and distribution. Yet other factors tended to increase costs. For example, during high water and slack times, power production was sacrificed to flood control and navigation functions. Finally, there could be no true comparability without similar markets. Costs would vary according to the particular mix of rural, small-town, large-city, and industrial customers. Thus, there was no way TVA rates could serve as an accurate benchmark for other utilities, especially in the early years when TVA's small local market was very different from other operating companies in the area.

Nevertheless, the yardstick had strong intuitive appeal—it seemed plausible, was easily communicated, and it was the president's pet notion.[43]

It came as no surprise that TVA adopted the yardstick as a rationale for the power program. The concept first surfaced in Lilienthal and A. E. Morgan's August 18 power policy statement, which called for the "comparison of operations with privately-owned plants." Both directors enthusiastically promoted TVA's ability to provide yardstick standards. Early in 1934, A. E. Morgan announced that TVA would promote the concept because the president had called for "a yardstick for power." For the next few years and as late as August 1937, A. E. Morgan endorsed the yardstick as long as "accounts were fully public, . . . costs . . . fairly reported, and . . . there were no subsidies." The difference between A. E. Morgan and Lilienthal, however, lay in experience. A. E. Morgan was naive about rate making and it was natural that he would promote the idea in an uncritical manner.[44]

Lilienthal embraced the yardstick even more quickly than A. E. Morgan did, but he should have known better. He knew the difficulties involved in calculating rates and comparing vastly different systems. Indeed, his old Wisconsin advisor, Martin Glaeser, recalled that as an early TVA consultant, he "sought to discourage the use of the yardstick analogy." To Glaeser, the yardstick was "a will-o'-the-wisp which lent itself admirably to propaganda purposes." Ed Morehouse also admitted that he "never thoroughly agreed with Dave Lilienthal that TVA retail rates were a yardstick" because differences in the way public and private companies financed their operations left little ground for comparison.[45]

Propaganda or not, the yardstick was made for Lilienthal's rhetoric. From fall 1933 until the first of 1935, he milked it for all it was worth. In all of his Rotary Club speeches he called it a "measure [of] the fairness of electric rates." In Memphis, he emphasized that the yardstick was part of "the President's plan." He preached the same message to the Atlanta lawyers in November, and in 1934 to the Academy of Political and Social Sciences in Philadelphia and the Boston League of Women voters. In November 1934 Frankfurter urged his friend to prepare a defense of the yardstick for the *Atlantic Monthly* or the *Saturday Evening Post*. As late as January 1935, in a debate with Wendell Willkie at the Economic and Harvard Business School Clubs of New York, Lilienthal continued to defend the concept.[46]

By mid-1935, however, Lilienthal shifted his interpretation. Now he spoke about the yardstick as an example of how innovative pricing could increase usage and continue to pay a handsome profit. Lilienthal was forced to back off from the comparative yardstick interpretation in part because of lengthy delays in developing a permanent allocation formula among power, navigation, and flood control. Without a sure allocation it was difficult to formulate a defensible rate base to use in the comparative calculus. In June 1935, Lilienthal also complained to Frankfurter about "the terrific barrage on our 'yardstick' all over the country" and wondered if his defensive posture was counterproductive. Perhaps more important, in late 1935 A. E. Morgan, again on the attack, had persuaded Roosevelt to question whether Lilienthal's yardstick really provided a fair comparison.[47]

On December 29, Lilienthal, perhaps mindful of Roosevelt's new doubts, added new twists in a speech to a national conclave of historians and political scientists. While continuing to acknowledge the comparative yardstick, he granted that comparisons might be limited by "underlying variables which affect every fair comparison." He emphasized that TVA was active "on several fronts" in developing "equally useful yardsticks." Yardstick now meant a model, and TVA was a model program that encouraged mass consumption, progressive labor policies, rural development, and an integrated watershed effort. Lilienthal went on to say that private industry could no longer justify its opposition to low rates by arguing that they "would be below the cost of distribution." TVA had demonstrated that low rates could stimulate demand and drive down unit costs enough to make them profitable.[48]

In the end, it was this version of the yardstick that fostered the development, as Arthur E. Schlesinger Jr. noted, of "a new attitude toward the setting of rates." Lilienthal had first embraced the more doubtful comparative model for good reason. It was too powerful a metaphor to pass up. Moreover, in the beginning, he was not sure that Llewellyn Evans's vision of low cost followed by high consumption would succeed. When it did, he jettisoned the original version, which had served well, in favor of another rendition to meet new realities.[49]

The appliance project was another public relations dream. A program that aimed at flooding the Tennessee Valley with inexpensive and reliable home and farm appliances, EHFA had great appeal and promised to stimulate the consumption so crucial to TVA's low rate strategy. Moreover, since the program promoted cooperation among appliance manufacturers, retail stores, and participating private utilities, it gave Lilienthal additional grounds for linking TVA's goals with those of business. He promoted EHFA with the same zeal and high expectations as he had the yardstick. In Memphis and Nashville, he called upon industry and government to "display qualities of statesmanship" by lowering rates and cooperating in an appliance program whereby "the private utilities and the electric manufacturers can both share in the benefits." In Atlanta, he announced that a low-cost appliance plan was "approaching completion, with the co-operation of many interests."[50]

With old friends, including National Recovery Administration head Donald Richberg and Morris Cooke, Lilienthal lobbied Roosevelt to establish EHFA by executive order and fund it from the National Industrial Recovery Act (NIRA). With typical enthusiasm, he asked for $200 million in NIRA credit and estimated that the program could easily sell more than four million appliances. On December 19 the president authorized EHFA as a Delaware corporation and TVA subsidiary, but approved only $1 million from the NIRA and $10 million in credits from the Reconstruction

Finance Corporation (RFC). He also limited EHFA to a year-and-a-half trial run in four Tennessee Valley states.[51]

The constraints did little to dampen Lilienthal's zeal. Frankfurter wrote in January 1934 that "the electrical appliances corporation . . . may well be the beginning of a tremendous thing." As EHFA president, Lilienthal spent much of the next few months on product and market development. Even before Roosevelt's order, he negotiated with General Electric and the National Electrical Manufacturer's Association to develop low-cost refrigerators, ranges, water heaters, and farm appliances. In January and February, the U.S. Department of Agriculture tested models, and in March, Lilienthal opened sealed bids on appliance prices in New York City. The meeting had mixed results. EHFA accepted all the ranges and water heaters, but none of the refrigerator bids came close to the unrealistic thirty-five-dollar unit estimate Lilienthal had given Roosevelt in January. Moreover, according to *Business Week,* most of the appliance models were not new but "merely the lowest-priced in the lines." Threatening to put EHFA into the manufacturing business, Lilienthal wrangled more reductions and a promise of new refrigerator designs. By May three refrigerators, seven ranges, and eight water heaters had been approved for EHFA financing.[52]

He was equally enthusiastic in public. To national audiences he touted EHFA as the answer to the excess generating capacity crisis and a way of improving life at home and on the farm. In addition to cheap appliances and low-cost financing, EHFA's education programs would promote more effective use of electricity. To expand EHFA's market and further reduce rates, Lilienthal struck a deal with Willkie to lower C&S rates in exchange for allowing the private companies to participate in EHFA. He also asked Eleanor Roosevelt to write a foreword to an EHFA pamphlet and developed a unique logo, a massive fist grasping an electric bolt. In April he told Frankfurter that the *Chicago Tribune* called the new logo "evidence of our intention of sovietizing [*sic*] the Valley and ultimately the country." He chuckled that "the revolutionary General Electric Company is asking permission to reproduce [the logo] in its advertising in the saintly Sat. Eve. Post."[53]

In May 1934, EHFA began with a publicity blitz in Tupelo. Soon, other EHFA offices and showrooms opened across the Tennessee Valley. In spite of a massive advertising campaign, the program foundered badly. In the summer of 1934, only 142 contracts worth $14,000 were executed. A year later, when the program ended, EHFA had let only 5,000 contracts worth $760,000, a far cry from the millions Lilienthal had suggested to Roosevelt in 1933. The program failed largely because he rushed into it without understanding market dynamics and popular demand. For one thing, EHFA limited its products to high-energy items like refrigerators, ranges, and water heaters, and refused to finance radios, irons, and washing machines. Moreover, many potential customers refused to participate because the new appliances were only scaled-back versions of current models and often were too small or poorly designed for those who could afford them. Other problems included increasingly unhappy local dealers whose profit margin was less on the EHFA models and who also resented sales competition from the utilities. The greatest obstacle, however, was economic underdevelopment. Even with reduced prices and finance charges, many Tennessee Valley residents still could not afford the long-term costs. Moreover, few could imagine paying for the high costs of electric water heating—even at TVA rates.[54]

By the summer of 1935 EHFA had reached the end of its trial run and was poised to go national. At the same time, the Supreme Court struck down the NIRA, thus invalidating Roosevelt's EHFA executive order. Lilienthal tried without success to get Congress to re-authorize EHFA under terms which would have retained its autonomy. Congress did so, but placed it under the RFC, thus severing TVA and Lilienthal's connections.

At first, it might seem that the EHFA failure was a serious setback for the man who invented the program and championed it for so many months. Nevertheless, while EHFA sold few appliances, it was successful, as Fields observed, in "easing [TVA's] political situation." Moreover, TVA's low rates and the lower C&S rates resulted in dramatic increases in power use throughout the Tennessee Valley. Consumers may not have had refrigerators or ranges, but they left the lights on and used other appliances such as radios, fans, washers, and irons. Lilienthal won with EHFA because, as with the yardstick, he capitalized on a concept which sounded good to the people. What mattered was that rates were low and residents found ways, even without heavy load appliances, to dramatically increase their use of power. Consumers were pleased and Lilienthal had proven his point—low rates stimulate high enough consumption so that utilities can keep profits up through lower unit costs.[55]

As successful as the "yardstick" and EHFA were in strengthening TVA's image, nothing was more crucial than Lilienthal's skill and resolve in fending off the relentless utility challenges, which he worried might lead to TVA being "swept completely out to sea, bag and baggage." Between 1934 and 1938, the Edison Electric Institute, a utility lobby, widely distributed seventeen anti-TVA pamphlets and articles. At the same time, TVA suffered thirty-four lawsuits and twenty-four injunctions, costing $500,000 in legal fees and more than $5 million in lost revenues. Although not directly involved in litigation, Lilienthal's presence was felt through men like Lawrence Fly and Joe Swidler, whom he handpicked for TVA's legal division. And every utility challenge, legal or otherwise, stiffened his resolve to make the power program succeed.[56]

The first serious challenge, the *Ashwander v. TVA* case, came in September 1934, when a group of Alabama Power stockholders claimed that TVA was unconstitutional and asked the court to cancel the January contract between TVA and C&S. The next February, Alabama Federal District Judge William Grubb issued an injunction annulling the contract and prohibiting seventeen Alabama communities that had signed TVA contracts from accepting PWA funds to build distribution systems. Grubb reasoned that TVA had overstepped its authority, moving beyond selling incidental power (that electricity produced as a by-product of constitutionally appropriate activities such as navigation or conservation). Later in the year, an appeals court overturned Grubb's decision, ruling that TVA had the right to sell whatever power it produced. In February 1935 the U.S. Supreme Court upheld the appeals decision, but narrowly fashioned the ruling to apply only to Wilson Dam power. Nothing was said about TVA's right to build other dams or its constitutional status. Regardless of the ultimate ruling, the suit had a profound effect on power revenues, which plummeted from $826,000 in 1934 to less than half that amount the following year. Although a vindication for TVA, the narrowly constructed decision only begged another assault.

That challenge came three months later. In May, 19 utility companies brought suit (henceforth referred to as the Tennessee Electric Power Company [TEPCO] suit) claiming that TVA was unconstitutional and asking for an injunction against the power program except for activities previously declared legal. In December 1936, Judge John Gore slapped another injunction on TVA, halting new construction and service extension and effectively freezing the power program. Six months later a circuit court vacated Gore's injunction and remanded it to the district court. In January 1938 a three-judge panel denied the injunction again and dismissed the suit. In January 1939, after a plaintiff appeal, the U.S. Supreme Court upheld the district decision, concluding that the utility companies had no standing to file a grievance since they were not guaranteed a monopoly in the first place. While neither decision ruled on TVA's constitutionality, the utilities and Willkie finally realized that the TEPCO dismissal signaled that TVA was there to stay.[57]

With legal challenges framing the power battlefield, Lilienthal marshaled his old boxing skills, thrusting, parrying, and always trying to keep the utilities and Willkie off balance. In the same speech he would both offer an olive branch and throw down the gauntlet. In negotiations, he often took one stand, only to do an abrupt about-face. Whether power pooling negotiations with the private utilities, the existence of surplus production capacity in the Tennessee Valley, territorial limitations, or responses to Willkie's offers to sell utility facilities to TVA: Lilienthal changed his mind on each of these issues. He differed with A. E. Morgan on the need for a definitive power policy precisely because he valued flexibility. Once a policy was made public, he feared, options would be limited and the utilities would be able to anticipate future moves. What seemed like vacillation or expediency, especially to A. E. Morgan, was part of Lilienthal's ongoing plan to strengthen his, and TVA's, position.

Negotiations were frustrating for Lilienthal and Willkie because both men were shrewd and stubborn. Between 1934 and early 1938 they held more than a dozen face-to-face meetings and exchanged over a hundred letters, telegrams, and telephone conversations. Willkie was put off by Lilienthal's position shifts, low offers for utility properties, and veiled threats that if he did not give in, PWA was always there with low-interest loans for local governments to build their own systems. He also tried in vain to get Lilienthal to promise that TVA would not raid communities served by his companies and would buy entire systems rather than dismantling utility networks in piecemeal fashion. To his disadvantage, Willkie often had difficulty controlling his own side, thus leading Lilienthal and Roosevelt to chide him for backtracking on agreements or, as an irritated Lilienthal once wrote, of his inability to "control [his] constituents."[58]

For Lilienthal, however, the uncertainty of the Ashwander and TEPCO cases, other legal challenges, and delaying tactics by local operating companies made it impossible to expedite the terms of the January 1934 agreement, which included sales of private utility properties in northern Mississippi, the Muscle Shoals area, and East Tennessee. By mid-1934 only a few Mississippi Power Company transfers had taken place. Indeed, while Knoxville voted for TVA power in 1933, TEPCO managed to stall the municipal takeover until 1938. It took five years for Memphis to get TVA power after a 1934 referendum, and two years for Chattanooga, which joined TVA as a distributor in 1937. The delays were frustrating for Lilienthal, because with each new dam, TVA's generating capacity increased. Only his success in selling power to Arkansas Power and Light, Monsanto Corporation, and the Aluminum Company of America (Alcoa) in 1936 and 1937 kept the critics from pointing the finger at TVA's overbuilt facilities.[59]

A good example of the dynamics of the Lilienthal-Willkie relationship was the debate over power pooling in 1936, which eventually included the president, his confidant Louis B. Wehle, A. E. Morgan, and Alexander Sachs of Lehman Brothers, who first proposed pooling to Roosevelt. By 1936 things were looking a little better for the authority. The Supreme Court ruled in TVA's favor in Ashwander, and the TEPCO case was yet to be filed. Moreover, TVA had extended its market: by the end of the year almost 10 percent of TVA power sales were to municipalities and rural cooperatives. Still, Lilienthal and Willkie were at loggerheads over the transfer of Alabama Power and TEPCO properties, territorial restrictions, and many lesser issues. And, since the Norris powerhouse would soon be on line, something had to be done about revising the January 1934 agreement, which itself contained some "pool" clauses including shared transmission lines and power exchanges. Perhaps the time was ripe for a new approach.

Sachs's proposal, based in part on the British Grid system, which Lilienthal had inspected in August 1934, was that TVA and C&S companies pool their power and distribute it at uniform rates to local buyers. In theory, everyone would benefit from the plan. Consumers would save on rates from coordinated distribution efforts and a cooperative effort would still much of the conflict between TVA and the private companies. Since the pool would buy power from the cheapest production sources first, the authority could continue its yardstick role. Moreover, pooling would open up large markets that TVA desperately needed to soak up new generating capacity. Finally, the companies would benefit by not having to invest in expensive new generating plants.

On March 26, 1936, Sachs spent nearly two hours describing his proposal to Lilienthal. The power director, aware that Roosevelt had suggested the meeting, listened carefully but responded guardedly. Two years earlier, after a visit to England, he expressed disappointment over high rates in the British system in a letter to Morris Cooke. The old reformer responded, "I am afraid you went over with the idea that you were going to find an electrical heaven." Lilienthal expressed the same concerns to Sachs and added that he was skeptical about private utility cooperation or that pooling would be politically acceptable to the public. Nevertheless, the next day Lilienthal talked about pooling with Willkie. As an alternative to Willkie's demand that TVA and C&S companies divide the region into exclusive service areas, Lilienthal suggested pooling all power and distributing it locally through private companies, municipalities, or cooperatives, with the proviso that any community served by a private company "could buy out the distribution facilities and purchase power from this pooled system." When Willkie balked, Lilienthal pointed out that large-scale municipal defections were not likely if private rates continued to drop. Willkie said he still feared massive buyouts. Lilienthal suggested the pool again in May, but Willkie continued in opposition because the proposal offered no protection for his companies against buyouts made possible by cheap PWA loans and grants.[60]

In August, Roosevelt again became interested in pooling. After talking with the TVA board and receiving a strong pro-pool statement from Lilienthal, the president invited more than a dozen public and private utility players to a September 30 conference. In addition to pooling, the invitees were asked about extending the soon-to-expire C&S-TVA January 1934 contract, which Roosevelt called "a rudimentary . . . pool." As Wehle, Roosevelt's mediator, recalled, the atmosphere was tense: with private representatives on one side of the room and government officials on the other, "weapons did not seem to have been left outside." Lilienthal and Willkie got into a heated exchange, the latter accusing TVA of "stealing our customers." The meeting ended when Roosevelt ordered further technical studies and asked Wehle to negotiate a truce and contract extension between TVA and C&S. After a week of fractious meetings, the two sides signed a ninety-day extension so pooling negotiations could proceed. The hoped-for peace was illusory, however, because Ickes's PWA, the object of much of Willkie's enmity, had not been included. Willkie and A. E. Morgan, now increasingly sympathetic to the utilities, argued that PWA grants would violate the truce, but Lilienthal disagreed. In the meantime, Ickes continued to dispense grants, including a $3 million allotment to Memphis. Immersed in a reelection campaign, Roosevelt refused to call a stop to the PWA announcements, which provided excellent political fodder throughout the South.[61]

Even before the power conference Lilienthal had second thoughts, and by year's end he was totally opposed to pooling. At first glance, his change of heart seemed opportunistic—he had proposed pooling to Willkie and had endorsed it to Roosevelt before the September conference. In reality, however, his shift was predicated on political considerations that, if he had persisted in a pro-pooling stance, he might have harmed TVA. In the first place, Lilienthal's original offer to Willkie was primarily a tactical counter to Willkie's insistence on limiting TVA's service area and restricting local communities from buying their own distribution systems. In his original offer to Willkie, Lilienthal could just as easily have proposed pooling and territorial limitations, but he did not. His offer was a "hardball," which he knew was not likely to be accepted. Indeed, he assured Senators Norris and La Follette in September that "the companies won't accept this proposal." When he heard Willkie complaining about TVA and PWA "stealing our customers" at the September conference, he must have realized that his earlier pooling ploy had succeeded.[62]

Lilienthal was also worried that Willkie seemed to have the support of Wehle, Sachs, and A. E. Morgan. The first two knew little about the larger context of the power struggle, and Lilienthal resented their sudden prominence, especially on Willkie's side—and A. E. Morgan was once again meddling in power affairs. In a twenty-two-page preconference memorandum prepared with extensive help from a former Insull vice-president and injudiciously leaked to the *New York Times,* A. E. Morgan insisted that a cooperative pooling agreement represented a "thoroughgoing reasonableness and fair-minded recognition of the legitimate interests of both sides." A. E. Morgan's collaboration with the former Insull executive and his increasing alignment with Willkie only angered the adamant pooling opponents, including La Follette, Norris, Mississippi Congressman John Rankin, and Chattanooga publisher George Fort Milton. At this juncture, Lilienthal could hardly afford to identify himself with any policy that suggested the utilities were acting with "reasonableness" and in "good faith." He had struck an adversarial pose vis-à-vis the power companies for years and, with another threat staring him in the face, it was hardly time to modify that position. To make sure his opposition was noted, the power director played an active role in the fall in developing a "power consumers' organization" in the Tennessee Valley which actively opposed the pool idea.[63]

Lilienthal's rationale for distancing himself from pooling was strengthened by Willkie's refusal or inability to delay the TEPCO suit. At the September 30 conference, Wehle heard Willkie say he could do nothing since "he represented only five of the nineteen complainant companies." Later that day, Wehle tried a second time to seek a delay, but again Willkie refused. In December, Judge Gore enjoined TVA from making any new contracts. Now Lilienthal could fully justify his change of heart on pooling. He wrote the president that TVA could not continue to discuss a policy that assumed trust and goodwill on both sides. Willkie had done nothing to forestall Gore's ruling, and the injunction was a real "breach of faith." Roosevelt agreed and on January 25 called a halt to pooling talks. To his friend, Wehle, who had tried hard to work out a plan, he confided, "I frankly see no possible use at this time in going ahead with conversations— and I think you will agree with me." Pooling was dead. Willkie's inability to delay the TEPCO proceedings and Gore's subsequent injunction only demonstrated the futility of cooperation, no matter how good pooling was in theory. Willkie and Lilienthal returned to their hard negotiations. Perhaps most important, the Lilienthal–A. E. Morgan feud escalated to new levels that at one point threatened TVA as much as any of the numerous court challenges had.[64]

Lilienthal and A. E. Morgan: A Tragic Confluence

The struggle between David Lilienthal and A. E. Morgan dragged on for five years. It was a tragic encounter between two dedicated men, and it almost wrecked TVA and drove both men to the edge of mental and physical collapse. Their feud was so dramatic that it was widely publicized at the time and has been the focus of numerous accounts of New Deal lore and history. In many ways Roosevelt was to blame because he confused both directors as to the direction of his support and allowed the exhausting conflict to continue until the spring of 1938. To a large extent, the struggle was a function of personality. Lilienthal and A. E. Morgan were different in many respects, but the characteristics they shared worked in an insidious fashion to exacerbate the polarities they brought to TVA.[65]

They were both hardworking, opinionated men, and often intolerant of those with whom they disagreed. One contemporary noted, "They were both prima donnas to a large extent." They were introverted, impatient, willing to take risks, and wanted things done quickly and on their own terms, and their orientation toward action often led to misunderstandings: A. E. Morgan's early take-charge attitude was an honest effort to get things going on the right track. Nevertheless, it disturbed Lilienthal and H. A. Morgan and drove them to permanent opposition to the chairman. In a like manner, Lilienthal's decision to publicize TVA's first rate structure in September 1933 before board approval offended A. E. Morgan. Each in his own way was an elitist: just as A. E. Morgan invested his social experiment with a sense of moral urgency, Lilienthal sensed that the project could not succeed without carefully cultivating powerful regional interests. Neither man had a systematic ideological bent: they were children of the Progressive belief in executive leadership and the role of professional knowledge in public life. Each was committed to administrative excellence through meritocratic service. They were suspicious of legislative politics, patronage, and "horse trading." Both directors were also inveterate communicators who used sometimes incautious rhetoric to share visions, persuade and, sometimes settle scores. They both used the word to escalate their own row, often in a manner calculated to savage the other as fiercely as possible.[66]

One of Lilienthal's self-appraisals in 1937 offered a list of personal characteristics. He described himself as "mentally on the quick side; [but] . . . [n]ot profound, nor capable of understanding subtle psychological analysis." Not interested in "new problems . . . unless they interest me greatly," he was "critical of slowness, . . . [and] generally impatient and restless." He concluded that he was "not a natural mixer" but had been "carried along so far by an intense and absorbing desire for achievement." Much later, A. E. Morgan offered his own self-appraisal: "When I have been under heavy stress for too long a time, . . . I find difficulty in controlling the course of my thoughts. That is, I cannot dismiss a subject from my mind, but it 'runs away with me,' keeping me awake at night. There is a lack of control which inclines me to lose my temper or to talk too much." The irony of both appraisals is they were strikingly close descriptions of both men.[67]

Nevertheless, they were very different in style and substance. While the young director may not have liked rough-and-tumble politics, he knew how to be flexible and pragmatic in response to political pressures. A. E. Morgan, on the other hand, was a strict moralist and as McCraw noted, "not just apolitical, but antipolitical." He was rigid, judgmental, and prone to dig in his heels when challenged on something he knew was right. As Wehle observed, "Morgan was an awkward fighter" and no match for Lilienthal with his "controlled, driving, effective intensity." These characteristics help explain A. E. Morgan's view of Lilienthal as unprincipled and consumed by "personal ambition." Lilienthal was ambitious and many of his actions, including some against A. E. Morgan, demonstrated an opportunistic and downright mean streak. Nevertheless, what A. E. Morgan failed to realize was that many of Lilienthal's so-called unprincipled actions were tactical maneuvers to win advantage for TVA. To A. E. Morgan, Lilienthal's hyperbole about the yardstick was propaganda. To the power director, it was a legitimating device. For A. E. Morgan, Lilienthal's negotiations with Willkie or an influential politician over a land settlement was proof of venal behavior. To Lilienthal, his back-and-forth with Willkie was just part of the negotiating ritual in a highly charged political atmosphere.[68]

They also differed in general outlook and in the manner in which they judged and related to others. Lilienthal made it a point to express his faith in the people's ability to make choices; the chairman stressed the things TVA ought to do *for* the people. While A. E. Morgan deserves credit for bringing many highly qualified and motivated people to the authority, he nevertheless had difficulty reading character and responding appropriately: he had all the necessary signals from his investigation of Lilienthal to have rejected him as a third director, yet he did not. He alienated McKellar from the beginning, dismissing him as another corrupt politician. Lilienthal saw this side of McKellar, but he cultivated and tolerated the powerful Tennessee solon into the 1940s. Finally, the chairman's ultimate fate was partly sealed by his misreading of Wendell Willkie. Lilienthal recognized the C&S president for what he was, a worthy but tenacious foe who fought as hard for the utilities as Lilienthal did for TVA. As A. E. Morgan's biographer noted, however, "Willkie hooked Morgan early on." As the years passed, A. E. Morgan's apparent identification with Willkie only strengthened Lilienthal's position.

There were also differences of substance. As Charles Poe wrote in *The Nation,* Lilienthal was a Jeffersonian and A. E. Morgan a Hamiltonian.

The power director saw TVA as an instrument for economic development with public power providing the major thrust. For A. E. Morgan, TVA was a social experiment and the Tennessee Valley a laboratory for character building or, in Lilienthal's derisively words, "social uplift." Public power was only one of many tools, and in fact, too great an emphasis on it might overshadow his overall grand plan. Lilienthal summed it up best in a conversation with Senator La Follette about A. E. Morgan: "Welfare work and economic revision are two different things—I don't have much confidence in the first." They also differed in their assessment and approach to the utilities. A. E. Morgan believed that cooperation and good faith efforts would lead to better service and cheaper power for everyone. He opposed the use of propaganda and coercion to run the utilities out of the Tennessee Valley. TVA, he thought, should carve out a modest fiefdom, perhaps as extensive as the Tennessee River watershed, and serve as a benign yardstick for everyone else. Lilienthal had no use for such notions. As an attorney, he felt comfortable in an adversarial role, a position an engineer like A. E. Morgan could never understand. Moreover, he had little faith that the utilities would ever cooperate and he hoped TVA would develop as large a role as it could. The best way to do that was through tough action, which included squeezing his enemies in any possible way in the hard-nosed competition for markets.[69]

The seeds of conflict were sown in the first board meeting, and Lilienthal and A. E. Morgan continued to differ over organization, power policy, and relationships with Willkie through the summer. However, as autumn came, the two directors became too busy to worry about each other, and A. E. Morgan saw a glimmer of cooperative spirit in Lilienthal and Willkie's January 1934 accord. While Lilienthal continued his low-intensity sniping, a truce of sorts held until mid-1935. Then, accusations that Lilienthal had made political appointments led A. E. Morgan to an ill-fated effort to deny Lilienthal reappointment to a full term. Once that plan failed, the skirmishes turned into two years of open warfare.

As a consummate professional, A. E. Morgan detested political appointments. In 1933 he told Roosevelt's patronage boss, James Farley, that all appointments be in accord with Section Six of the TVA Act, which prohibited "political test or qualification" in consideration for employment. While Lilienthal agreed with the merit principle, he was much more attuned to political realities. Norris, who wrote Section Six, felt that only Lilienthal could effectively ferret out applications planted by the utilities. In mid-1935 the power director wrote Frankfurter that "the Authority's policy with respect to political appointments has produced a great deal of antagonism against us" in Washington. Lilienthal deplored "the Y.M.C.A. atmosphere that was brought into the Authority's personnel work . . . [for producing] . . . a distinctly unfriendly feeling, much of which could be avoided." About that time, personnel director Floyd Reeves asked his assistant Gordon Clapp to explore patronage rumors. In July, Clapp told A. E. Morgan that Lilienthal may have made as many as five appointments in violation of

Section Six. Clapp cautioned Morgan, as Clapp later told Lilienthal, that whether they were political depended on a "judgment of motive and intent, . . . which could not fairly be made from the record of the facts as I knew them." Virtually everyone, including Clapp, concluded that the questionable hires were rare exceptions and all the less damaging since the inquiry also found that A. E. Morgan had appointed a friend of Eleanor Roosevelt's to a minor position. Lilienthal's lapses were perhaps judged more harshly by A. E. Morgan because two of the contested hires had congressional ties. In any case they spurred him into a campaign against Lilienthal's reappointment the next spring.[70]

While the record is sketchy, it is clear that A. E. Morgan's efforts were clumsy. He failed to realize that, in an election year, Roosevelt would be reluctant to remove anyone of Lilienthal's stature without strong cause. Then, in typical fashion, A. E. Morgan went about his mission in an awkward, desultory manner. He lobbied the president, Norris, Harold Ickes, and even H. A. Morgan, striking a sympathetic note with Ickes and, he thought, Roosevelt. However, instead of forcing Clapp's findings on Roosevelt and Norris, the chairman offered only vague reasons and accusations and then petulantly threatened to resign if Lilienthal was reappointed. There is some confusion as to whether A. E. Morgan tried to show Clapp's findings to Norris. He said he did, but Norris insisted that A. E. Morgan "never . . . [made] a charge or . . . claim that would have received any consideration by reasonable men."[71]

On April 21 Marguerite Owen told Lilienthal of A. E. Morgan's opposition to his reappointment. At that time he began to work incessantly to preserve his position. He arrived in Washington on April 23, prepared to stay as long as necessary. With the help of Frankfurter, Senator La Follette, and Benjamin Cohen, Lilienthal wrote Norris his side of the story. He told the senator that "the life of the project in which I believe with all my heart is at stake." He then accused A. E. Morgan of endangering the power program by cooperating with "a ruthless and well-financed antagonist." He wrangled four White House visits and arranged for Frankfurter, Norris, Philip and Robert La Follette, George Fort Milton, and H. A. Morgan to meet with the president on his behalf.

A. E. Morgan hardly knew what hit him. On April 30 Roosevelt asked the TVA chairman to stop his campaign against Lilienthal and on May 8 informed Morgan that he was going to reappoint Lilienthal. Norris, H. A. Morgan, and Milton all appealed to A. E. Morgan to quiet his opposition. Roosevelt asked Lilienthal to "think of going to see him, or writing him a note," and told him he was going to "sic [Milton] onto Morgan . . . and I'll sic [H. A. Morgan] on, too." On May 12 both Clapp and Reeves cornered A. E. Morgan and suggested that he resign rather than dump Lilienthal for someone less qualified. On the same day Lilienthal knew he was in when Roosevelt said that not to reappoint him would be "heralded . . . as a power company victory." Later in the afternoon, after a brutally frank visit with A. E. Morgan, Lilienthal heard the president say he was going to tell the chairman that he would consider any obstruction of the Lilienthal renomination to be a grave error. After talking to Roosevelt, a visibly shaken A. E. Morgan abruptly left Washington for Knoxville, and the reappointment controversy was settled—even if little else was.[72]

The next two years were hell—Lilienthal and A. E. Morgan disagreed on virtually every issue that came before the board, from contracts with the Aluminum Company of America (Alcoa) and Arkansas Power & Light to Lilienthal's efforts to drum up more power business. They even quarreled over how to amend old board minutes. The renomination fight had telling effects on the combatants. Before renomination, A. E. Morgan had been critical and suspicious of Lilienthal but reserved in action; afterward, he became an embittered man whose anger resulted in more intemperate public attacks and frequent physical and mental setbacks. Between the renomination and the first of 1938, A. E. Morgan missed almost 30 percent of all board meetings. Before the fight Lilienthal had acted with relative restraint: to be sure, he was rarely pleasant to A. E. Morgan and often downright rude. After May 1936, however, Lilienthal gave no quarter, and he began to go public.[73]

It took only a week after renomination for the battle to begin. On May 22 Lilienthal and H. A. Morgan, acting as board majority and in the face of A. E. Morgan's vigorous protest, created the position of general manager and appointed John B. Blandford Jr. in an acting capacity. The chairman was so incensed that he refused to sign the board minutes that day, in spite of the fact that Blandford had come to TVA as his personal assistant. By this time he trusted few people, least of all anyone supported by the other side. On June 4, still reeling, he informed the other directors he was leaving "for a needed rest . . . for several weeks" and curtly asked that "the Board make no decisions concerning matters of major policy during my absence."[74]

During A. E. Morgan's seven-week absence, the air was rife with rumor. Why had the chairman left at such a crucial time? Was he about to resign? Had the other board members advised A. E. Morgan of the fourteen meetings they held in his absence? The evidence is clear on the first two points. A. E. Morgan was thoroughly exhausted and spent most of the time at home in Yellow Springs, Ohio. He considered resigning, but decided against it. The third question was more problematic—in 1938 A. E. Morgan swore he received no notice of board meetings during his absence. The other directors testified to the contrary. The likely answer, as in most cases like this, lies somewhere in the middle. It is hard to imagine Lilienthal and H. A. Morgan holding fourteen "secret" meetings over seven weeks, especially with the number of A. E. Morgan loyalists in TVA's high ranks. Nevertheless, it is easy to assume that they were less than assiduous in keeping the chairman's office informed.

With A. E. Morgan gone, Lilienthal lost no time going after him. On June 12, barely a week after the chairman's departure, he dropped a bombshell with a lecture to TVA employees at the First Methodist Church in Knoxville, which, one paper speculated, seemed to portend significant changes at the authority. To Richard Niehoff, TVA's director of training and a staunch Lilienthal supporter, the speech, was "a shocking thing." It demonstrated Lilienthal's capacity to use words, not to heal, or sell, but to scorn and intimidate. He minced no words, calling A. E. Morgan's approach "'basket weaving' and all that it implies." With invective, Lilienthal said he had little "faith in 'uplift.'". . . "We should remember that this organization can be corrupted more quickly by a lack of a sense of proportion than perhaps any other way." In clear reference to the chairman he cautioned against "plans concocted by supermen and imposed upon the rest of the community for its own good," and of the "temptation to develop a kind of Alexander-the-Great complex among those of us who are carrying on this project." In a thinly veiled warning to A. E. Morgan supporters, he said that personal loyalties had no place at TVA: "There is only one kind of loyalty that I recognize, . . . loyalty to the job." Needless to say, there was some irony when he lectured his audience on "the need of humility," and the fact that personal loyalty "leads to intrigues, to cliques, to petty scheming." Lilienthal had many positive attributes, but humility was not one of them. Moreover, during their three-year feud, he had engaged in his own share of scheming against the chairman. Nevertheless, the gloves were off. As Niehoff recalled, the speech signaled Lilienthal's first "open challenge" to A. E. Morgan's leadership.[75]

While the speech cut to the quick, A. E. Morgan was most incensed by two decisions made by the attenuated board, a power contract with Alcoa and the Berry marble case. The Berry case highlighted the differences between the directors as well as any. A. E. Morgan was so consumed by the decision that he fought it all the way to its final resolution and beyond—it was the focal point of thirteen days of testimony during the 1938 congressional investigation of TVA. In 1934, George Berry, a prominent Roosevelt supporter and Tennessee Democrat, had bought marble properties in the Cove Creek basin. When the area was flooded in 1936, Berry submitted a multimillion-dollar claim for land that TVA geologists had deemed commercially useless. Under normal circumstances the board could have made a nominal settlement or condemned the land and let a three-person commission appointed by a federal judge determine the ultimate value. Lilienthal and H. A. Morgan were reluctant to take the latter route. They feared a local commission might judge in Berry's favor, especially since he was a prominent figure. Berry had also managed, through political contacts, to have his marble used in a Washington, D.C., public building, thus giving credence to the claim that the lode had some value. On July 13, 1936, the board struck an unusual conciliation agreement with Berry wherein a third party would make a nonbinding evaluation. The directors were confident that the agreed-upon conciliator, Dr. John Finch, head of the U.S. Bureau of Mines, would judge the claim worthless.

A. E. Morgan objected strenuously to any settlement, claiming that Berry had bought the land with intent to defraud (thus implying that Lilienthal and H. A. Morgan had made a political decision, or worse, participated in fraud). Lilienthal and the legal staff tried without luck to convince A. E. Morgan that proving fraud required more than a hunch. The case lasted until March 1938, when TVA attorneys finally uncovered evidence that Berry had acted in bad faith and the claim was denied. Nevertheless, the damage had been done and insinuations made. A. E. Morgan, the moralist, insisted that since Berry was dishonest there was no room for compromise: agreeing to continued negotiations was a sign of duplicity, or worse, complicity. Lilienthal, on the other hand, was a pragmatist. If compromise was necessary, so be it—Berry's character and unproven motives were irrelevant. The legal staff needed evidence of fraud, not just suspicions. It did not hurt to be circumspect with a strong presidential supporter, no matter how unsavory he might be.[76]

A. E. Morgan's efforts to derail the conciliation agreement spawned several other conflicts that summer and fall. In early August, Lilienthal and H. A. Morgan rammed through a board resolution that TVA would not agree to territorial restrictions on agreements with local governments. A. E. Morgan refused to send a telegram to the president advising him of the action, and the majority directors sent a pointed explanation to Roosevelt of A. E. Morgan's refusal to communicate the board decision. During the fall negotiations following the power pool conference, A. E. Morgan sided with Wendell Willkie on various points, including Willkie's continued insistence on territorial restrictions. On January 17, 1937, a few days before Roosevelt's decision to abandon pooling, A. E. Morgan lobbed a powerful bomb. On the front page of the *New York Times* he argued forcefully for a "basis of agreement between the TVA and the private utilities." Claiming that utility leadership now included "more public-spirited, forward-looking men," A. E. Morgan insisted that finding "common ground with the utilities" through "reasonableness, fair play and open dealing" was the only way to avoid the "bitter class controversies" of other countries. In an oblique swipe at Lilienthal, he decried government despotism and the chance that a "war to the death on certain large utility systems might discredit public ownership and set it back for a generation." A. E. Morgan echoed Lilienthal's "Alexander-the-Great complex" speech when he warned about "attracting people who are ruled by a Napoleonic complex which leads them to use any method at hand, including intrigue, arbitrary force and appeal to class hatred." If the article did not raise Lilienthal's ire, the next day's *Times* editorial that A. E. Morgan's statement was "a model of what a state paper should be" surely did.[77]

While A. E. Morgan continued to fight publicly, embarrassing the rest of the board and angering Frankfurter and La Follette, Lilienthal chipped away at the chairman's credibility. In mid-January he told the president that A. E. Morgan had caused many resignations at TVA and complained about his "utter lack of administration." Roosevelt listened and agreed, but defended A. E. Morgan for his "human engineer[ing] skills" and because "he builds good dams." With a second term assured and other distractions, such as the ill-fated Supreme Court–packing scheme, Roosevelt had become studiously uninterested in 1937 over the row at TVA. In typical fashion, all he would do was appoint a second-rate reorganization commission to study the authority. Nevertheless, Lilienthal continued his efforts. He wrote cousin Bernadine Szold in February, "The President . . . is wise to AE [Morgan], and has supported me, . . . so I must somehow manage to stand this miserable campaign. . . . But it is tough." The same month he wrote Norris and La Follette about A. E. Morgan's increasing identification with Willkie and, a week later, he and H. A. Morgan told Roosevelt that A. E. Morgan's cooperation with Willkie was "prevent[ing] the Board from carrying out its obligations to the President and the Congress." Lilienthal complained about A. E. Morgan to Frankfurter in March and to the reorganization committee in May that A. E. Morgan's "obsession" against the other directors was adversely affecting morale. Still, nothing happened.[78]

As fall came, A. E. Morgan became increasingly erratic, largely because the Berry case continued to gnaw. In early August, an article by him in the *Saturday Evening Post* warned "that some part of the program may try to run away with the show, menacing other aims of equal or greater importance." In large measure, though, the piece was moderate and did not add much fuel to the fire. However, a September *Atlantic Monthly* article did. In it he dutifully criticized the private utilities for past excesses and defended public power. Then, he took aim at Lilienthal. Private power abuses, he said, "have bred in some men an attitude of bitter hatred, and a conviction that the only course . . . is a war without quarter against the private companies." Arbitrary retaliation by public officials, he continued, "not only is unfair to legitimate private investors, but tends to substitute private dictation for democratic processes." In his most reckless charge, A. E. Morgan identified himself as a "minority [board] member" who differed with "the improprieties of [TVA's power] policy." A. E. Morgan's intemperate tone was bad enough—what damaged his position even more was that his article followed an August contribution in the same journal by Willkie. Once more, the proximity of the articles and the similar positions reinforced the suspicion that A. E. Morgan was in Willkie's pocket. Lilienthal immediately circulated a detailed analysis of the two articles which skillfully demonstrated their similarities. H. A. Morgan protested A. E. Morgan's *Atlantic* remarks to Roosevelt because the TEPCO case was soon going to trial. The president responded with a searing letter to A. E. Morgan demanding that he either substantiate his charges or retract them.[79]

Increasingly disturbed and alienated, A. E. Morgan abruptly turned TVA affairs over to Vice-Chairman H. A. Morgan in September and disappeared until November. The vacation did little to settle his troubled spirit. Immediately on return, he contacted TVA's lawyers, who were frantically preparing for the TEPCO trial the next week. According to TVA general counsel Lawrence Fly and John Lord O'Brian, the prominent Republican attorney who worked on the case with Fly, A. E. Morgan was severely disturbed. He accused them of keeping case information from him, persisted in a request to testify in spite of Fly's and O'Brian's decision to keep the directors off the stand, and tried to influence the testimony of certain witnesses. In a series of actions that seriously affected legal staff morale, A. E. Morgan's most outrageous question was, according to O'Brian, whether "the court . . . could not declare part of this project to be constitutional and yet enjoin the rest of it." When Fly told the other directors of A. E. Morgan's queries, they immediately told the president that the chairman had once more "exposed your Administration's conservation policies to grave danger."[80]

Denied the chance to testify in the TEPCO case, A. E. Morgan made a surprise appearance at the final hearings on the Berry case in Knoxville on December 20. His claim that "an effort was under way to defraud the government" clearly impugned the integrity of the other directors. During his appearance he also alluded to other evidence he would present at a congressional investigation. Two days later, Lilienthal and H. A. Morgan accused A. E. Morgan of "making statements with 'false and malicious' inference." They countered with a resounding vote of confidence in "our attorneys in their integrity and their ability" and charged that A. E. Morgan's actions were "unjust, unsupported by the facts, . . . and inconsistent with our conception of the responsibilities of public office."[81]

Something Has to Give

It seemed clearer than ever that any hope for reconciliation or a modus vivendi had been dashed. A much longer delay in resolving the conflict would endanger TVA and perhaps the president, who had lost enough political capital in 1937.

Although TVA had made giant strides by 1938, internal stress and the external assaults had taken their toll. Lilienthal and A. E. Morgan both suffered from physical and mental exhaustion. Even H. A. Morgan was feeling his age with increased absences due to illness. Pressure had also been mounting on the staff. In late December 1936, Bill Nichols, an early TVA power manager, warned Lilienthal that "TVA has lost some of its sense of direction, [and] that morale is rapidly going to hell." Walter Kahoe, an A. E. Morgan associate, recalled that in early 1937, he didn't "see how the TVA can continue to exist as a house divided. . . . [T]he morale has been lowered greatly, even in the last six months." "Our own TVA," he wrote in his diary, "is almost *bellum omnia contra omnes* [a war of all, against all]." Just one more aggravation, it seemed, and the entire house might tumble down. Roosevelt would have to act soon.[82]

CHAPTER 6

TVA: Vindication and Consolidation

It is terribly important that I shouldn't lose my nerve, for the
fact of the matter is that I am now the central point of this
enterprise, and if I begin to show signs of weakening or losing
courage, panic will spread throughout the whole organization.
—David E. Lilienthal, June 15, 1939

Roosevelt Takes Charge

January 1938 began with no letup in the struggle between the two
directors. After A. E. Morgan's attack at the Berry hearing in December,
Lilienthal and H. A. Morgan responded, first to the *New York Times,* and
then in a scathing communiqué to the president on January 18 in which
they defended A. E. Morgan's right to dissent, but attacked him for
"obstruct[ing] and subvert[ing] the decision of the majority." After listing a
long list of offenses, they accused the chairman of adopting a doctrine of
"rule or ruin," and promised that they would "continue to carry this project
forward in accordance with the law."[1]

In the meantime, things were breaking all around. Willkie, anticipating
an unfavorable district court ruling in the Tennessee Electric Power Company (TEPCO) case, offered to sell all C&S Valley holdings to TVA. After
seeing Roosevelt on January 18, Lilienthal rejected the offer, saying that
TVA only wanted "useful physical assets" and would buy nothing at inflated prices. Three days later the district panel dissolved the six-month-old
injunction and dismissed the suit. At the same time, congressional criticism
was growing. In late January, Lilienthal wrote Frankfurter about Congressman Maury Maverick's talk of the "public brawl" at TVA and asked him to
intervene with the Texas liberal. Two weeks later, during a six-week recuperation from illness, A. E. Morgan wrote Maverick about his version of
the TVA squabble. In his harshest words yet, the chairman told the congressman of "a practice of evasion, intrigue, and sharp strategy with remarkable skill in alibi and the habit of avoiding direct responsibility, which

makes Machiavelli seem open and candid." Using words like "deceit," "misrepresentation," "disorder," "waste," and "propaganda," A. E. Morgan assailed his fellow directors and insisted that he alone had tried to keep TVA on a straight and narrow path. He concluded by hinting of "many matters which concern me which I have not mentioned," and called for "nothing short of a Congressional investigation."[2]

Because A. E. Morgan was away and the letter to Maverick remained private, the conflict lulled in February. Then, on March 1, the Berry Commission ruled that the claims were worthless. A. E. Morgan publicly called the decision a vindication of his "effort to secure honesty, openness, and decency and fairness in government" in the face of deceit and maladministration, and again recommended a comprehensive congressional inquiry. That was it: as White House aide James H. Rowe Jr. wrote James Roosevelt, "the lid has blown off T.V.A." The president was furious and asked Lilienthal, "What the hell are we going to do about Arthur Morgan?" When Lilienthal offered to resign to avoid embarrassment, Roosevelt said no, the "only embarrassment is the embarrassment of having a befuddled old man on our hands." He immediately released the January 18 letter and A. E. Morgan countered by sending a copy of his letter to Maverick to the *New York Times*. When it appeared, Roosevelt asked Lilienthal what he thought about an open meeting in which each director would be asked to substantiate any charges he had made, thereby forcing A. E. Morgan to come forth or, best of all, resign. Lilienthal liked the idea and said Swidler and Owen had suggested a similar tactic: by this method, "calling on both sides to produce facts, [the president] would avoid any charge of prejudging the case." Soon, the press entered the fray and everyone knew something was awry in the Tennessee Valley. Conservative Senator Styles Bridges joined A. E. Morgan in calling for an investigation. So did virtually every major newspaper. Dorothy Thompson, a syndicated columnist, demanded an inquiry to keep a "distinguished public servant," A. E. Morgan, from being "railroaded out of office, 'purged,' and 'liquidated.'"[3]

Roosevelt scheduled the meeting for March 11. True to his erratic form, A. E. Morgan twice refused to come, saying in a first telegram that the conference would not serve "any useful purpose" and in a second that a congressional forum would be better than trying "to compose the issues in your office." An angry president sent a third message—this time A. E. Morgan acceded but the cards were badly stacked. He was physically and emotionally spent—Lilienthal wrote that "he really looked like hell" and had a "strained look in his eyes." Moreover, unlike Lilienthal, who had anticipated the meeting for weeks, A. E. Morgan, by his own admission, was totally unprepared. Perhaps most important, the president was now on Lilienthal's side. It would require extraordinary "facts" to change his mind.[4]

Friday came and Washington was abuzz. A furious debate over the coming investigation raged in Congress between Republicans, who could smell a scandal, and Senator Norris. At the other end of Pennsylvania Avenue, with reporters all around, the directors walked into a tense, taut White House. When the directors were ushered in, Roosevelt tried to lighten the atmosphere, charming a young stenographer, and telling the trio, "Smoking is allowed." In spite of the president's efforts, Lilienthal was "pretty tense" and left the session with a "terrible throat" after puffing up a storm.[5]

The hearing was a disaster for the embattled chairman. The president began amiably enough, explaining that he wanted to establish the facts regarding a number of charges A. E. Morgan had levied against the other directors. To each of the president's requests for facts, A. E. Morgan repeatedly replied that "I am an observer and not a participant in this alleged process of fact finding." He protested that he was disadvantaged since he was the only one not "fully advised of the purpose of the meeting." While A. E. Morgan persisted with vague accusations, Lilienthal responded with precise explanations of every issue, from the Berry case, to rate making, to industrial power contracts. At the end of six hours, Roosevelt told the men they would reconvene in a week to give the chairman a chance to "reply to very simple factual questions." If he could not, the president made it clear that resignation was inevitable. Lilienthal protested the delay, saying that A. E. Morgan's charges of "dishonesty and corruption" had to be substantiated or dropped because "almost 14,000 splendid men and women are under that cloud." Roosevelt agreed, but said he would "lean over backward" to avoid any appearance of a railroad job.[6]

The next session was no better—A. E. Morgan was even more obdurate. The president doggedly pressed for the facts, but A. E. Morgan rambled on with more vague allegations. The other directors listened and Lilienthal chimed in every so often with a sharp retort. To A. E. Morgan's protests that he was at a disadvantage because he was a layman and Lilienthal a lawyer, Lilienthal accused him of playing both sides of the street. Now "he speaks as a layman, . . . and yet he had no hesitation in disregarding the advice of counsel as to the conduct of [the Berry] case." Near the end of the meeting, A. E. Morgan revealed that he couldn't answer the questions because Marvin McIntyre, the president's secretary, had told him he could bring no documents to the meeting. Roosevelt immediately queried McIntyre about the charge which the secretary denied. Nevertheless, Roosevelt decided to give A. E. Morgan one last chance to sustain his "charges of dishonesty and want of integrity."[7]

Before adjourning, the president gave the chairman three days to provide the evidence. On Monday, March 21, 1938, A. E. Morgan refused again, saying "I feel impelled to say that I cannot participate further in these proceedings." Roosevelt immediately told A. E. Morgan to withdraw all charges or resign. Failing that, "in light of the record, . . . only two courses appear open—either your removal or your suspension as a member of the Board." After waiting two days for a response, Roosevelt removed A. E. Morgan from office for "contumacious" behavior. Neither Lilienthal nor H. A. Morgan uttered a word that day. They would not have to wait long, however, for a congressional inquiry involving almost as many enemies as friends.[8]

A Marathon Investigation

Roosevelt tried hard to head off a public investigation. He feared the press would make mountains out of molehills and that an inquiry into an enterprise as extensive as TVA was bound to turn up something, no matter how insignificant. Nevertheless, with A. E. Morgan and Republican legislators fanning the flames, not even George Norris was able to slow things down. In April, the U.S. Senate allocated $50,000 for the probe. Even TVA's friends at the *Christian Century* and the *New Republic* joined the bandwagon. The *Century* suggested that an inquiry would prove "to the entire country the baselessness of the charges of graft, inefficiency, and mismanagement." The *New Republic*, while insisting that "no investigation is warranted," nevertheless fueled negative images with its report on the "Hatfields and McCoys in the TVA, . . . Hatfield Morgan and McCoy Lilienthal."[9]

In the meantime both sides prepared for battle. In atypical fashion, Lilienthal took a few days off for a Caribbean cruise with Helen in late March. A. E. Morgan gathered over $28,000 in contributions from friends to help finance his campaign and tried unsuccessfully to gain access to TVA files and employee testimony. As Lilienthal explained to James Roosevelt, A. E. Morgan was now a "private individual" with no more right to access to official files than any other party "seeking to discredit [TVA's] operations." Contrary to the president's feelings, Lilienthal wanted to get on with the investigation. Quick attention and "close cross-questioning," he thought, "would deflate the whole business and make it out a clear case of difference of opinion on policy rather than dishonesty." In any case, there was not much either could do about timing. A joint resolution on April 4 authorized a special joint congressional panel and things were readied for a late May opening date.[10]

The investigation was long, sporadic, and tedious, and ran from May 25 to December 21, 1938. The seventy days of hearings, divided almost equally between Washington and the Tennessee Valley, produced over 6,000 pages of testimony, nearly 600 exhibits, and a 1,000-page report consisting of majority and minority opinions and technical reports. More than a hundred witnesses appeared, including the two directors, A. E. Morgan, and Wendell Willkie. A. E. Morgan was on the stand for ten days, Lilienthal for nine, and H. A. Morgan for four. The committee of six Democrats and four Republicans had an equal number of senators and representatives. With the exception of Chief Counsel Francis Biddle, later U.S. solicitor general and attorney general, the committee was not distinguished. According to historian Herman Pritchett, the chairman of the committee, Senator Victor Donahey of Ohio was "a weak and colorless figure with no particular ties to the Roosevelt administration." Indeed, the strongest members were Republican Representatives Charles Wolverton of New Jersey and Thomas Jenkins of Ohio, two men Roosevelt had tried to keep off the panel for "publicly prejudg[ing] the issues in the investigation." As much as he could, Democrat Biddle "did not," as Donald Davidson observed, "open trails into the bushes."[11]

The next months were trying for Lilienthal. Once more, he was forced to listen to A. E. Morgan's endless stream of accusations as well as answer Wolverton's scathing questions. He became so frustrated at one point that he asked Biddle if he could sue A. E. Morgan for libel. And, as he told Frankfurter, the distraction of the investigation made it difficult to concentrate on the Willkie negotiations, which one day seemed promising, and the next, "futile and deteriorating." The saving grace was that A. E. Morgan was his own worst enemy: he rambled and failed to develop an effective factual basis. Moreover, Lilienthal often proved him wrong in small but important details. A. E. Morgan's lone triumph came when he got the panel to allow TVA employees to confer with him without going through official channels. Lilienthal fared much better. He was always prepared and assertive, and never shy about doing battle with anyone— Wolverton, Jenkins, or even Biddle. The chief counsel noticed one small, but negative mannerism, however, "a trick of smiling slightly before answering a question, which gave him a suggestion of the supercilious."[12]

In late August Lilienthal was struck by a near-fatal attack of undulant fever. He was hospitalized, homebound, and convalescent at Captiva Island, Florida, for seven months. For weeks, he was depressed and uninterested in everything around him. As he told H. A. Morgan from a Washington hospital in November, "these last three months have been a nightmare." He tried to work but quickly became exhausted. By February 1939, he was improved, but weak and easily tired. About that time, perhaps because he felt better or was bored, he started his journal on a regular basis. For whatever reason, his thoughts showed an introspection not much evident since the 1920s. All the while, Helen kept him from diving too deeply into pools of fretful speculation. Once, after a restless day she turned to him and said, "For God's sake, wake up and use your first-class mind."[13]

The first day opened to a modest audience in the regal Senate Caucus Room. Apparently, in the intervening weeks since the blaring March headlines, interest in the TVA scandal had dwindled. After reading the bill of particulars, Donahey invited A. E. Morgan to speak. The former chairman destroyed any advantage he might have had with a six-hour statement delivered, as one observer noted, in "low, mumbling tones." Once again, his message was laced with generalities, such as the claim that "it is not any single act of misrepresentation and deceit from which the T.V.A. suffers, but a continuing habit of misrepresentation which is greatly in conflict with the public interest." The next day, Lilienthal took his turn. He said that A. E. Morgan's accusations implied that he and H. A. Morgan "were being charged with personal corruption and dishonesty." Continuing that he did "not intend to reply in kind to the personal attack leveled against me yesterday," Lilienthal pledged to discuss only matters of substance. He took each of A. E. Morgan's accusations and, at Roosevelt's suggestion, restated them in normal language and then gave his reply. By the time he finished, the tables were turned. Now, Lilienthal was the accuser and A. E. Morgan the accused. At one point, referring to the 1937 TEPCO case, he charged that the former chairman had "tamper[ed] with prospective witnesses, . . . and . . . obstruct[ed] and harass[ed] counsel and witnesses in the very heat of the trial of a crucial constitutional case."[14]

After two days in Washington, the hearings recessed until July 18, when they resumed in Knoxville. Out of the spotlight, the activities took on a different tenor. Committee attendance dwindled as Democratic and Republican representatives left to campaign back home. The only regular panel members were the chairman and the persistent Wolverton and Jenkins who mined every bit of testimony for a hint of scandal. However, nothing happened. A. E. Morgan continued with more of the same—it was becoming clear to almost everyone that he was confused and embittered. His dishonesty charges were less that than a sign of his disdain for the normal ambivalence of political decision making. At one point, A. E. Morgan accused Lilienthal of maladministration because he paid too little for land settlements rather than too much. Even the Republican questioning A. E. Morgan shook his head over this charge. Moreover, the hearing bogged down in thirteen endless days of testimony about the Berry case which had been decided to everyone but Berry's satisfaction earlier that year.[15]

Lilienthal took the offensive in late July. He continued to pick at A. E. Morgan's credibility in crisp lawyerly fashion. The former chairman had testified earlier that at a board meeting "about a week before" the 1935 Chattanooga public power election, Lilienthal had advocated a publicity stunt to influence the outcome of the election. The power director responded that A. E. Morgan was wrong because he, Lilienthal, had been in Florida convalescing from influenza three full weeks before the election. Indeed, the last time the three directors had all met together was January 8, hardly "about a week before" the March 12 election. The point, of course, was not that Lilienthal might not have suggested such a stunt. What was relevant was that Lilienthal once again caught A. E. Morgan in, if not a lie, then either sloppy documentation or senseless exaggeration. On other occasions he gave a bit, as in the case of A. E. Morgan's complaint that Lilienthal made the first TVA rate announcement before getting board approval. Lilienthal admitted jumping the gun, but reminded the committee that a short time later, A. E. Morgan had praised him in public for working out the power program "in a masterful way." On July 26, he stressed that he was proud of the power program for what it had done for the Tennessee Valley and of the authority for "tackling an old job in a new way." He hoped the committee would find that TVA was "an experiment in public administration of which every citizen will be proud."[16]

But for Wendell Willkie's November appearance, the hearings were virtually ignored by the press. After the last session in Knoxville on September 2, the investigation resumed in Washington in November, where it struggled through two dozen fitful sessions of technical testimony. Four days before Christmas 1938 Senator Donahey declared the committee's business at an end.

What did it all amount to? Not much. There were no stunning scandals, no evidence of gross corruption or maladministration. The nation heard of petty lapses such as verbal harassment of A. E. Morgan loyalists and the board's decision to make Knoxville the TVA headquarters rather than Muscle Shoals as specified in the act. Testimony uncovered ambiguities, including questions about TVA's rate base and the relevance of the yard-stick—but these issues had been debated for years. As usual, Willkie was eloquent, but his predictable litany that "T.V.A. should go out of the power business and confine itself to its functions of flood control, navigation, and soil conservation" was dated and irrelevant. There were issues that might have been explored more, such as TVA's industrial contracts with Alcoa and Arkansas Power & Light. Even if they had been, however, not much would have turned up. As Willson Whitman observed, "the hearings were a good show, with Dr. Arthur Morgan and Mr. Lilienthal, Attorney Francis Biddle and Mr. Wendell Willkie, playing heroes or villains according to the point of view."[17]

The final committee report was released April 3, 1939. Frankfurter told Lilienthal the most telling thing about it was that the *Washington Post* put the story on page 5. It was predictable in almost all respects. Five Democrats and one Republican gave TVA a clean bill of health on all charges. The majority views were buttressed by a series of positive technical reports on several issues raised in the hearings. The American Farm Bureau Federation reviewed the fertilizer program, and Leland Olds prepared an "Economic Analysis" of the yardstick. Leonard White, a Republican and political scientist from the University of Chicago, in his review of personnel policies, concluded "that appointments have not been made for political reasons or on account of political endorsements."[18]

The Republicans presented a minority report that criticized TVA for not having an "independent audit," "waste and inefficiency in the administration of power," and the board majority for "taking short cuts to make a showing for the T.V.A." They chided the Democrats for "important matters not investigated" and "failure to call witnesses" requested by the minority. In an individual dissent, Jenkins rebuked Biddle and his assistants for lack of "spirit and vigor" in pursuing various lines of inquiry. Nevertheless, the minority report failed to substantiate any of A. E. Morgan's charges.[19]

Lilienthal's reaction was surprisingly muted, perhaps because he was just back after his illness. He met with Brandeis the day after the report was issued and with Frankfurter the next day. Both justices seemed more elated than Lilienthal. He did venture, however, that "our troubles would certainly be less difficult and trying" now that the challenge had finally been stilled. Now he could turn his attention to finishing what he started back in 1933: consolidation of power in the Tennessee Valley.[20]

Settlement and Legitimation

The intense negotiations with Willkie had been overshadowed for some time by the TEPCO suit and the Lilienthal-Morgan conflict. In January 1938, however, the pace quickened and in less than twenty months, the long affair was concluded. Willkie's motivation for settling was simple: he saw the handwriting on the wall. There was little chance now for government relief. Roosevelt had been reelected by a landslide in 1936 and, in rejecting pooling in 1937, had signaled his antipathy toward the utilities. On the judicial front, a circuit court lifted the Gore injunction in mid-1937 and a district panel ruled in TVA's favor in the remanded case. A year later, almost to the day in January 1938, the Supreme Court finally laid TEPCO's claim to rest. While Willkie's support was stronger in Congress, that body also failed him; the congressional investigation had done little damage. Moreover, Willkie had no chance in the battle for the hearts and minds of Tennessee Valley citizens. Memphis, Chattanooga, and Knoxville all wanted public power and had only to ask for Public Works Administration (PWA) loans and grants to build or buy their own distribution systems. As Lilienthal remembered Willkie saying in 1936, it was impossible to compete where "some people seem to have the idea that your kilowatts are cleaner than ours." Finally, Willkie was wounded by his own side. As TVA became increasingly palpable, more non-C&S utilities began to strike their own deals with the authority, thus weakening the solidarity Willkie so badly needed.[21]

The administration faced its own pressures. In 1938, it found it could no longer steamroll its opponents. A nasty confrontation with United Mine Workers President John L. Lewis alienated many in organized labor. The court-packing scheme had angered Congress, and the public was restless over rising unemployment and lagging recovery programs. In spring 1938, a heavily Democratic Congress spiked administration efforts to create additional authorities and authorized the TVA investigation in spite of the president's wishes. In November the situation became more critical when the Democrats lost seven seats in the Senate and seventy in the House of Representatives. Although the Democrats still held both houses, some in the administration, particularly Commerce Secretary Harry Hopkins, thought it was time for more conciliation and less confrontation. There is some indication, moreover, that Lilienthal's lengthy absence from the negotiations because of illness was fortuitous. After five long years, Lilienthal and Willkie had reached a predictable impasse. Both men were stubborn, proud, and understandably reluctant to give in. New negotiators, however, might just break the logjam. According to observers, Julius "Cap" Krug and Joseph Swidler were instrumental in reaching a conclusive agreement on February 2, 1939. After the decision, Lilienthal told his old friend Ed Morehouse, "You have no idea how frightfully [Krug] and Swidler have been working. . . . They are both fine boys and I am proud and delighted with them."[22]

Throughout 1938 the two sides went back and forth. The major issues centered on price, the extent of the sale, and the question of whether TVA should be restricted to a fixed territory In January, anticipating the TEPCO decision, Willkie offered to sell all Tennessee Valley holdings if TVA would agree to permanent boundaries. Lilienthal rejected the offer, saying TVA was interested only in "useful" properties and not at all in territorial restrictions. By March, influenced by Roosevelt, who now thought Willkie's offer reasonable, Lilienthal agreed to negotiate for all TEPCO properties and small parts of Alabama and Mississippi Power. Later in the month, Lilienthal acknowledged that TVA would voluntarily set territorial limitations to coincide with Tennessee and parts of other states in the river basin. Willkie agreed and progress seemed assured. The negotiations, however, soon bogged down over terms. Willkie suggested a three-person board to help settle the price, but Lilienthal refused, saying that TVA could not delegate that responsibility. Willkie's accounting firm valued the properties at $94 million, which he rounded down to $90 million. TVA's estimate was $81 million from which Lilienthal deducted $24 million in depreciation for a $57 million total. When Willkie refused this offer, TVA raised it to $67 million—again, the C&S president refused.

Negotiations came to a halt. Distracted by the hearings and then devastated by undulant fever, Lilienthal stepped down as chief negotiator. Krug and Swidler took over, and they too locked horns with Willkie. Most talk about a fair settlement in November and December took place at the hearings when first Willkie and then Krug pleaded their cases to the committee. The problem was, however, that they were not talking with each other, but posturing before a less-than-interested Congress and American public. Nevertheless, a convergence of events and Krug and Swidler's determination soon brought a break. On January 30 the Supreme Court rejected the TEPCO suit. Within two days, the president announced that the Securities and Exchange Commission would not help with the TEPCO bargaining and, Willkie promised an end to litigation against TVA. After all-day sessions with Willkie on February 1 and 2, Krug and Swidler reported agreement on a $78.6 million settlement, halfway between the two previous best offers. TVA would pay nearly $45 million, and the rest would be covered by local distributors. Two days later, an excited TVA contingent crammed into Lilienthal's small Norris home to confirm the settlement by phone with Roosevelt and then with board action. The only casualty that day, according to Helen Lilienthal, was "a whole jar of cookies" for David Jr.'s camping trip—Joe Swidler had eaten them all![23]

Nevertheless, the deal was not complete. First, Lilienthal had to answer charges that Willkie had gotten the better end of the deal and the rumor that credit for the settlement should go to Harry Hopkins's "campaign to appease business." The *New Republic* made it clear in late February in an editorial that the real hero was "Mr. J. A. Krug, the thirty-two-year-old prodigy discovered by Mr. Lilienthal . . . [who] was in constant consultation by long-distance telephone with Mr. Lilienthal." The editorial continued that "Mr. Hopkins had no part whatever in the bargaining," and that Willkie's concessions were much greater than TVA's. For his part, Lilienthal grumbled in his journal that he would "have to fight off pride and resentment and restore my peace of mind and sense of balance."[24]

But a bruised ego was minor compared to getting Congress to pay for the agreement. In mid-March, taking leave from his recuperation, Lilienthal told Roosevelt that TVA needed help in getting a reluctant House to authorize adequate bond authority to pay for TEPCO properties. After listening to the president talk enthusiastically about a government-wide bond program for all revenue-producing federal agencies, the three directors nodded in agreement but insisted that "our program required very prompt action." Lilienthal was particularly concerned that Willkie would talk Congress into adding formal territorial limitations and got Roosevelt's assurance that he would veto such legislation.[25]

After returning for good from his convalescence in April, Lilienthal worked on the congressional bill. George Norris rammed through a $100-million bond authorization in the Senate, but the House stalled. Led by anti-TVA Kentucky Democrat Andrew Jackson May, the House authorized only $61.5 million and imposed several restrictions, including the dreaded territorial limitation. By early June, Lilienthal was disconsolate. He bemoaned his weeks of lobbying, calling them "the most dispiriting kind of work [involving] so many wasted hours, and so much distasteful work." On June 22 he reminded Roosevelt that the February TEPCO purchase agreement would expire at the end of the month and urged Roosevelt to apply pressure to get Congress to move. Once more he asked what the president would do if faced with a final bill mandating territorial restrictions. Sending a chill up Lilienthal's spine, the president answered, "Well, if that happens you come back and see me or give me a ring."[26]

The impression from journal entries and Richard Lowitt's account of the appropriation fight in his biography of Norris leads to the conclusion that Lilienthal was less effective than others in getting Congress to act. He disliked lobbying, mulled over resigning, and fussed that he was "impatient to be doing many other things." In part, his attitude stemmed from the lingering effects of his illness. It was also spurred by his disdain for congressional lobbying—he wrote once during the ordeal that lobbying was undignified "and not congenial to me at all." The onerous task also kept him from what he liked to do best: his last formal speech had been in February 1938. The real heroes were Congressmen Sparkman and Thomason, and Norris. Willkie's biographer Ellsworth Barnard also included Willkie and members of the Chattanooga Power Board who met with May and worked out a compromise. In the end, the final bill authorized only $61.5 million in bonds, but that was more than enough to cover the properties. All other restrictions on TVA were dropped, including territorial limitations. True, the bill required congressional permission for expansion, but everyone knew that TVA would have its hands full providing enough power just for the Tennessee River watershed.[27]

The compromise bill passed on July 15 and was signed into law on July 26. All that remained was the formal changing of the guard, and that took place with Wall Street panache on August 16. More than 250 people jammed the sixth floor of the First National Bank in Lower Manhattan to witness the exchange. Willkie was his usually exuberant self and quipped, "Dave, this is a lot of money for a couple of Indiana boys to be handling," as a multimillion-dollar check changed hands. Lilienthal, though, was uncharacteristically subdued. One of Willkie's biographers described him as "ill at ease, uncomfortable and sullen." Lilienthal attributed his reticence to "a flare-up of my undulant remnants" which put him in the hospital a few days later. He was also reluctant to say much "since both Willkie and I are pretty careful not to let the other fellow get in one word without answering it!" As the ceremony symbolizing six interminable years for both men began, Lilienthal reflected that "the entire last six years seemed to flash past as on a quickly moving film, too fast to see." And just like that, in two hours, the private utilities, Tennessee Valley citizens for more than three decades, were gone and a new power company was in charge.[28]

Lilienthal and Willkie had a remarkable relationship. They fought toe-to-toe for six years, with neither giving an inch most of the time. Willkie did everything he could to cripple TVA's power program and Lilienthal stopped at nothing to protect his charge. Yet, they walked away from the bloody fight with a mutual respect that held until Willkie's untimely death in 1944. That such respect endured was remarkable considering Lilienthal's personality. Somehow, he often evoked the worst in his adversaries and, in turn, demonstrated a ruthless ability to respond in kind—witness the savage nature of his dealings with Irving Rosenbaum and A. E. Morgan. Later, Harold Ickes, Kenneth McKellar, and Lewis Strauss would react in similar fashion, and would reap Lilienthal's scorn in return. But not Willkie—after it was all over, Willkie wrote a friend that "Dave is very able; also I have a good deal of affection for him."[29]

Perhaps the relationship remained positive because they were so much alike. Francis Biddle remembered Willkie as intense, possessed of a great "joie de vivre," and capacity to stimulate his listeners. Joe Swidler recalled that he was "a man of bluff manner, impetuous," and confident. Donald Richberg once described Willkie to Lilienthal as " 'arrogant,' 'cocksure,' a 'terrific talker,' and possessing 'that deadly charm.' " One would have to look long and hard to come up with better descriptions of Lilienthal himself. On the eve of Willkie's 1940 presidential run, Jonathan Daniels called the two men "strangely alike. Both were Hoosier boy orators. Both loved—and still love—to spout ideas." Finally, Willkie also had a creative way with words. He popularized the saying that "TVA waters four states and drains the nation," and also cleverly wrote that TVA's "yardstick is rubber from the first inch to the last."[30]

The sparring continued after the settlement. Almost immediately, Willkie charged that he had been forced to sell low because he could no longer compete with a subsidized government operation. He hoped the event would "arouse the American people against government invasion of their business." Lilienthal replied that the settlement was fair and that Willkie's rhetoric was "frightening potential investors in badly needed utility expansion." Perhaps the best insight into their relationship came from Helen Lilienthal. She remembered when David brought Willkie home once "to talk alone." Much to her dismay, her husband asked her to fix lunch, but she had little on hand. She scraped together something and later apologized for serving "the worst lunch I have ever given anyone." David told her not to worry—"neither of them had been conscious what they ate." Lilienthal and Willkie were absorbed in each other because of the dynamic tension between mutual respect and adversarial roles, and they thoroughly enjoyed it. When he heard of Willkie's death in October 1944, Lilienthal wrote of the "great tragedy of the loss of a terrifically vital personality." A few months from his own death thirty-six years later he remembered that "Willkie and I taught each other a lot during those years. I came to understand myself better because of that dead-earnest conflict."[31]

In the end, the August settlement signaled an end to eighteen hectic months, easily the most trying time of his public life. Between January 1938 and August 1939, Lilienthal weathered the final days of the battle with A. E. Morgan, the first of several confrontations with a hostile Congressional committee, a serious illness, and a settlement that guaranteed the success of the program he had fought for so long. Time was so precious and pressures so strong in these months that Lilienthal had little time for speeches—after two February 1938 addresses, he was absent from the circuit until November 1939. Nevertheless he always seemed to land on his feet. He was typically assertive, even arrogant: witness Biddle's observation of his demeanor at the hearings. And he could be transparently obsequious, just as he had been with Frank Walsh and Felix Frankfurter. In spring 1939 while at Captiva Island he wrote the first stamp collector in the land that he had started collecting stamps—Roosevelt wrote back with a twinkle in his words, "It is very good news to hear that you have started a stamp collection. . . . It will be grand to see you again." He also ingratiated himself in a letter to Eleanor Roosevelt in September thanking her for her "deep interest in the broad human and economic purposes of the authority" and "recent trip through the South" where she could come to know this vital region better. His greatest asset, as always, was his private life with Helen. As he thought in his end-of-year reflection in December 1939, "Every day, every crisis or victory or amusing or distressing incident adds to the store of things we have in common, adds richness to our joint life."[32]

Building and Administering a New Agency

It would be wrong to conclude that TVA's early success stemmed from the wisdom and heroics of the first directors alone. It did not. What the agency did on a day-to-day basis in building dams and providing services in the areas of power, fertilizer development, agriculture, and conservation resulted more from the efforts of a highly qualified and motivated cadre of

men and a few women than anything else. Lilienthal may have been an
exemplary leader and the two Morgans paragons of public virtue, but others, some anonymous, others not, provided the glue that held the organization together and protected it from outside predators. TVA's Personnel and
Legal Divisions were perhaps the finest of any federal agency. Without the
know-how to do the job, and do it well, Lilienthal's charisma and political
skills could never have prevailed.

All of the original directors believed in merit and tried to embody that
principle in everything TVA did. A. E. Morgan learned about merit through
the complex public works projects he had supervised for decades. As an
academic administrator, H. A. Morgan had been steeped in a tradition of
finding the best people he could for teaching, research, and public service.
And Lilienthal's experience in Wisconsin taught him there was only one
way to deal with the powerful utilities—with every ounce of expertise and
competence he could muster. It is also true that A. E. Morgan, and to a
lesser extent Lilienthal, were responsible for TVA's enlightened labor policies, including union recognition, collective bargaining, good wage scales,
wholesome working conditions at dam sites, and a thirty-three-hour week
on construction projects. Nevertheless, one must conclude that TVA's
people, not the special administrative genius or plan of any one of the directors, were mainly responsible for the spectacular record of good works in
the first half-decade.

In fact there were several factors that precluded what anyone might call
an integrated management plan. First, TVA was not only a new organization, but it was a new type of organization. There were no administrative
guidelines in the TVA Act, except that the board was responsible for all
staffing, organizational decisions, and the implementation of Section Six,
which prohibited political considerations in hiring. Second, there was little
time in the beginning for any of the directors to think about, let alone develop, a rational staffing plan. In June 1933, Floyd Reeves, four days on the
job as personnel director, told of "500 people a day . . . seeking interviews."
Two months later he wrote of a truck leaving "for Knoxville with our
50,000 applications" and of "1000 personnel applications appearing at the
[Knoxville] office each day." In August 1933, A. E. Morgan noted that TVA
had received 40,000 job applications in June and July. Norris was amazed
that A. E. Morgan had hired fourteen stenographers to answer job inquiries. In 1938, Gordon Clapp, then director of personnel, wrote Lilienthal
that it took two years simply to develop procedures necessary to comply
with Section Six. Third, the early board dissension and the concomitant
dividing of TVA functions put staffing and administrative decisions at the
mercy of the individual directors. Only A. E. Morgan's fortuitous choice of
Reeves and Reeve's decision to bring in Clapp helped bring some rhyme
and reason to the staffing process.[33]

Finally, in spite of their credentials and reputations as men of vision,
none of the first directors were traditional administrators. H. A. Morgan
was more philosopher than manager, and his meager administrative inter-

ests focused almost entirely on agriculture matters. A. E. Morgan was a brilliant technical manager—his TVA projects were almost always on time and under budget. However, he was virtually helpless in the face of the conflict and diversity inherent in a large organization like TVA. Lilienthal, on the other hand, developed somewhat of a reputation as an administrator, although to those who knew him best, he was no more a manager than the other two. As Pritchett marveled, "The wonder is rather that the end result was so good, and that the T.V.A. was able to . . . earn its reputation as one of the best administered federal agencies."[34]

In reality, the economic crisis deserved much of the credit. TVA benefited enormously from the availability of a large pool of eager young people, abandoned by the depression and drawn to an organization with an idealistic mission. Judging by their later accomplishments, TVA's young technical and managerial class had as much talent as any federal agency. Krug, in the Power Division, became Truman's secretary of the interior, and Henry Fowler, a young TVA lawyer, was treasury secretary in the Johnson administration. Lawrence Fly became chairman of the Federal Communications Commission, Swidler chaired the Federal Power Commission, and economist J. Hayden Alldredge served as chairman of the Interstate Commerce Commission. In addition, John Blandford, TVA's first general manager, was assistant director of the budget and then administrator of the National Housing Agency during World War II. Two staff attorneys, Bessie Margolin and Herbert Marks, went on to distinguished careers. Margolin, TVA's first woman attorney, held long tenure as assistant solicitor for the Labor Department, and Marks worked as general counsel for the Bonneville Power Project, the Atomic Energy Commission, and as an advisor to Dean Acheson. Three pioneer administrators, including Harry Curtis, Aubrey Wagner, and Gordon Clapp, later became members of the TVA board, and the latter two served as chairmen.

The early roster included others of literary and scholarly distinction. William I. Nichols, first head of electrical development, became longtime editor of *This Week Magazine* after leaving TVA. Former administrators Richard Niehoff and Harry Case of the Personnel Division, Herman Pritchett of the Social and Economic Division, Norman Wengert from Agriculture, Marguerite Owen, director of the Washington Office, A. E. Morgan's top aide Walter Kahoe, and Clapp contributed important book-length studies of one aspect or another of the TVA experience. How did they come to TVA? Krug, Fly, Swidler, and Owen were hired by Lilienthal, and Blandford was hired by A. E. Morgan. Floyd Reeves convinced a reluctant Lilienthal to hire Bessie Margolin. Clapp, who became as close as anyone to Lilienthal, was also handpicked by Reeves, his graduate professor at the University of Chicago—and, of course Reeves was one of A. E. Morgan's earliest choices.[35]

Lilienthal's views on management were pragmatic and progressive, and appealed to many who were attracted to TVA in the 1930s. In 1935, he mused that "the expert organizer" often confuses "an organization chart and an organization." For Lilienthal, "effective organization is about 90 percent personnel." The dilemma, however, was "that you don't want to build your organization around men because men lack any quality of standardization. . . [Y]et if you try to disregard the human factor and build your organization according to strictly administrative technique, you find yourself in an even worse difficulty." He often thought of how to reconcile objective considerations and human factors. Earlier the same year, he wrote Frankfurter that TVA's overly protectionist merit system policies were causing Congress to grumble. While acknowledging the justification, he criticized his fellow directors when he spoke of the "relatively large number of former business associates of Chairman Morgan in the engineering work, . . . and a relatively large number of University of Tennessee faculty people." He, on the other hand, had studiously "avoided bringing people from Wisconsin" (although he frequently used them as paid consultants). But, he concluded, his behavior "may exhibit too much concern about a criticism which has little real validity."[36]

In labor-management matters, Lilienthal supported the policies A. E. Morgan had already set in place. He told a Labor Day conclave in Detroit in 1935 that TVA's mission would fail without "fair and decent" labor-management relationships: "What permanent good will it do . . . to save our soil, to control floods, and to distribute cheap electricity if those goals are reached through the exploitation of labor?" He emphasized that TVA's labor policies encouraged every employee "to have a voice in management." Two years later at Chickamauga Dam in Chattanooga, he spoke of what happens when management loses "contact with the human beings who really make the machine go." Once again, "no amount of skill in administration and no perfection of organization can take the place of human understanding." Nevertheless, Lilienthal concluded by endorsing "sound organizational principles." He reminded his audience that "no man can be happy on his job if he doesn't know to whom he is responsible. . . . Vagueness and indefiniteness in organization due to faulty principles of administration will kill the effectiveness of any organization."[37]

In spite of *thinking* administratively, Lilienthal had little inclination for, or interest in, traditional management. In 1937 he admitted being bored with detail and frustrated by slowness, both traits antithetical to day-to-day managerial practice. His contemporaries at TVA, including Swidler, power engineer Roland Kampmeier, and almost everyone else, agreed that Lilienthal was not cut out, as Swidler remembered, "to running the details of a department." For Lilienthal, administration meant something different. He was there to establish and nurture "the cohesive force, the motivating driving force, behind this widespread organization." In an organization like TVA, dominated by "technical men and experts" as it was, "leadership [needed to] state the underlying social fundamentals of the work, so that each technician can get a feeling of pride and direction about his special responsibility." In a word, Lilienthal was the type of leader who gave direction, lifted spirits, and, as John Oliver remembered, "inspire[d] people to work over their heads." Swidler called it "program sense." Harry Case, not always a Lilienthal fan, called him a "man who . . . inspires an organization with his emotional fervor combined with a great deal of knowledge and intellectual competence." After a visit to TVA, Methodist Bishop G. Bromley Oxnam wrote of Lilienthal's responsibility for a spirit "in the offices, in the great powerhouses, in the staff. It was a friendly spirit, full of faith—a sense of teamplay, and of a game great and worth winning." In his excellent analysis of Lilienthal, Hargrove perhaps captured it best—"David Lilienthal was a rhetorical administrative leader."[38]

An important consequence, perhaps unintended, of Lilienthal's preference for administration by inspiration was a trend toward extensive delegation of authority and informal work ways. Pritchett observed that the first general managers, John Blandford and Gordon Clapp, strongly believed in decentralized administration. Clapp himself reflected that "the role of general management . . . is certainly not to attempt to keep a close check on everything. . . . That sort of concept would so hamstring the T.V.A. as to deprive it of the drive, imagination, and experience of its staff."[39]

Lilienthal felt much the same about management style. George Gant and Oliver, both later general managers, recalled an informal lunch ritual that went on for years at a downtown Knoxville "greasy spoon" where, according to Gant, "legal people and the personnel people and the General Manager's office would meet regularly with H. A. Morgan, Clapp, Lilienthal, and Harry Curtis." Lilienthal was "one of the boys" and everyone called him "Dave." After A. E. Morgan's departure, Lilienthal ran board meetings in an informal manner. Both Lilienthal and Oliver remembered the latter's first meeting in 1942. The chairman wondered at the time if the raucous give and take hadn't made the young budget officer turn "in his resignation . . . as he found that he had been engaged by a nut house." Oliver remembered it as an "unusual operation" and the "completely democratic way they went about talking through issues." And yet, for Lilienthal, friendliness and informality did not translate into intimacy. One associate characterized his inspiration as "charismatic detachment." He had few, if any, close friends, and did not, according to Swidler, "suffer needless intrusions." Kampmeier remembered him as a loner—on trips to Washington, the TVA entourage would sit around and play cards; everyone, that is, but Lilienthal, who would withdraw, "writing in his journal, . . . doing his own thing."[40]

Lilienthal's administrative style helped steer TVA away from a traditional authority structure for a number of reasons. First, the early division of responsibility resulted in a functional decentralization of authority. Each director ran his own show, and Lilienthal, in particular, delegated a great deal within the Power and Legal Divisions. Another reason his style caught on stemmed from the complexity and diversity of TVA itself. Clapp insisted that "no man in an agency with as broad a program as this . . . can possibly presume to sit in a focal position and pass authoritative judgments on everything." Third, widespread delegation was possible because, from top to bottom, TVA was blessed with a plenitude of talented people who needed little supervision once they had their marching orders. A final factor was the simple fact that Lilienthal's vision blended so well with that of his top managers. Their work was creative and useful, and as Biddle remembered about TVA staff spirit, "this enthusiasm was kept going not by the passing exhortation of improving talk, but by the concrete visible reality of building things that the inhabitants of the Valley needed." TVA employees believed in what they did, and they could see the fruits of their labor. It seemed natural that the best advice was "exhort 'em and let 'em go."—and Lilienthal was very good at that. It is easy to understand Maury Maverick's report of the TVA perspective "that all 'politicians' have red tails and work in sordid surroundings just as TVA'ers have wings and work in Green Pastures." His observation reflected Lilienthal's opinion of elected officials and the effect of his persuasive "administrative rhetoric" on thousands of TVA employees.[41]

Any story about David Lilienthal, or TVA for that matter, would be remiss without mentioning Gordon Clapp and Marguerite Owen. Each came on board early, Owen as director of the Washington Office and Clapp as Floyd Reeves's assistant. Owen, at one time a member of George Norris's staff, held her post for thirty-five years, until retiring in the late 1960s. Clapp became personnel director in 1937 and general manager in 1939. In 1946 he took Lilienthal's place as TVA board chairman, a position he held until 1954. They, along with the original three directors, were greatly responsible for TVA's early accomplishments. Clapp and Owen were equally influential in guaranteeing Lilienthal's success at TVA. "They were," as George Gant remembered, "able to help him choose between his good ideas and his bad ideas," a talent that the action-oriented, sometimes impatient director lacked.[42]

As TVA weathered its first shaky years, Clapp became a superb manager. Without exception, TVA old-timers remember him as TVA's "most able administrator," "an administrative genius," someone with the "unique talent of turning something you were having difficulty with into something that was easy more than almost anyone I ever knew." He was praised as a manager of impeccable honesty, credibility, courage, and a man who understood all of TVA's programs. As an administrator, he was fair and aboveboard, loyal, and dedicated to the proposition "If you've got a good man, let him alone." When comparisons arose between Clapp and Lilienthal, one observer noted that Lilienthal had "imagination and courage," while Clapp had "administrative know-how." Another called Clapp "the administrative man . . . , but [with] a warm feeling for people which really went, I think, beyond Lilienthal." One final observer called Clapp "a team player, [and] Lilienthal an individual star." Clapp was the administrative rock and moral foundation during most of Lilienthal's TVA days. As George Gant remembered, he "had such intelligence and integrity that, . . . when people had real problems they would go to Gordon Clapp. Blandford went to him, Lilienthal went to him. Even when he was a young man called 'that red headed boy in Floyd Reeves's office,' you know, this was the case, he was tough." Kampmeier recalled that "if Gordon was satisfied [with something

Lilienthal had pulled], I felt pretty good." Even Lilienthal called Clapp "a great stabilizer for me." Essentially, Clapp gave a stability to TVA which freed Lilienthal to practice the kind of administration he was best at—detached, inspirational, and rhetorical.[43]

If Clapp was "Mr. Inside," Marguerite Owen was "Miss Outside." There is unanimous consensus that her Washington job was central to the success of the young regional agency. Harry Case said she was "one of a small handful of people who were absolutely crucial to the history of TVA." Joe Swidler, a Washington insider at the time of his interview, called her TVA's main player in Washington. Lilienthal once volunteered that if he had to choose "the strongest, the most influential, the wisest friend the TVA had, . . . it would be Marguerite Owen. . . . I can't think of anyone else." In 1944, he wrote her father that "TVA would not be what it is today . . . if it had not had the benefit of her wonderfully clear head and good judgment." He continued that "since 1933, Marguerite has had a standing with a couple score Members of Congress that would have made Alice Roosevelt Longworth at the height of her powers seem like an extra girl on a bob-sled party." Ironically, A. E. Morgan gave Lilienthal the go-ahead to make this crucial hire in 1933, and based on the recommendations of both Norris and Tom Corcoran, he took the unusual step of selecting a woman. And it was a good choice. Richard Niehoff and Case showered her with praise, calling her astute, loyal, and consistent; a person of absolute integrity; and someone who knew Washington as well as anyone. Years later, even A. E. Morgan had praise for her.[44]

Virtually everyone agreed that she taught Lilienthal everything about Washington politics. Case thought she "probably saved [Lilienthal] from boners which could have come from his egocentrism." Niehoff said she was one of the few who could be blunt with the boss: In 1942 she chewed him out for "sign[ing] some very inadequate letters. Rude, almost. And more than once I've noticed your replies fail to respond fully to the inquiry." A few days later a chastened chairman wrote, "The thing is, you are right. And we are all going to try to do better." Owen's office was almost always the first stop for any TVA executive after getting off the train at Union Station. One former TVA executive thought that Owen "did a heck of a lot more than anyone else to build up Dave Lilienthal [and] give him national prominence." From Lilienthal's journal, it is clear that Owen was a key link in the Washington political game. She always seemed to wrangle White House appointments on short notice, to know the status of important legislative initiatives, or to be present at key hearings or meetings. Owen often helped Lilienthal with his speeches. He remembered that before his seminal grassroots speech in late 1939, she "argued it out with me and . . . did some of the actual draftsmanship."[45]

Owen and Clapp were extraordinary administrators. Without them, TVA would have prevailed, just as it probably would have without Lilienthal. Nevertheless, TVA was enriched and strengthened by their presence. So was Lilienthal.

Social Experiment to Corporate Reality

The year 1938 was a watershed for TVA. In the first six years no one, not even Lilienthal, could say for sure where the authority was heading, or even if it would survive. In that year however, the favorable TEPCO decision and the final settlement with the utilities gave the agency a secure basis for projecting a long-term future. The years had been exhilarating but harsh. TVA could take pride in its accomplishments and the strong esprit de corps of a highly competent work force. Not only was the authority "the apple of the [president's] eye," but it was the envy of public administration throughout the nation—TVA was a shining example of what enlightened public service was all about. The agency had demonstrated that large public entities could deliver complex services cheaply and effectively. Moreover, it had blazed new paths in power distribution, rate making, conservation, fertilizer technology, and watershed development.

This is not to say that TVA was without blemish. Even before A. E. Morgan's ouster, it had lost most of its visionary flare. Norris, Tennessee, originally an experimental community, turned into a segregated bedroom community for TVA administrators. Lilienthal's alliance with H. A. Morgan and the need to establish firm Tennessee Valley roots resulted in accommodation rather than the "derring-do" of a lively vision: TVA's closest allies were land grant colleges, the Farm Bureau, and the Extension Service, rather than upstart agencies such as the Farm Security Administration and Soil Conservation Service. After A. E. Morgan left, the notion of small-scale cooperative development gave way to an industrial policy favoring the Alcoas and Monsantos.

TVA also fell way short in the area of race relations. While the authority employed African Americans at a ratio equivalent to their numbers in the Tennessee Valley (about 10 percent), the vast majority were hired as low-level laborers. The 1938 investigation produced shameful testimony about TVA's lack of attention to matters of racial justice. For nearly a full day in August, Charles H. Houston, counsel for the National Association for the Advancement of Colored People, testified in great detail that TVA "has evolved no integrated Negro program, . . . regards Negroes as a labor commodity, and not as citizens, . . . has introduced new patterns of segregation," and that current "policies have resulted in closing the doors of opportunity to Negroes both for employment, for work advancement, [and] for apprenticeship training in the skilled crafts." Houston later charged that TVA delayed hiring African Americans on construction crews until two or three months after projects were started and none at all on reservoir clearing jobs. In the administration division the only African Americans included "a few Negro janitors" and the director of Negro training. TVA had no African American file clerks, secretaries, stenographers, administrators, or lawyers. A few days later, without disputing any of Houston's claims, Clapp responded that "the Authority in general does not feel that it has any special responsibility for attempting to revise or reconstruct the attitude of this area or any other area with respect to the racial question."[46]

There is little doubt that Lilienthal was fully aware of the situation and condoned it. He testified the same morning as Houston, following him almost immediately on the stand. Moreover, it is difficult to imagine that Clapp, by that time Lilienthal's right-hand man, would espouse a policy much different from that of the chairman. The best that can be said is that Lilienthal was a typical New Deal liberal on race. He felt uneasy about bias and bigotry and was glad when African Americans got an opportunity, such as when he gleefully watched blacks and whites participate in a TVA labor council meeting in 1943. Nevertheless, he failed to use institutional means to right wrongs. He never addressed the segregated situation at Norris, and once when daughter Nancy was disturbed by a "White Only" sign at Norris Lake, Lilienthal could do no better than counsel that segregation "should be approached as a fact," and that "there was no use pretending that there would be anything but social distinctions and with them segregation, perhaps for generations to come." He had little if anything to say, either, about TVA's decision to exclude Negro Land Grant Colleges from TVA's extensive network of agriculture programs. That was H. A. Morgan's call, not his.[47]

At TVA, Lilienthal moved a long way beyond the proactive state paternalism of Wisconsin. There, regulation had meant not just reacting to public demands and complaints, but interpreting citizen needs and taking action "regardless of public demand." Now he championed the next step, using state resources to influence and shape public demand and mass consumption. In a fanciful sketch of his differences with Willkie, Lilienthal talked of himself as *"new kind of business man . . .* But it [TVA] is more business than government—more likely to be the pattern (with economic regimentation . . . inevitable) than anything on American scene." His evangelical campaign to encourage greater power consumption symbolized the expansion of the benevolent state. Although nothing came of this, at least from Lilienthal, in August 1934, he even broached the idea to Frankfurter of a massive government credit program for "reestablishing and maintaining a stable purchasing power among the masses." In July 1937 Lilienthal shared his view of the activist state with TVA employees at Chickamauga Dam. He reminded them of their crucial role in public service since "government has taken on greater and greater responsibilities and is doing more and more of the things of the world."[48]

Lilienthal capitalized on his transformation from Progressive to state capitalist because of political skill, captivating rhetoric, a massive dose of chutzpah, and a lot of luck. Even in the early years, the authority had come, as Tugwell recommended, to "approximate a government." Far from harm's way in Washington, TVA became extraordinarily independent with its own merit system and immunity from General Accounting Office and

Bureau of the Budget strictures and rules. Through its linkages in the Tennessee Valley and constitutional considerations, TVA established similar freedoms from state and local jurisdictions—indeed, in its ability to dictate rates to local governments, TVA quickly became the senior partner in that relationship. Early on, in decisions to remove hundreds and then thousands of families from rich but doomed reservoir lowlands, the meaning of "the full power of the state" became painfully clear.[49]

At TVA, much more than in Wisconsin, Lilienthal was able to ride the wave of a merit-driven juggernaut. The scarcity of jobs, TVA's appeal, and more resources to hire the best than he could have hoped for up north made for a heady gathering of talent. Moreover, the fact that the other directors, particularly A. E. Morgan, had attracted extremely capable employees in engineering, personnel, and management, made the job of running a quality shop all the easier. TVA rarely lost momentum or face because of technical lapses or failures.

The Lilienthal-Morgan fight and its aftermath reflected several stark ideological differences. In many respects, their quarrel symbolized the juxtaposition between the traditional Progressivism of A. E. Morgan, from which he never moved, and Lilienthal's pragmatic statism, toward which he instinctively moved to remain close to a newly defined liberal center. Lilienthal's movement from Progressivism to practical liberalism, and the criticism he received from A. E. Morgan, reflected Richard Hofstadter's notion of the role reversal that took place between Progressives and conservatives early in the New Deal. Before the New Deal, Progressives were moralistic in their demands for justice and an end to the abuses of the established order, whereas conservatives were practical in their appeal to facts and institutional stability. During the New Deal, the Progressives became the pragmatists, and conservatives, the moralists protesting the loss of freedom and "socialist abuses." The Progressive Lilienthal was a moralist at first—like A. E. Morgan—but as he embraced statist norms, he increasingly became a practical man of action.[50]

The seesaw battle between A. E. Morgan and Lilienthal and the latter's eventual victory was symbolic of the transformation from the first to the second New Deal. The key figures of the first era, sometimes called the Columbia University crew, included Raymond Moley, Rex Tugwell, Adolph Berle, and Donald Richberg. They were visionaries who believed in social cohesion and cooperation. Their goal was to reshape American institutions with an eye toward transformation rather than mere reform. The second New Deal was typified by Frankfurter, Tom Corcoran, and Ben Cohen, realists, less concerned with grandiose visions and bent on solving problems in the best possible way. Their institutional center was Harvard Law School, and they favored adversarial action, whether in resuscitating competition in the marketplace or championing a litigious government. As Schlesinger observed, "Tugwell saw [the contrast between the first and second New Deals] as between men who had social vision and men who lacked it; Corcoran saw it as between men who disdained legal exactitude and men who valued it." A. E. Morgan fit in the first camp and Lilienthal the second, and Lilienthal won because the second New Dealers prevailed. Lilienthal also triumphed because A. E. Morgan was rigid and unable to adapt to new circumstances and realities. The youngest director, on the other hand, was flexible and did adjust. Lilienthal had embodied elements of both New Deals at first at TVA. He proclaimed himself to be a no-nonsense realist and championed adversarial practices from the beginning. However, his rhetoric reflected Progressive, even populist elements, and often a visionary flair. Lilienthal prevailed for many reasons, but an important one was his ability to keep his foot in both camps, to retain the loyalty and affection of fallen first New Dealers like Berle and Richberg, diehard Progressives like Norris and La Follette, and triumphant second New Dealers represented by his old mentor, Felix Frankfurter.[51]

Nevertheless, the transformation from social experiment to high-powered corporation had certain costs, as did the unfortunate circumstances that led to the necessary but tragic jettisoning of A. E. Morgan. Tugwell and Edward C. Banfield later wrote that "from 1936 on the TVA should have been called the Tennessee Valley Power Production and Flood Control Corporation." Its vision had narrowed considerably, perhaps the inevitable fate of any organization expected to excel in many areas. Even Lilienthal, the single-minded power director, sensed this new reality the day of the great transfer when he wrote of "a new power trust now, in the Tennessee Valley region" in his journal. In early November, Morris Cooke, sensing a disturbing narrowing of focus at TVA, wrote Lilienthal that he "had to win the power fight or you would have been sunk." Nevertheless, he continued, "you will be well advised to put the emphasis on other parts of your task, . . . [and] that except in the one matter of dams—acquired, built, building or to be built—you have given us laymen no picture of the size and length of your job." He warned finally, that he was disturbed over some evidence of "drifting policy" in TVA rather than a clearheaded vision of the future.

Without a doubt, TVA had achieved functional legitimacy by the summer of 1939. However, something was missing. A sense of vision, social purpose, and renewal had all been lost, or at least sublimated, during the hard years of fighting both inside and outside the agency. In all candor, Lilienthal, who had been relentless in pursuit of the electrical power objectives, was largely responsible for this narrowing of vision. More than a third of his forty-seven addresses between 1933 and 1938 were concerned with power. Nevertheless, concerns about old allies and new threats to TVA, along with his own doubts about TVA's narrowing path, set him to thinking about a new interpretation of his now-secure agency. That interpretation soon came, and, much to Lilienthal's surprise, it became a grand new warrant for TVA's existence.[52]

CHAPTER 7

Crafting a Vision

> Tom Corcoran and Ben Cohen had lunch with me on Thursday.
> Tom had had a talk with Senator Norris, upon whose sympa-
> thetic and sentimental shoulder Dave Lilienthal wept when he
> heard that the President was planning to issue an order that
> TVA report to him through me.
>
> —Harold L. Ickes, *The Secret Diary of
> Harold L. Ickes,* September 30, 1939

Pragmatic Myths

It is ironic that TVA's heroic vision was inspired in large measure by events that were less mythic or noble than plainly political. In early September 1939, Lilienthal found out that the secretary of the interior, Harold Ickes, had been plotting all summer to bring federal power programs, including TVA, under his control. Lilienthal knew he had a fight on his hands. Ickes was powerful and persistent, as were his allies Thomas Corcoran and Benjamin Cohen, both influential presidential advisors. The move was even more threatening, considering the looming international crisis. Soon America's industrial juggernaut might have to feed a war—if that happened, a coordinated energy policy would be essential.

According to Lilienthal, Ickes's threat made him "do some intensive thinking about" the future of TVA. Even before Ickes's assault he had been concerned about TVA's power company image. And, although "grass roots" had not always been part of his vocabulary, Lilienthal had always emphasized the role of local institutions in carrying out TVA's programs. As early as 1936, he told Wendell Willkie that TVA was pledged to "local participation and decentralization of those functions which can adequately be decentralized." Lilienthal's first mention of "grass roots administration" came in November 1939. The culmination of his effort, a comprehensive apologia, was finally published in Lilienthal's book *TVA: Democracy on the March* (hereafter referred to as *Democracy on the March*) in 1944. The book was a systematic integration of the ideas he had thought about privately and articulated in public since 1933. It also became a model for later efforts to bring TVA-like enterprises to watersheds across the globe.[1]

New Challenges

With the stroke of a pen and the exchange of $78 million in August 1939, TVA became the undisputed power king in the Tennessee Valley—it also became the largest public utility in the land. Convalescing from his long bout with undulant fever, Lilienthal found time to think about TVA in a post–power-fight era. He wrote Fred Arvin in February 1939 that he was sorry people thought of TVA mainly in terms of public power. To be sure, electricity was important because it "is something people understand and respond to." However, he had been concerned all along about the larger mission of "reviv[ing] Southern morale" and shaking off decades of "defeat and self-pity." "With the power program on its feet," he continued, he could now "devote more and more time" to articulating a wider vision. In April, he thought again about moving beyond power to an emphasis on "the *human* factor." He was taken by Willson Whitman's new book on TVA, *God's Valley*, which, while inaccurate in places, would "attract more interest and attention than almost anything we have done." By July, worn by endless negotiations over legislation to buy out Tennessee Power Company, Lilienthal thought that unless he could get back to "creating," he might resign. In mid-August, he published his first version of the new vision in the Sunday *New York Times* magazine. Lilienthal regretted "that the power phases of TVA have . . . overshadowed all else," and praised "the non-power activities," which were "producing results deserving of increasing public interest and respect." Programs in soil preservation, fertilizer, recreation, public health, and effective methods of "personnel selection and management," he continued, were all crucial to TVA's integrated method and "democratic way."[2]

A few weeks later Lilienthal learned of Ickes's plans for TVA. In some ways, the Lilienthal-Ickes conflict was a surprise. Donald Richberg was a common friend—both men had worked with him, albeit at different times, in Chicago. Also, as head of the Public Works Administration (PWA), Ickes, often helped TVA in the Commonwealth and Southern (C&S) battle by offering loans and grants to local towns and rural cooperatives to purchase their own distribution systems. Time after time a beleaguered Willkie would complain about how Lilienthal and Ickes had conspired to run C&S out of the Tennessee Valley.

But the feud was not altogether unexpected. Ickes was as notorious for his expansionist moves as Lilienthal was for his strident defense of TVA. The secretary of the interior was buoyed by recommendations of the president's Committee on Administrative Management regarding reorganization and consolidation of executive functions. Since other federal power projects were in Interior, Ickes reasoned, it just seemed logical that TVA might also belong there. Moreover, Ickes believed that TVA owed him since "the successful outcome of [Lilienthal's] negotiations with Willkie were due in large part to the [PWA] allocations." Personality was also a factor. Both men were strong-willed, volatile, and capable of brutally frank invective. Ickes was the legendary "old curmudgeon," and he could probably still remember that Lilienthal had lured Joseph Swidler away from Interior in 1933 after Swidler had been on the job only a few months.[3]

The conflict began in the spring of 1939, when Ickes added TVA to the list of programs he wanted for Interior. He succeeded in transferring the Federal Fisheries Agency and Biological Survey, and he had been pestering Roosevelt to give him Forestry and the Rural Electrification Administration (REA). As part of his REA pitch, Ickes argued that all federal power agencies, including TVA, "be set up in one strong organization in Interior." Happy with what he took as a positive response, Ickes raised the issue with Roosevelt three times that summer. In late June, according to Ickes, the president told him he would soon sign an executive order regarding TVA. Three weeks later Ickes offered to draft the order, but Roosevelt told him first to talk it over with Budget Director Harold Smith. In August, the frustrated secretary told Roosevelt he was preparing an order to bring TVA into Interior. The response this time was negative enough to prompt Ickes to complain, "It may be that I am just going to have a peep into the Promised Land but never set my feet therein."[4]

The battle began when Ickes's plan leaked out. Lilienthal and Gordon Clapp met with George Norris on September 8 at his Wisconsin summer home, and the senator wrote Roosevelt objecting to Ickes's actions. On September 23, TVA launched a counteroffensive. The first salvo was a forceful letter to Roosevelt from the TVA board with Lilienthal's clear imprint. Having to submit to the secretary of the interior, the letter argued, would result in "grave consequences," and "the loss to the cause of preserving our democratic institutions." Without independence "the experiment will be ended." In the board's mind, "there is no middle ground." To preserve TVA's "unified approach," it was essential to proceed freely and unfettered. For the first time "grass roots" was evoked to defend and describe "TVA's program of cooperation with local agencies." The board agreed that TVA should coordinate with other federal agencies, but insisted that they were already working hard at such cooperation.[5]

Two days later, on September 25, Lilienthal took command in Washington. First, he met with Norris. In addition to touching base with the White House, Norris conferred with Tom Corcoran the next day, and had long sessions with Ickes, Ben Cohen, and Corcoran on Wednesday and Friday. Norris held firm, and told Lilienthal, "I made it damn clear that I would never consent." Ickes and his crew were livid. Ickes reported Corcoran's sense that "Norris' mind had been thoroughly poisoned" through Lilienthal's manipulative practices. While Lilienthal knew how to handle Norris, he knew the senator need little encouragement. As Lilienthal summarized Norris's indignation, the senator knew "all about the TVA Act; . . . by God, he wrote it; . . . it was the very essence of the act that the TVA board should be independent."[6]

Lilienthal continued to monitor Norris's activities and, with TVA general manager John Blandford, met Budget Director Smith on Wednesday. He felt confident, sensing that Smith, while preferring to be neutral, would support TVA in the end. Lilienthal's position was strengthened by the fact that Blandford had long been courted by Smith and would soon take over as his assistant director. In a few days, Lilienthal found that his efforts had paid off. On October 2, Norris told him the president had assured him through Louis Brownlow that "The Ickes-Corcoran-Cohen proposal 'was on ice'. . . [and] was going to stay in the refrigerator." The next day, Roosevelt wrote Harcourt Morgan and assured him that "there was never any thought on my part of having the Secretary of the Interior determine policy matters affecting the TVA." He asked the board, however, to think about how to address the concern of the president's committee for better coordination and communication in the executive branch.[7]

While the president's memo seemed to resolve things, neither principal let up. On October 3, Lilienthal spent hours with Cohen and Corcoran "discussing" their role in the affair. In a "less and less judicial" manner, Lilienthal said he now knew about "the kind of maneuvering that had caused a large number of people in Washington . . . to lose their confidence in Corcoran and Cohen." Cohen admitted the issue could have been handled better and said the recommendations of the president's committee were the real culprits. Lilienthal left an overheated room vowing there was no way he would ever agree to limit TVA's autonomy. On October 12, Ickes asked Lilienthal to see him "about that TVA order," and on October 23 both men met loaded for bear. Lilienthal "looked forward to this meeting" expecting anything from "acid sarcasm to real abuse" and was ready to walk out if Ickes got out of line. Ickes thought the interview was one Lilienthal "rather dreaded but couldn't avoid." The diaries of both men agree that Ickes dominated the conversation and wasted no time lighting into the TVA director for using Norris to block a presidential order. How, asked Ickes, could anyone loyal to the president "try to block . . . what the President had decided that he wanted to do?" Lilienthal attempted to respond, but Ickes interrupted that any good lawyer "can find an argument to support anything you do." After more "berating" by Ickes, Lilienthal appealed to the notion of decentralization. Ickes dismissed the argument, concluding, "Some people believe in decentralization—break things down to the constables; others believe in good organization. . . . I prefer good organization." Soon after, Ickes abruptly ended the meeting with, as Lilienthal remembered, a dour "Good-bye and God bless you." Lilienthal exercised a good deal of self-restraint in what must have been a highly unpleasant encounter. Ickes wrote contemptuously that "Lilienthal really didn't put up much of an argument." Other interpretations might suggest that Ickes did not listen or that Lilienthal had difficulty getting a word in. One indication of Lilienthal's restraint was Ickes's admission that he was deliberately "contemptuous of [Lilienthal's] arguments and a little cavalier in my treatment of him."[8]

In spite of the ballistics, the feud ebbed for a time. In late 1940, however, it erupted with even greater fury, again prompting Ickes to try finishing what he had started in 1939. The catalyst for the second round was Lilienthal's much-heralded trip west to confer with the governor of California on water projects and to deliver a series of speeches up and down the coast. It was impossible to squelch the irrepressible Lilienthal—he was armed to the teeth and knew he would "be in for trouble . . . with [Ickes] and his gang" for talking about absentee government. The only thing better than one TVA would be several. With typical fervor, he preached to new audiences about the wonder of autonomous river authorities: three of his five speeches focused squarely on the issue, and his remarks in Portland about an independent Columbia River Authority were direct affronts to Ickes's efforts to develop the Columbia River through the Department of the Interior. Lilienthal also worked hard to reinforce the feeling of Governor Culbert Olson and his cabinet that California needed an independent Central Valley Authority rather than one run by Interior's Bureau of Land Reclamation (BLM).[9]

Ickes was furious when he found out about Lilienthal's trip. For one thing, the West was Interior's traditional domain. Federal dams and power projects belonged to Interior, and BLM was the most powerful federal agency west of the Mississippi. Lilienthal had gone too far. He was no longer defending his turf—now he was treading on someone else's. Arthur "Tex" Goldschmidt, an Ickes's aide, came back from a western trip with word that Lilienthal was "spreading the gospel" about three-man independent boards and that George Norris had jumped on the bandwagon. Ickes became even more angry when Olson showed up in Washington praising the TVA model. Olson visited with Ickes, but the governor was smitten by Lilienthal, who arranged a meeting with the president on December 19 and accompanied him to the White House. After Olson asked Roosevelt for help establishing an authority in California, the president told his visitors to work with Congress and Ickes on the idea of two multi-state authorities, Northwest and Southwest. In his usual fuzzy manner Roosevelt left the impression that he was committed to the idea and to Lilienthal taking the lead—Lilienthal gleefully wrote, "I could just see myself writing a TVA bill for the Columbia; boy, how Harold will go after me!" As before, however, Lilienthal, read more into the president's cryptic nods than he should have.[10]

The next day the TVA director presented presidential aide General Edwin M. "Pa" Watson with a draft memorandum for the president authorizing Lilienthal to take charge of the project. The draft was vintage Lilienthal: with no mention of Olson, Ickes, or any congressmen, it had Roosevelt giving him sole authority—"I should like to have you proceed with the preparation of draft of legislation providing for regional authorities. . . . You will also prepare a summary report to me respecting these proposals." Ickes immediately protested Lilienthal's presumptuousness to the president. A few days later, on December 28, Roosevelt reined in Lilienthal with a note that new "regional authorities should be sponsored by the Interior Department and not by any locality or by the TVA." He bluntly told him to patch things up with Ickes. Lilienthal reacted angrily, suggesting in his journal that Ickes had written that memo and pledging he would continue hitting "the 'absentee government' issue as hard as I can." The old boxer acknowledged that Ickes had "won the first round . . . . But he'd better keep his jaw well covered, for it's glass." Dutifully, Lilienthal went to see Ickes on January 21, 1941. This time, he remembered, things were "relatively mild and peaceful." They both made denials: Lilienthal, that he ever intended to sponsor authority legislation, and Ickes, that he ever "want[ed] TVA in the Interior Department." Ickes further revealed that the president had thought up "this TVA order as a sop to me for not getting the Forest Service." Neither believed the other a bit. Ickes noted that Lilienthal was "a coward," that he would "continue to make matters difficult for me" by hiding behind others such as Norris. Lilienthal wrote, "I did not move a muscle of my face" when Ickes denied his TVA designs. [11]

The issue, still, was far from settled. In May 1941, another round started, this one lasting until another uneasy peace in late July. In April, Ickes named Abe Fortas as Interior power coordinator in anticipation of bringing all federal power programs into the department. A few weeks later Roosevelt, not ready to make an overall energy coordination decision, appointed Ickes as national petroleum coordinator. At the same time, Lilienthal worked feverishly, building a coalition against the secretary's centralization plan and efforts to bring the Columbia River project into Interior. George Norris continued to be on Lilienthal's side, and the circle of allies expanded to include Federal Power Commission (FPC) head Leland Olds; former TVA power director Julius Krug, by then power coordinator for the Office of Production Management (OPM); John Lord O'Brian, OPM Chief Counsel; and Senator Homer Bone of Washington. Lilienthal also courted Assistant Secretary of State Adolf Berle and Bernard Baruch, the old war impresario to whom Ickes had also turned for support.

Incensed by Lilienthal and Olds's success at having Krug appointed to OPM in May and Lilienthal's meddling in the Columbia River matter, Ickes concentrated on Roosevelt and, by mid-July, had almost persuaded the president to appoint him national power coordinator. When they heard that a decision might be imminent, Lilienthal and Gordon Clapp, the new general manager, flew to Washington and were told "we were on [our] one-yard line." After meetings on July 18, with Norris, O'Brian, Harold Smith, and others, Lilienthal felt better, thinking that his efforts had moved them "almost to the mid-field." By the middle of the next week Lilienthal sensed that his team was now on "the other fellow's" ten-yard line. Norris, still the key to TVA's status, rebuffed Fortas and Goldschmidt and argued forcefully against Ickes's plan to Roosevelt. Lilienthal found out that important labor and business groups were lining up against Ickes. And, the secretary was becoming his own worst enemy. He first lost credibility by publicly levying charges against the FPC and the much-respected Krug. His second mistake was a horrendous meeting with Roosevelt on July 25, at which he remembered "plung[ing] in boldly, disregarding entirely what the President was trying to say to me." He attacked Krug, whom Norris had just commended to Roosevelt, and went after Leland Olds, one of Roosevelt's oldest friends. Ickes then threatened to resign if Krug continued and an overall power coordinator was not appointed. It was not a strategy likely to persuade—and it did not.[12]

By mid-August 1941, Lilienthal rejoiced that "the Ickes bushwhacking seems pretty well turned back." Even Ickes acknowledged in a bitter letter to Cohen that Roosevelt would never put him in charge of all power projects. Once more, Lilienthal and his allies had thwarted him. Moreover, Ickes's lapses of judgment as petroleum coordinator and his temper convinced the president that expanding the secretary's powers would be unwise. And so, except for occasional skirmishes, the great confrontation was over. In January 1943 Ickes complained to Roosevelt that Lilienthal had meddled with the War Production Board to curtail Interior's power projects. In late 1944 Lilienthal started up again with provocative speeches and articles championing TVA-like river authorities. In words bound to raise Ickes's ire, he contrasted the TVA with other "federal agencies concerned with natural resources" where everyone in the field "must report back to some bureau or department in Washington . . . . where the men live who make all the decisions of any consequence." Before leaving for Yalta in January 1945, Roosevelt asked his aide Jonathan Daniels to "try to keep Lilienthal from getting Ickes mad."[13]

Tex Goldschmidt recognized the irony of the spirited contest between Ickes and Lilienthal when he observed that "nobody won the battle." Lilienthal kept TVA intact but failed to inspire other river authorities. Ickes got control over Northwest power, including the great Bonneville project on the Columbia, but not TVA. While Norris could protect TVA, he was reluctant to back Lilienthal on the Columbia River for fear Ickes would not authorize much-needed Nebraska water projects. Also, the war gave both men much more serious things to worry about. As frustrating as the outcome may have been, the encounter spurred Lilienthal to a fuller articulation of the "TVA idea" he had already been thinking about. He admitted at the end of 1939 that Ickes's threat "was responsible for one of the best pieces of thinking and writing I have done on this job, the Grass Roots speech before the Southern Political Science Association on November 10."[14]

Serendipitous Response

Aside from self-prodding and the Ickes threat, others had encouraged Lilienthal to expand TVA's image. In November 1939, Roosevelt urged him to concentrate more on TVA's nonpower programs. A few days later Morris Cooke wrote that Lilienthal should counter the threat of a "drifting policy" at TVA with a more definitive vision. On November 12, Lilienthal gave his bold "Grass Roots" speech—it was just what he, Roosevelt, and Cooke, were looking for. The Knoxville speech was carefully planned for a sympathetic audience of TVA employees and social scientists. To ensure coverage, he sent 130 copies around the country. He was elated by the response. In spite of the length (his longest speech ever), he marveled that the audience was "close" and "fascinated, . . . interested from start to finish." In the next months his assessment was confirmed by a steady stream of praise from the likes of Berle; essayists Stuart Chase, Max Ascoli, and Max Lerner; and scholars Leonard White and Charles A. Beard.[15]

The speech was provocative and very different from past efforts. He had talked about participation, decentralization, and regionalism before, but always as a component of specific issues like electricity or economic development. This address brought all the concepts together under the umbrella of "grass roots" governance. As a committed statist, Lilienthal argued that big government was inevitable and desirable. As a cautious Brandeisian, however, he warned of the danger of ruling from a distant center. Using Tocqueville's distinction between centralized authority and centralized government, he suggested that the key was maintaining centralized authority and locally decentralizing administration. This was the essence of the TVA experiment, a national agency with power to act locally—"decentralized administration of federal functions." Grass roots administration involved decision making in the field, popular participation, and coordinating with state and local governments. Grass roots administration led to greater sensitivity to local needs and allowed quicker adjustments. The speech made little effort to wrestle with the conflict between bureaucracy and democracy. Lilienthal's discussion of democracy was hortatory—the most he allowed was that decentralized administration strengthened democracy. He was careful for the most part not to let his rhetoric say more than he meant. It was clear when he talked of "the active participation of the people," that *people* meant local and state governments and other valley institutions. His most egregious lapse was the claim that "ownership and the ultimate control of the local electricity distributions systems are vested in the people themselves." He knew better that these systems, while locally constituted, were controlled by TVA in the most crucial aspects of financing and rate making.[16]

Lilienthal soon realized that "grass roots" had been "a great success in directing attention to other matters" and gave him a chance to move beyond the same old issues he had been hammering at for years. Along with national defense, it became a regular topic in his speeches and in board discussions about program results: in 1940, five of his fifteen lectures broached the grass roots theme. It was also a topic of discussion in his voluminous correspondence with everyone from Eleanor Roosevelt to Frankfurter and Eric Fromm. In 1943 he and Fromm exchanged letters on the need for active participation in political and social life. Fromm concluded that Lilienthal's grass roots model was similar to his own thoughts in *Escape from Freedom,* "that the only solution for democracy in a highly industrialized society is the active participation of the average citizen."[17]

The November speech was hardly the end of his search for a "TVA Idea." In 1941 he wrote a devastating critique of James Burnham's controversial thesis in *The Managerial Revolution* that effective rule of private and state institutions such as TVA had passed from stockholders and elected officials to the managerial class that ran them. Not so, said Lilienthal—he called the book "superficial, pontifical, and as full of unsupported assumptions as a country dog is full of burrs." The threat of managerial dominance was real, but not inevitable, because "the American people do have a choice . . . between an exploiting managerial class and managers bound by the principles of public service and democratic methods." Countervailing forces such as "decentralized administration of centralized authority" and "independent unionism." were sure antidotes to managerial excess. In what Marquis Childs called an attack on Corcoran (he often fought more than one battle at a time), Lilienthal talked in the review about instances of "a kind of Phi Beta Kappa Tammany Hall," where former public officials use their contacts for private gain. Nevertheless, he concluded, in American public life there remains a strong commitment to the "principle that public office is a public trust."[18]

There were other stimuli in the early 1940s that led Lilienthal to think through the TVA way—Harold Ickes was hardly the only predator on the Potomac. In 1940 Norris successfully beat back an effort to put TVA under Civil Service. A year later, in June 1941, Lilienthal thwarted efforts by the General Accounting Office (GAO) to impose fiscal controls on TVA. Months later GAO tried, again unsuccessfully, to impose centralized travel rules on the authority. To Lilienthal, such rules constituted a double contradiction of the TVA way. Decentralization of authority within TVA was just as important as TVA's remaining a decentralized agency. If travel was necessary, he reasoned, the supervisor closest to the job was best qualified to approve it. Centralizing such decisions was inefficient and went against TVA's principle of trusting those who did the job.

Battles with Congress gave more grief, but they added grist to Lilienthal's thinking. In April 1942, he groaned that "the job of maintaining TVA's distinctive characteristics as a regional agency is a never-ending one." Legislation had just passed the Senate which made all federal agencies liable for torts and gave claim settlement authority to the U.S. attorney general. Lilienthal favored tort liability—TVA had been subject to citizen suits since 1933. However, the new bill took away TVA's right to manage its own claims. Here was yet "another instance of remote centralized government taking the place of regional decentralized government" and the loss of responsiveness and common understanding. After a visit to the attorney general's office, Lilienthal once more wangled an exception for TVA.[19]

The most pernicious effort to limit TVA was led by Senator Kenneth McKellar, who had been rebuffed in 1941 in an effort to stop the construction of Douglas Dam in east Tennessee. In 1942 the embittered Tennessee senator tried unsuccessfully to repeal TVA's authority to use its power revenues without congressional approval. A year later he failed in an effort to require TVA employees to stand for Senate confirmation. Although the battles with McKellar were bloody, for Lilienthal, they provided "a readymade and almost perfect vehicle for preaching the gospel of no politics in an important governmental enterprise."[20]

Lilienthal searched for the best way to spread the word. In August 1941 he wrote that TVA must move from public relations to public education. To him, the former was little more than "propaganda and information." It was often defensive and rarely had lasting impact. Education, on the other hand, meant not merely telling the "what," but also the "how," and instilling a sense of purpose in the people. At that moment, he rejected abstract "shotgun" approaches, topics such as "TVA and Democracy," in favor of communications directed to specific groups such as farmers, labor, and management. Almost a year later he pondered Woodrow Wilson's 1886 essay, "The Study of Administration." Lilienthal was struck by Wilson's observation that to achieve change, public officials "must first make public opinion willing to listen and then see to it that it listens to the right things." Through its programs and administrative method, he thought TVA had the "power to change the opinions of men about many fundamentals." Months later, thinking of the 42,000 TVA employees, he mulled over "indoctrinat[ing] a very large number of Valley citizens in the underlying purpose and function of the TVA." It was, he admitted a "devilishly intangible and subtle" task. Rejecting war and patriotism as primary motivating devices, Lilienthal chose to emphasize TVA's public mission and the effectiveness of offering jobs where employees worked "not simply to line the pockets of a boss." Even more important, perhaps, was the appeal to TVA's method of "working in harmony with nature" in "the development of resources for the good of a people of a region."[21]

A final factor that helped shape Lilienthal's thinking was a growing global concern. He had never been overly concerned with world affairs. However, in 1942 he concluded that unless his country "participate[d] in the problems of the world" after the war, there could shortly be yet another "devastating war." TVA had also become a mecca for hundreds of foreigners anxious to see if the authority could provide an example for their countries. By the early 1940s, Lilienthal had hosted delegations from Western Europe, Mexico, China, the Soviet Union, North Africa, and the Middle East. In November 1942 he talked to Jonathan Daniels at the White House, "very much steamed up," recalled Daniels, about making TVA "a model for the occupation and development of countries after this war." After a spirited discussion, Lilienthal asked what Daniels thought about his resigning from TVA and working with Herbert Lehman's Office of Foreign Relief and Rehabilitation. The presidential advisor told him he was skeptical about such an arrangement because he did "not think two Jews could be named" to feed Europe. Encouraged by the conversation, if not Daniel's words about a new job, Lilienthal became more enthusiastic about TVA's international

appeal. He spoke at length with Vice-President Wallace, and wrote
Roosevelt about TVA's role "in the rebuilding of a battered world." He
repeated the idea in January 1943 to Lyman Bryson at CBS, and to old TVA
friend and editor of *This Week* magazine Bill Nichols, sending the latter
extensive "excerpts from recent writings, etc., on the TVA idea in postwar
development."[22]

The Finished Product

Lilienthal first mentioned writing a book on TVA in May 1941 to Morris
Ernst. Ernst was supportive but doubted that Lilienthal had the time, and
suggested that Stuart Chase do the book instead. The book was still on his
mind late in the year, but McKellar's increasing attacks and the war buildup
were making that prospect less and less likely. Finally, in November 1942,
he and Harper & Row editor Ordway Tead sealed a deal. A month later, he
cleared his first paragraphs with Tead and prayerfully hoped that "McKellar
[would] just be reasonably quiet for the next six months." From January to
April he and Bill Nichols worked on basic themes. When he sent his first
draft to Nichols in January he wrote that it was "much less 'technical' and
'professional' than" Harper had wanted. Nichols responded that the draft
was still too narrow and technical and suggested that Lilienthal expand on
the TVA vision and its relevance as a model for the future. Nichols also told
Lilienthal to spend more time discussing values and morality. Lilienthal
was discouraged and defensive in response. By the end of March, however,
after another "McKellar rumpus," he took Nichols's advice, "trying now a
completely new way of stating what I want to communicate." After more
advice from Nichols, another bout of self-doubt, and a rewarding appropriations victory over McKellar in late May, Lilienthal was ready to "slav[e]
away at the book." That summer he experienced "about the hardest work
I've ever been through." Harper offered an extension until December 1943,
but Lilienthal declined. Gordon Clapp and Marguerite Owen spent endless
hours critiquing drafts, and finally, on October 9, it was off to the publisher
with a sigh of relief: "No matter what good may come of it or how it is
received, it was worth more than the cost, to me." He was elated when
Ordway, a tough editor, told him shortly thereafter that his manuscript was
acceptable "without qualification."[23]

Five months later *TVA: Democracy on the March* hit the bookstores,
and Lilienthal pressed hard to ensure maximum impact. He hired a pro-
moter and sent three hundred advance copies to everyone from old Tennessee banker ally Barrett Shelton in Alabama, to Frankfurter and Roosevelt.
Lilienthal enlisted an impressive cast of endorsees, including Vice-President
Wallace; G. Bromley Oxnam, American Methodism's most prominent
bishop; distinguished historian Charles A. Beard; and writers Stuart Chase
and Louis Bromfield. The hardback edition did well. While not making the
best-seller list, by January 1945 it had gone through seven editions, six

American and one British, and domestic sales totaled more than 12,000. By the end of 1945, the book had been translated into Hebrew, Chinese, German, Norse, and French. Lilienthal was elated, writing in June that "TVA's prestige and my own standing are the highest " since 1933. Nevertheless, the intense director was still not satisfied. Later that month, he asked an ailing Norris to help raise money to underwrite a paperback edition. After Norris agreed, Lilienthal was relentless, sending the old senator list after list of people to write for support including the editors of *The New Republic* and *The Nation*, Reinhold Niebuhr, Morris Cooke, farm-labor leader James G. Patton, and his old Valparaiso mentor, industrialist James H. McGill.[24]

After months of waiting, on December 6, Lilienthal signed with Pocket Books for a first printing of 150,000. He was doubly thrilled that day when he heard the National Education Association had called *Democracy on the March* "the most notable book of the year." Now, riding an even loftier crest, Lilienthal thought he could swing the ultimate deal, a personal foreword by Roosevelt. In spite of a concern earlier that year that the president had lost interest in TVA, he was confident about the endorsement. After all, Roosevelt praised the book in a September note—and Lilienthal had responded glowingly, "Your letter about the book . . . has set me up so that I hardly condescend to speak to ordinary mortals." In late December Lilienthal enlisted Daniel's help and wrote Roosevelt aide William Hassett requesting a presidential foreword or personal letter of endorsement. Not wanting to leave anything to chance, the brash chairman included drafts of both. Stephen Early told Lilienthal on December 28 that Roosevelt was pledged "never to write a foreword or endorse any single publication," and that Lilienthal could not even use the president's September letter. In typical fashion, Lilienthal tried to get others to change the president's mind. In January, Patton and Marshall Field, both strong Roosevelt supporters and erstwhile sponsors of the paperback edition, urged Roosevelt to reconsider. Once more Early declined, pointedly telling Patton that "the President's position . . . has not changed since" the letter to Lilienthal in late December. The next month the Pocket Book edition was released—without presidential remarks.[25]

With its dramatic litanies, evocative phrases, and lean prose, *Democracy on the March* is a superb example of American political rhetoric. This judgment is all the more remarkable considering it is so extensive—many times the length of the very best efforts by the likes of Patrick Henry, Abraham Lincoln, Woodrow Wilson, and Franklin Roosevelt. It accurately reflects the crisis themes, depression and war, which America had been struggling with for half a generation. *Democracy on the March,* like the mood then, is optimistic and heroic. The depression was years past, and the war tide was turning. It was time to think of a new world: as Lilienthal affirms in the first sentence, "This is a book about tomorrow." It was very much in the tradition of other ringing expressions of the time, including Pare Lorentz's documentaries of the depression, *The Plow That Broke the*

Plains and *The River;* Virgil Thomson's musical suites for those films; and Wendell Willkie's *One World.*[26]

There is no end to dramatic flourish in the twenty lean chapters. It is not too far-fetched to suggest parallels with the two-thousand-year-old songs attributed to another David. From the first sentence to the last— "They know it can be done, not only for the people but by the people"— there is a directness of expression that pulls the reader to the center. Lilienthal evokes a universal theme when he says, "I write of the Tennessee Valley, but all this could have happened in almost any of a thousand other valleys where rivers run from the hills to the seas." He encourages faith in technology in the credo "There is almost nothing, however fantastic, that (given competent organization) a team of engineers, scientists and administrators cannot do today." Later he seals his commitment to administration without politics, recasting Frank Goodnow's aphorism "There is no Republican way to build a road" into "A river has no politics." And, in a telling statement linking unified development and internationalism, the author affirms with a forceful and poetic combination of ordinary words, "in any perspective of time, unified resource development anywhere helps everyone everywhere."[27]

The chapter titles are carefully crafted. "A Seamless Web: The Unity of Land and Water and Men" recalls H. A. Morgan's "common mooring" philosophy. The last chapter is also suggestive—"It Can Be Done: Dreamers with Shovels." In the first phrase one hears the cry of a weary but optimistic people on the brink of a promising future. "Dreamers with Shovels" evokes an image of linking technology and democratic methods in pursuit of peace, prosperity, and a bountiful future. Finally, there is Lilienthal's masterful use of repetitive litanies. The first chapter opens with a simple statement: "This book is being written in the valley of a great American river, The Tennessee." This statement is followed by two paragraphs of sentences starting with "It is." The first talks of the setting—"It is about that river, and that valley. . . . It is about the rain. . . . This book is about . . . the men who work the land, . . . the women who tend the spindles or stir the kettles or teach the children." The second tells of the accomplishment: "This is the story of a great change. . . . It is an account of what has happened in this valley since 1933. . . . It is a tale of a wandering and inconstant river now become a chain of broad and lovely lakes."[28]

Democracy on the March is a dramatic synthesis of Lilienthal's TVA years—all the major themes and actors are present. The preface is generous to Norris "as one of the great men of America's history," and to Roosevelt "for his unfailing support of TVA's basic principles." H. A. Morgan is singled out as "the noblest and most comprehending man I have ever known, . . . a great teacher of fundamentals—for a whole valley." Lilienthal was as gracious to Clapp and Owen for their help on the book; the former for "ideas, . . . and . . . seminal intelligence," the latter for "rare critical judgment . . . and many productive suggestions." Although never mentioned by name, Ickes and McKellar are there in the book's fierce advocacy of decentralized administration and nonpolitical technical and professional decision making. The most notable omission, as one reviewer noted, is any mention of Arthur E. Morgan. Yet, while Lilienthal would be loathe to concede, even A. E. Morgan is represented. While Lilienthal was always the realist, *Democracy on the March* is, in Erwin Hargrove's words, "an idealized picture of harmonious material progress," not far in spirit from Morgan's "Bellamy-like" utopian images. One of the few critical reviews of the book called it a "Utopian picture of perfect co-operation" which might have been more thought-provoking "if viewed through less rosy glasses." There is no doubt that while he was scathingly critical of Morgan's notions of "social uplift, " Lilienthal clearly intended for *Democracy on the March* to "uplift" the morale and people of the Tennessee Valley. Finally, Morgan's unpolitic inclination to impose TVA's will from above provided the foil for Lilienthal to work out his "grass roots" doctrine—an agency pledged to cooperative rather than coercive relationships with the people and institutions of the Tennessee Valley. Even Wendell Willkie, mentioned only once, seemed to have a presence. Lilienthal followed his former antagonist's ups and downs after 1939 with mixed emotions and was aware of his great success with *One World*. Published in 1943, the book was a hit for two years and was hailed as a prophetic liberal statement. It is likely that Lilienthal also wanted to show the world that he could craft just as grand a manifesto.[29]

All the themes are here. TVA is characterized as an institution obligated to harmonize "the private interest . . . . with the dominant public interest." Lilienthal's faith in electricity is seen in the claim that "the quantity of electrical energy . . . is the best single measure of [the peoples'] productiveness . . . [and] potentialities for the future." He defends the yardstick "in its correct sense" as a demonstration of the principle of high consumption and low rates. Key elements of the 1939 "grass roots" speech are presented in greater detail—decentralized administration as an antidote to James Burnham's managerial elite, popular participation as a means of preserving democratic values, and decentralized decision making to ensure maximum flexibility and sensitivity to local conditions. *Democracy on the March* offers an expanded vision of the unity theme. Drawing from H. A. Morgan, Lilienthal writes about TVA as the first modern example of a public institution dedicated to integrating all of a region's resources. Such a task demands not only new organizational design but cooperation among people of many skills.[30]

Two other themes that Lilienthal had thought about privately but had given little public expression were introduced. Like Willkie's *One World*, *Democracy on the March* is a passionate defense of internationalism. In his evocation of images of faraway rivers such as the Yangtze, Ganges, Ob, Paraná, Amazon, and Nile, he sets forth a vision of TVA as a model for a world anxious for "democratic methods of consent and participation." Throughout the book, especially in the penultimate chapter, "TVA and World Reconstruction," Lilienthal argues forcefully, not merely against slipping back into isolationism but for transferring the "TVA Idea" to a wanting world. A final issue was concern for the influence of science and technology on public affairs. Like everyone else, Lilienthal was in awe of the magnificent engineering feats in the Tennessee Valley and concluded that those works were good. Of the more ominous doings at Oak Ridge, he knew little other than its insatiable demand for power. Nevertheless, he sensed enough to warn in *Democracy on the March* that humanity had a "choice: to use science either for evil or for good." A realist, he cautioned that "there is no technology of goodness. Men must make themselves spiritually free." An incurable optimist, though, he concluded that "men are not powerless; they have it in their hands to use the machine to augment the dignity of human existence." Little did he know that he would soon be a key participant in the most crucial debate of the century—stewardship of atomic science and technology.[31]

The Critics Respond

Democracy on the March was greeted with praise in journals as diverse as the *New York Times,* the *Christian Century,* the *American Sociological Review,* and the *New Republic.* Almost every reviewer, academic or popular, was taken by Lilienthal's optimistic and persuasive rhetoric. The usually staid *American Political Science Review* called it "a tract for the times, a ringing declaration of faith, . . . [and] the answer to pessimistic prophecies of the managerial revolution." The most critical review, in the *Engineering News-Record,* lamented that Arthur Morgan was not given his proper due and warned that an organization like TVA in the wrong hands "could have produced the post powerful and autocratic bureaucracy the nation has ever seen." Nevertheless, the same reviewer acknowledged that, "even after making a liberal allowance for the author's enthusiasm," the story was "an impressive one." Even *The Commonweal,* which wanted to be tough, relented. The review began with the observation that "few things can be more boring than a man with a pet idea. And it can be deadly when the idea is along panacea lines." It ended, however, with the reviewer acknowledging that the author "is a man of vision" who "comes through with the principal facts."

Virtually every reviewer focused on the "grass roots" method and its implications for democratic governance. Some, like Richard Rovere, praised Lilienthal's insights on harnessing technology for the common good. Rovere and the *Sociology and Social Research* reviewer were taken by the level of exposition. Rovere said the book did "credit to the literature of its day," and congratulated Lilienthal for catching "much of the poetry as well as the social import of the work in which he has played so large a part." The second reviewer noted that "the opening pages read like poetry in prose and are filled with drama." It did not hurt that two reviews, in the *New Republic* and the *Saturday Review of Literature,* were by friends, Jonathan

Daniels and Vice-President Wallace. It must have given Lilienthal satisfaction when Daniels, comparing *Democracy on the March* to *One World,* concluded, "Lilienthal . . . has written the tougher, better informed, more essential book about the world and its democratic possibilities." While Lilienthal did what he could to maximize the number of friendly reviews, there is little doubt that *Democracy on the March* was received well because it offered a creed with which a large portion of the press and academy felt comfortable. Moreover, Lilienthal was popular and credible, and he could write.[32]

Serious criticisms did not surface until the late 1940s. They focused less on the book than on the manner in which Lilienthal had misrepresented TVA's method of operation in the Tennessee Valley. Nashville Fugitive and Southern Agrarian Donald Davidson, who fired the first shot in 1948, barely mentioned *Democracy on the March*. Philip Selznick's 1949 classic *TVA and the Grass Roots* cited it twice, and Rexford Tugwell and Edward Banfield's extensive review of Selznick recalled the title only in parody, speaking of TVA as "democracy in retreat." Yet, each was a telling critique of Lilienthal's rhetorical web. From political, sociological, and organizational perspectives, all four concluded he had crafted an appealing, yet misleading "official doctrine" that protected TVA from criticism over the way it operated. Ironically, none of these critics argued at all from an anti-socialist perspective. Tugwell, Banfield, and Selznick were academic liberals, and Davidson, an English professor at Vanderbilt University, was part of a scholarly movement suspicious of any modernist intrusions into the agrarian South. Indeed, many of his fellow Southern Agrarians supported TVA.[33]

While Selznick was troubled over organizational aspects, and Tugwell and Banfield concerned themselves with political implications of grass roots philosophy, none of them questioned the fundamental transformation that Lilienthal celebrated. Davidson, however, did. His brief, sardonic review of Lilienthal's book reflected a deep concern about how TVA was running roughshod over traditional values and Tennessee Valley social structures: "Reading it, you were bound to feel that everything was hunky-dory in the Tennessee Valley. Tramp, tramp, tramp the boys were marching, though not to the old tune or in the same uniforms. All over the country people said what a wonderful thing it was that Mr. Lilienthal was doing for those poor fellows in Tennessee and Alabama." For Davidson, no amount of rhetoric about participation or decentralization could hide the fact that TVA was an alien influence, bent on turning his beloved pastoral society topsy-turvy. In less than a generation, TVA had rent the region's social fabric, weakened individual and community initiative, and displaced more than 70,000 citizens from 467,000 prime farmland acres. Worse, TVA was an occupying force—few key employees were sons of the Tennessee Valley. As Edward Shapiro and William Havard noted, Davidson's critique was a resounding repudiation of Lilienthal's vision of a new society. "Warmly humanistic in bias," perhaps, but, according to Davidson, TVA was infinitely more paternalistic than participative. *Democracy on the March* was a celebration of change and of technical and material progress, a set of values very different from those of Davidson, who championed an agrarian society and an enduring and constant social fabric.[34]

Selznick's criticisms arose from his study of the agriculture program. While supportive of TVA programs in general, he found that the grass roots method was less an empirical reality than a "protective ideology" to legitimate and justify TVA to regional and national interests. Selznick was not overly critical of the precise meaning of popular or democratic participation. For the most part, he assumed that Lilienthal meant balanced power-sharing relationships between TVA and an extensive array of local and regional institutions. He was troubled, however, by the lack of well-defined channels by which local interests could actually influence TVA, and also by the variable meaning of the policy "working through established agencies"—some agencies had balanced, even overly influential relationships with TVA while others were almost totally subservient. Selznick was also disturbed by the unexamined assumption that decentralized administration automatically led to meaningful participation and better decisions.

He argued that the claim of widespread grass roots participation in the agriculture program was a fiction. In the main, grass roots relationships were limited to interests that strengthened the authority. For example, TVA threw its lot in early with the white Land Grant Colleges, Agricultural Extension Service, and American Farm Bureau Federation, and at the same time, refused to work with Negro Colleges, Farm Security Administration (FSA), and Soil Conservation Service (SCS). Such a policy had two consequences. First, the chosen few were "coopted," becoming significantly involved in the TVA policy process. Second, limiting access to a few institutions subverted the notion of meaningful democratic administration, which "rests on the idea of broadening participation." Selznick concluded that the "eminently New Deal" agency found itself in the paradoxical position of joining with organizations representing established agricultural interests in fighting agencies such as FSA and SCS, which championed small holders and tenant farmers.[35]

Tugwell and Banfield agreed with Selznick's analysis, from his assessment of grass roots doctrine to the conclusion that TVA had seriously compromised its autonomy and liberal roots through cooptation. They added that TVA had forsaken its birthright as a instrument of comprehensive development and was nothing more now than "the Tennessee Valley Power Production and Flood Control Corporation." Their most telling criticism was of Lilienthal's claim that decentralized administration enhanced democracy. On the contrary, they concluded, "the way to get democratic administration is to begin by organizing a central government strong enough to eliminate those conditions which make much of our national life grossly undemocratic." The TVA experience proved the point: as a decentralized entity without direct Washington clout, TVA was compelled to team up with established forces and to ignore weaker, but no less deserving, interests. A greater Washington presence might well have encouraged more meaningful participation "through the play of political pressure from a variety of publics upon a government," which TVA had become.[36]

No doubt, much of the criticism rings true. TVA was a threat to Davidson's bucolic vision. The values of *Democracy on the March* are industrial, not agrarian. Jeffersonian virtues of a stable, independent, small-holding agricultural society held little appeal for Lilienthal. For him, progress came through change, quick action, and massive public intervention. Bigness in government was necessary, albeit a bigness tempered by proximity to the place where services were being provided. While Lilienthal worried about things that troubled Davidson, like the relocation of thousands of citizens from reservoir lands and the disappearance of family farms, he had no qualms about doing what was necessary. In 1941, he argued with the director of the populist Highlander Folk School that a massive relocation of people in poor counties might be better than "a continued pouring in of relief money." Later, when reviewing disturbing figures about the shrinking number of family farms in spite of TVA's farm demonstration program, he wondered if "we [ought not] face that unpalatable fact and build our farm policies . . . around the fact?" Lilienthal's pragmatism clashed strongly with Donald Davidson's idealism; so did his vision of a future very different from the past the ardent Southern Agrarian hoped to preserve.[37]

The most telling criticism, however, was of the manner in which Lilienthal had played loose and free with grass roots imagery. It was not so much that he used it to build an organizational doctrine. Selznick agreed that all organizations needed a distinctive self-understanding for stability, security, and to generate internal solidarity and external support. Lilienthal's problem, however, as Richard Lowitt observed, was in the careless use of "vague and ambiguous terms that allowed critics to prove their erudition." The critics were right. Lilienthal's claims that TVA was a thoroughgoing participatory organization and that it "shared power" were exaggerated. In fact, participation was selective, not universal, and the nature of the participative relationship varied widely, from the Farm Bureau with tremendous influence, to the local power boards with very little, to Negro and tenant farmer organizations with none at all.[38]

Why was Lilienthal not more careful and precise? Why did he mar his grand eloquence with generalizations and claims that could be easily discredited? In the first place, he knew the invocation of dramatic concepts such as the "yardstick" or "grass roots" governance worked. People were swayed by heady rhetoric just as they had been thirty years before when he invoked the stirring image of the "mission of the Jew." Second, Lilienthal had a strong aversion to arid intellectual games—the "splitting of invisible hairs," and "argufying over little points of difference." His concepts were self-evident to the "real world," which saw dense argument as "medieval scholasticism." A third reason for a failure of precision may have been that his rhetoric sometimes took on a life of its own, implying more than it ought and even convincing him of its import.[39]

Finally, it is likely that Lilienthal may never have clarified some of the concepts in his own mind. Take the key notion that "the people must participate actively" in Tennessee Valley development. If he mentions "the participation of the people" or some variant once, he mentions it a thousand times. However, in the index of *Democracy on the March,* the entry "participation by the people" has no page references and the reader is directed to the "grass roots administration" entry. Sometimes, the linkage is clear: "the people" is synonymous with local or regional institutions. On the other hand, he evokes "participation" so often, the reader wonders if he has a clear sense of the term. When Lilienthal flatly states that development is possible "if and only if the people of the region did much of the planning, and participated in most of the decisions," the reader must wonder if he is describing a radically participative institution, which, of course, TVA never was. Similar ambiguities frequently crop up in his journal. Once, he justifies the centralization of hydroelectric development as economically and technically necessary, but then describes participation as "having the public through the TVA develop the river in the economic way but directed toward the human end and objectives we have in our mind." What does "public through the TVA" mean? Of whose objectives does he speak—TVA's, Tennessee Valley institutions, or those of ordinary citizens? In late February 1945, more than a year after *Democracy on the March* was released, he referred to an educational conference of farmers at Muscle Shoals as a symbol of "the modern democratic process as I conceive of it: the citizen actually participating in decisions respecting technology." To the ordinary eye, this notion of participation seems more a case of "administrative involvement," the type of "participation" most removed in Selznick's spectrum from "substantive participation, involving an actual role in the determination of policy."[40]

In defense of *Democracy on the March,* however, one must move beyond these criticisms. Other issues are important, including the significance of the book as witness to a sea change in thinking about the role of big government and the fact that some of the negative assessments of TVA as a "democratic" institution may have failed to take political realities into consideration. First, *Democracy on the March* was an important witness to Lilienthal's own ideological transformation from Progressive to liberal statist and his effort to bridge the gap. It was a clear affirmation of the beneficence of state action and centralized authority, so unlike the traditional Progressive suspicion of centralized government. Yet, the book reverberates with the language of both movements. On one hand, there are Progressive words—citizen, democracy, service, participation, immoral, responsibility, and character. On the other, the book is rife with the vocabulary of bureaucracy—results, expertise, practical, technique, technology, methods, skill, and leadership. Thus, even as late as 1944, Lilienthal was still struggling to reconcile his Progressive roots with a new bureaucratic reality.

In spite of its flaws, in reality and in vague and ambiguous expression, grass roots administration was Lilienthal's way of reconciling a commit-

ment to central government authority and bigness with his earlier
Brandeisian leanings. Long a disciple of Brandeis, Lilienthal tried as best he
could with grassroots logic to meld the late justice's passion for decentralization with the corporatist framework of the modern state. Centralized state
authority and decentralized program administration was certainly a plausible way of reconciling the natural antagonism between the two traditions.

One must question the assessment that because grass roots reality is less
noble than Lilienthal's description of it, it is necessary to judge TVA harshly
as "democracy in retreat," or even dictatorial. The argument can be made
that TVA did much better than expected not only in surviving but in maintaining and fostering values compatible with democracy. It is true that
Lilienthal went along with TVA's alignment with powerful agricultural interests: he concurred in the decision to give conservative colleague H. A.
Morgan dominion over the agriculture programs. That, however, may have
been the price he had to pay for the freedom to fight on other fronts. H. A.
Morgan's support gave Lilienthal room to maneuver in his controversial
campaign against the utilities. And, as Wallace Sayre and others noted,
Lilienthal and TVA may have had no other alternative to forging bonds
with elite groups—the directors, after all, were committed to institutional
survival. The consequences of cooptation must also be considered. To be
sure, Selznick correctly concluded that TVA allowed powerful outside interests to influence its direction. However, as Schlesinger and Norman
Wengert note, influence is a two-way street. It is inconceivable to imagine
that TVA, with its dedicated staff and innovative methods of organization
and work, did not have as great an impact on traditional Tennessee Valley
institutions as those institutions had on TVA. As Schlesinger argued, "It may
well be that TVA dragged existing institutions of the Valley further along
than these institutions, through 'grass-roots democracy,' held TVA back."[41]

Then, there is the final judgment, more Tugwell and Banfield's than
Selznick's, that TVA betrayed its early promise by selling its soul as an integrated development agency and becoming little more than a power company. The force of this argument loses some strength in Tugwell's own admission that early on, no one knew precisely what Roosevelt wanted TVA
to be. The words of the Norris-Hill Act were heady and suggested an experiment unlike any before. Nevertheless, when it came time to mold an
organization, the original three directors were left to their own devices.
Others have argued that TVA's direction was stimulated more by political
and legal necessity than noble vision—but what public organization is not
moved by such forces? Lilienthal organized TVA around power because
cheap and abundant electricity caught everyone's imagination. He knew he
had a powerful set of symbols in the heroic symbol of massive dams taming
a fierce river and the brave fight against weakened but still powerful holding companies. Wengert also argued that TVA never lived up to the early
promise of a comprehensive development agency simply because it could
not. Conflicts with other agencies and jurisdictions and the distracting
battles in the first decade, both internal and those with Willkie, Ickes, and

McKellar, made it impossible for TVA to become the kind of organization some thought it should. The wonder is that TVA even came to approximate the admittedly exaggerated model of *Democracy on the March*. It also seems clear that Lilienthal was well aware of the charge that TVA lost its way after A. E. Morgan was fired and that he used *Democracy on the March* as a rebuttal to that argument. In 1960, in reaction to a reviewer's comments about Arthur Schlesinger Jr.'s "latest volume about the age of FDR," Lilienthal wrote that "the notion that TVA after Morgan's defeat became a soulless sort of institution with no impact on the non- physical life of people—I thought I had answered that in *TVA: Democracy on the March*."[42]

Finally, one can defend *Democracy on the March* on the grounds that it is nothing more than what Lilienthal intended, a spirited celebration and defense of TVA and its accomplishments. Lilienthal is honest about his intentions from the beginning, warning the reader that he "will find no tone of Olympian neutrality in this book. . . . The world badly needs conviction; it has had too much of the kind of impartiality that is inevitably irresponsible. In this book there are convictions stated and conclusions pressed." TVA made a significant impact on the Tennessee Valley—period. That was the tale he wanted to spin—in his own way. It is significant also that at the same time Lilienthal was preparing his manuscript, he was pressing Alfred Knopf to publish a photographic essay of TVA which would further the cause even more.[43]

Moreover, Lilienthal meant for his book to boost morale, and to pay tribute to the good citizens of the Tennessee Valley and to *their* part in transforming the region. For years he worried that Tennessee Valley people had labored under the double handicap of an outside image of backwardness and a low sense of self-esteem. In speech after speech he labored to change the oppressive myth, captured so aptly in Mark Twain and C. Dudley Warner's nineteenth-century description of east Tennessee, "[with a] reputation like Nazareth, as far as turning out any good thing was concerned." Lilienthal often expressed outrage in his journal about parochial and mean-spirited generalizations by outsiders about Tennessee Valley people. In July 1944, for example, he was outraged over Helen Gahagan Douglas's remarks at the Democratic convention celebrating "what 'we' had done in making a 'poverty-devastated,' etc., Valley over into a happy place in which to live." Such remarks only perpetuated the myth that TVA had to do it all since the people were fundamentally incapacitated. *Democracy on the March* was a celebration of both TVA and the people's triumph over the forces of nature and a long era of economic deprivation.[44]

A Basis for the Future

Democracy on the March was an important book for its time. It was a metaphor for what had transpired in the last decade: the rejection of narrow privatism for a vastly expanded public realm, the transformation of

Progressive liberalism into liberal statism, and the reality of government moving to center stage as an equal player in the economic life of the nation. The book was important for its vision of the future—a ringing rejection of isolationism after another great war, a warning of the threat science and technology might pose for human freedom, and an optimistic vision for a world tired of conflict and uncertainty. The book also had a personal significance. Lilienthal was often egotistical and driven, sometimes harsh, brutal with his pen and tongue, sycophantic, and always looking for the advantage, the opportunity—some would say the opportunistic edge. Nevertheless, he had been an extraordinary public servant for twelve hard, painful years. *Democracy on the March* was a valedictory of those years and it reflected his virtues—his exceptional ability to communicate, to motivate, to forge an optimistic vision of the future, and a commitment to public life and public service.

More than demonstrating his exceptional talents and insights, *Democracy on the March* was a powerful talisman for Lilienthal the rest of his life. The book solidified his reputation as a liberal spokesman and public administrator who made government work. Other New Dealers had written books, but none had written a more compelling treatise, one that was carried in the backpacks of many young soldiers and marines in the sweltering Pacific campaign. In addition, his perspectives on science and technology provided a sturdy foundation when he plunged into the treacherous waters of atomic politics two years later. His concern that a fatalistic acceptance of scientific outcomes would threaten public debate made him a champion of open discussions about atomic energy policies. On the other hand his optimism and faith in the capacity of ordinary citizens to make good decisions about science strengthened him, first at the Atomic Energy Commission and then as a concerned layperson, to argue forcefully for open debate about the atom.[45]

One can hardly forget *Democracy on the March*'s role as a mechanism for organizational empowerment. For better or worse, Lilienthal's model served as TVA's ideological and factual foundation for almost three decades. Until the early 1970s, when internal mismanagement in the nuclear program, the energy crisis, and an increasingly powerful environmental movement forced TVA on the defensive, the evocation of grass roots democracy, popular participation, and unified resource development was enough to still its strongest critics and to give strength to the faithful that their agency was still something special. *Democracy on the March* was the gospel. Aside from Davidson, Selznick, and Tugwell and Banfield, the academic community was remarkably quiescent about the TVA myth until the mid-1970s. It is remarkable that Lilienthal's book was accepted uncritically as a book of facts for so long. William Chandler, author of a devastating critique of TVA from a cost-benefit perspective, noted that an accurate accounting of TVA's accomplishments was long absent because *Democracy on the March* was so often relied upon as a basic source document.[46]

The intensity of some of the criticism levied against TVA in the past two decades gives witness of the power of Lilienthal's protective ideology. Grass roots rhetoric was always persuasive, perhaps to a fault. When cracks in the facade appeared, critics were overly harsh because their judgments about present failings were measured against a past that never really was. And those who really believed were more angry and disappointed than they might have been had their image of TVA not been so exalted. Perhaps it might have been better for TVA had it not enjoyed the protective aura Lilienthal had crafted in 1944.

There is a final legacy of *Democracy on the March* which extends beyond the author or the organization. It is a legacy of imagination and belief in the human capacity to organize itself in order to perform public tasks. Roscoe Martin aptly summed up TVA when he observed that "at the time of its establishment, the Tennessee Valley Authority was without precedent in the annals of man. . . . Never had there been in the United States or elsewhere, a series of multi-purpose projects designed to control and develop the water (and related resources) of an entire river system." In its time TVA was an environmental pioneer, a model of public service, an organization that tried new, humane ways of organizing work, and a public organization that envisioned the possibility of fuller popular participation and influence. Flawed as it might have been in expression, Lilienthal's imagery was appropriate witness to a venture that had never been tried before, and, more important, one that had succeeded beyond anyone's expectations. To be sure, his smooth and sweeping rhetoric covered a multitude of sins, including bureaucratic excess, technological arbitrariness, and insensitivity to public will. Nevertheless, the same rhetoric sparked controversy and debate about the pull and tug between democratic will and bureaucratic necessity: TVA has been more closely scrutinized, studied, and challenged than perhaps any other American public institution. That is a powerful legacy.[47]

CHAPTER 8

TVA: Wartime Administration and Expansion

I have refrained from much subjective talk about the war. . . .
But . . . it is the dominant note of almost every day of my life.
The war creeps in now into even the remote recesses of living
and thinking. You make no plans without feeling it. And that it
is the central and determining issue in everything connected
with my work goes without saying; that has been true with me
for two years now—longer than for most people.
—David E. Lilienthal, September 11, 1942

Vignettes of War

Lilienthal's wartime sketches provide vivid reminders of the great conflict
that touched the lives and hearts of every American. He was sensitive to the
uncertainties and dislocations of the times because TVA's agenda was vulnerable to the powerful Washington forces committed to shoring up the
nation's wartime capacity. He was also concerned because he did not know
how long the war would last, and he knew that David Jr. would be of draft
age in 1945. When he heard of the first hostilities in September 1939, he
wrote ominously, "What this means to all of us here, God knows. Reaction
and war are almost always synonymous." Ten months later, with his country more than a year from war, he reflected again on the rising tide of intol-
erance and recrimination. His first tale was of meeting a man in Nashville
"known as a violent anti-Roosevelt, anti-New Deal fellow" who belliger-
ently said, "There is no need for more than one party now. . . . Anybody
that talks about not following the President; well, a little hempen rope or
some barbed wire is the right treatment." He was bothered with Helen's
solution to simply do away with the Germans—all 80 million of them, a
conclusion he heard was "going on around the tea tables" in genteel societies all over the nation.[1]

A few months into the war he wondered, "What are people thinking
about this war?" An old Chicago friend, "about 52 or so" called to ask,
"Say, what should I do; . . . go into the service or take an emergency job in
Washington, or what in hell should I do?" Marguerite Owen told Lilienthal

that her brother, a promising young attorney, was "completely at sea" about the future and his own obligation. And Lilienthal himself, in the same journal entry, worried "about whether I ought not to be doing something closer to the fighting." Waiting in a crowded Washington Union Station a few days before Christmas 1942, he was captivated by "soldiers . . . by the hundreds. . . . Some rather bedraggled, . . . Some very jaunty"—Canadian, Venezuelan, British, Free French, "a Polish officer painstakingly writing out a telegram." Then, he noticed a group marked with "P-W." These are the "deserters, prisoners of war," surrounded by armed guards, "on their way to general court-martial. . . . What was the history back of their standing there," he wondered, "with those hideous signs on their backs, on their chests, even . . . on their legs?" Sitting at home in Norris listening to the radio in February 1944, he was jolted back to a recent New York excursion with Nancy where at "Sardi's . . . , a young Marine private came to our table for a while," a shy young man named Stephen Hopkins. His memory of that night darkened when Walter Winchell announced that "word has just come that Steve Hopkins, youngest son of Harry Hopkins, has been killed in action in the South Pacific."[2]

There was also a quiet war going on in Lilienthal's mind. At the same time that he was struggling to develop a more comprehensive vision of TVA, the war forced him to focus almost entirely on power. Between 1940 and 1945, TVA's capacity increased from under a million to more than 2.5 million kilowatt hours, as the aluminum industry and the army plant in Oak Ridge demanded more and more electricity: during the war, over 75 percent of all TVA power was used for defense. He rationalized the conflict between his vision, so forcefully articulated in *TVA: Democracy on the March*, and the reality of TVA's role, predicting that wartime capacity would quickly be absorbed after the war by the peaceful growth and development of the Tennessee Valley.[3]

Lilienthal knew the new challenges were different. No longer was TVA on a precarious edge. The legal battles and power fights were distant memories. TVA was entrenched and accepted, even by old foes. So was he. In March 1940 he spoke to the National Industrial Conference. Fearful of a repeat of the "chilly, hostile treatment" he had felt at an appearance at the Economic Club and Harvard Club of New York in 1935, he was pleased by the "good reception" and concluded that "TVA is now an established concern . . . , no longer an active issue in the same sense as in the previous years." The same year, in October, he reveled in the increasing number of "visits from industrial big shots, who are coming to see that the TVA is here, [and] . . . that perhaps there may be something . . . they can learn." In April 1940, he beamed after a well-received speech to a group of southern newspaper editors, when TVA information director Bill Sturdevant called the talk part of "a campaign for the 'dehorning of Dave.'" Gleefully accepting the publisher's accolades, he mused, "You get some idea of the extent to which the dehorning has been successful." The final mark of legitimacy came in September 1941, when Harcourt Morgan resigned as chairman and Lilienthal took charge of the organization he had dominated since Arthur Morgan's departure. Frankfurter congratulated him, "Such fruition of wise and devoted public service which the chairmanship will doubtless afford is very heartening." TVA had made it—so had Lilienthal. It was time to get ready for war.[4]

Preparations

Lilienthal's activities in 1940–41 gave dramatic testimony to the degree to which the Roosevelt administration had focused on preparing for war. In retrospect, there seemed little doubt that the key question was not *"Will* we go to war?" but *"When?"*

On paper, national preparedness seemed well organized. Immediately after the German invasion of Western Europe in April 1940, President Roosevelt established the National Defense Advisory Commission (NDAC) by authority of the National Defense Act of 1916. Soon after, Congress passed the first peacetime Selective Service Act and Roosevelt exchanged fifty old destroyers with Great Britain for several island naval bases. In March 1941, Congress approved the Lend-Lease Act, and several organizations, including the Office of Production Management (OPM), supplanted the loosely organized NDAC. All the while, scores of business executives were trooping to Washington to form the famous dollar-a-year corps. OPM, under the leadership of General Motors executive William Knudsen and a multitude of high-powered volunteers, was placed in the Executive Office of the President and given the job of organizing a wartime economy.

In spite of these actions, official preparations were haphazard and were characterized by one observer as "backing into the war." The administration said one thing and did another. It talked peace and rearmed, criticized munitions makers and threw money at them, preached defense but prepared for offense. NDAC had little authority to coordinate. Even OPM was plagued by constant conflict between Knudsen and Associate Director Sidney Hillman, a diehard advocate of organized labor. Moreover, OPM had little control over War Department procurement and resources and eventually gave way to the War Production Board (WPB) in January 1942 because it was unable to push the automobile industry into total wartime production. The "organized chaos" could be traced, as usual, to Roosevelt, who let his "war government of high-strung individualists . . . fight it out . . . [and then] somehow managed to settle [the disputes] and go his own way."[5]

In many respects TVA had an advantage over other civilian agencies in preparing for war. It had already forged a national defense mandate, partly from statutory requirements, and partly, as one critic noted, because "TVA methodically aggrandizes and enlarges its roles as [a] national security institution—*far beyond* original statutory intent."[6]

The 1933 act authorized TVA to take custody of the old nitrate works at Muscle Shoals and be prepared to produce munitions chemicals such as ammonia, nitrates, and later, phosphorus. Some officials, including TVA Solicitor James Fly, Arthur E. Morgan, and Lilienthal, tried to move beyond a passive, custodial role. In 1934 Fly told the board that TVA had "such a direct interest in and relationship to the national defense as to justify and require affirmative action to carry out these provisions." Later, Fly and his staff used defense obligations to defend TVA and the power program against the Ashwander and Tennessee Electric Power Company suits. In 1935, A. E. Morgan and Lilienthal justified an accelerated power program in the interest of national defense. Morgan told Congress that "an adequate supply of electric energy comes pretty close to being a matter of national defense." Later, Lilienthal, testifying before the House Military Affairs Committee, recommended a stepped-up power program because of the "troubled state of affairs in Europe." The 1934 and 1936 annual reports also emphasized that TVA's program, including its navigation, flood protection, and power aspects was a vital element of the national defense effort.[7]

By the late 1930s, it was increasingly obvious that defense needs might affect several of TVA's peacetime activities. At a Regional Planning Council meeting in December 1938, Authority officials identified several areas where they might be asked to make a significant contribution. In addition to chemicals and power, the council talked of strategic minerals, navigation, agriculture, and forestry as likely targets. TVA became concerned that defense pressures would force them to convert most of their then phosphorus-based fertilizer program to wartime nitrates and ammonia. As it turned out, the fertilizer program continued through the war, with 42 percent of TVA's phosphate fertilizer being shipped to allies under Lend-Lease. Moreover, TVA produced more than 100,000 tons of ammonia and ammonium nitrate for munitions and supplied 60 percent of the phosphorus for incendiary bombs, tracer bullets, and smoke screens.[8]

The most vexing problem was power. In May 1940, Roosevelt's call for a 50,000-plane air force had serious implications for TVA: the aircraft industry depended on vast quantities of energy for aluminum production, and the largest aluminum plant in the world was in Alcoa, Tennessee, just south of Knoxville. The Aluminum Company of America (Alcoa), still an industrial monopoly, built the plant in 1914, and had drawn most of its power until the mid-1930s from its own hydroelectric facilities on the Little Tennessee River. Although TVA helped satisfy Alcoa's appetite for power after 1935, aluminum production remained unpredictable and seasonal— everything depended on the availability of nonguaranteed power and climatic and stream-flow factors. Roosevelt's call for 50,000 combat aircraft guaranteed that the gap between power needs and production would grow even more. The crisis was compounded by a two-and-a-half-year drought in the Tennessee Valley, from March 1939 to December 1941, which threatened TVA's ability to provide enough power for all of its customers.[9]

Lilienthal wasted no time cozying up to the "Washington warlords." On May 28, 1940, shortly after NDAC was established, Lilienthal met with

Adolf Berle, and then the president's chief defense aide, Harry Hopkins, about TVA's wartime role. After telling Lilienthal that plans were still fluid, Hopkins urged him to quickly work up specific proposals for the president about increasing TVA's power supply. Lilienthal let Hopkins know that he had little faith in Harold Ickes's loosely organized National Power Policy Committee (of which Lilienthal had been a member) and their "interconnection scheme," an attempt to resurrect the old power-pool notion. The only way to get power quickly was through more generators and turbines. He then emphasized TVA's independence, telling Hopkins he "had long since decided that the only way you could survive in the Federal service was to tend to your own knitting and to fight off bitterly anybody who interfered with your getting your work done."[10]

In mid-June, Lilienthal was in Washington again, this time lobbying for the first of TVA's emergency projects. He met first with NDAC's head of industrial materials, Edward Stettinius, former board chairman of United States Steel, and then saw the president. Contingent on Stettinius's approval, Roosevelt authorized Lilienthal to proceed with Cherokee Dam, a steam plant at Watts Bar, and extra generators at existing hydroelectric sites. After meeting with Stettinius and his chief advisor, industrialist Gano Dunn, and becoming a little irritated with the latter's resistance, Lilienthal was amazed to see the projects quickly approved. On June 22, Lilienthal counseled Stettinius, who was upset because a Senate subcommittee on deficiency appropriations had turned down the request for extra TVA power. He told the industrialist that Congress was behind the times, but that the public would soon insist that the president take charge of getting the country ready for war. With typical scorn, he thought of the problems his executives faced with Congress in going "through a long and to them stupid and meaningless process of persuading a bunch of uninformed and often wholly political minded ex-district attorneys and promoted precinct captains."[11]

The fight for this first project exemplified Lilienthal's keen pragmatic instinct. Without hesitation, he closed ranks with the folks who once had vehemently opposed TVA. On July 9, Stettinius and Lilienthal visited Judge Clifton Woodrum, chairman of the House Appropriations Committee, who immediately called his committee into session. Answering only a few questions himself, Lilienthal was delighted to hear Stettinius, Knudsen, and Dunn, whose engineering firm had worked for Commonwealth & Southern against TVA, carrying the banner for public power. The distinguished witnesses forcefully emphasized that they had "found no other place as favorable as TVA for this large block of power increase." A Washington labor paper noted the irony of "the extraordinary . . . conversion of bitter foes of the Tennessee Valley Authority into ardent supporters." After the hearing, and quick approval in both houses, Lilienthal marveled at the "great vindication . . . to have your . . . bitterest enemies carry the ball for you; those are some of the sweets of a hard, long job that I had never expected to taste." A few days later, Hopkins praised him for "showing the country and these industrialists that an agency like the TVA . . . can honestly and effectively work with men with conflicting social objectives, but with coincident objectives as to defense."[12]

By early 1941, however, it was obvious that the first emergency project was not enough. The War Department again asked Alcoa for more aluminum, and Alcoa turned again to an increasingly strapped Authority. Again, TVA, with OPM's support, recommended a second emergency plan for 116,000 kilowatts from four new dams in North Carolina and Georgia. This time, facing a doubling of demand for aluminum along with the continuing drought, the projects were approved with so little controversy that Lilienthal barely mentioned his testimony on behalf of this project.[13]

In addition to meeting the war challenge, Lilienthal turned again to speechmaking. After 1938–39, when he gave only two speeches each year, he scheduled fifteen formal addresses in 1940, sixteen in 1941, and another twenty in 1942. The speeches, more than half outside the Tennessee Valley, trumpeted TVA's commitment to the war effort. While four concentrated on grass roots, ten were patriotic testimonials about the will and capacity of the country and TVA to prevail in the coming crisis. In June 1940, before a national CBS radio audience, Lilienthal pledged that TVA and the Southeast could "transform our peacetime economic institutions so that the needs of defense shall be met quickly and effectively." TVA was a key to regional readiness: it produced munitions in Muscle Shoals and electricity for defense needs. Moreover, TVA engineers and technical staff had investigated and tested new ways for a "more extensive processing of the raw materials resources now available." A unique method of using domestic talc for electrical and ceramic products, treating vermiculite so it could be substituted for cork insulation, and new ways of processing magnesium and asbestos deposits; all were dramatic reminders of TVA's contribution. In conclusion, he reminded his audience that in spite of technical prowess and capacity, "the will, the inner flame, must be there or all the engines of defense will be without avail. . . . This will be our greatest asset of defense: that on the farm, in the mine and factory, in places of business, the people of this country shall feel deep in their hearts that they have . . . a future that is worth every effort to improve and every sacrifice to defend."[14]

On his West Coast tour in December, he devoted two of his four speeches to patriotism and national defense. In Eugene, Oregon, Lilienthal invoked Walt Whitman's theme of "celebrating America" and said it was time to snap out of the "national jitters" plaguing the country: "Jitters," he said, "in the face of danger are not in the American tradition. Whitman would have roared his disapproval." After dismissing charges that "we are torn with disunity, rife with disloyalty, bankrupt, and soft" as "rubbish," Lilienthal asserted that "it is also important to remember how strong we are." After a lengthy paean to TVA for what it had done to help make democracy work and to prepare for war, he continued, saying that America has a "solidarity, a unity of spirit and purpose that we can brag about." Indeed, he said, "we today ought to revive that good old-fashioned custom of bragging about America." He repeated the message over and over. In

1941 he reiterated his message to university convocations in Minnesota, Alabama, and Tennessee; the Knoxville Rotary Club; and another CBS broadcast May on "The TVA and National Defense."[15]

The task of preparedness increasingly pulled Lilienthal away from the office. Of his thirty-five trips in 1941, only seven were in the Tennessee Valley. The other twenty-eight included speeches in Florida, appearances in Minneapolis, Chicago and other midwestern points, Atlanta and Little Rock, and three trips to New York City. He was in Washington twenty-three times, for anywhere from one day to several week-long stays. These prewar years offered a big challenge—much to do and a lot of turf to protect. The most serious crisis arose in mid-1941, when it became clear that the first two emergency projects would still fail to satisfy Alcoa's voracious appetite. Now, Lilienthal faced his greatest challenge, fitting in the last piece of the wartime power puzzle with the most controversial proposals of all, Fontana and Douglas Dams. He faced the prospect of hard bargaining with Alcoa over their Fontana site in the North Carolina mountains. He also had to endure the righteous temper of Kenneth McKellar over TVA's decision to build Douglas Dam forty miles east of Knoxville in the middle of East Tennessee's agricultural heartland.[16]

Alcoa: State Capitalism and Industrial Cooperation

In the 1930s, TVA and Alcoa shared a rocky but symbiotic relationship. In 1935, George Norris denounced the Mellon-owned monopoly for siding with the utilities to keep TVA from building new dams. However, the next year Alcoa gave the authority a big boost by agreeing to rescue TVA from the embarrassing prospect, brought on by injunctions against expanding local services, of a large power surplus. In 1936–37 Alcoa contracted for 100,000 kilowatts of excess TVA power and continued with yearly contracts the rest of the decade.[17]

TVA had long coveted the Fontana site, home of one of the heaviest rainfall areas in America, for its unified river control plan. In 1936, negotiations with Alcoa broke off after Congress failed to appropriate funds for the project. In 1941, Fontana became an issue again. After failing to secure government loans, Alcoa announced in February it would not build at Fontana. By May, it was obvious that more power was necessary than the second emergency project could provide. In spite of the drought, TVA had supplied Alcoa with 150,000 kilowatts of power over contract; however, it was becoming more difficult to do so. Things were so desperate in mid-May that Lilienthal seriously considered Bernard Baruch's idea of using ocean liners, aircraft carriers, and diesel electric locomotives to generate electricity. He was amused by the prospect of "telling [Alcoa] that they are about to buy a string of nice, shiny, streamlined locomotives and parade them into . . . their pot rooms . . . , especially when they realize that the power will cost them about two cents a kilowatt compared to five mills."

He was peeved, though, because the company had "known for 18 months that it must operate its production facilities 100 percent, and yet neither has 100 percent year-round power supply nor pays any attention to our insistence to them and to the Defense Commission people that provision should be made for that kind of power supply."[18]

Pressured by Senator Harry Truman's special committee on military contract abuse and its own inability to meet government demands, Alcoa agreed to reopen Fontana negotiations. Lilienthal and Alcoa Board Chairman Arthur Davis met in Washington on Friday, June 28, and into the next week. At first, Lilienthal worried that the company's public willingness to sell and private stubbornness over terms would allow Alcoa to accuse TVA "of impeding the national defense, of being a dog in the manger, of neither building it ourselves nor permitting them to build it." The crux of Alcoa's proposal was to give TVA the site without charge in exchange for two concessions: First, Alcoa would receive all additional power produced by its two downstream dams as a result of Fontana Dam's presence. Second, all the dams in the system, both TVA's and Alcoa's, would be treated as a unified management system, and extra power generated from the coordinated system would be divided equally At first the TVA team was confused by the proposal, according to Lilienthal, "a very difficult and subtle thing to catch," but the TVA negotiators finally figured out that such terms would allow Alcoa to realize a $15 million windfall profit.[19]

Lilienthal countered with an offer to buy the site for cash and give Alcoa half the benefits accruing to its two projects from Fontana. He accepted a unified operation, but denied Alcoa's claim to extra benefits from the TVA system since those would result from Fontana, not Alcoa's dams. The difference between the two proposals, according to Lilienthal, was "between dividing 60,000 kilowatts and dividing 20,000 kilowatts . . . which [if] capitalized, would require an investment of about $25 million." Lilienthal answered Davis's negative response to his proposal by insisting that TVA "never would accept any proposition that gave him a nickel's worth of benefit from the effect of Fontana on Government dams below." After more give and take, the two parties compromised. TVA retained full control over the total system but allowed Alcoa the extra benefits accruing to its two dams and 11,000 kilowatts of primary power, much less than Alcoa's original demand. The accord was signed in mid-August, appropriations were approved in the fall, and construction began on January 1, 1942. Lilienthal was elated because the agreement put "TVA virtually into partnership with a huge private concern. . . . So far as I know, there is nothing like that anywhere in America." His assessment was seconded by Alcoa's historian, who wrote of the relationship "as a model of the way Government and industry can sometimes work in harmony for the mutual benefit of each." Again, another sign of Lilienthal's developing statist philosophy—a respectable partnership between public and private enterprise.[20]

In spite of his new cooperative spirit, Lilienthal remained wary of monopoly. During a visit with Department of Justice trustbuster Thurman

Arnold, he reflected that the Alcoa relationship was "a beautiful and illuminating example of the power of a monopoly even at a time of national peril and even when pitted against a governmental organization like the TVA which has no fondness for monopolies." However, as a pragmatist, he was critical of useless trust-busting: he opposed old TVA ally Senator Lister Hill in his effort to publicly finance Reynolds Metals in order to establish the first competitive aluminum smelters since the nineteenth century. He feared that effort would do little to stimulate competition or lower prices—and he was right. The price of aluminum remained stable during most of the war, mainly because there was no slack in demand and the companies had only one customer—the military. By the end of 1943, Alcoa still controlled 93 percent of all ingot production. Lilienthal was also critical of other efforts by Truman and Harold Ickes to build government aluminum plants and lease them to private industry. He objected because Alcoa would "operate the plant and the Government take all the risk, with the Aluminum Company in a position to buy the plant back [after the war] . . . at practically nothing." "What," he wondered, was "the mysterious barrier to [the Government] doing the whole job and taking the whole financial responsibility, both the risk and the benefits?"[21]

An Enemy for Life

By the end of 1941, Lilienthal had his hands full with Kenneth McKellar's campaign, first against the Douglas Dam decision and then, against everything Lilienthal and TVA stood for. Up to that time, the two men had maintained a civil relationship. Lilienthal consulted McKellar in 1933 about TVA appointments and rate decisions. In subsequent years, he praised the senator and kept him abreast of TVA matters. McKellar responded with gestures of appreciation and support. After reviewing the September 1933 rate schedule, he praised Lilienthal for "doing a splendid work." In April 1934, McKellar wrote Roosevelt that Lilienthal was "splendidly equipped for the great work he is doing." In 1937, in response to several letters critical of Lilienthal from a Knoxville lawyer friend, McKellar was noncommittal, stressing that he was "not taking the part of anyone. . . . I am simply using every endeavor I can to get the dams built."[22]

Nevertheless, the seeds of conflict with TVA were present early on. McKellar had always disliked Arthur Morgan, especially after Morgan lectured him in 1933 that politics would play no role in TVA appointments. In fall 1933, he publicly announced that he would "be the first to praise Professor Morgan if he will stop making long-winded and perfectly useless speeches and get down to work on his job." In 1935, he wrote George Fort Milton, editor of the *Chattanooga News,* that Morgan was "the most blundersome man in the world . . . [and that] if we get any of these dams started we shall do it in spite of Mr. Morgan instead of by his help." McKellar later complained on the Senate floor that "I do not know of a man I have recommended who has been appointed by the T.V.A.; not one."[23]

There was another, perhaps more compelling reason to anticipate McKellar's ire—his deep resentment that George Norris received most of the credit for TVA. A few years before McKellar's death in 1957, he wrote a bitter memoir in which he recalled that "from 1916 to 1932, if Mr. Norris aided in the remotest kind of way my fights for these dams on the Tennessee River, I never heard of it." He charged that on a 1933 trip to Muscle Shoals with Roosevelt, "Senator Norris virtually took charge of the President." Before he knew it, Norris had taken his Tennessee River bill and introduced it as his own—"I never," he recalled, "was more astonished in my life." His bitterest complaint was that Norris took "credit for the building of these dams on the Tennessee River when he had nothing in the world to do with it except possibly he voted for the dams if he happened to be in the Senate Chamber at the time."[24]

Certainly, these reflections were written long after the events and represent the sad efforts of a man lost in his twilight years. Nevertheless, McKellar's animus grew as he watched TVA thrive under the watchful eye of someone not even from the Tennessee Valley. In early 1942, Lilienthal recalled Arkansas Congressman Clyde Ellison's remark that McKellar was "insanely jealous of the credit Norris has received for the TVA, [and] has taken occasion to show that jealousy through the years." In February 1943, McKellar accused Roosevelt of taking "away from me the credit that was due me for more than a quarter century's work on these dams and for some unaccountable reason [throwing] the credit in the lap of Senator Norris who could not have gotten a dollar for those dams . . . to save his immortal soul." It did not help, either, that Lilienthal and Norris had become close. Once, after hearing Norris's words of praise for Lilienthal, Allen Drury remembered a frustrating McKellar blurting out, "You see? You see? He will not defend himself, but gets othuhs [sic] to dew [sic] it. Smaht [sic] strategies! Smaht [sic] strategies!" By 1941, McKellar may have been recalling his lawyer friend's 1937 warning about Lilienthal—"I know you don't like A. E. Morgan but he is not half as bad as Lilienthal."[25]

The Lilienthal-McKellar feud began in May 1941, when power demands prompted TVA engineers to push for Douglas Dam, a project they had just put on hold the previous month. The French Broad River site had strong hydroelectric potential. It was also less than twenty-five miles from the nearly finished Cherokee project, making it easy, as Norris noted, to quickly transfer "the same crew, the same management, the same organization, and the same material." Nevertheless, TVA had at first tabled Douglas because it would inundate 30,000 acres of rich farmland and incur the wrath of powerful interests such as the Stokely canning company. Throughout the summer, TVA officials studied and deliberated. Lilienthal readied a proposal, although in the summer he was still publicly committed to another plan involving two dams on the Holston River. After reviewing the situation further, OPM insisted that TVA proceed with Douglas because it would provide more power in less time than any other option. Finally, in September, Lilienthal submitted his proposal to Congress—without consulting McKellar.

Reaction in East Tennessee was swift. The pro-TVA University of Tennessee president took, as Lilienthal recorded "a terrific shot at us in a public letter." People around Dandridge, the community closest to the site, also complained, and McKellar joined in opposition. On September 30, Lilienthal wrote the senator a thorough, professional missive, explaining that Douglas would provide more and cheaper power and would be generating a year earlier than the Holston alternative. McKellar fired back a mean response. Blasting the chairman for his "discourteous letter," McKellar insisted that he "was entitled to some consideration" because of his long support for TVA. He accused Lilienthal of going ahead with Douglas without consulting him and promised the proposal would "have the most vigorous opposition from me that I am capable of giving to it." Lilienthal first regretted that he had not gone to the senator "and laid the whole case before him months ago." He tried to patch things up with another letter, thanking McKellar for "always [having] dealt with me in a kindly and generous spirit, minimizing my faults (of which I have many) and always giving me the benefit of the doubt." It did not work.[26]

Despite plea after plea, from Roosevelt, Vice-President Wallace, military brass, and top OPM officials Batt, Knudsen, and Krug, McKellar refused to budge. In solidarity with their powerful colleague, the House and Senate Appropriation Committees also refused to act. Meanwhile, Lilienthal had to endure one after another of McKellar's blistering attacks. By the end of October, he was shaken by "as critical and unpleasant an issue as I have had to face for a number of years." Now, McKellar threatened to cut off all TVA appropriations until Douglas was withdrawn. Throughout December, even after Pearl Harbor, McKellar held firm. On December 11, at his Appropriations Subcommittee hearings, he again unmercifully skewered TVA and OPM officials, prompting Marguerite Owen to write that McKellar's "choler appeared to be inexhaustible, and his diligence in obstruction . . . unremitting." On Christmas day, Lilienthal tried to write himself out of a creeping bitterness, by admitting his anger "at McKellar and the damned canners and their selfishness" and resentment of "the processes of democracy that will permit one man . . . to block the wishes of those responsible for the war." He pledged, however, that he would "not let any one thing, however important, however infuriating and wrong and evil, destroy my perspective."

Finally, in mid-January, after more presidential pressure and press accusations that he was "sabotaging the national defense effort," McKellar relented. With the reality of the war finally sinking in, the House and Senate approved Douglas, and Roosevelt signed the bill on January 30, 1942. Marguerite Owen immediately teletyped Knoxville—DOUGLAS DAM BILL JUST SIGNED. START DIGGING. The dam was finished a little over a year later in record time, just before the spring rains.[27]

Douglas signaled the completion of TVA's comprehensive river plan. It was a splendid accomplishment, and Lilienthal could be proud of his rule. Nevertheless, the cost was high. McKellar was not inclined to forget or forgive—his war with TVA and Lilienthal had just begun. For the next three years Lilienthal had to endure and thwart vicious personal attacks, as well as the infamous "McKellar Amendments" designed to cripple the political inviolability and independence of the agency. Spring 1942 was the worst of times. Still smarting from his humiliating defeat over Douglas, McKellar introduced legislation requiring congressional approval for all TVA operating expenses and a bill transferring TVA condemnation cases from court-appointed commissions to local citizen panels. While both bills failed, McKellar's legislative maneuvering gave him a chance to zero in on his real target—Lilienthal. However, Lilienthal held his own, and his tongue. At a Senate Appropriations Committee meeting in March, Lilienthal recalled that McKellar "completely lost his temper." He was pleased because he had kept his composure, and the rest of the committee (which, in typical fashion, he labeled "the Committee of Destructive Criticism and Opprobrium") treated him respectfully. McKellar's attacks became so strong that in May Norris had to defend Lilienthal on the Senate floor. Calling McKellar's attacks more "in the nature of a stump speech," Norris praised Lilienthal for his patience in the face of McKellar's bullying questioning: "never once did he resent such a method of interrogation." Moreover, he "would put [no other public official] above Mr. Lilienthal for honesty and integrity."[28]

Lilienthal fought back in the Tennessee Valley. In late March he went to McKellar territory—"west Tennessee, where we are weakest in public esteem." He inspected tornado damage, talked to farmers in the Jackson area, and took a planeload of journalists to examine the spectacular Kentucky Dam project at the mouth of the Tennessee River. He also spoke to the Jackson Rotary Club, and was pleased that they approved his criticism of McKellar's "pop pistol politics." In April he headed south to Columbus and Tupelo, Mississippi, to preach "the gospel of no politics in an important governmental enterprise." Finally, in Chattanooga in May, he attacked the senator with a hard-hitting denunciation of "political management." Without mentioning McKellar by name, he repeatedly invoked the ugly possibility of TVA's becoming an agency more influenced by politics than business principles. Half-a-dozen times, he asked his audience if they wanted the alternative—a politics-ridden TVA. At the same time, in towns like Decatur, Alabama, and Columbia, Tennessee, local civic clubs were sponsoring full-page advertisements in local papers with "Save TVA From Politics" themes.[29]

In 1943 and 1944, McKellar repeated his attacks, adding riders to the TVA appropriation which threatened the authority's independence. While causing uneasy moments for Lilienthal with temporary victories in committee and even in the Senate, each year he failed. Nineteen-forty-three proved to be a relatively painless year. The House passed the TVA Appropriations

Bill without a dissenting vote. McKellar was slowed by illness that spring and, Lilienthal surmised, pressure from E. H. "Ed" Crump's Memphis political machine to tone down his attack. Spring 1944 was another matter. After a February exchange in committee, Lilienthal wrote that McKellar was "more violent and virulent than ever." It was so bad that Lilienthal finally looked "him straight in the eye," and said, "Senator, you are an old man, and probably haven't much time to live. You are doing a fellow human being an injustice in your position toward me. You don't want to carry that on your soul when it comes your time to go." McKellar was so distraught, Lilienthal remembered, that he shouted back, "God damn, God damn, I have had enough of this. I am God damn tired of this, and I won't stand for it any longer." The next day, and for days after, it continued. Nevertheless, McKellar failed again. The Crump forces did what they could to back McKellar away from his futile fight. Drury remembered that the Senate, led by Lister Hill, came to see McKellar's opposition for what it really was, "simply a feud against Lilienthal who apparently hasn't yielded to pressure the way he was expected to."[30]

It would be wrong to dismiss McKellar's chances in his fight with Lilienthal. If Lilienthal had been his only foe, he might have prevailed. As Dean of the Senate, he had many weapons— seniority; formidable parliamentary skills; support back home in East Tennessee and the Crump machine in the West, at least until his anti-Lilienthal antics became embarrassing; a junior colleague, Tom Stewart, who detested Lilienthal almost as much as he did; and the traditional bonds of loyalty in the exclusive Senate club. Nevertheless, he was often betrayed by his careless temper. Moreover, there were far more daunting obstacles to his old-style method of combat. For one thing, the public attitude toward big government had changed. As one contemporary observer sympathetic to McKellar noted, "McKellar knows the Tennessee voter will reflect that Crump and McKellar are but transients whereas the Federal government goes on forever." He also had to face a formidable array of executive offices and agencies pledged to do everything possible to win the war. The powerful dollar-a-year men were not about to abandon a valuable comrade-in-arms such as Lilienthal to the winds of political vengeance—even if just a few years earlier that "comrade" had been anathema to their beliefs about the limits of public action.[31]

Mission Accomplished

There is little question that TVA performed superbly in preparing for and carrying out its war mission. In 1941, the Federal Power Commission reported that without TVA power, the nation would have fallen short of meeting key defense needs. OPM also concluded that TVA was better prepared than any other organization, public or private, to mobilize resources quickly and efficiently. Perhaps for that reason, 1942 represented the zenith of TVA's wartime effort. By the year's end all the emergency projects—seven dams, a large steam plant, and eleven additional generating units—were under way. Three dams authorized before the emergency were on schedule, and TVA could report a record 42,000 employees. By mid-1943, however, other decisions mandated a diminution of TVA's warrior role. In October 1942, much to Lilienthal's consternation, the WPB deferred further construction on TVA projects, except Fontana, not slated for completion before 1944. And in July 1943, the War Department told TVA that it no longer needed its ammonium nitrate.[32]

In spite of McKellar's distractions, Lilienthal continued pushing the war effort in 1942. Eight of his twenty speeches focused on patriotism and defense issues. In Asheville in July, he told the North Carolina Press Association they had four wartime functions; reporting, criticizing, clarifying and unifying. He urged the journalists to report "fully, fairly, and impartially without fear or prejudice." After all, he emphasized, "the only way the public can really determine who can be trusted and who are fools . . . is for you to report what they have to say." He stressed that "the right and even the duty to criticize seems to me more important in time of war than at any other time," and that "there is no sacred class in America that should be exempt from public criticism." Admitting that he had often been targeted by the press, he said, "(a) I have had plenty criticism from the press, some of it far from factual; (b) I never enjoyed any part of it; and (c) Much of it was good for me and good for the TVA; None of it did any permanent harm." In October he exhorted several thousand workers at the Douglas site "to rededicate ourselves to the task to which we set our hand only eight months ago," and reminded the throng that they were not just "spectators up in the bleachers watching a war" but just as much a part of the war effort as those in combat.[33]

As in mid-1941, he arranged in 1943 for Robert L. Duffus of the *New York Times* to tour the Tennessee Valley and write about TVA's war role. On March 28, Duffus's article, "Our River of Power Flowing to War" appeared in the Sunday magazine. Duffus's piece was a rousing panegyric. Observing the Tennessee Valley ten years after the founding of TVA, he wrote of "an amazing spectacle" which "takes the breath away." It was a tale of the Cherokee Dam miracle, where the "world's record was broken," and then of Douglas Dam where "it was broken again, . . . finished in twelve months and nineteen days." He reported on the growth in TVA capacity: "On the morning of Pearl harbor, . . . [TVA had] 1,000,000 kilowatts of installed power. This morning it has more than 1,500,000. On New Year's Day, 1944, or earlier, it will have 2,000,000." Its power is everywhere, "flow[ing] into the great aluminum plants, . . . [helping] make delicate instruments at Knoxville, . . . boilers . . . at Chattanooga, . . . and [rushing] with the speed of lightning into the huge Vultee [A-31 bomber] factory at Nashville." The article was anything but tough-minded, but, as Lilienthal calculated, it served TVA—and himself—well.[34]

The other wartime activity Lilienthal was concerned with, and then, to his consternation, shut out of, was the secret military plant in East Tennessee which needed, as he observed with amazement, "twice as much [power] as the city of Memphis." All spring and summer 1942 TVA officials helped the army, WPB, and private contractors look for an isolated site close to water and with access to 150,000 kilowatts of power. Authority officials were not enthusiastic about the project because it threatened yet another power crisis. Lilienthal was perturbed over the WPB order in fall 1942 curtailing TVA projects since "the 'mystery plant' . . . [was going] to require fantastic amounts of power." In addition, TVA was disturbed because no one, not even Lilienthal, was told much about the enterprise other than it would produce some kind of "product for war purposes," At a September TVA board meeting, Lilienthal suggested that given "the shortage of management, the shortage of competent contractors," TVA should take charge of the "mystery plant." A month later, Under Secretary of War Patterson bluntly told him that the project involved requirements far beyond TVA's capacities. In mid-1943, Lilienthal protested the army's decision to build their own steam plant on the site. Nevertheless, after conferring with Patterson, TVA officials quietly backed down.[35]

In 1943, Lilienthal's attention to wartime matters began to wane. Between 1943 and 1945, only one of his twenty-six public addresses touched on defense, and, after 1943, he had much less contact with Washington wartime officialdom. What happened? To an extent, Lilienthal, a man who thrived on confrontation and challenge, found that by the end of 1942, the most important battles, other than his feud with McKellar, had been decided. While the 1942 WPB decision to defer TVA projects rankled, the authority wangled a deal with Congress in 1943 which allowed it to keep the unexpended balance of the 1943 budget for any projects that might be reinstated. Moreover, with his superb general manager, Gordon Clapp, Lilienthal could depend on things running smoothly. There was also the McKellar distraction. In the first half of every year during the appropriations season he was preoccupied with trying to stave off the increasingly vitriolic senator's attacks. In 1944, after a contentious bout with McKellar, Lilienthal recorded that "I am quite weary, of course. This is wearing business." With things more in order than during the first three years of the war push, Lilienthal found time to focus on his book, which demanded more of his time and attention. That he was indeed consumed by this project was evident in a note in his journal—"The fact that I made only two journal entries from May 28 to October 10—a period of some four and one-half months—was chiefly due to my absorption in writing the TVA book."[36]

The pattern of his addresses reflected new directions. No longer as concerned about the war, he turned more to issues central to TVA: Democracy on the March. Two addresses in 1945 dealt with the challenge of science and technology to democracy, and seven in 1944–45 focused on America's future in the postwar era. His 1944 commencement address to the College of the City of New York, "The Grand Job of Our Century" was a moving example of the new agenda. He reflected upon "the greatest paradox of all—that the splendor of a creative age should follow close upon a nightmare of destruction," and exhorted that "beyond the war there opens before us an historic opportunity." America has "the skills and organization and technology." All it needs is the will to avoid petty arguments over "meaningless slogans and catch-phrases, . . . vague abstractions . . . such as 'free enterprise,' 'collectivism,' 'reactionary,' or 'radical.'" Once again reflecting the new statism and its ties to the industrial sector, Lilienthal warned against "neatly segregating 'public' works from 'private' enterprise as if they were not both parts of the same living tissue of community existence, interacting and wholly interdependent." He called upon the graduates to make the right choice between "resting on our laurels, holding fearfully to what we have; or [being] a land that forever renews its youth by magnificent dreams, noble plans, and great deeds."[37]

In late 1944 and early 1945, he reintroduced the river authority concept, another topic of *TVA: Democracy on the March*. In May he flew to St. Louis to monitor a devastating flood and was flattered when the *St. Louis Post-Dispatch* quoted him in calling for a Missouri Valley TVA (MVA). Roosevelt's message to Congress in September recommending consideration of an MVA, along with favorable editorials in *Collier's Magazine* and the *New York Times,* encouraged him more, as did strong congressional opposition in November to Corps of Engineer flood control legislation that would have threatened MVA's chances. In December he gave a radio talk in St. Louis, encouraging serious dialog about an authority in the region, and in January he published an article, "Shall We Have More TVA's?" in the *New York Times Magazine*. Other than these efforts, however, he seemed strangely detached from what, in 1941, had been a burning issue for him.[38]

The last three years of the war provided a transition for Lilienthal. Making time to think, write, and talk about new ideas, he backed off from his frenetic pace. After 1942 he made fewer public appearances and he was no longer as enthusiastic about issues such as "more TVAs" as he had been before. But, just as he was concerned in *TVA: Democracy on the March* with the nation's future, he was also pondering a future that might or might not include a continuing commitment to TVA.

The End of an Era

Lilienthal's change was also occasioned by increasing fatigue and growing frustrations. By late 1942, he was fed up with all the Congressional "diehards and reactionaries," and the fact that "like the elephant, the reactionary never forgets; but even the elephant, with his tiny brain and huge, clumsy body, does learn—which is more than you can say for a reactionary." His friend and mentor George Norris was defeated in November after forty years in Congress. At Roosevelt's suggestion, Lilienthal tried to persuade the old senator to take another national position, but Norris, depressed and weary himself, seemed only interested in moving back to Nebraska. Lilienthal was also upset because he felt that the president, concerned only with "winning a military victory," was too distracted to take time to use his considerable charms on Norris. Lilienthal was also tired of the constant fight with WPB and observed that "WPBers are mostly of the same stripe as these foolish and bitter utility men who are out to destroy everything we have tried to do."[39]

In March 1943, he mentioned "a heavy and persistent pall of gloominess." The escalating clash with McKellar started him worrying about "hav[ing] such little capital saved . . . [and wondering] how I would earn a living if I found I couldn't go on with TVA." Similar signs of dejection cropped up in the fall after his frenetic summer when he was finishing *TVA: Democracy on the March*. He was also depressed by what he feared was another spell of undulant fever. In January 1945 Lilienthal exhibited an atypically cavalier attitude toward his official responsibilities, spending most of the first three weeks in January, usually a crucial time for cramming for appropriation hearings, in New York City socializing, going to plays, and promoting his book. He broke away to return to Washington for the hearings, but on January 18, a day after the hearings, he was back in New York.[40]

In spite of a changing sense of obligation, Lilienthal carefully guarded his TVA position. In April 1943, he turned down a tempting offer to become WPB's labor-management relations vice-chairman. A year later he declined an army request to lead the rebuilding of Italy's electric power-industrial infrastructure. He suspected that this offer was "part of somebody's idea of a way to solve the McKellar opposition." His caution served him well later that year when assistant president for the home front, James F. Byrnes, urged Roosevelt to appoint Lilienthal chairman of the Surplus Property Board (SPB) to avoid a reappointment fight in 1945. On November 17, Byrnes tried unsuccessfully to talk Lilienthal into taking the SPB position. He then advised the president "he would have to 'turn on the charm'" when they met with the TVA chairman the next day. When he walked into the Oval Office, Lilienthal was on guard, reminding himself, "if I were to make my 'No, thank you, sir' stick, I mustn't let [the president's] delightful and flattering greeting 'get me.'" According to the crusty Byrnes, Lilienthal outmaneuvered the president by a mile. After listening to Roosevelt's effusive flattery, Byrnes recalled that "Dave soared to heights of eloquence. He said if he had ever done anything of value with TVA, it was entirely due to the [president's] inspiration." Then, Byrnes continued, "the President took off. . . . I was left alone, grounded with my sordid appointment to the Surplus Property Board. . . . Lilienthal told the President . . . he would consider the appointment further, but, once away from the charm, he declined." Later in the day Roosevelt asked Byrnes how he had done—Byrnes glumly replied, "Overdone!"

Nevertheless, in late February 1945, Roosevelt thought once again of moving Lilienthal, this time to head up a yet unauthorized Missouri Valley Authority. Both his wife, Eleanor, and Jonathan Daniels tried to talk him out of it.[41]

Needless to say, Lilienthal was concerned about his future. Roosevelt told him bluntly in November that "they won't confirm you next spring—and McKellar will say you are personally objectionable to him, and that will be that." After Lilienthal stubbornly insisted that he did not want to "run away from this issue," a frustrated president replied, "Well, you know how it will be when the time comes. I'll get mad and send your name up regardless and fight it out, . . . and we'll probably lose." In the next few months, however, there were few clear signals either way. During February Appropriations hearings McKellar was civil, causing Lilienthal to worry that others would think he had made a deal with the senator. Two weeks later, however, McKellar was his usual choleric self. Lilienthal was relieved, noting that "to win my renomination and confirmation at the price of even appearing to have made some kind of trade would be to injure the TVA seriously, and cost me peace of mind and esteem." Behind the scenes both pro- and anti-Lilienthal forces worked on Roosevelt. Stirred up by Lilienthal's January "Shall We Have More TVAs?" article, Harold Ickes joined up with McKellar in what Jonathan Daniels called "an alliance of antagonism . . . against Dave." At the same time Tennessee's rising star, Representative Estes Kefauver, gave Roosevelt a strong endorsement for Lilienthal's reappointment. The reply was noncommittal, suggesting that Roosevelt was having second thoughts about whether Lilienthal's renomination was worth the fight.[42]

All bets were off when Roosevelt died on April 12. Lilienthal's first reaction, according to Daniels was "that Throttlebottom in the person of Truman [would] be President." Daniels also revealed in his memoirs, but not to Lilienthal, that with peace negotiations pending in the Senate, Roosevelt had decided not to antagonize McKellar by reappointing Lilienthal. In spite of the new uncertainty, Lilienthal kept his humor. When he realized that Truman's elevation also meant McKellar would become president pro tempore of the Senate, he wrote, "When I pick enemies, I make 'em good!" Unlike Roosevelt, Truman took little time making up his mind. After a visit from powerful Alabama Senators John Bankhead and Lister Hill in support of Lilienthal and impassioned letters from McKellar and Stewart opposing the nomination, the president called Lilienthal in May 1 and told him the job was his. All he had to do was assure the president "that you will carry on the TVA for me in the same fine way that you did for my predecessor." Lilienthal was impressed at the lack of concern for the "'rap' he, as President, was assuming in naming me in spite of the President of the Senate." It was, as the chairman remembered, "an admirable performance. Simple. No mock heroics. Nothing complex. Straightforward." At the same time, Truman "with eyes twinkling behind his thick lenses" told Jonathan Daniels, "McKellar will have a shit hemorrhage."[43]

The approval process was swift and surprisingly smooth. Editorial endorsements were, as Lilienthal wrote, "almost without exception highly favorable, and from throughout the country." The liberal *Nation* featured an endorsement by a conservative Alabama newspaper editor who minced no words in saying that progress in the Tennessee Valley was largely a function of "the personal efforts of David E. Lilienthal." Nominated on May 3, Lilienthal appeared before the committee on September 14 and was approved by a vote of thirteen to two. On September 21 the Senate passed his nomination on a voice vote with only McKellar and Stewart voting "no." The next day, after taking his third TVA oath, he was amazed at "what actually happened with what Justice Byrnes predicted to the late President would happen as recently as November." His triumph was complete when on May 28, the often anti-TVA *Time* magazine lauded Lilienthal and told of McKellar's announcement of defeat "in one last flow of thin and bitter accusation." The "quiet, smooth-faced TVA Chairman, David Eli Lilienthal" had beat odds many felt he could never overcome.[44]

The rest of his TVA tenure was anticlimactic and without controversy. The European war ended a day after he took oath and the Pacific conflict less than two months later. Under Clapp, TVA ran smoothly and without distraction. Lilienthal spent considerable time educating the new president about TVA and telling him about the river authority concept. In October, Lilienthal accompanied Truman to the dedication of the crown jewel of TVA's river projects, the spectacular Kentucky Dam. In early August, Lilienthal wondered, now that the crisis with McKellar and a new president was over, if he shouldn't "be getting on to some other work?" Perhaps it was time for "a fresh viewpoint in TVA."

With children in college and the reality of caring for Helen's aging mother and his folks, he fretted again about personal finances. Yet, he stopped to ask himself, "Is there anything you could have done, in the whole wide world, that could be more useful, more honorable, or more satisfying?" His answer was a resounding "Hell, no." He thought he would wait a bit longer because "there is my luck, which is tremendous. Perhaps it will decide what to do next, and especially when. It's worked before."

In these later years, Lilienthal could look back with pride and satisfaction. As much as anyone else, he was responsible for willing and moving TVA to survive and then to flourish. To be sure, others—the Morgans, Norris, Roosevelt, Clapp, and Owen—helped guide the authority through countless crises. Nevertheless, Lilienthal was the one constant factor combining prodigious energy and political acumen. He also had the uncanny ability to inspire and engender support from a people very different from himself and wary of the new technologies and ideas about governance he brought to the Tennessee Valley.

There was irony in his accomplishments, however. In TVA's first half-decade, Lilienthal, with his singled-minded attention to power, was largely responsible for the authority's losing much of its original vision and developing a reputation of being little more than a giant public utility. In 1939, because of the prodding of others and his own thinking, he attempted to expand TVA's horizons, talking about grass roots administration, and encouraging innovative management within the organization. Yet, only a few months after his attempt to forge a new vision, in November 1939, he found himself again concentrating mostly on power matters. He was so successful in his second power mission that by 1945 TVA's productive capacity was almost triple that of 1939. Lilienthal assumed that postwar demands would absorb the great wartime capacity of TVA's generators and turbines and that the authority could move on to some of the expansive themes he talked about in *TVA: Democracy on the March*. What he did not realize was that World War II power would indeed be absorbed and that demands would increase even more, but largely because of the insatiable appetites of state institutions such as the Atomic Energy Commission; by the late 1950s, more than half of all TVA power was sold to federal agencies. Thus, grass roots ideology lived on, but primarily as the handmaiden to the technological requirements of other state enterprises.[45]

President Truman authorizing transfer of Manhattan Project assets to the Atomic Energy Commission. Front row, left to right, Carrol L. Wilson, President Truman, and Lilienthal; back row, left to right, Sumner T. Pike, K. D. Nichols, Robert P. Patterson, Major General Leslie Groves, Lewis L. Strauss, William W. Waymack, December 1946. Courtesy of Stock Montage.

Senator Kenneth McKellar confronting Lilienthal during Atomic Energy Commission confirmation hearings, March 1947. Courtesy of Stock Montage.

Joseph A. Volpe Jr., deputy counsel and later chief counsel, Atomic Energy Commission, late 1940s. Courtesy of Joseph A. Volpe Jr.

Lilienthal on cover of *Time* magazine, © August 1947. Courtesy of Time-Warner Incorporated.

Arnold Newman portrait of Lilienthal as chairman of the Atomic Energy
Commission, probably 1948. Courtesy of the National Portrait Gallery,
Smithsonian Institution; gift of the family of David E. Lilienthal Sr. Copyright ©
1996 by Arnold Newman.

Meeting at Lake Success, New York, on international control of atomic energy: Sir George Thompson, United Kingdom; General A. G. L. McNaughton, Canada; Lilienthal; and Professor Dmitry V. Skobeltzyn, USSR (left to right), June 1947. Courtesy of the History Division, U.S. Department of Energy.

First Atomic Energy Commission headquarters, 1901 Constitution Avenue, N.W., formerly U.S. Public Health Service, now Department of Interior South, late 1940s. Courtesy of the History Division, U.S. Department of Energy.

Lilienthal at luncheon with actor Adolphe Menjou, late 1940s. Courtesy of the History Division, U.S. Department of Energy.

Lilienthal speaking at Oak Ridge on occasion of opening of the community to the public, March 1949. Courtesy of the History Division, U.S. Department of Energy.

Senator Bourke B. Hickenlooper, 1949. Courtesy of U.S. Senate History Office.

"Incredible Mismanagement" hearings, Lilienthal in center, June 1949. Courtesy of the History Division, U.S. Department of Energy—picture taken by U.S. Information Agency.

David and Helen Lilienthal chatting with David Jr., late 1940s. Courtesy of the Public Policy Papers, Seeley G. Mudd Manuscript Library, Department of Rare Books and Special Collections, Princeton University Libraries.

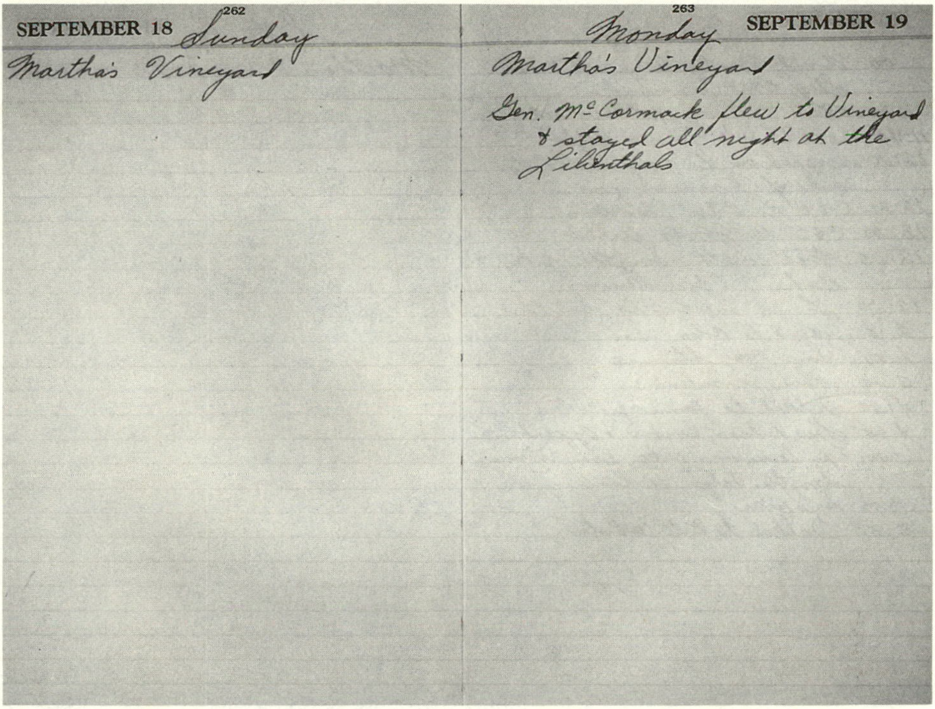

SEPTEMBER 18 *Sunday* 262

Martha's Vineyard

263 *Monday* SEPTEMBER 19

Martha's Vineyard

Gen. McCormack flew to Vineyard
& stayed all night at the
Lilienthals

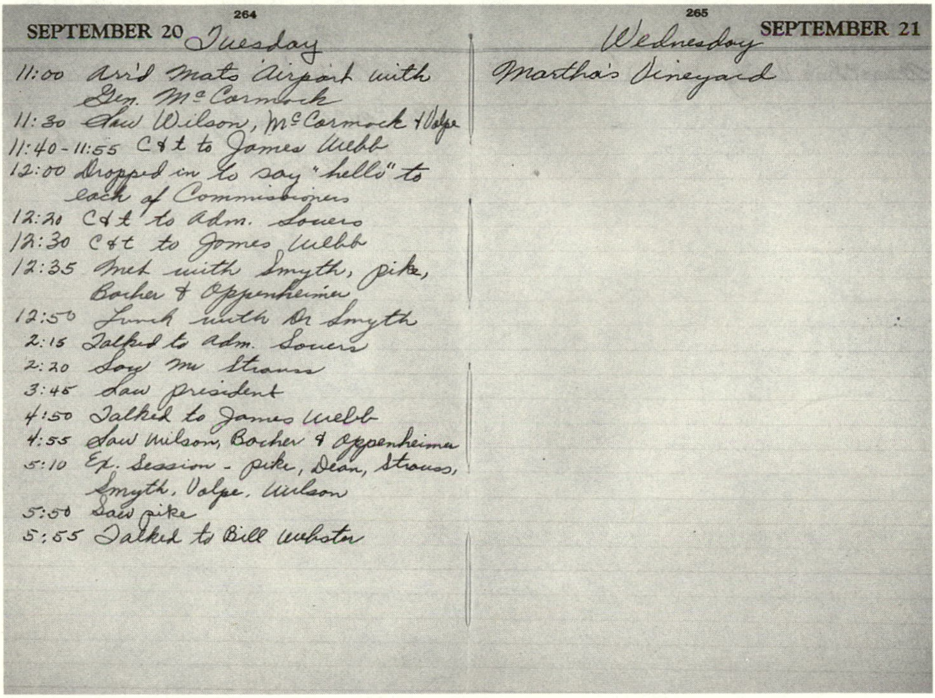

SEPTEMBER 20 *Tuesday* 264

11:00 Arr'd Mats Airport with
      Gen. McCormack
11:30 Saw Wilson, McCormack & Volpe
11:40 – 11:55 C&t to James Webb
12:00 Dropped in to say "hello" to
      each of Commissioners
12:20 C&t to Adm. Souers
12:30 C&t to James Webb
12:35 Met with Smyth, Pike,
      Bacher & Oppenheimer
12:50 Lunch with Dr Smyth
2:15 Talked to Adm. Souers
2:20 Say Mr Strauss
3:45 Saw president
4:50 Talked to James Webb
4:55 Saw Wilson, Bacher & Oppenheimer
5:10 Ex. Session - Pike, Dean, Strauss,
      Smyth. Volpe, Wilson
5:50 Saw Pike
5:55 Talked to Bill Webster

265 *Wednesday* SEPTEMBER 21

Martha's Vineyard

Lilienthal's official Atomic Energy Commission calendar for September, 18–21,
first Soviet nuclear explosion crisis, 1949. Courtesy of the National Archives.

Editorial cartoon in the *New York Herald Tribune,* November 1949. From *New York Herald Tribune,* November 6, 1949; © 1949, *New York Herald Tribune,* Inc. All rights reserved. Reproduced by permission.

Lilienthal, Glenn T. Seborg, and Lewis L. Straus at ceremony honoring 25th anniversary of the Atomic Energy Act, 1971. Courtesy of the History Division, U.S. Department of Energy.

Lilienthal home, 88 Battle Road, Princeton, New Jersey. Photograph by the author.

Lilienthal and the Shah of Iran tasting sugar cane in the Khuzistan, probably late 1950s. Courtesy of the Public Policy Papers, Seeley G. Mudd Manuscript Library, Department of Rare Books and Special Collections, Princeton University Libraries.

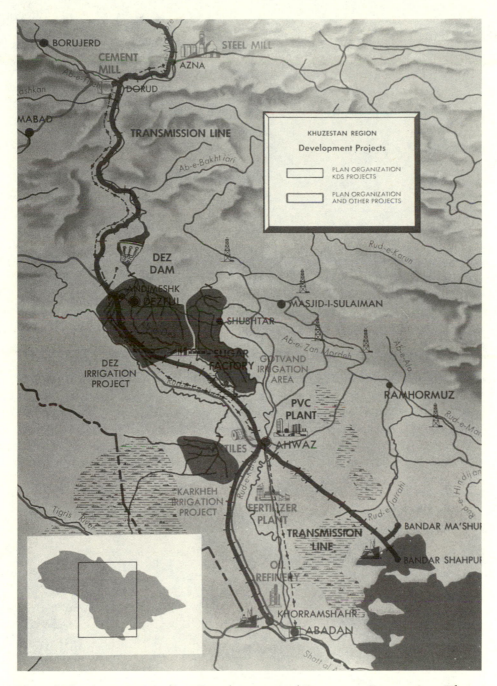

Map of Khuzistan Project from Development and Resources Corporation, *The Unified Development of the Natural Resources of the Khuzistan Region*, 1959.

Robert McNamara, President Johnson, Walter Rostow, John McNaughton, and Lilienthal on Air Force One en route to Guam Conference with Vietnamese leaders, March 1967. Courtesy of the Lyndon B. Johnson Presidential Library. Yoichi R. Okamoto, photographer.

The Atomic Trust: Bright Fires, Bright Hopes

> God grant that in the coming year I may by a bit lessen the
> cloud of dread that hangs over the world since Hiroshima. For I
> am sure that if we have some wisdom and patience, and divine
> guidance, we will find, we mortals, that the cloud has indeed a
> lining of silver.
>
> —David E. Lilienthal, December 31, 1946

Premonitions

David Lilienthal discovered the power of the atom the same day
most other Americans did—on August 6, 1945. To be sure, he knew that
the nearby government facilities, shadowed by rugged Black Oak Ridge,
were "something of great portent." Since 1942, the mysterious project
northwest of Knoxville, called the "Shangri-la" plant by Lilienthal, had taken
an ever-increasing portion of TVA's power. However he, like others close to the
secret activities, not only in eastern Tennessee, but in northern New Mexico
and eastern Washington State, could only wonder and speculate.[1]

Lilienthal sensed that something significant was happening. Repeating
the themes of *TVA: Democracy on the March* at the University of North
Carolina in May 1945, Lilienthal warned that it was by no means certain
"that scientific research and technology will work for good." Research must
have moral purpose and be channeled through democratic processes "to
nourish and strengthen the human spirit." Recalling Czech playwright Karel
Capek's spiritless robots in *R.U.R.,* he emphasized that "research must have
a 'soul'" to forestall "one catastrophe after another, one war after another,
each more horrible and mechanically perfect than its predecessor."[2]

In June, with Hiroshima more than a month away, he asked bluntly at
his daughter Nancy's Radcliffe commencement, "Are machines to control
men, or are men to control machines?" Again, he concluded that through
"science and the skills of management," modern citizens "can deliberately
and consciously direct and shape the course of events." On August 7
Lilienthal wrote about the new technology "that no such control over the

destinies of us all can be left in the hands of private corporations." Already, he knew the TVA controversy would pale when "compared to the debate and decision affecting this undertaking."[3]

In September, the University of Chicago invited him to an atomic energy conference that included University of Chicago President Robert Hutchins, a pair of his faculty members, Robert Redfield and Charles Merriam, theologian Reinhold Niebuhr, Chester Barnard, chairman of New Jersey Bell, and Manhattan Project pioneer Leo Szilard. James Franck, another atomic scientist and chair of a committee that had recommended international control of the atom well before Hiroshima, was also there. Lilienthal immediately took the scientific community to task, demanding that they make it "plain to the American people . . . that you fellows have other things cooking . . . that may be just as bad or worse [than the atomic bomb]." The next day he warned that "unless the people are properly informed, . . . policy regarding the atomic bomb will be neither sound nor enduring." Secrecy and censorship result in an atmosphere in which "scientists are prevented from speaking out." Such "pre-audit over the opinions of men of high professional standing will create a paralysis. . . . First, it will be mental. Then it will be ethical, moral." He concluded by cautioning "the scientists that they are . . . the trustees of a great moral responsibility in this issue of whether they shall insist on the duty to speak out so the public may know." Open debate, public choice, a modern sword of Damocles— Lilienthal had found a reality, an atomic reality, for the abstractions of science he had been talking about since *TVA: Democracy on the March*. It was the opening to the future he had been looking for.[4]

New Directions: The Board of Consultants

During the latter part of 1945, Lilienthal concentrated on TVA business. Only once after September did his journal note the controversies over the atom. In early January 1946, that changed. Secretary of State James F. Byrnes was pressed by Congress and an upcoming meeting of the United Nations Atomic Energy Commission to clarify Truman's international position on atomic energy. Shortly before leaving for the first United Nations General Assembly meeting in London, Byrnes asked his under secretary of state, Dean Acheson, to chair a task force to develop recommendations on the issue. After consulting his committee, made up of Vannevar Bush, former director of the wartime Office of Scientific Research and Development (OSRD); James B. Conant, president of Harvard University; General Leslie Groves, head of the Manhattan Project; and John J. McCloy, former assistant secretary of war. Acheson decided to appoint a small consultant group to bring in fresh perspectives and assess the technical issues involved.

According to Acheson, his assistant Herbert Marks, who had worked for Lilienthal in Chicago and at TVA, suggested that the TVA chairman lead the consultant group. Acheson liked the idea and quickly enlisted Lilienthal. In short order Acheson and Marks filled out the rest of the committee. Lilienthal suggested Chester Barnard, a telephone executive and author of the landmark book *Functions of the Executive*, and General Groves proposed Harry A. Winne, a Manhattan Project veteran and vice-president of General Electric. J. Robert Oppenheimer, the genius of Los Alamos and father of the bomb, and Dr. Charles Thomas, vice-president of Monsanto and distinguished plutonium chemist, rounded out the group. Oppenheimer and Thomas were the only two in the group who had witnessed the first atomic explosion at Trinity Site, New Mexico, on July 16, 1944.

Lilienthal called the invitation "one of the most flattering proposals ever made to me, and yet one of the most humbling possible." Sensing the assignment might permanently turn their colleague's head, Gordon Clapp and H. A. Morgan opposed Lilienthal's accepting this new job, but to no avail. For the next two months Lilienthal and his committee worked overtime developing a policy that, they hoped, would protect the national interest and achieve international control over the most dangerous aspects of atomic energy.[5]

Lilienthal immediately grasped the problem. The atomic energy debate had raged back and forth between proponents of the May-Johnson bill, which authorized military control over the atom, and those of the McMahon bill, which favored civilian control. Security and secrecy were key issues, and Leslie Groves remained the master of the atomic universe, doling out information, even to Congress, with great parsimony. For Lilienthal, the emphasis on secrecy was problematic. Democratic policy could not be forged without open debate—that he had made clear in Chicago. Equally compelling, however, was his hunch "that in the real sense there are no secrets (that is, nothing that is not known or knowable)." Hoarding scientific findings, even given a government monopoly, was bound to fail. According to Lilienthal, his board was charged with developing "a position . . . that will 'work' and have a good chance of being accepted, especially by Russia"—a policy they could carry first to Acheson's group, then the president, and ultimately the American people and the world.[6]

On January 23, the Board of Consultants received its charge from Acheson's group. For Lilienthal it was "one of the most memorable intellectual and emotional experiences" of his life. In the afternoon the consultants met with Conant, who urged them to develop "an explicit schedule" to safeguard the American advantage and security until all controls were in place. When Conant left, the board pledged to "liberate all our discussion from idea possessiveness," and to avoid a watered-down, "pork barrel" report. After a secret briefing by Oppenheimer, Lilienthal urged his colleagues to keep "the scope manageable [and] not [to fall] into the illusion that there is 'a' solution, one answer that we must seek for and that will answer everything." Facts, instead of dogma, should light the way. Lilienthal felt good about making "headway on that proposition, even in two days' discussion."[7]

The board began in earnest on January 28 in the oak-paneled top floor of the American Trucking Association in Washington, D.C., the former OSRD headquarters. There, in New York City, and in Tennessee and New

Mexico, for two grueling months, Lilienthal was at his best. He marveled that he had shown "far more patience than anyone would have guessed." He was proud of his ability to judge "the people I was trying to keep together, . . . unsnarling differences that developed," and ensuring that "all five men participated actively, . . . rather than one or two doing the work." A year later all the consultants but Oppenheimer confirmed Lilienthal's self-assessment at the Atomic Energy Commission (AEC) confirmation hearings. Winne denied that Lilienthal had been "domineering and difficult to work with," noting that "anyone coming into our deliberations 95 percent of the time would have had difficulty in determining who was Chairman." Thomas called Lilienthal "a catalytic agent; in getting people to work well with each other, . . . never [trying] to impress his views or arguments on any of us." Barnard, in defending the report, emphasized that "this is not a report on Mr. Lilienthal, but a report of five men, and I never was on a report in which all five contributed as they did to this." In response to Senator Brien McMahon's query about Lilienthal's being a "dominating kind of fellow," Barnard answered, "sometimes I was irritated . . . because I thought if [Lilienthal] might take hold of it a little stronger, we would make a little better progress."[8]

If anyone shaped the report, it was Oppenheimer, who represented a scientific community committed to civilian and international control. Lilienthal was smitten by the scientist. He was "impressed with his flash of mind" and later confided to Marks, "he is worth living a lifetime just to know that mankind has been able to produce such a being." Leslie Groves, no friend to either man, quipped that "Lilienthal got so bad he would consult Oppie on what tie to wear in the morning." Oppenheimer guided his colleagues, along with Herbert Marks and Carroll Wilson, Vannevar Bush's former OSRD assistant who was now seconded to the board, through a complex atomic primer. His lecture on January 28 was a brilliant soliloquy on the atom—so much that for Lilienthal, "no fairy tale [of] rapture or enchantment . . . can . . . compare."[9]

On January 31 and February 1, 1946, the consultants pondered their options. Should they recommend keeping the atomic secret or giving it to the world? Should they despair for lack of solutions to unbridled nuclear competition or should they call for a worldwide ban on the bomb? Oppenheimer suggested an international agency to control all atomic activities that could produce weapons materials. His colleagues agreed in principle to an organization in which positive development instead of negative policing framed the control question. Sensing consensus, Lilienthal asked each man to prepare part of the report and to return in ten days. So began the formation of a plan that carried the name Acheson-Lilienthal, but perhaps "bore the stamp of Robert Oppenheimer more than that of any other single individual."[10]

The committee reconvened February 12 with a mishmash of papers and memoranda. Lilienthal's introduction brought together the familiar themes of public involvement, affirmative policy, and concern for flexibility in reaching international accord. Other parts of the "notebook" included Oppenheimer's essay on technical matters, a memorandum from Wilson on raw materials and refining, and contributions by Winne, Thomas, Barnard, and Oppenheimer on international control and security. After days of discussion in New York and a tour of Oak Ridge and Los Alamos, the consultants reached consensus. First, they rejected a ban on the bomb—there was no way to force the genie back into the bottle. Winne emphasized that "if [a ban] was the aim of this board of consultants, this was no place for me because I thought . . . development had to go forward." They agreed with Lilienthal's concern that atomic policy remain in civilian hands. Their firmest accord was on Oppenheimer and Thomas's notion of a strong international atomic authority to control both the destructive and constructive aspects of the atom. Once sure that talk had run its course, Lilienthal asked Marks and Wilson to prepare a draft for Acheson's committee.[11]

When they met again on February 25, Lilienthal recorded that "we now have arrived together—a beautiful demonstration of what well-directed discussion can do." After ten more days, the board was ready. The finished product was a model of collaboration. Oppenheimer was responsible for the lucid technical discussion and the inspiration for international control. According to Hewlett and Anderson, Lilienthal "helped give the passages on the international authority a ring of practicality," and his rhetoric lent a style not often found in official reports. Thomas's strong doubts about effective international inspection were stressed. And, through their contributions, particularly through their wholehearted approval of the draft, Winne and Barnard, both staunchly cautious businessmen, gave the work a legitimacy that would be difficult to shake.[12]

On March 6, Lilienthal prepared his board for the presentation to Acheson's committee and suggested they take turns reading the draft aloud at the meeting the next day. They each took an assignment and waited anxiously. The importance of the moment was not lost on the chairman: "I didn't sleep well last night. . . . I find myself in the midst of wholly strange and fearsome things. And as a result of the past six weeks, these seem quite close and real."[13]

On March 7, they met in the magnificent tapestry-draped conference room at Dumbarton Oaks. Acheson made a few remarks and then turned to the consultants. Lilienthal characterized the report as "a place to begin, a foundation on which to build" and introduced the first reader, Chester Barnard. The telephone executive read Section I, which rejected the notion that a policelike inspection system could alone control the proliferation of atomic weapons.[14]

Oppenheimer, Winne, and Thomas read Section II, a discussion of workable, international safeguards. They emphasized the need for an early warning system to keep rogue nations from building nuclear weapons. Security was relatively easy, they continued, because uranium, the only natural substance that could maintain a chain reaction, was scarce. Then, they introduced the possibility of denaturing fissionable materials, making them useless for bombs. They argued that radical new discoveries that might undermine security were unlikely, and that a positive, cooperative approach rather than unbridled competition would better promote control. The heart of this section proposed that all nations be barred from any atomic activity with potential military application and that such authority be vested in an international organization. Because all reactors produce weapons-grade material as a by-product, this meant that even nuclear power generation would come under the proposed agency.

The final section, read by Winne, Barnard, and Lilienthal, invested the proposed "Atomic Development Authority" (ADA) with control over raw materials and ownership of all processing and production facilities. ADA would also license, regulate, and inspect allowable national activities. Lilienthal concluded that ADA must be truly international and accountable to the UN Security Council. Most important for any plan to succeed, the new agency must evolve out of dialogue, not dictate. Without fanfare, Lilienthal finished, looked up, and said, "This, gentlemen, is our recommendation of a plan for security in a world of atomic energy."[15]

Acheson called the report "a brilliant and profound document." After lunch, the criticisms began. Groves and Conant questioned the ability to control raw materials. Others observed that classified data was in the draft and that international inspections had been downplayed. The most serious concern was the lack of a transition plan for shifting knowledge and authority to international hands. Bush was strongly opposed to transferring American secrets without adequate safeguards. Moreover, there was no statement stipulating that the United States could cancel the agreement should its security be compromised.[16]

In spite of Bush's and McCloy's praise that it was "the best proposal that has ever been put forward," Lilienthal's committee was crestfallen when its "baby" came under fire. The consultants were also disturbed by the insistence that a schedule for the transfer of atomic technology to international control had to be spelled out. They worried that a timetable would signal American mistrust of the Soviet Union and endanger the plan's success. After discussion, however, the board reluctantly agreed to add a section on transfer and several other suggested changes.[17]

By Saturday, March 16, 1946, the revision was ready. Inspection of raw materials was emphasized, classified data was eliminated, and a transition plan was added. That, said Lilienthal firmly, was as far as they would go. Bush and Groves protested that the transition section was not sufficient: they wanted an explicit schedule. Lilienthal, now very tired, became belligerent and argued that too much detail would signal that the U.S. was more interested in playing by its own rules than in cooperating. He was discouraged and wondered if "all our work might be wasted." The impasse continued into Sunday morning, when Acheson's secretary suggested a coffee break. Acheson recalled that he "collected Conant, Oppenheimer, Lilienthal, and Groves" and told them to work it out. Within minutes of reconvening, they reached an agreement. Acheson's people, as weary as the rest, were satisfied that the new schedule provisions were explicit enough. By late afternoon, the State Department committee signed a letter of transmittal to Secretary Byrnes and Lilienthal marveled at what "now seems nothing less than a miracle."[18]

Newspapers got wind of the plan on Tuesday from congressional sources. Reaction varied widely. The *Chicago Tribune* and *Washington Times-Herald* were predictably critical, while the *Washington Post* and *New York Times* were positive. Dorothy Thompson called it a "daydream," and others, including the Federation of American Scientists, endorsed it heartily. Dozens of magazines and journals reviewed the report. The State Department found the "weight of opinion . . . heavily in favor of the Committee's Report." After first feeling dismay when neither he nor his board were cited in initial releases, Lilienthal was happy when later reports acknowledged their role and when he realized that "our long work has met with a grand response all over."[19]

It was remarkable that the praise was so strong. The report shattered the nation's sure sense of national security with its gloomy claims that "there can be no adequate military defense against atomic weapons" and that atomic secrets were only transitory. It went against common sense in recommending the internationalization of its most dramatic advantage over the Soviets. And it flaunted popular notions when it proposed government ownership of the means of extraction, production, and manufacture of a revolutionary technology that had already cost taxpayers nearly $2 billion; and the idea that the United States should cooperate with the Soviet Union, already the new enemy in the eyes of millions of Americans.[20]

Why the acclaim? It was positive in part because of the stature of the men who forged the plan. Lilienthal, Groves, and Oppenheimer were popular figures; Barnard, Winne, and Thomas were prominent industrialists; Acheson and McCloy were high-ranking diplomats; and Conant and Bush were executives of prestigious private institutions. Moreover, the report offered hope to a world spent by the most destructive war it had ever known. It was also heralded because it took the same position as that of many other Americans—former New Dealers, atomic scientists and other liberal groups—who were fighting for civilian control of the atom. The lucid prose and logic was compelling. International cooperation might be idealistic and a nuclear ban even more so. But the other alternative, an unbridled arms race, was almost unthinkable. Secrets could be kept briefly but this advantage would fade as other nations discovered their own atomic power.[21]

Lilienthal's buoyancy was short-lived. On March 17, the same day the Acheson-Lilienthal Report became official, Byrnes appointed seventy-six-year-old Bernard Baruch to lead the U.S. delegation to the United Nations Atomic Energy Commission. Many, including Lilienthal, felt the appointment was driven by political considerations—and it was. But it was necessary politics. As much as Truman disliked Baruch, he had to have someone

Congress would trust and who could deflect criticism of the administration's atomic energy policy.

Lilienthal was worried that his vision was in jeopardy. Baruch was too old, vain, ignorant about atomic energy, and not an internationalist. Most important, perhaps, Lilienthal was fresh from an exhilarating association with a group that had grown close in its adventure with the atom. How, he wondered, could Baruch take charge of international atomic politics, especially with a staff that included cronies from World War I War Industries Board days, a Wall Street investment banker, and one technical person, a mining engineer, who used to work for Baruch?[22]

The next three months were frustrating for Lilienthal, Acheson, and the president. Stung by the word that the Lilienthal-Acheson Report was official doctrine, Baruch stressed that he was too old to be "a messenger boy" for someone else's policy. After badgering Truman about who was in charge of setting the American position, Baruch elicited a frustrating "Hell, you are!" from the president. On the same day, March 24, 1946, Lilienthal assured Baruch that the policy was only a beginning and that there were many "important details we didn't fill in." When Baruch insisted on help from those who "knew how to fill it in," Lilienthal refused to cooperate and recommended Oppenheimer and Thomas instead. Later in the conversation Baruch told Lilienthal, "Don't think, young man, you won't be pulled back into this," and asked, "When are you coming to Wash. to go over this with me?" On April 16, Lilienthal again refused Baruch's entreaties, this time so firmly he thought, that "my guess is that I'm not too likely to be called upon again by him." Weeks later Baruch called Lilienthal "sour" for not cooperating, and about the same time Oppenheimer refused to join the Baruch bandwagon.[23]

Lilienthal's refusal to cooperate was, according to Baruch's biographer, a sign of "bruised egos" and Felix Frankfurter's bias. As significant, however, were Lilienthal's and Oppenheimer's assumptions that changes should take place *after* the plan had been presented to the UN by trained diplomats, not before. What galled most was that Baruch's group seemed like ill-informed Johnny-come-latelies who said they would do whatever they thought was necessary to shape the international blueprint.[24]

By early May, Baruch's team had floated several amendments but had not yet come up with a coherent policy. On May 7, Acheson told Lilienthal that the president had rejected Baruch's idea, totally contrary to the report, of a disarmament conference. Baruch also proposed that the United Nations stockpile atomic bombs and that uranium mines be left in private hands, along with removing the veto power of the five permanent members of the Security Council on atomic energy decisions and spelling out sanctions against nations that violated international policies. Alarmed that these changes would invite a Soviet veto, Acheson and Lilienthal agreed to bring their committees together with Baruch on Saturday, May 17.

Lilienthal felt good after the meeting. John Hancock, Baruch's main advisor, "ran the show . . . and did a good job." Baruch showed *"none of* the complaining . . . I had heard reports about." Moreover, Lilienthal's consultants "stood right up to all the questions, and resisted any of the efforts to develop differences among us." However, there was little give. Every point on one side was met with objections by the other. Herbert Bayard Swope, one of Baruch's inner circle who had served with him on the old War Industries Board in 1917, complained that the report failed to spell out sanctions for violating ADA policies. To Lilienthal this peroration was "a stuffy, pompous lecture, . . . mischievous in the extreme." Thomas, McCloy, and Winne protested that making an issue of penalties might scare the Soviets away—but no one on Baruch's side was swayed. Baruch's objection to the internationalization of uranium mines and his proposal for removing the Security Council veto were met with coolness by the other side.[25]

The bickering continued until a frustrated Acheson asked, "Where do we go from here?" Baruch flustered the under secretary by peevishly putting his hand on Lilienthal's knee and announcing, "This gentleman . . . told me quite frankly . . . back in March that it would take me eight weeks . . . to understand this subject, and it is going to take even longer. . . . I am not ready to make a recommendation to the President." He then looked over at Harry Winne and said, "Write down what your Report means to you." The consultants were "flabbergasted." The two days of discussion seemed all for naught. For hours, "until after midnight," Lilienthal's people slaved away on yet another summary, which was given to Baruch on Sunday morning. Needless to say, the board was, as Oppenheimer reflected, "heavy of heart," and not sure what was to come of its work.[26]

Nevertheless, after another month of negotiations between Baruch, Acheson, Byrnes, and the president, a proposal emerged. The Acheson-Lilienthal Report, along with several of Baruch's ideas, formed the basis of the UN report. The most important addition spelled out penalties for treaty violations, "dominion over" rather than ownership of uranium mines, a more detailed section on transition to international control, and the removal of the Security Council veto power over ADA decisions. Lilienthal was bothered by the mine ownership issue, but after reviewing a copy of Baruch's United Nations speech, he wrote that "it was our Report to the 'T'." After Baruch's June 14 speech, Oppenheimer and Thomas, who had approved Baruch's fourteen points but feared Lilienthal's reaction, called to urge him to go along.[27]

In spite of all the struggle, hope for approval faded quickly. On June 19, 1946, the Soviets called for an immediate ban on nuclear weapons, future safeguards, and a refusal to give up the veto power—in other words, nothing compatible with the American position. On July 24, after fruitless debate, the Soviets rejected the U.S. plan. A gloomy Oppenheimer told Lilienthal, "So Dave, we have failed." Lilienthal was upset at the news, but more so by Oppenheimer's report that Baruch was still angry with the TVA chairman for not working with the U.S. delegation. When Oppenheimer told him that Baruch had recommended Groves for the new Atomic Energy Commission, Lilienthal was bitter because "it was [Baruch's] intention that

O[ppenheimer] get this word and that he pass it on to me, to show how B[aruch] was 'punishing' and 'finishing' me for my intransigence."[28]

The proposal failed at the UN for many reasons. Lilienthal's group had good reason for resisting the Acheson Committee's insistence on a detailed transition schedule and Baruch's plans for sanctions and veto removal. Each of these items seemed a mark of American arrogance and raised special problems for the Soviets. Moreover, there was good reason for dismay over Baruch's appointment: a seasoned diplomat might have fared much better.

Nevertheless, the possibility of failure had been present from the beginning. In the first place, the president had always been terribly ambivalent about the internationalization of the atom. As Paul Boyer concluded, "Truman vacillated in ways that reflected the larger uncertainty of the American people." On the one hand, he insisted publicly "that a fundamental objective of U.S. policy was to devise a system of international control." On the other, he remained deeply suspicious of the Soviets and understood that, given the drastic demobilization after the war, nuclear supremacy gave the nation a comfortable edge against the mighty Red Army. Second, no matter how reasonable the idea of international control seemed when compared with an unlimited atomic arms race, or how true it was that atomic secrets could not be held very long, it was questionable whether, in the increasingly partisan American political arena, a radically new policy would succeed. It is also clear that Truman had little leeway in selecting his United Nations representative. The president may been ambivalent about internationalizing the atom, but he had to placate critical domestic opinion. Baruch did so as no seasoned diplomat could have.[29]

Moreover, while the Acheson-Lilienthal Report was lucid and visionary, it assumed too much. In its defense, all the consultants had been asked to do was assess the technical feasibility of international control. They did that in fine fashion. It was technically possible to institute an ADA with international public service values and it was logical to include major atomic energy activities under ADA authority. Even a schedule for transferring authority while ensuring national security made sense.

Political feasibility was another matter. The consultants were naive in expecting the ADA to be a true, international public service corps. They failed to see that the United Nations was already more like a bazaar than a unified international body. Second, the board was technically correct in recommending that the ADA control all activities that could produce weapons material. Such a policy, though, would have threatened the Soviets, who had grave energy deficiencies. Internationalizing domestic power plants would have deprived the Soviets of a cheap source of power and much of their economic independence.

The most important issue concerned the transfer of atomic assets. For political reasons it was essential to include a timetable. The problem, however, derived from the one-sided concern with American security and the lack of sensitivity to Soviet concerns. Under the proposal, the Soviet Union would have to "hand over control of her nuclear raw materials and her atomic development work to A.D.A." without any quid pro quo. At the same time, the United States would continue to stockpile nuclear weapons until the final transition stage. Thus, the paradox of failure: in order to meet domestic expectations, the United States had to offer a plan that the Soviets probably could not accept.[30]

Two additional factors were relevant. Both Lieberman and Blackett contended that American leaders never expected the Soviets to agree to an international agreement. Therefore, there was little risk in making high-minded offers. Even the smallest chance that the Soviets might accept the American proposal was reduced by restrictions added to the consultant's report by Acheson's and Baruch's groups. In a real sense, the hopeful and sincere language of the final report, much of it still Lilienthal's, made the contrast between a flexible United States and an intransigent Soviet Union even more dramatic. Blackett wrote that those who truly believed in an international plan—Lilienthal was certainly among that number—were sacrificed to the wiles of others who knew that the Soviets would never agree, and that such refusal would constitute a diplomatic coup for the United States.[31]

The second factor flowed from George Kennan's gloomy cable from Moscow in February 1946, which reported the Soviet fear of "foreign penetration," and "contact between the Western world and their own." Soviet paranoia was so strong that they were "committed fanatically to the belief that with the United States there can be no permanent *modus vivendi.*" Lilienthal read the report in March but took the challenge as one of opportunity rather than despair. None of the consultants had had much experience in international affairs. In *TVA: Democracy on the March,* Lilienthal wrote glowingly of a new internationalism in the postwar era, but he had little understanding of the difficulties in exporting his idealized liberal vision to a world far different from his own. He and his fellow consultants were part of a large group of Americans who wanted to believe that cooperation would open up the Soviet Union and reduce its isolationism. That, perhaps, was why the Acheson-Lilienthal Report seemed one of willing and hope—willing the creation of an international body to control the frightful threat, and hoping the Soviets would accept a proposal that met U.S. security needs but neglected their own. Even in his optimism, however, Lilienthal slept little the night after reading Kennan's report.[32]

A National Figure

By mid-1946, the Acheson-Lilienthal Report had fallen on hard times, but Lilienthal's star continued rising. When Harold Ickes resigned at Interior in February, word got out that Truman was thinking of Lilienthal as a replacement. Dave and Helen beamed at the irony of replacing his old foe. As he was involved with the Board of Consultants, however, he asked Marguerite Owen to spread the word that he had "no interest in becoming a member of this Cabinet."

During his time on the consultant board, he was feted by luminaries outside the atomic arena. In New York, at an April FDR memorial dinner,

Lilienthal soaked up praise from Senator Claude Pepper, Max Lerner, Paul Appleby, and Sidney Hillman. The next day over lunch, Clare Boothe Luce told him he was "the only living New Dealer . . . who is still popular." Lilienthal was amused that he had "become something of a phenomenon— a minor one perhaps—but something rather extra; somewhere between a prize fighter who reads the classics, say and a man who can wiggle his ears." In spite of this self-deprecation, he was beginning to think of a grander stage than TVA—Clapp and Harcourt Morgan had been right in fearing the defection of their friend and colleague.[33]

Lilienthal remained a popular public speaker. In 1946, he spoke to groups as diverse as the New York *Herald Tribune* Forum, the American Library Association, the American Chemical Society, and the National Municipal League, in addition to addressing a national CBS radio audience on "You and the Atom." In September he received the Catholic Committee of the South's award for "significant contribution to the progress of the Southland."[34]

His familiar message now had an atomic flavor. In Buffalo in June, he told the American Library Association that "the machine is neither good nor evil in itself," and that this reality had an "immediate and critical application in the field of atomic energy." Everything depended on "those who direct its course and use and define the purposes for which it is put." A few days later, at a Congregational Christian Churches national gathering, he argued that mankind could "choose deliberately and consciously whether machines or human beings come first," and he spoke of making "practical application of a faith in the supreme worth of men and the human spirit." In illustration of "practical application," Lilienthal cited his consultants as men who believed that "the purpose and direction of technology may safely be entrusted only to those who have a deep faith in the human spirit."[35]

In the meantime, after a long and tortuous legislative battle, Truman signed the Atomic Energy Act on August 1, 1946. The law authorized a civilian commission and a five-member board selected by the president. Its authors called it "a radical piece of legislation. . . . Never before in the peacetime history of the United States has Congress established an administrative agency vested with such sweeping authority and entrusted with such portentous responsibilities." The act decreed a government monopoly on ownership, production, and processing of all fissionable materials, and authorized the Atomic Energy Commission (AEC) to do the work or contract it out. The commission was given strong powers in the area of patents and licensing, and authority to supply fissionable materials such as radioactive isotopes to researchers, including foreign governments, who met safety and security standards. To ensure civilian control, easily the most contentious issue, the act gave the commission control over all military applications and custody of atomic weapons, both assembled and unassembled. The AEC was required, however, to consult regularly with a Military Liaison Committee (MLC) and the AEC Division of Military Application, which was to be directed by a military officer. Moreover, the act specified that the FBI had certain responsibilities in personnel security matters. Finally, the act ordered the transfer of all public property related to atomic research, production, and processing to the AEC. This included Manhattan Project assets worth over $1.5 billion; major works in Hanford, Washington; Los Alamos, New Mexico; Chicago; and Oak Ridge, Tennessee; as well as a multitude of smaller facilities across the nation. It was little wonder the bill's authors concluded that "the field of atomic energy is made an island of socialism in the midst of a free enterprise economy."[36]

Speculation about who Truman would pick for the AEC was rampant even before the act was signed. One of the names that frequently surfaced was that of David E. Lilienthal. Truman was set on a politically neutral commission, and Lilienthal, although clearly a New Dealer, had pointedly stayed above Democratic party politics. Moreover, the new commission needed both leadership and someone who understood the atom. By late July, Lilienthal, aware that he might be a prime candidate, decided that "if I am offered the chairmanship, . . . I will accept." In hopes that Baruch might help out, he swallowed his pride and spent three days at the old man's Adirondacks retreat to talk about the atom. He knew that Baruch's invitation came "at an important time, for the decision about the chairmanship of the Atomic Energy Commission will probably be made in the next few days."[37]

Recommendations had bombarded the White House since early summer. Thorfin Hogness, chairman of the executive committee of the Atomic Scientists of Chicago, suggested Lilienthal, Chester Barnard, Adlai Stevenson, former Securities and Exchange Commission Chairman Sumner Pike, and scientists Edward U. Condon and Harold C. Urey. On July 8, Senator Brien McMahon's staff recommended Lilienthal, Pike, Condon, Frank P. Graham, president of the University of North Carolina, and Lewis L. Strauss, former aide to President Hoover and partner in Kuhn, Loeb and Company. Later that month the National Committee for Civilian Control of Atomic Energy named Lilienthal and six others, including Barnard and Pike. Commerce Secretary and former Vice-President Henry Wallace, Interior Secretary Cap Krug, Congressmen Albert Gore Sr., Adolph Sabath, and Vannevar Bush all urged Truman to appoint Lilienthal.[38]

Truman, however, was cautious. In late July he secretly appointed Pike and Strauss. He asked Harvard President Conant to chair the commission, but Conant declined, as did nuclear pioneer and MIT President Karl Compton. Truman waited. Reluctant to name Lilienthal, he told Bush, "I don't want to take the chance of getting a dud in [TVA]." Now deeply interested, Lilienthal, hung on every rumor about appointments. After hearing that Pike had been appointed and Conant offered the chairmanship, Lilienthal peevishly wrote that the Harvard president was "being pushed by the Army, particularly Groves, who is determined to continue to run things." Minutes later Krug called to say that Truman hesitated because he was unsure about Lilienthal's replacement at TVA. Lilienthal said that Frank Graham or Gordon Clapp would be strong candidates, but Krug replied that the president wondered whether Clapp "had the strength to beat off political attacks."[39]

As the summer passed, Baruch told Lilienthal he had spoken to Truman and offered to see his nomination through the Senate. By mid-September there were still "no hints or feelers or anything." In a defensive catharsis, Lilienthal wrote, "I think I would be relieved if I didn't have to face [the nomination]." Finally, on September 20, 1946, Truman offered him the chairmanship. Lilienthal brashly answered that he would accept if an adequate TVA replacement could be found, if he could advise Truman on "TVA's current problems and opportunities," and if the president would appoint five commissioners who could work together. Truman immediately agreed to the first two points, and, without revealing names, told Lilienthal that two commissioners were already in the fold but that the chairman would be consulted on the others. Piqued by Truman's refusal to reveal the names (which he already knew), Lilienthal told the president he "didn't particularly relish this unwillingness." He also let Truman know, "with a laugh," that he knew he was only "a third or fourth choice." It was what he wanted, though, "a job that needs doing even more than the TVA job." And he knew he could "do it as well or better than anyone else."[40]

He worked for a month on the matters he and the president talked about. On September 21, he talked for hours with Clapp about the transition. Only then did he realize how much H. A. Morgan, Marguerite Owen, and Clapp resented his change of loyalties. Clapp was blunt, "TVA is the most important thing in the world and we were jealous of this other thing, that it could attract and interest you." Lilienthal asked Clapp why he or Owen had never mentioned it. Clapp said he was "so upset by the whole thing and especially the way you handled the acceptance of the assignment that I didn't want to have to think about the Report or anything about it."[41]

By Wednesday the twenty-fifth, however, Clapp and Owen were hard at work helping their chief with a "state of TVA" memorandum. After working from two in the afternoon until two the next morning and all Thursday morning, they sent a draft to Clark Clifford at the White House. The rhetoric was vintage Lilienthal. Decentralization "is perhaps TVA's most important contribution to the country and to your administration." Even now, TVA was besieged by a coalition of private interests and "Washington bureaus and departments who are not in sympathy with the decentralized methods TVA represents." The Corps of Engineers, Reclamation Service, and Soil Conservation Service were "enemies in combination" and "reactionary interests." Independence was crucial in getting the job done, retaining a committed staff, and keeping faith in the Tennessee Valley. The message concluded that "as long as the exasperations of red tape and the burdens of bureaucracy are kept at a minimum, [the staff] will continue to do a job that cannot be destroyed by any enemy, in which the people of the United States can take satisfaction, and of which the President can be proud."[42]

The next day Truman told Lilienthal he agreed with the memo and urged him to get on the new appointments, especially at TVA. Finding willing candidates for either agency was not easy. Frank Graham and former

TVA general manager Jack Blandford both said no to the TVA position. Lilienthal flew to Louisville to talk with publisher Mark Ethridge and then to Michigan to confer with Michigan State University President John Hannah. When they declined, Lilienthal convinced a reluctant Clapp to relinquish the general managership for the perils of the board. The AEC search went a little better. William Batt, former vice-chairman of the War Planning Board, said no, but on October 18, William Waymack, editor of the Des Moines *Register and Tribune,* said yes when Lilienthal made "about the best presentation of this sort of thing I have ever managed." A week later, former Los Alamos physicist Robert Bacher, after an intense session with Lilienthal and Clifford and arm-twisting by Oppenheimer, agreed to fill the last slot. Lilienthal finally had his man at TVA and a commission he was comfortable with—four Republicans and one independent—himself. On October 28, the president introduced his nominees to the nation and made it clear that all atomic activities would soon be transferred from military to civilian control and that he expected full cooperation from the War Department.[43]

The next three months were frantic. While their appointments still awaited Senate confirmation, the five commissioners faced the challenge of organizing and staffing a new agency and preparing to accept an awesome technology from the military. They were blessed by strong press support. Ironically, only the Hearst papers and the *Daily Worker* spoke in opposition. All five knew, though, that future praise would have to be earned.[44]

Lilienthal had "a hell of a good time. . . . The panic and doubts, so acute a couple weeks ago—where are they now?" His November energy level was high. In addition to two speeches in Philadelphia, he met with Baruch and *New York Times* editors in New York, presided over his last TVA meeting, spent two days at Oak Ridge, and endured a long day closeted with General Groves, U.S. Attorney General Tom C. Clark, FBI officials, and Senator McMahon. He reveled in a luncheon where he talked to a group of high-powered journalists, including Walter Lippmann, Eric Sevareid, Martin Agronsky, Al Friendly, Arthur Krock, David Lawrence, Marquis Childs, and Joseph Alsop.[45]

Lilienthal knew that enthusiasm was not enough. An agency was waiting to be built, and that meant a capable and trustworthy staff and adequate offices. When Truman introduced his five nominees, they had no staff, no office, nothing. In quick order, Lilienthal's "homeless five," appointed Joseph A. Volpe Jr., Groves's former aide, and Wilson and Marks as the commission's first staff members. A few days later, Lilienthal enlisted TVA executives Richard Niehoff and Paul Ager to work on personnel and budget matters. In November, Wilson, temporary general manager, found offices in the new War Department Building.

Nevertheless, organization went beyond staffing and offices. For Lilienthal, the key to success was consensus, forged by listening, cooperation, and trust building. He could remember the contrast between the first five years at TVA, when rancor and mistrust had prevailed, and his last seven after A. E. Morgan's departure. In November 1946, the commissioners quickly agreed on two of Lilienthal's chief concerns. The AEC would avoid politics: no patronage and decisions free of partisan politics. The commission also decided to continue the army's practice of contractor operation. Contracting would allow the AEC to tap the vast store of scientific and engineering expertise in private industry, a work force they could hardly expect to duplicate. Relying on private industry would also allow greater decentralization, which was just what Lilienthal wanted.

Their first meeting in a drafty Oak Ridge building on November 13 set the tone. In response to Lewis Strauss's request to begin "with a moment of silent prayer for divine guidance," Lilienthal turned to Strauss and said, "Lewis, you just took your oath yesterday and it is fresh in your mind but it goes for all of us on this difficult and portentous assignment, 'So Help Us God.'" According to Lilienthal, "the meeting went beautifully, with a fine spirit, clear discussion, . . . without chatter or steam-roller methods." Later, after a successful social outing, he wrote that if this spirit was "carefully nourished and worked at—this I know how to do, . . . this can carry us over many of the difficulties inherent in a five man board."[46]

The camaraderie continued the rest of November. The commissioners traveled to the far-flung corners of its empire. In spite of a painful back, the chairman continued molding "five men, strikingly different men, into the unity that will make our very considerable task a possible one." For six days they slept, ate, flew, and learned together. Waymack, Strauss, and Pike had their first look at Los Alamos and the Oppenheimer genius in California. They spent a few hours in Cheyenne with Harry Winne, who briefed them on Hanford. and in Chicago. where they discussed the new Argonne Laboratories. What might have bound them most closely was the perilous flight over the Rockies, where their army plane almost went down because of ice. Lilienthal noted the gruff Sumner Pike's comment during the flight, "Someone better tell Harry to warm up the second team."[47]

By early December, it appeared that Lilienthal's team-building effort was successful. On December 2, Strauss wrote Clifford, "I have never been more impressed with a man [Lilienthal] in all my experience. . . . I see in him also the qualities of discriminating judgment, firmness and courage, which unless I am badly mistaken, mark a truly great man." These were strong words from the commissioner who was to become a frequent and sometimes bitter dissenter. That December Lilienthal was thrilled to have achieved "such great respect, affection, . . . and a real common purpose," a unity that held nearly a year.[48]

Other matters were not resolved so smoothly. In early December the commission appointed a General Advisory Committee (GAC), which included Oppenheimer, Enrico Fermi, Conant, and nuclear scientist Glenn Seaborg. However, they still lacked a general manager. The problem, according to Lilienthal, was finding someone "with industrial experience who won't be *too* business-minded, . . . [and with] some sense of public policy and its primacy." On December 4, he told a search committee that a strong manager was essential because he did not want to be a "super-general manager." As always, Lilienthal was the inspirer who planned to use, according to Hewlett and Anderson, "his sense for publicity, his flair for the dramatic . . . to project the life-and-death issues of atomic energy into the lives of average Americans." Finally, in late December, the commission offered the position to Carroll Wilson, who had done well in the temporary position. The decision was quickly approved by Clifford and Truman.[49]

The most onerous task was "the transfer." In early December the commission and Groves agreed on a transfer date of December 31. That, however, was the only point of agreement. There were three complications. First, both Groves and Lilienthal had outsized egos and they had already developed an adversarial relationship because of sparring earlier in the year. Second, the transfer was difficult for Groves because the Manhattan Project was his creation. This psychological tie had nothing to do with policy, but it made the move all the stickier. To Groves, the commissioners were interlopers and amateurs who knew little about nuclear policy—and he was largely correct. None of the commissioners, not even Lilienthal, realized the enormity of their task. After one frustrating meeting with the military, Lilienthal noted that the commission "got a look-see at what we have undertaken, and one or two were pretty worried, if not rattled." He reported Waymack's frustration, "We pull at a worm, like a robin, and the whole earth explodes and out comes a two-headed elephant."[50]

The third conflict was over policy. In spite of Truman's decision, the military tried as hard as it could to keep control of weapons and facilities. The commission said no. Then, they tried to name Colonel Kenneth Nichols to head the AEC Division of Military Applications and to make it a line position. The commission, in accord with their decentralization policy, balked—all division heads held staff positions; all operations and administrative responsibilities remained in the field. Besides, the commission questioned Nichols's qualifications. On a cold and miserable weekend a few days before Christmas, Lilienthal traipsed from meeting to meeting, with Secretary of War Robert Patterson, Navy Secretary James Forrestal, Admirals Nimitz and Ramsey, and finally Vannevar Bush, to protest the nomination. His determination worked, and Nichols was not appointed. On February 1, 1947, U.S. Air Force General James McCormack Jr., a man Lilienthal respected, was named to head the division.[51]

On December 23, Marks finished an executive order on the transfer. There was compromise regarding property rights, but the commission held firm on raw materials and weapons. It allowed the War Department to keep the intelligence gathering function, but insisted on unrestricted access to all intelligence records. Knowing that strong publicity might expedite the process, Lilienthal persuaded Truman to have an official transfer ceremony. At 2:50 P.M. on New Year's Eve 1946, the "'papers' of the old melodrama" were signed and the deed was accomplished.[52]

The end of the year was good for Lilienthal. He was tired, and his back still hurt. However, he and Helen had made a successful move from Norris earlier that month to a home north of the District line in Bethesda, Maryland. He had even brought part of the cherished garden he had tended with such care in Norris with him. Nancy and David Jr. were home for Christmas, and the parents were pleased when David concluded, as Lilienthal remembered, "this was a rather good family to grow up in."[53]

It was a good time to reflect on present successes and a hopeful future. He noted in an end-of-year journal entry that the TVA experience was "never far from the way I do things." Lilienthal was confident that he could "do a job of organization, and think in organization terms," and "to be able to 'take it.'" In the future, he hoped to inform "the American people of what lies ahead for them as a result of the entry of this new source of energy and means of learning about the world." In the next months he would be able to test his ability to "take it." He would also begin to bring the American people into partnership of a venture that had been the province of a chosen few.[54]

This I Do Believe

Optimism aside, Lilienthal was aware that concerns over his nomination were growing as confirmation hearings neared. In a November editorial, Ickes accused Lilienthal of stalking the nomination "with a single-minded purpose that would not take 'no' for an answer." Lilienthal's acceptance of the position with "deep humility" was "bunk," said Ickes, because "Mr. Lilienthal is not capable of 'deep humility' except when he contemplates [his] reflection in a mirror." *The Nation* called it a "splenetic assault," and reminded Ickes that he had little room to talk about humility. Lilienthal thought the piece "quite childish . . . just plain funny," not worth answering.[55]

On December 21, 1946, Morris Cooke warned Lilienthal that Senators Robert A. Taft and Kenneth D. McKellar were plotting against the nomination. More disquieting, however, was a spate of anti-Semitic protests over the appointment of "three (3) JEWS to the Atomic Commission." Lilienthal incurred FBI wrath when he supposedly "leaked" FBI files: Marquis Childs ridiculed the bureau for combing over Lilienthal's background so thoroughly that "one of the Atomic Commissioners [Lilienthal] was amused to find included in his dossier the fact that in 1926 he had written a magazine article for the Outlook [sic]." Finally, just days before the hearings, Bourke Hickenlooper, chair of the Senate Section of the Joint Committee on Atomic Energy (JCAE), complained to Forrestal that the MLC had been ignored by the commission and "he and his Senate associates are very much concerned about a pacifistic and unrealistic trend in the Atomic Energy Commission"[56]

Confirmation hearings for the commissioners and the general manager opened January 27, 1947, and continued until March 6. They generated more than eight hundred pages of testimony from forty-eight witnesses and the nominees. Lilienthal testified seven days. Twenty-five witnesses favored, and seven opposed, his nomination. The committee received over 3,000 communications on the nominations—2,604 favorable. Polls also reported strong support for Lilienthal: 73 percent of respondents said they knew of his appointment. Of that number 47 percent approved the nomination, 18 percent opposed it, and 35 percent had no opinion. Confirmation seemed a foregone conclusion, and yet, the first day of hearings, Lilienthal wondered if "we shall find it necessary to ask that our names be withdrawn."[57]

Why the self-doubts? First, there was Senator McKellar's bitter opposition. Although not a JCAE member, he participated as a matter of senatorial courtesy. Of 834 pages of testimony, he was interrogator in 409. Yet McKellar was only part of the problem, and, ultimately, a minor one. At first, however, he was much on Lilienthal's mind. On January 28 he wrote, "McKellar is yet to come"; the next night, "Tomorrow McKellar."[58]

Other factors were more serious. *Time* correspondent Frank McNaughton observed, "there are a lot of other maneuvers than McKellar's, and they are the ones that have Lilienthal and his backers rocking on the ropes." Republicans were in control of both houses of Congress the first time since the late 1920s and eager "to get rid of New Dealism once and for all." How better to begin that task than by rejecting a popular New Dealer?[59]

The case against Lilienthal was helped by constant FBI gossip. Denying that Lilienthal had ever been investigated, the bureau still managed to provide a fifteen-page document detailing his "left wing" associations. At least four times during the hearings, J. Edgar Hoover wrote Truman aide Harry Vaughan with "additional information which has been brought to my attention concerning David Lilienthal." Other information was passed back and forth between the FBI and Hickenlooper, his aides, and other Republican senators.[60]

Lilienthal's personality was also a problem. His ego was large, he had played hardball for years, and along the way, he made many enemies, including some in Congress. Republican Senator Styles Bridges, a former member of the New Hampshire Public Service Commission at the same time Lilienthal was in Wisconsin, remembered him, according to McNaughton, as "'a ruthless sonofabitch' . . . utterly convinced of the rightness of his stand." Bridges also recalled the Lilienthal-Morgan feud as one where Lilienthal had "utterly sacked and ruined . . . Morgan." Lilienthal's reputation for protecting TVA against congressional efforts to submit the authority to General Accounting Office or Civil Service regulations provided additional grist for the mill. In addition, his strong air of confidence always left a definite sense of arrogance, even among supporters.[61]

The hearings opened on January 27 with flashbulbs, a jammed room, and considerable uncertainty over whose ox was about to be gored. Lilienthal immediately took "the offensive, . . . believing deeply in something and showing it." He spoke of the "terrible responsibility; not only because of the great scope of powers vested, but because errors of judgment . . . can mean missed opportunity for the people of this country." He deflected Republican charges that the AEC had kept MLC and JCAE representatives at arm's length by promising that members of both groups would always have access to the commission. He praised General Groves, affirmed the Baruch Plan, and called for the eventual privatization of commercial atomic energy projects.[62]

Lilienthal closed with a hard-hitting statement on security. Protesting punitive attitudes, he said the AEC would face an impossible task unless "there is a great deal more than just a police force or security force on the commission, and threats of prosecution." He noted that Groves insisted on rigid control of scientific information but at the same time had authorized publishing "the official Army report on the bomb," the Smyth Report, which represented "the principal breach of security since the beginning of the atomic energy project." He called, finally, for an advisory body to study security in light of American traditions to prevent "something . . . that the American people will not stand for." Lilienthal smugly wrote that his testimony "certainly worked to stop the hysteria that . . . the civilian Commission can't be trusted with the 'secret.'"[63]

McKellar's attack lasted six days. On January 27, he questioned Lilienthal's qualifications and said that General Groves should have been appointed chairman. Any persuasive force he might have had was dashed by his inane contention, repeatedly voiced, that Alexander the Great's Macedonian scientists were the first to try to split the atom. Ignoring McKellar's historical allusion, Lilienthal agreed that Groves deserved much credit, but pointed out that the nomination was, after all, the president's to make.

The brunt of the assault took place Friday, January 31, and for two days the following week. McKellar drifted from one accusation to another and often appeared disoriented and unprepared. There was no mistaking his venom as he accused the nominee of being against a government of law, disregarding congressional directives, and displaying left-wing sympathies. Once he asked if Lilienthal was a Communist, since his parents had been born in what was now Communist Czechoslovakia. Another time he accused Lilienthal of protecting Communists at TVA. Later, in a rasping frenzy, he demanded to know if Lilienthal had ever corresponded with Commissars Bulganin, Mikoyan, Malenkov, Stalin, Molotov, Kaganovich, or Zenonik (to which last name, Lilienthal replied, "That's hard on the dentures, Senator"). McKellar also implied that Swidler, Marks, and Melvin Siegel, all former members of the TVA legal staff, had been "tinctured with communism."[64]

Lilienthal patiently parried each attack. After Friday's session he reflected, "Everybody gave me credit for holding my temper, but I don't really deserve any." Things changed Tuesday as Lilienthal trembled with rage. From his first sentence, McKellar badgered the nominee unmercifully about his parents, and for not carrying detailed figures about TVA in his head. He then shifted to political loyalty, sneering, "The truth is your sympathies are very leftist, are they not?" Lilienthal said he would be glad to respond and McKellar savagely replied that "it is very important what your views are on communistic doctrine." With that, the unsuspecting senator allowed Lilienthal to make one of those relatively rare statements, according to Jeffrey Brand, "that capture the attention of the American people."[65]

According to Alfred Friendly of the *Washington Post,* Lilienthal "suddenly wheeled in his chair to face his antagonist, . . . [saying] in a voice which was low, but electric with fervor: 'This I DO carry in my head, Senator.'" In a few minutes he offered his own philosophy of democracy, which Senator McMahon immediately called "a statement . . . of a very real American." Lilienthal looked at McKellar and said that "my convictions are not so much concerned with what I am against as what I am for." Calling democracy an affirmative doctrine, he continued, "I believe in . . . the fundamental proposition of the integrity of the individual," and the responsibility of public and private institutions to secure that integrity. He contrasted this belief with Communism, where "the state is an end in itself, and that therefore the powers which the state exercises over the individual are without any ethical standard to limit them. That," he emphasized, "I deeply disbelieve."

The remainder of his soliloquy was a forceful attack on the growing Red hysteria. In a measured cadence, he said, "It is very easy to talk about being against communism. It is equally important to believe those things which provide a satisfying and effective alternative. Democracy is that satisfying, affirmative alternative." The very center of the "affirmative alternative," he continued, consists of the belief "that the individual comes first, that all men are the children of God and that their personalities are therefore sacred." Democracy also implies a "deep belief in civil liberties . . . and a repugnance to anyone who would steal from a human being that which is most precious to him—his good name—either by imputing things to him, by innuendo or by insinuation."

Lamenting that such things often are "done in the name of democracy," Lilienthal stressed that they threatened to "tear our country apart and destroy it." Again, positively, he said, "I deeply believe in the capacity of democracy to surmount any trials that may lie ahead, provided only that we practice it in our daily lives." Recognizing the need "to ferret out the subversive and anti-democratic forces," he decried hysteria or innuendo or other means which "besmirch the very cause that we believe in." He concluded by condemning "administrative agencies acting arbitrarily, . . . or . . . investigating activities of legislative branches" which fail to protect the good name of individuals "against besmirchment by gossip, hearsay, and the statements of witnesses who are not subject to cross-examination." Pausing for a second, he sat back in his chair, looked up at the panel and said— "This I deeply believe."[66]

The room was absolutely still—as it had been throughout his statement. The *New York Times* said it was delivered "in a way that cast a spell of solemnity over the Joint Congressional Committee." After a few moments, McMahon gave his assessment. Then, as if nothing had happened, McKellar continued with more questions about Communists in TVA, the competence of its legal staff, and the correspondence with Russian commissars. At the end of the session the room broke into pandemonium. Senator John Bricker motioned Lilienthal to the bench to shake his hand. Senator William Knowland called the remarks "the finest definition of democracy I have ever heard in my life." The press crowded close to congratulate him and get copies of the transcript. By nightfall the "credo," as it was called, was broadcast across the nation and by the next morning was all over America's front pages. Lilienthal savored the telegrams and letters that compared his definition of democracy with those of "Lincoln, Jefferson, Tom

Paine." It was an extraordinary moment of political rhetoric, perhaps not a Gettysburg Address, but certainly one of the best of the century.[67]

It may have been suggestive enough to influence the style and cadence of the "Truman Doctrine" speech a little more than a month later. Clifford recalled that early drafts of that speech were "written in a weakly worded, bureaucratic style." On March 5, 1947, Dean Acheson added "a more forward-looking statement," beginning with "I believe it must be the policy of the United States to give support to free peoples who are attempting to resist subjugation by armed minorities and outside forces." Clifford and aide George Elsey wanted something even "punchier, more dramatic, more memorable." On March 10, the two thought of beginning each key sentence with "I believe that . . . " Two days later, Truman gave his speech, which included the three sentences that Clifford and Elsey also called the credo:

> I believe that it must be the policy of the United States to support free peoples who are resisting attempted subjugation by armed minorities or by outside pressures. I believe that we must assist free peoples to work out their own destinies in their own way. I believe that our help should be primarily through economic and financial aid which is essential to economic stability and orderly political processes."[68]

Lilienthal's speech reflected his complex nature. He was actor, showman, rhetorician—but he also believed those words. He carefully stressed the most fundamental American values—individualism, patriotism, faith in god, civil liberties—in a positive manner before he took deliberate aim first at Communism and then the violations by his own government against individual liberties. The circumstances surrounding the delivery revealed even more. It was widely assumed that the speech was spontaneous. The press described it so, and Lilienthal wrote that McKellar "was responsible for my getting off, quite spontaneously a statement of my democratic faith." According to associates, however, the speech was not unrehearsed. Frankfurter called it a "carefully prepared rhetorical manifesto." Baruch remembered that he had advised Lilienthal to "seize the opportunity to state his own convictions" and that soon after he delivered "that memorable statement of his philosophic faith which stirred the nation." Joe Volpe recalled that he and Lilienthal had talked the night before about taking "advantage of some opening that McKellar would give him," and a few minutes later Volpe heard Lilienthal say "'I got it! I got it!', and he started scribbling something in shorthand, and sort of outlined to me what he might say, and sure enough, when McKellar gave him the opening there it was." No doubt there is some truth here—as Willson Whitman noted, "Anybody as smart as David Lilienthal of course would know that McKellar's nagging would afford plenty of opportunity for such a statement." Whatever the truth, Lilienthal's decision not to deny the image of spontaneity speaks amply to his self-promoting style and even to a bit of self-deception.[69]

Although he won that skirmish, two months passed before the confirmation vote. The toll on Lilienthal was heavy. He reported "lows" and grinding fatigue. He worried about the growing Republican opposition and shrill anti-Semitism. Perhaps most taxing, he and his fellow commissioners faced a never-ending stream of challenges. They were upset when Secretary of War Patterson unexpectedly appointed General Groves to the MLC, and on April 3, they faced the unenviable task of telling Truman how low the nuclear stockpile was. Lilienthal's frustration was heightened by the fact that he, the other commissioners, and Wilson could only wait for the crucial votes, first in committee and then in the full Senate.[70]

In spite of McKellar's badgering and Hickenlooper's doubts, the hearings were Lilienthal's to lose. McKellar failed to shake the testimony of the distinguished witnesses who came to praise Lilienthal. Nor was he able to capitalize on a group of disgruntled former TVA employees who appeared at his request. Even A. E. Morgan's testimony was a warmed-over version of his old, bitter accusations. Only Meads Leitzell's testimony seemed to threaten, but even that faded.[71]

Leitzell, Lilienthal's secretary in Chicago, helped prepare the Commerce Clearing House (CCH) *Public Utilities and Carriers' Service,* which Lilienthal edited in the late 1920s. During the hearings, Hickenlooper heard that Lilienthal had violated Wisconsin conflict of interest laws by drawing CCH compensation after his appointment to the Public Service Commission. Leitzell subsequently testified that her former boss had told her to tell callers he was no longer connected to the *Service* even though he continued to receive CCH payments. The day after Leitzell's testimony McKellar presented other documents that showed that Lilienthal had received CCH checks after joining the commission. Lilienthal was floored, and agonized about "how determined and ruthless" his opponents were. He had hoped his grilling was over, but the senators wanted to hear his side. On March 3 and 4, he wearily explained that Philip La Follette knew and approved of the arrangement; that others in Wisconsin reviewed the plan and a copy of the agreement was in the official Wisconsin executive files. His testimony was bolstered by a telegram from La Follette, which called Lilienthal's record "wholly honorable."[72]

There was more to the Leitzell episode than the testimony revealed. While Lilienthal's deal with La Follette was legitimate, it nevertheless seems clear that he violated the spirit of the agreement by continuing to keep close watch on his Chicago practice. Correspondence leaves little doubt that Lilienthal ran his office with a strict hand long after settling in Madison. Telephone and supply use, Christmas bonuses, and sometimes harsh criticism of Harry Booth's and Joe Swidler's actions: nothing much escaped his attention. If the committee had called Harry Booth, who was apparently disgruntled with Lilienthal, things might have turned out very differently.[73]

Outside the hearings, however, criticism was rising. On February 10, Styles Bridges attacked Lilienthal, and other senators, including Majority Leader Wallace White, Republican Whip Kenneth Wherry, and a half dozen Democrats followed his lead. Meanwhile, everyone wondered where "Mr. Republican" Robert Taft, and Arthur Vandenberg, the widely respected Michigan senator, stood. In committee on February 21, Vandenberg tipped his position by reading a forceful letter in support of Lilienthal from MIT President Karl Compton. A few hours later, however, Taft called Lilienthal's "confirmation a real threat to our national safety." Now, even with Vandenberg's implicit support, there was real doubt about Lilienthal's chances for winning in committee.[74]

But the tide began to change. Moderate Republicans, including Nelson Rockefeller and Senator Henry Cabot Lodge Jr., spoke up for Lilienthal. The press came to his defense with few major dailies other than the Hearst chain, the *Chicago Tribune*, Washington *Times-Herald*, and San Francisco *Chronicle* in opposition. At the same time, mainline religious and scientific groups joined in support. Finally, on Monday, March 10, even a reluctant Senator Hickenlooper, feeling strong sentiment for Lilienthal in his state of Iowa, voted for Lilienthal. A few minutes later the panel endorsed him eight to one; the only dissenter was John Bricker, Taft's Ohio colleague.[75]

One hurdle had been cleared, but victory was still questionable. For starters, Lilienthal and his fellow commissioners were stunned by a confidential FBI report that accused Oppenheimer's wife Kitty of radical connections and his brother Frank of a Communist past. They realized that none of them stood a chance if the report got out. Even without this fuel, the fire continued to rage. Bricker questioned Wilson's and Lilienthal's "loyalty to our form of government." A bipartisan Senate group proposed turning all atomic energy affairs over to a board led by Secretary of State George C. Marshall. Bricker tried to recommit the nominations pending an extensive FBI investigation, a move defeated by only thirty-eight to fifty. In early April Bridges urged Truman to withdraw the Lilienthal nomination in favor of Bob La Follette, Forrestal, Baruch, or Byrnes. Meanwhile, Taft continued his attack, charging that the Acheson-Lilienthal recommendations would lead to Soviet control over American atomic energy plants. The cruelest cut of all was the accusation that Nancy Lilienthal was a left-wing labor agitator who would soon join her father at AEC. Only a firm denial from Lilienthal and Nancy's resignation from the Department of Labor stilled those rumors.[76]

In spite of Taft, Bridges, and Bricker, two Washington papers predicted a successful Lilienthal vote. The key was Arthur Vandenberg. A few minutes before the April 3 recommittal vote, Vandenberg gave an impassioned speech on the Senate floor which thwarted the recommittal. In the hushed chamber, Vandenberg defended Lilienthal against left-wing charges and reminded his colleagues that being "in the top bracket of all Communist Blacklists . . . demonstrates that I am not calculated to be soft on such a subject." Taking a swipe at those who wanted a return to military control, he emphasized that "in peacetime we cannot drive science into its laboratories with bayonets." A week later, the Senate voted: four commissioners and Wilson were approved by voice vote for eighteen-month terms. Lilienthal won the same length term, by a vote of fifty to thirty-one.[77]

The next few days were bittersweet for the new chairman. He caught up on his sleep, and on April 12 and 13 took a cruise on the Secretary of Navy's yacht with Vandenberg, who asked, "What keeps a man in public service with that kind of provocation?" A few days later he was reminded that even sweet victory could not mask the lingering hostility. On the House floor on April 15, Nancy and Helen were attacked by those who could not get their father and husband. Chicago Republican Fred Busbey called Nancy "an active and sympathetic pro-Communist leader of the United States Workers' Local 10." He then suggested that the fault lay with the mother, not the father, "for Mrs. Lilienthal is reliably reported to have belonged in the middle thirties to several front organizations." Not wanting to forget the real target, Eugene Cox, a Georgia Democrat, added that "the appointment of Mr. Lilienthal to the Atomic Energy Commission is one thing that only God Himself can explain."[78]

Riding a High: April 1947–May 1948

Lilienthal's first year as chairman resulted in large personal triumphs and modest success at AEC. Popular *Collier's* magazine published two of his articles. He was on the cover of *Time* in August 1947, and later competed for the magazine's man-of-the-year award. His disappointment at not winning was tempered by the knowledge that Henry Luce favored him, and that the honor eventually went to America's undisputed hero, George C. Marshall. He was mollified by the publication in late December of Willson Whitman's flattering biography, *David Lilienthal: Public Servant in a Power Age.*

On April 19, he broke a self-imposed silence with his first speech since November. On the road for nearly two of the next thirteen months, he gave twenty-five speeches, including three national radio broadcasts and one on NBC television. He spoke to a half dozen media organizations, including the American Society of Newspaper Editors, the National Press Club, and the Inland Daily Press Association. Prestigious forums sponsored by the *Manchester Union-Leader* and the *New York Herald-Tribune* afforded further opportunities, as did appearances before the Detroit Economic Club, the American Farm Bureau Federation, and the Council on Foreign Relations. There was even a triumphant return to Indiana and a national broadcast from Wabash College in Crawfordsville.[79]

Lilienthal touched on familiar themes, but with a difference. Before, he had talked about the atom without an institutional base; now, he was first among equals among the atomic caretakers. He had also been bloodied— the confirmation process had been a rude initiation into the dark side of nuclear politics. He spoke with firsthand experience of the curses of ignorance, innuendo, and fear. In his first effort, a dramatic appearance before the American Society of Newspaper Editors, Lilienthal pulled no punches in what one newspaper man called "the most important speech of [Lilienthal's] life." He charged the American press with "a heavy and . . . sacred responsibility" of educating the America about atomic energy. In a speech repeatedly interrupted by applause, he left no doubt of his scarifying confirmation experience, telling the editors, "had it not been that the press . . . is overwhelmingly fair, decent, independent, and above narrow partisanship, your present speaker would almost certainly not be talking to you tonight."

Holding up a tiny vial of uranium with enough energy to run Washington for a day, he hammered home the point that the American people had a right to know and make decisions about the atom. The war was over. It was high time to think about "how much secrecy the American people and its representatives will accept in peacetime." He emphatically denied that atomic energy decisions were merely technical or industrial: "They are human decisions, decisions about human organization, about our way of life." Moreover, repeating the consultant report, he stressed that "this scientific knowledge . . . is not an American monopoly; . . . knowledge about atomic energy is part of a basic store of knowledge that is worldwide, and that other nations, including Russia will inevitably . . . learn . . . what we know." Departing from his text, he criticized the Soviets and domestic foes of an international agreement and hoped that "the time will come when in spite of all political obstacles to the free flow of news, in spite of iron curtains and iron heads, the peoples of the world will also come to realize that there is no security for anyone unless international agreement safeguards the whole world." The people of the United States had a right to know; the people of the world had a right to international security; the press, and recalcitrant "iron curtains," and "iron heads," were morally bound to respect and ensure those rights.[80]

He repeated the message over and over. A month later the Inland Daily Press Association heard that "we cannot make wise decisions . . . unless the public has an understanding of the fundamental facts" about international control, about the need for government monopoly, and about the possibility that the atom might soon contribute to the "everyday life, health, and prosperity." At another media gathering in January 1948, Lilienthal asked the press to ensure "that your public servants, legislative and executive, are held to the highest standards of performance, . . . [and] that atomic energy shall never become the victim of petty politics or narrow partizanship [sic]." In November, he told a national conclave of educators that they had to inform the American people or democracy "is doomed to perish." A few days later, at the annual American Society of Mechanical Engineers meeting, he emphasized that "technically trained men" had a special responsibility in this educational process.[81]

The Wabash College speech in September, before a packed house and a national CBS radio audience, was described by the New York Times as "a fighting speech." Disturbed by the shrill security debate, Lilienthal condemned the "growing tendency . . . to act as if atomic energy were none of the American public's business." "Of course," he continued coyly, the argument is usually "put more discreetly. It is said that the subject is too 'technical'. . . —or that 'national security' requires that the public be kept in the dark." Such thinking was "plain nonsense, . . . dangerous to cherished American institutions and for that reason dangerous to genuine national security." To be true to democracy, atomic policy making must be the province of "an informed lay public," not scientists and bureaucrats. Ultimately, "the strength of democracy" lay in open debate and public responsibility. In December, before the Mechanical Engineers, he argued that secrecy and security were not synonymous, and denied that "the more secrecy the more security." "Secrecy, applied in a stupid and hysterical and demagogic way," he continued, "can actually impair and weaken our security" by impeding the flow of scientific information and dialogue, and hence the ability to make further progress in the field.[82]

His confidence grew daily. After the American Society of Newspaper Editors speech, Dwight Eisenhower congratulated him, telling him, "You can count on me," and Supreme Court Justice Robert Jackson said the "audience hardly moved, the whole while." Lilienthal, as always fascinated by effect, wrote about the "thrill in holding a great audience . . . intently through 30 minutes." After the *Herald-Tribune* talk in October, former assistant attorney general Thurman Arnold told Lilienthal his speech had "wowed" them. In February 1948, Edward R. Murrow called a draft of Lilienthal's talk to the Radio Executives Club "magnificent." After that address, John Daly told him he "had the best stage presence in America." No shrinking violet, Lilienthal wrote in October, "I am about as good a public speaker, with as much to say and an effective, persuasive, emotion-inspiring way of saying it, as there is in the country."[83]

Talking about enlightened security policy and democratic methods was one thing. Achieving them was another. The lofty rhetoric of the lecture halls met its match on the treacherous Washington playing fields. Nevertheless, Lilienthal fought hard to develop security policies that respected the rights and reputations of innocent men and women. He struggled against a rear-guard military effort to retake control of the nuclear arsenal and against a wounded but still dangerous Leslie Groves. His relationships with the Republican Congress were tenuous, but by mid-1948, he established a working relationship with Hickenlooper and could count on Vandenberg's support. Within the commission he enjoyed the constant support of three commissioners, and Strauss's vote on all but one issue.

The security issue was most vexing. It was emotional, touched on substantive policy issues, and involved factors beyond the commission's control. Moreover, everyone, including the FBI, Congress, and the military wanted in on the game. One day in June 1947 the security bugaboo hit Lilienthal full in the face. He wrote that "Thursday of this week was one of those bad days when I wonder why in the name of hell and good sense I am willing to have anything to do with so ugly and insane an enterprise." He was struck first by the case of a couple, "their income . . . cut off and future clouded," waiting months for FBI clearance so they could work at the Brookhaven Laboratory. Later that day he was troubled by a proposal authorizing him to summarily dismiss any employee. Not only did such procedures deny basic due process, but worse, they "confer[red] the kind of power that is bad for the best [of] people."[84]

Another thorny issue that day related to sending atomic isotopes to European allies for medical and industrial research. At first opposed to the idea, Lilienthal realized by this time that sharing such materials, while a calculated security risk, was overshadowed by the "restoration of the international fraternity of knowledge." The question of instability and tension in Western Europe which arose in the context of security, however, depressed Lilienthal, making him "low as a duck's instep."[85]

The biggest blow came from headlines about security problems. At lunch on June 5, Strauss and Hickenlooper warned Lilienthal that J. Parnell Thomas, chairman of the House Committee on Un-American Activities, was about to publish an article on security breaches at Oak Ridge and call for a return of the atomic program to the army. That afternoon the FBI reported that two army sergeants had walked off with classified "souvenir" documents from Los Alamos in March 1946. While disturbed about the impact of these events on the commission, Lilienthal noted the irony of Thomas's call for military control at the same time "we find this young soldier [sic] walks off the premises, in Army hands, with hot documents." It was easy to speculate on the "coincidence" of the two releases. Walter Williams, Oak Ridge manager, suspected the AEC was being set up and warned Wilson that if the commission did not act, military control might be restored.[86]

Relationships with the military posed other problems. Preoccupied with organizational matters and confirmation hearings, the commission had little time to develop constructive relationships with the MLC. Still smarting from the transfer, many in the War Department found it doubly hard to stomach the commission's zealous commitment to a "civilian trust." The presence of strong personalities on both sides—Groves and Lilienthal most notably—along with growing Soviet pressures on Eastern and Central Europe and the uncertainties surrounding the formation of the new Department of Defense, only added to the tensions.[87]

To everyone's surprise, the first meeting with the MLC on April 30, 1947, went smoothly. There were disagreements about military access to restricted information and questions about why the armed forces had not yet established long-range nuclear explosion detection devices, but discussion was civil. Aware of the tensions, USAF Generals Lewis Brereton, who was MLC chairman, and James McCormack Jr., director of Military Applications, planned the first meeting carefully. Lilienthal was bothered only by the tenor of discussion "fascinating and horrible, but oh, so impersonal."[88]

However, even Brereton and McCormack found it impossible to keep General Groves in check and Lilienthal from reacting. The commissioners were still smarting over Patterson's appointment of Groves to the MLC. They were also bothered by Groves's position as commander of the Armed Forces Special Weapons Project (AFSWP), the unit in charge of all military applications of atomic technology. Holding these positions, the general had a strong voice in both policy and operations. Besides, Groves was a legendary figure with strong support from Congress, the joint chiefs of staff, Secretary of War Patterson, until his retirement in July 1947, and after that Kenneth Royall, first secretary of the army.

By midyear, Lilienthal was stalking the general. On June 30 Eisenhower told him that if Groves caused any trouble, "let me know, . . . and we will take him off." At a July 14 cabinet meeting, Attorney General Tom Clark reported that Lilienthal had accused Groves of spreading stories about lax security at Los Alamos and Oak Ridge. The same day, Lilienthal confronted Groves at an AEC-MLC meeting. The latter had asked for the meeting to find out more about the Los Alamos case in order to be better prepared to brief the press and Congress. Lilienthal, on the other hand, saw a chance to "smoke him out," and show that Groves had leaked information about the security lapses. Lilienthal rejected Groves's denial that he had talked to the press about the issue, and was perturbed by the general's assertion that "he talked to Representative Thomas . . . and always talked to newspapermen— and gave notice he intended to continue to do so." Late that afternoon Lilienthal marched his fellow commissioners and Brereton to Patterson's office and demanded that Groves be removed from the MLC. Patterson listened but denied the request, asking them to wait a few days until after congressional inquiries over the Oak Ridge and Los Alamos controversies.[89]

Nothing happened and the conflict simmered. At a July 30 MLC meeting Lilienthal goaded Groves about "thousands of [unaccounted] blueprints" during Manhattan Project days. In August, Groves fought back, suggesting that the commission and the new secretary of defense, James Forrestal, ask the president to return all weapons to the military, and for the rest of 1947 he tried to consolidate control by shifting more operational authority from Los Alamos to AFSWP Command Headquarters at Sandia, New Mexico. In September, Brereton advised Lilienthal that Eisenhower, chairman of the Joint Chiefs of Staff, might relieve Groves of the AFSWP Command, but was not keen on dismissing him from the MLC. On October 15, Lilienthal met with Army Secretary Kenneth Royall and Eisenhower—the news was not good. In the morning, Royall said he was unwilling to remove Groves from either the MLC or the AFSWP, insisting that "Groves was the best-qualified man in the Armed Forces," that his removal could start a political firestorm. and the three chiefs of staff wanted to keep him. Lilienthal countered that it was difficult to meet the civilian mandate with Groves around and threatened to take it to the country. Royall shut him off, saying there was no issue, only a matter of selecting the best qualified man for the job. Later, Lilienthal heard Eisenhower say he would have backed Lilienthal "but the others [members of the joint chiefs of staff] took a different view, and that's the score."[90]

By early 1948, however, Lilienthal's efforts and other factors, including Groves's abrasive personality, began to take effect. In January, Forrestal's staff recommended abolishing the AFSWP and transferring its functions to the MLC and the individual services. Later that month, Bush, Conant, and Oppenheimer met with Forrestal, and Lilienthal learned from Oppenheimer that the secretary was likely to act. On February 2 Groves announced his retirement and Lilienthal's long duel with the general was over. On March 11 President Truman marched in Lilienthal, Royall, and General Kenneth D. Nichols, Groves's replacement at the still-functioning AFSWP and told them he wanted an end to the squabbles between the commission and armed forces which had embarrassed the administration in 1947. He knew

Lilienthal and Nichols disagreed over custody, but he expected cooperation. As one might expect, Lilienthal and Nichols interpreted the president's words differently. Where Lilienthal saw them as a reaffirmation of civilian control, Nichols took them to suggest a future transfer of nuclear weapons to the military. The civilian-military control issue seemed to have a life of its own.[91]

Lilienthal's congressional relationships were touchy but, given the conservative tenor of both houses, generally good. As always, he showed disdain for the legislative process, writing of having "had too much of the legislative branch," and asking why he should "work so desperately hard while these thin top-soil boys [members of Congress] make it impossible to do a job?" Nevertheless, he was a skillful advocate. In response to Congressman Thomas's accusations of lax Oak Ridge security and the Los Alamos thefts, Lilienthal masterfully calmed the storm. In a July memo and in hearings, he convinced JCAE that security lapses could be traced to poor inventory control by the Manhattan District. The problem only seemed serious, he explained, because a diligent commission staff had worked overtime to uncover all discrepancies, present and past.[92]

Lilienthal often found himself at odds with JCAE Chairman Bourke Hickenlooper. In October 1947 one of the senator's staffers reported that both Lilienthal and Joe Volpe got a "chewing out" for "horrible Congressional relations." The senator told Forrestal in February 1948 that Lilienthal's speeches about future uses of atomic power and "his constant reference to control . . . 'by the people'" all seemed to point to "the perpetuation of Mr. Lilienthal in power," and "the general underlying idea of statism." Nevertheless, Lilienthal tried to nurture the relationship. In July, he praised Hickenlooper for restoring funds to the commission's appropriation, telling him "if it were not for your effectiveness frankly I don't know *where in hell* this work would be." Next April he took Hickenlooper's side against Truman in a dispute regarding executive branch documents. Citing the special relationship between the commission and JCAE, Lilienthal persuaded the administration to let AEC furnish the committee with certain files. The end of April, Hickenlooper took the lead in proposing a two-year extension for all five commissioners beyond the initial eighteen months. While resisting Truman's demand for five-year terms, Hickenlooper felt the wrath of many Republicans opposed to any kind of Lilienthal reappointment.[93]

By the end of May 1948, much of the conflict had abated. No more incidents of the magnitude of the Los Alamos theft or Parnell Thomas's accusations made the news. In December 1947, the commission established one of Lilienthal's objectives, a lay security board to help set personnel security standards in accord with democratic norms. Lilienthal was proud of his role in shaping policy regarding sharing radioactive isotopes. After several frustrating months, a Joint Policy Committee, made up of representatives of the State Department, JCAE, and Lilienthal, agreed on January 7, 1948, on a pact with Great Britain and Canada on technical cooperation. Groves's retirement and Truman's call for an end to the nuclear tug-of-war between the commission and military in March boded well for Lilienthal. And, within the commission, things seemed to be running smoothly. Aside from Strauss's opposition to sending isotopes to European allies, Lilienthal could still count on constant support from his colleagues.[94]

While frustrated by the difficulty of recruiting good scientists and growing concern at Oak Ridge over impending labor contract negotiations, Lilienthal prided himself on other personnel matters, particularly keeping patronage requests at bay. In June 1947 he told Clifford that under no circumstances would he hire anyone "if the man recommended doesn't meet qualifications, or there isn't any appropriate place for him even though he is qualified." In a most unexpected move, Lilienthal even asked his personnel head, Fletcher Waller, "if we are doing everything possible to recruit able women for some of our key positions . . . [and] if we cannot encourage this among our contractors." An early feminist he was not, but, as usual, he was not averse to suggestions even as audacious as this one.[95]

Gathering Clouds

There was another, less positive side. Lilienthal fretted over personal finances, and by April 1948 thought of returning to private life where "probably the income would be greater, and . . . the pressure . . . less." He and Helen were troubled because he could no longer confide in her as before. Unlike TVA business, most AEC doings were confidential, and Helen made it clear that she did not want to be a wife who "doesn't fit into the life work of her husband." Moreover, their home in Bethesda was isolated, the children were gone, and friends were harder to come by than in Tennessee. Lilienthal could no longer rely on the richness of his private life to sustain an increasingly trying public life.[96]

Internal problems also stalked the chairman. The General Advisory Committee regularly complained that the commission failed to provide direction. In August 1947, GAC Chairman Oppenheimer told Robert Bacher that the commission was derelict in "reaching broad determinations of technical policy." He also wrote of a rift between Lilienthal and the influential Conant "in which the gulf between them looked very broad and Dave manifested no great desire to bridge it." Later in the fall, the GAC complained that coordination lapses among field laboratories had resulted in serious delays in research. Finally, problems with contractors plagued efforts. Monsanto refused to sign a new contract to run the Oak Ridge plants in May 1947, and a permanent replacement was not found until the next January, when Union Carbide took over. In Hanford, construction delays by General Electric slowed the development of advanced reactor facilities.[97]

The frustrations were partly rooted in Lilienthal's managerial philosophy. Steeped in his "grass roots" philosophy and a commitment to public-private partnerships, he pressed hard to decentralize decisions in the field, maintain a small headquarters staff, and contract out most work. As Hewlett and Duncan observed, however, this "kind of organization . . . demanded imagination and creativeness"—and one might add experience and attention. Both Lilienthal and general manager Wilson were imaginative and creative. But Wilson had limited managerial experience, much less than a master like Gordon Clapp. Moreover, Lilienthal had little interest in day-to-day management issues. His 1947 December journal summation reflected his priorities. He wrote that the year had been exciting. The thrill he "felt most" was in his speeches, and "almost as exhilarating, . . . the writing of these speeches." Almost as an afterthought, he concluded that "there has been exhilaration, too, in seeing a floundering, mediocre organization change into something quite remarkable." Much later, Volpe observed that Lilienthal "was never one who rolled up his sleeves and did the nitty-gritty of a particular program or project." Most comfortable in "selling" ideas and concepts, Lilienthal left the important details of administration to Wilson, who found the challenge almost overwhelming.[98]

The commissioners also were bothered by their anomalous position. Appointed by the president to a civilian agency, they found themselves overwhelmed by military issues. At first they hoped the atom might soon be adaptable to peaceful uses, but in July 1947, Oppenheimer told the commission that atomic power plants were many years away. Lilienthal wrote that Oppenheimer's statement "not only discouraged hope of atomic power in any substantial way for decades, but put it in such a way as to question whether it would ever be of consequence." He expressed his feelings in the same December 1947 summation: "The pain of contemplating the grim aspect of my work, concentrating . . . on . . . an instrument for the annihilation of human beings on a scale and in a manner that would make Sherman think his definition of war was a great understatement." Even though he tempered these thoughts with his remarks about more rewarding activities, Lilienthal must have sensed that the commission would continue to face the same issues in the months and years to come. It was frustrating that he had to find his greatest sense of accomplishment in speeches full of hopes and promises not likely to be soon realized.[99]

Lilienthal press
conference after first
trip to Vietnam,
February 1967.
Courtesy of Lyndon
B. Johnson
Presidential Library.
Yoichi R. Okamato,
photographer.

Note from President Johnson to Lilienthal at cabinet meeting, December 1967. Courtesy of the Public Policy Papers, Seeley G. Mudd Manuscript Library, Department of Rare Books and Special Collections, Princeton University Libraries.

THE WHITE HOUSE

Dave —

I'll call on you for 10 min

When he & his team conclude 10 min from now. You may want to jot down an outline, for you to follow.

Lilienthal reporting about Vietnam trip to Johnson Cabinet, December 1967. Courtesy of the Lyndon B. Johnson Presidential Library. Yoichi R. Okamoto, photographer.

Lilienthal in conference with President Johnson before trip to Vietnam, April 1968. Courtesy of Lyndon B. Johnson Presidential Library. Yoichi R. Okamoto, photographer.

Gerald Levin, Development and Resources Corporation manager and executive, 1968–1971, present chief executive officer of Time Warner-Turner, 1995. Courtesy of Gerald Levin.

Andrea Pampanini, D&R Executive Vice-President, 1971–77. Photograph by the author.

John Macy, D&R President, 1975–79. Courtesy of U.S. Office of Personnel Management.

The Shah of Iran and his generals, probably 1960s or 1970s. Courtesy of James A. Bill.

The Shah aboard USS *Kitty Hawk*, 1974. Courtesy of U.S. Navy.

David and Helen, 1978. Courtesy of the Lilienthal family.

Lilienthal at Topside, July 4, 1975. Courtesy of Time-Warner Incorporated and the estate of Alfred Eisenstaedt. © Time Inc.

Judge Robert Taylor, General Counsel Herb Sanger, Retired General Counsel Robert Marquis, and Lilienthal at TVA Reunion, May 1979. Courtesy of the Tennessee Valley Authority.

Lilienthal gravesite, Martha's Vineyard. Photograph by the author.

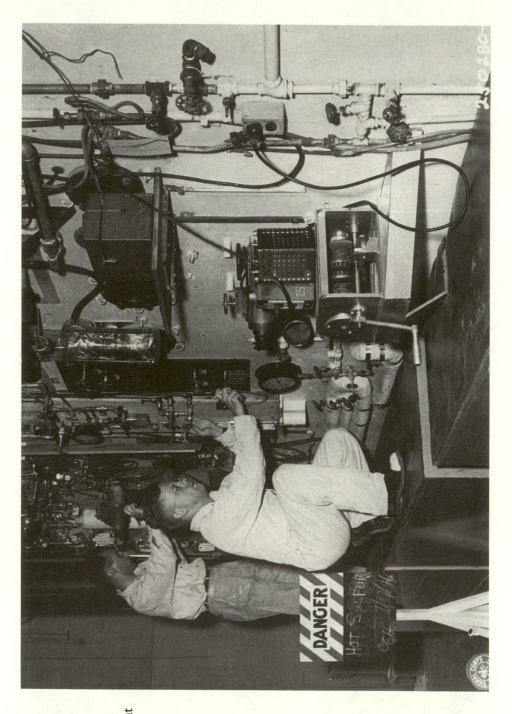

Production of radioactive isotopes at Oak Ridge National Laboratories, about 1946. Courtesy of the U.S. Department of Energy.

CHAPTER 10

The Atomic Trust: Reality

The resignation of David Lilienthal from the Atomic Energy Commission—and from government service after 20 years—is in itself only a footnote to history. But it is one of those footnotes which somehow encompasses a whole span of history and reminds us . . . how great has been the change in our way of living and our way of thinking over a period of time as brief as 20 years.
—Joseph C. Harsch, *Christian Science Monitor,*
November 25, 1949

Atomic politics were quite different from those of state regulation or regional government. Neither rhetoric, innovation, nor leadership skills worked as they had before. Lilienthal's appeals to public involvement and his protests of excessive secrecy and the effect of security on democratic processes were overshadowed by new crises abroad and rising anti-Communism at home. By early 1947 the heady optimism about forging world peace began to fade. By mid-1948, it had all but disappeared. Americans read with alarm of the rise of Communism in places like China, France, Italy, and Czechoslovakia, where their boys had sacrificed so much just a few years earlier. In the United States, national leaders sounded the alarm. With Winston Churchill's warning about "an iron curtain" falling across Europe still echoing, the president invoked his "Truman Doctrine" to contain the spread of Communism in Greece and Turkey in March 1947. Barely a month later, Walter Lippmann picked up Bernard Baruch's warning that "today we are in the midst of a cold war" and sent it across the nation in his widely read columns.

In early June, two weeks after the unprecedented appropriation of $400 million to Turkey and Greece, Secretary of State George C. Marshall unveiled another massive plan, this time for reconstructing war-torn Western Europe. The Soviets left no doubt that the Americans' concerns were well placed. In September, at the UN General Assembly, Soviet Deputy Foreign Minister Andrei Vishinsky accused the U.S. of warmongering. Three weeks later, Moscow attacked the Marshall Plan and reestablished the Comintern, the dreaded instrument for spreading Communism around the world, under its new name Cominform. Within months, Hungary and Czechoslovakia disappeared behind the Iron Curtain, and in June 1948, the Soviet Union imposed its nearly year-long blockade of Berlin. Americans were also aware that on the other side of the world powerful Chinese Communist forces were advancing relentlessly against the inept Nationalist armies. In response to these and other crises, President Truman had little choice but to increase the Pentagon's 1949 defense budget by more than 30 percent to $13 billion.[1]

In the meantime, an insidious theory of conspiracy had already worked its way into the American psyche. Shaken by the 1946 revelation of a Canadian spy ring that fed important atomic secrets to the Soviets, Americans became increasingly aware of the threat of subversion when President Truman issued an order in March 1947 mandating extensive loyalty checks in the federal government. Concerns reached a new high a year later when Whittaker Chambers accused Alger Hiss of spying for the Soviet Union, and then again in early 1949, when eleven American Communists were accused of violating the Smith Act and forced to undergo a ten-month showcase trial and the conviction of all eleven.[2]

Lilienthal was frustrated because he found himself spending more and more time on military matters. For the most part, that was what Congress wanted. And even though the president strongly encouraged Lilienthal to focus on the peacetime atom, White House visits almost always seemed to dwell on atomic weapons and national defense. No matter how much Lilienthal complained about military encroachment or overzealous security measures, no matter how often he spoke of the positive side of the atom, it made little difference. Those in charge were interested in weapons, and with the advance of fusion science, the even more ominous prospect of the "super" bomb. The General Advisory Committee's (GAC) warning that peaceful uses of the atom were a long way off further dampened his hopes. So did the ineffectiveness of the Industrial Advisory Committee he had announced with great fanfare in a speech to the Economic Club of Detroit in October 1947.[3]

Organizational pressures were relentless. The GAC criticized the commission in June 1948, calling the chairman's emphasis on decentralized management inefficient and counterproductive. Congress increasingly objected to the way the commission conducted its business, so much so, that by mid-1949 even Arthur Vandenberg's support had wavered. The resignation in late 1948 and early 1949 of Lilienthal's two choices to the original commission, Robert Bacher and William Waymack, further distressed the chairman, and introduced two new commissioners, neither of whom was shy about straying from his lead. And Lewis Strauss became more of a divisive force, no longer casting opposing votes in the privacy of the commission but now dissenting in public.

Organizational Crises

After a relatively calm spring, the summer of 1948 brought challenges to Lilienthal's cherished organizational assumptions. The most devastating was a GAC critique of the commission's organization and effectiveness. Since the fall of 1947, Congress and others had raised questions about AEC's strategy of maintaining a small central staff and allowing most operating decisions to be made in the field. In spring 1948, Donald F. Carpenter, a Remington executive and new chairman of the Military Liaison Committee (MLC), toured the field offices and returned disturbed about AEC management. He found that the decentralized structure placed almost impossible demands on the general manager. To achieve better overall control, Carpenter recommended greater centralization in Washington, giving division directors line authority over the field, and making them directly responsible to the general manager. On June 3, the commission reacted defensively to these recommendations, calling them impractical and impossible to implement.

The issue did not die there, however. The GAC came to Washington the next day with similar concerns. After lengthy discussion on Saturday, June 5, following a review of Carpenter's report, the committee detailed three of their number to compose a statement and authorized Oppenheimer to present it to the commission. Later in the day the physicist told the commission that "the situation is extremely serious" and "the original decision . . . to decentralize . . . was a mistake." After recommending a major reorganization based on "line rather than a staff organization . . . [and] functional rather than a geographic arrangement," Oppenheimer warned that the GAC could "be of little use to the Commission under the present organization."[4]

Coming unexpectedly from the supposedly sympathetic GAC, and immediately on the heels of Carpenter's critique, the statement devastated the commissioners, especially Lilienthal. Late that afternoon he angrily accused the scientists of complaining about things that happened in every organization. In frustration he wrote that "able men can run *any* kind of organization," but only with able help. Angry or not, Lilienthal reflected the real impact when he wrote late that evening, "I feel pretty *low*, frankly, but I will pull out of it."[5]

He ignored the criticism for days. Joe Volpe said later that Lilienthal "didn't think those long-hairs knew what they were talking about," and "brushed it off." On June 9 Lilienthal referred to the meeting as "the beating we took from the [GAC]." Oppenheimer followed up in a June 18 letter, emphasizing that the GAC was unanimous and that the commission should not "disparage or discount the sense of discontent, nor to ascribe it entirely to [committee] naivete." He reminded Lilienthal that GAC members were well versed in "administrative problems not too unlike those with which you are faced." His letter concluded that "organizational changes [constitute] only one part of what needs to be done." Better relationships with Congress and the MLC were essential. So was "the establishment of accountable and *intelligible* administration." Calling the challenge a "job for a man," Oppenheimer assured Lilienthal that the GAC thought he could do it.[6]

After hearing about Lilienthal's anger from Bob Bacher, Oppenheimer told Lilienthal on June 25 he regretted that only negative issues had been discussed and that the last thing GAC wanted to do was to destroy the commission's confidence. The GAC was proud of what AEC had done and was confident of its ability to meet future challenges. Somewhat mollified, Lilienthal admitted that "the medicine they administered so crudely and cruelly is having a good effect. . . .We are re-examining our organization." Ruefully, he wrote, the criticisms "made it clear that I must be much more active in [commission] management matters." This was a role he wished he could have avoided.[7]

After an intense summer, Carroll Wilson presented a plan in September which addressed the GAC's criticisms. He recommended dividing major responsibilities into five centralized divisions—Production, Military Applications, Reactor Development, Research, and Biology and Medicine—each assuming line authority over field activities. The general manager's office was strengthened by adding a deputy, and some security clearance activities were delegated to the field. In spite of concern by Lilienthal, Bacher, and Strauss that the director of the Military Applications Division remained a military officer and Strauss's objection to delegating clearances to field offices, the commission authorized the changes, effective September 15. In October, the GAC expressed a few concerns, but they were largely satisfied. The changes were reflected when employment at AEC headquarters rose from 361 in August 1947 to 699 a year later.[8]

About the same time, Lilienthal was shaken by serious run-ins with unionized contractor workers. Long a friend of labor, the chairman was now compelled to take the other side. Once again, the exigencies of military need and security forced him to a position he would have preferred not to take. Pressures built throughout spring 1948 between Oak Ridge contractor Union Carbide and the United Gas, Coke, and Chemical workers. Lilienthal realized, however, that the demand for enriched uranium would force him to take Carbide's side if necessary. He also knew that the presence of a Republican, Bourke Hickenlooper, as chairman of the Senate Section of the Joint Committee on Atomic Energy (JCAE) necessitated such a position. This stance was all the more difficult because Lilienthal saw Carbide as a "hard-boiled and . . . antediluvian chemical corporation" on labor matters.[9]

On May 18, he met with a joint labor-management group in Washington and emphasized that despite his pro-union record, national security made it necessary to back Carbide in keeping up production. To a local union spokesman who asked what the "little people" would think, Lilienthal testily responded that in the Tennessee Valley, there were no "'little' people—they were just people, and fine people." He was little comforted a few days later when Carbide officials expressed amazement that "this New Dealer had 'told off' labor to its face." He knew what would happen: the company would "break the strike, . . . and the way they will do it will grind my soul, and threaten my reputation as a labor man."[10]

On June 1, the commission publicly defended the contract system and offered a lukewarm endorsement of Carbide's position. Two days later Lilienthal heard that the Oak Ridge locals had rejected the company offer by a margin of thirty to one and authorized a strike on twenty-four-hour notice. The same day he spent two hours with the American Federation of

Labor (AFL) Executive Council and Oak Ridge union representatives defending AEC policy. In a highly charged atmosphere he stressed that as long as Carbide stayed "within reasonable bounds" he would back the company. In reply to questions by AFL President William Green and southern representative George Googe about what would happen if there was a strike, Lilienthal bluntly replied, "George, those plants must be operated, and whatever it takes to do it, that's what we must do." His own positive assessment of his performance was validated by the Council's decision that day to defer a strike until "every possible orderly means is exhausted." This small victory provided little personal consolation when on June 8, five hundred Oak Ridge Union workers opposed reconfirming any of the commissioners. Lilienthal reflected that while "the Oak Ridge thing hurts quite a bit, I don't seem to be too upset." Nevertheless, on June 15 the unions finally accepted Carbide's terms and a strike was averted.[11]

Lilienthal's pro-labor reputation was tarnished further in 1948 when leaders of two unions, the United Electrical Workers (UEW) and United Public Workers (UPW) refused to sign loyalty oaths required by the 1947 Taft-Hartley Act. Feeling there could be no question of loyalty at AEC installations, Lilienthal and AEC director of labor relations Oscar Smith worked assiduously, but to no avail, to convince the unions to submit affidavits. The situation was aggravated when General Electric (GE) failed to cooperate: at a September 23 meeting with the AEC, GE refused to withdraw UEW recognition at the Schenectady Knolls Laboratories without explicit commission orders because their contract with UEW prevented them from doing so. Lilienthal thought, however, that GE balked because of potential problems at other facilities where UEW also represented the work force. He and the other commissioners were dismayed to find that GE really wanted to get rid of all unions, and the company hoped that House Committee on Un-American Activities (HUAC) hearings in Schenectady would do just that. In spite of lecturing GE officials about AEC's commitment to loyal unions, Lilienthal sensed his words had fallen on deaf ears.

Having no other option, on September 27, Lilienthal advised the University of Chicago and GE, the prime contractors at the Argonne and Knolls labs, that they would soon have to withdraw recognition from UPW and UEW. UEW President Albert J. Fitzgerald attacked Lilienthal immediately, and on September 30, Congress of Industrial Organizations (CIO) President Philip Murray publicly went after Lilienthal. Lilienthal exacerbated the situation in an October 6 letter to Murray, claiming that while noncompliance was one reason for denying recognition, there was also evidence "of alleged Communist affiliation or association of various officers of UEW and UPW." On November 1, after a month of futile correspondence with Fitzgerald, Lilienthal ordered GE to "withdraw and withhold recognition from the United Electrical, Radio, and Machine Workers of America, CIO." Aware of the company's anti-union bias, he reminded GE President Charles Wilson that AEC had no objection to his company's extending recognition to any union willing to swear to "full and unqualified adherence and loyalty to the interests of the United States." The labor rights tug-of-war gave

Lilienthal little joy. He resented the contractors' refusal to act on their own and later admitted that his actions were "something I hated and will never entirely live down."[12]

One bright note for Lilienthal during the second half of 1948 was a final settlement of the squabble over weapons custody. In spite of Truman's attempt to settle the matter in March, things flared up again because of MLC chairman Carpenter's assertiveness and the growing Berlin crisis. The military argued that having control over weapons would permit better hands-on experience as well as quicker response time in case of a national emergency.

The commission still contended that basic policy was at stake. Throughout May and June, the two sides debated the issue. In late May, AEC and the MLC reviewed the custody question again. Thinking he had met commission objections, Carpenter had General Nichols present a transfer recommendation. The commission demurred and asked for advice from GAC and Los Alamos officials. On June 18, the two groups met again. Carpenter stressed that in light of international crises, including the ominous Berlin standoff, weapons should be in military hands, and he offered a joint recommendation to the president to that effect. Again, the commission balked, with Lilienthal arguing that a joint recommendation was inappropriate—the president must have the full range of options in front of him. Sensing that public opinion still favored civilian control, he insisted that any custody decision must be made openly. On June 30, the commission met with Secretary of Defense Forrestal and agreed that each group would prepare its own statement for Truman.[13]

The advantage was Lilienthal's—he knew sentiment was on his side. Clifford told him on June 30 that Truman, along with Budget Director James Webb and Secretary of State Marshall, favored civilian control. All he needed was the chance to put the two positions before the president. That opportunity came on July 21 when a large delegation from both sides filed into the Oval Office. For Lilienthal, "it was one of the most important meetings I have ever attended." Accompanied by the entire commission, the chairman seized the high ground by taking the chair directly in front of the president. Then he manipulated Forrestal into presenting his position first. Soon after, the military custody advocates self-destructed. Much to Truman's dismay (and Lilienthal's delight), Carpenter read a long letter and then started reading additional memoranda from the service secretaries and the Joint Chiefs. Truman interrupted, "I can read," and brusquely asked for the documents. Realizing Carpenter's blunder, Lilienthal made a very short presentation. He emphasized the president's commitment to civilian control and admitted that trying to enlighten him on broad policy issues was a little "like trying to teach grandmother how to spin." After three or four minutes Lilienthal sensed "the 'Judge' was inclined in the direction of our arguments," and he stopped talking.[14]

The other side blundered on. Air Force Secretary Stuart Symington continued, Strauss remembered, with a "rambling and discursive statement" that irritated the president. Reacting to Symington's criticism of a Los

Alamos scientist who did not think the bomb should be used, Truman snapped, "I don't either. I don't think we ought to use this thing unless we absolutely have to." A few minutes later Army Secretary Royall blurted out that after spending all that money on atomic weapons, "if we aren't going to use them, that doesn't make any sense." Sensing that the military had failed to make its case, Lilienthal kept quiet and simply handed the commission's letter to Truman. While Strauss felt that "both sides understood the status quo was maintained," the president was silent until July 23 when he announced publicly that the commission would maintain custody. For the remainder of Lilienthal's term, military control, at least with respect to custody, was no longer an issue.[15]

The Errant Commissioner

One of Lilienthal's most difficult challenges in his last seventeen months at AEC was the intensifying conflict with Lewis Strauss. While insisting he was only one of five commissioners, Lilienthal worked hard at being *primus inter pares*. His views on decentralization held until the GAC took exception to that policy, and he prevailed, perhaps to a fault, in keeping the commissioners out of day-to-day management. His views on security, civilian control, and the export of radioactive isotopes also prevailed. For a while Lilienthal maintained unity. Waymack, Pike, and Bacher almost always followed, with the latter confining his attention mostly to scientific issues. Strauss, on the other hand, found himself increasingly at odds with the chairman over style and substance. Ironically, much of the conflict arose from coincidence of personality. Both men had large egos and a capacity for arrogant bearing. Each was sure of his own position and stubbornly defended it. The major difference lay in Strauss's rigidity in following his principles—Lilienthal was more flexible and accommodating, traits Strauss often interpreted as expedient and unprincipled behavior, much as A. E. Morgan had years before.

Unlike his colleagues, Strauss was an ideological conservative. When Truman appointed him, Strauss reminded the president he was a "Black Hoover Republican." He had worked for Herbert Hoover for three years after the Great War and kept in close touch with his mentor afterwards. Between wars Strauss had been a partner with the Kuhn, Loeb investment firm and became a lay expert on cancer radiation therapy after both parents died of the disease in the 1930s. By 1939, Strauss knew many of the leading physicists, including atomic pioneers Leo Szilard and Niels Bohr, and was a major financier of physics research. In the naval reserves since 1926, Strauss rose to rear admiral during the Second World War in the Bureau of Ordnance. Unlike Lilienthal, Strauss was a practicing Jew and, according to his biographer, tended to be both "dogmatic and suspicious." Lilienthal was able to moderate Strauss's conservative tendencies for a while, but by mid-1948 they began to dominate.[16]

Their relationship was positive at first. Strauss praised Lilienthal in a

1946 letter to Clark Clifford. Lilienthal was also taken by Strauss's "light and warm" wit. During the confirmation struggle, Strauss frequently interceded on Lilienthal's behalf. In December 1946 and March 1947 he dutifully tried to persuade Senator Taft not to oppose Lilienthal. When the senator came out against Lilienthal, Strauss told the chairman, "Dave I have failed you." Immediately after Lilienthal's moving response to Senator McKellar during the confirmation hearings, Strauss was so impressed that he said, "That was history; the tide is turned." As late as June 1948, the Strausses and the Lilienthals shared an amiable weekend at Strauss's comfortable country estate in northern Virginia.[17]

Yet, the seeds of conflict were always present. Although Strauss, with his extensive wartime experience, was the only commissioner schooled in security matters, Lilienthal, with virtually no experience, almost immediately took the lead on that issue. It helped little, either, that their positions were diametrically opposed: Strauss was deeply committed to a strong security program, even erring in the direction of too much security if necessary. Lilienthal, on the other hand, wanted as much openness as possible in the atomic debate.[18]

Nevertheless, Lilienthal kept the peace well into 1948. For more than a year Strauss cast only two negative votes. In June 1947, the commission recorded its first dissenting vote, a minor one according to Lilienthal, when Strauss voted against a security clearance for a Brookhaven scientist. The first serious disagreement came two months later, in August, as the commissioners met at the posh Bohemian Groves Camp in California to talk over an isotope exchange program with the European allies. With the awesome redwood background, the commission listened as Strauss argued passionately that the program posed a serious risk to the country. The other commissioners disagreed, arguing instead that security risks were outweighed by the need to build the allies' goodwill toward the United States and by the possibility of scientific advancements. Disturbed by this "first internal rift," Lilienthal was doubly riled that Strauss insisted on going public with his differences. Such a move, Lilienthal felt, only weakened the commission's authority.[19]

In September, Lilienthal felt he had to act. Not only did the *New York Times* and James Forrestal know of the rift, but Strauss was pressuring his colleagues to rethink the exchange program. On September 25, Lilienthal confronted Strauss. The chairman explained that he had no objection to internal dissent, but carrying disagreements outside the commission or obstructing commission decisions would destroy the "family feeling" he tried to foster. Strauss apologized profusely and assured Lilienthal he was "through with it. I will forget it, or try to, though I am still not convinced I'm not right." While satisfied with Strauss's response, Lilienthal was skeptical: "I doubt that he will be able to drop it entirely; but here's hoping."[20]

For almost a year his optimism held—until July 8, 1948. That day, Lilienthal recorded ominously, "Had the first dissenting vote today for a year." The issue again was international cooperation, and the dissenter, Strauss. In response to Strauss's objection to the exchange program,

Lilienthal quoted Herbert Hoover to the effect that keeping promises, such as the cooperative agreement, was "the very fabric of civilization." Lilienthal added that he "thought it would be unthinkable to be in the position where it could be said we were 'welshing.'" Strauss angrily reacted and asked if it was the commission's policy to foster a program "to facilitate the production of atomic weapons by Britain?" Lilienthal retorted that Strauss was rash and inaccurate, and vowed in his journal to "to be much more stern and 'chairmanish' in handling Commission meetings, [and] to cut off diversions."[21]

A few days later, Lilienthal learned from Robert Lovett at the State Department that Strauss was "active all over the place" in opposition to the British agreement. Disturbed by Strauss's public opposition, the commissioners confronted him on July 20. After more than an hour of tense discussion, Lilienthal thought they had convinced him. But it was just wishful thinking. That day Strauss had protested to Hickenlooper aide Fred Rhodes. Two weeks later he sent Republican presidential candidate Thomas E. Dewey a detailed report about his concerns.[22]

Strauss became increasingly divisive within the commission. On August 18, he objected to a draft of a speech Lilienthal was to give on August 21 in New York City on international cooperation. Strauss told Lilienthal that his remarks misled the public into believing the cooperative agreement was more extensive than it really was. Chiding Lilienthal that "the frankness of the rest of the speech makes this omission notable," he urged him to admit that the British program was "primarily engaged in the attempt to make atomic bombs." Strauss suggested that Lilienthal was out of order in announcing that the cooperative program would soon be reviewed. That responsibility, he felt, belonged to "the President or the Secretary of State." Although heeding the suggestion to stress the limited nature of the program, Lilienthal ignored the other criticisms. He announced the upcoming review and did not mention British efforts to build a bomb. Later in the month Strauss criticized the staff for not keeping the commissioners informed about the cooperative program and accused them of rationalizing away errors of judgment.[23]

At year's end, Lilienthal sent a cheery memorandum to the commissioners about improving communications. To Strauss, Lilienthal's words appeared to be a thinly veiled criticism of his activities. At one place in the memo Lilienthal praised a new method of informal reporting because it kept the commission from meddling in managerial decisions "which it has deliberately delegated, and does not wish to mess into, for good and sound reasons." He suggested that the plan would not work "if each member of the Commission did not carefully restrain his special interest in this and that item, as it came up in the Commission report." In the margin of his copy, Strauss noted both statements with pointed question marks. Suspicious by nature and increasingly alienated from his fellow commissioners, he could have hardly failed to get the message.[24]

His suspicions intensified, as did disagreements with Lilienthal. Using "memoranda for file" to record his positions, Strauss reflected an increasing uneasiness over the commission's activities. In a December executive meeting, he and Lilienthal squared off on Alger Hiss. In January he joined Bacher in objecting to staff involvement in activities that he felt ought to have been handled by the commissioners. In February 1949, he noted for the record that Carroll Wilson had left his briefcase with top secret material at the Capitol. In early spring he deposited memoranda that revealed his deep displeasure with the way the commission had handled Hanford cost overruns, the lack of concern about keeping stockpile figures secret, and the decision to ship radioactive isotopes to the Norwegian army. On May 19, he was so agitated over the growing gulf with the rest of the commission that he prepared a list of "things done or attempted" by the commission and general manager over his objection, and asked his secretary to keep it handy in case he needed it in a hurry. Thirteen items made the list, including opposition to the exchange program, poor control over fissionable materials, security differences, shoddy management, and the fact that none of the commissioners knew of or had approved a British liaison office in the AEC building.[25]

Increasingly isolated and publicly recognized as the commission's "loose cannon," Strauss became even more defensive. At the height of the JCAE investigation of the AEC in June, he wrote a friend in New York that he was being sorely tested by some members of Congress and the commission "for having the effrontery to disagree with my colleagues on certain important issues." He claimed that he had "become the target of a sort of midget smear campaign, the thesis of which is that I started the investigation and that I am running it from the sidelines." On June 14, reacting to calls for his resignation, he wrote Truman a plaintive note asking the president to support him at his next news conference. Strauss even suggested the text for the president's statement.[26]

Lilienthal was beside himself and frustrated over his inability to control, let alone trying to persuade Strauss to moderate his positions. In January he wrote that he was unhappy over Strauss's attitude and that his "respect for him has suffered a considerable blow, not because of his *views,* as such, but the air of circumlocution." Less than a month later, after a series of sharp confrontations over the international agreement with Canada and Great Britain, Lilienthal came home from the office "pretty much in the dumps." The depth of his frustration was evident in a carefully edited-out journal vow, "not to let any provocation from my slippery playmate [Strauss] at 1900 Constitution [AEC headquarters] induce me to hate, or malice, or a sense of revenge."[27]

Wearing Down

Between June 1948 and June 1949, Lilienthal worked at a dizzying pace. He was on the road for fifty-six days, four more than the previous seventeen months. His itinerary included virtually every commission facility east of Chicago and an exhausting twelve-day tour in April 1949 of Hanford,

Oak Ridge, and the Argonne Laboratories. He continued to speak widely, and several of his addresses were reprinted in journals such as the *Bulletin of the Atomic Scientists,* the *New York Times Sunday Magazine,* the *Saturday Review of Literature,* and the *Commercial and Financial Chronicle.* Public exposure gave him personal satisfaction and the feeling he was doing what he ought to do as chairman. Creating words to be spoken was perhaps his greatest reward. In May 1949, after four days working on speeches, he wrote of the "hard work, with agonies . . . that rival physical torment at times," but, he continued, the process "has satisfactions that are full compensation." He was elated that speechmaking gave him and Helen "things to do together, which in appropriate moderation, is excellent for a marriage."[28]

The themes of his speeches were much the same. Openness and public education were the keys to democratic governance in an atomic age. But the tenor in some of his addresses had changed. There was a more combative edge, even in his more reflective efforts. At the University of Virginia commencement in spring 1948, Lilienthal criticized his generation and the present one for being most concerned with "tak[ing] care of number one," and urged the graduates to "be an active, living part of your times." Quoting Albert Einstein, that "politics is more difficult than physics," he suggested that responsible citizenship involved paying attention to "physics and politics, or more accurately science and government." Science, he contended, "is a dominant fact with which your generation must reckon." Being attentive to this realm means keep[ing] informed of the essentials, of the basic facts. . . [and] . . . *"the use to which science is put."*

Politics, on the other hand, is threatened by an unsettling reality—"our concept of what constitutes a decent society, our deepest moral convictions, our ideas of self-government, these are all the targets of the fury of extremism, of fanaticism, both abroad and at home." To combat these dangers requires "steadfastness and faith," and "great skills in self-government, great judgment and open-mindedness in the development of public policies." Invoking Thomas Jefferson, Lilienthal called for a "citizens' universal public service, . . . a fluid kind of citizen-service in which men and women move from private life into public service, . . . and then back to private life." Such movement would result in "private citizens experienced in firsthand knowledge of public affairs," and "public servants whose judgment will be enriched by recent experience in the day-to-day problems of private affairs." Lilienthal was elated over the coverage, including the publication of the address in the *New York Times* Sunday magazine. A few days later, again thinking of the current legislative process, he thought of "an additional angle"—term limitations for all Congressional offices. That way, "Congress [would be] refreshed with men closer to the stream of ordinary life; would end the terrible evils of seniority power in the only way I can ever see it ended."[29]

In September, the gloves came off. According to the *Washington Post,* Lilienthal "lashed out against attacks on scientists from 'petty or prejudiced or malevolent sources'" in a speech to the American Association for the Advancement of Science. Atomic progress was stymied because of the "increasing unwillingness of specially qualified scientists, engineers and management experts" to work for the government because of security restrictions and careless charges against individual loyalty. Again, he challenged the conservative strategy of hoarding secrets: "The notion that our atomic energy leadership depends upon a 'secret formula' locked in a vault, is nothing less than a gigantic hoax upon the people of this country." Maintaining that leadership requires "the very best qualified people. . . . We must have more of them . . . right away. Otherwise we face the imminent threat of stagnation." Coming on the heels of HUAC investigations of atomic scientists and Hickenlooper's denial that scientists were leaving government because they feared smear tactics, Lilienthal knew the speech would anger many in Congress. Republican HUAC member John McDowell said he didn't "think [Lilienthal] is telling the Truth. It's a 100 per cent political statement." Scientists, heartened by Lilienthal's remarks and similar ones by Truman about the same time, struck back, claiming that many of them were leaving government because of unreasonable questions about personal loyalty.[30]

Next June, in the face of increasing appeal to the "atomic shield" as the basis of national defense, Lilienthal answered with a scathing commencement talk at Michigan State University. He bluntly asserted that "neither the atomic weapon nor any other form of force constitutes the source of American strength." He then denied that "the strength of America" lay in its economic system. Echoing his "this I do believe" soliloquy, Lilienthal argued that "the basic sources of the strength of American civilization . . . are ethical and spiritual." The armament of America resided in the faith of its people in fair play, "the free inquiring mind," and "human dignity and the freedom of the individual." This, he concluded, "is the wellspring of our strength, this . . . is the spirit of democracy."[31]

Energized by speechmaking, Lilienthal was buoyed by other events, especially Truman's stunning upset of Dewey. At midyear he had been relieved by the adjournment of the Republican Congress, but sobered by the prospect of the Republicans' winning the presidency in November. On a night train to Chicago on Election Day, Lilienthal heard the next morning that not only was Truman leading, but Democrats Paul Douglas and Adlai Stevenson had won in Illinois. When he arrived at his hotel his first act was to write jubilantly, "Dewey has just conceded the election to Truman! And the Democrats control the Senate *and the House!*" Now, things might be different. In February 1949 he was encouraged by a positive *Newsweek* article about AEC, and his picture on the cover of the issue.[32]

Other circumstances worried and wore, though none more than the paradox of his own position. Lilienthal preached peace, but the atom of war held center stage. He wanted, perhaps more than anything else, Joe Volpe remembered, to take the atomic debate to the public—"He really wanted to open up and say more than he could." However, the limitations of national security and partisan politics severely limited his options. In September 1948 *Life* published "A Progress Report on Atomic Energy," a dialogue between Lilienthal and poet Archibald MacLeish. Based on a lengthy interview and a painstaking editorial job by Lilienthal, Helen, and his aide Frances Henderson, the finished product revealed a measure of frustration over atomic policy. Although the interview echoed the substance of his speeches, Lilienthal seemed more tentative and less positive about his role and the future. MacLeish, the artist, who characterized Lilienthal's words as "spoken thoughts," cut through the rhetoric, to the heart of the matter.[33]

Lilienthal began, grimly asserting, "We're worse off . . . than we were three years ago. Worse off because we've stopped thinking about the whole problem." Basic atomic policy decisions were being made behind closed doors. In response to MacLeish's contention that American policy was contradictory, preaching international control and building a nuclear arsenal at the same time, Lilienthal responded that the weapons approach was only a means of "buying time for the working out of a decent and human solution of a very difficult problem." One could only hope, he continued, that American preeminence in weapons and peaceful applications would lead to international control and peace. MacLeish then demanded "practical proof that the atomic age. . . can be not only peaceful . . . but free." After a long pause, the chairman replied bluntly that he did not know if the nation could succeed "without crippling our democratic institutions," and that "we'd be the blindest kind of fools if we didn't recognize that we *could* fail."

Lilienthal then emphasized the potential fatal flaw in atomic policy—government monopoly and secrecy. Both were necessary, but both threatened national and democratic principles. After more give and take, MacLeish concluded that "our whole hope for peace . . . [depends] . . . on the ability of this country to attain your interim objective. There are reasons, in your judgment, for believing that we may fail." He then asked if there were ways out of the dilemma of security. Lilienthal answered, "I have no doubt of it whatever." MacLeish asked, "Will we?" Lilienthal answered, a bit less surely, "We will if we see what the problem is. And see it in time." MacLeish wrote that they both sat quietly "looking at that doubtful future somewhere in the shadows . . . of the room." Then he asked, "On the basis of those answers, do you want to revise your estimate of the chances of success?" Lilienthal "laughed for the first time in a long day of talk," replying in a tentative voice, "Yes, I'd say we'll make it."[34]

In December 1948 Lilienthal did something that flew in the face of his commitment to openness. He persuaded Truman to quash an article on atomic energy in the *Saturday Evening Post* by MLC member Rear Admiral William S. Parsons. Parsons's manuscript tried to allay the "reservoir of unjustified fear" among Americans regarding the unknown horrors of the atomic weapon. In November and early December he shared his work with Oppenheimer, Waymack, Bacher, and Strauss, and received clearance from military authorities and AEC. On December 12 the commission met with Parsons about the article. According to the admiral, the commissioners "overwhelmed me in praise" but thought the article "*so* authoritative that, while it would be rightly believed by the American people, it might also have the effect of decreasing the fear of the atomic power of the United States in the Politburo." Lilienthal argued "that the American people should be kept in a state of 'benign' ignorance of the facts, on the chance that the Politburo are [sic] also ignorant." At the end of the meeting, Parsons assured the commissioners, several now swayed by Lilienthal, that he would not publish his article without additional clearance. Leaving nothing to chance, Lilienthal sent a memorandum to Clark Clifford opposing publication on the grounds that it would be unwise for a top ranking military official to downplay the value of the atomic bomb as a military weapon— exactly the same thing Lilienthal had tried to do in public. In spite of George Elsey's protest to Clifford that he saw nothing wrong with the manuscript, Clifford recommended on December 29 to Truman that the article not be published. The president agreed immediately.[35]

There is no evidence that Lilienthal puzzled over contradictions between his behavior in this incident and his oft-repeated public stance. Perhaps he saw a difference between the freedom of civilian policy makers and military advisors to speak out. Perhaps he saw Parsons as an interloper in his own prophetic mission. He had always preferred being the point man for the causes he championed, and it is possible that he saw the "peaceful and open atom message" as his alone.

A second factor bothering Lilienthal was his relationship with the president. It was nothing he could pinpoint. To be sure, he saw Truman less, and almost always about national security, but he was close to Clifford. Moreover, Truman was a Lilienthal liberal—the president reflected a "Middle West kind of progressivism, a kind of twentieth-century version of Populism." He was a man like Teddy Roosevelt, Norris, Bryan, or the senior La Follette, who "could not communicate with the more recent progressives with their great emphasis on language that seemed to him highfalutin and crackpot." And yet, in the fall of 1948, Lilienthal thought about voting for Dewey. His feelings made little sense, as he recalled "nothing but good experience with [Truman]." In spite of this, "the collection of faces in Washington these days has rather got me down."[36]

Lilienthal was also frustrated because Truman seemed less favorably inclined toward his agenda. On February 9, 1949, Lilienthal came to the White House to discuss the new AEC appointments. Not only did he wait for twenty minutes, but the president never broached the issue, talking about everything else, including TVA as an international model. At a May meeting with the five commissioners, the same thing happened. Lilienthal wanted to discuss atomic policy; Truman, again, focused on the TVA and international development. The new appointments bothered him the most. In early February he learned that Truman was thinking of appointing Gordon Dean, Senator McMahon's former law partner. The chairman bluntly told Clifford "that under no circumstances should the appointee appear to be, or in fact be, a political appointee." Later that month, he told the president that Dean had neither the experience nor training to be on the commission and that "his chief qualification was that Brien McMahon had sponsored him." Truman noted that the points were well taken and Lilienthal wrote, "I had a feeling by this time that Gordon Dean would not be appointed." Three months later, much to Lilienthal's dismay, Truman appointed Dean. The chairman reacted bitterly: "We will just have to make the best of what is clearly a second—or third—rate appointment to a first-rate responsibility."[37]

In late spring, personal tragedy struck. Lilienthal learned that Harcourt A. Morgan had been diagnosed with a malignant tumor, and he immediately wrote that "he has been a colleague, brother, and father, and most of the things that I know, or think I know, I have learned from him." Of all his mentors, H. A. had given the most. Through the AEC years he was the one TVA link Lilienthal kept up with a steady stream of letters and visits. In early May, Lilienthal told his elder friend, "You are my idea of a man." James Forrestal's suicide in May also hit hard. Although not close to the former secretary of defense, Lilienthal identified with Forrestal as an intense man, like himself subject to tremendous pressures of office. After passing Bethesda Hospital with its flag at half-mast, Lilienthal reminded himself not to "let this political fracas get you down." The next day, Truman, sensing "what was bothering me," told him to ignore the pressure or "you'll get like Forrestal."[38]

By the end of 1948, pressures were mounting. As early as August he mentioned resigning to Ed Murrow, a possibility reflected in the journal with increasing frequency. In a plaintive 1949 New Year's Day memo to the commissioners, Lilienthal admitted his failure to enhance public understanding of the atomic enterprise. He noted that "there seemed nothing I could try to do that had greater importance than to endeavor . . . by speeches, writings, etc., to try to plug this matter of public understanding." He concluded that "the results . . . have been disappointing and short of any reasonable goal." His solution was weak and uninspired—a public relations czar whose sole responsibility would be "to inform the public, to disseminate information that will foster public understanding and technical advance." This was a major concession by the man who believed that preaching about democracy and the atom was his responsibility.[39]

The job also took a physical toll. Joe Volpe revealed that in spite of his image as a workaholic, Lilienthal's pace slowed as his AEC tenure wore on. In late summer 1948, the Lilienthals spent more than five weeks on Martha's Vineyard, a tradition that began that year and lasted the rest of their life together. Next February and March, less than six months later, he and Helen escaped for nearly three weeks to Captiva Island. In all of 1947 Lilienthal had taken only two weeks of vacation. His fatigue was obvious in a March 1949 notation, "Pretty tired. Especially considering I'm just back from a holiday."[40]

Management pressures continued to mount. Determined to stay out of day-to-day administration, Lilienthal was forced time and again to attend to organizational crises. Upon returning from Captiva Island in March, he was hit with reports about cost overruns by GE's plutonium-processing facilities at Hanford. After intense scrutiny, Lilienthal became convinced that the problem was due to poor cost-control efforts and technical problems in handling toxic materials. Two days later, on March 20, he wrote that he was disappointed in commission management. He harkened back to the early TVA years, remembering that "organizationally [it] was a mess at the beginning, and for years, and yet its essential vitality and drive pulled it through." He reminded himself again that he had to avoid the "details of management," or risk "crack[ing] wide open, and hav[ing] to quit, or [being] so worn down that I will quit in disgust."[41] In late spring 1949, tensions started building again. Lilienthal hoped that the new Democratic Congress and the ascension of Senator Brien McMahon to the JCAE Chair would reduce some of the partisan pressures. Instead, they continued to mount.

"Incredible Mismanagement"

Helen and David Lilienthal marked the end of April 1949 with two rites of passage—the purchase of a home in the District, their first since Madison, and a down payment on nine acres on Martha's Vineyard. They were also pleased that Fred Arvin had dedicated his biography on Herman Melville to Lilienthal, who was ecstatic about a rough draft of his second book, *This I Do Believe*. About the same time, however, new rumblings about security were promising a miserable summer.[42]

The issues that sparked the controversy seemed minor. One involved an apparently settled AEC fellowship policy; the other the misplacement of a few grams of fissionable material at the Argonne Laboratories in Chicago. However, in the Washington tinderbox, they were enough to start a firestorm over AEC leadership. In late May, Senator Bourke Hickenlooper accused Lilienthal of "incredible mismanagement" and demanded that Truman fire him. Within days the JCAE opened hearings on the senator's charges, which lasted nearly the entire muggy summer.

The first controversy concerned an AEC graduate science student fellowship program. In June 1948, the commission had debated over whether to award fellowships to students with doubtful security backgrounds. Lilienthal convinced his fellow commissioners, except Strauss, not "to countenance the idea that political acceptability should be a criterion in our public support of education" and to consider applicants on academic merit alone. When he learned of the decision, Hickenlooper asked for an explanation. After receiving a legal opinion requested by Strauss in September, Lilienthal wrote the senator that the AEC had no legal obligation to run security checks on students if restricted data was not involved. Therefore, the balance between security and academic freedom could be maintained by restricting checks only on applicants whose research involved sensitive material. Hickenlooper delayed his response until January and again asked about the policy, at which point Lilienthal requested an immediate hearing. Once more, Hickenlooper, perhaps realizing his tenure as JCAE chairman was nearly over, did not respond. A reasonable observer might have assumed that while the senator disagreed with the policy, he had decided the issue was not worth a confrontation. That was not the case.[43]

In late April the controversy erupted. Senator Clyde Hoey of North Carolina blasted Lilienthal for giving an award to a professed Communist to study at the University of North Carolina. Four weeks later the press found that another fellow had once failed an FBI check. Starting on May 7, the broadcast media, led by Fulton Lewis Jr., joined the attack. Pundits from ABC, NBC, and CBS followed suit—only CBS's Murrow and ABC's Elmer Davis defended the program. The print media was equally critical, with only the *New York Times* and the *Washington Post* favoring academic freedom over security.

The pressure on Lilienthal was enormous, but he held to principle as long as he could. On Monday, May 16, at a JCAE session, he defended the program by appealing to the principles of academic freedom and nongovernmental interference in higher education: he offered an unqualified "I would" to Republican Representative Charles Elston's question as to whether he "would keep a Communist in school and let the Government pay?" Wednesday, he warned at the American Booksellers Association convention that "the direction and control and policing of thought and inquiry and education at the hands of political leaders will wither and kill the program of science and technology." But he could not withstand a Senate Appropriations Subcommittee threat the next day; without loyalty provisions, AEC would not receive a dime. Realizing he was stymied, Lilienthal finally gave in. That night he vented his frustrations about how hard it was to "mollify these fellows without giving up all sense of principle." Two days later, May 22, he wrote, with an eerie sense of the coming McCarthy days, "Now we have called a retreat—agreeing to loyalty oaths—but that won't appease those who want to drive me out. . . . Nor will it allay the almost hysterical fear of Communism . . . that underlies this. *A historic pattern is woven into the course of things*" (emphasis added).[44]

His dramatic about-face was precipitated by another bombshell. On May 18 a small amount of enriched uranium was reported missing at the Argonne Laboratories. The charge was all the more serious because the time lag in reporting the loss seemed inexcusably long. Thirty-odd grams of enriched uranium oxide, stored in a vault in September 1948, was missing the next February when the vault was opened. It took more than five weeks for the news to reach Washington and another ten days for the FBI and Carroll Wilson to be notified. While JCAE chairman McMahon was notified in late April, the rest of the committee learned of the loss the same day it became public. Needless to say, neither the JCAE nor the Senate Appropriations Subcommittee were amused by the delays. Still smarting from the scholarship pummeling, Lilienthal could do little but glumly agree that "the lab's property accounting procedures and our own are sloppy and lax."[45]

On May 22, the roof fell in. First, Forrestal committed suicide. Then, Lilienthal's most consistent Republican supporter, Arthur Vandenberg, announced he would probably not vote for Lilienthal again. Most devastating, however, Bourke Hickenlooper fired his broadside, demanding Lilienthal's resignation on the grounds of "incredible mismanagement." Emboldened by a flood of mail critical of Lilienthal, Hickenlooper blasted the chairman about the scholarship program and the missing material. He hinted, without elaborating, that "in addition to these two highly publicized fiascos . . . there is now perhaps even more serious evidence of malad-ministration."[46]

Lilienthal recognized the moment as "a tormenting business, and hard on Helen to boot." After a pep talk from Truman the next day and a forty-five-minute attempt to mollify Vandenberg, he took the initiative. He scheduled a press conference to refute the charges, but backed off when McMahon insisted that the proper forum was the JCAE. Frances Henderson suggested that he write the new chairman and demand time to answer the allegations. On May 25, Lilienthal worked feverishly to turn his original statement into a request for a hearing. He asked McMahon for a thorough investigation of Hickenlooper's charges, saying that they involved "nothing less than the security of this nation and the peace of the world." Lilienthal suggested several "tests" to judge the commission: how much better off the nation was regarding "the production and improvement of . . . complex scientific weapons," the "production of fissionable materials," the progress of "basic and applied research," and the state of security. He was proud of his record and asked the JCAE to call "not only the Commission, its staff, and principal industrial and university contractors, but also other citizens of the highest renown . . . for their testimony and appraisal." The next months were not easy, but as he had before, Lilienthal found the high ground from which to fight this last battle with Congress.[47]

McMahon wasted no time, gaveling his committee to order the next morning and calling Lilienthal to testify. Thus began three months of grueling, disruptive hearings, equally divided between open and closed sessions. The public record ran nearly 1,300 pages in length and included twenty-eight witnesses. Lilienthal sat through all but one hearing and testified on twelve days. The Washington office was virtually paralyzed because Hickenlooper, playing his cards close to his chest, or as some said, because he had no idea what he was doing, forced a large group of AEC officials, sometimes more than fifty, to show up every day in case their testimony or crucial information was needed.

Lilienthal asked the committee to "make a full report to the American people" and to let them make up their own minds about the charges. He asked for an expanded list of witnesses, including Dwight Eisenhower, Secretary of State Acheson, members of the General Advisory Committee, the top officials of major corporations ranging from General Electric to Standard Oil, experts in atomic research, and high-ranking university administrators from Harvard, MIT, California Institute of Technology, and the Universities of California and Chicago. He concluded by emphasizing that the commission welcomed rigorous scrutiny of his five tests, when measured where we started from "and the progress that has been made."[48]

His quick counter worked. Hickenlooper responded that he was "not prepared to present in any orderly fashion any evidence, but I shall be in a very few days." Lilienthal was ecstatic. That night he wrote, "The awful nightmare feeling . . . is over." Recounting the bright lights "and the biggest press turnout I can remember," he reveled that "Hickenlooper folded. . . .

The newspapermen enjoyed it, and you could hear Pete Edson [of the *Washington News*] say, clear around the room: 'Why, the ———.'"[49]

The next two sessions turned out even better. First, the missing uranium, minus a few grams attributed to wastage, had been found on May 27 in a misplaced disposal canister—there was no evidence of espionage, only careless handling. Buoyed by support from the Federation of American Scientists, Lilienthal gave a joint AP-UPI interview on May 30 and described himself as "pretty damn mad." He accused Hickenlooper of using "words calculated to arouse fear and distrust and a feeling of approaching collapse," and predicted that the attack of "scares and frights" could result in a "death blow" for the AEC unless it was defused responsibly.[50]

Meanwhile, Hickenlooper continued to dawdle. On June 1 McMahon asked him once more to state his case. Again, Hickenlooper stalled, first promising that "I shall produce the proof before this committee," and then demanding twelve sets of commission documents (including all the minutes of the commission, the MLC, and the GAC) "for examination." The rest of the morning and the next he queried Lilienthal in a desultory fashion about employees, high turnover rates, and emergency security clearances. Lilienthal deftly responded that turnover was largely a function of low salaries and scientists' aversion to security measures. To Hickenlooper's badgering over turnover rates, Lilienthal answered wryly that pregnancies had caused some turnover and that "this may be evidence of incredible mismanagement, but not on the part of the Commission."[51]

In response to Hickenlooper's charge that the numerous emergency clearances endangered national security, Lilienthal countered by distinguishing between security as "fences, padlocks, and safes, and of the examination of the backgrounds and loyalty of individuals," and security as "whether the country's strength is increased by the actions of the Commission." In response to Representative Henry Jackson's question as to whether as many bombs could have been made had the commission not issued emergency clearances, Lilienthal answered unequivocally, "No, the Commission could not." Once more Lilienthal was clever, almost to a fault. He piqued Hickenlooper first by noting that even Dwight Eisenhower had been cleared on an "emergency" basis. A few minutes later he quoted Hickenlooper's earlier statement that "the percentage of undesirable people who have occasion to have access to restricted data [in AEC] is remarkably low and indicates a standard that probably could not be excelled."[52]

By the end of the June 1 session, Representative Chet Holifield concluded that if the criticisms were valid, they should fall equally on all the commissioners. Jackson added that he found it strange that the turnover data had been widely available for some time and wondered why Hickenlooper had not raised questions earlier. In any case, the evidence showed that turnover rates in other agencies, including the Manhattan Project, were even higher. At the end of testimony on June 2, Lilienthal reminded the assemblage of Hickenlooper's lack of focus: in response to Republican Representative Sterling Cole's concern that the hearings might interfere with commission work because of the number of staff at the hearings (twenty-nine that day), Lilienthal asked for advanced information about subsequent hearings. Hickenlooper pleaded "the difficulty of trying to prepare a presentation and getting the supporting data only a short time before the meeting," but promised to cooperate as much as he could.[53]

While the accusations bothered Lilienthal, his aggressive counterattack and Hickenlooper's vacillation turned the tide. Before May 26, press and radio editorials ran against Lilienthal at about a five-to-four margin. After the first week of hearings, opinion changed dramatically, with pro-Lilienthal commentary outnumbering criticisms by about five to three. On May 27 the *New York Herald-Tribune*, generally a pro-Lilienthal paper, wrote that Hickenlooper had abandoned his original charges. Next day, the *Spokane Spokesman-Review,* which had been critical earlier, lamented the politicized turn in the hearings. In the week following June 2, the press became more suspicious of Hickenlooper's motives. Traditionally liberal papers such as the *Washington Post, Raleigh News and Observer,* and the *New York Post* and the *New York Times* criticized the senator for failing to back his charges. More impressively, newspapers that had been critical of the scholarship program or the missing uranium and had called for an investigation, including the *Philadelphia Bulletin* and the *Philadelphia Inquirer,* the *Omaha World-Herald,* the *Hartford Courant,* and the *Christian Science Monitor* also began questioning Hickenlooper's judgment.

By the first week in June, commentary ran more than two to one in Lilienthal's favor or critical of Hickenlooper. Joseph Alsop typified the mood, observing that "with considerable pomp but little precision, Senator Bourke B. Hickenlooper fired a barrage of peanuts at David E. Lilienthal." On June 1, the Headline Writers Association of America telegraphed the Iowa Republican State Committee, "If you can't elect a senator with a shorter name than Hickenlooper, the least you can do is to keep him out of an argument with Lilienthal." On Saturday, June 4, as he lazed in the sun at home, Lilienthal wrote that he was "relaxed and reassured deeply by the events of the past few days," and pleased that instead of a long ball, Hickenlooper had only popped "a short one to the infield."[54]

Nevertheless, the hearings droned on. From June 9 until the end of public hearings on July 11, press and radio comments continued in Lilienthal's favor. In spite of having an indexed portfolio of forty-three issues and charges, ranging from "Mr. Lilienthal's evasion of controversial correspondence," to "Lesbians" (at Los Alamos), Hickenlooper was unable to make his accusations stick. Nevertheless, the sessions were not comforting to Lilienthal. Some findings proved downright embarrassing, including GE's cost overruns at Hanford. It was irritating that the commissioners, with the exception of Strauss, had to replay the old issues about security, isotope exchanges, and the missing Argonne material. Also, the broad focus of the charges often deteriorated into a nitpicking investigation with trivial questions about how unrestricted sites were guarded at Argonne and the construction of garbage can pads at Oak Ridge. Lilienthal became increasingly disgusted, and wrote one day that "hearing gets duller by the day. Down to garbage cans yesterday—even lower, the slab beneath them!"[55]

The final days of the public hearings belonged to Lilienthal. On July 6, he quoted from the Book of Matthew that "a good tree cannot bring forth evil fruit, neither can a corrupt tree bring forth good fruit," and continued that "it is the theme of our presentation that very bad management can hardly produce over-all good results." In the last sessions, JCAE was bowled over by favorable testimony. Robert Bacher, respected by everyone, testified first. Then came General James McCormack Jr., director of military applications, and Mervin J. Kelly, executive vice-president of Bell Laboratories. The most impressive lineup came the next day: James Parker, president of Detroit Edison; Isaac Harter, chairman of the board of Babcock & Wilcox; Lee DuBridge, president of the California Institute of Technology; and the much-revered Enrico Fermi from the University of Chicago—witness after witness affirmed great progress in atomic science. By July 11, the open hearings crept to a close. Hickenlooper's bang was little more than a whimper. Mistakes, and even poor managerial decisions, were noted, but the charges of "incredible mismanagement" were smothered by testimony about impressive accomplishments. In late October, former commissioner William Waymack wrote Lilienthal that he should be happy Hickenlooper's "attack was begun so stupidly—to start big and wind up little is dumb." He gleefully offered Lilienthal the prayer: "Dear Lord, if I must have enemies send me dumb ones."[56]

Nevertheless, the hearings had a devastating effect. Lilienthal first wondered how he could stay on the commission with the "innuendo and fear," and then worried about making "a living, me with practically no reserves and a new house." On June 11 he recalled the nightmarish month and regretted blowing up at his colleagues because of "too much sleeping pills and strain." On July 1 he wrote H. A. Morgan that he always managed "to pick up some of the sweetest play-mates: AE [Morgan], Wendell [Willkie], McKellar, . . . and now Looptheloop Hickenloop."[57]

It was not so much the viciousness of the proceedings as the pettiness. However much a critic, Hickenlooper was not mean-spirited like McKellar. It helped little either that the hearings uncovered an embarrassing tale of overruns on projects that might have been better monitored by Washington. Lilienthal was bothered finally about the fact that he had lost the unanimity of spirit among his fellow commissioners, and perhaps even majority control. Through the summer Strauss continued his protest. Much to Lilienthal's dismay, he testified four times during the hearings about his opposition, twice in closed sessions from which the chairman was excluded. Nor was Lilienthal so sure about the loyalties of Henry D. Smyth and Gordon Dean, who had joined the commission in late May.[58]

On October 12, the JCAE voted along party lines that Hickenlooper's charges had no basis. The majority vindicated Lilienthal, acknowledged his distinction between security "by achievement" and "by concealment," and judged AEC successful in both areas. While recognizing the cost overruns, the report noted that the overall overrun rate at Hanford on fifty-seven projects was very small. It absolved the commission of blame regarding lapses of security, emergency clearance policies, and missing uranium. The report concluded, taking a cue from Lilienthal, that "the committee has before it an indictment which, on the one hand, says the results are good but which, on the other hand, insists the management is bad. How may good results and bad management coexist?" Moreover, the AEC was praised by the MLC, the GAC, the president, and the Department of Defense. Finally, the report noted that there was no evidence of an implacable rift—of five hundred recorded commission votes, there had been only twelve dissents. The minority report, which Vandenberg told Lilienthal had to be written for political reasons, was weak. Three pages long, it changed Hickenlooper's tune, now "direct[ing] these criticisms to the Commission as a whole," and weakly concluded that "we believe that the investigation was thoroughly warranted and that it has already produced some constructive results."[59]

Even as unequivocal vindication the report provided little comfort. By October, Lilienthal was becoming sure that the end to his government service was very near.

Endgame

Hickenlooper's accusations and the hearings shattered any hope Lilienthal might have had for remaining at AEC. In spite of Truman's support, a Democratic majority in Congress, and a favorable public image, the chairman was now damaged goods. Yet another controversy had marred atomic politics—the AEC was skittish and uncertain with two new members, and Lewis Strauss was also eager to resign; Lilienthal was exhausted and unnerved. At best his victory was pyrrhic.

Yet, the summer had its positive side. David and Helen Lilienthal settled into their home on Albemarle Street, and David Jr., a recent Harvard graduate, signed on with the *St. Louis Post-Dispatch*. On July 28 the galley proofs of *This I Do Believe* arrived. In early August Nancy was married to Sylvain Bromberger at her parents' home, a match that gave Helen and David much satisfaction. On August 18, they began their Martha's Vineyard vacation. The next month David worked a bit on commission business, but mainly tried, as he told "Doc" Morgan, to get "the misery and torment of the last few months quite out of my system." Stimulated by neighbors such as the Thomas Harte Bentons, the Roger Baldwins, and the Robert Duffuses (the men were, respectively, a painter, cofounder of the American Civil Liberties Union, and a *New York Times* columnist), the Lilienthals pondered their future. David hoped he could finish his present term, which ran until June 30, 1950, but he knew things might come to a head sooner. Helen was blunter: "If we have another [crisis], I'll resign." David admitted to "a funk, a blue, blue one about making the change to 'private' life." Things were uncertain, but the Vineyard seemed to raise spirits and brighten horizons. Then came the night of September 19.[60]

After a delightful evening with friends, Helen and David rounded the last curve on the narrow road before turning into their driveway. There, alone in the swirling fog, stood General James McCormack. After driving to the house and visiting with Helen a few minutes, the two men excused themselves. Over a couple of beers McCormack gave Lilienthal the chilling news—the Soviets had exploded their first nuclear device. An air force WB-29 reconnaissance plane picked up radioactive traces in the North Pacific on September 3 and, after two weeks of analysis, Washington was sure of what had happened. No matter how much he had prepared for this news, Lilienthal knew "the shock and impact, the recriminations, the whole box of trouble it portended."[61]

Lilienthal's reaction was typical of his behavior those last months at AEC. As he came to bed, Helen asked, "Are you troubled, disturbed?" David responded "Oh some; one of those things. Probably be back by night." After a restless night, he flew to Washington early, hoping he could get back that evening. September 20 was a whirlwind. Between his arrival at 11:00 A.M. and a last meeting at 5:55 P.M., Lilienthal conferred with the commissioners, Oppenheimer, Bacher, Wilson, Admiral Sidney W. Souers of the National Security Council, and Under Secretary of State James Webb. He spent a half-hour with Truman and urged him to make the findings public. His notes showed his intensity: "May I have permission to state views, despite fact that you have reached conclusion? . . . Advantages [of making announcement] would be three in number. First, would show Pres. knows what is going on in [Russia]; . . . Second, Pres. knowing and saying so would show him not scared . . .; third, would show Pres. will tell people when things come along they need to know that won't hurt being told." In spite of the plea, Truman kept quiet until September 23. Late that day, Lilienthal allowed himself to be persuaded that things were under control and that he should return that evening to his last week of vacation. It is difficult to imagine David E. Lilienthal leaving a crisis like this to others. However, it is easy to understand why he did so this time—the month of sea and sun had not really rejuvenated his body or soul. And, Washington no longer appealed—it repelled.[62]

When Lilienthal returned from vacation, he seemed refreshed. On October 13, he and Berlin Airlift hero General Lucius Clay, received Freedom House Awards in New York. Sensing this might be one of his last public appearances, Lilienthal spoke out forcefully, defending the principle of the summer hearings and the vitality of "the questioning process," but belittling the trivial nature of some of the "examination questions," such as those about Oak Ridge garbage cans. Then he suggested that the Russian achievement, hardly three weeks public, should force Americans to ask whether atomic weapons provided the best way of defending against Communist expansion. His answer to the question "What do we do now?" included stopping "this senseless business of choking ourselves by some of the extremes of secrecy," cooperating more with Great Britain and Canada, intensifying efforts to find peaceful atomic applications, and developing "our greatest weapon, . . . working faith in the spirit of men that we call democracy." He closed by citing the paradox of the atomic bomb—while it is erroneous to consider it "just another weapon," it is equally wrong to see it as "a simple and quick and cheap solution of our problems." Vigilance requires all free people to recognize Anne O'Hare McCormick's warning: "A solved problem only puts us in a little better position to attack the next one, [and] that responsibility has no limits and no end."[63]

Both he and Helen relished the moment. The *New York Times* commented that "it is good to turn . . . to Mr. Lilienthal's emphasis last night upon 'the very fundamentals of democracy—the need of the people for essential information by which they may steer their own course.'" However, optimism faded as pressures mounted to respond to the Soviets with an even more powerful weapon. Within the commission, Lilienthal was rapidly losing control. Strauss was pushing for new and troubling solutions to Soviet advances, and one of the newest commissioners, Gordon Dean, had started to openly challenge the chairman.[64]

Washington was abuzz about the Soviet explosion. What should be done?—greater production of fissionable materials, more atomic bombs, or thermonuclear devices many times more powerful than the atomic bomb? The fusion possibility was first raised by Wilson at a JCAE meeting on September 27. Two days later, with Lilienthal absent, the commission talked among themselves about an appropriate response. By the next morning Strauss drafted a memorandum to his fellow commissioners urging "a quantum jump in our planning . . . an intensive effort to get ahead with super." In the next ten days, Strauss lobbied anyone who would listen. At the same time, scientists long involved in fusion research, including E. O. Lawrence, Luis Alvarez, and Edward Teller, began pushing their own thermonuclear agenda.[65]

At first distracted, Lilienthal was more concerned after his vacation with new questions about British-Canadian relationships and Truman's refusal to approve a supplemental AEC fund request. Nevertheless, the fusion debate soon got everyone's attention—including Lilienthal's. Barely having a chance to digest Strauss's memo on Monday, October 10, he listened to Lawrence and Alvarez urge the commission to proceed with the H-bomb, and then wrote in dismay, "Is that all we have to offer?" On October 12, Dean urged him to act on Strauss's recommendation. Hoping to head off a panicky JCAE decision fueled by Lawrence, Alvarez, and Teller's aggressive lobbying, Lilienthal asked Oppenheimer to call a GAC meeting at the end of October to prepare a recommendation for the president.[66]

At the opening session on October 29, Lilienthal, not yet sure where he stood, asked the GAC and others, including Generals Omar Bradley and Lars Norstad, to help decide whether the nation should go all out for a fusion project. Emphasizing that their charge was to review "what constitutes the best possible assurance of the common defense and security," the chairman wondered if "expanded production plus the change in program emphasis plus super [the H-bomb] provide that? Or put another way, are we, should we be, in an all-out arms race?" The meeting was dramatic, with an austere Oppenheimer at the head of the table, the aging Conant "looking almost translucent, so gray [and] Bradley very G.A.R.-ish." Opinion about

"Campbell," Lilienthal's code name for the Super Bomb (a pun on Campbell's soup[er]), was divided at first. All Bradley could say was that it would have psychological value, to which Lilienthal retorted that experts said the same thing about the atomic bomb and look how thin that argument was. GAC member Hartley Rowe called the Campbell a Frankenstein, and Conant lamented that "this whole discussion makes me feel I was seeing the same film, and a punk one, for the second time." Isidor Rabi and Enrico Fermi made the obvious point that regardless of moral considerations, fusion research would continue. At the end of the first day Lilienthal thought that as many as five GAC members were in favor of proceeding with the project. By Sunday, the tide had turned—all eight recommended against additional development. Six members, including Oppenheimer and Conant, voted against further development, citing the threat of extreme nuclear contamination, the fact that the weapon could only be used for mass destruction, and the absence of nonmilitary applications. Fermi and Rabi concurred but suggested that the United States should try "to secure from the Russians a promise that they would not develop" the super.[67]

The GAC recommendation quickly galvanized opinions. Strauss became more resolved and began worrying about Oppenheimer's loyalty. Soon after, Dean switched to Strauss's side. Lilienthal, on the other hand, accepted the GAC decision, first hesitantly and then without reservation. On Tuesday, November 1, he had told Acheson that the GAC recommendation "did not seem very attractive or useful" unless coupled with a bold new initiative for world stability and peace. On a plane from Chicago two days later, Lilienthal sketched his thoughts. By this time, his views had gelled. He preferred to link rejection of the bomb with a "Pact for World Survival," *but* the issue was so important that linkage was no longer an absolute. At a commission meeting later the same day, Lilienthal announced he was "flatly against" the H-bomb project. By the weekend he had convinced himself to "disassociat[e] from a means of deception [continuing reliance on big bombs]." The next day, November 7, he took the fight to Dean, who had announced he would publicize his pro–super-bomb position. Dean complained of being ganged up on at a commission meeting that day by Lilienthal, who pointedly said that "we have gathered here because Mr. Dean has some serious doubts about the validity of the GAC conclusion." Nine people, with Strauss absent and the rest being against the fusion bomb, tried with no avail to convince Dean.[68]

At that point, Lilienthal realized the best he could send Truman was a divided recommendation. The rift was just too deep. However, the lobbying activities of the pro-fusion scientists, and Senator McMahon's increasingly vocal support for the project, made a report to the president all the more urgent. On Wednesday, the commission finalized their draft and Lilienthal took it to the White House late in the afternoon. Lilienthal, Smythe, and Pike asked Truman to rule "against the development of a 'Super' bomb," and to emphasize that "the development of this weapon is [not] consistent with . . . world peace or our own long term security." Dean and Strauss urged the president to proceed after attempting to make the

Soviets reconsider an international control agreement. In his commentary, Lilienthal argued that the super would add nothing to overall strength, and would detract from "the strategy of peace of your Administration." He stressed that producing a weapon of unlimited destruction would lead the rest of the world to conclude that "we are going far beyond any possible military needs, [and] . . . are resigned to war." In opposition, Dean wrote that renouncing development would guarantee the Soviets a monopoly, and that the "weapon might be the occasion for supplying a hypodermic in the realm of international cooperation." He concluded that the new bomb was necessary "for reprisal," even as "a decisive weapon."[69]

The president immediately called Lilienthal, Acheson, and Secretary of Defense Louis Johnson together as a Special Committee of the National Security Council (NSC) to make a recommendation on the super. Regrettably, that group, owing to the frequent absence from Washington of one or another member and, according to Acheson "the acerbity of Louis Johnson's nature," took nearly three months to get a report to Truman.[70]

Could Lilienthal have forged a consensus? Probably not. He was dispirited, and the mood had changed dramatically. A year, perhaps even months earlier, he would have taken his failure to achieve agreement as a black mark. This time, after dropping the split decision off at the White House, he exulted, "I feel wonderful." Strauss's continued opposition was trouble enough, but by the end of October, Dean was writing long memoranda to his fellow commissioners obliquely criticizing Lilienthal's "hands off" management style. On November 5 Lilienthal wrote plaintively to former commissioner Bill Waymack that "the Spirit we had the first 6 or 8 months would help now, but it's not that, and nothing I can do seems to change it much: two direct pipe lines [in seeming reference to Strauss and Dean] is about two too much, for one thing." Even if Lilienthal had sensed an eventual consensus, time was short. Super-bomb proponents were pushing McMahon and others on the JCAE. Lilienthal thought Truman had to have some basis to resist "a blitz to get a quick decision."[71]

Lilienthal's friends were also concerned. John Manley, associate director at Los Alamos and GAC secretary, wrote in his diary that at the GAC meeting, Pike said Lilienthal no longer had much drive. Pike feared, said Manley, that telling the chairman this would only "enforce the conviction of Mr. Lilienthal that he was physically not equal to the task of carrying on the Chairmanship." Oppenheimer was worried "as to whether Lilienthal had enough drive, stamina and courage left to get enthused about the matter of the super-bomb and to carry it through." And everything was colored by Lilienthal's announcement to Truman on November 7 that "it was time to look for a successor."[72]

The decision to resign was predictable. Lilienthal had explored the lecture circuit with W. Colston Leigh in late October, and Robert Hutchins offered him the dean of law position at the University of Chicago in November. Four days after telling Truman of his plans, he chatted with an equally restless Clark Clifford about practicing law together. On Saturday, November 18, in the face of growing controversy, Clifford told him to give

Truman a firm letter of resignation, or face the possibility of having "to leave under fire." The next day Lilienthal wept as he composed the letter, but concluded that he had "no regrets; just the usual one that after so long a time, such a change stirs something in me." On Monday he resigned, effective December 31, and two days later Truman graciously announced the decision. Public response was overwhelming. Scores of papers were full of praise about Lilienthal—only a few were critical. Lilienthal was thrilled that Wednesday broadcasts and Thursday papers were "very friendly, nice touch, no talk of my 'running out.'" Even Hickenlooper and the critical *Chicago Tribune* were gracious. Eleanor Roosevelt, in a *Washington News* column, lamented the "loss of a courageous public servant," and Adolf Berle wrote Lilienthal, "I have come to regard you . . . as a great fixture in management of huge and dynamic government enterprise." By Friday, job and lecture offers were pouring in.[73]

No one was more pleased than Helen. On November 26, she recounted in a letter to Nancy and David Jr. that on Wednesday afternoon, she had opened the door to a young reporter who asked, "'Is Mr. L. home?' I said 'No.' He said 'Do you think he will come home?' 'Well,' I said, 'he always has so far.'" The reporter then asked if she had heard the resignation news, to which Helen replied "Oh, I've heard rumors, but I've learned not to pay too much attention to rumors about my husband." That evening she watched a broadcast with Lilienthal and Edward R. Murrow—she "sat in the room with . . . an engineer. . . . [David] told the press my comment about a tin cup [Helen joked that she was going to give him a tin cup as a resignation gift] and they added the pencils." The last lines of the letter were reassuring signs of their faith in the future and the direction of his thinking: "But I think he really is not worried about the future. he is determined to take on nothing that will prevent him doing the sort of public jobs from time to time he may have a chance to do." The future seemed to be taking care of itself. Lilienthal lacked no end of prospects. *Life, Collier's*, and *Reader's Digest* all made lucrative offers. Other offers and feelers poured in from prestigious law firms, banks, and universities.[74]

Perhaps his greatest pleasure that fall came in seeing *This I Do Believe* in print. Helen had worked more than a year weaving her husband's speeches since 1933 into a thematic whole. The book began with his memorable words at the 1947 confirmation hearings and concluded with a ringing endorsement of democracy, American style. All the themes were there: public involvement, TVA-style decentralized administration, faith in people, and universal service. So were the villains—oppressive secrecy and security, and the problem of congressional domination of executive decision making. Noted by publications such as the *New York Times,* the *Annals of the American Academy of Political and Social Sciences,* and *Christian Century*, the reviews, with a few exceptions, were mainly positive. One called the thin volume "inspirational," another, "packed with ideas for putting democracy into greater practice." Norman Cousins labeled it a primer for the young, and the *Annals* reviewer predicted that it would become "another book in the Bible of democracy." In the *New York Herald Tribune,* Henry

Steele Commager recommended that every congressman ponder Lilienthal's thoughts on "the invasion by Congress of what is properly the executive department." The *Review of Politics* praised the book as "words of hard-won wisdom that we will continue to ignore at our own peril," and for suggesting a healthy circulation of elites through decentralized administration and the idea of the citizen-servant.[75]

In spite of the accolades, there were critical undercurrents in the reviews. Some reviewers noted the lack of depth, continuity, and concrete examples about strengthening democracy. Cousins wrote that "not enough attention has been given to the basic conditions that make a democracy possible," and Commager noted that it "deals with a miscellany of subjects held together, rather tenuously, by the common theme of making democracy work." Others complained that the optimistic tone "reflect[ed] an almost religious faith," that obscures an "appraisal of the obstacles confronting modern democracy." The *Canadian Forum* was incensed by Lilienthal's statement that "it would be wholesome if we were to revive that good old-fashioned custom of bragging about America." The reviewer asked, "When has that custom ever been allowed to die? . . . Certainly not in this book," and continued that "the most distressing. . . feature [is that the book lacks] . . . even the beginning of an attempt to think on anything but the national level." The *Christian Science Monitor* also questioned the call to "bragging," complaining that Lilienthal's recommendations about "a greater America" could have been much more specific.[76]

The positive reception of *This I Do Believe* reflected the strength of Lilienthal's words, reputation, and Helen's editing skills. The critical undertones of the reviews suggested there was some truth to Lilienthal's concern that the manuscript needed a more explicit theme. About the time of publication, he worried that the book might be seen as "a collection or compilation of twice-told things." Unfortunately, it was to an extent. Worse, some of the old themes, the argument that low power rates led to higher consumption and even lower rates, for example, were only well-worn truisms. One chapter optimistically mentioned "the coming of electricity from atomic power" almost as a foregone conclusion. Certainly Lilienthal might have been optimistic before Oppenheimer advised him mid-1948 that peaceful power was many years away, but not after—and the book was published more than a year after Oppenheimer's gloomy news.[77]

The real import of *This I Do Believe* was perhaps best captured in an exchange of letters between Frankfurter and British Broadcasting System (BBC) executive George Barnes in January 1950. Barnes wrote that he had considered asking Lilienthal to give the Reith lectures, but had second thoughts after reading *This I Do Believe*, which seemed to be a book "of a tired man who is merely giving fresh shape to the ideas he had propounded with much greater force and clarity while he was in T.V.A." He asked the Justice, "Am I right to be so critical of the book? Does it fairly represent him as he is now?" Frankfurter praised Lilienthal but told Barnes that twenty years on the firing line "takes the stuffings out of a man," and that

Lilienthal "need[ed] the refreshment of spirit which can only come from adequate leisure and a long stretch of freedom." Frankfurter was clear that he did "not think that in the immediate future [Lilienthal] will be ready for such searching reflections on the meaning of his experiences as could be distilled into fitting Reith Lectures."[78]

This I Do Believe was a commendable volume, and Lilienthal was pleased that it provided Helen an outlet for her literary skills. Nevertheless, given their decision to use only material from the speeches and David's fleeting attention to the manuscript, there was only so much she could do. In the end, the book was only a modest success, one hardback edition and nothing in paperback. It is interesting to note that in all the later journals there are only two references to *This I Do Believe,* in contrast to scores to *TVA: Democracy on the March.*

In December Lilienthal began to wind down commission business. By January 1950, as Hewlett and Duncan noted, "Lilienthal had all but retired from the scene." Routine business was handled by Acting Chairman Sumner Pike. Lilienthal spent much of January working on a lecture circuit agenda and finalizing a $60,000 contract with *Collier's*. He took off two weeks, spending a few days with his parents in Daytona Beach, giving two speeches before local groups, much to Leo and Minna's delight; then spent a week on Captiva Island, Helen and David's favorite winter getaway.[79]

At Truman's request, however, Lilienthal remained active in the H-bomb talks. Indeed, when Lilienthal proffered his resignation, he assured the president that the Special NSC Committee report would be ready by December 31. Lilienthal even promised to stay on a couple of weeks after if necessary. On December 22, however, he informed Truman the report would not be ready on time, and the president asked him to extend his tenure to February 1. Since Clifford had announced that as his departure date, Lilienthal suggested it might be better if he left on February 15.[80]

At first the prospects for a cautious approach to fusion seemed hopeful. Acheson was sympathetic to the idea that a comprehensive approach to national and world security and not just a single weapon would be the best way to proceed. However, the committee delayed meeting until December 22, at which time Johnson and the military representatives enraged Lilienthal when they described the decision as merely technical. Lilienthal responded with the larger philosophical and moral arguments, a position that now even to Acheson "appeared less persuasive as one examined it critically." Meanwhile, other informal groups from the military, national security agencies, and the AEC were staking out their positions.[81]

By mid-January, the tide turned decisively in favor of fusion. The military took a firm position. In the break between sessions, JCAE members visited the field and talked with H-bomb advocates and appeared ready to approve the project. Even the State Department, more reluctant perhaps because of Acheson, was ready to go along. Lilienthal's opinions carried little weight anymore. Acheson's committee, which might have provided a base for the departing chairman, had met only once, and then inconclusively. Lilienthal seemed less and less interested in affairs of state, spending more time exploring future opportunities and on his own private affairs in Florida than on the one issue he was still involved with, the H-bomb.

Even when in Washington, his efforts seemed desultory and half-hearted. Lilienthal visited with Acheson and Truman, and only weakly defended his position. On Friday, January 27, the JCAE heard from the commission. Lilienthal's testimony regarding the issue was pallid compared to past performances. When he finished, he turned things over to Commissioner Harry Smyth and left. When committee members pressed the other commissioners on how they now felt about the Super Bomb, all they did was repeat their position from their recommendation to Truman on November 9.

The denouement came on January 31 when the NSC committee met for a second time. Two days before, Lilienthal wrote of the coming showdown. Recognizing that this might be his last chance, he hoped for a decision affirming "that gadgets won't give us security alone." The meeting was tense. Acheson proposed going ahead and making the decision public. Johnson objected to a provision that production be delayed until research was completed. Lilienthal then launched into an extended statement in which he seemed to reverse himself on whether or not to build the Super Bomb. The central questions were not moral, nor did they focus on whether "we should build the super bomb or not build it." Instead, Lilienthal pleaded that the central problem lay in putting the cart before the horse—deciding to approve a vast new weapons system before evaluating present weaknesses and coming to grips with overall defense policy. Acheson found little to disagree with, but realized that two facts demanded immediate action: "Delaying research would not delay Soviet research." Moreover, "the American people simply would not tolerate delaying nuclear research in so vital a matter."

After editorial changes, the paper was signed by the committee, including, much to Acheson's surprise, Lilienthal. The three, along with Admiral Souers, walked over to see Truman. Lilienthal asked again to express his concerns. Before long, Truman silenced Lilienthal, observing that since the issue was now public, he had no option but to move ahead. Later that day he instructed State and Defense to proceed. Needless to say, the departing chairman was disappointed but not bitter. He praised Acheson and Truman in the journal and that evening asked disillusioned GAC members not to resign in protest.[82]

Lilienthal's last two weeks passed quietly. On February 14 he told Truman he would continue to support the administration's atomic energy policies. After a round of parties that day and the next, he said his farewells and took the long walk down the steps of the old Public Health Building at 1900 Constitution Avenue. That was his last farewell to full-time public service, but by no means an end to a concern with atomic politics, which he considered an important public issue until the last summer of his life.[83]

A Whole Span of History

On February 15, 1950, Lilienthal's official public life came to a close. Nearly twenty years had passed since that enthusiastic but tentative move from the comforts of established law practice to the uncertain circumstances of public life in Wisconsin. Between March 1931 and February 1950, Helen and David experienced and shared in a major transformation of American life. They witnessed the miasma of economic depression and Philip La Follette's heroic but often futile efforts to use government to hasten the recovery. They shared an uncertain adventure with a new, obscure public agency and saw that agency become a worldwide symbol of beneficent public enterprise. And they suffered through the painful years of the late 1940s, a time when the atomic promise burned brightly at first, but when in the end, the fire of thermonuclear oblivion seemed even more possible.

Lilienthal exemplified three public roles; administrative champion of positive government, rhetorical leader, and disciple of openness and turbulence. His role as advocate of positive government was best captured by Joseph C. Harsch's November 1949 editorial in the *Christian Science Monitor*. To the columnist, Lilienthal represented the transformation of the American "way of living and . . . thinking" since the 1930s. His enemies despised him because they saw "in him the symbol and the heart of the thing they have most wished to keep from the American scene." To be sure, Roosevelt was the grand architect of the change from a "private enterprise capitalist country" to one where the norm was no longer "capitalism in its original or dominant form." But Lilienthal was a doer, one who, as Bishop G. Bromley Oxnam said, melded "faith, purpose, and action" into successful public-regarding enterprises at TVA and then, in his bittersweet years at AEC. Harsch continued that "the ideas Mr. Lilienthal executed have come to be such an established . . . part of our national existence that most Americans . . today no longer realize that only a generation ago the idea of government in business seemed to a majority of Americans either absurd or vicious." In the end, Harsch applauded Lilienthal and noted that "he is the logical target of all believers in the lost cause. From that kind of personal battle he steps aside."[84]

The greatest weapon in his arsenal, the one that abetted his powers of persuasion best, was his brilliant rhetoric. Bishop Oxnam described Lilienthal as an administrator who "caused words to unbend." Less poetically, but with more precision, Jameson Doig and Erwin Hargrove called him one of America's finest twentieth-century "Rhetorical Leaders," a man who used voice and pen "as the chief means of winning support for and creating cohesion within the organizations he led." From the "Mission of the Jew" speech at DePauw to his incisive style as essayist for *The New Republic* and scholarly writing for the *Harvard Law Review* in the 1920s; from the uncanny brilliance of *TVA: Democracy on the March*, arguably the best crafted defense of positive government since the *Federalist Papers* to his frenetic stump in the late 1940s on behalf of open atomic policy making, Lilienthal used language to maximum advantage.[85]

To be sure, his rhetorical skills did not always prevail. He toyed with the "grass roots" notion at AEC, but it failed in a far-flung bureaucratic empire without popular sources of support. Moreover, he often came under the spell of his own rhetoric. Joe Volpe praised Lilienthal's effort to speak out about America's passage through the Scylla and Charybdis–like straits of atomic policy, but he also felt that in his opposition to the H-bomb Lilienthal "got caught up a little bit" in his own rhetoric. According to Volpe, "They [also referring to Oppenheimer and his opposition to the H-bomb] preached these lofty ideas. They got engaged in kind of believing their own rhetoric. But, . . . they never stopped to think that there was simply no way anyone could stop research and development."[86]

As self-beguiling, or perhaps even self-serving, as his rhetorical skills may have been, they were the key to his commitment to the public realm. Looking back, it hardly seemed likely that AEC could have provided a platform from which to encourage openness and debate. Neither grass roots rhetoric nor reality was appropriate in a necessarily secretive agency with no natural constituency. Moreover, there was no need for such a doctrine to serve as a protective ideology. AEC, as an agency, had few natural enemies (in comparison with TVA in its first decade) and was more consistently supported by the president than TVA had been in the 1930s. Whereas the authority was a symbol of regional progress, AEC evoked the image of national will locked in a deadly race with the Soviet Union.

Nevertheless, Lilienthal's five-year association with the atom was marked by a firm commitment to open debate and public access. He was first concerned with the destructive consequences of secrecy—the public realm was diminished when the free flow of knowledge was impeded, even by positive government. At the Chicago conference barely a month after Hiroshima and Nagasaki, he stressed that "unless the people are properly informed of the facts, the resulting public policy regarding the atomic bomb will be neither sound nor enduring." Yet, he was also a realist. Two years later he complained to Archibald MacLeish about "the paradox of secrecy in science, secrecy in a democracy. They just don't go together. But . . some secrecy is essential." At AEC, he made every effort to minimize the need for clearances and to counter the continual interference of the FBI in gathering "derogatory information." He stressed that abusing security regulations could lead to the sad situation where important decisions about people were made on the basis of "caution, not justice" and that careers could be ruined by innuendo.[87]

Lilienthal often went public with his concerns. He persuaded conservatives such as Arthur Vandenberg to back civilian stewardship of the atom. In 1949, he defended the fellowship program as long as possible. Ultimately, he set an important standard for discourse about government secrecy. According to Robert Goheen, Lilienthal confidant and former president of Princeton University, the legacy of openness may have been Lilienthal's greatest contribution to debate over the atom.[88]

Lilienthal was equally concerned with technological determinism as a threat to openness. He first became disturbed over the impact of technical decisions on patterns of human organization when he found that TVA agriculture policies had resulted in greater concentration of land ownership. At AEC, he was bothered that atomic energy policies seemed so complex that few would even attempt to influence their direction—in the end, fatalism and paralysis of action threatened to allow technology to determine its own destiny. Nevertheless, Lilienthal insisted that the only way to combat this threat was through open debate by educated citizens who could reject the notion of technological control.

In the end, Lilienthal could offer only vague suggestions about controlling technology. His greatest contribution in this area may have been his testimony that while modern men and women have to live with the uncertainties of science, they were not bound to accept the inevitability of any outcome, whether it be nuclear war or the determinism of a brave new world. He wrote of this faith a few months before leaving AEC:

> Men like myself can devote themselves to the development of force and destructive power, and still retain a repugnance . . . for force and military matters. If this can be done, then for once, the lover of persuasion, agreement, and goodwill will be in a position to make use of these qualities, because the lowest common denominator, i.e., those who put their faith on power, will know that we do not regard ourselves as "too good" to develop power, and develop it to use if we must—and yet *not* be poisoned by the very power we have developed—poisoned so that we have become like the very thing we hate and seek to protect the world from.

No doubt, his AEC experience was frustrating and with only minor triumphs. Nevertheless, he tried to balance the necessities of power and the requirements of democratic life through openness and turbulence. That was his greatest public legacy.[89]

A Continuing Interest as a Citizen—Atomic Politics

One day in May 1950, after finishing up some loose ends at AEC, Lilienthal wrote, "It's like me, though. When I'm through with something, I'm through." Nothing was further from the truth. Almost immediately after leaving AEC, Lilienthal began talking about the atom in a way he been unable to as chairman. While he assured Truman that he would not criticize the administration after leaving, he did just that. Early in 1955, a perturbed Truman noted that "Dave was always a controversial figure—I'd hoped one of firm convictions on certain subjects. After reading some of his pieces in slick magazines I'm not so sure!"[90]

In March 1950, in his first speech as a private citizen, Lilienthal rejoiced in leaving "that neutron-infested squirrel cage in Washington." Finally, he could engage in a less circumspect discussion of what secrecy really meant—

censoring vital public debate about the role of the atom in national defense. In June 1950, after the near-loss of Korea, he wrote of the danger of slighting conventional preparedness for a weapon that could rarely be used. In an early 1951 *Collier's* article, Lilienthal charged "that the [A-]bomb has been overvalued . . . as a guarantee of victory." And the much ballyhooed H-bomb, still "a remote possibility," promised no better. Lasting peace would come only after costly conventional rearmament. He argued that using nuclear weapons was often inappropriate for military and moral reasons. Simply put, "The very force of an A-bomb [even more so an H-bomb] limits" its purposes "and . . . restricts its flexibility." The only justification for the bomb was "if we are certain that its use is vital to our national existence."[91]

Ironically, liberals criticized his first speech. In it, he had scolded several scientists, including Leo Szilard, for "predicting that a hydrogen bomb would result in the 'end of the world,'" and complained that such predictions bred only "hopelessness and helplessness.'" Freda Kirchwey, a *Nation* editor, wrote that "if people, facing squarely the hazards Mr. Lilienthal wishes to play down, realize that human survival requires a solution of the potential conflict, . . . then much good can result from such revelations as were broadcast by the four physicists." The *Christian Century* called his talk "an effort to soothe the [legitimate] fears of the public." Unfortunately, neither of the two journals nor the *New York Times* understood Lilienthal's real concern, that such talk might encourage drastic civil defense policies, or as the scientists recommended, "the decentralization of coastal cities . . . [and] transplantation . . . of thirty to sixty million persons within ten years." Lilienthal feared that "mass evacuation drills and homes built underground in remote deserts" could tempt Americans to believe that the atomic crisis had been solved. Nothing, he argued, was further from the truth. Nevertheless, Szilard fired back in the *New York Herald Tribune* that regardless of the implications of the scientists' warning, "It is the people who will pay the price, and it must be their decision to pay it, and they will have to discuss it before they will be able to decide." Ironically, those words could have been Lilienthal's a few months earlier.[92]

Lilienthal took up another cause in the summer 1950 *Collier's* articles when he suggested an end to the government's atomic monopoly. To some, the call for privatization was a surprise, but it should not have been. Two years earlier, in a speech on atomic energy and industry, He predicted that while free enterprise was not yet possible in nuclear science, "areas will [soon] appear . . . that can be separated off and left to the usual forces of the competitive system." He then detailed the areas where he thought "private business can operate in substantially the usual manner."[93]

In the June article, Lilienthal was blunt: "No Soviet industrial monopoly is more completely owned by the state than is the industrial atom in free-enterprise America." In July, he called for atomic competitiveness. Charging that the AEC was only a "munitions trust," he recommended legislation that would maintain the military monopoly but institute a workable system of industrial information declassification, private reactor development, and isotope and tracer production. He also recommended tax incentives to encourage more private involvement in atomic energy. In a clever swipe at the secrecy syndrome, Lilienthal noted the absurdity of keeping secrets from American industry that had already been discovered by the Soviets.[94]

In his first years of retirement he kept an eye on internal AEC politics. He regretted that Truman had passed over Sumner Pike and appointed Gordon Dean as chairman. To Lilienthal, Dean was "a lightweight . . . with a bad sense of administration." He was concerned that Dean's ascent meant a wholesale change of personnel, from secretaries to key people such as Frances Henderson, Joe Volpe, and Carroll Wilson. While confining his concerns to the journal and private correspondence, Lilienthal went public on one procedural matter. In July 1951 on "Meet the Press," he roundly criticized the commission for releasing too much information about recent atomic tests. When James Reston pointed out that he seemed to have changed positions, Lilienthal told the panel he was firm on secrecy regarding information that might be useful to the Russians. Reston failed to note in follow-up that Lilienthal had also been accused of releasing information that might have helped the other side. Dean wrote Strauss that many of Lilienthal's friends, including Oppenheimer, Bacher, and Lee DuBridge, had "expressed shock" at his criticism and dismissed the charge as "entirely an emotional reaction."[95]

Lilienthal's criticism of the commission was a sign of a desire to keep a hand in the atomic debate. It also seemed to constitute an effort to move to a more centrist position on certain issues. In the same interview he said that the 1946 Lilienthal-Acheson report was not "a good idea now." A few minutes later he tried, not without confusion, to clarify his H-bomb position. He first insisted he "was not opposed to the development of a hydrogen bomb," and then, almost in the same breath, that "I was opposed to the hydrogen bomb." What he meant, he elaborated, was that, while not opposed to the weapon in principle, he was reluctant to approve an all-out program before a full assessment of defense policy. Lilienthal answered yes to Ernest Lindley's question of whether he now would favor the H-bomb given "a more-rounded military development." His change in position was fortuitous in light of the challenge he was about to face in the shrill debate over J. Robert Oppenheimer.[96]

Between 1950 and 1952, Lilienthal spoke out on atomic policy with little fear of retaliation. In 1953 things changed. Once again, it was necessary to defend his record as AEC chairman. Many factors intervened, including the explosion of "Joe 4," the first Soviet thermonuclear device, and Joseph McCarthy's escalating search for Communists in government. Most important, however, was the reemergence of Lewis Strauss in the atomic debate and his renewed attack on Oppenheimer. It took little imagination for Lilienthal to realize that if his friend was under fire, he also might be at risk.

In spite of Stevenson's defeat in November, Lilienthal felt good at the beginning of 1953. He was happy as "the top brass of a private business," and even more so with his lucrative stock option plan. In February, however, a storm began brewing on the atomic front which Lilienthal sensed he would have to weather. On February 11 Gordon Dean, whom Lilienthal had come to respect, announced he would soon retire as AEC chairman. By itself, the news was not alarming, but less than a month later Eisenhower picked Lewis Strauss as his special assistant for atomic energy. Harry Smyth, still a commissioner, confided to Lilienthal in late March that Strauss told the commission that if he could not find a replacement for Dean, "he would take it himself"—and he did in June.

In May trouble arose with an anonymous *Fortune* article that accused Oppenheimer of trying "to reverse U.S. military strategy." Full of innuendo, the article prompted Lilienthal to call it "nasty and obviously inspired." He worried that the piece might signal "the beginning of a campaign of revenge for the way the Hickenlooper investigation against me fizzled out." Anticipating Strauss's appointment, Lilienthal wondered if he should not search out "the relevant documentation, at the Commission, before L. [Strauss] gets in there and God knows what will happen to the files." In late June, as Strauss was taking over, Lilienthal was in Washington poring over classified documents, especially those dealing with disagreements between the old and new chairmen.[97]

The terms of engagement changed quickly after the *Fortune* article and Strauss's takeover. Things began to happen that prompted Lilienthal to start building his own defense. In July, on the Vineyard, an FBI agent told him that Strauss had blocked Carroll Wilson's appointment to a World Bank position because the new chairman had doubts about Wilson's loyalty. To Lilienthal this was a grave injustice. He insisted that the FBI get the views of people who could speak positively about Wilson and counter the negative perceptions people like Strauss who acted in a "mean, vindictive, devious and small" manner. Lilienthal thought, "When the word gets around, in the Commission staff, and in the scientific community, about this, I can't feel that it will make [Strauss's] tenure any happier. I hope it doesn't."[98]

In mid-September, *Time* lavishly praised the new chairman. The article was a masterful combination of backhanded compliments and innuendo. Strauss was lauded as an atomic pioneer, "one of a little band of men . . . who caught the threat of Communism when others heard only what they wanted to hear." At AEC he "stepped into this general atmosphere of baseless hope and emotional hand-wringing with a sense of purpose and humility." Lilienthal, on the other hand, was "known for his good and peaceful works, . . . who rebelled inwardly at the job of making bombs, who traveled the land to deliver esoteric speeches lamenting secrecy." The implication was clear: Lilienthal had been out his element at AEC, while Strauss was a valiant soldier, outnumbered, but never outmaneuvered by those who failed to understand the Soviet threat. Strauss was credited with pushing through the atomic explosion detection program and foiling the release of critical secret information. Strauss was further praised for getting the thermonuclear project going despite overwhelming resistance. While never accusing Lilienthal or Oppenheimer of wrongdoing or disloyalty, the article clearly implied that some of their decisions were questionable. The article also noted that the United States took seven years to develop a thermonuclear device after the first atom bomb while the Soviets did it in just four. Again, no blame was assessed, but the finger was clearly pointed.[99]

Lilienthal was angry, not at the "eulogy of L.L.S." (although that did not please him either), but of "the plain and intended effort . . . to smear me and Oppenheimer." He wrote an immediate response, which appeared in the *New York Times* on October 4. With characteristic zeal he called for greater candor and openness, saying there was "no greater risk in a democracy than lack of public understanding and public support of basic policies." He countered the implication that he and Oppenheimer had endangered national security and wrote forcefully that the whole point of the H-bomb debate was to force a comprehensive examination of defense policy. Lilienthal pointed out that the Korean crisis documented "what a sorry substitute [A-bombs] are for a comprehensive system of over-all defense." He then posed the key question about the arms race: Where does it stop? Now that they have the H-bomb, he asked, "Will our Government now set out to make a bomb . . . bigger than the Russian H-bomb? . . . Will such a super-super-bomb, if we make it, bring us any closer to peace or safety?" In conclusion, he returned to his common theme: "The ultimate source of our strength . . . is not in weapons. . . . [Real strength,] the firm foundation of our faith in our free institutions, is knowledge and understanding."

Lewis Strauss was not pleased. After seeing a draft of the article, he wrote *Times* managing editor Julius Adler that it was "mildly infuriating." He questioned Lilienthal's "assumption that with the necessary information the public can make wise decisions," and pointed out that "with all the information which Dr. Oppenheimer possesses (which is complete) he has consistently made very disastrous guesses." Strauss concluded that "Mr. Lilienthal is a poet and what he writes reads extremely well but it doesn't make any sense and it is dangerous." Two days later he sent another letter to *Times* publisher Arthur Hays Sulzberger complaining that Lilienthal had wrongly attributed the atomic explosion long-range detection (LRD) program to the British. That day he told his fellow commissioners the same thing. Strauss was piqued because he had always taken personal credit for the LRD program. For someone else to be given credit, especially the British, and by the likes of Lilienthal, was doubly insulting.[100]

Following the *Time* skirmish, Lilienthal took a positive position toward the new administration after Eisenhower's "Atoms for Peace" speech at the United Nations in December, praising the president's call for world cooperation and a pooling of resources for atomic development. Finally, Lilienthal thought, a president felt secure enough to offer ideas not unlike those his consultant group had proposed in 1946. Eisenhower seemed to have rejected Strauss's tunnel vision and the mind-set of those who saw atomic energy only in terms of armaments. In a December 13 *Washington Post* article, Lilienthal called the speech "a courageous effort to establish a basis for some degree of mutual faith" between West and East. Later in the month, before a national NBC audience, he called for the approval of Eisenhower's plan. For a moment things seemed hopeful, but the Oppenheimer controversy came to a head again. On December 23, 1953, the AEC announced the suspension of the physicist's clearance, subject to an unprecedented security investigation.[101]

The crisis had been building for years. From the time of his appointment to the Manhattan Project in 1942, Oppenheimer had been highly controversial. Even earlier, he, his second wife Kitty, and his brother Frank had been known for their left-wing friends and associates. While cleared for Manhattan, and again as a key commission advisor until the end of 1953, Oppenheimer had still remained suspect. During Lilienthal's AEC days, his greatest sin, according to detractors, was a consistent opposition to the thermonuclear project, a position he shared with Lilienthal, other commissioners, and his General Advisory Committee (GAC) colleagues. Equally important for Strauss was the fact that Oppenheimer had more than once humiliated him in public. Strauss never forgave the physicist's dismissal in the June 1949 congressional hearings, of Strauss's opposition to exporting radioactive isotopes. Using words designed to belittle, Oppenheimer admitted that isotopes could be used for atomic energy. He also added that one could also "use a shovel . . . [or] a bottle of beer for atomic energy" but no one would recommend export restrictions on those items. The audience laughed, but Strauss was not amused.

After Lilienthal's departure, Oppenheimer continued to chair the GAC until August 1952. However, in the face of a more cautious commission and a more conservative administration, he became increasingly critical. In 1952 he opposed Edward Teller's campaign for a second weapons laboratory. Through chairing a State Department disarmament strategy committee, he became a forceful spokesman for "Operation Candor," which advocated greater openness on disarmament issues, including hard data on weapons, increase rates, and proliferation. While the committee was originally Truman's, Eisenhower enthusiastically received its report in February 1953. But Operation Candor was anathema to Strauss and other cold warriors—something had to be done to discredit Oppenheimer, to reduce his aura of charm, which had extended even to a Republican president.[102]

As Operation Candor gained administration support through the Spring, Strauss became increasingly disturbed. In May he told the FBI he was suspicious about Oppenheimer's Communist sympathies. He also informed Eisenhower that he could not lead the AEC if the physicist was involved in any way. Much to Strauss's dismay, Dean renewed Oppenheimer's consultant contract just before he stepped down on June 30 and Eisenhower did not object. Soon after, however, Oppenheimer's star began to fall. Premier Georgi Malenkov's August announcement that the Soviets had detonated a thermonuclear device less than a year after the first American H-bomb explosion quickly muted enthusiasm for Operation Candor. Then, on November 7, the FBI received a letter charging that "more probably than not, J. Robert Oppenheimer is an agent of the Soviet Union." It was not the first letter of this sort, but this one was different—it was from William Borden, former staff director of Congress's Joint Committee on Atomic Energy (JCAE) under the Democrats. As Philip Stern noted, Borden's charge was the "trigger" Strauss had been looking for. Eisenhower, who had resisted the negative feedback on Oppenheimer for a long time, was impressed that a man of Borden's stature would make such claims. Early in December he told Strauss to withhold Oppenheimer's clearance pending a formal inquiry. On December 21 Strauss confronted Oppenheimer with the president's directive and tried to convince him to accept the decision voluntarily to avoid a hearing. The next day a still stunned Oppenheimer told Strauss he would fight the charges. Even before this confrontation, Strauss initiated a comprehensive surveillance of Oppenheimer and his family, including wiretaps at home and work, and electronic bugs in his attorneys' offices. The great physicist was covered. All he could do was wait for the Personnel Security Review Board hearing in April 1954.[103]

When Joe Volpe told him Oppenheimer's clearance had been lifted, Lilienthal met with Oppenheimer's attorneys, Lloyd Garrison and Herbert Marks, in January 1954 to review the charges, and in February issued an affidavit defending Oppenheimer's character and loyalty, and his role in the 1949 H-bomb debate. Lilienthal then traveled to Washington in April to prepare his testimony for the special board chaired by Democrat and University of North Carolina President Gordon Gray. The day before his appearance he spent hours going through classified files to refresh his memory. Little did he realize that several key documents had been withheld.[104]

Tuesday, April 20, was trying. Since the proceedings were secret, Lilienthal had no idea how intense they were. Gray and Roger Robb, the board's chief counsel, ran the hearings more like a criminal trial than an objective inquiry. Oppenheimer's attorneys were disadvantaged because, lacking clearances, they had to leave the room every time confidential information was introduced. To add to the indignity, the hearings were held in one of the rundown temporary buildings still scattered around the Washington Monument. Moreover, on April 20, Lilienthal had to wait all day to complete his testimony. After testifying an hour in the morning, he agreed to defer to Enrico Fermi and James Conant. He took the stand again at 3:30 in the afternoon and testified until Robb suggested at five that they recess until the next day. Lilienthal asked the board to continue after a short break so he could finish up. His request was a serious mistake—already tired and irritated from waiting and more than two hours of testimony, Lilienthal laid himself open to Robb's predatory style. When the session ended three hours later, Lilienthal was outraged. Robb had successfully raised doubts about how much Lilienthal remembered or wanted to remember about events in the late 1940s.[105]

Robb was restrained in the morning. He asked Lilienthal about the commission's 1947 decision to clear Oppenheimer of charges of which he had already been exonerated by the Manhattan Project. In the afternoon, before the break, Robb reviewed the 1949 GAC deliberations on the H-bomb—still nothing of controversy. After the break, he stepped up his attack. Angered at the sight of Garrison leaving because a classified document had been introduced, Lilienthal sparred first with Robb and then Gray. Irritated at Robb's persistent question about identifying his chief H-bomb advisors, Lilienthal testily answered, "I rather you would not push me after I said I don't remember." Robb shot back, "I am sorry I have to push you because I want to get responsive answers."

About 6:00 P.M. Robb set the first of two traps to discredit Lilienthal's testimony, asking him if he and Clark Clifford had talked in 1947 about a special review of the Oppenheimer charges. Having just reviewed those files, Lilienthal answered: "No, we did not."; "No, I believe not."; "I am not sure, but I have no recollection of it." Laying the second trap, Robb asked "whether or not in March of 1947 you had the old Manhattan District files" at the AEC? Lilienthal answered, yes, because of Truman's December 1946 transfer order "we were supposed to have them." Robb then lowered the boom, introducing a memorandum indicating that the Manhattan files were with the FBI, not the commission. To Gray's query as to whether he had ever seen those files, Lilienthal replied weakly, "I am beginning to doubt it." Without hesitation Robb then sprung the first trap, introducing documents that demonstrated that Lilienthal had talked at least twice with Clifford about convening a special security board over the Oppenheimer issue.

As Robb chided Lilienthal for his lapse, Garrison and Lilienthal realized that crucial documents had been withheld the day before. Garrison blasted Robb for trying "to make the witness look . . . in as unfavorable a light as possible, and to make what is a lapse of memory seem like a deliberate falsification." Lilienthal was furious over Robb's tactics and retorted that "the board wants the facts, and the facts are in the file, and I asked for the file so I could be a better witness, and it was denied me." In spite of Gray's promise to take Garrison's protest into account, the damage was done. Neither Lilienthal's testimony nor that of the other thirty-nine witnesses would keep the board from a seemingly foreordained conclusion. After two more weeks of testimony and three of deliberation, the board recommended the permanent suspension of Oppenheimer's clearance on the questionable grounds that he had impeded the development of the H-bomb and the less deniable charge that he had at times met with persons of questionable loyalty. At no time did it offer sufficient proof of disloyalty or espionage. A month later Strauss had his due—the AEC accepted the Gray board's recommendation on a four-to-one vote. The most brilliant American nuclear physicist was persona non grata in official atomic circles for the rest of his life.[106]

The remainder of 1954 was difficult for Lilienthal as an atomic partisan. Most of the time he managed to keep his anger and bitterness confined to his journal. Nevertheless, he relished news about turmoil at AEC over the Oppenheimer matter and of other Strauss decisions. "The high point of" one day in June "was an unexpected visit with Gordon Dean . . . [who said] that the atomic energy program is in grave and deep trouble" because Strauss had alienated top staff and fellow commissioners. In September, he recognized his "just plain grumpiness" over what had happened and talked his feelings out with Helen to keep bitterness from overwhelming him.[107]

His last challenge that year came with the publication of James R.

Shepley and Clay Blair Jr.'s book on the hydrogen bomb. Favorable to Strauss, the book charged Lilienthal and Oppenheimer with endangering national security because of their opposition to the thermonuclear program. While he told Truman the book was "a wicked job, politically-inspired, with not even a bowing acquaintance with the truth," Lilienthal decided not to respond publicly. In his journal, he accused Strauss of "encourag[ing] the book." Although the AEC chairman had "asked Shepley to 'suppress' the book," Lilienthal still blamed Strauss—"he read the MS; he didn't try to get the falsities corrected, and the implication of trying to suppress it is that the story is true, but embarrassing to those who opposed him." Lilienthal was pleased when Dean and New Mexico Senator Clinton Anderson attacked the book in public. His last public statement that year was a letter to the *New York Times* accusing Strauss of bringing partisan politics to AEC, something Truman had never intended when he signed the Atomic Energy Act into law in 1946.[108]

Aside from backing Adlai Stevenson's 1956 pledge to stop H-bomb tests, Lilienthal was quiet about the atom until 1963. His near-decade of silence was punctuated by Gordon Dean's death in a 1958 airplane accident. Lilienthal finally admitted "a great respect for Dean. . . . The high point in his career . . . was his appearance before the . . . Gray panel. . . . His performance . . . was *much* better than mine." This was quite a tribute considering his earlier efforts to keep Dean off the commission. Between 1954 and 1962, Lilienthal was preoccupied with his own company and confined atomic opinions to his journal. Now Princeton neighbors, he and Oppenheimer visited often, worrying over disarmament and test ban treaties. Lilienthal also became concerned with "the atomic pork barrel" and the unrealistic prospects for commercial nuclear power. By 1962 he was raring to go again, looking for a forum to advance a new atomic agenda and to question those who were pushing too hard for "'the peaceful atom,' or disarmament."[109]

Late that year Princeton University officials gave him his chance with an invitation to give the Stafford Little Lectures in February 1963. In January he and Helen went "through a husband-wife routine begun nearly forty years ago; whipping out the final versions of a piece of thinking and writing." His friend and Lazard general counsel Nate Greene, Joe Volpe, and son David also critiqued the drafts. All three disagreed with his views on disarmament, but Lilienthal felt he had to say his piece and "take the consequences." In the first lecture on February 11, he threw down the first of several gauntlets that would soon earn him the enmity of Congress, the private power industry, nuclear policy experts, and many in the scholarly community. The first two lectures focused on international policies and emphasized that neither nuclear superiority nor disarmament would provide the ultimate answer to world peace and security. Nuclear weapons were different from conventional ones only in their power. Hence, it was wrongheaded to seek peace through nuclear solutions alone, whether weapons superiority or disarmament. Quickly dismissing the argument for peace through nuclear superiority, Lilienthal focused mainly on the disarmament talks in Geneva. He suggested that, far from relieving international tensions, the talks might generate even greater ill will and mistrust. Charges of bad faith could push both sides to the brink. And, casting the talks as humankind's last hope could encourage false expectations and, should they fail, even greater disillusionment.[110]

In his second lecture he repeated that the atomic sword of Damocles was not the cause, but only a symptom, of the threat of war. For Lilienthal, the solution was the reduction of animosities and suspicions within and across national boundaries. Reaching back to H. A. Morgan's "common mooring" philosophy, he called for programs that encouraged interdependence and global communities of interest. Trade, economic development of poorer countries, and meeting food, health, and education needs throughout the world were key aspects of such a policy. Only then could "disarmers" be successful and the nuclear threat vanish into the past. Lilienthal was pleased that he could still "hold an 'audience' so that at times 'they' seem quite unable to move until you choose to release them." Friends and associates, including Oppenheimer, Bernard Baruch, and his physician, Dana Atchley, a distinguished New York internist, praised the lectures. Eugene Rabinowitch, founder and editor of the *Bulletin of the Atomic Scientists,* agreed that disarmament was an example of "barking up the wrong tree" and congratulated him for taking a politically unpopular position. E. B. White at the *New Yorker* wrote that "to be against disarmament . . . is like being in favor of influenza. . . . You've done a great service . . . to dispel these fantasies of life." Once more, he was in the thick of an issue—and he loved it.[111]

The third lecture on February 19 stimulated a quite different response. Turning to domestic policy, he pondered "what the peaceful atom means for us today, and the realistic prospects in the immediate future." If the first two lectures challenged sacred cows, this one slaughtered a few. His message was blunt: cheap nuclear power was a chimera. Moreover, even if cost-competitive with coal, oil, or falling water, Lilienthal doubted that atomic power was "just as good." Too many questions lingered about risks to human populations and waste disposal.

Whether for personal reasons or deeply felt principle, Lilienthal now had a chance to criticize the AEC as he had been criticized in 1954. He had defended the enthusiastic prognosis for the peaceful atom in the mid-1940s and the AEC's decision to commit resources in that direction. Then, there was hope for energy "produced so cheaply and abundantly as to 'cause profound changes in our present way of life.'" Now, things were different. The peaceful atom no longer held miraculous promise, and there was no excuse for spending vast sums of public money on questionable projects such as the breeder reactor. Nor could he understand why the commission continued to stockpile far more uranium than it would ever need. He charged that "a kind of Parkinson's Law of Research has developed" where "research expands as fast as money for that work is made available." Concerning the "atomic political pork barrel," he lambasted Congress for "force-feed[ing] atomic energy," and suggested that when the time comes, the development of the peaceful atom will happen whether government is involved or not. Lilienthal scoffed at rumors of a fuel shortage and concluded that atomic energy was "not now needed for civilian purposes." His plans for the AEC seemed a call for dismemberment: nuclear decisions should be taken in the context of a comprehensive energy plan, not by an agency biased toward one energy source. Many AEC functions should devolve to the private sector or other federal agencies. Things had changed drastically in atomic politics, he concluded, but "the Atomic Energy Commission, has hardly changed at all."[112]

At first the third lecture seemed to have little impact. The *New York Times* had been silent for months because of a strike and, aside from copies Lilienthal had sent out, the lectures suffered a limited circulation. In the meantime, Lilienthal took off for three weeks to celebrate the completion of his new development corporation's project in Iran. He returned on March 26 to a firestorm. Within days JCAE chairman John Pastore angrily told him the lecture had "caused us here no end of trouble." The senator ordered Lilienthal to "come down to answer some questions; [warning,] maybe we will take you apart but you don't mind that." Lilienthal refused to come immediately but promised he would the next week. He realized the seriousness of this "voluntary involuntary appearance" when on Friday, March 29, the JCAE executive director told him the committee had authorized a subpoena compelling his attendance on April 4.[113]

Two days of angry hearings preceded his appearance. Executives from North American Aviation, General Electric, and General Dynamics lambasted the lecture. Frederic de Hoffmann of General Dynamics called it "emotional and . . . devoid of technical context." Even former Argonne Laboratory director Walter Zinn, Lilienthal's old ally, questioned his conclusions and motives. In a biting critique, Zinn told the panel, "I actually think that the main stream has been diverted and left Mr. Lilienthal high and dry." Lilienthal entered the fray ready to fight. As he entered the room, he saw a familiar sight—"A crowded standing-room hearing room; a belligerent scowling Committee, . . . the press, lobbyists, angry AEC Commissioners."[114]

Lilienthal stood his ground for two tough hours. Of the five JCAE members present, Pastore and Representative Chet Holifield, always a solid Lilienthal supporter, were most critical, and a new congressman, John Anderson of Illinois, most supportive. Attention focused on Lilienthal's views on safety and waste disposal, and the role of government in nuclear affairs. He carried the day on the first issue but not the second. With respect to safety, Lilienthal persuasively criticized Consolidated Edison's plan and the AEC's seeming acquiescence to the building of a nuclear plant in densely populated Queens, New York, calling such a move "a very risky business." Both Pastore and Holifield defended the commission for waste and reactor safety research, but Lilienthal stuck to his guns. He admitted progress but rejoined that attitudes were pretty much the same as "15 years ago. . . . 'Put it [nuclear power plant] in an inaccessible place and hope nothing will happen.'" Lilienthal adamantly concluded that he "would not dream of living in the Borough of Queens if there were a large atomic powerplant in that region."

He was less convincing in his views on the role of government in nuclear science, perhaps because his rhetoric outdistanced the facts. Pastore asked Lilienthal about his notion that government get out of nuclear research and development, confessing, "That is the thing that shook me." Lilienthal denied he had said that "government should pull out entirely." What he meant was that government should be involved, but only "in areas where private industry has neither the resources . . . nor the funds." A few minutes later, Holifield asked if projects like TVA and Lilienthal's public works programs in Iran were not reason enough for government intervention? Are not there certain jobs, continued Holifield, "that the Government can do better than individual entrepreneurs?" Lilienthal quickly agreed. Holifield, and then Pastore, criticized Lilienthal's claim that AEC had created a national brain drain by monopolizing scientific talent. The California representative noted that AEC employed only 1,296 scientists and engineers, lagging behind Defense with 47,800, Commerce (6,186), the National Aeronautics and Space Administration (5,093), TVA (1,780) and Fish and Wildlife Bureau (1,338). Pastore chastised Lilienthal for claiming that America's scientific "needs are relatively impoverished, neglected, and starved" because two-thirds of all scientists and engineers work for atomic energy, space, and defense agencies. Pastore called the statement disingenuous, pointing out that the atomic share was only 1 or 2 percent. Lilienthal replied weakly that since this figure was from the president's economic report, "if there is anything clever or misleading about it . . . it is President Kennedy's misleading and cleverness."[115]

His testimony had a mixed impact. Congressman Anderson said Lilienthal had "performed a real public service . . . . [and that] a little skepticism is indeed a healthy thing." Holifield, on the other hand, told him he had "hurt the program, hurt it badly." In the end, Lilienthal's testimony had no earthshaking consequence. Of the twenty-seven witnesses, twenty-six were from industry, and none of them deviated from the view that nuclear power and government support were good for the country. Nevertheless, Lilienthal was happy to act as a "knowledgeable *private* citizen . . . prepared to say what you think and then be willing to absorb this kind of going-over." He still had what it took to fend off hostile questions, and was pleased that part of his testimony made a difference for at least a few citizens. In January 1964 Con Edison withdrew its application for the Queens project and Lilienthal noted that he had been asked by the *New York Times* to comment "since it was your statement of opposition to the plant that started the controversy about its safety."[116]

After the April testimony, Lilienthal spent two months working the lectures and other material into a new book, *Change, Hope, and the Bomb*. The reviews were mixed, but generally critical. Some reviewers favored his call for drastic reform of the AEC and congressional relationships. Others, including Adolf Berle, praised Lilienthal for criticizing the disarmament crowd for thinking there was only one solution to the nuclear problem.[117]

The severest criticism referred to Lilienthal's tendency toward overstatement and glibness. The most benign critics called the book a "wonderful mixture of four parts wisdom and one part nonsense" and accused him "of

falling victim . . . to the oversimplified thinking he so brilliantly scores."
J. David Singer, distinguished international relations professor at the University of Michigan, called it "little but polemic and platitude." The *Journal of Conflict Resolution* accused Lilienthal of "carry[ing] pragmatism to an anti-intellectual extreme" and "spend[ing] so much time on ridicule and caricature." The problem, said one reviewer, was that "what may have been telling rhetoric for a public lecture . . . appears unjustly harsh in print." This time, rhetoric failed. In the past, his readers recognized the inspirational intent of his books while forgiving analytic lapses. This time the subject was too serious to allow inspiration to hide inadequate conclusions. In his review, Singer charged that Lilienthal and Lewis Strauss, who had just published *Men and Decisions,* demonstrated "undisciplined mental processes, the conceptual skills of an average undergraduate, and most serious, an ignorance of their ignorance." Singer scored Lilienthal for confusing negotiated and unilateral approaches to disarmament and for condemning them both. Others criticized the flowery prose, calling his claim that hope "'lies . . . in the vivid life-giving imagination-stirring waves of change upon change that are the chief characteristic of our times' poetically persuasive," but smacking of an "optimism . . . based on faith rather than reason."[118]

What offended many was his sweeping attack on scholarship, science, and American universities. However insightful some of his points, the message was damaged by a mean-spirited anti-intellectual tone. On the first page he set the mood by emphasizing that his insight was based "not in the theories and abstractions that are found in books, but in real life." Barely a page later he wrote, "A thousand books by a thousand learned soothsayers of our Fluent Society [were] not as meaningful" as his own practical experiences. He later ridiculed "technicians and experts and specialists [who] took over the Atom" for not developing a holistic view of nuclear policy. Lilienthal then launched an attack on scientists and their universities. He criticized them for naively "espousing the doctrine of panacea: that in human affairs 'A Solution can be found,'" calling their efforts a "revival . . . of the old technocrat dogma: that all problems are basically technical, susceptible of . . . final solution." Another target was the rising "Scientific Establishment." Reeking with sarcasm, Lilienthal tagged this emerging elite "the new doctrinaires of the nuclear world, the new scholastics." In particular, he went after Herman Kahn, whom he referred to as "a high priest of the emerging cult of game-theory and operational analysis as a guide to human affairs." Lilienthal then criticized universities as handmaidens to government and chastised them for accepting huge sums of money for work that had no relation to the academic function. In a last shot, he asked "to what extent are decisions . . . about nuclear weapons or missiles . . . based on experts . . . no one knows except when they choose to write a book or appear on a TV panel?"[119]

The Economist called him an "embittered father denouncing his child to everyone who will listen." Singer accused Lilienthal of profoundly misstating the role of science, especially social science, and of confusing "the work of the military think-factories with 'empirical studies.'" He pointed out that regardless of what Lilienthal thought of theory and abstraction, even *Change, Hope, and the Bomb* could hardly escape some degree of generalization. The *Journal of Conflict Resolution Review* also criticized Lilienthal for his "cranky credenza on scientists and experts" and for not being aware that many universities, including Princeton, had already initiated evaluations of their relationships with the federal government. In retrospect, it is clear that the Stafford Little Lectures and *Change, Hope, and the Bomb* had many challenging insights, and it is interesting to note that none of the reviews spoke to his warnings about the safety of nuclear plants and the problem of nuclear waste. Perhaps one could appreciate those early warnings only in the wake of the Three Mile Island incident, Chernobyl, and the still unsolved mystery of what to do with tons of spent atomic fuel. Nevertheless, Lilienthal's tendency to let a sometimes embittered rhetoric rule over substance once again lessened the impact his message might have had.[120]

His last nuclear skirmish that year was a November address to the American Nuclear Society. He again attacked the AEC and Chairman Glen Seaborg for "prejudging the New York application [for the Queens plant] in the most forceful possible form." He advocated dividing AEC into one agency to promote nuclear power and another to regulate safety. He continued, as he had in April, to champion coal as "the best way to meet the rapidly increasing energy requirements of the country." Lilienthal acknowledged that "the antagonism so obvious in that crowded hall was understandable and anticipated," but nevertheless he had to say his piece. AEC and industry reaction was swift. Seaborg denied the New York accusation, and corporate representatives claimed that pollution problems from coal and oil-fired plants were much more severe than those of nuclear power plants. Within days, Westinghouse Corporation urged the industry to "launch a 'national campaign' to 'rebut' [Lilienthal] and educate the public." For better or worse, however, the controversy was set aside in the wake of the Kennedy assassination on November 22, 1963.[121]

In his later years, Lilienthal could be satisfied with his efforts in atomic politics. He was influential in raising questions about the safety of nuclear power plants in heavily populated areas, and his recommendations regarding the AEC and JCAE were finally implemented in 1974 when the AEC was split into the Nuclear Regulatory Commission and the Department of Energy, an agency with a comprehensive energy focus. The same year the JCAE was disbanded. Lilienthal continued as an elder statesman, occasionally writing an op-ed piece for the *New York Times,* and speaking from time to time. His last notable appearance was in 1976, when he testified on the dangers of nuclear proliferation before the Senate Government Operations Committee.[122]

CHAPTER 11

Midcentury Passage:
Transformation and Transition

> I've had a number of careers; why one more? . . . Perhaps part of
> the answer is in the picture I have of myself as wanting to interpret
> my times. That is the kind of "memoir" I'd like to write. And to
> do this, about a time when business is so important, and an
> understanding of men of business so essential, . . . you must
> associate with them, . . . and yourself share the life, or what you
> say won't be authentic.
>   —David E. Lilienthal, December 20, 1952

New Beginnings

In 1950, David Lilienthal celebrated his fiftieth birthday. The years
that followed were as varied as any before. He plunged into the business
world, much to the amazement of old foes and dismay of some liberal
friends who wondered how he could move so easily into circles where his
name had once been anathema. Unlike before, when he rarely traveled
abroad, Lilienthal became a peripatetic globetrotter. Between 1950 and
1960, he averaged almost two months a year overseas. In 1959 alone, he was
abroad more than four months—all but a few days on business. He revived his
TVA ties and continued speaking out on the atom. And, unknowingly,
Lilienthal remained the target of FBI gossip through the 1950s as the occasional subject of inquiries about his loyalty and his new foreign agenda.[1]

Lilienthal began the decade as an enthusiastic speaker under contract
with the W. Colston Leigh Agency. He soon tired of the lecture circuit and
returned with enthusiasm to writing. He revised *TVA: Democracy on the
March* and wrote a passionate defense of free enterprise entitled *Big Business: A New Era.* In 1963, the Princeton University Press published *Change,
Hope, and the Bomb.* In addition to occasional pieces in the *New York
Times,* the *Washington Post,* and *Foreign Affairs,* Lilienthal published a
dozen articles for *Collier's Magazine* on atomic energy, India and Pakistan,
and American business. Even Helen broke her long writing silence in 1952

with a saucy piece in the *Atlantic Monthly* called "Climbing the Family Tree." With wry irony she took aim at the Daughters of the American Revolution (DAR). She confessed that she had never been a member because it was "a rather subversive organization," having been sired by real revolutionaries—"rude forefathers." She noted that one could not "be too careful what you join," especially when "Congressional committees are backtracking . . . into a man's antecedents." Anyway, she concluded, by her figures, she was "related to everyone alive now who has English . . . blood." Hence, what was the big deal about DAR's exclusionary policies? "I guess," said Helen, "I can boast about my family too." [2]

It was also a time of personal changes. His old ally and friend, Harcourt A. Morgan, died in 1950, his father in 1951, and his mother in 1956. He became a grandfather when David married Peggy, a young mother with two children, and again when David and Peggy, and Nancy and Sylvain bore their own children. Lilienthal also cherished an intense relationship, almost partnership, with his son. David and Helen moved to New York in 1952 for five exciting years. In 1954 Lilienthal wrote that "living in New York . . . is another part of this appetite for new experience." They rented from actress Katherine Cornell before moving to a fashionable Sutton Place highrise. Their social circle included Truman Capote, James Thurber, John Gunther, and John D. Rockefeller III. In 1953, Lilienthal enjoyed being wooed as a potential mayoral candidate. Several prominent New Yorkers, including Adolf Berle, Henry Fowler, David Dubinsky, and La Guardia Republican Newbold Morris, pressured him to run on a fusion ticket. While flattered, even tempted, Lilienthal finally declined and asked Fowler to issue a legal opinion that he had not met residency requirements as "an easy way to put an end to the pressure." By 1957, the temptation of a more leisurely pace prompted the Lilienthals to move to a red-brick Georgian home in a prestigious Princeton neighborhood. [3]

Lilienthal experienced serious physical problems in the 1950s and a continuation of the emotional ups and downs that had haunted him for years. Insomnia became a regular visitor; so for a while did mysterious intestinal pains. His 1955 Vineyard vacation was marred by despondency, an "ugly cloud of uneasiness and corrosive anxiety" that took all the joy from that time with Helen. Two years later, he recorded, "From mid-October of 1957 until mid-summer 1958, illness, disability and disengagement were my lot." He first suffered a serious infection picked up in Iran and then a painful bout with Bells' palsy which hospitalized him all of April. But he weathered these afflictions and progressed along his "venturesome road to change." [4]

Perhaps most important, the 1950s gave Lilienthal a solid foundation for the future. The fortunate confluence of business experience and exposure to the wider world helped inspire his Development and Resources Corporation (D&R), an idealistic firm dedicated to combining private and public initiative in international economic development projects. What better model to emulate than his beloved TVA—integrated development and grass roots attentiveness across the globe? The second rock of his foundation was financial independence. His association with Lazard Frères and a fortuitous bull market in the mid-1950s gave him his long sought-after fortune and the means to strike out on his own. In 1949, his last year at AEC, the Lilienthals' net income was less than $30,000. In 1955 it was more than $110,000. By the end of 1955, a stock option with Lazard appreciated to a net gain of almost $1.5 million.[5]

A New Dealer on Wall Street

When David Lilienthal left public life in February 1950, his future was uncertain. He signed lucrative contracts with *Collier's* and W. Colston Leigh and vaguely contemplated "consulting." By May 1950, he finished his first lecture tour and decided that after October he would cut back on appearances. He enjoyed the publicity and crowds, but complained that taxes ate up his fees and the hectic schedule stole his energy. Late in 1952 Bill Leigh begged Lilienthal to get back on the circuit, telling him he "was the 'greatest earner' he could remember . . . , excepting only Mrs. Roosevelt when she was the President's wife," and that "he could have booked [Lilienthal] to earn $250,000 in that one year."[6]

By May 1950, however, his new career began to emerge. He opened a consulting office in Washington and became a part-time advisor for the Carrier Corporation. Earlier that spring, influential New York advertising executive Albert Lasker introduced him to André Meyer, managing partner of Lazard Frères investment banking firm. Within weeks, Meyer signed Lilienthal to a part-time retainer with a vague promise to share in future capital gains ventures. Lazard officials admitted that they didn't quite know how they were going to use him other than capitalizing on his name and reputation: one partner, George Murnane, told Lilienthal to "keep yourself uncomplicated, 'floating,'" because he had held "a great position of trust, [had] done two huge jobs, [and has a] brilliant name." Murnane later averred that Lilienthal was just the kind of person who would appeal to "important business people" to "discuss the larger aspects of their problems."[7]

His move into business should not have puzzled Lilienthal's liberal friends. As always, he was interested in something different and being *active*—neither law nor higher education, two other options, would satisfy those requirements, but business could. After his first day with Carrier, he reveled, "I like the fact that Carrier is an outfit that is *doing* things. I like getting into a plant . . . , walking around among men who are operating lathes and welders, rather than being confined to inchoate or idea situations." More important, perhaps now he could make money. In the 1930s and 1940s Lilienthal worried constantly about supporting his family on a modest public salary. Joe Volpe later confided that after his friend left office, he "was very much concerned about making money." Indeed, in a 1951 *New Yorker* interview Lilienthal rashly blurted out, "One reason I'm happy these days is that I'm making a lot of money," a statement he later denied to alarmed friends.[8]

However, there were other reasons for the new venture. Even in the early days, Lilienthal had never been antibusiness. True, he fought the railroads and opposed the utilities in Chicago, Madison, and the Tennessee Valley. But he did so only in his official capacity as labor lawyer and utility reformer. Like millions of Americans he bought and sold stock and worried about the market. Excepting the utilities, his experience with Tennessee Valley businesses, especially the aluminum companies and other war industries, had been positive. Later, he worked closely with AEC contractors, including Union Carbide and General Electric, and was close to giants of industry such as Chester Barnard, who convinced him of the integrity of corporate America. Neither could he forget the support he received from scores of top businessmen in his confrontations with Congress in the 1947 confirmation hearings and the 1949 Hickenlooper investigation.

Moreover, as Joe Volpe observed, Lilienthal wanted to be where the action was. After all, for nearly eighteen years he had helped run two of the largest public enterprises in the country. In the 1951 *New Yorker* article he reminded his interviewer that "in the past twenty years, I've come to know some of the shrewdest and most resourceful people in America," people who could help gauge "whether this or that possibility might be a good short-term or long-term investment." Perhaps most important, as the epigraph to this chapter suggests, he could hardly resist getting to know an old foe better: life truly "wouldn't be complete, living in a *business* period . . . unless I had been active in that area." His inclinations in 1950 were no different from what they had been in 1923 when he joined the labor struggles; or in 1931, casting his lot with a rising tide of Progressivism; or two years later at the beginning of Roosevelt's experiment in state capitalism.[9]

Still, he was uneasy about the move. He fretted for two years over his ambiguous situation at Lazard. Lewis Strauss wrote that Lilienthal was embarrassed at receiving regular checks "for which he thought he was performing no service." On one hand, Carrier President Cloud Wampler warned him that Lazard only wanted his "name and reputation to be used as a come-on" for wealthy investors. André Meyer, on the other hand, discouraged him from accepting retainers with outsiders such as Carrier and later, RCA. Lilienthal was also bothered because living in Washington kept him away from "the [Lazard] team," not being around "when ideas come up for informal discussion . . . [and] when negotiations are undertaken." In April 1951 he decided to spend alternate weeks on Wall Street, and he and Helen moved to the city in late 1952.[10]

It was not easy either, to shake two decades of being in the limelight and making momentous public decisions. He was disappointed that his *Collier's* articles did not receive much press coverage. By the late 1950s, however, he solved that problem by eschewing the popular magazines for occasional pieces in the more influential Sunday *New York Times Magazine*. He was not disappointed either with profiles in the stylish *New Yorker* three times between 1951 and 1961.[11]

Moreover, many business decisions seemed trivial to him. Lilienthal railed at having to court boorish business executives. More haunting was the thought of losing his public-mindedness. In April 1952 he wondered if he was "not doing a successful job" in either business or public affairs. In mid-1952 he told Felix Frankfurter how difficult the adjustment to private life had been and about "wasting talents on ordinary mundane matters." Image was also a problem. It was bad enough that he was not courted by the press, but it was worse when friends misinterpreted his new career. When the 1951 *New Yorker* interview appeared, Helen warned him that the statement "Lilienthal had changed" and the remark about making "lots of money" might upset his friends. Sure enough, former TVA associate Ted Schultz soon wrote Lilienthal that the article "had given a number of [his] friends down there quite a scare." Lilienthal stewed "that if I let people down who have come to put their trust in me, . . . the whole world would crumble for me." On December 17 he complained to TVA chairman Gordon Clapp that "considering the fact (which I don't advertise, naturally) that I'm giving one-third of my time to non-compensated pro bono things, the picture of me [in the article] has a certain irony."[12]

At the end of 1952, Lilienthal concluded that his first two years in business "were really shadow-boxing." He recalled the end of 1951 as "the bluest funk, the most miserable period of acute unhappiness," and admitted that even a year later, "I haven't had peace of mind, and I am not yet engaged in anything that consumes me with interest." Nevertheless, by this time his opportunities were beginning to expand. Earlier in the year André Meyer asked him to run a small moribund business in which Lazard owned considerable stock. And, he began to formulate an apologia of big business, an effort that resulted in a controversial book whose conclusions again raised the eyebrows of old friends.[13]

Minerals Separation and *"Big Business"*

Lilienthal was well advised by his Lazard tutors. To a man, they told him he would never get rich on a big salary—Uncle Sam's tax rates were too steep. While Lasker, Meyer, and others counseled that prosperity came only through capital gains on stock appreciation, Lilienthal wondered throughout 1951 and 1952 when he was going to get his chance. In September 1951 he rejected an offer from David Sarnoff to supervise RCA's color television effort because he "wanted something which RCA could not provide: capital gains." A short time later, he grumbled to Lasker after turning down Sarnoff that "while I am waiting for a capital gains to cash in on, if one ever comes, I must eat."[14]

The opportunity for "capital gains" began inauspiciously in January 1951, when Meyer asked Lilienthal to run a small company in which the firm had a substantial investment. Led by nonagenarian Seth Gregory, Minerals Separation North American Corporation (MSNA) specialized in licensing its own metal-processing patents. Lazard was concerned because MSNA had become extremely passive. Founded in 1916, MSNA reported its last dividend in 1923 and had not been listed in Moody's investment manual since 1933. More disturbing yet, many of the patents would pass into the public domain in a few years, leaving MSNA without a profit basis. In June, Lazard convinced Gregory to allow Lilienthal to explore getting MSNA's iron ore flotation process into production. For the next seventeen months Lilienthal worked hard to make MSNA viable. Frustrated by Gregory's insistence on "sitting and waiting for the companies to embrace our process," Lilienthal approached several steel companies, all of whom told him that the flotation process was not economically viable. In February 1952 Lazard bought all MSNA stock and appointed Lilienthal CEO and director. Later that year, the new CEO shut down the New York offices and consolidated corporate quarters in Florida, and in August, he eased Gregory into an honorific consultant position. Still, nothing developed with the flotation process, and Lilienthal remained a salaried executive without stock options.[15]

In November 1952, things changed dramatically. Convinced that MSNA lacked the resources to expand to production and sales, André Meyer merged it with recently acquired Attapulgus Clay Company. The board asked Lilienthal to continue as chairman and, more important, agreed to give him a three-year option on 50,000 shares of stock at about five dollars a share. For the next year, Attapulgus Minerals and Chemicals Company (AMCC) gave him a workout he never forgot. By the end of 1953 Lilienthal deserved every bit of advantage the bargain purchase of 10,700 shares that year had given him. Both Jim Adams, a Lazard partner on the AMCC board, and André Meyer kept close tabs on their sometimes beleaguered charge. Soon after the merger, Meyer exploded over a poor sales forecast for 1953, a display that tempted Lilienthal to "mental pictures of walking into André's office and telling them all what they could do with this clay." Lilienthal quietly tried all year to make something of the company with its four hundred employees and $4.6 million in sales. He was on the road frequently, if not at Attapulgus headquarters in Philadelphia, then at the clay mines in Florida or selling the product in New York or Texas. The first months were heady. He enjoyed "seeing people and punching up the management side of things . . . [and thinking of]. . . new ways to make use of . . .[a] rather prosaic material, clay." Nevertheless, the company took more time than he anticipated. L. R. Streander, former Attapulgus Clay head and president of AMCC, offered little leadership. Moreover, Lilienthal found it difficult to adjust to the normal ups and downs of production and sales—after disappointing September sales, he wrote that he was "discouraged and alarmed" and thought maybe it was time to move on "to something more useful in the world." Adams reminded him that short-term crises called for "perspective *and* action: doing something about your work," not despair and gloom.[16]

Perhaps sensing Lilienthal's frustration, Lazard replaced Streander with Wright Gary, a successful CEO with another Lazard Company, in November 1953. Lilienthal was pleased, noting "the end of the terrible frustration . . . of trying to run a company that I should not have to consider running." He remained board chairman until June 1954, when he was elevated to chairman of the executive committee of another company, Minerals and Chemical Company of America (MCCA). In December 1955, Lilienthal resigned as chairman, but remained on MCCA's executive committee and that of a later firm, Minerals and Chemicals Philipp Corporation, until it was absorbed into the billion-dollar Engelhardt Corporation in 1967.[17]

From 1954 on, Lilienthal was involved less and less with MSNA's successor companies. He attended board meetings, occasionally traveled for the company, and even tried, unsuccessfully, to effect a merger in 1962 with a Utah company he had worked with earlier. For the most part, however, he had little to do with internal company affairs or the MCCA and Philipp mergers in 1954 and 1960. Ironically, he made his fortune in 1954–55. From January 1954 to July 1955, his stock (37,500 shares by 1954) appreciated to over $41 a share. Needless to say, Lilienthal was both elated and baffled. In January 1954 when the stock jumped from $10 to $13, a Lazard partner told Lilienthal he was "having just about every possible experience with that company, including one of those unexplained ups in prices." In late November after it had risen to $28, he fretted that perhaps "it had risen too rapidly, without anything more than prospects" and that the price might sink just as quickly. By late 1954 he felt he had made it in business and wrote that "what counts in acquiring a business reputation is not sitting on boards but making money." Savoring his success, he concluded that "I'm no longer David Lilienthal, the 'controversial' public servant, but . . . someone who succeeds in their [the bankers] own game, and so an almost respectable and possibly even respected individual."[18]

Assessing Lilienthal's success as an "entrepreneur," as he liked to call himself, is difficult. He worked diligently at MSNA and for a year with the successor company. However, Attapulgus really took off after Wright Gary came aboard and Meyer orchestrated mergers that resulted in a company with $280 million in sales in 1961. David Morse, one of Lilienthal's advisors at AEC and D&R, reflected that his friend was not really a businessman and "at Lazard he had made his fortune without knowing how he made it." Joe Volpe disagreed and said that Lilienthal did have business sense. Yet, even Lilienthal confessed once to Edwin Newman on NBC television that "well, I suppose it [making a million dollars] must have been a fluke." Clearly, however, he never distinguished himself as a detail man, nor as someone who understood the ins and outs of corporate finance. His year as chairman of the board of AMCC was frustrating and he was relieved when Gary took over in late 1954. Nevertheless, Lilienthal was astute in picking his mentors. Knowing André Meyer led to financial independence and eventually to Lazard's backing for D&R. And, the experience helped him learn to fend for himself, a skill he had not mastered as head of large public institutions. His experience with "business life . . . full of creative, original minds" also gave him a new perspective on a major force in American life, a vision he reflected in his controversial writings on private enterprise.[19]

There is little doubt that Lilienthal's association with Lazard, Carrier, and RCA stimulated his thinking about big business. Three months after starting with Minerals Separation, he wrote, "This morning suddenly got an 'idea'—a big special issue of *Collier's* devoted to my 'Big Business for a Big Country' theme." In an outline, he sketched out several articles. The Sherman Anti-Trust Act was a major obstacle to economic development. He argued that regardless of the sentimental view toward small business, "we *are* going to have size—have it now—must have it." Big business has delivered higher production and competition, effective research, and better employee security. Borrowing from the TVA philosophy, he concluded that "the formula for best results [was] size plus decentralization." For the next nine months he thought, jotted, and wrote. *Collier's* jumped at the prospect, seeing the work as a chance, as the editors later wrote, "to hasten the establishment of a more realistic attitude on the part of government toward Big Business." In February 1952, he told a delighted Cass Canfield at Harper & Brothers that he would have a book on the subject later that year.[20]

That spring, Lilienthal was ebullient but cautious about the project. John Kenneth Galbraith's new book, *American Capitalism: The Concept of Countervailing Power,* seemed to validate his own thinking "as the basis of a whole new philosophy." After reading rough drafts of Lilienthal's work, Joe Volpe warned that the articles were unduly polemical and would alarm many of his supporters. Lilienthal agreed to tone down the rhetoric and clarify that he wasn't against all antitrust legislation. Nevertheless, he stuck to his conclusions and enthusiasm for "Bigness." With some trepidation he sought out Frankfurter's counsel. He was relieved when, "without waiting to hear my particular slant," Frankfurter lashed out at the way antitrust litigation was clogging up the courts.[21]

The five-week series began on May 31. Apocalyptic in tone, Lilienthal wrote that only "America's mastery of productivity . . . stands between freedom and the tidal wave of Communist militarism." In one rhetorical flourish after another, he maintained that the key to productivity was "Big Business." "Bigness" provided the context for innovation, research, competition, consumer choice, and enhanced national security. The great increase in material wealth, a result of bigness, promised even more individual freedom and happiness. And bigness promised a measure of personal security that Americans had never enjoyed before.[22]

To Lilienthal's dismay, there was little reaction to the articles. Complaining that the press ignored his writing because *Collier's* had identified itself too closely with the series, Lilienthal huffily wrote he was glad he "reserved the right to do a book—[because] . . . a magazine is an ephemeral and largely ineffective way to have ideas 'take.'" There were a few responses, however. In late May, in Senate hearings on Monopoly and Cartels, Senator Russell Long wondered if Lilienthal's preference for bigness implied a call for more government monopolies. About the same time, former President Hoover wrote *Collier's* that "it is still a puzzle as to exactly what [Lilienthal] proposes—if anything." Old friends were also disturbed. Bill Waymack congratulated Lilienthal on the series, but hoped the book would do better at addressing "ways of counterbalancing and neutralizing the dangers and evils of economic giantism." Morris Cooke, his old public power ally, was shaken and wrote one friend that the articles were "completely inexplicable to me," and another that Lilienthal "minimizes what will be the losses and dangers to our democratic system if we follow . . . his program." To Lilienthal, Cooke wrote of "bewilderment," and asked plaintively, "Am I really old-fashioned?" Lilienthal deigned to reply in substance, and simply wrote his friend, "you shore [*sic*] *aren't* 'old-fashioned'!" Cooke's concerns seemed to be vindicated when General Motors sent a sixteen-page summary of the articles to employees, suppliers, and customers, with the suggestion "to contemplate The [*sic*] wonders Bigness has been able to accomplish."[23]

Published in early 1953, *Big Business: A New Era* went through three printings and was picked up by Pocket Books. Within weeks, more than a dozen journals and distinguished pundits, including Peter Drucker, Richard Rovere, and Samuel Lubell, reacted in reviews. Like *TVA: Democracy on the March*, *Big Business* was a rhetorical manifesto, long on anecdote, unsubstantiated conclusion, and disdain for academic language and theory. His objective was to create a groundswell of opposition to traditional antitrust legislation and a push for a positive "New Economic Policy." For Lilienthal, "The Sherman Act *forbids* '*restraint* of trade'—a double negative. The new law . . . should expressly *foster* the '*development* of trade'— a double affirmative." A Basic Economic Act would judge business not in terms of bigness—monopoly or oligopoly—but whether or not it furthered the public interest. He concluded that bigness provided the most "efficient way to produce and distribute basic commodities, . . . strengthen the nation's security, [and] . . . promote human freedom and individualism." He also argued that because of a significant diffusion of power, large corporations no longer posed a threat to American life. Government, organized labor, stockholder power, and socially aware corporate managers promised to counter the advantage of "bigness." Moreover, "the saving factor of diversity in the American temperament" would prevent any single economic force from dominating.[24]

Lilienthal's call for a new Basic Economic Act to supplant outmoded antitrust laws was a vague but innovative twist on industrial regulation: "The legal test Bigness would have to face would thenceforth be whether the particular aspect of size challenged by the government does in fact *further the public interest.*" Henceforth, American corporations would have to demonstrate how much they contributed to the nation's prosperity. Lilienthal denied *Time*'s assessment that his new policy meant a planned economy, but even so, there was more than a hint of national industrial policy championed decades later by financiers such as Felix Rohatyn, another longtime Lazard partner. Finally, in a strong attack on "latter-day Luddites," he argued that in deploring materialism, certain groups had confused means with ends. For Lilienthal, the material accomplishments of corporate America were not ends in themselves. Material goods were only the *means* for "further[ing] the highest values known to men." "The ends," he concluded, "are the use and purpose to which we put these material things."[25]

Some reviewers described the book as an important contribution to the

postwar debate on capitalism. Richard Rovere called it "an immensely
stimulating work, and [one that] may turn out to be an immensely important one." Most reviewers applauded him for criticizing attacks on business on the grounds of "bigness" alone. On the whole, however, critical
assessments prevailed. From pens on the left, such as that of T. K. Quinn of
The Nation and Samuel Lubell, and those on the right, especially Peter
Drucker and the anonymous reviewer for *American Mercury, Big Business:
A New Era* was described as a superficial essay with little rigor or empirical
grounding. Lubell wrote of "the noises emanating from the Brandeis grave"
in reference to the irony of a Brandeis disciple now championing a cause
the old justice had fought all his life. Writing in the *Yale Review* and echoing the liberals, Drucker was aghast at Lilienthal's naive acceptance of the
goodness of big business. For Drucker, the book was a "pamphlet" smacking "of the zeal of the convert." Quinn and Lubell were disturbed by the
uncritical assumption that large organizations could indeed maximize individualism and human freedom. Lubell accused Lilienthal of failing to address "the quite real problems of social, political, and human control created by huge administrative units." Quinn wished Lilienthal "had started
somewhere near the bottom of [a large organization] so that he might have
a mental picture of what they are like viewed from the bottom up."[26]

What might have troubled Lilienthal most, if he read the reviews, was
the unfavorable comparison of *Big Business* to Galbraith's *American Capitalism.* It was particularly galling given his bias against the dismal science
of economics. Writing soon after Galbraith's book was published, Lilienthal
offered a backhanded compliment. He was relieved that Galbraith's ideas
paralleled his, but observed that the book was "messed up with the jargon
of the economist." A year later, in *Big Business,* he charged that economic
theory merely confused the public and haughtily advised economists to "accept a measure of responsibility . . . to see to it that their students . . . and
the public generally are able to distinguish between what is taught and used
as a theoretical device, and what is operating fact." A few pages later, in his
only reference to Galbraith, he challenged the economist's claim that where
large firms dominate, it was difficult for new competitors to enter the market, declaring, "Nothing could be farther from the reality." Reviewers who
compared the two books differed with Lilienthal's assessment. In the *New
Republic,* Richard Lester called Lilienthal's book "more superficial and
dogmatic than Galbraith's well reasoned volume." Former TVA assistant
general counsel Frank Towsley, writing in the *Columbia Law Review,* said
that Galbraith "is the one who is being 'realistic' with his concern for developing countervailing power . . . for the protection of the public welfare, . . . [a
concept] Lilienthal certainly does not stress the need for." Drucker's comparison was even more forceful. Ticking off a long list of recent "liberal" books
on business, he observed that "not all the liberal writers who have discovered Big Business share [Lilienthal's] uncritical and two-dimensional approach." He went on to praise Galbraith's theory of "countervailing powers,"
for being far more profound, even if too sophisticated "to be fashionable."[27]

The reviews spoke volumes about Lilienthal. In all fairness, the book was a dramatic addition to an important debate. Published by America's foremost trade press, Lilienthal wrote with passion, and—if one did not probe too deeply—his arguments seemed persuasive. But, in his rush to sell another idea, he allowed rhetoric to run roughshod over careful exposition and analysis. There is no better example of Lilienthal's bias than his criticism of Galbraith's "jargon"-laden style. Most reviewers praised *American Capitalism* for its elegance. The *American Economic Review* concluded that the volume had "a profoundly satisfactory style, easy, lucid, witty." The *New Republic* deemed it a "highly readable essay." In the *New York Herald Tribune,* Samuel Lubell called the book "not too technically written, . . . and one of the most provocative economic essays" since Keynes. The *New York Times* praised it for demonstrating that "economics can be written with style."[28]

The critics were fair in describing *Big Business* as provocative but superficial. For one thing, Lilienthal had promised to seriously evaluate the "hazards of bigness," such as concentration of power, bureaucratic inefficiency, and the negative effect of organizations on individualism and freedom. But, in the book, he offered only a glib and abbreviated discussion and denied the "hazards." If his journal had not reflected that Lilienthal labored many months on the book, one might conclude that it had been prepared in haste. However, haste was not the culprit; the problem was the preference for rhetoric over reasoned discourse.

Two examples should suffice. Lilienthal tried to allay the fear of big business by claiming "a decided trend—'trend' is perhaps not a strong enough word to describe it" to a new sense of social responsibility among "top bosses." A few pages later, though, he wrote that "it is certainly not true that all, *or perhaps even a majority* [emphasis mine] of the top officers . . . of the five thousand larger corporate enterprises of the country as yet accept . . . the idea that broad public accountability is part of the modern responsibility of business." Later, in criticizing Galbraith's warning that dominance by a few large firms makes it more difficult for new companies to enter an industrial sector, Lilienthal offered warrants that did not even relate to Galbraith's conclusion. Instead of furnishing examples, even anecdotal, of new firms which had broken through, Lilienthal proceeded to discuss, as if in refutation of Galbraith's hypothesis, the manner by which large companies had successfully diversified into other fields—Celanese from textile fibers to chemicals, Schenley from distilling to pharmaceuticals, and Glidden from paints to mining and metal processing—a line of reasoning not remotely related to Galbraith's claim.[29]

In retrospect, it is not difficult to understand why Lilienthal wrote as he did. Once committed, Lilienthal tended to support ideas passionately and without question. His support of bigness was no less intense than past commitments to labor, public power, and atomic energy. Even the ideological embrace of big business was understandable. Richard Hofstadter, Arthur Schlesinger Jr., and Jordan Schwarz recognized that Lilienthal had embraced a New Deal ideology that emphasized practical action, expertise, and economic development—an ideology that had no quarrel with bigness, or in many respects, business. As Hofstadter commented, "Lilienthal's more recent defense of big business does not represent a conversion to a new philosophy but simply an ability to find in private organization many of the same virtues that as TVA administrator he found in public enterprise." Schwarz noted that "the New Dealers did not like certain capitalists, but they had nothing against capitalism."[30]

That Lilienthal may have erred in his assessment of bigness was due in part to the fact that he had never been part of a large organization from the bottom up. Indeed, his own business experience was anomalous. He worked for one of the foremost investment firms in the world, a company more interested in dealing and leveraging than in production and the coordination of thousands of employees—a far cry from the bigness he professed to understand. Even his direct experience was with a small company. By the time Metals Separation evolved into a large corporation, Lilienthal was far removed from day-to-day management. Finally, it is important to note that in spite of the dismay of liberal friends that he had changed sides, nothing was further from the truth. By 1950 Lilienthal already had an appreciation for business people through the giant industries he courted at TVA and AEC. In spite of grass roots rhetoric, Lilienthal had been a proponent of bigness since the TVA days—first as director of the largest public power producer in the nation and then as leader of an industrial monopoly over the greatest source of power in the world. Indeed, his move from liberal Progressivism to benevolent statism in the early 1930s may have been more difficult than the move from public bureaucracy to Wall Street corporate life.

Internationalism and the Inspiration of TVA

During his years at the AEC, Lilienthal had had little time to think about TVA. In 1950, he began to drift back to those roots cautiously, not wanting, as he told H. A. Morgan, "to stir up my pal McKellar, and make Gordon [Clapp] and the rest have to suffer from their being seen with me." His relationship with TVA was far different from his relationship with the post-Lilienthal AEC. For the next dozen years, indeed for the rest of his life, Lilienthal was a gray eminence who offered counsel and defended his beloved creation during eight years of a hostile Republican administration. Most of his actions on behalf of TVA took place behind the scenes, and never in the kleig lights of Congressional hearings.[31]

Aside from keeping in touch with Clapp, Washington office director Marguerite Owen, and sometime TVA general counsel Joe Volpe, Lilienthal often tried between 1951 and 1955 to rally support for a new way of financing capital expenditures. Under the 1933 TVA Act, capital funding was restricted to Congressional appropriations. Basking in the warm glow of national approval and Democratic presidents, TVA had had little problem at first in raising the money it needed. In the early 1950s, however, political support had slipped. TVA was now just another middle-aged agency, a Republican administration was in office, and growing demands were forcing the authority all too often to an increasingly reluctant Congress for money for new plants. At first, Lilienthal tried to convince the TVA brass to sell the power system to municipalities and electric cooperatives who could legally finance capital needs through bonds. In spite of his considerable influence, neither top management nor the power staff accepted the idea, preferring, instead, the old familiar approaches. In August 1951, Clapp scolded Lilienthal in an angry letter, telling him that "the purpose of [Lilienthal's] discussions . . . on refinancing TVA was 'journalistic,' that is a *Collier's* article."[32]

By mid-1953, support for TVA had eroded. Eisenhower called the authority an example of "creeping socialism" and the House Appropriations Committee refused to fund a new steam plant near Memphis. Lilienthal groused that his recommendation had been "delayed and slow-motioned by staff members who just couldn't believe that getting funds . . . from Congress would ever have to be changed. Now," he said, "it is too late for TVA itself to make such proposals." The next year, 1954, was even more of a nightmare when Herbert Vogel, a Republican and Corps of Engineers general, replaced Clapp as board chairman. To stem TVA's growth, the Eisenhower administration proposed the Dixon-Yates plan, which would force TVA to distribute privately produced power. Once more Lilienthal intervened, trying to convince TVA to back a self-financing plan and using his Lazard sources to line up private support for the move. In September 1954, George Woods, president of First Boston Corporation, reacted positively to selling bonds for a new Tennessee public power corporation, confessing, as Lilienthal reported, that "the utility business would be wild if they thought I would join in something like this." Still, TVA would not budge.

The following January, after hours of talk, he gave up: "The boys in the TVA power staff, plus (General Counsel) Swidler, are just reluctant to do things differently than they have been doing them. . . . They believe that somehow things will work out." Four years later, in the wake of the Dixon-Yates failure, Congress finally authorized TVA to issue its own bonds. Lilienthal was pleased, but still convinced that his idea of allowing municipalities and cooperatives to sell bonds was still a better one. As he noted then and later, the interest on municipal bonds would have been much less than what TVA would have had to pay on the open money market.[33]

Lilienthal's ties with TVA extended beyond occasional forays into Authority business and the satisfaction of being a senior statesman. For the former chairman, the inspiration of a TVA global model proved far more important. When he left AEC, he had little experience in the international realm, spending most of his time at TVA and AEC on domestic politics. At TVA, foreign relations mainly meant hosting a steady stream of foreigners who came to see the Tennessee miracle. During Lilienthal's atomic energy career, first as State Department consultant and then at AEC, international affairs mainly involved abstract discussions about the nuclear balance of power. Nevertheless, Lilienthal had evinced some interest in the outside world. In 1934 he spent a month in England exploring the British electrical grid system, and in Mexico in 1941 he visited with the powerful minister of hydraulic resources, Adolfo Orive de Alba. A year later, and then again in early 1943, Lilienthal wrote notes to Roosevelt suggesting that TVA was a wonderful international example for the United States. In 1946 he planned a trip to France (subsequently canceled) to meet the French minister of planning, Jean Monnet, and in October 1949 Jawaharlal Nehru invited him to India. Nearly all of his final meetings with Truman in 1949 centered around Lilienthal's plans for a trip around the world and an extended visit to India. Moreover, he had made an impassioned plea in *TVA: Democracy on the March* for the continuation after the war of an American global presence, and he envisioned that presence in terms of TVA-style development.

His first post-AEC global venture was in May 1950, when he and Helen took a five-week vacation to France and England. Because of his reputation, he was quickly drawn into the debate on the Schuman Plan, a bold initiative for integrating Western European coal and steel industries. At a party his first night in Paris, Lilienthal met Jean Monnet, the father of the plan, and talked at length, along with Averell Harriman, about the project. Subsequently, he spent much of his vacation in long discussions with the French Lazard partners, and with French and English officials, including Monnet and British prime minister Clement Atlee, discussing the nuances of the plan. The dialogue was an eye-opener—journal entries reveal an amazement that politics elsewhere was just as complex and confusing as back home. The trip also gave him a much-needed ego boost after the battering he had taken in 1949. Everyone wanted to meet the American miracle worker. And more than one person echoed Atlee's remark to Lilienthal, "You have provided inspiration for many of us with your work." He was especially flattered when the British press noted that he, along with a Britisher, had been "the only names mentioned to be head of the European coal-steel business."[34]

Late that year Lilienthal began planning his and Helen's trip to India and other points east. He had become fascinated with the developmental problems of the huge subcontinent and wondered how the West could help steer India away from the Chinese Communist model. Lilienthal thought he could bring his business and TVA experience to bear on the problem. In January he cleared the project with Lazard and talked *Collier's* into picking up the tab for an around-the-world trip. At the same time he offered Secretary of State Acheson his services as a private "unofficial" ambassador. Assistant Secretary of State George McGhee told him that "at this particular time you can render a service no one else can, going as a private citizen."[35]

On February 2, 1951, Helen and David were off again. In the next six weeks they visited thirteen cities in seven countries. Alighting for a few days each in Italy, Egypt, Thailand, Hong Kong, and Japan, then they crisscrossed the Indian subcontinent for almost three weeks, exploring the tinderbox West Pakistan border, visiting at length with Nehru, the Pakistani prime minister and other officials, inspecting Indian development projects, and enjoying the comforts of Nehru's official residence as guests. The trip was a kaleidoscope of new adventures and insights. He observed after a bone-chilling night in "the best hotel in the Punjab" that it reminded him "of the decayed splendor of a Mississippi Delta hotel of my early TVA days." Lilienthal saw the legacy of centuries of Muslim-Hindu conflict in the stalemate between India and Pakistan over Kashmir and the division of Indus waters, and he agonized over the omnipresent poverty, hostility, and seeming despair. Early in the trip he called "himself a chauvinist American, . . . [seeing] no evidence that [the Pakistanis] have the requisite management ability, the moral power, the leadership, the sense of responsibility, *or* the resources to crawl out of this morass." His frustrations were tempered after visits to impressive dam projects in the Punjab and Orissa, and the massive Tata Steel Works in Jamshedpur, India—as always, a dam was an important talisman for Lilienthal. His view of India further brightened when he met young Indians who had trained at TVA, and after a visit to the Damodar Valley Corporation, a regional river enterprise that had drawn heavily from TVA technical expertise[36]

The most telling insights came from long conversations with Nehru, in which Lilienthal tried to "understand what America's role in Asia should be." The prime minister pulled no punches. After a long night of talk and a second evening of dinner conversation, the tired guest hoped for "no further conversation with the P.M." Nevertheless, Nehru continued on well after midnight. Lilienthal was receptive to Nehru's critical evaluation of American foreign policy in every respect but one, China. He bridled at Nehru's positive view of China and the notion that Chinese hostility toward the United States was largely America's fault. Lilienthal had no doubts about America's Korean response or its critical stance toward China, whose "blasts at us, are full of . . . bitterness." He was taken, though, by Nehru's critique of the way America aided other nations. All too often, in global relations "people set out to *answer* questions without having knowledge and understanding requisite to frame the question they are seeking to answer." The next evening he told Lilienthal that Americans in India "*see* many things . . . *but* they are not receptive to what they see, they don't imbibe the things they see, are not receptive to things outside themselves."[37]

Whereas the European trip introduced Lilienthal to a wider world, the Indian adventure helped foster a global perspective, and started him thinking what his role might be in the international arena. The immediate effect was the publication of two articles for *Collier's*. The first, in June 1951, was a measured text with an alarmist title, "Are We Losing India?" In it he urged a large increase in technical and humanitarian aid. Lilienthal called Nehru a "practical man" with an eye toward the future and deep roots in the past. He reported Nehru's defense of China and defended India for following its own course even when it did not coincide with American policy. Lilienthal concluded that slavish agreement was much less important than "a good working relation with a vast and struggling young nation."[38]

The August article, "Another 'Korea' in the Making," focused on the explosive Indian–West Pakistani border. After reviewing arguments on both sides, Lilienthal concluded that peace depended on recognizing the partition, rejecting a permanent armed truce, and developing a structure of interdependence between the two nations. To achieve these ends, he recommended a bilateral treaty regarding the Indus River basin waters. The agreement would involve compromise over Pakistan's advantage in canals and irrigation systems and India's control over river headwaters. The proposals were received positively by both sides. Within a year the World Bank funded a study to explore the feasibility of the proposal. For years Lilienthal enjoyed being the only person both sides could trust and acting as an informal sounding board for World Bank, Indian, and Pakistani officials as the agreement moved slowly toward resolution. Lilienthal was enormously pleased when Pakistani President Mohammed Ayub cabled him the day a treaty was finally signed in September 1961, "You have cause for legitimate pride in fulfillment of your cherished desire for harmony and understanding between the two neighbors."[39]

The Indian trip also prompted Lilienthal to think again about the relevance of TVA to the developing world. Preoccupied with the war and then his atomic energy vocation, Lilienthal's first insights about TVA and world reconstruction in *TVA: Democracy on the March* never really took root—at least not until India. Something there, perhaps his encounter with young Indian technicians who had studied at TVA or the efforts of the Damodar Valley Corporation, stimulated him to a new vision.[40]

Four months after returning from India, Lilienthal started revising *TVA: Democracy on the March* with an eye toward an international theme. In October, he reminded Truman that George C. Marshall had recently called TVA a "model for the whole world." He told the president that the TVA idea fit well with the new Point Four foreign aid program. In April 1952, during a short vacation, Lilienthal began thinking of the future. He fretted over turning down international jobs, but told himself those jobs would interfere with his consulting work at RCA and get in the way of opportunities at Lazard. Furthermore, he dismissed international work because he lacked the resources to do the job right on a sustained basis. But, he kept telling himself that since TVA was "the most important thing in my life, . . . something that grows out of that might be another great adventure for me." After a lengthy conversation in June 1952 with his confidant at Lazard, Nate Greene, he jotted down "DEL, Inc." Throughout 1952 and into 1953, Lilienthal continued to think of his future and how to give the "TVA model" an international context. In February 1953, as he finished up the galleys of the TVA book, he reminded himself how many of his ideas, including the Indus River proposal and the 1946 plan for an Atomic Development Authority, were "outgrowths of my TVA experience."[41]

In May 1953, the Twentieth Anniversary [of TVA] Edition of *TVA: Democracy on the March* was published. The new edition was identical to the first except that it added a new preface, a chapter on "The TVA Idea Abroad," and an extensive appendix describing nearly twenty international projects "which appear to approach . . . the TVA conception." The new chapter described Supreme Court Justice William O. Douglas's experience in Central Asia, where he had constantly been asked "Why can't we have a TVA?" Lilienthal told of TVA interest in Mexico, Pakistan, India, Scotland, France, and Japan, and of the way his Indus River proposal had been influenced by TVA. "TVA," he concluded, "has rendered its greatest service in safeguarding and nurturing freedom in the world . . . [through] its high symbolic value 'in a thousand valleys' beyond the seas." If no one else was convinced by the rhetoric, Lilienthal was. By October, he started fleshing out his new future. Worrying about all the TVAs springing up around the world without his involvement, he thought he "ought to be working at that sort of enterprise . . . so that I could make a living that way." All he needed was a nudge in the right direction—and the nation of Colombia provided it.[42]

By the early 1950s the Cauca Valley in Colombia was ripe for regional development. Colombia had been the subject of the first World Bank country study in 1949 prepared by one of FDR's early advisors, Lauchlin Currie. Even earlier, in 1928, Cauca Valley elites had commissioned a study on agricultural resources and had fostered a strong sense of regional identity for years. Geographical factors like the isolation forced by high mountain ranges and distinct patterns of crop specialization further strengthened regional unity. In early 1954 a confluence of factors brought Lilienthal to Colombia. Military dictator Gustavo Rojas Pinilla was "looking for a development project that would bring credit to his young regime." Also, the most influential governor in the Cauca basin, Diego Garces (whose brother Bernardo was the Cauca Valley Corporation's [CVC] first executive director and a member of the D&R Board), and the regional director of the Cauca Valley Chapter of the National Association of Industrialists asked Rojas to invite Lilienthal to Colombia.[43]

As far back as August 1953, Lilienthal's New Deal acquaintance Milo Perkins had indicated that Colombia might ask Lilienthal to consult on an economic development project. In November Lilienthal attended a lecture by the Colombian ambassador because he understood he might be invited to work on a project in the Cauca Valley. In the middle of December, Perkins called and said a letter from Rojas Pinilla was in the mail. After several delays, Lilienthal and Helen left on February 12, 1954 for three weeks in Colombia.

When he arrived, Colombia fascinated him as "a frontier country, a *new* country . . . The place is changing like mad." His naiveté about Latin America was evident. He innocently asked why Communism was a threat in an overwhelmingly Catholic nation. He was disturbed by the "filth of the place," but nothing dampened his desire for action. He proudly declared "I am not a scholar, nor scientist. . . . [M]y experience has been in getting things done." After the second week of his whirlwind visit, he told Rojas Pinilla that the Cauca Valley needed a regional development project and promised to put together a plan in the next few months.[44]

Lilienthal's first international report, submitted in June 1954, a year before D&R became a reality, was another rhetorical masterpiece. "Plan Lilienthal" was "based upon the TVA experiment." In it, Lilienthal called for a "Second Liberation" equal to Bolivar's, which offered hope for "rapidly advancing the agricultural, industrial and educational welfare of the entire Colombian people [and which] lies in the creation of a regional development corporation." The language was straight out of *TVA: Democ-*

racy on the March and his new faith in big business. He spoke of the yoking of *"private* business activity . . [and] . . . *public* development"; that the "regional agency should be a *demonstration* area"; that "the development of that stream [the Cauca River] is inseparably inter-related to the land; [and] that the agency should also generate electric power."

The most curious aspect of the report was the linkage between development and a guarantee of fair and stable coffee prices. In his argument, Lilienthal reflected either amazing brashness or naiveté, or perhaps both. He reminded Rojas Pinilla that America was unhappy with high coffee prices and might take punitive action against Colombia. He then noted that if the American people knew that their "proceeds of purchases of coffee . . . are [to be] used for such a development program . . . as I here suggest, the chance . . . of winning American public opinion to the cause of fair and compensatory coffee prices as a long-term policy, is improved." Lilienthal made two puzzling claims: First, that America would tolerate higher coffee prices if his plan was accepted. The second related to the issue of "fairness." At one point, he spoke of "fair and compensatory coffee prices" as if they were synonymous. However, he defined fair prices earlier as "those fixed in a free competitive market rather than by arbitrary political pressures, boycotts or governmental 'ceilings.'" Accepting this definition, one may have "fair" or "compensatory" prices, but not both. Did Lilienthal deliberately dissemble? Probably not—once more, his rhetoric ruled. And he probably sincerely believed that the American people would sacrifice for another TVA on foreign shores.[45]

A few months later, with Lilienthal present, Rojas Pinilla established a provisional CVC Board and ordered it to draw up statutes and a program. For the next two years the board relied heavily on Lilienthal, and, after D&R's incorporation, Clapp, for direction. Lilienthal worried that the official charter had not been signed by mid-1955 and that the World Bank was about to pull out of Colombia because of maladministration in the military regime. He flew to Colombia in July 1955 and was instrumental (according to his journal) in finally getting the charter signed.

Once signed, CVC began to take shape. In July 1956, however, Rojas Pinilla withdrew support from the key Calima hydroelectric project, a move that threatened the heart of the plan. Again, Lilienthal intervened. He and Clapp, now partners, warned the general that the World Bank would not approve the cancellation of the Calima project. Rojas Pinilla refused to budge, and Lilienthal and Clapp resigned as CVC consultants effective in October. Early that month the Cauca Valley press loudly protested the pending end of the Lilienthal arrangement. In a letter to Bernardo Garces, Gordon Clapp offered to extend D&R's contract if the government reinstated the Calima project. The letter demonstrated the degree to which Lilienthal and Clapp were willing to play hardball to defend their concept of development. Nevertheless, Rojas remained firm, and the crisis continued. The CVC board resigned in February 1957, and Bernardo Garces in April. Lilienthal despaired, "Anyway: [CVC] is finished." But the corporation found new life when Rojas Pinilla was overthrown in May 1957.[46]

The CVC was a well-documented success. For Lilienthal, it was an enduring example of development done the TVA way. He sincerely believed his touch made it possible. In 1961 in Bogota he thrilled to "hear an idea of mine that later became the CVC, the subject of exegesis." Six years later, enthusiastic about a new CVC contract with D&R, he said that "it would be great if after almost fifteen years my child, the now sturdy CVC, would again become an important part of my work." Lilienthal did play a crucial role in the project. His plan, reputation, and strong personality helped mobilize Colombian elites who were already sold on regional development. Moreover, in the early years D&R helped CVC decide which foreign firms would receive contracts. In reality, the TVA technical ethic was carefully nurtured in the Cauca Valley. Over time, CVC, much the same as TVA before, accommodated various interests, shifted focus, and adjusted programs. Lilienthal was always pleased with the results. He returned to Colombia frequently and established lifelong friendships. In 1968 he contributed $25,000 to the University del Valle. And yet, even with CVC there was disappointment. In 1973, D&R Executive Vice-President Andrea Pampanini reported to Lilienthal that the CVC had turned down a D&R proposal because of "a quite bitter disagreement in regard to the payment of a retainer fee of $25,000 to D&R" some years past. [47]

Clearly, the 1954 Colombia adventure provided the stimulus for Lilienthal to form his own company. After a promise of financial support from Lazard in exchange for profits on venture capital projects, Lilienthal wrote on Monday, May 23, 1955, that he had "crossed the Rubicon, today" with a memorandum to Meyer setting forth his plans for a "resources development service agency." By the end of the week he was thinking of the challenge of "weav[ing] my way through the very real dangers of trying to combine the objectives of a banking group and my own objectives of trying to do some building of the life of ordinary people here and there on the globe." Typically, at a time most men were thinking of retiring, David Lilienthal was beginning a challenge that was to span the far corners of the globe.[48]

CHAPTER 12

Lilienthal and the World

An article might be called "The Fallacy of Good Intentions," the notion that a foreigner because of his good intentions can go into a country like Persia, or Colombia, for that matter, and directly influence the political and social consequences of economic development.

—David E. Lilienthal, May 5, 1958

An Idea Becomes Reality

The 1950s was an exhilarating time. Business boomed, anxieties about the world lessened, and international tensions eased. Eisenhower made peace in Korea, Communist aggression in Eastern Europe and China was replaced by an uneasy peace between East and West, and America reached out to a world it had once shunned. The dramatic fifteen weeks that framed the birth of the Truman Doctrine and the Marshall Plan testified to the nation's will and faith in good works abroad. The president's Point Four program, which called for "a bold new program . . . for the improvement and growth of underdeveloped areas," gave the country even more resolve to put a strange new ally called "foreign aid" to work.[1]

Lilienthal was swept along by the times—he made his million and became an internationalist. He conferred with Jean Monnet, Clement Attlee, and Jawaharlal Nehru, and mediated the Indian-Pakistani dispute and forged a regional development plan in Colombia. On May 23, 1955, Lilienthal told André Meyer he was ready to form a unique "organization to provide development services to underdeveloped countries." Soon after, he recruited Gordon Clapp, then assistant administrator of New York City, as president of his new Development and Resources Corporation (D&R), and he presented Meyer with an expansive statement about the "joint venture between myself and Lazard." D&R would incorporate Lilienthal's "government development experience" and Lazard's "private business and financial talents" to stimulate economic development abroad. In exchange for benefits from international "business opportunities" uncovered by D&R, Lazard agreed to support the company and underwrite losses for three years. The incorporation was approved in June 1955, and one thousand shares of voting stock were divided equally between Lazard Frères and Lilienthal.[2]

The company started quietly. Other than announcements in New York business pages, Clapp and Lilienthal "discouraged publicity, articles, speeches, etc.," preferring to work through their own and Lazard's reputations. The International Bank for Reconstruction and Development (World Bank), impressed by Lilienthal's work in Colombia, introduced the partners to potential clients in Iran and Italy. In the fall, D&R announced its first projects, a $45,000 contract with the Cauca Valley Corporation of Colombia and a $15,000 agreement with the Puerto Rican Water Resources Authority (PRWRA). In 1956, D&R signed other pacts with an Italian development corporation and the first of its contracts with Iran for the massive development of Khuzistan Province.[3]

In the early years, Lilienthal and Clapp operated with a small cadre. Their first addition was their General Counsel Nathan Greene, whom they brought in from Lazard. In the spring of 1956, former TVA general managers John Oliver and John Blandford took over as executive vice-president and chief representative in Iran, respectively, and William Voorduin, the former head civil engineer for TVA, became vice-president for engineering. By summer of 1957, D&R had thirty employees and ninety local hires in Iran. Ten of its employees were former TVA men, including four of the five corporate officers. By 1958, the payroll had grown to include 64 employees and 437 local hires. D&R moved its Agriculture Department to northern California in 1965 because of the difficulty of attracting agriculture specialists to the New York City area. By the late 1960s D&R employed more than 200 professionals and support staff, mostly in California, New York City, and Iran.[4]

Until Clapp's fatal heart attack in April 1963, The two men worked together closely. Clapp was Lilienthal's sounding board and confidant—they shared the vision, traveled the same roads servicing clients, and they stood together on principle. In 1956, they resisted Rojas Pinilla's interference with the Cauca Valley Corporation. In 1960, neither hesitated a bit before canceling an attractive contract with Argentina when they found that their Italian partner, ITALCONSULT, had bribed a local official.[5]

Yet, they were very different in temperament. Lilienthal was the idea man and catalyst, always ready for action. No one at D&R could sketch a bigger vision or project greater confidence. No one could match his gold-plated name when it came to opening doors to audiences with sovereigns, presidents, and prime ministers. Between 1955 and 1960 he averaged three months a year abroad, including nine trips to Iran, seven to Italy, four to Latin America, and trips to Africa, and Asia east of Iran. As Oliver noted, "D&R wouldn't have been possible without Dave." But, he continued, "the guy who did the work was Gordon Clapp." John Burnett, another D&R

executive, recalled that Clapp made the nine-to-five decisions. Burnett also recalled that where Lilienthal was optimistic and charismatic, Clapp was cautious and precise, always formal in manner, and always with a strong moral compass. Clapp, as his brother Norman remembered, did what no one else could do—bring Lilienthal down to earth when he took off on his flights of fancy.[6]

Although the two shared a deep, mutual respect, their relationship was often strained—Clapp was formal and reserved; Lilienthal was full of himself and had his own agenda. Lilienthal felt his partner was too cautious about D&R's capabilities. For example, Clapp was much less sanguine about the company's entrepreneurial mission. Once, in a staff meeting, he remarked "that the price . . . of working hard at something that would or might make money . . . was more than he. . . was willing to pay." Lilienthal was also bothered by his friend's rigidity. More than once he opposed Clapp when he pushed Iran to the wall on contract provisions or overdue payments. In 1962, he was so worried over slow contract talks that he vowed "to take over from Gordon . . . [in] reaching a workable agreement." For his part, Clapp was frustrated by Lilienthal's impatience and refusal to be a team player. Joe Volpe, who worked on D&R legal matters, recalled that Clapp complained when Lilienthal made grand and unrealistic plans and then expected others to do the impossible. Some felt that keeping Lilienthal in check wore Clapp down. Burnett, Volpe, Oliver, and even Lilienthal noticed Clapp's growing fatigue. Yet, he remained loyal all those years. John Oliver recalled asking Clapp after an argument with Lilienthal, "Is this burden really necessary?" After a moment, Clapp replied, "Yes, John, he is."[7]

While Lilienthal certainly contributed to Clapp's frustration and fatigue, there was another source—Iran. D&R might have one other contract or a dozen, but Iran was always the company's main source of income. Nevertheless, the Persian connection was a mixed blessing. Payment delays frequently resulted in serious cash flow problems, and agonizingly slow contract negotiations brought on many anxious moments. Sooner or later every D&R executive was drawn into the Iranian vortex. Some, like Blandford, resigned in frustration; others, like Voorduin, were worn down by the grinding pressure. For nine years Clapp bore the brunt of the Iranian burden. Lilienthal conversed with the Shah; Clapp worked out the fine points with mercurial ministers and functionaries. Clapp was D&R's point man in Iran, and he shielded his boss from many maddening details.

D&R and Iran: Noble Intentions, Questionable Outcomes

Iran was Lilienthal's consuming passion from 1955 to 1978. Iranian contracts sustained D&R, and the Khuzistan project gave him an opportunity to bring the TVA idea to life again. There were other rewards, including true Iranian friendships and an ego-boosting relationship with the Shah.

Lilienthal made twenty-nine trips to Iran between 1956 and 1977—the Shah received him twenty-three times and he and Helen were guests at Persia's lavish 2,500-year celebration at Persepolis in 1971. Whenever the Shah was in the United States, at his embassy, at the White House, or elsewhere, Lilienthal was always invited and recognized as a special friend. In Iran, he was received with respect by prime ministers, ministry heads, and friends like Abol Hassan Ebtehaj and Mehdi Samii, who introduced him to their country and remained true the rest of his life.[8]

D&R's Persian connection arose from the turbulence of Iranian politics and renewed Western interest in Central Asia. The short-lived Mossadeq regime, accompanied by the nationalization of the Iranian oil industry in 1951 and increased Soviet and indigenous Communist activities, raised Western anxieties. The United States was disturbed because Iran's traditional Western protector, the British, had declined in influence. In 1953, the CIA helped overthrow Mossadeq and restore Mohammad Reza Shah to the Iranian throne, thus beginning twenty-five years of official American support of the Shah's regime. American aid to Iran doubled to $110 million in 1954, more than 60 percent of Iranian government expenditures. In 1952, the United States had ten technical officials in Iran; by 1956, that number had skyrocketed to more than three hundred.

The World Bank also had a stake. Iran was one of the bank's original targets, but instability, corruption, and the Mossadeq interlude had kept it from tendering a loan. The Shah's return promised stability, and his appointment of Ebtehaj as managing director of the national development agency Plan Organization (PO) signaled a new commitment to economic development. An international economist and banker, Ebtehaj was respected in the West for his technical knowledge and incorruptibility. Even better, the Shah promised that neither he nor the omnivorous bureaucratic fiefdoms would interfere in PO activities.[9]

In May 1955 Ebtehaj asked senior World Bank official Hector Prud'homme to head his technical bureau and search for the very best foreign advisors. Soon after, World Bank President Eugene Black and Prud'homme arranged for Lilienthal and Ebtehaj to meet in Istanbul in September. The two dynamos took to each other immediately. D&R wanted a big contract, and Ebtehaj needed someone like Lilienthal to legitimate his operation. Lilienthal described Ebtehaj as "positively incandescent, impetuous, full of feeling." Ebtehaj later told Helen Lilienthal that in David, "I knew I had found the best man in the world to carry out my old dreams in Khuzistan." They shared a grand vision of large-scale and massive development and cultural transformation—according to James A. Bill, they were both "technical missionaries." Regardless of the venue, the Tennessee Valley or Khuzistan, what mattered was the swift marshaling of resources and action without political interference. After their visit, Ebtehaj invited Lilienthal to Iran and flew home to secure the Shah's approval.[10]

Before their first visit in February 1956, Ebtehaj wrote Lilienthal and Clapp about his vision for developing the Khuzistan, a remote southwestern province on the Iraqi border. World Bank officials were cautious. Prud'homme wrote Black that his perspective on Lilienthal's visit depended on "whether what he may propose relieves us of some of the burden we are now carrying, or adds to it." The month-long tour was a whirlwind. Ebtehaj escorted Lilienthal and Clapp in and out of ministerial offices. They took the overnight train to Khuzistan and returned to an audience with the Shah. Lilienthal was predictably optimistic. He dismissed advice that nothing could be done because of high temperatures and soil salinity, saying, as Ebtehaj remembered, that experts had predicted similar things about the Tennessee Valley. Lilienthal told Ebtehaj that all the ingredients for success were present and that a project at the site of an ancient civilization would be an inspiring national symbol. For Ebtehaj, Lilienthal's vision confirmed "all the dreams I had concerning Khuzestan." No doubt, Lilienthal had also convinced himself. In March, he wrote Eleanor Roosevelt that "two of the President's 'boys'" were going to restore western Persia "to the verdure of trees and grain that it had many centuries ago," a job her husband said "he would love to tackle as he flew over its barren plains" during World War II.[11]

After meeting the Shah, Lilienthal and Clapp signed a two-year $813,000 contract on March 14 with Iran's Plan Organization "to plan and help carry out a long-range program of agricultural and industrial development of the Khuzestan region, along TVA lines." The unique contract, which delegated executive authority to D&R, covered mapping, dam site and power use surveys, soil and salinity studies, minerals inventory, and review of industrial development potential, including the feasibility of the Shah's pet idea, a fertilizer plant. Needless to say, the partners were thrilled over the "degree of responsibility quite extraordinary for private individuals in their own countries, to say nothing of a foreign country so strange and new to us." Lilienthal was little concerned by troublesome signals. Both Prud'homme and Ebtehaj warned him that unless D&R was "prepared to take full responsibility . . . nothing would happen." Neither was he perturbed over a stormy confrontation between Ebtehaj and ministers over PO's privileged status, and Ebtehaj's feeling that someone had to challenge "the stupidity, corruption, and nonsense of 'these fellows.'"[12]

D&R moved quickly, dispatching Voorduin to Iran in May for preliminary surveys, and in mid-June signing a contract supplement for $3 million. In December PO extended D&R's authority to all Khuzistan projects and established the Khuzistan Development Service (KDS) as D&R's agent in Iran. Throughout 1957, Lilienthal and Clapp's vision grew and reinforced Ebtehaj's notions of massive development. In April, Lilienthal urged the Shah to "action even before the investigation and initial report were completed." By mid-1957, D&R recommended a huge irrigation program, regional power distribution projects, sugar cane plantations, petrochemical works, including fertilizer and polyvinyl chloride (PVC) plants, and the Dez hydroelectric project, which Lilienthal called the "keystone in the arch of the Khuzestan region."[13]

Meanwhile, the World Bank, which had just finalized a $75 million nonspecific loan to Iran, was becoming alarmed at the turn of events, fearing that Ebtehaj's plans were too ambitious and a threat to Iran's fragile economy. The bank was troubled that many of D&R's recommendations were flawed by questionable assumptions and slipshod analyses. The most bothersome concern was the economical viability of the Dez Dam. Growing evidence suggested that it and the accompanying irrigation project were too costly when compared to thermal generating plants and surface water diversion schemes. Moreover, bank officials were disturbed that D&R had encouraged Iran to resist their advice to proceed cautiously and pare down the project. In April 1957 Burke Knapp, the bank's associate director, warned Ebtehaj that excessive spending might trigger serious inflation. The PO director angrily responded that without quick action, "Iran will surely die."[14]

The seesaw battle, between the bank on one side, and D&R and Iran on the other, continued for two and a half years. D&R pushed for a Dez Dam loan in the summer of 1957. The bank said the company had not adequately addressed cost-benefit issues and resettlement plans, and that it had failed to relate the project to regional goals. The bank went on to say that it "would consider whether the project was bankable" only after a comprehensive report. Lilienthal responded with persuasive rhetoric. In Tehran in September he told Ebtehaj, "God must have intended that a dam be built in that great gorge." To the Shah, he called the Dez project a "heroic structure" and compared it to the pyramids. Unlike those ancient monuments, "built to glorify dead kings, this huge work will be devoted to the living" and "a symbol of the way in which an ancient nation is moving into the future." In a few days he was on his way home with another $6.5 million. In October, Lilienthal announced that Iran would provide more than $38 million for the Dez and other Khuzistan projects. Lilienthal was in action, barely a year after Voorduin's preliminary surveys.[15]

The bank accused D&R of "retreat[ing] to arguments such as the effect on public psychology of the building of a great dam." In October, Black admonished Ebtehaj, and in a San Francisco speech chastised developing nations for their impatience. Then, the bank decided to teach D&R and Iran a lesson, using its best weapon—a bureaucratic stall. For months, the bank tormented D&R with constant requests for new information or revisions, and delayed its required field trip until September 1958. Then, the bank dallied several more months before making a final decision.[16]

Meanwhile, Lilienthal, Clapp, and Ebtehaj fought back. In March 1958, Iran snubbed the bank by committing another $13.1 million to Khuzistan, and Lilienthal continued his assault. In April 1959 he told the bank that in Iran's case, political issues were as important as technical judgments. He also threatened to withdraw if a loan was not approved, an event that could prove embarrassing to the bank. In Iran, he used similar tactics to keep the Persians on track. In October 1958 he warned Ebtehaj that D&R might back out unless the bank acted soon. In March 1959, he repeated the threat to the Shah, the prime minister, and the PO's Economic Bureau, which had begun having second thoughts about the Dez price tag. At the same time, Lilienthal and Clapp presented their final report, a two-hundred-page recommendation on "The Unified Development of the Natural Resources of the Khuzestan Region." The document was as much poetry as technical exposition. In the introduction, the consultants noted that "Persia's dream of Khuzestan restored was [until recently] still but a vision; today it is a dream no longer." Later, they emphasized that however significant the project's tangible results, intangibles were even more important. The most compelling fact was that the inspiration for "restor[ing] and expand[ing] a once flourishing valley to its once great glory, is wholly Persian in its origin." Moreover, the unified Khuzistan project would be "truly productive" and "understandable by people of all kinds, the powerful and humble, those well educated and those who are not."[17]

In spite of Lilienthal's efforts and Iran's objections, the bank rejected the Dez loan in May 1959. Dismayed at first, Lilienthal was buoyed when Assistant Prime Minister Khosrow Hedayat told him, "We want the Dez," and the Shah promised to find the money by "deferring or canceling other things, or by getting World Bank loans . . . for *other* things, and re-allocating those funds for the Dez." Hedayat promised Clapp another $10 million in September, and the bank's resolve soon crumbled. In part, Iran's stubborn commitment to the project helped change minds. Knapp wrote Black that while "the Dez Project is too big, too expensive, and too much beyond Iran's prospective capacities," Iran was likely to go ahead anyway by diverting funds to Dez now covered by other bank loans. Another factor was the bank's grudging respect for what D&R had done in a difficult situation. In a May 1959 letter to Knapp, Prud'homme said that Lilienthal and Clapp had done wonders in the midst of the "debilitating Iranian inability to take decisions." If Iran went on without them, "the Khuzistan operation is again due for Mr. [Eugene] Black's chamber of horrors." With the $75 million loan in 1957 and additional loans of $72 million in 1959, the bank could hardly afford for the Iranians to foul up. Prud'homme concluded that it might be best to help find other financing to ensure Lilienthal and Clapp's continuing involvement in Iran. Prud'homme also wrote Ebtehaj that Dez was not feasible, but that, nevertheless, it had a priceless ingredient, the "management and inspiration of Lilienthal and Clapp." In May, Knapp told Lilienthal he felt foolish about turning him down and hinted that the bank might fund other projects and let Iran shift its own money to the Dez.[18]

In June, D&R officials lobbied the bank to change its mind, and the next month it finally relented: at staff meetings then and in September, an alternative plan was approved to fund Dez and reduce the irrigation program to a pilot project. In late August, World Bank officials told the PO and D&R that the dam was being reconsidered, and in early 1960 a $42 million loan was approved. Much amended from original plans, the final program still included the Dez Dam. Now, Clapp and Lilienthal could make their vision of Iranian development, TVA-style, a reality.[19]

As bright as D&R's future seemed, there were darker currents that challenged Lilienthal more than the World Bank ever did. Just as his triumphs, the completion of the Dez Dam in 1963 and Lilienthal's special status with the Shah, were defining elements of the Iranian experience, so were the more unsavory aspects of the relationship. In concentrating almost all of his attention the first few years on setting up the Khuzistan project and wrestling with the World Bank over funding, he ignored other dynamics of Iranian politics which kept D&R in a frustrating and precarious situation.

There had been many warnings about Iran. In 1957, the House Committee on Government Operations concluded that U.S.-Iranian programs were rife with slipshod management and bureaucratic corruption. Between 1958 and 1961 Lilienthal was cautioned about Iran at least five times, by Ford Foundation staff, the Pakistani Foreign Minister, Walter Lippmann, Edward R. Murrow, and Eleanor Roosevelt. American pundits warned of Iran's potential instability. In London, in November 1959, Murrow advised his friend he was dealing with "a rather brittle regime." Manzoor Qadir, himself a member of the Pakistani elite, told Lilienthal that he was appalled by the ostentatious Iranian elite and their lack of concern for the poverty-stricken masses.[20]

Economic crises posed the first challenges to PO's effort to execute its lofty plans. In a 1958 staff memo, Clapp was warned that by 1962, PO revenues would fall $323 million short of planned expenditures and that D&R could expect severe cutbacks. By 1959 high inflation forced the Iranian government to accept austerity measures in return for assistance from the International Monetary Fund. In February 1960, PO economic advisor Kenneth Hansen told Khuzistan Development Service officials that even with the Dez loan, "DRC-KDS can look forward to no cessation of financial troubles during 1960–62." Falling oil prices and increasing competition from other government programs for shrinking resources were steadily eroding PO's position.[21]

Political pressures continued to build. Lilienthal faced strong resistance at PO in September 1957, when its Chemical Committee insisted on building a urea fertilizer plant instead of a demonstration project he recommended to determine "the *best kinds* of chemical fertilizer . . . and then to *see to it that they are well used,* by farmers through education, etc.—a TVA sort of approach." In April 1958, Lilienthal was floored when the High Council of Ministers rejected a proposal, sponsored partly by Lazard Frères and endorsed, he thought, by the Shah, to set up a local development bank. A few months later, Lilienthal became aware of PO staff criticism of D&R's autonomy and more High Council grumbling that Khuzistan was absorbing too much of Iran's limited resources. As long as Ebtehaj was in charge, however, D&R was relatively safe from outside predators and criticism inside PO. Money was no problem, either—while projects might be scaled back, Ebtehaj was a stickler for paying contractors on time. According to his biographer, if payments "were not made within five days of receiving the relevant accounts, the person responsible for such payments was dismissed."[22]

Things changed drastically with Ebtehaj's forced resignation in early 1959. As effective as he had been, his departure was not unexpected. Both the Shah and traditional bureaucratic elites had become concerned that the maverick had extended his power base too far. His reliance on public-

minded foreign experts like Lilienthal and Clapp in a land with few techni-
cal-managerial resources and little sense of public service led to accusations
that he was "'anti-Iranian' and a foreign 'stooge.'" His rejection of bureaucratic politics in favor of "rational development" alienated ministers who
also objected to his superior attitude and the siphoning of funds from their
own coffers. By January 1959, Ebtehaj was rapidly becoming persona non
grata. He tangled with Prime Minister Manouchehr Eqbal over oil revenues and made no secret of his opposition to growing military expenditures, which included an embarrassing dressing down of a visiting American admiral. The last straw, however, was Ebtehaj's opposition to a Ministry
of Industry and Mines plan for a fertilizer plant in Shiraz. Not only did the
project challenge PO's prerogative as sole source for industrial development programs, but it was scheduled to cost 50 percent more than a similar
plant in Khuzistan. It helped little that one of the Shah's mistresses was
involved in the negotiations for the Shiraz plant. Shortly after taking his
vociferous opposition to the Shah, legislation was drawn up stripping Ebtehaj
of his powers. Two days later, on February 14, Ebtehaj quit. With the resignation, the Shah eliminated his most distinguished potential rival and started
taking control of economic planning and development policy himself.[23]

Ebtehaj's resignation was a watershed. No longer could D&R depend
on a stable and politically neutral host. The PO was immediately plunged
into traditional bureaucratic politics and behind-the-scenes manipulation.
Many who were offended by D&R's unprecedented autonomy, now saw a
chance to get back at the foreigners. Lilienthal's continuing relationship
with the Shah helped little, either. On one hand, many officials objected to
the special relationship and did what they could to undermine D&R whenever they could. On the other, as James Bill makes clear, the relationship
had a Janus-faced quality that Lilienthal never understood. In his eyes, the
Shah was a grateful patron who appreciated and supported D&R's efforts
in Khuzistan and later in other areas. To the monarch, Lilienthal was an
important apologist for Iran who warranted a certain level of support for
his Iranian ventures. Nevertheless, the Shah did little to stop the never-
ending harassment and humiliation exacted on D&R by powerful groups
whose support he also needed. Lilienthal never realized the Shah's role in
Ebtehaj's leave-taking, nor did he wonder much about Ebtehaj's arrest in
November 1961 and his seven ensuing months of solitary confinement. At
first, he puzzled over the seeming contradiction between charges against
Ebtehaj that he had illegally engaged D&R in Khuzistan "and the fact that
the Shah, the Prime Minister, and the rest are praising that venture so lavishly." But even that concern passed quickly.[24]

For some months, D&R's work in Iran continued as it had under
Ebtehaj. The dedicated PO cadre tried as long as it could to deflect political
interference. When a second Khuzistan contract was finalized in 1962,
however, D&R ceded much of its unique authority to Iranian agencies associated with the project. In part, the change represented bureaucratic efforts to gain greater control over the process. But D&R was also commit-

ted to a systematic "Iranization" of its organization and wanted to shift more of the executive and subcontractor financial burdens to Iran to minimize the effect of late payments on D&R's cash flow problem. Other changes in the Khuzistan program resulted from reactions to economic difficulties and accommodations with the World Bank necessary to land the $42 million Dez loan: a large irrigation project was postponed, the PVC project was abandoned, and several rural development and public health programs were scaled back. Even the Dez Dam completion date was pushed back from 1962 to 1963. Nevertheless, work on the Dez continued, and in March 1963, at the grand dedication of the Pahlavi dam and reservoir, Lilienthal was able to report his "great experience," seeing that "'our' dam now controls the Dez River."[25]

There were other signs of D&R's shifting fortunes. While D&R extended its Khuzistan contracts for several additional years, first with PO and then the regional Khuzistan Water and Power Authority (KWPA), payment delays, tortuous contract negotiations, and discouraging encounters with officials became the order of the day. The $10 million promised in September 1959 shrank to $2.5 million, with a vague promise that the rest would soon follow. In October 1959, Lilienthal complained to Ebtehaj about "the deterioration of the kind of drive from the Iranian side that we experienced under him," and "how harassed we had been about the advance payments, the delays and uncertainties." In November Lilienthal and Clapp sat through an hour of discussion in Farsi in the prime minister's office, punctuated only by a brief summary translation for their benefit. Year after year, D&R was reduced to the humiliating ritual of begging for agreed-upon sums and then threatening to withdraw if payments were not forthcoming. By early 1967, the cash flow problem was so severe that Lilienthal lent $50,000 of his own money to meet the payroll.[26]

D&R, and then KWPA, rapidly became pawns in Iran's political games. In April 1961, Deputy Prime Minister Ahmad Aramesh, the head of Plan Organization, criticized KDS for its extravagant programs. A year later he accused D&R of taking $100 million from PO without accounting for "a single rial," a charge that prompted more questions from American congressmen already concerned about D&R's financial doings in Iran. Lilienthal exploded with anger that spring when an Iranian official confided that D&R was being singled out for criticism as a way of bringing pressure on the U.S. government. For some time, D&R's relationship with KWPA was secure because Lilienthal's close friend Abdol Reza Ansari was managing director. In early 1964, however, the Ministry of Water and Power took over KWPA and all hopes for autonomous and apolitical development in Khuzistan vanished. Ansari found it impossible to maintain his independence or to protect D&R. Company morale plummeted in June 1965 when another foreign firm was chosen to work on two other dams in D&R's 1959 Khuzistan report. A second blow fell a year later when the Ministry of Power and Light named a new KWPA managing director who was opposed to regional autonomy. By mid-decade, Lilienthal seemed resigned to these not very pleasant circumstances, musing that "I have worked my way out of the quagmire of resentments and anger, to a plateau where I can see things more clearly."[27]

In spite of the mounting frustrations, Lilienthal remained enthusiastic about the Shah, who knew that nothing fueled Lilienthal's energies and aroused his sense of loyalty more than praise and attention. Every chance he had, the Shah lauded his special American friends. In 1962, at the Council on Foreign Affairs, he called Lilienthal and Clapp's work in Iran as "grandiose and spectacular as your own TVA." Five years later at a White House State dinner he singled out Lilienthal, saying, "A mark of the spirit of your country toward mine and one of the greatest contributions your great country has made to my government and my people has been that of this very distinguished citizen, who has wrought such wonders in your country."[28]

Lilienthal responded in kind. As Bill noted, he "developed a strong loyalty to Pahlavi rule and became an extremely effective voice for the shah in the United States." In *Foreign Affairs* in October 1959, Lilienthal wrote about a "green and flourishing Khuzestan region" with "its origin in the imagination, the sense of history and the judgment of Iranian leadership." The Persians would succeed because they had sustained "an atmosphere of urgency and singleness of purpose." Five years later, at Columbia University, he reiterated his faith in Iran and spoke of the events that had "transform[ed] the Desert to a Garden." In less than eight years Iranians were in charge of most of the technical responsibilities, a feat hardly imaginable a few years earlier. In addition, the future was secure because of the "superior quality of young Iranians . . . attracted to public service." And his optimism extended to all Iranians. The Khuzistan peasants, he concluded, had "already demonstrated their ability to apply improved farming practices," so much so that the region would soon compete "with the Imperial Valley of California" in food production. In 1967, he gave Iran's nascent agribusiness efforts a ringing endorsement at the National Industrial Conference Board in New York City, asserting that "Iran stands apart from the other countries of the Middle East." Its "politically stable regime" has engaged in "rational organization and exploitation" of national resources and has "avoided . . . . regional power struggles, ideological quarrels and military adventures." In late 1969 he defended Iran's agriculture reform efforts to a skeptical Robert McNamara, president of the World Bank, who argued that the reforms had undermined the stability of rural life by inadequately supporting small landholders and overly emphasizing corporate farms and agribusinesses.[29]

Lilienthal's approbation of the Shah was even stronger. He confided to his journal that the Shah had a strong "sense of social mission." Another time, he wrote, "I really believe in this man." After the Shah's 1962 Council on Foreign Relations speech, Lilienthal called it "an absolute knockout, a smash hit." He was no less enthusiastic in public. At an Iranian embassy gathering with U.S. business leaders in 1958, he was thrilled that he "was talking for the Shah," who was sitting in the front row. To D&R employees in Khuzistan in 1960, Lilienthal called the Shah "one of the most capable practical and economic leaders . . . anywhere in the world." Comparing him with Lincoln, he cited the Shah as "an example of a leader with a warm heart who has a concern for people—for the poor people, for all of the people of his country." At a 1967 White House dinner he talked for fifteen minutes with Mrs. Johnson about "what a remarkable man the Shah was." The next night he offered more words of praise at a special dinner at Averell Harriman's New York mansion.[30]

In a sense, it is ironic that Lilienthal, who had been so wise on his own political turf, was such an easy mark for the Shah of Iran. There is solace in knowing that Lilienthal was not alone. A substantial portion of America's political and business elite, including Republicans, Democrats, liberals, and conservatives, followed the Shah without question for a quarter of a century. Lilienthal distinguished himself, however, by allowing yet another masterful power broker to cast a spell on him. The venue again was a far-away land plagued by instability and bureaucratic intrigue—Vietnam. This time the seducer was an American president—Lyndon Baines Johnson.

A Chimera: Peace in the Midst of War

Lilienthal had known Lyndon Johnson since the late 1930s, when the young Texas congressman became an instant TVA fan. Before going to the Senate in 1948, Johnson served briefly as a supportive House member on the Joint Committee on Atomic Energy. Other than being invited to a dinner for Nigeria's president in the late 1950s, Lilienthal had no contact with Johnson until the 1960 Democratic Convention in Los Angeles. At the time, Lilienthal, an unofficial Kennedy supporter, concluded that Johnson "seems to be spoiled by his period of unquestioned 'leadership' in the Senate, so he seems to resent critical questions."[31]

For the next five years, Lilienthal kept in touch with the Kennedy-Johnson administrations. In 1961, Under Secretary of State Chester Bowles tried unsuccessfully to recruit him, first as assistant secretary of state for Latin America and later as ambassador to Thailand or the Congo. He piqued Lilienthal's interest with the Thai offer, suggesting that the assignment would allow him to "create the atmosphere and steam behind the development of the Mekong River, a big Southeast Asian TVA." Lilienthal served on the Peace Corps Advisory Committee and was an occasional guest at White House state dinners. His first contacts with President Johnson included a White House luncheon for the Shah in June 1964 and a private meeting afterwards to lobby on Iran's behalf. While Johnson had little idea how he could utilize Lilienthal's talents, he knew his guest appreciated flattery and praise. As Lilienthal remembered, the president told him that "what is going on in Iran is about the best thing going on anywhere in the world."[32]

Johnson's interest in a peaceful thrust for his Vietnam policy evolved from both moral and political considerations. Like Lilienthal, the president believed in regional development. He had been proud of his own efforts to develop a "little TVA" on the Texas Colorado River in the 1930s and 1940s. Moreover, he was taken by the potential of the Mekong Delta on a trip to Southeast Asia in 1961. The idea surfaced again in 1965 at Johns Hopkins University, when he called for a billion-dollar development program for both North and South Vietnam. In summer 1966, John Macy, Johnson's personnel advisor, suggested that Lilienthal would be a good choice to head up a Vietnamese peace initiative. Not long after, in late August, Helen picked up the phone and told David, "with a resigned look, 'The White House calling.'" On September 7, Lilienthal talked to presidential assistant Robert Komer in Washington about leading a "joint postwar development effort" in South Vietnam. For the next two months Lilienthal thought hard about the assignment. On one hand, the Iran job had become more difficult, and he was wary of "an unappetizing job [in Vietnam], with an absolute minimum of apparent prospects for doing something effective." On the other, when the president calls, patriotism "strongly favors accepting the responsibility."

After a fall summit on postwar economic planning in Manila with Prime Minister Nguyen Ky, Johnson moved quickly. On December 16, the White House announced that Lilienthal would "lead a nongovernmental American team to work with Vietnamese experts on long-range planning for the Vietnamese economy." With this decision, Johnson hoped to appeal to a growing chorus of critics of his Vietnam policy. In addition, the administration thought that talking peace might influence South Vietnam to do the same and perhaps entice North Vietnam into a cooperative venture. It is also likely that Johnson, for all his cynical image, had his own vision of peace and prosperity in the region. Who could represent him better than David Lilienthal, the symbol of TVA and a consummate American liberal?[33]

Ignoring the cautions of family and friends that he was taking on an impossible, even immoral, assignment, Lilienthal threw himself into the project. Between February 1967 and April 1969 he made four trips to Vietnam to rally his American and Vietnamese colleagues, and to act as official spokesman for "The Joint Development Group" to both sides, including Ambassadors Henry Cabot Lodge Jr. and Ellsworth Bunker, General William Westmoreland, Agency for International Development (AID) officials, and the Vietnamese high command, headed by Ky and Nguyen Thieu. He also accompanied Johnson in March 1967 to meet with Ky and Thieu in Guam. Back home he became an strong advocate of the prospects for economic development once peace was secured and even to a certain extent while the war was going on. Television interviews with Bill Ryan, Hugh Downs, Edwin Newman, and Helen Meyner, New York City talk show host, reinforced his belief that something good would come from U.S. efforts in Indochina. Flattering articles in *Business Week,* the *New York Times,* and *U.S. News and World Report* about Lilienthal's initiative, and his own writing, especially a forceful piece in *Foreign Affairs* in January 1969, helped fuel his optimistic outlook.[34]

The project began in earnest in January 1967 with Washington briefings and skull sessions with a newly assembled D&R Saigon staff to ready Lilienthal for his February trip to Vietnam. His old friend and secretary of defense Clark Clifford assured him of the president's humanitarian motives and told him that "nothing you have ever undertaken . . . compares in importance to your present involvement in Southeast Asia." Komer reviewed the administration's mandate for preparing a "rational plan" for the use of native and foreign resources, encouraging the Vietnamese to think positively and creatively about the future, and demonstrating that the U.S. has a "constructive purpose . . . in Vietnam and in Southeast Asia." The Joint Development Group, Komer continued, could not expect much help from official sources and should stay away from them as much as possible. Most significantly, Lilienthal was advised to "start from the arbitrary assumption of a 'peacetime environment' rather than to try to start from where we are today." To his own staff, Lilienthal emphasized that the Group would look beyond South Vietnam to a regional vision. As always, he hoped to involve the Vietnamese as much as possible and to move beyond studies and surveys to action.[35]

As an anonymous report (probably Komer to Johnson) observed after the February trip, "Lilienthal put in a vigorous two weeks in Vietnam." With bombs dropping in the background, he immediately took to Professor Vu Quoc Thuc, his Vietnamese counterpart, and visited with Ambassador Lodge, Ky, Westmoreland and a bevy of Vietnamese ministers and AID officials. He spent days touring the Delta, Cam Ranh Bay, and other military posts. After being angered by a rude press at a military briefing, Lilienthal listened with little sympathy as *New York Times* correspondent Jon Randal told him the press was hostile "because we all believe our Government is and has been lying to us." While disappointed that present Mekong Delta activities seemed to be an "international pork barrel," he returned home, according to Komer's report, "extremely enthused, . . . [with no more doubts] about the basic potential of Vietnam's economy or of the Vietnamese ability to make their contribution." He also appeared ready to do "a little educational missionary work among those friends of his who do not understand the Vietnam problem." The report concluded that "a pat on the back from you would probably move him a long way [toward defending Administration policy]."[36]

Lilienthal did not disappoint the administration. In a White House press briefing after his return, he radiated enthusiasm. He had learned a great deal "and almost all of it was encouraging." The Vietnamese were positive and among the hardest-working people he had ever seen. He was impressed with the "fantastically productive resources," especially "the Delta of the Mekong River"—a land "like Texas with a lot of water and no oil. And there may be oil too, for all we know." On NBC television in March, he said he anticipated few problems in converting to peacetime development. Many capital needs would be met by the massive American military-built infrastructure. Moreover, he was sure that substantial investment capital would materialize "out of hiding" from ordinary Vietnamese citizens waiting for stability and peace. Regarding war damage, Lilienthal concluded that "this is not a ravaged country" and that "economic development can proceed without the kind of ravaging that we think of in terms of World War II, for example, or World War I." The following month, he disagreed with the press that the Guam summit had little substance. To Helen Meyner he insisted that the meeting "was a great turning point in the history of the processes of democracy." The Guam postwar planning agreements, a new constitution, and recent elections were all "exciting thing[s]; this is what will put an end to this war."[37]

In November 1967, Lilienthal returned to Vietnam to present a preliminary report prepared by D&R and Vietnamese professionals and Saigon graduate students. Although pleased with the document, he recognized a subtle shift in morale. "Among the Americans," he sensed "a more sober, somber feeling." He was disturbed when Professor Thuc told him that Vietnamese members of the Joint Development team had become prime Viet Cong targets. Nevertheless, power meetings with Bunker and Vice-President Ky, a lavish presentation of the report to President Thieu, and the attendant publicity, even from the Viet Cong, helped him forget his new concern that "the war looks interminable." He was also heartened when the Vietnamese Group, on its own, enlarged D&R's forty-page presentation by another hundred pages.[38]

Lilienthal returned home to a delighted White House. On December 6, he briefed the president, talked to the Cabinet, and held a national press conference. The president bluntly told him why he was the center of attention: "'I want the country to hear the whole story, the constructive things, the building things. You tell Sarnoff [president of NBC],' he said, 'and Stanton [president of CBS] to get you on one of these panel shows and tell the country what you told me and told the Cabinet.'" In the briefing, Lilienthal recounted the recent events and his faith in Thieu, Ky, and the new Cabinet. South Vietnam had leadership, abundant local capital, an optimistic and resourceful population, and a strong infrastructure relatively unscathed by the war. He also mentioned a topic dear to his heart, impending Vietnamese legislation for a Mekong Delta Authority. Other than being peeved because the *New York Times* failed to cover the briefing, Lilienthal was at the top of his form. Perhaps, just perhaps, the Vietnam venture was going to pay off.[39]

Unfortunately, December 1967 was the apogee of Lilienthal's hopes for, and influence over, peacetime planning in Vietnam. The January 1968 Tet offensive dashed all hopes for peace and the chance for cooperative efforts with the North. Moreover, Tet brought the booming Delta economy to a standstill, thus dampening hopes that some progress might be made while the war was going on. Lyndon Johnson's March announcement that he would not run again raised even more doubts about the postwar development strategy. With a lame-duck president, it was unclear to South Vietnam and the American civilian establishment in Saigon which elements of the administration's Vietnam policy would survive. For the South Vietnamese government, now under increasing military pressure, peace seemed even more remote. For agencies like AID and Defense, it was a good time to resist a maverick organization like D&R competing for its own niche in the region.

For the next two years Lilienthal struggled to finish the postwar study and to expand D&R's role into the implementation stage, mainly in the Mekong Delta. In May 1968, at Johnson's request, a skeptical Lilienthal traveled to Vietnam to reassure the Joint Group and President Thieu of "the firmness of US support in the present period . . . and in the developmental period that the post-war will bring." He found it hard to be positive after an unsettling talk with Johnson left him sensing that "the feeling of 'withdrawal'. . . is definitely in the air." Saigon's siege mentality also made him wonder, "How can we do very much in a country that is, by this night's measure [fierce bombing which woke him up], still so far from anything resembling 'postwar' or 'long-term' development?" Uncharacteristically, he turned down a press conference, wondering what he would say "that wouldn't be falsely optimistic." Nevertheless, his meeting with Thieu went well. The president assured him that D&R would have a key role in Vietnam's future and that he felt the prospects were good for a Mekong Delta Authority. Lilienthal was so excited he wrote that night, "It could just happen that the President will . . . set up the Mekong Delta Development Authority *soon.*" He was also encouraged that Professor Thuc had been appointed minister of state and was interested in negotiating a new contract with D&R.[40]

Nevertheless, Lilienthal should have trusted his sense of the situation when he arrived in Saigon, rather than listening to the false hopes of an embattled Vietnamese president. While continuing the Joint Development Study, D&R failed to negotiate other contracts with AID or South Vietnam. In July 1968, his representative in Saigon, Tom Mead, reported that local support for the Joint Development Group was slipping and Thuc no longer seemed interested in involving D&R. More disturbing, Mead told him that conflicts between Cambodia and Vietnam had stalled regional Mekong Delta discussions and that South Vietnam, increasingly distracted by the war, had tabled consideration of a Mekong Delta initiative. At the same time, Lilienthal spent time fighting efforts by Herman Kahn's Hudson Institute and the Department of Defense Advanced Research Projects Agency to bring a twenty-man team to Vietnam to combine pacification programs with some of D&R's efforts. After threatening to leave immediately if D&R's work was undermined, Lilienthal met with AID officials in Washington and forced them to drop Kahn's project. White House Vietnam policy expert William Leonhart assured him "that Defense, State and the White House will give you what you think you need to do what the President asked you to do two years ago."[41]

Stopping Kahn was little more than a pyrrhic victory, however. D&R negotiations with AID and the U.S.-backed four-nation Mekong Delta Committee were deadlocked, and in September World Bank President Robert McNamara told Lilienthal the bank would finance no Mekong projects. At two October meetings with Leonhart, Lilienthal volunteered to help the stalled Paris peace talks, offering to present an economic development plan to North Vietnam. After receiving no response, he reacted disconsolately: "Right now a dead calm has come over Washington, and if I were to talk to Rusk or Rostow I would feel I was talking to ghosts."[42]

Nixon's victory was the final blow. D&R was alone—no patron, a different party in power, and increasing uncertainty in Saigon. In January, a bitter Lilienthal told departing AID Director James Grant that "bit by bit AID's mission [in Vietnam] was contracting out this and that piece" of work that should have been assigned to the Joint Group. By April, when Lilienthal traveled to Vietnam for the last time to present the final report to Thieu, and two weeks later in Washington when he made the same presentation to President Nixon, D&R was nothing more than a handmaiden, carrying out "specific studies as AID might from time to time request." The press showed little interest in the meetings, and Nixon made no effort to encourage Lilienthal about the future except to ask if he was "going to continue on this job." By October, D&R's Vietnam show was over. Mead wrote his boss that neither South Vietnam nor AID was interested in continuing with D&R beyond the final contract date. On April 15, 1970, D&R's presence in South Vietnam came to an end.[43]

One could not fault Lilienthal for lack of optimism or loyalty. Even after it became clear that D&R would not be involved beyond the Joint Development Group study, he remained positive about the chances for peace and meaningful economic development. In 1969, in *Foreign Affairs,* he wrote that "the prospects for rehabilitation and growth in Viet Nam in a peaceful environment are favorable . . . . [and] it is reasonable to expect that the country can achieve economic independence within ten years." Even after Tet, he was sanguine about the possibility of an extensive Mekong Delta project. He even wondered if linking up with the North might not provide "the most productive opportunity for economic liaison." It does not "seem impossible," he speculated, "to achieve the necessary cooperation in human terms." In a March interview with Edwin Newman, he was predictably positive—Vietnam's economic outlook was "certainly not a gloomy one . . . . [nor was it] a destroyed or devastated country." Human and fiscal capital were abundant; "there's a lot of savings, a lot of mattress money, . . . but mostly it's because of the people. They are the most hard-working people, and ingenious." *Newsweek,* however, raised an obvious point that Lilienthal never allowed himself to consider, that the entire plan was based on "a highly controversial assumption: that the ultimate peace settlement in Vietnam will result in a non-Communist regime in Saigon." As late as 1973, long after D&R's contract had expired, Lilienthal pleaded for the United States to "participate and contribute to reconstruction and rehabilitation [in Vietnam] because we are a moral and humanitarian people." And he still wondered if "the Mekong [can] be made to serve as a unifying political mechanism for gradual political and joint action in that region."[44]

Six hundred pages long, the report entitled "The Postwar Development of the Republic of Vietnam" was a monument to unfounded assumptions and exaggerated optimism. In a foreword to the 1970 published report, Lilienthal concluded that "though the end of the war is not clearly in sight, it is at any rate closer than it was when we last reported" and thus, it is time for many of the postwar programs to "be made ready for implementation." Ten chapters long, the study included detailed recommendations for everything from monetary and fiscal policies to industrial, institutional, and agricultural development and social services. Almost a fourth of the document focused on the issue dearest to Lilienthal's heart, regional development with an explicit set of recommendations for the Mekong Delta.[45]

In retrospect, after the U.S. retreat and collapse of the South in 1975, the report seemed Pollyannaish and an abstract academic treatise. Between 1967 and 1969, however, there was little to suggest that such a drastic outcome would come to pass. Given the possibility that some kind of peace, however tentative or sporadic, might be achieved, several recommendations were quite realistic. Albert Williams Jr. argued that the recommendations to reduce public-sector involvement in economic affairs were wise. Such efforts, including privatizing state enterprises, extensive reduction of economic regulations, simplifying the tariff system, and encouraging export industries over import substitution strategies, would allow the state sector to concentrate on the war and help cut down on official corruption.[46]

At times, however, the report contradicted Lilienthal's optimistic tone. His constant assurance that the war had done little damage was belied by evidence that infrastructure war damage amounted to more than $250 million. The fatal flaw, however, was in the conflict between the report's basic assumption, the possibility of real peace, and the reality of indefinite conflict. Just as the government of Vietnam, the United States, and the Joint Development Group could hardly foresee a total collapse of the South, it was just as unrealistic to think of a "full-fledged peace" in the near future. So was the idea that certain programs could be implemented during hostilities. First, it was unlikely that a nation spending 80 percent of its budget on military affairs would have much left for anything else. Given the realities, Williams argued that the recommended $2.5 billion ten-year U.S. aid package would have to be at least doubled. Also, the high priority placed on infrastructure was unrealistic, given that such targets are always primary in wartime. And, until the burdens of national security were eased, there was little hope that Vietnamese officials would have much inclination to focus on anything but the war. Williams was critical, finally, of the report's recommendation that aid be concentrated in technical and capital assistance instead of in balance-of-payments support. The latter could have an immediate and widespread impact providing foreign exchange assistance to the small-business sector. Technical assistance, however, would perpetuate the practice of providing "technicians who bring U.S. solutions in search of Vietnamese problems." Moreover, hopes for massive capital assistance seemed absurd in light of U.S. efforts to scale back its highly visible presence.[47]

Innocence Abroad: A Requiem for American Liberalism

In a way, it is difficult to explain Lilienthal's naiveté about Iran and Vietnam, both of which eventually became quagmires and political liabilities for which he and his country paid dearly. How could an impeccable liberal fail to heed warnings about the dark corners of the Persian empire? Why did he ally himself with an unpopular policy with a country that was on the verge of spinning out of control? And, why did he keep the faith so long with the Shah and Lyndon Johnson, especially after both regimes repeatedly frustrated his efforts?

In part, he loved the limelight and the blandishments of the mighty. His immediate sense of camaraderie with the Shah was tonic to someone long absent from the corridors of power, and Johnson's 1966 invitation was the first presidential call in nearly two decades. No doubt, the Shah and Johnson capitalized on Lilienthal's ego and his reckless willingness to tackle tough issues. Lilienthal was a patriot, though—when a president called, he could hardly say no. His unflagging attachment to both men was driven by another lifelong axiom: honorable men keep their promises, no matter how difficult the circumstances. It is also likely that Lilienthal saw Vietnam as a respite from the growing frustrations in Iran. A week before Komer's call in August 1966, he wrote that he was "sour about Iran at this point." From then until late 1969, he went to Iran only twice and paid less attention to D&R's projects there than he had before. Finally, there were rivers to tame and regions to develop. Iran first, and then Vietnam offered the chance to pick up where he had left off at TVA. What greater incentive could there be for an old "river rat"?[48]

There were other factors that influenced his decision to cast his lot with the Shah and Johnson. His words and actions reflected the dominant U.S. postwar foreign policy doctrine—belief in the inexorable progression from technical assistance to economic development to political development characterized by stability, peace, a strong civic culture, democracy, and friendship with the United States. The doctrine was saturated with optimism and moral fervor. Where there was a will there was a way, and "the American Way" could, and should, be shared with the world. And, as always, Lilienthal convinced himself of these truths as much as he did anyone else.

His experiences in Iran and Vietnam were poignant examples of Robert A. Packenham's metaphor of "liberal America encounter[ing] an illiberal world." No doubt Lilienthal was an astute political player at home. Nevertheless, his liberalism failed him as he faced a world with very different values. As American historians Louis Hartz and Carl Degler have observed, American liberalism was rooted in the precepts of John Locke—equality, individual liberty, and a rational secular outlook. In time, this outlook evolved into the rationalism of due process, the judgment of individual merit, and confidence in technological achievement. Moreover, America's revolution was conservative, not radical. The founding fathers rebelled to return to traditional English values, not to adopt radically different ones. Just as important, American liberalism arose in a context with few major constraints. There were fewer class or caste barriers to hinder mobility or create implacable social oppositions, and natural and human resources were more plentiful than they had been in any modern national setting. Finally, the absence of divisive ideologies, the stuff of radical revolution and reactionary response, made it possible for American leaders to embrace a pragmatic philosophy in solving the nation's problems.[49]

This was Lilienthal's faith and TVA was his testimony. The Tennessee Valley flourished because due process protected its chief agent of development, and merit and technical considerations won out over venal politics. There were no class barriers, only people working together to forge their own destiny. Moreover, the resources needed to do the job were abundant, and the absence of ideology allowed TVA to maximize its position through swift, practical action. Years later, he took the same creed on the road to Iran and Vietnam.

According to Packenham, the American credo generated four proverbs about third-world involvement. First, "Change and development are easy." Because economic and political development were relatively easy at home, it was logical to think that the right mix of U.S. goodwill and assistance, and native determination would lead to similar results abroad. The second tenet "All good things go together" led to the assumption that "good things" like technical assistance, economic development, and political development were all part of an inevitable process. A corollary followed that the greater the aggregation of "good things," the more likely the success; hence, the comprehensive approach was the most effective of all. American liberalism's third proposition was that "radicalism and revolution are bad." Since the United States had succeeded without radical solutions, other nations could develop without them as well. Moreover, given the linkage between technical assistance and economic and political development, revolutionary solutions with all their pain and grief were unnecessary. The fourth proposition, "Distributing power is more important than accumulating it," was derived from the United States' pluralistic and federal roots. Concentrating power stymied democratic development. Dispersing power, on the other hand, enhanced citizen empowerment and participation, and strengthened voluntary associations, all key aspects of Tocqueville's American democratic model.[50]

To Lilienthal, the rest of the world seemed an extension of his own. The Shah was an Asian Lincoln or Roosevelt. In 1958, in response to Iranian ministerial criticism of D&R, he mused, "We'll substitute TVA for D&R and the High Council for our own comptroller general, or Harold Ickes, or the Chicago *Tribune*, and the parallel with our TVA experience is remarkable." At his first meeting with Ky, Lilienthal equated the prime minister's concern for vocational education to Lincoln's land grant college policy. A month later on Guam, he likened the new Vietnamese Constitution to the

American Articles of Confederation, both models of compromise forged in the midst of war. Given these images, it is easy to see why Lilienthal thought he could transplant his nation's economic and political miracles. A 1971 *Nation* observer aptly captured this faith when he wrote that Lilienthal's international activities "admirably illustrated" the "common denominators" of the new American empire with its emphases on "expansionism, profound faith in technology, and a conviction that the good life requires economic development."[51] Lilienthal believed that "change and development are easy." His optimistic report about Khuzistan to Ebtehaj after a brief visit spoke to his faith in technological achievement: in the stark Khuzistan plains "in the middle of absolute nowhere," technology would triumph—green the desert, transform ancient feudalism, ward off powerful bureaucratic intrigues—and stand as a symbol of goodwill and good intentions. Even to anthropologist Grace Goodell, a harsh Lilienthal critic, "The technocrats who planned and ran the [Khuzistan] scheme were on the whole well-meaning, genial, even kind men." Lilienthal's decision to work in Vietnam was another mark of his unswerving faith in economic and social transformation. Son David warned his father that planning for peace would have little effect in a nation consumed by war and that his activities would only support the war. In 1964, at Columbia University, Lilienthal articulated this first tenet of the liberal credo. For him, the first pillars of successful development included "a deep faith that men can create beneficial change" and "change can come quickly." A year later at Brandeis University, he spoke of a new era "sweeping the world" recognizing and taking advantage of "the latent capacities of all men." For Lilienthal, it was a glorious "time of renaissance" and home and throughout the globe.[52]

There was little doubt, either, that for Lilienthal, "all good things go together." It was enough that the Shah and President Johnson spoke of good intentions. Likewise, if economic and political development were positive forces, it was logical to assume they were closely linked. Giving the Newton Baker Memorial Lecture in 1960, he said that American economic policies abroad could "yield better results, for the underdeveloped peoples, and results consistent with our own ethical and democratic standards." In his conclusion he stressed the linkage again: through altruistic technical assistance policies America "could provide an example by which the rapidly emerging nations of the world could weigh and judge the virtue of making increasing freedom for the individual with justice for his neighbor—the cornerstone of their own evolving societies." Lilienthal's battle with the World Bank over the size of the Khuzistan project testified to his uncritical faith that there could never be too much of a good thing. He never understood, that in a land with limited resources, a vast project such as Khuzistan posed a real threat to other hopes for development.[53]

Like most of his countrymen, Lilienthal believed that "revolution and radicalism are bad." Nevertheless, he was never a strident anti-Communist. In 1960, he spoke against using economic aid "to stop the spread of Communism in underdeveloped countries," adding his "voice to those who challenge both the wisdom and effectiveness of these ideas." Seven years later, he cautioned his staff against allowing the Vietnam project to degenerate into anti-Communist propaganda. Lilienthal's perspective on revolution took two forms. First, he refused to recognize the intensity of revolutionary oppositions. In Iran, he never took the radical forces on the left or right seriously: neither the Communist Tudeh party nor the fundamentalist Muslims were of any consequence to him. In Vietnam, he failed to gauge the deep ideological opposition of the Viet Cong and Northern Communists to the Southern regime and their foreign protectors. As late as 1973, Lilienthal thought the North and South could reach an accommodation. He also articulated a definition of revolution that echoed his own TVA rhetoric. For Lilienthal, authentic revolution arose not from "rising expectations." Instead, true revolution, "the prime mover in the changes sweeping the world," consisted "of a rising sense of men's power, of rising demands that heretofore unrecognized creative energies be given an opportunity to find fulfillment." Such revolution inhered not in ideology, but in the liberating process of economic development that leads inexorably to unleashing the "unlimited latent capacity of the average man."[54]

Lilienthal's belief that "distributing power is more important than accumulating it" was perhaps strongest held of all. In Iran he never gave up on a TVA-like project in Khuzistan. In Vietnam he was inspired by the vision of a grand regional project encompassing the entire Mekong Delta. When he spoke of "recast[ing] the thinking that denies the latent capacities and power of peoples in underdeveloped or impoverished regions," he evoked an image of distributing power by empowering ordinary people. His conclusion that nothing would happen "unless the Iranians who lived on the land and in the towns participated actively in this development and were prepared in a few years to run it themselves" was yet another call for distribution. He never understood that philosophies of regionalism and active local participation were alien to elites who had ruled from the center for centuries and to the vast majority of citizens who had never experienced anything remotely resembling "grass roots participation." Besides, the notion of sharing power was anathema to rulers who were sure that such a policy would lead to their own loss of control and ultimate destruction.[55]

A final factor contributing to Lilienthal's willingness to commit his reputation and energies to Iran and Vietnam was his compelling optimism. Rooted deeply in his soul and liberal mien, his positive outlook had contributed substantially to many successes. No challenge was too daunting. No area was too desolate, no canyon too deep, for one of the largest thinarch dams in the world. Nor were ideological differences so great that a successful plan could not be worked out even in a tiny, war-torn corner of the world. He was sure that both Iran and Vietnam were firmly on "paths to change" that included such objectives as popular participation and fairer distribution of income and goods. Lilienthal's optimism was infectious. It nourished his spirit and strengthened his staff over many rough years. Sometimes, though, this optimism was counterproductive. At times it caused misjudgments, goading him into action when he might better have exercised caution and prudence. Other times the optimism fed and reinforced the "up" side of an increasingly rapid alternation of mood, from troughs of personal despair and anxiety to compelling episodes of activity and motion.

A Personal Toll

Lilienthal's emotional ups and downs were partly due to the extraordinary pressures he faced in the 1960s. The decade began with the news, covered in detail in the *New York Times,* that his boyhood friend Fred Newton Arvin had been arrested and dismissed from Smith College for homosexuality. Lilienthal contributed to his destitute friend's legal fund. He also tried to boost a shattered morale, telling Fred he had "never . . . known a more creative intelligence . . . [and that] there is no one in America of greater talent and literary comprehension." Near the end of 1960, Lilienthal admitted he was "baffled and grieved about [Fred's] grave troubles . . . [and that] so ugly a charge shook me as greatly as it utterly puzzled me." Three years later, Fred died after a painful bout with pancreatic cancer. Lilienthal was generous in his private eulogy: "My boyhood friend suffered through most of his life; but he did something great with his talents, something that will outlive him."[56]

Fred was not the only personal loss. Four of Lilienthal's confidants followed in rapid succession. Gordon Clapp died unexpectedly a month after Fred in April 1963, and Nate Greene, D&R's first legal counsel, died in October. Felix Frankfurter died in February 1965, and Edward R. Murrow two months later, exactly two years after Clapp. Lilienthal was most open about his feelings about Frankfurter. Upon hearing the news, he wrote, "Felix, the fountain of life that flows forever, is dead." As tears "overwhelmed me, such as I can't remember has ever struck me," Lilienthal tried to think of Frankfurter's great contribution to American life. "But," he added sadly, "that is no help, that solace, in the irrevocable moment of finality."[57]

If Frankfurter's death was painful, Clapp's was devastating. At first, he was numb, grieving over "so close, so intimate a friend, so much a part of me suddenly gone: I simply can't take it in." In June 1963, he apologized to Ebtehaj for not responding earlier to his condolences, saying that "the tragic event, was too close in time, and I found I could not say what I had in my heart." In his note, he praised Clapp's "goodness and greatness" and lamented that "the world of America, of Iran—all men—are deprived of a rare and talented spirit." In his journal he wrote a few times about missing Clapp, and in the late 1970s, he was grateful that D&R's last president, John Macy, was so much like Clapp. Nevertheless, Lilienthal kept most of his grief to himself. In August 1963, he refused to write a biographical essay on Clapp for the *Public Administration Review,* offering only to contribute a "brief, essentially personal foreword about Gordon" to someone else's eulogy. Those close to both men, including Helen, Oliver, and Norman

Clapp, felt Clapp's death hit Lilienthal very hard. It was also a great blow to D&R.[58]

The most traumatic event was a loss of another kind, a long and painful alienation from David Jr. over Vietnam. The conflict was exacerbated by strong tensions between Lilienthal and daughter-in-law Peggy, and his son's struggle to become a writer. From late 1956 until mid-1959 David Jr. worked for D&R but resigned to move to Martha's Vineyard to write and run a small weekly paper. Two years later, Lilienthal convinced his son to move to Princeton to help him prepare the journals for Harper & Row. After publishing his first short stories and novel in 1962, David told his parents in April 1963 that he would continue editing the journals but would move back to the Vineyard. Each move reflected the frustrations of the parents and their son and daughter-in-law. The elder Lilienthals had mixed emotions. The father was much taken by the idea of his son working beside him and felt he had *"real* executive talent." At the same time he was proud of his writing ambitions and he and Helen continued to support him and his family financially whenever they could. However, neither he nor Helen were pleased when David Jr. asserted his independence by moving away— both times they felt Peggy had unduly influenced the decision.

Peggy, on the other hand, wanted a family life independent of a domineering father-in-law. She was frustrated because they often clashed over issues and she felt David Sr. had dominated her husband. The son was caught in the middle. There is little doubt that he deeply loved both his father and wife. The problem, however, was that both father and wife were assertive, strong-willed, and volatile. He was further frustrated because his writing was not an easy vocation. Without independent means, it was difficult to reject his parents' support. Somehow, though, he had to accommodate his wife's concerns.[59]

Tensions rose again in 1964 when Lilienthal became upset over Peggy's arrest at a civil rights demonstration in Williamston, North Carolina. He had long felt that the southern civil rights struggle sometimes disparaged his adopted homeland and ignored equally deplorable situations in the North. Lilienthal was also critical because he feared Peggy's activism would interfere with David's writing career and his work on the journal. In August, he was disturbed when Peggy brought a black family up from North Carolina to live with them on Martha's Vineyard. Nevertheless, he admired her resolve. By September her southern guests had won him over with their "reserved and somber" demeanor and genuine interest in his notions of economic development. In October, however, Lilienthal refused to underwrite Peggy's expenses for a southern voter registration project.[60]

The civil rights conflict was nothing compared to the vehement reaction to his Vietnam assignment. While daughter Nancy and her husband Sylvain also opposed his participation, Lilienthal was wounded most by his son's opposition, first in impassioned letters, then his resignation as journal editor, and finally by David and Peggy's decision to move permanently to Florence, Italy, partly in protest against America's Southeast Asia policy. In

December 1966 David Jr. argued passionately against his father's taking the job. He was blunt in response to his father's plea that "I badly need a dare, a challenge," retorting, "his isn't a challenging job; it is an impossible one." He begged his father to go to Vietnam first and assess the situation, but the elder Lilienthal had already made his decision.[61]

In early 1967, the feud escalated beyond disagreement to tragic breach. The mood was precipitated by the publication of their son's second novel, which he dedicated to his parents. Set in an unnamed Caribbean nation, *The Tour* was a harsh satire of the real war 10,000 miles away. Helen's feelings about the book were unequivocal: to her husband, she said, "It will make a great movie; not a 'pleasant' book." She pointedly told her son, "I have read your *book* to the *bitter end.*" The father had mixed feelings. On one hand, he "found [the book] as good, indeed better than, say Evelyn Waugh or Graham Greene at their best." On the other, he, like Helen, was deeply disturbed by the "bitter[ness] about almost everything, whether in exposing sham, tearing people into little bits, [or] portraying by parable the ugliness of what we are doing in [Vietnam]." Lilienthal was troubled that he found no "escape hatch, some tiny note of affirmation, some relief from the anger and violence, hatred and frustration." In a letter to cousin Dee Szold, he touted his son as a great writer but lamented "how remote from my own experience of life (and yours) is the bitterness and the scorn."[62]

The feud continued to escalate. In late January 1967, David Jr.'s daughter Pamela (whom Lilienthal could not remember "ever exchanging a dozen words with me on any subject") wrote her grandfather that she was "appalled and 'ashamed'" by his association with President Johnson. A month later David Jr. told his father they were moving to Florence in the summer, but that he would continue editing the journals. After a month of angry telephone exchanges over Lilienthal's response to Pam and the war, Peggy told her father-in-law she had burned the copies of the journal her husband was editing "as a symbolic act, the only way we could separate ourselves completely from you and what you are doing."[63]

That stunning call was followed a few days later with an elegant, powerful letter from David Jr. detailing his objections to his father's participation in Vietnam. In a loving, yet critical missive, rich with the familiar Lilienthal cadence and passion, the son pulled no punches. Arguing that all positive actions in the midst of a conflict contributed to the goals of the war, he concluded that his father "support[ed] the war—all of it, including the bombing, including the mining of rivers, including whatever may be done further tomorrow and next week and next month." He told his father that if he did not support the war, he should "denounce the bombing publicly and denounce any other military activities which you may now privately deplore." He continued, asserting that in Vietnam or any country at war, "any development program will be coercive." That "is a contradiction of everything you have heretofore done." Near the end of the letter, he told his father, "Vietnam has divided us. . . . I love you as my father and I respect you, too, and I love you now nonetheless and always will." Nevertheless, "I cannot [continue to] work on the Journals. I must withdraw from our contract." In his view, "Vietnam [was] not an issue . . . on which reasonable men may honestly hold differing views. . . . Vietnam lies outside the experience heretofore of our generations. . . . [I]t is the curse of our time now." He concluded with a heart-wrenching plea: "You must believe me that I could not write you like this nor say these things without conviction hardwon and from the depth. And great sorrow."[64]

In response, Helen penned a lengthy and sometimes angry reply, making clear that her loyalties were with her husband: "But you must know that we share everything, that we always have and always will; that what he knows, I know; what affects him, affects me." After a rousing defense of her husband's motives, reputation, and all he had done on behalf of the public interest, she closed with a mother's benediction: "I wish only for your well-being, your happiness, the welfare of your family. I love you as I always have and always will, steadfastly and forever." The son's letter had a devastating effect on Lilienthal. He asked Helen not to send her "magnificent letter" and he decided "not [to] reply to David's letter, nor acknowledge its receipt, believing any further discussion . . . would be futile, even harmful." For three months he suffered, once writing, "It hurts, the whole chapter hurts. Deep down."

The most painful wound of all was the isolation from the man, once his closest confidant, and now his most eloquent critic. Even worse, David Sr. had to live with his son's admission that he had been responsible for letting Peggy destroy the journal pages. Finally, in mid-June, days before their departure to Florence, father and son met and, as best they could, put things straight between them. Lilienthal was relieved that his son did not share Peggy's feeling that the father had ruined his life. David Jr. was clear that he did not want to talk about his wife, who "has given me far more than I have been able to give her." Although there were many subsequent bumps in the road, the relationship between the Lilienthals, their son, and Peggy, improved over the years. Ten years later the father finally admitted to his son that "your intense feeling about my having anything to do with the Vietnam disaster was confirmed by events." He added, however, "that being the kind of guy I am I could not do otherwise."[65]

These enormous personal pressures, along with the challenge of trying to keep D&R on course, were accompanied by a dramatic personality change. All his life Lilienthal had been plagued by recurring episodes of emotional highs and lows. With the exception of the painful times during the 1930s, the episodes were brief and usually followed by extended bursts of high energy. In the 1950s he suffered a few lapses and some insomnia. But as late as 1961, he reported, "I'm functioning . . . with more vigor, less fatigue, less tension. . . . The emotional ups and downs—especially the latter—I face up to quite well . . . [and] get through them better."[66]

As the 1960s progressed, however, moments of gloom began to intrude more often and their toll was devastating. In his journal he increasingly noted episodes of gloominess and dejection, "feeling terribly let down" or "a sense of emotional nothingness." More often, he logged his entries in the darkest hours of the night while waiting for sleep that never came. While still capable of enormous bursts of energy and activity, even in his seventh decade, his thoughts and actions told of a troubled soul. After 1960, his private jottings reflected insecurities and a sense of self-pity he had never before reported. Journal entries were laced with bitterness and sarcasm toward people and events—he had been sharp before, even critical, but never like this. Personal relationships also suffered. Close colleagues were hurt by wide and abrupt swings of emotion that sometimes brought pain and confusion. John Oliver, John Burnett, his California water resources expert, William Warne, and one-time Iran representative Ross Pritchard were all "fair-haired" men who ultimately lost the boss's favor and ultimately their jobs at D&R.[67]

To an extent, Lilienthal's pattern of mood swings was a natural physical progression. When he was younger, long periods of intense activity were interrupted by relatively short, but sometimes fierce, "lows." By middle age, the late 1950s, and early 1960s, the valleys appeared more often, and as the 1960s progressed, Lilienthal seemed to fall into a pattern of "rapid cycling," shifting "back and forth from deep depression to startling euphoria or extreme irritability, sometimes in a matter of days or even hours." While medical authorities suggest that rapid cycling can take place with little or no external provocation, there is little doubt that extreme stress is also a significant trigger. The decade was highly stressful for David Lilienthal, and his mind and body responded in predictable fashion. It is remarkable, considering the progression of his condition and the intensity of external provocations, that he continued to function at D&R, sometimes brilliantly and with the great prescience he had demonstrated in earlier times. That he was able to do so at the close of the decade, when the walls seemed to be closing in on him, is even more remarkable.[68]

Crucial Decisions

For a decade, D&R had contracted with no more than four countries at a time. Most of the projects, including those in Iran, Italy, Colombia, Ivory Coast, and Puerto Rico, focused on rural water and land development. By the spring of 1970, D&R had twenty-five contracts, including its first entrepreneurial effort, a Colombian cut-flower enterprise aimed at the U.S. market. D&R experienced modest financial success until 1969. It recorded a small profit the first year, and thereafter, annual net income ranged from $40,000 to $180,000. Because of the uncertainty of some of the contracts and the strong dependence on Iran, D&R kept all profits in a contingency fund for several years. In 1959, for example, when all Iranian project money was funneled through D&R, income soared to more than $23.3 million, all but $15,000 of it from Iran. By the mid-1960s, with the completion of the expensive Khuzistan Dez Dam, revenues dropped to a yearly range of between $2.1 and 4.1 million.[69]

By mid-1969 D&R was in serious trouble. The year-end financial report showed the first loss in fifteen years. Cash flow problems intensified as Iran and then the Ivory Coast delayed payments for months at a time, and New York banks refused to extend credit. Internal management problems mounted with the departure of key executives, some of whom left voluntarily, while others resigned or were fired in the wake of Lilienthal's shifting moods. D&R was also rocked with serious disagreements between the California office, which never had been properly socialized into the D&R philosophy, and Lilienthal and his new representative in Iran, Ross Pritchard.[70]

The crisis began in January with the news that there would be no new bank loans. At the same time, André Meyer chided Lilienthal that D&R's chances for survival depended on developing a keener business sense. The next month, Gerald Levin, Oliver's new assistant, told Lilienthal that "cash flow crises, have jeopardized our fundamental ability to meet our payroll and pay our creditors." D&R's net income had plummeted simultaneously with "bountifully rising operating revenues." Levin also warned that reserve levels in Iran had sunk so low that the company was "powerless in any threat to shut down our operations since the cost of bringing our staff home on short notice exceeds our present borrowing limit." Moreover, D&R's other projects, including Peace Corps training contracts and the near-moribund Vietnam program, still "our third largest revenue source," had extremely low "profitability" potential. Levin estimated that D&R needed an immediate and "substantial infusion of working capital . . . rang[ing] anywhere from $500,000 to $1,500,000." A week later, Meyer repeated the message and added that he had little confidence in John Oliver's ability to lead D&R out of its financial bind. Two weeks later Oliver "resigned," Lilienthal assumed the presidency of the firm, and Gerry Levin took over as general manager.[71]

To top off the managerial and fiscal crises, D&R faced several demoralizing setbacks in generating new business. Another dismal memorandum from Levin in June 1969 reminded Lilienthal that D&R had not succeeded, much to André Meyer's disappointment, in any money-making "entrepreneurial" activities. The shutdown of D&R's urban department in May 1969, just two months after Lilienthal had bragged about it to Edwin Newman, was a devastating blow, especially since he had hoped U.S. projects could provide financial security against third-world uncertainties. In a January 1970 progress report to André Meyer, Lilienthal complained that D&R had been unable to take advantage of energy projects in the Western United States and mineral explorations in Western Australia in the late 1960s for lack of capital. Perhaps most ominous, Lilienthal's relationship with Meyer was wearing dangerously thin. In another testy encounter in March 1970, Meyer complained that D&R had shown little appreciation for Lazard's support over the years. Lilienthal responded that Lazard had taken more out of the company than it had put in and brusquely told Meyer that if he would not help D&R find a new partner, Lilienthal would do it himself.[72]

CHAPTER 13

Life at a "High Trot"—Unfinished Business

> Now as I approach my eightieth birthday I reconfirm my belief
> in man's infinite potentialities for living and loving. I can say
> with a whole heart that I have lived the kind of life I most
> wanted, a life of taking chances, of not playing it safe, of being
> not merely an observer but a combatant in the arena of action.
> —David E. Lilienthal, 1979

A New Start: Enter the Rockefellers

D&R had been hobbled from the beginning by financial restrictions. The
company made money, but not enough to attract new investors or for corporate development. Lilienthal's fortune was never large enough to build
D&R into a major consulting firm. With the exception of the corporate share-
holders, Lazard and Utah Construction, the other stockholders, including
Gordon Clapp, John Oliver, and John Burnett, were men of modest means.[1]

Lilienthal worked hard in 1969 to find a partner who could provide
a much-needed infusion of managerial and financial resources but allow D&R to preserve "its distinctive character and essential autonomy."
In July, he asked Sol Linowitz, former chairman of Xerox, for help.
After several false starts, Linowitz told Lilienthal and André Meyer early
in 1970 that International Telegraph and Telephone Corporation (ITT) and
Nelson Rockefeller's oldest son, Rodman, president of International Basic
Economy Corporation (IBEC) were interested in acquiring D&R. Meyer was
frank with Linowitz: "The only solution for D&R is an arrangement with
another company. . . . Lazard is not going to invest further in D&R, . . . but I
am going . . . to help . . . David; he does not have the people to run the
company."[2]

In mid-April, after ITT dropped out of the running, Lilienthal and Rodman Rockefeller met for the first time. Much later, Rockefeller admitted "it
was almost inevitable that the two corporations would get together." D&R
needed a financial base and IBEC could use Lilienthal's gold-plated reputa-

tion. According to Andrea Pampanini, IBEC's liaison and D&R executive vice-president from 1971 to 1977, Rockefeller also hoped Lilienthal could settle a long-simmering dispute his company had with the Iranian government over a failed housing project. For his part, Lilienthal was pleased "because the stated overall objectives of IBEC and D&R appear much the same." In addition to manufacturing and retail sales, IBEC had housing projects for low- and middle-income markets and agribusiness ventures, mostly in Latin America. A week later, Lilienthal asked for more "discussion dealing in specifics of IBEC and D&R's widely different but . . . complementary areas of activity and expertise."[3]

As they talked and negotiated, D&R's situation continued to deteriorate. Long delays in Iranian and Ivory Coast payments forced the company into an embarrassing inability to pay a large bank loan, the first it had negotiated in some time. By late summer 1970 Lilienthal once again had to cover D&R's payroll with his own assets. At the same time personnel woes mounted. Lilienthal was increasingly concerned about the inexperience of Gerald Levin (now company vice-president) and was disappointed when Alexander Trowbridge turned down the D&R presidency. A slew of key employees, some with the company since 1956, resigned in the face of organizational uncertainties and Lilienthal's mercurial moods. Then, in July, ten engineers in the California office offered to buy out the Iranian engineering contract and take it over themselves—Lilienthal refused, angrily calling the proposal "blackmail." By early September, the California office was in full revolt and posed a serious threat to the IBEC talks. Levin acted quickly, firing the ringleaders and placing then-loyalist Harald Frederiksen in charge. The action temporarily stilled the California unrest, and redeemed Levin in Lilienthal's eyes.[4]

Negotiations picked up in late August, but were still too slow for Lilienthal. In addition, he was annoyed by IBEC's close scrutiny of D&R's personnel and financial affairs. In late September he pointedly wrote, "When do I start asking similar questions about *their* human capabilities, that will be the decisive factor in making this a congenial 'home' for D&R's people?" On the other hand, discussions with Rockefeller and Pampanini gave him "someone of intelligence and ideas and comprehension—to *talk* to, and with. . . . I really think it is the filling of this void that the IBEC partnership will produce is the greatest good for me." He was also thrilled over the prospect of IBEC's "ability to strengthen D&R's fiscal and accounting management resources." Finally, on October 28, 1970, IBEC agreed to buy D&R's common stock, leaving the preferred shares with the present owners, Lilienthal, Walt Seymour, and Lazard Frères. Lilienthal continued as D&R president and was named to the IBEC board. At last the future seemed secure—new backing promised opportunities Lilienthal had only hoped for in recent years.[5]

At first the partners had mixed feelings about the merger. On his first trip to Iran with Lilienthal in November 1970, Pampanini was impressed by the Khuzistan miracle and by the fact that everyone bowed down to

Lilienthal—"Iranians falling before him like sheaves of wheat." Upon re-turning he told Rockefeller that IBEC had made a good deal. Soon after joining D&R in January 1971, however, Pampanini realized that D&R was broke—$500,000 in bad debts were still on the books, and negotiations over unsettled Iranian accounts had been stalled for some time. In addition, many contracts were in a shambles because English and Farsi versions said different things. In the past, Lilienthal had gone directly to the Shah to resolve conflicts. Pampanini soon found, however, that animosities at the ministry level over Lilienthal's end runs were increasing at an alarming rate.[6]

Lilienthal was happy at the "prospect of getting myself less entangled in the recurrent crises of 'meeting a payroll'" and the chance to back away from day-to-day details. He was shocked, however, by Iran's angry reaction to the failed housing project and worried that the IBEC relationship might affect D&R's ties with its best client. Lilienthal felt better when IBEC agreed to scale back its claims and "leave half of [a] $750,000 [settlement] in [Iran] for investment." At the merger ceremony in January, he was optimistic that D&R might be able to "impart to those in IBEC who are looking for new, invigorating ideas—and Rodman Rockefeller is certainly doing just that."[7]

D&R's future looked brighter than it had in years. Lilienthal's resolve was still strong, and for a septuagenarian, his stamina remarkable. New projects in Brazil beckoned, as did other hydroelectric initiatives at home. In Iran, D&R expanded contract services beyond the Khuzistan, including an ambitious civil service reform program. Yet, in spite of all the energy and optimism, the next eight years were to be as challenging and difficult as any in the past.

The IBEC partnership failed to develop the way everyone had antici-pated. While Rockefeller and Lilienthal genuinely liked each other, their relationship was stormy. Although Rockefeller assiduously respected D&R's autonomy, Lilienthal never felt comfortable with a younger "boss" who, he thought, lacked vision and experience. In addition, in the 1970s, IBEC had its own fiscal crisis. Because of business downturns and poor management, net income in 1971 fell nearly $6 million from 1970, and in 1972 IBEC recorded a $14 million loss. Between 1973 and 1977 IBEC revenues plummeted from $312.9 million to $83 million. In that time, the company reported small profits three years (the highest, $2.7 million) and two large losses (a high of $16.7 million in 1975), mainly because of other housing project failures in Brazil and Puerto Rico.[8]

The Brazilian Connection:
Another Go at Latin America

By 1970, D&R had been involved in Latin America more than any other region. The firm executed projects for the Inter-American Bank for Regional Development (IBRD), nine nations, and Puerto Rico. Of all the projects, the only sure successes were in Puerto Rico, Colombia, Nicaragua, and the

IBRD report on economic integration. D&R's long contract with the Puerto Rican Water Resources Authority, originally Clapp's initiative, provided a steady source of income most years. In Colombia, in addition to the Cauca project, D&R helped establish a development corporation in the Bogota area and the Colombian Agrarian Reform Institute. Although Pampanini thought D&R's Nicaraguan tax reform project a moral disaster because of the Somoza family dictatorship, Lilienthal called the program "a good story." In 1961 Lilienthal was clear about his feelings toward Latin America: "I don't warm to the Latinos as I do to the Persians, but perhaps that is because I don't see much of the latter, really. And yet I don't know when I have been happier . . . than in the Cauca Valley."[9]

Elsewhere, either projects never materialized or host countries failed to follow through. In 1961 the IBRD rejected D&R's recommendation for a loan to Haiti to purchase the country's major power producer, an American company. In grudging concession, Lilienthal reflected that the bank's response was appropriate since "the President of Haiti was 'pretty awful,' not someone to be entrusted with anything." The same year, at the request of the Agency for International Development, and they thought, with Senator J. W. Fulbright's endorsement, Lilienthal and Clapp put together a regional development plan for the Dominican Republic which was received enthusiastically on the island. Yet, months passed, then years, and D&R heard nothing. When U.S. Marines invaded the island in 1965, Lilienthal told Fulbright that although "we spent a good deal of time and money, somehow nothing happened. . . . I thought I ought to give you this background; perhaps the 'brains' will want to do something . . . as a demonstration of our good will." Much to his dismay, Fulbright denied knowing about the original effort and told Lilienthal, "I don't know anything about what's going on down there, except what I read in the newspapers."[10]

The tale of missed opportunities continued in Peru in 1964–65. At President Fernando Belaunde's request, Lilienthal and Oliver spent a week in December assessing the Piura region and recommending that "an autonomous regional agency was the best instrumentality for getting the most value out of the natural and human resources of that region." In February 1965, on a day already scarred by Felix Frankfurter's death, Lilienthal heard that a key World Bank official had submitted a negative report on the project. In July, he returned to Lima hoping to salvage something, but he found that Belaunde was no longer interested. Lilienthal returned home, out of sorts and empty-handed.[11]

Five years later, in 1970, Latin America beckoned again. One could see his eyes light up as he wrote about the Amazon: "My god, to a river man such as I am, what a stirring in the innards . . . at that picture of a river and a basin, a valley bigger than big. At last our chance, my chance, to have something important to do with the future of that colossus of rivers." His enthusiasm was spurred by a proposal from a Brazilian engineering firm (SERETE) that D&R join them in a regional planning project in the Amazon. This opening led Lilienthal to five years of work in Brazil and eight grueling trips across the subcontinent. In this, his last bow in Latin America, there was a curious combination of hope and finality. Lilienthal was past seventy. The IBEC partnership was disappointing. Although Iran brought increasing frustrations, Lilienthal saw Brazil as "'another Iran'—a *major, long-term* task comparable to that thus far successful and accepted . . . by Iranians and the professional world." The TVA dream was alive again. Everywhere in Brazil people asked him about a TVA for their country. Maybe, just maybe, he could make that dream come true one last time.[12]

In those years, D&R executed two major contracts and formed a partnership with other firms to pursue development and entrepreneurial schemes. The first venture, SERETE, never lived up to D&R's expectations. The contract failed to include a guaranteed-payment clause, and SERETE gradually took over more of the work, forcing D&R "to 'play second fiddle' to a great degree." In mid-1972, however, Lilienthal's great Brazilian opportunity arose. Pampanini's indefatigable promotional efforts and the magic of Lilienthal's name resulted in a summons from high Brazilian officials for D&R to develop a comprehensive project in the Sao Francisco River Valley. Lilienthal was promised carte blanche, and Brazilian President Emilio Medici told him that "anytime there is a problem, DEL should come to him." In September, Lilienthal signed a $1.5 million contract with the government which required him to devote at least eight weeks a year personally to the project.[13]

In January 1973 Lilienthal directed an exhaustive survey of the Sao Francisco Valley. He wondered whether his recommendations should follow Brazil's traditional sectoral approach, dividing development responsibilities among several agencies, or stress integration with a single regional agency. He quickly answered this question with another: "Why should this government reach out for me, one who stands for a different way of developing a region than the 'sectoral' one, if they didn't consider that with the present method the full potential of that vast region isn't being reached?" His preliminary report to Medici in March called for "a unified development approach to the entire Valley" with a powerful regional agency invested with planning, program coordination, and execution, and resource regulation and management responsibilities. Lilienthal advised the president that the new agency must "involve the people" and be organized as a government corporation with headquarters in the valley.[14]

D&R staff immediately started work on a final report, but the enthusiasm soon turned into frustration. The Brazilian government moved slowly on the proposal and by spring 1973 was behind $210,000 in its monthly payments—it was beginning to look like another Iran. During a visit in May to speed things up, Lilienthal was assured that legislation would be introduced in July and the project would probably start in January 1974. On another visit in September he learned that several ministries opposed the plan, and he immediately took his concerns to Medici, who assured him, "I will remove the differences." Lilienthal delivered the final report in March 1974. Unfortunately, a new administration with other agendas took over a few days later.[15]

Although the proposal was codified in July 1974 with the formation of the Development Corporation of the Sao Francisco Valley (CODEVASF), it was a hollow victory. In May 1974 the new government had already canceled D&R's contract, and despite promises to the contrary, never engaged the company again. CODEVASF rapidly became a casualty of Brazil's sectoral political tradition. The Sao Francisco disappointment was heightened by a third failure. In Summer 1973, D&R acquired 20 percent of the stock of Development and Systems Corporation (DeS), a multinational Brazilian-based company. Lilienthal and others at D&R hoped DeS would lead to other development projects and profitable risk capital opportunities. Because of bad management, DeS was moribund by late 1974. Lilienthal realized DeS's demise spelled the end of D&R in Brazil: Vice-President Harald Frederiksen told Lilienthal in May 1975, "With the laws in Brazil, the lack of a solid partner and sponsor [like DeS] has prevented D&R from access to about 90 percent of the jobs we were pushing and had hopes for." D&R finally closed its Brazil office in July 1975.[16]

In assessing this disappointing outcome, one must note that Lilienthal and his staff had been well advised about Brazilian politics. They knew that two earlier Sao Francisco Valley development agencies had failed. Moreover, Lilienthal had been warned in 1973 by economist Stefan Robock, that "Brazil has been operating on a 'sectoral basis' since the 16th Century and isn't likely to change now just because you recommend it." Nevertheless, he dismissed Robock's counsel and the earlier lessons, telling himself the previous failure "was not due to inconsistency between the TVA concept and Brazilian conditions, but a failure to recognize how its central theme is necessary for overall development here." Once again, the liberal credo led him astray. For Lilienthal, local conditions and realities were irrelevant to the task at hand. Development was development wherever it occurred. If the American model worked once it could work anywhere. All that was necessary was an appropriate vision, competent technical assistance, and national will.[17]

Hopes at Home: A New Domestic Cause

In 1970, D&R did a study for New York City on long-term power needs, and the next February Lilienthal listened as Ford Foundation President McGeorge Bundy asked him to lead an effort to "shape and reshape the country's mind on the whole set of environment issues." At first flattered, he wrote that he was "*eager* to do a big job in this country, utilizing . . . D&R . . . for the undertaking." In a week, he withdrew from discussions when it became clear that the foundation wanted him, not D&R. The experience was not a total loss, however, because it started him thinking that "D&R *is* equipped to do professional work . . . in the environmental impact area, ... [and] with some working capital support from IBEC, . . . could develop a substantial position in that field." In mid-1973, D&R staff talked with Atomic Energy Commission Chairman Dixie Lee Ray and her staff about what Lilienthal hoped would lead to a "continuing assignment with AEC, and one in which the D&R energy management experience . . . could be used." When the commission offered only a small contract, D&R said no, "that DEL wants flexibility to puruse [sic] energy issues without being tied to AEC." [18]

In addition, Lilienthal went public. In June 1971, he predicted in the *New York Times* that the environmental movement would be the next grass roots force in America, thus "repudiat[ing], with very serious consequences, the Government bodies as the source of protection in this field." In mid-1975 and early 1976, he reentered the "atomic spotlight" with a *Times* editorial and testimony before the Senate Government Operations Committee on the dangers of nuclear proliferation. In an op-ed piece he spoke of the proliferation of atomic energy plants around the world. In spite of official assurances, he warned, little had been done to prevent environmental contamination and the conversion of fuel into weapons-grade material. In the editorial, he called for an international effort to find a way to render nuclear wastes harmless and recommended that the International Atomic Energy Agency take possession of all used fuels. Once more, being in the spotlight gave him "great satisfaction out of this business of coming out of the too 'low profile' period."[19]

Lilienthal's testimony on January 19 was a powerful elixir. He thrilled at "facing again the senior circle of a Senatorial Committee, back of me the hubbub of a crowded standing room of spectators and a jammed press table." In a forceful voice, he called the U.S. "the atomic patsy of the world . . . [for] putting into the hands of our own commercial interests and of foreign countries [great] quantities of bomb material." He recommended that the U.S. institute an immediate export ban on nuclear materials and technology until effective international safeguards could be devised. For days, he reveled in follow-up interviews with the *Wall Street Journal* and *Newsweek* and a feeler from senior staffer Paul Leventhal about serving as a consultant for the Senate Government Operations Committee. In March, the *Bulletin of the Atomic Scientists* praised his testimony and said that if the country had heeded the Acheson-Lilienthal plan thirty years earlier, the world would not be facing continuing nuclear peril.[20]

After six years of hit-and-miss efforts to find a niche in the energy field and his own reemergence as an energy spokesman, Lilienthal, with the help of a new member of the D&R team, John Macy, finally came up with a comprehensive energy initiative for D&R in March 1976. Hired in late 1974 to run a civil service reform program in Iran, Macy, former head of Lyndon Johnson's Civil Service Commission, quickly gained Lilienthal's confidence. He became the first person since Clapp who could be frank with his boss and also moderate his frenetic tendencies. In January 1975, Lilienthal called him "a kindred spirit" who reflected "the level of professional and intellectual competence and excellence such as Gordon [Clapp] exemplified." Another time he recognized Macy as "a center of gravity, of force for me." In December 1975, Macy became D&R's last president, a position he held with Lilienthal's full approval the rest of their tenures at D&R.[21]

As part of their plan, Lilienthal took charge of selling D&R's virtues in the field to energy-related government agencies and private businesses. Walt Seymour, who had retired in 1973, was hired in April for two months to explore coal-based programs. Lilienthal participated in an energy colloquium on the *McNeil-Lehrer Report* in May, gave an extensive interview in June with syndicated columnist John Cunniff which resulted in a widely disseminated three-part series, and wrote an extensive article for the July *Smithsonian*. Once more, Lilienthal talked of optimism and action. America "needs . . . more, not less energy." There is no need "to be timid and fearful of growth," for the country has enormous untapped resources. Citizens, local communities, and forward-looking companies must hurry to exploit "additional sources of energy, safe ones, bearing a minimum risk of pollution." A new initiative to produce synthetic oil and gas from coal, "a far better designed atomic energy industry [and]. . . a genuine all-out solar energy program" were all part of his package. Lilienthal was particularly intrigued with developing "to the full the wasted energy of the water in our rivers and canals." After the McNeil-Lehrer program he was thrilled that he had "moved D&R affirmatively into the role of a business that is 'available' for the promotion of waterpower, power from smaller installations, an idea that has great appeal to me."[22]

For the next two years Lilienthal worked hard on the idea of developing small hydroelectric dams. At first, the prospects seemed good. A December 1976 *New York Times* op-ed piece set the tone for the project, and Allis-Chalmers, the nation's major turbine manufacturer, expressed interest in a joint venture. In late 1976 Lilienthal and Macy concentrated on a new "Energy Venture . . . to increase the national supply of energy . . . [from] existing or undeveloped installations on the nation's streams and waterways." Lilienthal and Macy would lead the new corporation, D&R would provide engineering services and "Rockefeller interests, . . . possibly Lazard Freres, . . . and the Allis-Chalmers Corporation" would provide initial capital. To bolster D&R, Lilienthal hired Gordon Clapp's brother, Norman, as a new energy vice-president. Clapp, former director of the Rural Electrification Administration and recent member of the Wisconsin Public Service Commission, was well known in energy circles. By May, D&R seemed to be on its way. The Federal Energy Research and Development Administration (ERDA) approached Lilienthal about helping "formulate a program for development of small hydroelectricity," and D&R signed its first contract with Paterson, New Jersey, to develop a small hydro project.[23]

Unfortunately, Lilienthal and Macy had been far too optimistic. In February 1977, President Carter's energy advisor, S. David Freeman, told Lilienthal that "in Washington everybody thinks that waterpower is a thing of the past" and suggested, half in jest, that the only way to "attract any attention to it'" was to call "waterpower a form of solar energy." A peeved Lilienthal then recalled that ERDA's water power expertise was indeed in its solar and geothermal energy section. Lilienthal and Macy were further disappointed when the financing fell through. In March, Allis-Chalmers vaguely promised seed money and IBEC flatly refused to participate, causing Lilienthal to grouse "over the Rockefeller prissiness about financing a really important idea." On March 25, Macy wrote disconsolately that "at this stage no commitment has been made to any program . . . in this field." Nevertheless, D&R would continue to "perform its customary consulting services to clients interested in small hydro" and would tell Allis-Chalmers and IBEC that it reserved the right to explore other options with outside groups.[24]

ERDA prospects also faded. After a conversation with Acting Administrator Robert Fri, it became clear to Lilienthal that the agency had approached him mainly as a courtesy to a few congressmen interested in the issue. Nevertheless, in a June 1977 meeting, Fri told Lilienthal that ERDA would soon initiate a demonstration hydro project. Lilienthal sensed that ERDA support was only skin-deep because he saw "no enthusiasm for such a program from the five or six senior staff who sat with Bob Fri." Later that month Fri told Lilienthal he was leaving ERDA, but that he would "move ahead [on a D&R demonstration project proposal] while I am here." A skeptical Lilienthal complained that when "[Fri's] 'people down the line' see it and wrap it in typical contract-officer barbed wire and time delays— that will be a different story." Sure enough, a few days later, the head of the Geothermal office told him that any decision would take months to make. The irony of the situation was obvious—and sad. ERDA, along with the Nuclear Regulatory Commission, had been carved out of the old AEC. Now, the former AEC chairman, who had pushed hard to divide the old commission, found he could not even get his foot in the door. Times had changed.[25]

For the rest of the year and into 1978 D&R had little success. Lilienthal met with General Electric and Niagara Mohawk Utility officials and lobbied New York Governor Hugh Carey on water power and a project to provide the Northeast with power from Appalachian coal. Nothing happened. Nor was there much support from Allis-Chalmers. In their first meeting since March, Lilienthal told company executive Thomas Dineen in December he had not found "additional financing . . . to balance and complement the Allis-Chalmers role in the new venture." Under these circumstances all Dineen would promise was $200,000 for D&R for two small demonstration hydro projects. By the end of the year, Lilienthal, Macy, and Clapp were terribly discouraged. Lilienthal noted the paradox of the situation when he confided to his journal that "the amount of approval increasing by the day in my small hydro concept in letters and editorials is in contrast to the fact that so little *revenue* has been produced."[26]

Clapp's first-year progress report in March 1978 was dismaying. D&R had spent $146,000 promoting small hydro and realized only $60,000 in revenue. The Paterson contract and another with the Appalachian Regional Commission to market coal were the only viable projects. The Allis-Chalmers demonstrations were yet to begin, and nine other projects, including five ERDA grants, were awaiting approval or funding. Clapp indicated that D&R was budgeted "on the basis of getting at least three of these studies funded." At year's end, however, only two had been approved. In a glum litany, he reported that there was still not much demand for small hydro, and that D&R was at a disadvantage in competing for "specialized economic analyses . . . such as rate design, anti-trust, and power requirement questions in the regulatory process" because the company simply did not have the staff. Moreover, he reported that D&R faced stiff competition from organizations such as universities and traditional engineering firms that already had "long-established consulting relationships" with the utilities.[27]

Nevertheless, Lilienthal kept going. In March, in *Business Week,* he warned that increasing reliance on foreign oil was a critical problem, scolded the energy industry for its "unfashionable" lack of interest in hydro power, and called for federal demonstration projects "not to show that it can be done, but to show how quickly it can be done." In an April interview with the *National Journal,* he criticized the Carter administration for insisting on more demonstration projects: "The idea of having to prove that water running down hill produces energy seems very much a 'Washington angle'—demonstrating something that has been around and at work for hundreds of years." Optimistically, though, he predicted more movement in the area "as hydropower 'is approached on a private investment basis.'" But, the market did not pick up. In August 1978, Dineen told Clapp that Allis-Chalmers could no longer afford to support D&R because the two-year-long "promotion of small standardized turbines has as yet resulted in no completed sales." Niagara Mohawk's rejection of a D&R proposal in September 1978 to conduct Hudson River Basin studies sounded the death knell for the company's efforts to establish a secure financial base for its energy efforts. In early 1979, D&R had seven active small hydro projects, but the anticipated income for all seven was less than $170,000, nowhere near earlier $2 million estimates.[28]

Why did D&R fail in an area where Lilienthal had so much experience? In 1987, Norman Clapp speculated that his boss was much "more optimistic than he should have been . . . [about] small hydro." Even small projects were expensive, and long-term success depended on the questionable assumption that oil prices would continue to rise. With the federal government, states, and local communities reluctant to sink scarce resources into an uncertain energy source, it was hardly reasonable to expect firms like Allis-Chalmers or IBEC, which was already floundering, to risk their money on a concept that might not pay off. Lilienthal's basic approach posed another problem. "Dave," remembered Clapp, "was much more interested in the public policy and the social aspects of his ideas than he was in the nitty-gritty of engineering." He was a keen advocate, but he failed to develop the technical capabilities necessary to compete for limited opportunities. Both John Silveira, D&R's vice-president for engineering, and Rodman Rockefeller unsuccessfully tried to steer Lilienthal in this direction. John Macy might have done better, but Macy was in Iran most of the time trying to keep D&R's projects going in the midst of economic and political turmoil over there. In the end Lilienthal failed to recognize that all the rhetoric, innovation, and optimism in the world would not make up for inadequate technical and human support. Finally, he failed because he had little left of that most precious commodity, political clout.[29]

Other factors clouded Lilienthal's judgment. Clapp thought "Dave's interest in small hydro was partly nostalgic." He had built an organization and a reputation before on hydroelectric power—why not ride that crest again? In a conversation with the head of the Corps of Engineers, Clapp recalled Lilienthal telling the general that he hoped to "rehabilitate hydro-electric power in the public mind." His new interest was also a diversion from the Iran headaches. In June 1976, just as he had in 1967 when he turned to Vietnam, he confided in his journal that "somehow the zest for Iran has declined." Lilienthal was also concerned about his and D&R's future. According to Clapp, Lilienthal lived for a "feeling of being signifi-cant [and] of doing important things." Clapp agreed with the assessment of David Morse, D&R's general counsel in the last years, that Lilienthal nei-ther knew when nor how to stop. There was a sense of urgency because of the uncertainties in Iran. In a dismal report from Iran in April 1976, Macy warned Lilienthal that D&R's position in Iran was deteriorating. Lilienthal agreed that "the danger signals are flying" and "we had better bear down on our alternative, i.e., the United States." Two years later, he wrote Macy that small hydro was all the more crucial "in the context of the fading prospects outside the U.S. for D&R." As thin a reed as it was, by late 1978, small hydro seemed the only hope he had.[30]

Iran: The Last Chapter

D&R gained a new lease on life in the 1970s. Company revenues, mostly from Iran, soared from $2.7 million in 1972 to more than $6 million in 1976 and 1977. Profits rebounded after the early 1970s to a record $220,500 in 1976. In the first half of the decade D&R signed several large new contracts outside Khuzistan. Lilienthal's new burst of energy was part of the reason for the new business. The Shah also made sure his American friend had enough reason to continue as his irrepressible promoter in the United States. Even the Khuzistan project, which had languished for years, received new money to expand the Pahlavi dam power network, irrigation projects, and the agricultural research program at Safiabad. The Ministry of Agriculture extended a $2 million contract to set up several additional agriculture research centers, and in 1973, the Ministry of Water and Power awarded D&R $2.5 million to develop a multi-year national water plan. In spite of failing in a scheme to bring private insurance companies to Iran and in convincing the Shah that a watershed stabilization program was essen-tial to alleviate reservoir silting, Lilienthal was pleased with his efforts. He was more elated when D&R landed a public-sector management reform contract in 1974 and the Karkheh River Basin project the next year.[31]

Alarmed by increasing bureaucratic bottlenecks, the Shah told Lilienthal in April 1974 he wanted to "improv[e] efficiency in government." Taking this cue, Lilienthal initiated talks with the Ministry of Interior and soon had a $400,000 Public Sector Management Program (PSM) contract authorizing D&R to prepare recommendations for strengthening and improving "Iranian Public Administration; the Iranian Civil Service; and the Iranian Civil Service Code." In spite of being a firsthand witness to the savaging of Ebtehaj's Plan Organization in the 1950s and 1960s by the old-line ministries, Lilienthal was now optimistic about reforming those same organizations. With typical confidence, D&R declared it would help "create an administrative structure . . . adapted to the nation's needs, and responsive to its goals, . . . define an underlying 'theme' . . . [to] encourage a spirit of public service, . . . public esprit de corps and pride, . . . [and] strike a balance . . . between bureaucratic controls required to protect the public interest . . . and initiative required to keep pace with the rapid tempo of Iranian development." With bravado, Lilienthal told Interior Minister Jamshid Amouzegar he was ready "to accept the responsibility" even though his efforts would "be controversial and stir conflict tween government agencies and within the private sector as well."[32]

By mid-December, a small advance team had a set of preliminary recommendations, including the possible formation of "an Iranian . . . Hoover Commission." The key reform issues included delegating authority and decentralization, both to the provinces and within ministries, greater coordination among ministries below cabinet levels, privatization, higher salaries, and stronger public manpower-training programs. The report suggested that the project begin with a test-case investigation of a single ministry. In January, Macy took over and assembled a ten-man team, made up of five D&R regulars and five public administration specialists, to finish phase one.[33]

In spring 1974, Lilienthal pushed another project. He had been bothered for some time that the Khuzistan work had lost its original integrated approach and taken on a "project" mentality. While many of the original programs had been cut or reduced because of Iran's recurring fiscal crises, D&R was also at fault. For all of Lilienthal's concern for integrated development, the California office, which handled most of the infrastructure programs, had a definite bias toward looking at assignments as discrete projects rather than in terms of overall economic development. Organized well after D&R's first decade and never adequately socialized into the firm's TVA-like ideology, the technical staff there worked in a way that continually frustrated Lilienthal.[34]

While flying over Khuzistan in May, Lilienthal was struck by the contrast between progress in central Khuzistan and the barren reaches of the Karkheh Basin in western Khuzistan, which had been part of the original plan but never developed. A few days later he told the Shah it was "gratifying to see so much productivity [in Khuzistan] but I am an impatient man. . . . [T]he contrast between the Dez region and the Karkheh explains my impatience and dissatisfaction." Within weeks D&R was in serious discussions with the Ministries of Agriculture and Energy about Karkheh development. Leaving nothing to chance, Lilienthal broached the issue again with the Shah in November. Pulling out a copy of the 1959 "Unified Development" report, he pointed to a map of the region and said that the entire basin "was part of D&R's original plan. . . . But nothing has been done in the Karkheh Valley." In response to the Shah's query about future possibilities, Lilienthal answered that D&R would soon have a proposal ensuring that the Karkheh would be "treated as was the Khuzistan region, as a single comprehensive job." Lilienthal then said the new initiative would prevent floods in the South and provide economic development for "some very poor people, very poor." The Shah responded, "Yes, poor; and very close to the Iraq border." Lilienthal thought to himself, "The political point, of course, had been made without my mentioning it. But he will not need to be reminded again."[35]

In March 1975, the Ministry of Energy awarded a $4.5 million Karkheh Basin contract to Development & Resources/Iran (DRI), a new company made necessary by new legislation requiring foreign companies in Iran to have majority local ownership. Although he favored the new arrangement, Lilienthal felt anxious as he pondered turning "D&R's new responsibilities in Iran to Iranians who may not share our views about development or even about integrity."[36]

In spite of Lilienthal's energetic salesmanship and the Shah's subtle patronage, there were disturbing signals that should have tempered D&R's high spirits. KWPA relationships had already turned sour in late 1970 when Lilienthal complained to Director A. A. Shahgholi about shoddy work at the Pahlavi Dam. Shagholi demanded that D&R submit all future correspondence in Farsi, and he told a seething Lilienthal, "'You have been here for so many years; you should be able to speak Farsi." A year later, in September, Shahgholi ordered D&R to pay KWPA $5.3 million for unauthorized billings between 1962 and 1968. Although KWPA reduced the claim to $450,000 in 1972, and finally settled for $182,000 in 1976, the dispute cast a constant pall over KWPA relationships. KWPA stalled on virtually every contract negotiation for the next few years and continued delaying payments to D&R more every year.[37]

Lilienthal had ample warnings about the growing contradictions in Iranian society. In October 1972, he and Helen visited a fundamentalist Muslim religious ceremony in Meshed, where he was taken aback by the emotional scene, asking, "Am I the fellow who told prospective visitors to Iran that modernization has about taken over, that they are just too late to see the Persia we saw sixteen years ago . . .?" How can these people "be *part* of the same world of 'spectacular progress' the Shah declaimed about yesterday?" Iranian friends also warned him of corruption and repression at the other end of the social spectrum. After yet another caution from Ebtehaj in 1974, Lilienthal dismissed the advice, reasoning that "if there was any strain of the dictator in the Shah or the secret police were as horrible as is sometimes charged, surely Ebtehaj wouldn't be allowed to talk this way in Iran and outside." Another friend, Plan Organization director Khodad Farmanfarmaian, told him in April 1971 of the "hard core of opposition . . . within the Plan Organization Staff [against D&R]." Many of these people were resentful that in spite of promising to "work yourself out of a job, . . .

after fifteen years you are still here, and doing more than ever." In a letter to Mehdi Samii that summer, Lilienthal explained away the "explicit resentment" against D&R because of his ability to get things done by working directly through the Shah.[38]

By 1975, there were more than warnings. Iran's much-vaunted economic and social revolution had turned into a nightmare. Economic and social dislocations caused by the rash and inept policies of the 1960s and 1970s led to public protest and an increasing reliance on the oppressive SAVAK secret police. Failed agriculture policies forced an alarming migration to the cities, and the emphasis on economic growth instead of development triggered a spectacular surge of inflation. The unprecedented military buildup diverted even more funds from vital social services essential for an ever-growing impoverished mass. By 1977, military and security expenditures claimed more than 40 percent of the national budget. More ominous, xenophobic sentiments were on the rise, and even an old friend like D&R was suspect.[39]

Government programs were failing left and right. The Khuzistan agribusiness initiative that Lilienthal had pushed since the late 1960s was an unmitigated disaster and was abandoned in 1976. The failure hit Lilienthal particularly hard because he had sponsored one of the major investors, Hashem Naraghi, a California almond grower. In May 1975, Ebtehaj told Lilienthal that Naraghi had abandoned his large holdings, leaving a considerable debt. He mused to an irritated Lilienthal, "Naraghi's operation was to be one of the great demonstrations about Khuzestan's productivity, and this is a kind of black eye, don't you think?"[40]

After 1975, D&R increasingly felt the effects of the Iranian crisis. In October 1975, Pampanini told Macy that KWPA was plagued by demoralization, lost of status, and a serious "cannibalization by other Ministries." Programs were "behind schedule or barely operational, and D&R has become increasingly vulnerable to criticism and finger pointing." In January 1976 Macy warned Lilienthal that "the general climate . . . is not very good. There is increased awareness of the financial difficulties with high commitments and falling revenues." In the same letter, he reported that $500,000 had been cut from D&R's Public Sector Management program. Three months later, Macy wrote New York that Iran was behind in its payments a record $1.5 million, KWPA contract talks were stalled, a Farm Management Program (FMP) was in trouble, and funding cuts at the Safiabad agriculture research program had forced D&R to reduce its staff there to one person. In early 1977, past due accounts rose to $1.7 million, and D&R was severely embarrassed when Samii at the Agriculture Development Bank canceled the FMP for nonperformance. On top of that, the National Agriculture Research Program at Safiabad had suffered even greater cuts. Even the Karkheh Basin Project, which had done well, was beginning to be troublesome. In May 1977 Project Director John Williams complained about the lack of support from California and offered to buy the company's interest in the project, a request Lilienthal answered by telex with "'no sale' of D&R 'at any price.'" At the same time, the DRI partners, unhappy with the lack of cooperation from California and feeling a rising anti-American sentiment, were begging D&R to reduce its ownership in DRI from 40 to 10 percent.[41]

Lilienthal's reaction to the alarming developments was oddly mixed. On one hand, he acknowledged to Macy that "the posture of D&R would appear to have reached . . . a pretty low point." A few lines later, however, he counseled his beleaguered president that "despite our financial difficulties and the dispiriting situation . . . in Iran there are some positive factors. If 'positive factors' is too optimistic, let us say 'positive potentials.'" Nevertheless, pressures continued to build. In May 1976 when Mehdi Samii called, Lilienthal bitterly reproached him, "You in Iran wouldn't treat a family servant who has been with you faithfully for a long time the way we have been treated." Next month, he contemplated Macy's return to the states "from what seems a long and not completely successful stint in Iran. . . . He hasn't thus far been able to remove the ugly massive cloud of unpaid accounts, and the health of several other programs leaves much to be desired." Lilienthal's thoughts that day were all the more remarkable because he rarely wrote anything negative about Macy, so unlike his treatment of virtually every other D&R associate—including Gordon Clapp.[42]

In spite of the crisis, several of D&R's programs flourished. The water plan program with the Ministry of Water and Power was successful enough for D&R to anticipate a contract extension in late 1978. In spite of chronic payment delays, Lilienthal and Macy were pleased with the PSM program. The first phase, the preparation of a set of "proposals and recommendations in principle" for reforming Iranian public administration, led to a thirty-three-month contract to help implement some recommendations, including regional decentralization of national activities and a comprehensive managerial training program. While phase two did not meet all objectives, Iran was pleased enough in May 1978 to authorize a three-year contract extension.[43]

In the midst of the turmoil and unrest, D&R executives seemed oblivious to the growing social and political turmoil. To be sure, they were aware of the financial crisis because of its negative impact on D&R's work and profit margin. But no one realized that the financial stress was merely a symptom of far more serious conditions. From time to time they mentioned issues that should have alarmed them—wondering if SAVAK, the Iranian secret police, had infiltrated the PSM project or what to do should they uncover government corruption. And they were repeatedly warned by Minister Amouzegar that D&R should keep a low profile on the PSM project because "there was little popular appreciation of foreign advice." But these concerns were either brushed aside or ignored. Month after month, Macy's letters to Lilienthal revealed virtually nothing about the unraveling of a nation.[44]

All that changed with Macy's "Confidential Letter #1" to Lilienthal on April 27, 1978. "The political and economic atmosphere," he said eerily, "does not possess the same clarity and distinct colors." For the first time, he mentioned political unrest and religious riots and the government's inability to switch from "industrial and physical emphasis to human and agricultural priorities." That summer, Lilienthal heard that high officials, perhaps even the Shah, were trying to distance themselves from D&R by blaming the company for silting at the Pahlavi Reservoir and the failure of the agribusiness project. In late August, a disturbed Macy called Martha's Vineyard to report that the Iranian Cabinet had just resigned, hundreds had died in a movie theater fire in Abadan, and martial law had been declared across the nation. Still, Lilienthal remained hopeful, thinking that the turmoil might well only mean delays in contract decisions and funding. "A takeover of the Throne," he thought, "seems to me most unlikely."[45]

Throughout the fall, Lilienthal moved in and out of denial. In November he was buoyed when a Muslim fundamentalist general strike failed. At a December board meeting he responded to D&R's new Iran project director, Jack Vaughn, who painted a "black picture of the prospects for the Shah," that he doubted "if the picture is as black as that." A week later he was hopeful again when a "blood bath" on a religious holiday failed to materialize. Maybe, he thought, "the Iran middle class . . . has begun to realize that a mob can attract attention but a mob can't run a country." Yet, Macy, once as optimistic as his boss, continued to write about the rampant violence and disorder: KWPA was on strike, and mounting opposition to foreigners made relationships with any Iranians increasingly problematic.[46]

By late December 1978 it was all over. On December 26, Vaughn telexed Lilienthal that Iran had canceled the PSM contracts and was defaulting on all outstanding payments. On December 29 Lilienthal recorded "one of the saddest entries I have ever made in these journals: the Shah is leaving Iran; the long campaign has succeeded." The first week in January a beleaguered Vaughn got through on the phone that the Khuzistan project was also finished. A few days later a deeply depressed Lilienthal admitted that Vaughn had been right in December—"I was very, very wrong." Throughout January, Macy gamely tried to pull things together, but D&R had left nearly $2 million in assets in Iran and had only thirteen small projects promising less than $700,000 remaining at home. At a special D&R board meeting on February 7, the last he was to attend, Lilienthal, along with Macy, Clapp, and Vaughn, resigned and recommended that D&R be dissolved. Much to his chagrin, Rodman Rockefeller, whose father Nelson had died ten days earlier, refused to liquidate the company in order to allow "for the transfer, assignment or termination of contracts . . . to assure the least unfavorable outcome."[47]

For some time Lilienthal's only solace was Helen, his children, and his close cousin, Beatrice Tobey. David Jr. wrote his father that "good work is never work wasted" and that "I am sure that you have nothing but a decent and prideful satisfaction in the record you and the company made there." He finished, praising his father's "toughness" and "spirit" and for "steady[ing] others and help[ing] them keep their nerve and do what had to be done." His last words were so much a part of the Lilienthal spirit: "A program ends but the work does not; the work goes on." A week later a grateful father responded that the letter "did what no doubt you intended it to do." He was deeply moved that nowhere in the letter was there any hint of "I told you so; how wrong you were. . . . [I]nstead you gave me credit for trying, and for not folding in the face of what I might have thought a 'waste' of twenty-five years." He concluded in typical fashion that "keeping my spirit and convictions, looking ahead as I now do . . . is [due to] the kind of confidence expressed in your magnificent letter." D&R's painful ordeal was over, but Lilienthal continued to grieve. Helen Lilienthal reported that "so depressed was he by the events in Iran that for weeks at a time he would say nothing to me on the subject." Yet, she said, "his spirits were never daunted for long." He kept on going, "developing new ideas and . . . planning future work."[48]

No account of the Iranian story would be complete without examining Lilienthal's unflinching support of the Shah to the end. Moreover, there is value in looking more carefully at the disappointing results of D&R's work in Iran, especially in the Khuzistan and assessing the extent to which Lilienthal and his exceptional team were to blame for what went wrong. From his spirited defense of the 2,500th anniversary of Persia in 1971 to his words, "I felt as if I had been physically wounded," on hearing of the Shah's exodus, Lilienthal remained loyal. Iran could not have asked for a better spokesman. Everywhere he went, Lilienthal praised the Shah's "thorough-going . . . program of social justice that has transformed Iran from an almost feudal nation . . . to a modern society." At an Asia House Iranian Investor's Conference in March 1976, he defended Iran against charges of public corruption, telling his audience, "not once was it ever so much as hinted that someone needed to be an intermediary for pay, that influence was needed or to be used."[49]

In late 1977 Lilienthal clashed with U.S. Ambassador William Sullivan at the Tehran embassy in what Macy called a "frosty" session. In response to the ambassador's "cynicism" over "the true objective of the country," Macy reported that his boss strongly defended Iran and offered "his favorable judgment concerning current trends as well." Three weeks later, Lilienthal called Jack Watson at the White House asking for "a chance to give the President our positive and affirmative impressions about Iran and the Shah, as a contrast to the negative, doleful report he would get from his Ambassador."[50]

His most impassioned defense of the Shah and Iran came earlier that year in a letter to David Jr. Perhaps emboldened by his father's recent admission that going to Vietnam was an error, David Jr. had pleaded with him to distance himself from the regime because "the Shah seems a very different fellow now." Iran, he continued, has developed into "an American military client state, bristling with weapons, truculent, infamous for its repression and secret police." He reminded his father that he had rightfully been "an enthusiastic booster for Persia" over the years, but things had changed drastically—"And you are still [a] foreign agent." To be sure, David did not expect his father to leave Iran or "tell the Shah how to run his country." At the very least, however, he could speak out about American policy with its "dreary supercostly military sales game, the emphasis on police training, ... [and] the cold war antiCommunist rhetoric as a cover for Lord knows what unholy examples of corruption and careerism." Lilienthal protested that he was not a foreign agent but only "a private citizen working for certain objectives in that remarkable country." The Shah was, and continues to be, a friend, he said, and "I have been enthusiastic about Persia." He went on to cite the PSM project, which the "Shah INVITED AND URGED me to provide for him and his Government" as "part of the transition from authoritarism [*sic*] TOWARD democracy." He concluded, noting that "singling out Iran [for its arms buildup] may be myopic." After all, "the whole world, the USSR and Israel included with USA are knocking ourselves out" in the arms race.

Perhaps recalling the alienation engendered by another letter a decade before, both men wrote much more conciliatory letters the second round. Once more, the father defended Iran's leaders for their commitment to the PSM project with its emphasis on "'democratization' and 'people-involvement.'" He also reminded his son that his stand in Congress against nuclear proliferation in 1976 ran directly counter to Iran's efforts to develop its own nuclear industry. In any case the last thing he wanted was to "discourage your full expression of our concerns. For if they concern you, then, both as your father and as one who so deeply respects and loves you, they concern me." This time the ties between father and son were not broken— they were strengthened.[51]

Even at the end, Lilienthal never broke with the Shah nor blamed him for D&R's demise. In his eyes, the real devils were revolutionary elements and the bureaucracy. In late December 1978, Lilienthal wrote that "the Communists have registered one of their greatest gains." A month later he mused that "it took a bloody revolution and a 'holy war' by Moslem professionals . . . to give D&R as decent a burial as possible." When all was said and done, however, it seems likely that Lilienthal finally placed the lion's share of the blame on the backs of the highest elite, including his friends and the byzantine bureaucracies that had done so much to thwart Lilienthal's efforts in his beloved Persia. In March 1979, Macy wrote that the Shah was truly committed to "democratization in Iran" through his administrative reform program. However, he continued, "there were counter forces, including those in the public sector, that were unable to apply the designs for change." He approvingly quoted an Iranian friend in his conclusion: "It was the bureaucracy in its refusal to work and its political demands that halted the Shah's revolution." There is little doubt, considering how close they had become, that Macy's assessment was not far from Lilienthal's. Indeed, after his last meeting with Abdol Hassan Ebtehaj in October 1979, Lilienthal concluded that "the 'revolution' was made almost inevitable by the blind greed of the 'very best' of the Westernized Iranians." In a judgment laced with irony, Lilienthal concluded that "development became for [Ebtehaj] a technical achievement, not a human goal."[52]

In assessing Lilienthal's role in Iran, one must conclude that he and his associates deserve much of the responsibility for what went wrong with many of the projects there. They came, assuming that western ways and grand development schemes could be easily adapted to the "wasteland" they saw and that Iran could easily be transformed into a modern civic society. The most poignant witness to the guile of good men with honest intentions was Lilienthal's bitter reproach to Ebtehaj at that last visit: "I complained that no one had every explained to me during all those many years that the 200,000 mullahs I now hear were functioning throughout the country had great political power." Years later, in a sad letter to Helen, Ebtehaj said he "was grieved to read David's comments . . . about his last conversation with me" and that he had kept "David . . . fully informed of my views and of the situation."[53]

In truth, the centerpiece of the Khuzistan project, the Pahlavi Dam, was an extravagant investment for Iran. Cheaper irrigation could have been provided by stream diversion projects and strengthening the traditional *qanat* system. Thermal plants fueled by abundant flared natural gas would also have been much more economical. The agribusiness debacle in the Khuzistan was another failure for which D&R must bear some responsibility. According to anthropologist Grace Goodell, who spent years studying Khuzistan rural life in the 1970s, the ill-fated project failed miserably. Agricultural production was less than it had been under traditional methods, and by 1975, two of the four large farms, including Naraghi's, declared bankruptcy and left, owing tremendous debts. The regime's effort to rationalize the agricultural sector seriously disrupted the values, economic circumstances, and social structures of the rural underclass D&R was so keen on helping. Goodell, who was befriended by Lilienthal in Iran, estimated that 75,000 peasants were displaced from traditional lands and communities and forced to move to sterile model towns or leave the region for good in search of economic opportunities elsewhere. Many were not compensated for their confiscated lands and others were idled by the diminished need for labor on the large mechanized enterprises. D&R's reputation was also sullied by its longtime relationship with the Safiabad research farm, which, according to Goodell, became a place of "pervasive corruption [which] prevented serious research." Instead of experiments in small plots and herds, "the Iranian technocrats used the farm to sell first class milk, butter, cream and cheeses, the finest cuts of beef, pork, and lamb, and vegetables and fruit hardly available elsewhere in Iran."[54]

One must temper this assessment, however, by noting that Lilienthal's perspective on Iran was not much different from that of most of the major players in the U.S.-Iranian drama that played from 1952 to 1979. Every American president in this period, with the one exception of John F. Kennedy, courted the Shah and depended on his regime as a bulwark against Soviet designs in Central Asia. The Shah also enjoyed tremendous support from political elites of both parties and the cream of America's business establishment. It is difficult to imagine how Lilienthal, very much a part of this coterie, which included the Rockefellers, World Bank executives, and friends like George Woods of First Boston Corporation and David Morse, a prominent Manhattan attorney, could have reacted any differently.[55]

Lilienthal was also bound by economic necessity. Diversification efforts in other countries were modestly successful, but Iran was always there to guarantee D&R's survival, even though the company was vulnerable to economic uncertainties and the personal agendas of Ebtehaj, the Shah, and countless other high-ranking officials. Moreover, as naive and unaware as Lilienthal and his associates were about Persian culture and politics, they were decent and well-intentioned men who tried hard to correct some of the problems that contributed to later failures. Lilienthal was deeply troubled, for example, that watershed protection programs were virtually ignored in the Khuzistan and other places. By 1971 more than 300 million tons of silt clogged the Pahlavi reservoir, and some observers, including Goodell, estimated that the "dam's original life expectancy of eighty years had been revised to thirty." In spite of strong pleas to reinstate erosion control programs in the early 1970s, no one, not even the Shah, listened. In late 1976 in Lilienthal's next-to-last audience with the Shah, he spoke at length, and at no small risk, about the failure of Iranian agriculture policies. He was blunt about the disappointing results in the Khuzistan, especially the agribusiness corporations "beset by greed," and KWPA, which no longer had an "interest in agriculture, not even . . . . at Safiabad." After the Shah failed to respond, Lilienthal realized that "I am not going to make any friends in the official hierarchy by reminding them of the failure of agriculture in this country, or the downgrading of Khuzistan."[56]

A final testimony to Lilienthal's decent instincts was his willingness to speak against nuclear proliferation. In early 1974 the Shah announced that Iran had committed to a nuclear power generation program. Almost immediately, Pampanini and John Silveira suggested to the Ministry of Energy that they avail themselves of Lilienthal's expertise, and in May, Lilienthal managed to broach the subject with the Shah. In May 1975 Amouzegar, Samii, and Ebtehaj urged him to "make himself available for counsel to the new atomic energy program" and asked for a memorandum to the Shah detailing his views. Lilienthal reluctantly agreed, but worried, "[I] may have opened a pandora's box for myself." Always loyal, however, he concluded that he had "an obligation to try to help the Iranian beginnings in this tricky field." The following January, however, he advised Congress to institute an immediate export embargo of nuclear materials and technology. In response to his son's critical January 1977 letter about Iran, he replied that his testimony "ran counter to Iranian policy and potentially 'endangered' D&R's position on its development activities of our principal client and the views of the Shah toward me." Although Iran and the Shah took no action in response to Lilienthal's recommendations, by early 1976 it seemed obvious that certain aspects of the friendship were becoming increasingly tenuous.[57]

In retrospect it seems clear that whatever his errors of judgment and perception, Lilienthal was an honest man who tried to be faithful to a country he dearly loved. It is easy to believe that he never offered a bribe and that he would have dismissed any of his employees who did. Moreover, his loyalty to, and defense of, Iran was genuine, much more than self-aggrandizing flattery. He really believed that what he did there would eventually result in a better life for all Iranians, and until nearly the end, he was sure that D&R would succeed in its vital mission. Nevertheless, he was foiled by his inability to see below the surface of a culture very different from the one he had helped transform more than four decades earlier.

The Last Years

The last decade of his life was a difficult time for David Lilienthal. His health rebounded in the first years and his chronic insomnia eased some. By the late 1970s, however, the afflictions of old age, an increasingly painful arthritic hip condition, a minor heart attack, and prostate surgery, intruded more. Even after he lost his company, though, he kept a regular vigil in a New York office until June 1980, when he faced a long convalescence for double hip-replacement surgery in June and a cataract operation in November.

The pressures of business took their toll. According to those close to him, including Rockefeller, Frederiksen, and Morse, Lilienthal became harsher and more unpredictable in his personal relations. He often clashed with Rockefeller about IBEC's lack of support and the feeling that he had not been treated right by the parent company. One sign of his volatility came in late 1973, when he became upset that he had not resisted the sale "of the flower project in Colombia (a Levin project and a good one)." Just two years earlier he had indicated he was greatly pleased when Pampanini had arranged the sale. After Frederiksen resigned in 1975 after serious conflicts with his boss and Rockefeller, Lilienthal became obsessed that his former vice-president's new company was deliberately stealing business and luring key staff away from D&R. In an October 1976 meeting Frederiksen tried to smooth over their differences. Lilienthal refused to listen, and according to Frederiksen, became extremely rude.[58]

Lilienthal was also afflicted by an increasing sense of loneliness and isolation. Clapp, Oliver, and Burnett were long gone, and Gerald Levin, his last young confidant, left D&R in 1971. Although he genuinely liked Rockefeller, their clashes over corporate matters checked a deeper relationship. While he thought a great deal of Pampanini, there was little time for intimate discussions since his executive vice-president was constantly on the road looking for business and putting out fires in Iran. The steady attrition of staff in New York, due to Pampanini's cost-cutting efforts and the decision in 1974 to move the operational activities to California, where most day-to-day decisions were being made, only exacerbated the situation. In March 1975, a doleful Lilienthal, who Norman Clapp remembered, "needed to be with people," wondered how he would "transform the New York office (jokingly referred to as the home office) into something alive. . . . Miss Baron [his longtime secretary] and I will be rattling around in an empty lot of space, and I will have no contact with professionals except as they come to see me."[59]

Much of his behavior these years can be explained by the personality quirks that had driven him for seven decades. Optimism, a restless spirit, and a huge concern for his public persona had always contributed to his successes. In the 1970s these traits turned on him, resulting in more failures

than successes. His emotional highs and lows seemed to transform themselves, as they sometimes do, into an obsessive sense of purpose. David
Morse concluded that "the double tragedy was that . . . [Lilienthal] never
knew when to quit. . . . [His] dreams were too big. . . . He was a workaholic,
he was driven, and never was satisfied." Morse remembers many a night
finding his friend in an almost-deserted dining room in New York's Century
Club. "Dave," he concluded, "never could savor things." Frederiksen also
thought that over the years Lilienthal became more driven by the TVA idea
and his journals, which he would write in for hours. Rockefeller said it
best: Lilienthal was always haunted by *inquieto,* inquietude—"He was
never satisfied or pleased with the way things were going."[60]

To a large extent, his driven spirit manifested itself in an almost obsessive concern for his public image and posterity. In 1966, Lilienthal started
deeding his personal papers to the Firestone Library at Princeton, and in
1974, donated many of the D&R records to the library, along with $50,000
for cataloging. Tom Mead, a longtime D&R employee in Vietnam, Africa,
and Iran was paid by the firm to work at Princeton for a year to prepare a
comprehensive annotated history and bibliography of D&R's activities in
the Khuzistan. In his last years, Lilienthal was often disturbed over lack of
public attention. After a 1976 address in Washington, D.C. to a national
planning conference, he grumbled over the "complete and total disregard
of the speech by the press in Washington or New York." He was upset in
1971 and 1976 when volumes 5 and 6 of the Journals received scant reviewer attention. In November 1971, he penned an embarrassing note to
New York Times columnist Scotty Reston, wishing that he "or someone as
understanding as you are . . . were to do a review of my recent volume of
Journals, which so far has not been reviewed in the *Times.*" The paper
finally responded in January 1972, but only with the sparse comment of an
anonymous reviewer that the journals "were obviously written for others
to read in his lifetime. Circumspect and unsensational, they present the
Lilienthal he wants us to see. . . . They provide valuable material for the
study of the subtle relationship between infiltration and co-optation, between changing the system and being changed by it." In late 1976 he worried about the same lack of response to volume 6, wondering why a book
like *The Letters of E. B. White* received more attention than his. After all,
he noted in a petty tone, many of White's descriptions of rural Maine were
"nowhere as well written as Thoreau, or to be honest about it, some of
David Lilienthal's entries about the moors of Martha's Vineyard."[61]

Yet, in spite of these tribulations, the old Lilienthal still shone through.
Sensing the malaise of the decade, he became an avid spokesman on behalf
of the American Commonwealth and a champion of its potential. From a
homecoming commencement address at DePauw University in 1970 to one
of his last public speeches, the Gordon Clapp Lecture at Lawrence University in Appleton, Wisconsin, in September 1976, he remained a staunch
optimist and prophet of a great "Coming American Renaissance." Echoing
the themes of *This I Do Believe,* he reminded his audiences that America
still had the greatest potential and future of any nation on earth. To his

Lawrence audience he proclaimed that "a capacity for peaceful self-correction and renewal is one of the greatest talents of our democratic society." Earlier in the year, before the American Philosophical Society in Philadelphia, he acknowledged the difficult times, but saw them "as a new beginning, another of those times of rebirth that marked the American past . . . which generated . . . a resurgence of spirit and achievements in human progress which most of the people of the world have looked at with admiration, and, indeed, envy." While his optimism sometimes seemed to turn to desperation, it did not always. When it did not, he could still speak convincingly of affirmation and faith, of trust in people and public and private institutions alike.[62]

Moreover, it was a time for family reconciliation. Although David and his family continued their life in Florence, they and the elderly Lilienthals visited frequently in stopovers to, or from, Iran. Letters between father and son were filled with mutual respect. Even David's January 1977 letter about Iran created only a momentary ripple as both men remembered the pain of the earlier exchanges over Vietnam. The Lilienthals enjoyed visits with their grandchildren on Martha's Vineyard and supported David's children with a generous loan in 1974 to Mike to start a pottery business and buying a house on Cape Cod for Pamela in 1976.

The bond with David had never been stronger than in the summer of 1979, when father and son spent six weeks on the Vineyard hammering out Lilienthal's last manuscript, "Atomic Energy: A New Start," for a book that Harper & Row asked him to do. Lilienthal called his son "a guide and an intellectual catalyst [and] the best, the most sensitive, the most effective partner I have ever had." The message of their last collaboration was clear. It was futile to rely on energy conservation alone to meet the energy crisis. Support for coal, solar energy, hydroelectric, and even nuclear research was essential. Nevertheless, the United States should do everything possible to move away from relying on the light-water technology that had dominated the nuclear industry from the start. Admitting his "role in this inadequately considered rush to adopt the light water method of atomic energy production," he argued that "our new objective must be to find a safer, 'healthier' method of producing peaceful energy from the atom by a method that also minimizes or eliminates the present risk of furthering the spread of nuclear weapons." Much to his delight, this last public testimony was not ignored as his later journals had been. It was reviewed extensively in newspapers across the nation and in the *New Yorker,* the *Christian Science Monitor,* the *National Review,* and yes, even the *New York Times.* What was even sweeter was that most of the reviews were positive and receptive. In early 1981, the *Monitor* recommended it as one of the "Notable Books of 1980" in Nature and Science.[63]

In spite of the crushing disappointment of Iran and increasing physical problems, Lilienthal remained active in 1979 and 1980. He spent as much time as possible in his New York office, including a week with Helen in May 1979 in the Tennessee Valley as an honored TVA guest, and even managed a trip to Northern Quebec to inspect the massive James Bay hydro-electric project. He also became an active trustee for Princeton Theological Seminary's Center for Theological Inquiry. His main hope was that the center would "throw some light on the practical problem facing the world, how to understand Islam and the misuse—as I saw it—of the political and military power of the Islamic religious leaders."[64]

After hip surgery in June 1980, he spent four months recuperating and planning his next projects. By late October, he was back in his office working, as he told IBEC President Dick Dilworth, on "acquiring surplus hydro-electricity from Quebec for New York." A letter to David in late December reflected the old spirit. Barely a month had passed since cataract surgery, but he was already in a new Broadway office "with a great view of mid-Manhattan," which he shared with Donald Straus, an old friend from AEC days. He was looking forward to lectures at the University of Texas and Brown University, meetings in January with TVA distributors, and, he told his son, "the New Englanders want me to help on the idea of a bond between Eastern Canada's energy resources and New England—an idea I'm fathering."[65]

On January 13, the ebullient octogenarian had his cataract surgery dressing removed in Manhattan and retired to his hotel in anticipation of working the next day. Sometime during the night he died in his sleep.

Ten days later, after a private family interment on Martha's Vineyard, several score of friends, family, and associates made their way to Miller Chapel at the Princeton Seminary for a service of remembrance. Three friends and associates, John Macy, Dick Dilworth, and Donald Straus, offered eulogies. To Straus, Lilienthal was unique because he was an "innovator, thinker, problem-solver, fighter philosopher, doer, pragmatist, moral leader, and compassionate friend." Dilworth reminded the gathering that "in a dangerous and wicked world, it is indeed fortunate that in each generation a few, all too few, people like David come amongst us, else suffering humanity would be the poorer." The colleague who knew him best the last years, John Macy, summarized the life of this remarkable man best: Dave was "a combination of tenderness and toughness, a man of almost romantic values. . . . He was a man of peace who sought reconciliation, ... a generator of ideas, ... [and] he advocated action." Macy continued that Lilienthal "was a communicator par excellence [sic]. . . . Yet he was impatient with those who *only* communicate." Finally, it was clear that Lilienthal "was a constant and unabashed patriot . . . . [and] a model of public service at TVA and AEC for generations of public servants who followed."[66]

CHAPTER 14

Assessment

Disputes always seemed to surround him and he was attacked bitterly by critics. Though he was a man of compassion, he never skirted a fight in defense of the American commonwealth and its future. David Lilienthal was a special citizen.

—*New York Times*, January 17, 1981

A Present Witness

This study would not be complete without examining Lilienthal's role in the human radiation experiments sponsored by several government agencies, including the Atomic Energy Commission (AEC), from the early 1940s until well into the 1970s. What did Lilienthal know and how did his commission react to the Manhattan Project experiments that had performed clinical tests on more than six dozen human subjects, most without informed consent and few that promised therapeutic benefits to the patients? Some of the "nuclear guinea pigs" were volunteers, and others were chosen because they were deemed terminally ill. Seventeen were mentally disabled children. Some were given oral doses of radioactive iron and polonium, while others were given radiation x-ray treatments above approved occupational limits. The most dramatic interventions included more than two dozen injections of uranium, polonium, americium, and plutonium compounds to determine the rate at which radioactive substances were excreted from the body.[1]

The answer regarding Lilienthal's involvement cannot yet be definitively settled. It appears, though, from papers released so far by the Department of Energy under the direction of President Bill Clinton's Advisory Committee on Human Radiation Experiments that Lilienthal's commission demonstrated a strong ethical presence and acquitted itself well over these highly questionable programs. According to Joseph Volpe, deputy general counsel to the AEC at the time, the five commissioners found out about the experi-

ments after taking over the Manhattan Project in January 1947 and immediately became concerned about moral and legal implications.[2]

In late January, the AEC Interim Medical Committee recommended to
the commission that clinical testing programs be continued, including tracer
injections "of polonium, radium and uranium in human and animal subjects" at the University of Rochester and similar experiments at the University of California, Berkeley on the "metabolism of fission products,
protoactinium, uranium, neptunium, plutonium, americium and curium."
Two weeks later, on February 6, AEC general manager Carroll Wilson wrote
Interim Committee Chairman Stafford Warren that AEC attorneys would
be taking a closer look at the clinical testing program. A month later the
legal department recommended that all clinical tests should proceed under
strict conditions of informed consent, and in mid-April, word leaked that
the commission would forbid any clinical tests without a therapeutic basis.
On April 30, Wilson formally advised Warren that the commission would
extend medical research contracts, including programs involving "clinical
testing." He stipulated, however, that any such "treatment . . . will be administered to a patient only when there is expectation that it may have
therapeutic effect," and that "each patient should be clearly informed of
the nature of the treatment and its possible effects, and [should express] his
willingness to receive the treatment." Wilson further required that two phy-
sicians certify in writing that the consent guidelines had been followed.[3]

In June, the commission authorized a formal Medical Board of Review,
which immediately reaffirmed the need to continue "the application of
atomic energy to medical and biological problems . . . [and] recommend[ed]
that in so far as it is compatible with national security, secrecy in the field of
biological and medical research be avoided." In August, Lilienthal pushed
for even stronger administrative support, an Advisory Committee for Biology and Medicine "of a stature comparable to our General Advisory Committee," and "a Director of Biology and Medicine, operating on a level
with the [other AEC division directors]." The commission needed more
help than it now had, said the chairman, in determining which projects
should remain under the exclusive purview of the agency and which ones
ought to be joint ventures. He was also concerned with "obtain[ing] the
fresh approach and advice of groups not previously associated with the
[Manhattan] project." In November 1947, the new Advisory Committee
reinforced the April order on therapeutic effect and informed consent, a
policy that held through the remainder of Lilienthal's tenure.[4]

That the commission acted so quickly was a tribute to their resolve and
willingness to tackle a controversial issue. In the first place, it was not easy
to make quick decisions on any issue. Volpe remembered that the situation
was in constant flux. The transfer of assets was slow, and the commissioners and their small staff were overwhelmed each day by new revelations
about the vast and secretive empire they had inherited. Moreover, centralized project monitoring was difficult because of the extensive distribution
of radioactive isotopes, the decentralized nature of the experiments, the

multi-institutional sponsorship of several of the projects, and the lack of adequate written documentation on many experiments. Placing restrictions on clinical testing was also difficult because the experiments were seen as crucial for establishing safer conditions for a growing work force facing nuclear hazards. In the third place, the commission's decision was bold because neither informed consent nor therapeutic effect was as strongly held a principle as it later became. Robert Schlinker, of the Argonne Laboratories, noted recently that in the 1940s, the physician-patient relationship was very different from today's "partnership" model: the physician's word was final, and patients were often seen as incapable of making informed decisions about their own treatment. The consent issue was further muddled in some cases because even mentioning plutonium by name was considered a breach of security. It also seems the case that therapeutic effect was a much less sure principle then. In a 1948 *Science* article on medical ethics, for example, the author grants the principle of informed consent. He continues, however, that while therapeutic effect is important, "It is also a matter of common understanding that an individual may justifiably permit a physical evil on himself for the good of another or for the good of humanity."[5]

Even with the commission's resolve, however, however, there is evidence that anywhere from two to twenty-two human experiments took place after Wilson's April 30 letter to Warren. Two experiments, the last of eighteen plutonium injections (the only one known to have involved informed consent) and a singular americium injection, were administered after the letter. In addition, one, two, or five non-therapeutic polonium injections and up to fifteen finger x-ray experiments may have been given after April 30. One source states that four of the five polonium injections had been administered by December 1945, but others give unspecified 1947 dates. The finger x-rays, reported as 1947 experiments, had to have been administered before July 9, 1947, the date of the program's report. Because of a lack of written documentation, the exact dates are unknown.[6]

In assessing the state of the human radiation experiments on Lilienthal's watch, it is important to be candid about two curious exceptions to the otherwise positive assessment of his role in, and sensibilities about, the experiments. Sometime in late 1949, the Oak Ridge Subcommittee on Human Applications reinstated a Massachusetts state school study which had been halted in 1946 where both "normal children" and "mentally deficient subjects" consumed cereal containing radioactive calcium. Considering Lilienthal's increasing detachment from commission affairs as early as summer 1949, it is likely he had no knowledge of this breach of the 1947 policy. No one knows why Oak Ridge gave the green light for the clinical tests, which actually began in 1950. It may have been a function of the commission's inability to properly control the nearly eight thousand shipments of medical therapy isotopes that had been dispersed by the end of 1949. This experiment may have also been difficult to rein in because of the confusing array of institutions, including AEC, the Quaker Oats Company, Massachusetts Institute of Technology, Harvard Medical School, and Walter E. Fernald State School, with a stake in this particular project.[7]

The other question relating to Lilienthal's sensitivity to testing is related by Kurt Vonnegut, who was in the early 1950s a public relations specialist at the General Electric AEC contract laboratories at Schenectady, New York. Vonnegut recalled that Lilienthal, just having left AEC, spoke to a group of scientists at the labs, depressing everyone with his "gushing" story "about his egg man, who had a malignant throat tumor the size and shape of a summer squash." Vonnegut continued that "this man, who was about to die, was urged to drink an atomic cocktail. The tumor disappeared entirely in a matter of days. The egg man died anyway. But Lilienthal and others like him found the experiment encouraging in the extreme." A quarter of a century later, a chastened Lilienthal, after reading Vonnegut's commentary, wrote in his journal that "my own recollection of that and other lectures I made . . . coincides pretty much with the sour picture Vonnegut wrote." In spite of these two "incidents," it seems clear that Lilienthal acquitted himself in this sordid tale of government excess. John Abbotts, a staff member of U.S. Representative Edward J. Markey (D-Mass.), who held hearings on the experiments six years before the Clinton Administration finally broke the silence, confided to this author that nothing has tarnished Lilienthal's reputation and that probably nothing would.[8]

The Public Life

David Lilienthal was an extraordinary American. He was a rhetorician, entrepreneur, charismatic leader, and a quintessential twentieth-century liberal moralist. He was also a larger-than-life individual whose sharp ego frequently hurt those he cared for (and sometimes those he opposed) in indiscriminate ways. He was an impatient man who expressed disdain for academic discourse and the spinning of theoretical webs that interfered with the "action" he so dearly loved. His greatest shortcomings, however, came by way of two of his most important strengths, his optimism and ability to persuade. All too often, he believed that sheer force of will and a positive outlook could prevail over seemingly impossible odds. That attitude served him well at TVA, where he succeeded when many thought he would not. It was less effective during the atomic years, when he was disappointed by the rejection of the Acheson-Lilienthal plan for the internationalization of the atom, and then by his and Robert Oppenheimer's quixotic crusade against thermonuclear weapons. His blinderlike optimism failed him miserably in his later years, in Vietnam, Iran, and even at home in his futile crusade for small–hydro power development.

His rhetoric often served his ends in dramatic fashion as in the 1939 "Grass Roots" address and *TVA: Democracy on the March*. But it also had a double edge. Sometimes it seduced him into embracing a perception of the world and his role which was far different from both realities. In 1960, at a Carnegie Institute of Technology management symposium, he advised that multinational corporations needed to cultivate "a lively awareness of politics in the broadest sense" overseas. He also insisted that overseas managers must have a keen grasp of the "meaningful art of trying to understand the ways, the thoughts, and the whole culture of the people who speak another tongue." Moreover, they must make a concerted effort to gather vital information about "the details of the laws of the country, of its institutions, of its attitudes." There is little doubt that Lilienthal believed what he preached to this gathering—yet, the evidence suggests many a slip 'twixt the cup of advice and the lips of practice: neither Lilienthal nor many of his D&R colleagues ever learned Spanish, Portuguese, or Farsi, the tongues of the lands in which they most frequently toiled. It was also obvious that no one at D&R really understood the compelling realities of the Shah's Iran. Indeed, in the end it became clear that they barely understood the elites with whom they had worked for nearly a quarter of a century.[9]

Ironically, Lilienthal prevailed at home and failed abroad because he never changed his mode of public action. All his life he was, in Glendon Schubert's words, a larger-than-life "Administrative Platonist." The Platonist, according to Schubert, is an idealistic social engineer who sees the executive as the key to effective policy making and "the legislature as an inadequate, incompetent source of public policy." The world of the administrative Platonist requires "a highly moral official world, personified in the image of the Good Administrator. The public interest is created by the imaginative manipulation of not-too-stubborn facts . . . by administrative Philosopher Kings." It is difficult to imagine a better description of Lilienthal's administrative style.[10]

At home, Lilienthal was a consummate "Administrative Platonist." For nearly two decades, he served three executives with unflagging loyalty while regularly expressing contempt for the legislative process, first in Wisconsin and then Washington. As Platonist, Lilienthal became a masterful administrative manipulator, standing firm when he could and bending in the wind where necessary. His courting of traditional interests in the Tennessee Valley, seen by Selznick as cooptation, and his close ties with corporate America, first at AEC and later as a private citizen, attested to his keen instinct to realize his ends and those of the public and private organizations he led.

What Lilienthal failed to realize later on, particularly in Vietnam and Iran, was that administrative Platonism is more likely to prevail where the executive office offers a strong and unambiguous source of the moral will so necessary for the good administrator. Lilienthal badly underestimated the moral authority and real power of both Lyndon Johnson and his Vietnamese allies, and of the Shah of Iran. In neither situation was he able to function within the context of "a highly moral official world." There was certainly very little official morality in the Shah's realm, even less after Abol Hassan Ebtehaj left Plan Organization. And for all the power and glory of the Shah's empire, it crumbled in an instant in the late 1970s. Johnson's Vietnam policy was terribly flawed from the beginning, and public sentiment constantly eroded the moral legitimacy of his policies in that tragic land. In the end, Johnson, like the Shah, was forced to abandon his position as the nation's leader. In both cases, Lilienthal was left wondering why things had gone so badly. In Vietnam it shattered his hopes for lucrative contracts and the chance to develop yet another river; in Iran, it cost him his company—and months of personal bitterness and hurt.

A final fascinating and positive aspect of Lilienthal's public persona was his ability to engender almost universal respect from those he worked with, including friends he clashed or crossed swords with, and even foes. Oral history interviews, both those done by TVA and by University of Memphis historian Charles Crawford, reveal a strong admiration for Lilienthal among most of the pioneer administrators, even many in A. E. Morgan's camp. Likewise, it is striking to see the deep sense of veneration among D&R veterans, including those who differed strongly with Lilienthal or who left under fire. John Oliver, John Burnett, Gerald Levin, Rodman Rockefeller, and even Harald Frederiksen all agreed that working with Lilienthal was an exhilarating adventure, even in the rockiest of days. Joseph Volpe, whose time with Lilienthal spanned the AEC and D&R years, offered the most compelling explanation—"My fascination with Lilienthal was that he was always involved in something interesting—and I like to be involved in interesting things." Levin, currently CEO of Time Warner-Turner, described his former boss as "omnipresent. . . . He had a sense of constant change . . . [and] was always pushing ideas." Even though Levin left, in part because he felt he had been demoted in 1971, he confided to the author that "in my own case, it became clear that I had to go. [Lilienthal] was overpowering, and in the end it became difficult for me to separate my ideas from his." Lilienthal was compelling for many people, for many years, in many venues.[11]

The Private Life

Lilienthal's private side was just as tumultuous. He was legendary as a whirling dervish, ambitious, driven, brilliant, a man with seemingly inexhaustible energies. But his frenetic pace, often lasting for months, was always punctuated by illness, or bouts of mental or physical exhaustion—usually accompanied by a long trip or convalescence, usually to the beaches of western Florida or later to the Caribbean. This pattern continued his entire life, and by his twilight years, it seemed he might have reached the limits of his prodigious energy and the therapeutic effect of periodic repose. What fueled this drive with its seemingly contradictory creative and destructive effects?

Edward Falck, a brilliant TVA rate engineer, and Rodman Rockefeller, Lilienthal's nominal boss in the 1970s when D&R was bought by the IBEC Corporation, suggested that his religious background was a root factor. Both men wondered if Lilienthal's intensity did not reflect a deep concern for his own Jewishness, even a need, as Falck suggested, to overcome a sense of inferiority occasioned by his Jewish experience. While one can never know, it is likely that "the Jewish Factor" was not the central force that shaped his life. Clearly, anti-Semitism was not part of his formative experience, and when it raised its ugly head at TVA and AEC, it never gave him much pause for thought. In Valparaiso, he was a Jew, as Fred Arvin was an Episcopalian. At DePauw, he used his Jewish background to his advantage. Moreover, his letter to Uncle Adolph in 1923, embracing heritage but rejecting creed, and his behavior the rest of his life made it clear that he neither shrunk from his Jewishness nor wore it on his sleeve. He was religious but not in a defensive manner. As he wrote in 1965, "I have been accepted as a man, well-known to be a Jew in origins, but accepted as a man: among my young fellow students, by the young woman I married in my early twenties, by the farmers and business people of the strongly Protestant and Anglo-Saxon South, by three Presidents, by Cardinals and Archbishops of the Roman Catholic faith and Bishops of the Methodist Church, by college Presidents, by two Moslem Kings and by many Moslem peasants and officials, by fellow Jews." Methodist Bishop G. Bromley Oxnam wrote of Lilienthal's efforts, as chairman of Dean Acheson's advisory committee in 1946 and later at AEC, to consult with religious leaders of all faiths about the atomic burden. Oxnam observed that Lilienthal's "thought is grounded deep in religious and moral considerations." He even "regard[ed] him as one of the truest Christians I have ever known." His speeches— many delivered to all manner of religious bodies—Protestant, Catholic, and Jewish—were full of references to a common American faith that sustained the democratic spirit. As Jordan Schwarz aptly observed, "Lilienthal's religion was American liberalism: it gave him the freedom not to be a Jew."[12]

Lilienthal developed as he did, in part because he was his parents' child. His ambition and drive, brilliance and intelligence, and ego—or self-concern—could be traced in less intense form to Leo or Minna, or to both parents. Moreover, if anything fueled his insecurity, it was not religion but the memory of a meager family life, constantly shadowed by Leo's commercial ineptness and financial insecurity.

Perhaps the greatest explanation for his restless spirit and drive lies in the combination of strong ambition with a fortunate confluence of personal relationships that both inspired and abetted that ambition. In his early years, Fred Arvin, James H. McGill, and the "big rawboned teacher" easily come to mind. Felix Frankfurter and Donald Richberg were important in his formative adult years, and people like Philip La Follette, George Norris, Morris Cooke, H. A. Morgan, Gordon Clapp, J. Robert Oppenheimer, and yes, A. E. Morgan, Wendell Willkie, and Lewis Strauss, fed his energies during his public life. In his later years that web extended to include André Meyer, Ebtehaj, John Macy, and again, Gordon Clapp. Most important, there was Helen, whose patience and constant forbearance allowed her husband to follow his dreams wherever he wanted.

In his private life, Lilienthal could be immensely thoughtful and generous toward those he cared for. His children and grandchildren all benefited from Helen and David's largesse, even in the rocky times when they differed over issues such as Vietnam and race relations. The Lilienthals were equally generous with frequent monetary and securities gifts to David's brother Allen, cousins Beatrice Tobey and Bernadine (Dee) Szold, and boyhood friend Fred Arvin when they needed help. Lilienthal was just as thoughtful with his pen. To friends, he wrote scores of eloquent congratulatory notes during good times and consoling messages in sad times. In 1964, he wrote a terminally ill Edward R. Murrow that "of all the men who have commanded the ear and eye and heart of their fellows with the coming of electronic communication, you are the only one who still has the direction, the freshness, the individualness that you learned . . . in the hardboiled idealism of your youth. No one and nothing has ever really scared you and never will." In probably his last written word, Lilienthal told Robert Moses as he looked out over the mid-Manhattan skyline from his hotel room that he was reminded of "Steichen's . . . portrait of the young Robert Moses [and how it] foretells the city he made come alive. What a combination of dreamer and gutsy fighter in that face!"[13]

The Legacy

What then is Lilienthal's enduring contribution to the American commonwealth? First, there is the ambivalent circumstance of his long international crusade in his last three decades. Lilienthal is an important example of the best and the worst impulses of post–World War II American internationalism. His steadfast honesty in his international dealings is an important legacy. He was appalled by the thought of money changing hands for favors, a standard that cost D&R at least one potentially lucrative contract in South America. So too, were his extraordinary efforts to win a peace on the Indian-Pakistani border, standing up to Colombian dictator Rojas Pinilla in the early 1950s, and influential testimony to Congress against nuclear proliferation in 1976—the latter two acts taken at great risk to Development & Resources Corporation. Another admirable trait was his refusal to pander to the anti-Communist strain of American internationalism. While as anti-Communist as any American might be, Lilienthal steadfastly refused to allow his work to become an instrument of the cold war. He defended Jawaharlal Nehru when many accused the Indian leader of being another Red voice. He spoke against the shrillness of anti-Communist rhetoric, and emphasized to his D&R team in Vietnam that under no circumstances would he allow them to become a propaganda tool for the American government.

But he was also a dramatic example of what was wrong with American peacetime efforts abroad. Like most of his peers who served abroad, he spoke only English, and he associated almost exclusively with those at the very highest political and economic strata. He presumed to be able to "read" the pulse of a nation by visiting local markets, and he had little but contempt for scholars who tried to teach him the finer nuances of these foreign cultures. His wrongheaded assumption that American liberal principles would be easy to transplant into cultures very different from his own was a serious, even fatal flaw—but one he shared with virtually every postwar administration, the World Bank, and the myriad private institutions and individuals concerned with remaking the third world in the image of the West. The gospel of large-scale, top-down development, and the vision of genuine democratic reform were, in the end, only illusory hopes that could never be realized.

On the positive side, his writings and speeches are important in both style and content. *TVA: Democracy on the March* is an important contribution to American political rhetoric, as is the "Grass Roots" speech and the 1947 "This I do Believe" soliloquy. The seven-volume *Journals of David E. Lilienthal* have already served as an invaluable source for a multitude of historians, social scientists, and other writers, and will continue to do so for the indefinite future. One cannot forget, either, that Lilienthal popularized the "grass roots" maxim and that his controversial exposition of that concept set into motion a fierce debate about bureaucracy and democratic participation which has not yet been resolved. Lilienthal was also indirectly responsible for the genesis of another significant concept into the American vocabulary—cooptation, which Philip Selznick coined to describe TVA's method of securing support for its early, sometimes tenuous, programs.

While Lilienthal was hardly a systematic or original thinker—he might be best characterized as an extremely gifted pamphleteer—there was one constancy in his works, which extends from his earliest words in "The Mission of the Jew" to his last small book on atomic energy. He was always confident that the American commonwealth could work its way out of difficult corners and trying times. He often sounded Pollyannaish, but his speeches in the 1930s were balm to the anxious citizens of the Tennessee Valley and TVA employees. His confidence in the people's judgment in the AEC days was an important counter in the battle against forces that sought to privatize discussion about the atom. In the late 1960s and 1970s, his frequent witness that "we Americans have every reason to be positive, hopeful and optimistic, to be proud and reassured," or that "I don't join in this chorus of self-derogation, of reaching deeper and deeper into the dark caverns of despair" was a refreshing counter to the demoralizing shadows cast by Vietnam, Watergate, and the devastating energy crisis.[14]

There is a final legacy of no small import. Lilienthal was a model public administrator and an inspiration for present times where higher public service is better characterized by "revolving door tenure" than commitment and constancy. The best example of Lilienthal's penchant for public service was his "capacity for self-distancing," the ability, as Richard Sennett describes it, of "public behavior . . . [or] action at a distance from the self, from its immediate history, circumstances, and needs." For almost twenty years, Lilienthal was able to consistently "self-distance" himself through a discipline and impersonality that often seemed ruthless and cold. Yet, he also had the uncanny capacity to engender a wide and enthusiastic following. With a few words he could evoke an enduring loyalty—his first re-

marks, not part of the formal address, to his Rotary audience in Chattanooga in September 1933 are apropos: "My friends of Tennessee. It would
not be human for me not to be touched by the friendliness of your greeting.
A few weeks ago I was a stranger in your gates—already you are treating
me as your neighbor. Today there is no east or west or north or south. We are
all Americans, working together for the common security and well being."[15]

His capacity for self-distancing was a fortuitous gift through which he
could channel his exceptional talents. It also served to moderate the deeper
and darker impulses that manifested themselves over the years in frequent
ups and downs and frenetic highs and abject crashes. It was not a perfect
governor, to be sure. Sometimes his almost uncontrollable drive resulted in
errors of judgment and untoward behavior toward others. Sometimes it led
to dreadful days and weeks of anxiety and psychological paralysis. Nevertheless, it worked most of the time to help him for nearly two public decades and three more on his own to prevail in battle with powerful external
forces and his own personal demons.

Lilienthal helped preside over two public institutions for nearly seventeen unbroken years. The record is even more remarkable considering that
both agencies were extremely crucial to the success of the Roosevelt and
Truman administrations, and they both embraced highly controversial mandates. Regardless of TVA's current state of disrepair, or of the present controversies surrounding the AEC human radiation experiments, it is important to remember that Lilienthal tried to make both institutions work for
all Americans. George Will recently wrote that "disunion is not a danger
today. Decay is. That is a pity because public works are the sort of things
government is good at. The Tennessee Valley Authority and the Interstate
Highway System were not just good in themselves. they were good for the
morale of government, which periodically needs some inspiriting successes."[16]

Perhaps the most fitting epitaph for David E. Lilienthal was penned by
Arthur E. Schlesinger Jr. in a letter to Helen a few days after her husband's
death: "Dave was one of the remarkable men of the century—remarkable
especially in his unflagging and unquenchable commitment to the possibility of constructive work—so rare in an age given over so sadly to the work
of destruction."[17]

Notes

Abbreviations

AA	Development and Resources Corporation papers, held by Arbor Acres Corporation, Glastonbury, Connecticut
AB	Adolf Berle papers. Franklin Delano Roosevelt Presidential Library, Hyde Park, New York
AP	Private papers of Andrea Pampanini, New York City
BH	Bourke Hickenlooper papers, Herbert Hoover Presidential Library, West Branch, Iowa
CC	Clark Clifford papers, Harry S. Truman Presidential Library, Independence, Missouri
DEL	David E. Lilienthal papers, Seeley G. Mudd Manuscript Library, Princeton University
DELAEC	David E. Lilienthal Atomic Energy Commission office files, National Archives, Washington, D.C.
DOE	U.S. Dept. of Energy, Central Information Center, Las Vegas, Nevada
DRC	Development and Resources Corporation archives, Seeley G. Mudd Manuscript Library, Princeton University
FBI	Documents released by Federal Bureau of Investigation pursuant to author's Freedom of Information Act request regarding David E. Lilienthal
FDR	Franklin Delano Roosevelt presidential papers, Franklin Delano Roosevelt Presidential Library, Hyde Park, New York
FF	Felix Frankfurter papers, Library of Congress Manuscript Division, Washington, D.C.
FFHLS	Felix Frankfurter papers, Harvard Law School, Cambridge, Massachusetts
GN	George Norris papers, Library of Congress Manuscript Division, Washington, D.C.

GRC	Gordon R. Clapp papers, Harry S. Truman Presidential Library, Independence, Missouri
HAM	Harcourt A. Morgan papers, University of Tennessee, Knoxville
HD	History Division. Dept. of Energy, Germantown, Maryland
HH	Herbert Hoover Presidential Papers, Herbert Hoover Presidential Library, West Branch, Iowa
HI	Harold Ickes papers, Library of Congress Manuscript Division, Washington, D.C.
HST	Harry S. Truman presidential papers, Harry S. Truman Presidential Library, Independence, Missouri
LBJ	Lyndon Baines Johnson Presidential Papers, Lyndon Baines Johnson Presidential Library, University of Texas, Austin
LS	Lewis Strauss papers, Herbert Hoover Presidential Library, West Branch, Iowa
MC	Morris Cooke papers, Franklin Delano Roosevelt Presidential Library, Hyde Park, New York
MCK	Kenneth D. McKellar papers, Memphis Public Library, Memphis, Tennessee
MVC	Mississippi Valley Collection, John Willard Brister Library, University of Memphis, Memphis, Tennessee
NA	1938 Tennessee Valley Authority investigation exhibits, National Archives, Washington, D.C.
RO	J. Robert Oppenheimer papers, Library of Congress Manuscript Division, Washington, D.C.
TVA	TVA Lilienthal papers (microfilm), Seeley G. Mudd Manuscript Library, Princeton University
UJ	Unpublished journal of David E. Lilienthal, Seeley G. Mudd Manuscript Library, Princeton University
WB	World Bank archives, Washington, D.C.
WN	William I. Nichols papers, Library of Congress Manuscript Division, Washington, D.C.
WW	William Waymack papers, Iowa Historical Society, Iowa City

Introduction

1. David E. Lilienthal, *The Journals of David E. Lilienthal,* vol. 1, *The TVA Years, 1939–1945* (New York: Harper & Row, 1964), xi, 1–2. DEL: Lilienthal to Lamb, sometime in 1922 and May 1921.

2. Lilienthal, *The Journals of David E. Lilienthal,* vol. 3, *Venturesome Years, 1950–55* (New York: Harper & Row, 1966), 589. Lilienthal, *Journals* 1:xii. WN: Nichols to Lilienthal, Dec. 14, 1943.

3. Interview with Sylvain Bromberger, Martha's Vineyard, Mass., July 25, 1986. Lilienthal, *The Journals of David E. Lilienthal,* vol. 4, *The Road to Change, 1955–1959* (New York: Harper & Row, 1969), 163. DEL: Lilienthal to Canfield, May 28, 1960; David E. Lilienthal Jr. to Lilienthal, Nov. 17, 1961. John Gorham Palfrey, "Personal Battles in the Public Interest," *New York Times,* Nov. 15, 1964, sec. 7, 1, 70. "Public Servant," *The Economist,* Sept. 11 1965, 999. "The Sweet Draught of Power," *Time,* Jan. 15, 1965, 91–92. C. Herman Pritchett, *Journal of Politics,* May 1965, 427. The first two volumes were published with considerable fanfare and reviewed in more than a dozen additional publications.

4. Both his shorthand entries (those still extant) and the transcribed typescripts are in his papers at Princeton. After 1939 all transcribed journal material was kept in

a set of identical loose-leaf binders, hence the ability to compare the yearly volume of entries. DEL: UJ, June 5, 1958, and July 5, 1964.

5. DEL: David E. Lilienthal Jr. to Lilienthal, Nov. 17, 1961; UJ, Mar. 18, 1962, and Oct. 7, 1966 (Currie quotation from second UJ entry). Interview with Harald Frederiksen, Washington, D.C., Aug. 11, 1986.

6. James R. Newman, "Failing Safe," *New York Review of Books,* Nov. 5, 1964, 15–17. In my estimation Newman's point would have been well taken had it referred to volumes 5–7. It is not, I believe, accurate in reference to volumes 1 and 2. Since there are scores of less than flattering entries throughout the journals, it seems unlikely that someone like Lilienthal would have written down what he knew would eventually be published. The last three volumes are more problematic. My hunch is that at times he was so obsessed by the journal that he used no caution in his remarks. In any case, many unflattering remarks have been edited out of these volumes, including volumes 5 and 6, which he helped edit. It is to the Lilienthal family's credit that the unpublished portions of the journals (most of them from volumes 5 through 7) have been opened to the public.

7. Joseph C. Harsch, "Lilienthal: A Whole Span of History," *Christian Science Monitor,* Nov. 25, 1949, 1.

8. Louis Hartz, *The Liberal Tradition in America* (New York: Harcourt, Brace & World, 1955), 5–10, 10, 14, 16, 270–71, 284–86; quotation on 286. Hartz's book is the classical analysis of the roots and manifestations of American liberalism. Much of my initial stimulation for this volume came from this work. Other important works that deal with liberalism are noted throughout the text. James A. Bill, *The Eagle and the Lion: The Tragedy of American-Iranian Relations* (New Haven: Yale Univ. Press, 1988), 178–82, 203, 320–21, 356–60, 429.

Chapter 1. The Formative Years

1. The quotations and genealogical information are from two documents still in the possession of the family: Helen Lilienthal's "Background," and another document presumably by her, "Told by Hermine Lilienthal Szold (Mrs. Jacob)."

2. Information about the Rosenak family is from three documents prepared by Helen Lilienthal: "Genealogy of Rosenak family," "Remarks on the Rosenak-Lilienthal-Szold family," and "Extracts from memorandum of Max Rosenak, Sept. 1953."

3. Helen Lilienthal, "Background," 5. Interview with Helen Lilienthal, Martha's Vineyard, July 24–26, 1986. DEL: Helen Lilienthal interviews with Leo Lilienthal, June 20, 1934, and Minna Rosenak Lilienthal, Dec. 1, 1937. "Genealogy of Rosenak family." Lilienthal, *Journals* 3:529; family interview with Minna Rosenak Lilienthal, Dec. 1, 1937.

4. Lilienthal, *Journals* 3:140; Helen L. Lilienthal, "Background," 5–6. According to local historians, neither Morton, Ill., nor Valparaiso, Ind., had Jewish synagogues while Leo and Minna lived there. The nearest houses of worship were in Peoria and Gary. Telephone interviews with Morton historian Jeanne Baker, Feb. 15, 1990, and Porter County, Ind., historian George E. Neely, Feb. 20, 1990.

5. H. Lilienthal, "Background," 5–6.

6. H. Lilienthal, "Background," 1, 7–8. "Leo Lilienthal Dies in Florida: Had Local Store," *Michigan City News-Dispatch,* Apr. 11, 1951, 1.

7. "To Raze Birthplace of David Lilienthal," *Tazewell County News,* Oct. 19, 1961, A-4. Telephone interview with Jeanne Baker, Feb. 15, 1990. H. Lilienthal, "Background" and *Family Chronicle,* introduction, n.p. Over the years, Helen

Lilienthal wrote an extensive family history, first hers, and then that of her own family. It has no title so, for purposes of identification, I have called it *Family Chronicle*. When citing this document and her other family writings, I have corrected typographical and spelling errors. I have done so because these documents are rough typescripts and drafts originally intended for family use only—Mrs. Lilienthal allowed me to use the material wherever I saw fit. If she had followed her original plans to publish some of this material she certainly would have done a thorough job of proofing her work just as she did when she edited her husband's writings.

8. The summer 1913 departure date is based on information from Arvin's incomplete manuscript, which noted that they left "the summer . . . before I entered high school," and from a local article indicating that Leo Lilienthal had serious financial setbacks in February 1913. "Will Dissolve Partnership," *Evening Messenger*, Feb. 4, 1913, 1. Information regarding Valparaiso population and George Norris is from George E. Neely interview, Feb. 20, 1990. The Fred Newton Arvin quotations and much of the information about Valparaiso are from Arvin's incomplete manuscript sent to Lilienthal shortly before Arvin's death in March 1963: see pp. 40–42, 49, 56, 86 (copies at Smith College and in DEL), and Lilienthal, *The Journals of David E. Lilienthal*, vol. 5, *The Harvest Years, 1959–1963* (New York: Harper & Row, 1971), 442–43.

9. DEL: Arvin, 52–55, 58. Lilienthal, *Journals* 1:147.

10. Lilienthal, *The Journals of David E. Lilienthal*, vol. 7, *Unfinished Business, 1968–1981* (New York: Harper & Row, 1983), 436. H. Lilienthal, "Background," 1. Arvin MS, 85.

11. Arvin MS, 83–84, 86.

12. Arvin MS, 82, 84. Arvin's life was never easy. Always a compulsive worrier whose timidity overshadowed everything, he suffered through one marriage before coming to full terms with his homosexuality, and was disappointed in a short but intense affair with Truman Capote whom he idolized from the late 1940s until his death. In September 1960 he was arrested for possession of pornographic materials. In the process his sexual preferences became public, he had a nervous breakdown, and was forced into a humiliating resignation from the Smith College faculty. See Gerald Clarke, *Capote: A Biography* (New York: Simon and Schuster, 1988), passim. Lilienthal did not know that Arvin was gay until the scandal, but both he and Helen helped their friend through the painful times. Lilienthal privately recorded his tribute to Fred after reading Fred's deathbed manuscript: "I have a feeling that in these few hours of reading his extraordinary memoir I have traveled back to another world, an aspect of boyhood I didn't recognize when first I passed that way." Lilienthal, *Journals* 5:443.

13. After Lilienthal moved from Valparaiso, he and Fred carried on a lively correspondence in which they continued their intellectual quest by trying to stump each other with questions. In one letter from Fred to Dave on Jan. 19, 1915, Fred answered Dave's queries regarding the authorship of "Faust," the composer of the opera of the same name, who Caedmon and Bede were, and the definition of pantheism. Fred's questions to Dave included "Who was Cecil Rhodes?" "Where is Antioch? (or was)," and "Who was the 'Master of those who know?'" This letter is in the DEL collection.

14. Arvin MS, 58–58a. Interview with George Neely, Feb. 20, 1990. Jonathan Daniels, *White House Witness: 1942–1945* (Garden City, N.Y.: Doubleday and Company, 1975), 101.

15. Arvin MS, 86. George Neely, in a letter to the author, May 11, 1990. Joseph Decker, *Souvenir Book of Valparaiso* (Valparaiso: n.p., 1911). "Will Dissolve Partnership," *Evening Messenger*, Feb. 4, 1913, 1. Lilienthal's Shoe Store adver-

tisement, *Evening Messenger,* Mar. 8, 1913, 2. H. Lilienthal, "Background," 1. *Caron's Michigan City Directory* (Louisville, Ky.: Caron Directory Co., Oct. 1, 1916), 219. Citations provided by Patricia A. Harris, curator/director, Michigan City Historical Society, in letter to the author, Feb. 28, 1990.

16. H. Lilienthal, "Background," 1. DEL: UJ, Dec. 13, 1979, and Apr. 28, 1980; Lilienthal, personal notes, Sept. 12, 1920. Lilienthal, *Journals* 7:156. Jack Slater, "A Conversation with . . . Social Catalyst of a Golden Era," *Los Angeles Times,* June 12, 1977, part 9, 8. Dee was much involved with the radical movement of the times. She was featured in the movie *Reds* as one of the old-timers who reminisced about John Reed.

17. Transcript of David E. Lilienthal, Elston High School, Michigan City, Ind. Jean Seyring, librarian, Elston High School in a letter to the author, Feb. 23, 1990; *The Elstonian* II (Published by the senior class of 1916), 27; *The Elstonian* I (Published by the junior class of 1915), 86; DEL: UJ, Mar. 2, 1980.

18. *The Elstonian* II (1916), 16–17, 20–21, 27, 74, 76, 82, 89, 90.

19. H. Lilienthal, "Background," 1–2. DEL: UJ, May 7, 1980. *Caron's Michigan City Directory,* 219.

20. Helen L. Lilienthal, "Told by Hermine Lilienthal Szold."

21. H. Lilienthal, "Background," 6. Lilienthal, *Journals* 3:537. Telephone interview with Allen Lilienthal, July 9, 1987.

22. Lilienthal, *Journals* 3:537.

23. Henry Steele Commager, "Introduction," in Lilienthal, *Journals* 1:xvi.

24. MVC: interview between Charles W. Crawford and David E. Lilienthal at Princeton, Feb. 6, 1970, 1–3.

25. Lilienthal, *Journals* 7:787. DEL: UJ, May 7, 1980.

26. Lilienthal, *Journals* 1:533.

Chapter 2. DePauw College, Harvard Law School, and Helen

1. Helen Lilienthal, *Family Chronicle,* 58–60, 68A, 84–84A, 90, 94A–94B, 96, 111, 112B, 114–18, 117A, 120. interview with Helen Lilienthal, Martha's Vineyard, July 24, 1986.

2. Helen Lilienthal, *Family Chronicle,* 121–22.

3. DEL: unpublished journal (UJ), May 15, 1980, and Dec. 7, 1917; Lilienthal to Lamb, Oct. 1919. interview with Helen L. Lilienthal, Hightstown, N.J., June 30, 1988. Helen Lilienthal, *Family Chronicle,* unpublished ms, n.d., 122.

4. Helen Lilienthal, *Family Chronicle,* 122–23, 122A. interview with Helen L. Lilienthal, Hightstown, N.J., June 26, 1988. The Mirage of 1918 (Anderson, Ind.: Herald Publishing Co., 1918), 204. *The Mirage of 1919* (Anderson, Ind.: Herald Publishing Co., 1919), 182.

5. DEL: Lilienthal to Lamb, Apr. 6, 1918; Sept. 1, 1919; one in Oct. 1919; one in Oct. 1921; two letters sometime in 1919; and one sometime in 1920 or 1921.

6. DEL: Lilienthal to Lamb, Nov. 1919, Feb. 1921, and one letter sometime in 1920 or 1921.

7. Interview with Helen Lilienthal, Hightstown, N.J., June 20, 1987. DEL: Lilienthal to Lamb, sometime in 1922, sometime in 1920. Interview with Helen L. Lilienthal, Martha's Vineyard, July 24–26, 1986.

8. Alumni information was provided by the DePauw University Library. Eric F. Goldman, *Rendezvous with Destiny* (New York: Vintage Books, 1958), 99–100. Margaret Mead, *Blackberry Winter* (New York: Simon and Schuster, 1972), 98–99.

9. Helen Lilienthal, *Family Chronicle,* 126. DePauw Univ., "Official Transcript of David E. Lilienthal". DEL: Lilienthal, "General Academic Interests" (Rhodes Scholarship candidate statement), n.d. (written sometime in the fall of 1919).

10. "Registration Is Held for Student Council Officers: Both Parties Confident," and "Are You in Favor of Clean Politics?" *DePauw Daily,* Apr. 15, 1919, 1, 4. "Conservative Victory Won on Thursday: Lilienthal 266, Guild 120," *DePauw Daily,* Apr. 18, 1919, 1. "Lilienthal Is Scholarship Candidate," *DePauw Daily,* Oct. 16, 1919, 1. DEL: Lilienthal to Lamb, sometime in late 1919 or early 1920.

11. DEL: Lilienthal, "General Academic Interests"; Lilienthal to Lamb, Sept. 1919. "Lilienthal Is Appointed Boxing Mentor at DePauw," *DePauw Daily,* Jan. 16, 1920, 2. "They Will Box Like Dempsey," *DePauw Daily,* Feb. 11, 1920, 3. John Brooks, "A Second Sort of Life," *Business Adventures* (New York: Weybright & Talley, 1969), 273.

12. DEL: Lilienthal, "General Academic Interests." "Lilienthal Easily Wins. DePauw Orator Adds Another Victory to College Record. Has Eight Points Margin," *DePauw Daily,* Feb. 25, 1918, 1. "Galsworthy Play Enacted by Duzer Du: Lilienthal Scores Hit," *DePauw Daily,* Mar. 22, 1919, 1. "The Amateur Accepts the Challenge," *Theatre Magazine,* June 1920, 542.

13. Lilienthal, *Journals* 1:5–8. DEL: Lilienthal to Lamb, June 17, and July 12, 1918.

14. Lilienthal, *Journals* 1:2–3, 7; DePauw Univ., "Official Transcript." DEL: Lilienthal to Lamb, July 10, 1919, and July 1920; Lilienthal, personal notes on labor leaders he had seen or heard, Sept. 12, 1920; UJ, Dec. 25, 1920. H. Lilienthal, "Background," 2.

15. Lilienthal, *Journals* 1:7, 10. DEL: Leo Lilienthal to David Lilienthal, Jan. 16, 1921, Lilienthal to Lamb, sometime late 1919, other letters Apr. and June 1920. H. Lilienthal, "Background," 7.

16. DEL: Lilienthal to Lamb, Sept. 1919, another letter sometime late 1919, other letters Oct. and July 1919. Lilienthal, *Journals* 1:11. Interview with Allen Lilienthal, June 9, 1987.

17. Helen Lilienthal, *Family Chronicle,* 122. DEL: Lilienthal to Lamb, Nov. 1919, June and Apr. 1920.

18. Lilienthal, *Journals* 1:6. DEL: Lilienthal to Lamb, Apr. 1920, and Sept. 1919. As a layperson, I am reluctant to use clinical terms such as "manic-depressive" and "obsessive-compulsive." Nevertheless, his dramatic ups and downs, reported by friends and frequently recorded in the journal, and his perfectionist drive and single-minded attention to certain issues such as his journal, suggest that he struggled at times with his emotional equilibrium. In addition, there are objective indicators of severe mental stress, including his own admission that he had suffered a "nervous breakdown" in late 1933. However, the physician he consulted at the time was Dr. E. B. Freeman, a Baltimore internal medicine specialist. (see DEL: Lilienthal to Arvin, Apr. 28, 1934; Lilienthal to Freeman, July 28, 1934; also see two receipts for fifty dollars each, Freeman to Lilienthal, July 2 and 10, 1934; Freeman's specialty was confirmed by the Baltimore Medical Society). After 1950, his longtime physician was Dr. Dana Atchley, a well-known internist at New York Presbyterian Hospital. At various times later in life Lilienthal took Sodium Amytal and Miltown and suffered from chronic insomnia (DEL: Lilienthal to his physician Dana Atchley, dated only as 1964).

19. I am indebted to my colleagues at the University of Arkansas, Jacob Adler and Daniel Levine, for helping me understand Lilienthal's religious perspective better; DEL: Lilienthal to Lamb, two letters, Nov. 1919.

20. "Lilienthal Speaks on 'Mission of the Jew,'" *DePauw Daily,* Dec. 20, 1917, 2. "Lilienthal will be DePauw's Orator," *DePauw Daily,* Dec. 22, 1917, 1.

"Lilienthal Easily Wins," *DePauw Daily,* Feb. 25, 1918, 1. "Wins Third in Contest," *DePauw Daily,* May 6, 1918, 1. *The Mirage of 1918,* 146.

21. DEL: UJ, May 15, 1980. Lilienthal, *Journals* 1:6–7.

22. DEL: Lilienthal, "The Mission of the Jew," printed copy of speech first delivered on Dec. 19, 1917.

23. Interview with Helen L. Lilienthal, July 24–26, 1986.

24. DEL: Lilienthal, "General Academic Interests"; Lilienthal to Lamb, July, Nov. 1919, two letters, Dec. 1919; Lilienthal, "Notes on Labor Leaders," Sept. 12, 1920; Lilienthal, "School Notes," n.d. (probably early 1920). These notes only included the title and a short excerpt from his labor problems paper. The title was "The I.W.W. *versus* the A.F. of L., a Comparative Study." DePauw Univ., "Official Transcript." Lilienthal, *Journals* 1:9.

25. Lilienthal, *Journals* 1:3.

26. DEL: UJ, Apr. 28, 1980; Lilienthal to Lamb, Aug. 24 and 8, 1918. Lilienthal, *Journals* 1:7.

27. Lilienthal and Bernadine Szold wrote frequently during the DePauw days. Most of Bernadine's letters relate to family affairs and her theatrical work with the Workers Institute in Chicago. DEL: Lilienthal to Lamb, sometime in 1919; Simons to Lilienthal, July 15, 1919—the job offer is mentioned in this letter; Lilienthal to Lamb, May 1920; Szold to Lilienthal, May 5, 1920.

28. Lilienthal, *Journals* 1:7, 9–10.

29. DEL: Lilienthal to Lamb, July and Nov. 1920; UJ, Dec. 25, 1920.

30. Lilienthal, *Journals* 1:4–5. DEL: Lilienthal to M. Feuerlicht, Jan. 29, 1918.

31. Lilienthal, *Journals* 1:7. DEL: Lilienthal to Lamb, Aug. and July 1919.

32. DEL, Lilienthal to Lamb, Oct. 1919. Lilienthal, *Journals* 1:11. "Student Cribbing Exposed: Entire University Upset," *DePauw Daily,* Apr. 1, 1919, 1. "To Bridge Gap Between Profs and Students: Proposal Made by D. E. Lilienthal Last Night," *DePauw Daily,* Apr. 4, 1919, 1. "Faculty Will Consider Draft of Honor System: Hope Early Adoption," *DePauw Daily,* May 13, 1919, 1. "Students Vote for Adoption of Honor System," *DePauw Daily,* May 22, 1919, 1. "Will Soon Vote on the Honor System," *DePauw Daily,* Oct. 14, 1919, 1.

33. DEL: Lilienthal to Lamb, Feb. 1920, and two letters May 1920. "Grave Mistake Says Lilienthal," *DePauw Daily,* May 14, 1920, 1. "The Will of DePauw," *Student Voice,* May 15, 1920, 1.

34. Lilienthal, *Journals* 1:7. DEL: Lilienthal to Lamb, Dec. 1919; July and Aug. 1920; UJ, Dec. 25, 1920.

35. Lilienthal, *Journals* 1:2, 10. DEL: Lilienthal, "General Academic Interests"; Lilienthal to Lamb, Dec. 1919; Arvin to Lilienthal, Apr. 24, 1920.

36. Lilienthal, *Journals* 1: 9–10. DEL: Lilienthal to Lamb, Sept. 1919, May and Aug. 1920.

37. Joel Seligman, *The High Citadel: The Influence of Harvard Law School* (Boston: Houghton Mifflin Company, 1978), xiii, 20–21. Lilienthal, *Journals* 1:11. Arthur E. Sutherland, *The Law at Harvard* (Cambridge: Belknap Press of Harvard Univ. Press, 1967), 226–27, 232, 238.

38. DEL: Arvin to Lilienthal, Apr. 24, 1920; Lilienthal to Lamb, Oct. 1921. Lilienthal, *Journals* 1:12.

39. Harvard Law School, "Official Transcript of David E. Lilienthal." The law school grading scale was 75 and up = A; 70–74 = B; 66–69 = C+; 62–65 = C; 55–61 = D; and below 55 = F. DEL: Lilienthal to Lamb, Aug. 1921; Lilienthal to Frank Walsh, Oct. 19, 1921, and Aug. 19, 1922; Roscoe Pound to Lilienthal, Oct. 10, 1921.

40. DEL: Leo Lilienthal to David Lilienthal, Jan. 16 and 28, 1922; Lilienthal to Lamb, two letters, Jan. 1922.

41. DEL: Lilienthal to Lamb, Oct. 1921.
42. Lilienthal, *Journals* 1:12–13. DEL: Lilienthal to Lamb, Feb. 1922.
43. Lilienthal, *Journals* 1:13. Lilienthal to Walsh, Oct. 19, and Dec. 5, 1921, Feb. 1, Aug. 19, and Nov. 14, 1922; Lilienthal to Lamb, Feb. 1921; Dec. 1921 or Jan. 1922; Nov. 15, 1922.
44. DEL: Lilienthal to Frankfurter, May 1, 1921; Lilienthal to Lamb, May 1921.
45. DEL: Lilienthal to Lamb, Jan. 1922.
46. DEL: Lilienthal to Lamb, Jan. 1922 and Oct. 1921.
47. DEL: UJ, Dec. 31, 1923. Lilienthal, "Labor and the Courts," *New Republic,* May 16, 1923, 314–16.

Chapter 3. A Young Professional Makes His Mark

1. DEL: correspondence between Lilienthal and Walsh, Nov. 14 and 15, 1922.
2. Thomas E. Vadney, *The Wayward Liberal: A Political Biography of Donald Richberg* (Lexington: Univ. of Kentucky Press, 1970), 9–34, 44ff., 66–68. Quotation from Donald R. Richberg, *My Hero: The Indiscreet Memoirs of an Eventful but Unheroic Life* (New York: G. P. Putnam's Sons, 1954), 112–14.
3. Lilienthal, *Journals* 1:14. DEL: Lilienthal to Richberg, Dec. 13 and 21, 1922; Mar. 17, 1923; May 3, 1923.
4. DEL: Walsh to Richberg, Dec. 12, 1922; Frankfurter to Richberg, n.d.—sometime late 1922 or early 1923; correspondence between Richberg and Lilienthal, Nov. 24, 1922, Mar. 23, May 7, and July 31, 1923. See also Vadney, 53, *Wayward Liberal,* and Richberg, *My Hero,* 121, 126. Lilienthal, *Journals* 1:14.
5. Helen Lilienthal, *Family Chronicle,* unpublished ms., n.d., 126B. DEL: UJ, Jan. 4, 1924.
6. Helen Lilienthal, *Family Chronicle,* 127. DEL: UJ, Jan. 4, 1924.
7. Irving Bernstein, *The Lean Years* (Boston: Houghton Mifflin Company, 1960), 48–49, 53–54, 59, 60–66, 84, 87–94, 97. Goldman, *Rendezvous with Destiny,* 222, 228. Vadney, *Wayward Liberal,* 44.
8. Taft quoted in Arthur M. Schlesinger Jr., *The Crisis of the Old Order, 1919–1933* (Boston: Houghton Mifflin Company, 1957), 113, see also 51. Goldman, *Rendezvous with Destiny,* 237. Bernstein, *The Lean Years,* 200, 209–12. Richberg, *My Hero,* 117. Lilienthal, "Labor and the Courts," 314.
9. DEL: Richberg to Hassenauer and Lilienthal, Dec. 17, 1923; Lilienthal to Richberg, Dec. 23, 1923; UJ, Jan. 3, 1926.
10. Vadney, *Wayward Liberal,* 5, 8, 13–15.
11. Vadney, *Wayward Liberal,* 20, 35, 42–43. Lilienthal, *Journals* 1:9–13. DEL: Lilienthal to Lamb, Aug. 1920.
12. Willson Whitman, *David Lilienthal: Public Servant in a Power Age* (New York: Henry Holt and Co., 1948), 5. Vadney, *Wayward Liberal,* 32–34. Lilienthal, *The Journals of David E. Lilienthal,* vol. 2, *The Atomic Energy Years, 1945–1950* (New York: Harper & Row, 1964), 21. "Has the Negro the Right of Self-Defense," *The Nation,* Dec. 23, 1925, 724–25.
13. DEL: UJ, Dec. 31, 1923, and Jan. 3, 1926; Lilienthal to Helen, n.d., probably sometime 1924 or 1925; Lilienthal to Arvin, Aug. 1, 1924, Oct. 7, 1924, and May 24, 1926. Helen Lilienthal, *Family Chronicle,* 131.
14. DEL: UJ, Jan. 1, 1925. Lilienthal, "Dawes: First Aid to Swindlers," *The Nation,* Oct. 15, 1924, 414–16.
15. Lilienthal, *Journals* 1:14–15; *Michaelson et al. v. United States ex rel. Chicago, St. P., M. & O. Ry. Co.,* 266 U.S. 42, 45 *Supreme Court Reporter* (1924), 18–21. Richberg, *My Hero,* 124–25.

16. In The Supreme Court of the United States, October Term, A.D. 1923;
    Michaelson et al. v. United States," "Brief of Petitioners" (after issuance of writ of
    certiorari), 1–80.

17. Richberg, *My Hero,* 124. 45 *Supreme Court Reporter* (1924), 21. Lilienthal,
    Journals 1:21.

18. DEL: R. Berle to Lilienthal, Mar. 27, 24.

19. DEL: correspondence between Frankfurter and Lilienthal, June 4 and 6, 1924
    (Holmes quotation from second letter). *Gompers v. United States,* 233 U.S. 604
    (1913); 45 *Supreme Court Reporter* (1924), 21.

20. Lilienthal, *Journals* 1:15; *Railroad Labor Board v. Robertson, Same v. Mcguire,*
    nos. 4282, 4326, *Federal Reporter, 2d Series* (1925): 488–96.

21. In the Supreme Court of the United States, October Term, A.D. 1924; *D. B.
    Robertson, Appellant v. Railroad Labor Board, Appellee,* 1–143.

22. Lilienthal, *Journals* 1:15; *D. B. Robertson v. Railroad Labor Board,* 45 *Supreme
    Court Reporter* (1924), 624.

23. Lilienthal, "The Power of Governmental Agencies to Compel Testimony,"
    Harvard Law Review, Apr. 1926, 694–724.

24. Richberg, *My Hero,* 119–24. Richberg, *Tents of the Mighty* (New York: Willett,
    Clark & Colby, 1930), 141ff. Lilienthal, "Appendix A: Property Rights in
    Constitutional Law," in "Outline of Argument in Behalf of National Conference
    on Valuation of American Railroads," Donald R. Richberg, General Counsel.
    Before the Interstate Commerce Commission, Finance Dockets nos. 3908 and
    4026, July 1, 1926, 82–83. Lilienthal, "Valuation by the Interstate Commerce
    Commission for Recapture of Excess Earnings," *Journal of Land & Public Utility
    Economics* , May 1927, 222–24.

25. Bernstein, *Lean Years,* 215–20. Richberg, *My Hero,* 127–28. Vadney, *Wayward
    Liberal,* 52–53. Richberg, *Tents of the Mighty,* 130.

26. DEL: Lilienthal, "A Practical Plan for Railroad Peace," (Chicago: mimeographed,
    Mar. 1924), 1–7. Lilienthal, "Needed, A New Railroad Labor Law," *New
    Republic,* Apr. 9, 1924, 923–25; Lilienthal, "Labor and the Human Problems of
    Railroading," *Machinists' Monthly Journal,* May 1924, 197–98, 237–39.

27. Bernstein, *Lean Years,* 216–18. Richberg, *My Hero,* 126–28.

28. DEL; UJ, Dec. 31, 1923. Lilienthal to Arvin, Mar. 3, 1925. Income tax returns for
    1926. Lilienthal, *Journals* 1:16.

29. DEL: Lilienthal to Arvin, Mar. 16, 1926; Lilienthal to Helen, Aug. 17, 1926;
    Lilienthal to Irving Rosenbaum, Aug. 5, 1926. Richberg, *My Hero,* 126.

30. DEL: UJ, Jan. 1, 1927; Lilienthal to Helen, Aug. 3, 17, 18, 1926; Kixmiller to
    Lilienthal and Rosenbaum, Aug. 17, 1926. Lilienthal and Rosenbaum, "Motor
    Carriers and the State—A Study in Contemporary Public Utility Legislation,"
    Journal of Land & Public Utility Economics, July 1926, 257–75.

31. Richberg, *My Hero,* 126. DEL: income tax returns for 1925–1930.

32. DEL: Lilienthal to Arvin, Nov. 9, 1926.

33. DEL: income tax returns; Lilienthal to Rosenbaum, Apr. 7, 13, and 27, 1927;
    Sept. 26, 1927; Oct. 1, 1928; unsigned contract between Lilienthal-Rosenbaum
    and Commerce Clearing House, Sept. 6, 1927; "Commerce Clearing House. Inc.,
    was entirely within its legal rights in terminating payments to Rosenbaum in Jan.,
    1929," document setting forth Commerce Clearing House's side of conflict, no
    author, n.d., probably sometime in 1929.

34. DEL: correspondence between Lilienthal and Rosenbaum, Apr. 29, 1927; Dec. 9,
    1927; Mar. 13, 1929; Lilienthal to Kixmiller, July 8, 1930.

35. DEL: Lilienthal to Rosenbaum, Dec. 8, 1927; Dec. 9 and 24, 1928.

36. DEL: "Commerce Clearing House. Inc."; Lilienthal to Kixmiller, July 8, 1930;

correspondence between Lilienthal and Rosenbaum, Jan. 29 and 30, 1929; Mar. 13, 15, and 19, 1929.

37. DEL: Lilienthal to Arvin, Mar. 16, 1926; Petrillo to Lilienthal, Oct. 1, 1928; correspondence between Lilienthal and Frankfurter, Oct. 5 and 16, 1928; miscellaneous materials from box 48.

38. DEL: Lilienthal to Arvin, Mar. 19, 1929; miscellaneous materials from boxes 49 and 50.

39. William Z. Ripley, "From Main Street to Wall Street, *Atlantic Monthly,* Jan. 1926, 94–108. Lilienthal, "The Regulation of Public Utility Holding Companies," *Columbia Law Review*, Apr. 1929, 408, 432–40. Lilienthal, "Recent Developments in the Law of Public Utility Holding Companies," *Columbia Law Review,* Feb. 1931, 195.

40. Lilienthal, "The Regulation of Public Utility Holding Companies," 412. Lilienthal, "Recent Developments," 191–92, 197–98.

41. James C. Bonbright, "'Recent Developments in the Law of Public Utility Holding Companies'—A Comment," *Columbia Law Review,* Feb. 1931, 208. James C. Bonbright and Gardiner C. Means, *The Holding Company: Its Public Significance and Its Regulation* (New York: McGraw-Hill, 1932), 200–201. William E. Mosher and Finla G. Crawford, *Public Utility Regulation* (New York: Harper & Brothers Publishers, 1933), 582–83. Mosher and Crawford were both active in the utility reform movement, and their book was the best study of utility regulation at that time. In their extensive bibliography, Lilienthal's essays were the only academic/law journal articles on holding companies cited. Ripley's essay and another 1928 essay by Philip Cabot of the Harvard Business School are listed, but both of them were published in the *Atlantic Monthly.* DEL: A. Berle to Lilienthal, June 29, 1929.

42. Lilienthal, "The Federal Courts and State Regulation of Public Utilities," *Harvard Law Review,* Jan. 1930, 379–423. DEL: Frankfurter to Lilienthal, Dec. 20, 1929, and Jan. 3, 1930.

43. Lilienthal's publications after graduation from law school until his acceptance of the Public Service Commission position in Wisconsin in 1931 include the following:
"Is the Presidency a 'Hazardous Occupation'?" *Outlook,* Aug. 22, 1923, 621; "Oklahoma—A Test of Our Theory of Constitutional Government," *Outlook,* Oct. 10, 1923, 216–17; "New Unionism for Old," *The Nation,* Oct. 24, 1923, 466–67; "Economics—Antiquarian and Academic" (book review), *The Nation,* Dec. 19, 1923, 716–17; "On a Hoosier Farm," *American Review,* Jan./Feb. 1924, 39–48; "Facts and Fancies in Constitutional Law," (book review) *Outlook,* Feb. 6, 1924, 232–33; "Needed, A New Railroad Labor Law," *New Republic,* Apr. 9, 1924, 169–71; "Labor and the Human Problems of Railroading," *Machinists' Monthly Journal,* May 1924, 197–98, 237–39; "Dawes: First Aid to Swindlers," *The Nation,* Oct. 15, 1924, 414–16; "The Tennessee Case and State Autonomy," *Outlook,* July 29, 1925, 453–54; "Terry Teaches Us a Lesson in Government," *The Independent,* Oct. 31, 1925, 503–4, 512; "Has the Negro the Right of Self-Defense," *The Nation,* Dec. 23, 1925, 724–25; "A Trial of Two Races," *Outlook,* Dec. 23, 1925, 629–30; "Osteopathy and the Law," *Osteopathic Workshop,* 1926, 603–8; "Strikeless Railroads?" *Survey Graphics,* Mar. 15, 1926, 690–92; "The Power of Governmental Agencies to Compel Testimony," *Harvard Law Review,* Apr. 1926, 694–724; "Making Scholarship Popular," *American Review,* Apr. 4, 1926, 306–10; "For 'High Crimes and Misdemeanors,'" *The Independent,* June 5, 1926, 653–55; "Thomas Jefferson One Hundred Years After" (book review), (with H. Lilienthal) *Outlook,* June 30, 1926, 322–24; "Motor Carriers

and the State—A Study in Contemporary Public Utility Legislation," (with I. Rosenbaum) *Journal of Land & Public Utility Economics,* July 1926, 257–75; "Motor Carrier Regulation by Certificates of Necessity and Convenience," (with I. Rosenbaum) *Yale Law Review,* Dec. 1926, 163–94; "Motor Carrier Regulation; Federal, State, and Municipal" (with I. Rosenbaum), *Columbia Law Review,* Dec. 1926, 954–87; "Motor Carrier Regulation in Ohio" (with I. Rosenbaum), *University of Cincinnati Law Review,* May 1927, 288–335; "Valuation by the Interstate Commerce Commission for Recapture of Excess Earnings," *Journal of Land & Public Utility Economics,* May 1927, 222–24; "Clarence Darrow," *The Nation,* Apr. 20, 1927, 416–19; "Motor Carrier Regulation in Illinois" (with I. Rosenbaum), *Illinois Law Review,* May 1927, 47–81; "The Regulation of Motor Carriers in Pennsylvania" (with I. Rosenbaum), *University of Pennsylvania Law Review,* June 1927, 696–722; "Public Utility Legislation of 1927" (with I. Rosenbaum), *Journal of Land & Public Utility Economics,* Nov. 1927, 434–37; "Court Review of Orders of the Ohio Public Utilities Commission" (with I. Rosenbaum), *University of Cincinnati Law Review,* May 1928, 225–54; "Issuance of Securities by Public Service Corporations" (with I. Rosenbaum), part I, *Yale Law Journal,* Apr. 1928, 908–34; "The Regulation of Public Utility Holding Companies," *Columbia Law Review,* Apr. 1929, 404–40; "The Federal Courts and State Regulation of Public Utilities," *Harvard Law Review,* Jan. 1930, 379–423; "Law and the Engineer," *Electrical World,* May 24, 1930, 1041–42; "Recent Developments in the Law of Public Utility Holding Companies," *Columbia Law Review,* Feb. 1931, 189–207.

Lilienthal was also largely responsible for preparing the following legal documents for Donald Richberg:

"Brief of Petitioners" on the merits for the U.S. Supreme Court, Sam Michaelson, Dan Cullen, Fred Henstra, Ole North, Art Daniels, Joe Richie, Matt Anderson, John Hagen, Arley Martin and Clarence Michaelson, Petitioners, vs. The United States, ex rel. Chicago, St. Paul, Minneapolis and Omaha Railway Company, Respondent, October Term A.D. 1923, no. 246 (80 pp.); "Brief of Appellant" on the merits for the U.S. Supreme Court, D. B. Robertson, Appellant, v. Railroad Labor Board, Appellee, October Term A.D. 1924, no 739 (143 pp.); "Appendix A: Property Rights in Constitutional Law," in "Outline of Argument in Behalf of National Conference on Valuation of American Railroads," Donald R. Richberg, General Counsel. Before the Interstate Commerce Commission, Finance Dockets nos. 3908 and 4026, July 1, 1926 (84 pp.).

44. DEL: Lilienthal to Dean Ralph C. Heilman, July 29, 1930; correspondence between Lilienthal and W. L. Ransom, Dec. 8 and 15, 1930; miscellaneous materials from boxes 49–50; Richard Ely to Lilienthal, Sept. 7, 1929; correspondence between Lilienthal and Frankfurter, Oct. 10 and 31, Nov. 7 and 12, 1929. Lilienthal, "Law and the Engineer."

45. Helen Lilienthal, *Family Chronicle,* 133–45B. DEL: miscellaneous notes from box 51; Lilienthal to Arvin, Oct. 29, 1927.

46. DEL: UJ, Feb. 24, 1980.

47. DEL: UJ, Jan. 1, 1925; correspondence between Lilienthal and Rosenbaum, Jan. 27, 1927, and Mar. 19, 1929; correspondence between Lilienthal and Arvin, Oct. 16, and Nov. 16, 1925; May 24, and Aug. 17, 1926; Jan. 27, and Oct. 29, 1927; Dec. 27, 1928; Jan. 3, 1929; correspondence between Lilienthal and Freda Kirchway, Dec. 14 and 16, 1925.

48. DEL: Lilienthal to Arvin, Oct. 29, 1927. Richberg, *My Hero,* 127.

Chapter 4. The Wisconsin Public Service Commission

1. Helen Lilienthal, *Family Chronicle*, 147.
2. Arthur M. Schlesinger Jr., *The Crisis of the Old Order: 1919–1933*, 100–101. David P. Thelen, *The New Citizenship: Origins of Progressivism in Wisconsin, 1885–1900* (Columbia: Univ. of Missouri Press, 1972), 1–33, 290–91. Forrest McDonald, *Let There Be Light: The Electric Utility Industry in Wisconsin, 1881–1955* (Madison, Wis.: American History Research Center, 1957), 115. Goldman, *Rendezvous with Destiny*, 132. Allen Fraser Lovejoy, *La Follette and the Establishment of the Direct Primary in Wisconsin: 1890–1904* (New Haven: Yale Univ. Press, 1941), 76–96; William E. Mosher and Finla G. Crawford, *Public Utility Regulation*, 22–23.
3. Schlesinger, *Crisis*, 102, 125. Richard Hofstadter, *The Age of Reform: From Bryan to F.D.R.* (New York: Alfred A. Knopf, 1981), 280, 282–83. Donald Young, ed., *Adventure in Politics: The Memoirs of Philip La Follette* (New York: Holt, Rinehart and Winston, 1970), 114–15. John E. Miller, *Governor Philip F. La Follette, The Wisconsin Progressives, and the New Deal* (Columbia: Univ. of Missouri Press, 1982), 10.
4. Miller, *Governor Philip F. La Follette*, 8–9. Robert C. Nesbit, *Wisconsin: A History* (Madison: Univ. of Wisconsin Press, 1973), 476–77.
5. The Unofficial Observer [Jay Franklin], *American Messiahs* (New York: Simon and Schuster, 1935), 111–12; Young, *Adventure in Politics*, 144; Miller, *Governor Philip F. La Follette*, 8–11; quotation from "Outlines Tasks of Legislature," *Milwaukee Journal*, Feb. 1, 1931, main sec., 10.
6. McDonald, *Let There Be Light*, 120, 212, 270–71, 275, 305, 308–10; Mosher and Crawford, *Public Utility Regulation*, 22–23, 40, 53, 560. See also G. Lloyd Wilson, James M. Herring, and Roland B. Eutsler, *Public Utility Regulation* (New York: McGraw-Hill Book Company, 1938), 8–12, 17–18, 35, 58.
7. McDonald, *Let There Be Light*, 322. "A New Railroad Commission," *Milwaukee Journal*, editorial sec., Feb. 6, 1931, 6. "Mayor Hoan on Utility Rates," *Milwaukee Journal*, Mar. 24, 1931, editorial sec., 2. "Hoan Extends Utilities Fight," *Milwaukee Journal*, May 2, 1931, main sec., 1. Young, *Adventure in Politics*, 169. Richberg, *My Hero*, 126–27. Helen Lilienthal, *Family Chronicle*, 145–50. DEL: 1931 Notes; Income tax returns; UJ, Dec. 25, 1931. Jerold S. Auerbach and Eugene Bardach, "Born to an Era of Insecurity: Career Patterns of Law Review Editors, 1918–41: *American Journal of Legal History*, Jan. 1973, 5.
8. Young, *Adventure in Politics*, 169–70. La Follette recalled that Lilienthal made the decision in Madison after talking with Helen by phone. Both Lilienthals write in different sources that they decided to go to Madison only after Dave returned to Chicago. Helen Lilienthal, *Family Chronicle*, 147–48.
9. "Rail Job Given to Kronshage," *Milwaukee Journal*, Feb. 6, 1931 main sec., 1. DEL: "Announcement, by William Kixmiller of Commerce Clearing House, Inc.," n.d. See *United States Supreme Court Reports*, 75 Law Ed., October Term 1930, U.S. 282–83:257. Also 75 *Lawyer's Edition*, October Term 1930, U.S. 282–83:1427, both by the Publishers' Editorial Staff, Lawyers Cooperative Publishing Co., Rochester, N.Y., 1931. DEL: Kixmiller to Lilienthal, Feb. 5, 1931; undated and unattributed memorandum, probably Lilienthal to Kixmiller, late Aug. 1932. BH: typed report regarding Leitzell testimony and background on issue, n.d. U.S. Congress, Senate Section of the Joint Committee on Atomic Energy, *Confirmation of the Atomic Energy Commission and the General Manager*. Hearings, 80th Congress, 1st. session, 1947: 588–93, 637–38, 783, 805–34. Lilienthal, *Journals* 2:152.
10. Lilienthal, *Journals* 4:211. Helen Lilienthal, *Family Chronicle*, 150.

11. Lilienthal, *Journals* 1:17. Mosher and Crawford, *Public Utility Regulation,* xiii, 560.

12. Academy of Political Science, "Public Control of Power," *Proceedings* 14–1 (1930–32), v–xi, 3–210. Mosher and Crawford, *Public Utility Regulation,* 183, 185–93. Felix Frankfurter, *The Public and Its Government* (New Haven: Yale Univ. Press, 1930), 100, 105.

13. Eli Winston Clemens, "Public Utility Regulation in Wisconsin since the Reorganization of the Commission in 1931" (Ph.D. dissertation, Univ. of Wisconsin, 1940), 34–35. Mosher and Crawford, *Public Utility Regulation,* 72, 185–93. Henry C. Spurr, "What the New Governors Think of State Regulation," *Public Utilities Fortnightly,* Apr. 2, 1931, 390–400 (reports of changes in state law and rate cuts were reported in virtually every issue in 1931). "Give the Commission a Chance," *Milwaukee Journal,* Nov. 13, 1931, editorial sec., 12. Martin G. Glaeser, "Progressive Ventures in Commission Regulation; the New Measures in Wisconsin," Part 1, *Public Utilities Fortnightly,* Feb. 4, 1932, 146.

14. "Phil's Sec'y. in Hot Charges on Wis. Press," *The Progressive,* Sept. 19, 1931, 1. The *Milwaukee Journal* is the source for the following editorial section citations: "A New Railroad Commission," Feb. 6, 1931, 6; "And Now the Utilities Duck," Apr. 24, 1931, 4; "Gov. La Follette on Power," May 4, 1931, 4; "Final Link in Power Plan," May 12, 1931, 6; "No More 'Yes, Yes' Regulation," Feb. 16, 1932, 8; "Lilienthal and Smith on Utilities," Oct. 11, 1932, 10; "Keep Commissioner Lilienthal," Jan. 4, 1933, 10; "Only Mr. Lilienthal Will Do," Jan. 24, 1933, 8; "The Governor's Utility Battle," May 8, 1933, 8.

15. DEL: "Realism in Regulation," speech by William L. Ransom, Chicago, Mar. 20, 1931; Lilienthal to Ransom, Apr. 11, 1931. Lilienthal, *Journals* 1:18 (Frankfurter quotation).

16. *The Progressive,* Feb. 7, 1931, 4. "Utility Control Bill Attacked," *Milwaukee Journal,* Apr. 24, 1931, main sec., 6. "Governor's Utility Program is Attacked," *Public Utilities Fortnightly,* Mar. 5, 1931, 312. "Power District Bill is Signed," *Milwaukee Journal,* Apr. 16, 1931, main sec., 19. "The Power Plan Complete," *Milwaukee Journal,* June 26, 1931, editorial sec., 4. "Roll Call on Utility Bills," *The Progressive,* June 27, 1931, 3. DEL: UJ, Apr. 29, 1931. George E. Doying, "What State Lawmakers Have Done for and to regulation in 1931," Part 1, *Public Utilities Fortnightly,* Dec. 10, 1931, 727–28. Lilienthal acknowledged that he had considerable help from George Mathews of the commission in drafting the provisions on depreciation and securities. Mathews later provided leadership in helping pass the 1933 Wisconsin securities regulation bill.

17. Glaeser, "Progressive Ventures," 144–54. DEL: UJ, Dec. 25, 1931.; "Utility Control Attacked," *Milwaukee Journal,* Apr. 24, 1931, main sec., 6.

18. Glaeser, "Progressive Ventures," 144–54.; "Utility Control Bill Attacked," *Milwaukee Journal,* Apr. 24, 1931, main sec., 6.; "Wisconsin's New Utility Law," *Milwaukee Journal,* July 8, 1931, editorial sec., 2. "Fact-finding Basis for Control of Public Utilities," *United States Daily,* Feb. 26, 1932, 1.

19. "Utility Control Bill Attacked," *Milwaukee Journal,* Apr. 24, 1931, main sec., 6. DEL: UJ, Apr. 29, 1931. "Utilities Back Revised Bill," *Milwaukee Journal,* Apr. 30, 1931, main sec., 4. "Gov. La Follette on Power," *Milwaukee Journal,* May 4, 1931, editorial sec., 2.

20. "Utilities Back Revised Bill," *Milwaukee Journal,* Apr. 30, 1931, main sec., 4. "Tax Exemption Bill Is Signed," *Milwaukee Journal,* May 29, 1931, main sec., 3. DEL: UJ, Dec. 25, 1931; Lilienthal to Mauritz Hallgren, July 13, 1931. "Wisconsin Adopts Strict Power Rule," *New York Times,* July 5, 1931, sec. 2, 2. "Wisconsin Tests Utility Control," *New York Times,* Oct. 11, 1931, sec. 2, 1.

21. In July 1931 the PSC billed the Wisconsin Telephone Company $1,000 for

investigation expenses. The company filed a formal complaint with a state court, which ruled that the discretion granted the PSC to exempt utilities from paying investigation costs was an unconstitutional delegation of legislative power. While the case made its way through the appeals process (the Wisconsin Supreme Court ruled in favor of the commission early in 1932), Lilienthal took no chances. He asked La Follette to include a revision of the law in a late 1931 special session of the legislature. After detailed correspondence with Richberg and James Landis (who advised him that "the more one gets away from stereotyped language, the more you will convince a court that the statute in your phraseology 'means what it says'"), Lilienthal proposed an amendment that could withstand constitutional challenge. After an excruciating struggle in the senate (the house was no problem), where the utilities fought the proposal, the bill passed by one vote. DEL: UJ, Dec. 25, 1931; correspondence between Lilienthal and Richberg, Oct., 13 and 25, 1931; between Lilienthal and Landis, Oct. 13 and 17, 1931. "Utility Inquiry Upheld," *New York Times,* Jan. 13, 1932, 40. J.D.C., "The Attitude of the House of La Follette Toward Regulatory Reform," *Public Utilities Fortnightly,* May 27, 1931, 687. Mauritz A. Hallgren, *The Nation,* Apr. 29, 1931, 474.

22. "State Will Investigate Big Insull Subsidiary," *Milwaukee Journal,* June 12, 1931, market sec., 1. "Utilities Must Reveal Owners," *Milwaukee Journal,* June 16, 1931, editorial sec., 1. "Hoan Extends Utilities Fight," *Milwaukee Journal,* May 2, 1931, main sec., 1. "Cities to Join in Phone War," *Milwaukee Journal,* May 17, 1931, main sec., 6. "State Telephone Quiz Starting," *Milwaukee Journal,* Mar. 20, 1932, main sec., 2.

23. DEL: Kronshage to La Follette, Dec. 17, 1931. Clemens, "Public Utility Regulation in Wisconsin," 5.

24. Helen Lilienthal, *Family Chronicle,* 150. DEL: UJ, Dec. 27, 1931.

25. "A Revision in the Managerial Methods of Wisconsin Municipal Plants Is Suggested," *Public Utilities Fortnightly,* May 14, 1931, 635. DEL: Lilienthal to Morris L. Cooke, Nov. 30, 1931; Lilienthal to Loomis, Nov. 4, 1931.

26. "Wisconsin Tests Utility Control," *New York Times,* Oct. 11, 1931, second sec., 1. "Lilienthal Hits Utility Session," *Milwaukee Journal,* Oct. 28, 1931, main sec., 2. "Utilities Liquor 'Em Up?" *Milwaukee Journal,* Oct. 29, 1931, editorial sec., 6. "Utility Building Plan Must Hereafter Be Approved by the Wisconsin Commission," *Public Utilities Fortnightly,* Oct. 1, 1931, 442. Miller, *Governor Philip F. La Follette,* 22–23. "Utilities Must Pay Quiz Cost," *Milwaukee Journal,* Jan. 12, 1932, main sec., 1. "Sure to Sign New Measure," *Milwaukee Journal,* Jan. 15, 1932, main sec., 2. "Stalwarts Seek Salary Report," *Milwaukee Journal,* Dec. 3, 1931, main sec., 10. DEL: UJ, Dec. 25, 1931. "Pass the Utility Bill, *Milwaukee Journal*, Dec. 28, 1931, editorial sec., 8.

27. "Order Inquiry of 2 Utilities," *Milwaukee Journal,* Jan. 6, 1932, main sec., 1. "Utility Agrees to Cut Rates," *Milwaukee Journal,* Jan. 15, 1932, markets sec., 8. DEL: Lilienthal to A. Berle, Feb. 13, 1932; Lilienthal to Ripley, Feb. 19, 1932. "Fact-finding Basis for Control of Public Utilities," *United States Daily,* Feb. 26, 1932, 8. "The State Commission in the Role of Public Utility District Attorney," *Public Utility Fortnightly,* Apr. 14, 1932: 476–78.

28. Lilienthal, *Journals* 1:24–25.

29. "Suburban Gas Quiz Ordered," *Milwaukee Journal,* Apr. 2, 1932, main sec., 8. Lilienthal, *Journals* 1:24–25. "Won't Let State Insull Firms Pay Receivers," *Milwaukee Journal,* Apr. 16, 1932, markets sec., 9. FFHLS: Lilienthal, "Statement on Middle-West Receivership," Apr. 15, 1932. Lilienthal, *Journals* 1:25.

30. "Commission Cuts Dividends of 7 Big Utilities," *Milwaukee Journal,* July 15, 1932, main sec., 1. "Orders 7 Utilities to Halt Dividends," *New York Times,* July 16, 1932, financial sec., 15. "Utility Men Score Wisconsin Board," *New York*

Times, July 17, 1932, sec 4, 1. DEL: Lilienthal to Financial Editor, *New York Times,* July 22, 1932. "Wisconsin Orders Based on Inquiry," *New York Times,* July 27, 1932, financial sec., 25.

31. DEL: author unknown, probably Lilienthal, "The Work of the Public Service Commission During Governor La Follette's Administration," memorandum dated sometime after July 1, 1932. "Progressives Were Sponsors of Commission," *The Progressive,* July 16, 1932, 1. "Over $3,000,000 Saved Public by La Follette Body," *The Progressive,* Sept. 17, 1932, 1. Public Service Commission of Wisconsin, *Biennial Report of the Public Service Commission of Wisconsin,* from July 1, 1930, to June 30, 1932, Madison, 1932, 15.

32. DEL: correspondence between Lilienthal and Frankfurter, Apr. 22, 25, and 27, 1932.

33. DEL: correspondence between Lilienthal and Kixmiller, Aug. 20, 22, and 27, 1932; Harry R. Booth to Lilienthal, Aug. 30, 1932; Lilienthal to Kixmiller (no authors listed, assumed from text), "Memorandum," n.d., probably end of Aug. 1932.

34. DEL: Kronshage to La Follette, Dec. 17, 1931; Lilienthal to Frankfurter, Apr. 27, 1932; UJ, May 4, 1932. Lilienthal, *Journals* 1:26 (this entry is published under Jan. 24, 1932. The original unpublished journal entry is dated May 4, 1932, the same entry as the previous reference).

35. "Wisconsin Utility Body Rate Cuts," *The Progressive,* July 16, 1932, 1. DEL: Kronshage to La Follette, Dec. 17, 1931; UJ, Dec. 27, 1931, and Feb. 21, 1932.

36. Goldman, *Rendezvous with Destiny,* 105–7. DEL: UJ, Feb. 21, and Apr. 24, 1932.

37. DEL: correspondence between Lilienthal and Bonbright, Feb. 4 and 18; Apr. 18, 21, and 23, 1932; Morehouse to Bonbright, Apr. 25, 1932; Lilienthal to Bonbright, Apr. 23, 1932. "Steady Return Called Raise," *Milwaukee Journal,* May 1, 1932, main sec., 2.

38. "17-Year Profit Reached Total of 35 Millions," *Milwaukee Journal,* Apr. 1, 1932, main sec., 1. "Patrons Pay for Research," *Milwaukee Journal,* Apr. 14, 1932, main sec., 2. "Phone Inquiry Hits Material," *Milwaukee Journal,* Apr. 21, 1932, main sec., 16.

39. "Study Methods in Phone Costs," *Milwaukee Journal,* Apr. 25, 1932, main sec., 2. "State Revises Phone Profits," *Milwaukee Journal,* Apr. 26, 1932, main sec., 4.

40. Lilienthal, "Wisconsin's Latest Steps in Utility Reform," *Electrical World,* Mar. 12, 1932, 486. M. W. Childs, "Wisconsin Now at Grips With Its Biggest Problem, Effective Regulation of Public Utilities," *St. Louis Post-Dispatch,* Apr. 17, 1932, part 2, p. 1. "Steady Return Called Raise," *Milwaukee Journal,* May 1, 1932, main sec., 2. "Utility Rate Inquiries May Consider Falling Private Profits," *Milwaukee Journal,* May 1, 1932, main sec., 2. DEL: Lilienthal to Bonbright, May 6, 1932.

41. Public Service Commission of Wisconsin, *Before the Public Service Commission of Wisconsin: Testimony in the matter of the State-Wide Investigation on the Commission's own Motion of the Rates, Rules, Practices, and Activities of the Wisconsin Telephone Company,* Madison, May 11–19, 1932, 765–1690.

42. *Before the Public Service Commission of Wisconsin,* 1226, 1502–3, 1601.

43. DEL: correspondence between Lilienthal and Frankfurter, June 15 and 20, 1932. William A. Prendergast, "The 'Economic Emergency' as a Factor in Rate Making," *Public Utility Fortnightly,* Sept. 1, 1932, 244. "State Prepares Phone Orders; Cut Expected," *Milwaukee Journal,* June 25, 1932, main sec., 1.

44. "State Phone Rates Cut $1,500,000," *Milwaukee Journal,* July 1, 1932, main sec., 1. "The Real Significance of the Wisconsin Telephone Case," *Public Utility Fortnightly,* Aug. 4, 1932, 174.

45. "Bringing Down Telephone Rates," *Milwaukee Journal,* July 5, 1932, editorial sec., 10. "Wisconsin Reduces Phone Rates 12%," *New York Times,* July 6, 1932, financial sec., 34. "General Economic Data Held Admissible in a Rate Case," *Public Utility Fortnightly,* July 7, 1932, 54. "Temporary Order Cuts Wisconsin Phone Rates," *Public Utility Fortnightly,* July 21, 1932, 117–18. "Wisconsin Telephone Rates," *New York Times,* July 8, 1932, 16. "Objections Filed against Rate Reductions," *Public Utilities Fortnightly,* Aug. 8, 1932, 233. "No Retrial in the Wisconsin Emergency Telephone Rate Case," *Public Utilities Fortnightly,* Aug. 18, 1932, 236. "State Denies Telephone Company's Plea on Rates," *Milwaukee Journal,* July 26, 1932, market sec., 1. "Telephone Cut Goes to Court," *Milwaukee Journal,* July 28, 1932, main sec., 1. "Geiger halts Telephone Cut," *Milwaukee Journal,* July 30, 1932, main sec., 1.

46. "Editorial," *Telephony,* July 16, 1932, 7–8.; "Putting Prices Below Cost," *Nation's Business,* Aug. 1932, 15. Prendergast, "Economic Emergency," 243, 249. M.M., "Was the Wisconsin Rate Order a Gesture or an Omen?" *Public Utilities Fortnightly,* Sept. 15, 1932, 341. Henry C. Spurr, "'Value of Service' as a Basis of Rate Making," *Public Utilities Fortnightly,* Sept. 29, 1932, 369, 372.

47. "Telephone Company Granted Writ to have Rate Slash Delayed," *Milwaukee Journal,* Sept. 22, 1932, main sec., 2. "State Wins Right to Appeal Phone Case Direct to U.S.," *Milwaukee Journal,* Oct. 24, 1932, main sec., 1. "Court's Action on Other Cases," *New York Times,* Dec. 13, 1932, financial sec., 35. "Returns Case to Trial Court for Rehearing," *Milwaukee Journal,* Mar. 27, 1933, main sec., 1. Clemens, "Public Utility Regulation in Wisconsin," 12, 248–49. *Wisconsin Telephone Co. v. Public Service Commission* 287 NW 122; 287 NW 167. July 11, 1939. James C. Bonbright, *Principles of Public Utility Rates* (New York: Columbia Univ. Press, 1961), 85–86, 261.

48. Clemens, "Public Utility Regulation in Wisconsin," 56–57.

49. "Progressives' Parley Meets at Washington," *The Progressive,* Mar. 14, 1931, 1. DEL: Donald R. Richberg, chairman, "Report of Committee on Public Utilities of the Progressive Conference," Oct. 8, 1931. Milton W. Harrison, quoted in J.T.C, "What the Progressive Conference Committee Proposed to Do About the Utilities," *Public Utilities Fortnightly,* Nov. 12, 1931, 680. *Traffic World,* Oct. 24, 1931, 889–90. *The Nation,* Oct. 28, 1931, 446. *New Republic,* Nov. 28, 1931, 284.

50. DEL: Lilienthal to Richberg, Aug. 7, 1931. Goldman, *Rendezvous with Destiny,* 236–37.

51. DEL: Richberg to the Members of the Committee on Public Utilities of the Progressive Conference, Oct. 1, 1931; correspondence between Lilienthal and Richberg, Oct. 7 and 9, 1931.

52. Lilienthal, *Journals* 1:19–20. David Lay, "The Association of Commissioners Grows a Left Wing," *Public Utilities Fortnightly,* Nov. 12, 1931, 580–83.

53. Lilienthal, *Journals* 1:20. "Utilities Liquor 'Em Up?" *Milwaukee Journal,* Oct. 29, 1931, editorial sec. 6.

54. DEL: correspondence between Lilienthal and Ransom, Oct. 28 and 31, 1931.

55. DEL: Lilienthal to Ransom, Nov. 3, 1931; Lilienthal to Maltbie, Dec. 8, 17, and 28, 1931; Lilienthal to Seavey and Maltbie, Jan. 20, 1932; "A Communication from members of the California, New York and Wisconsin Commissions, To the Members of the National Association of Railroad and Utilities Commissioners respecting the conduct of the affairs of the Association," Jan. 31, 1932.

56. "A Communication . . ."

57. DEL: John J. Murphy, "A Response to A COMMUNICATION FROM MEMBERS OF THE CALIFORNIA, NEW YORK AND WISCONSIN COMMISSIONS TO THE MEMBERS OF THE NATIONAL ASSOCIATION OF RAILROAD AND UTILITIES COMMISSIONERS RESPECTING THE CONDUCT OF

THE AFFAIRS OF THE ASSOCIATION," n.d. (sometime after Jan. 31, 1932). National Association of Railroad and Utilities Commissioners, *Proceedings of Forty-Third Annual Convention* (Richmond: National Association of Railroad and Utilities Commissioners, 1932). Paul A. Walker, "The Purposes of the Conventions of the National Association of Railroad and Utilities Commissioners," *Public Utilities Fortnightly*, Jan. 7, 1932, 34–36.

58. DEL: Murphy, "A Response," 264, 276–77.

59. DEL: Murphy, "A Response."

60. DEL: Lilienthal to Frankfurter, Nov. 11, 1932. "Closer Watch Over Utilities," *Milwaukee Journal*, Nov. 19, 1932, market sec., 10.

61. DEL: correspondence between Lilienthal and Cooke, Jan. 19, 22, and 26, Feb. 4 and 8, Mar. 24, 1931. William Z. Ripley, "Liberal Viewpoint on Regulation," *Public Utilities Fortnightly*, May 5, 1932, 584, 588. DEL: "Summary of Proceedings at Round Table Conference on Regulation Held at Hotel Pennsylvania," New York City, Apr. 8 and 9, 1932. "Economists Assail Utilities' Policies," *New York Times*, Apr. 9, 1932, financial sec., 19. "Attack on Control Splits Utility Men," *New York Times*, Apr. 10, 1932, main sec., 7. DEL: "List of Those Who Have Accepted the Invitation to Attend the Conference on Regulation of Public Utilities in New York City, Apr. 8–9, 1932," n.d.

62. DEL: correspondence between Lilienthal and Frankfurter, Nov. 9 and 14, 1932; Lilienthal, "Holding Companies and the Public Interest," address to the Annual Meeting of the American Bar Association, Oct. 11, 1932; Landis to Lilienthal, Jan. 3, 1933. "Bar Association Hears Lilienthal on Regulation," *Milwaukee Journal*, Oct. 11, 1932, main sec., 5. "Lilienthal and Smith on Utilities," *Milwaukee Journal*, Oct. 11, 1932, editorial sec., 10. "Bar Group Lays Rise in Gangs to Dry Law," *New York Times*, Oct. 12, 1932, main sec., 3. M.M., "Alternative Proposals for Regulating the Holding Company," *Public Utility Fortnightly*, Nov. 24, 1932, 635–37. "Wider State Curbs on Utilities Urged," *New York Times*, Oct. 16, 1932, financial sec. 1.

63. "Named to Aid Power Probes," *Milwaukee Journal*, Jan. 13, 1933, market sec., 8. "Suggested Fund for Rate Cuts," *Milwaukee Journal*, Jan. 25, 1933, main sec., 7. Elmer Bown, a professor at Duquesne University, had suggested a "surplus accumulation in an earlier publication. See C. Elmer Bown, "Economic Aspects of Rate Regulation," *American Bar Association Journal*, July 1932, reported in F.X.W., "How Far Should 'Value of Service' Be Considered as a Basis of Rate Making?" *Public Utilities Fortnightly*, Dec. 8, 1932, 703.

64. Young, *Adventure in Politics*, 162–65, 177. La Follette quotation in Miller, *Governor Philip F. La Follette*, 24. Arthur M. Schlesinger Jr., *The Coming of the New Deal* (Boston: Houghton Mifflin, 1959), 301.

65. Young, *Adventure in Politics*, 178–80. Miller, *Governor Philip F. La Follette*, 3, 6, 25–27. Hofstadter, *Age of Reform*, 154–55.

66. Young, *Adventure in Politics*, 177–78. Miller, *Governor Philip F. La Follette*, 29.

67. "State GOP Platform Adopted by Convention," *Milwaukee Journal*, June 8, 1932, main sec., 3. "Platform of Democrats Adopted at Green Bay," *Milwaukee Journal*, June 12, 1932, main sec., 3. "Let the Commission Alone," *Milwaukee Journal*, July 8, 1932, editorial sec., 12. "Distortion Laid to La Follette," *Milwaukee Journal*, Aug. 25, 1932, main sec., 4.

68. "Back to the Job, Commissioner," *Milwaukee Journal*, July 14, 1932, editorial sec., 10. DEL: UJ, Aug. 10, 1932.

69. Lilienthal, *Journals* 1:27. DEL: UJ, Sept. 9, 1932; Helen Lilienthal, *Family Chronicle*, 152.

70. DEL: UJ, Sept. 9, 1932; Lilienthal to Frankfurter, Sept. 21, 1932. Lilienthal, *Journals* 1:27, 29.

344   Notes to Pages 60–62

71. Lilienthal, *Journals* 1:29. "Praise from Outside," *Capital Times,* Oct. 2, 1932, editorial page. DEL: UJ, Oct. 13, 1932 (both the Republican and Democratic platform statements on utilities were attached to this entry). "Mr. Kohler and Mr. Schmedeman?" *Milwaukee Journal,* Sept. 22, 1932, editorial sec., 12. "Schmedeman Right on Utilities," *Milwaukee Journal,* Sept. 26, 1932, editorial sec., 8.

72. Helen Lilienthal, *Family Chronicle,* 153. "Security Sales Evils Assailed," *Milwaukee Journal,* Jan. 30, 1933, main sec., 3. "Must Tighten Lid on Selling," *Milwaukee Journal,* Feb. 3, 1932, market sec., 10. New Blue Sky Bill Is Passed," *Milwaukee Journal,* May 4, 1933, market sec., 8. Lilienthal, "Reconciling Holding Companies with Public Interest," *Electrical World,* Oct. 29, 1932, 588–91. "Keep Commissioner Lilienthal," *Milwaukee Journal,* Jan. 4, 1933, editorial sec., 10. "Only Mr. Lilienthal Will Do," *Milwaukee Journal,* Jan. 24, 1933, editorial sec., 8. "The Governor's Utility Battle," *Milwaukee Journal,* May 8, 1933, editorial sec., 8. DEL: UJ, June 3, 1933; Lilienthal to Maltbie, Dec. 27, 1932; correspondence between Frankfurter and Lilienthal, Jan. 4 and 7, 1933.

73. DEL: Lilienthal to Frankfurter, Jan. 17, 1933. "Lilienthal Foes Seek Removal," *Milwaukee Journal,* Jan. 17, main sec., 9. DEL: UJ, June 3, 1933; Lilienthal to Frankfurter, Jan. 7, 1933.

74. "Utility Probe Plans Halted," *Milwaukee Journal,* Jan. 14, 1933, main sec., 12. "Governor's Message Assures State He Will Not Permit Deficit," *Milwaukee Journal,* Jan. 27, 1933, main sec., 14.

75. "Vote to Make Utilities Pay," *Milwaukee Journal,* Feb. 2, 1933, market sec., 1. "State Inquiry Awaits Budget," *Milwaukee Journal,* Feb. 8, 1933, main sec., 5. "Back to the Spoils System?" *Milwaukee Journal,* Mar. 12, 1933, editorial sec., 10. "Test Looming on Lilienthal," *Milwaukee Journal,* Apr. 23, 1933, main sec., 9. "Senate Close on Lilienthal," *Milwaukee Journal,* May 9, 1933, main sec., 11. DEL: UJ, Oct. 13, and Nov. 5, 1932; June 3, 1933; Frankfurter to Lilienthal, Jan. 4, and Apr. 28, 1933. Raymond Moley, *The First New Deal* (New York: Harcourt Brace and World, 1966), 332. Lilienthal, *Journals* 1:30.

76. Helen Lilienthal, *Family Chronicle,* 148. DEL: UJ, Jan. 27, 1931.

77. DEL: Berle to Lilienthal, Sept. 22, 1932; Frankfurter to Lilienthal, Jan. 4, 1933; Lilienthal to Berle, Nov. 4, 1932; UJ, Oct. 13, 1932; and June 3, 1933 (Lilienthal only referred to Mr. X by that name in the original typescript. Sometime later, as evidenced by his handwriting, he came back to that entry and tried to remember who Mr. X was. While not sure, he thought Mr. X might have been Milo Maltbie); correspondence between Lilienthal and Bonbright, Apr. 27 and 28, 1933.

78. DEL: UJ, Nov. 5, 1932, and June 3, 1933; correspondence between Lilienthal and Frank McNinch, Feb. 27 and 29, 1932; correspondence between Lilienthal and Berle, Nov. 4 and ?, 1932; Lilienthal to Frankfurter, Nov. 9, 1932, and May 18, 1933; Lilienthal to Bonbright, Apr. 27, 1933.

79. "Washington Report Involves Lilienthal," *Milwaukee Journal,* May 9, 1933, main sec., 11. Lilienthal, *Journals* 1:32, 38, 102. Senator Norris was the source of the Roosevelt quotation. DEL: Lilienthal to Frankfurter, June 2, 1933.

80. "Lilienthal Answers Power Trust Attacks," *The Progressive,* May 13, 1933, 1. DEL: correspondence between Lilienthal and Forrest Allen, May 20 and 25, June 1, 1933.

81. The story of Morgan's investigation is reported, with slight variation in three sources, including Arthur E. Morgan, *The Making of TVA* (Buffalo: Prometheus Books, 1974), 21–23; Thomas K. McCraw, *Morgan vs. Lilienthal: The Feud within the TVA* (Chicago: Loyola Univ. Press, 1970), 17–18; Roy Talbert Jr., *FDR's Utopian: Arthur Morgan of the TVA* (Jackson: Univ. Press of Mississippi,

1987), 91–93. There is one point in both Morgan and McCraw's account which is probably incorrect. Both sources say that Algo Henderson talked with Lilienthal on his trip to Madison. Helen Lilienthal notes in her *Family Chronicle* that "we learned later that A. E. Morgan had sent a friend of his to Madison to look into Dave" (154). This suggests that Henderson did *not* talk with Lilienthal at that time.

82. Morgan quotation from Talbert, *FDR's Utopian*, 93. Interview with Helen Lilienthal July 24–26, 1986, Martha's Vineyard, Mass. Lilienthal, *Journals* 1: 33. Helen Lilienthal, *Family Chronicle*, 153.

83. Lilienthal, *Journals* 1:33–34. DEL: Lilienthal to Frankfurter, June 2, 1933; UJ, June 3, 1933. Morgan, *The Making of TVA*, 23. Talbert, *FDR's Utopian*, 93.

84. "Wisconsin in Muscle Shoals," *Milwaukee Journal*, June 5, 1933, editorial sec., 8. "Wisconsin Loses, the Nation Gains," *Capital Times*, June 5, 1933, editorial page. "Editorial Topics of the Day," *The Progressive*, June 10, 1933, 3. "Lilienthal Drafted by U.S. for Tennessee Board Job," *Milwaukee Journal*, June 4, 1933, main sec., 1. DEL: correspondence between Lilienthal and Frankfurter, June 6 and 9, 1933.

85. DEL: telegrams, Lilienthal to La Follette, Lilienthal to Frankfurter, June 10, 1933; UJ, June 22, 1933.

86. "Clear All Wires," *Milwaukee Journal*, May 14, 1933, main sec., 3. Hofstadter, *Age of Reform*, 263. DEL: UJ, Sept. 9, 1932; Lilienthal to Arvin, Jan. 15, 1932. Lilienthal, "Fact-finding Basis for Control of Public Utilities," *United States Daily*, Feb. 26, 1932, 1.

87. "Utility Control Trouble Cited," *Milwaukee Journal*, Mar. 24, 1933, main sec., 5. "Stalwart Dem 'Deal' Is Bared," *The Progressive*, May 13, 1933, 1.

88. DEL: Lilienthal to Arvin, Jan. 15, 1932; Lilienthal to Richberg, Oct. 7, 1931.

89. Lilienthal, *Journals* 1:37–38.; Talbert, *FDR's Utopian*, 94. Arthur M. Schlesinger Jr., *The Age of Roosevelt*, vol. 3, *The Politics of Upheaval* (Boston: Houghton Mifflin Company, 1960), 233–35. Jordan A. Schwarz, *Liberal: Adolf A. Berle and the Vision of an American Era* (New York: Free Press, 1987), 14–15.

90. Helen Lilienthal, *Family Chronicle*, 150. Telephone interview with Allen Lilienthal, June 9, 1987.

91. DEL: see for example correspondence between Lilienthal and Booth and Swidler, July 22, 23, and 24, 1931; Lilienthal to Booth, Aug. 1, 1931; Lilienthal to Leitzell, Aug. 10 and 13, 1931.

92. Clemens, "Public Utility Regulation in Wisconsin," 11. CC: State of Wisconsin, In assembly, *Jt. Res. No. 132, A.*, June 6, 1933.

93. William E. Leuchtenberg, *Franklin Delano Roosevelt and the New Deal: 1932–1940* (New York: Harper & Row, 1963), 342–43.

94. Lilienthal, *Journals* 1:34.

Chapter 5. TVA: The Tumultuous Years

1. Goldman, *Rendezvous with Destiny*, 255–68. Roosevelt quotation in Marguerite Owen, *The Tennessee Valley Authority* (New York: Praeger Publishers, 1973), 13–14. Leuchtenburg, *Franklin D. Roosevelt and the New Deal*, 41–62 (quotation on 61).

2. Whitman, *David Lilienthal*, 1, 10. Helen L. Lilienthal, *Family Chronicle*, 154–55. Lilienthal, *Journals* 1:32–39. DEL: Lilienthal to Allen, June 22, 1933. Thomas K. McCraw, *Morgan vs. Lilienthal: The Feud within the TVA* (Chicago: Loyola Univ. Press, 1970), 27. Alfred Lief, *Democracy's Norris: The Biography of a Lonely Crusade* (New York: Stackpole Sons, 1939), 482.

3. There are several sources that report on the first board meeting. Harcourt Morgan
   and Arthur Morgan told their versions during the 1938 TVA Investigation Hearings.
   Lilienthal made his observations in his journal and in a later interview. Good second-
   ary sources include Talbert and McCraw. Joint Committee on the Investigation of the
   Tennessee Valley Authority, Congress of the United States, *Investigation of the
   Tennessee Valley Authority*, part 1, (Washington, D.C.: GPO, 1939), 98–99, 289–
   90 (hereafter cited as *Investigation*). Lilienthal, *Journals* 1:39. MVC: Charles W.
   Crawford, interview with David E. Lilienthal, Feb. 6, 1970, 3–6. McCraw,
   Morgan vs. Lilienthal, 26–27. Talbert, *FDR's Utopian*, 101–2.
4. Rexford G. Tugwell, *The Battle for Democracy* (New York: Columbia Univ.
   Press, 1935), 23. McCraw, *TVA and the Power Fight: 1933–1939* (Philadelphia:
   J. B. Lippincott Co., 1971), 1–25. Schlesinger Jr., *Coming of the New Deal*, 319–
   25. Schlesinger, *Politics of Upheaval*, 377. Raymond Moley, *The First New Deal*
   (New York: Harcourt Brace and World, 1966), 332. Roosevelt quoted in
   Goldman, *Rendezvous with Destiny*, 263. Rexford G. Tugwell and Edward C.
   Banfield, "Grass Roots Democracy—Myth or Reality?" *Public Administration
   Review*, Winter 1950, 47. McCraw, *Morgan vs. Lilienthal*, 1–5. Donald
   Davidson, *The Tennessee: The New River, Civil War to TVA*, 2 vols. (New York:
   Rinehart & Company, 1948), vol. 2:226–27.
5. Schlesinger, *Coming of the New Deal*, 325. Mary Earhart Dillon, *Wendell
   Willkie: 1892–1944* (Philadelphia: J. B. Lippincott Co., 1952), 48. McCraw, *TVA
   and the Power Fight*, 51, 53. Schlesinger, *Politics of Upheaval*, 363.
6. C. E. Allred, S. W. Atkins, and G. H. Hatfield, *Tennessee, Economic and Social,
   Part II—The Counties* (Knoxville: Division of University Extension, 1929), 47–
   48.
7. Waldemar Kaempffert, "Power for the Abundant Life," *New York Times
   Magazine*, Aug. 23, 1936, 21.
8. Descriptions of the Morgans are abundant. The best description of A. E. Morgan
   is, of course, in Talbert's biography, *FDR's Utopian*, especially the introduction
   and first three chapters. Talbert discusses the influence of Frederick Taylor and
   Edward Bellamy in these chapters. He also discusses Morgan's written works on
   Bellamy in the epilogue. Other accounts of both men include chapter 2 of
   McCraw, *Morgan vs. Lilienthal*, 6–23, and Willson Whitman, *God's Valley:
   People and Power along the Tennessee River* (New York: Viking Press, 1939),
   125–52, and passim.
9. Lilienthal quoted in Whitman, *David Lilienthal*, 11. "Mr. Lilienthal and the
   Professors," *Chattanooga Daily Times*, Sept. 29, 1933, 4.
10. Many of the personal insights were drawn from interviews by Charles Crawford
    and are held by the Mississippi Valley Collection at the University of Memphis:
    the first quotation is from Harry L. Case, Jan. 1, 1980, 7, 8; the second is from
    William Hays, Dec. 29, 1970, 24; see also Crawford interviews with Louis Eckl,
    June 16, 1979 and Harry Case, Mar. 6, 1970. Other interviews were done for the
    TVA Oral History Collection, TVA Employee Series, see Mark R. Winter,
    interview with Harry Wiersema, July 17, 1981, 2, 3. Interview with Mr. and Mrs.
    John Oliver, Chattanooga, Aug. 4, 1987.
11. G. Bromley Oxnam, *Personalities in Social Reform* (New York: Abingdon-
    Cokesbury Press, 1950), 104. Max Freedman, ed., *Roosevelt and Frankfurter:
    Their Correspondence, 1882–1945* (Boston: Little Brown, 1968), 138, 341, 447–
    49. Lief, *Democracy's Norris*, 482. McCraw, *TVA and the Power Fight*, 31.
    Talbert, *FDR's Utopian*, 148. MVC: Crawford interviews with Walter Kahoe,
    Apr. 26, 1971, 17, and Joseph Swidler, Dec. 8, 1969, 15–16. Interviews with
    Edwin Falck, Washington, D.C., July 21, 1987, and Roland Kampmeier, Chatta-
    nooga, Tenn., Aug. 4, 1987.

12. Ellsworth Barnard, *Wendell Willkie: Fighter for Freedom* (Marquette, Mich.: Northern Michigan Univ. Press, 1966), 108. Whitman, *God's Valley,* 125–52.

13. Helen Lilienthal, *Family Chronicle,* 157A–72.

14. DEL: Lilienthal to Frankfurter, June 9, 1933. MCK: McKellar to Lilienthal, July 8, 1933. MC: Lilienthal to Cooke, June 30, 1933, Cooke to Lilienthal, July 5, 1933 (two letters, same date). FFHLS: Lilienthal to Frankfurter, June 22, 1933.

15. Whitman, *David Lilienthal,* 13. Morgan, *The Making of TVA,* 28, 172. MVC: Crawford interviews with John Session, Dec. 9, 1971, 5; and David E. Lilienthal, Feb. 6, 1970, 24.

16. McCraw, *Morgan vs. Lilienthal,* 21, 31. Owen, *The Tennessee Valley Authority,* 46. MVC: Crawford interview with David E. Lilienthal, Feb. 6, 1970, 20–21. *Investigation,* 98–99.

17. NA: *Investigation,* Exhibit 13; TVA Board of Directors Minutes, July 30, 1933. *Investigation,* 99–102. Owen, *The Tennessee Valley Authority,* 46. Harold L. Ickes, *The Secret Diary of Harold L. Ickes: The First Thousand Days, 1933–1936* (New York: Simon & Schuster, 1954), 119. Talbert, *FDR's Utopian,* 103, 106.; C. Herman Pritchett, *The Tennessee Valley Authority: A Study in Public Administration* (Chapel Hill: Univ. of North Carolina Press, 1943), 187–88. McCraw, *TVA and the Power Fight,* 20.

18. *Investigation,* 103–9. FDR: Harcourt Morgan and Lilienthal to Arthur Morgan, Aug. 3, 1933; Arthur Morgan, "Memorandum on Progress toward Organization to Aug. 5, 1933," Aug. 5, 1933. Pritchett, *The Tennessee Valley Authority,* 154.

19. "Dr. A. E. Morgan's Letter Assailing Intrigue in the TVA," *New York Times,* Mar. 7, 1938, 6. *Investigation,* 109, 337. MVC: Crawford interviews with Lilienthal, Feb. 6, 1970, 15; and J. Dudley Dawson, June 20, 1969, 1. McCraw, *Morgan vs. Lilienthal,* 32. Owen, *The Tennessee Valley Authority,* 47. Pritchett, *The Tennessee Valley Authority,* 154–58. Talbert, *FDR's Utopian,* 103.

20. North Callahan, *TVA: Bridge Over Troubled Waters* (South Brunswick, N.J.: A. S. Barnes and Company, 1980), 99. *Investigation,* 310–11. McCraw, *Morgan vs. Lilienthal,* 30–32, 48. Morgan, *The Making of TVA,* 27–35. Talbert, *FDR's Utopian,* 151–52. Richard O. Niehoff, *Floyd W. Reeves: Innovative Educator and Distinguished Practitioner of the Art of Public Administration* (East Lansing, Mich.: Univ. Press of America, 1991), 213–19. Jordan A. Schwarz, *The New Dealers: Power Politics in the Age of Roosevelt* (New York: Alfred A. Knopf, 1993), 219.

21. Interview with Roland Kampmeier, Chattanooga, Tenn., Aug. 4, 1987. Morgan, *The Making of TVA,* 108. Oxnam, *Personalities in Social Reform,* 90. MVC: Crawford interviews with Joseph Swidler, Dec. 8, 1969, 15–16, and Lilienthal, Feb. 6, 1970, 11–12, 28. Helen Lilienthal, *Family Chronicle,* 161D–161E. Whitman, *David Lilienthal,* 11, 72

22. McCraw, *Morgan vs. Lilienthal,* 34. Whitman, *David Lilienthal,* 11–16; Whitman describes certain details of the speeches in Chattanooga, Memphis, and Nashville. "Valley Board Won't Act As Dictator Here," *Knoxville News-Sentinel,* Aug. 1, 1933, 1, 10. "TVA Pledges Cooperation," *Knoxville Journal,* Aug. 2, 1933, 1. DEL: Address of David E. Lilienthal before the Rotary Club of Chattanooga, Sept. 28, 1933, 1–9; Address of David E. Lilienthal before the Rotary Club of Memphis, Oct. 17, 1933, 1–9; Address of David E. Lilienthal before joint meeting Rotary Club, Chamber of Commerce and Exchange Club of Nashville, Tennessee, Nov. 7, 1933, 1–9.

23. Lilienthal, "T.V.A. Seen Only as Spur to Electrification of America," *Electrical World,* Nov. 25, 1933, 687–90. This article is a reprint of Lilienthal's speech "A Five-point Program for the Electrification of America," before the Lawyer's Club,

Atlanta, Ga. "Lilienthal Urges Electrified Nation," *New York Times,* financial sec., Nov. 11, 1933, 23.

24. MVC: Crawford interview with Joseph Swidler, Dec. 8, 1969, 8. "Here to Cooperate," *Knoxville News-Sentinel,* Aug. 2, 1933, 4. *News* quotation from Whitman, *David Lilienthal,* 14. "City's Cheap Power Hope Rests Upon Legislature; Lilienthal Defends T.V.A.," *Chattanooga Daily Times,* Sept. 29, 1933, 1. "Mr. Lilienthal and the Professors," *Chattanooga Daily Times,* Sept. 29, 1933, 4. "Mr. Lilienthal's Address," *Nashville Tennessean,* Nov. 9, 1933, 4. "The TVA and Our Investments," *Memphis Press-Scimitar,* Oct. 18, 1933, 4.

25. DEL: correspondence between Frankfurter and Lilienthal, July 29, and Aug. 18, 1933. Letter from Frankfurter to Brandeis, Aug. 12, 1933, quoted in Nelson L. Dawson, *Frankfurter and the New Deal* (Hamden, Conn.: Archon Books, 1980), 82.

26. Jean Christie, *Morris Llewellyn Cooke: Progressive Engineer* (New York: Garland Publishing, 1983), 11, 129–30. MC: Lilienthal to Cooke, June 30, 1933, Cooke to Lilienthal, July 5, 1933 (two letters); Carl Bock (Morgan assistant) to Cooke, July 11, 1933; Cooke to Morgan, n.d., around July 20, 1933; Cooke to Lilienthal, July 26, 1933 (two letters); Philip S. Broughton (Morgan assistant) to Cooke, July 28, 1933; Cooke to Lilienthal, Aug. 29, 1933.

27. FDR: Morgan to Lilienthal, n.d., around July 15, 1933.

28. FDR: Lilienthal to Morgan, July 21, 1933.

29. DEL: Arthur Morgan to H. A. Morgan and Lilienthal, Aug. 14, 1933; Lilienthal, "Memorandum in Opposition to PROPOSAL OF CHAIRMAN A. E. MORGAN FOR TERRITORIAL DIVISION AGREEMENT AND 'COOPERATION' between Tennessee Valley Authority and Private Utilities," Aug. 16, 1933; Lilienthal to Helen Lilienthal, Aug. 15, 1933; Lilienthal to Frankfurter, Aug. 18, 1933; Talbert, *FDR's Utopian,* 142–43.

30. Talbert, *FDR's Utopian,* 144. McCraw, *Morgan vs. Lilienthal,* 57–59. *Investigation,* 785. NA: *Investigation,* exhibit 38, "The Power Policy of the Tennessee Valley Authority," Press release of Aug. 24, 1933.

31. Joint Committee on the Investigation of the Tennessee Valley Authority, Congress of the United States, *Report of Chief Engineer* (hereafter cited as *Report*) (Washington, D.C.: Government Printing Office, Apr. 3, 1939), 243. Pritchett, *The Tennessee Valley Authority,* 82.

32. *Report,* 244. MVC: Crawford interview with Joseph Swidler, Oct. 29, 1969. McCraw, *TVA and the Power Fight,* 26–27, 59–62 (the latter pages offer an excellent summary of the original rate fixing process). Morgan, *The Making of TVA,* 22, 27.

33. *Investigation,* 755–78, 786. MVC: Crawford interview with Edward W. Morehouse, July 30, 1971, 16–17, 19. *Report,* 245.

34. "Tennessee Project Held Rate Yardstick," *New York Times,* financial sec., Sept. 14, 1933, 35. NA: *Investigation,* exhibit 7: TVA Press Release—"Electric Rates Announced," Sept. 14, 1933; exhibit 10: TVA Press Release—"Basis of Rates Announced," Sept. 15, 1933.

35. McCraw, *TVA and the Power Fight,* 59–60. Lilienthal, *Journals* 5:164. "Muscle Shoals Electric Rates Set New Low; $1.50 to small User, Against $4.50 Here," *New York Times,* Sept. 15, 1933, 1. "At Muscle Shoals," and "Utility Issues Hit by Federal Rates," both in *New York Times,* editorial sec., 12, and financial sec., 19, 21, respectively, Sept. 16, 1933. *Chicago Tribune* quotation in "Muscle Shoals as a Yardstick For Electrical Rates," *Literary Digest,* Sept. 30, 1933, 9. *Investigation,* 769–70, 786–88. NA: *Investigation*; exhibit 30C, Zinder to Lilienthal, Sept. 7, 1933.

36. Morgan quoted in *Investigation,* 784. DEL: Lilienthal to Arvin, Nov. 26, 1933.

MVC: Crawford interview with Joseph Swidler, Oct. 29, 1969, 16–17. *Report*, 247. Lilienthal, *Journals* 1:713.

37. The substance of this discussion is taken from "Appendix: Conferences in 1933 between Lilienthal and Willkie," in Lilienthal, *Journals* 1:711–15; see also DEL: "Lilienthal-Willkie Correspondence—1939–1933," n.d. (after Aug. 1939); "Contest of the corn-feds," n.d., additional Lilienthal notes on their relationship. McCraw, *TVA and the Power Fight,* 63–66.

38. DEL: Lilienthal to Helen Lilienthal, Apr. 1934; Lilienthal to Arvin, Apr. 29, 1934; TVA desk calender, Jan.–Mar. 1934; Lilienthal to Dr. E. B. Freeman, July 28, 1933; Lilianthal [*sic*], Mr. David E., "medical report," Mar. 20, 1936, no Physician name on report. Helen Lilienthal, *Family Chronicle,* 171–71B.

39. Talbert, *FDR's Utopian,* 137–38, 156. *Investigation,* 957–64, 1014–16.

40. DEL: Lilienthal to Frankfurter, Apr. 29, 1934. Pritchett, *The Tennessee Valley Authority,* 68–69. In 1934 virtually all Wilson Dam power was sold directly to Alabama Power and Light Co.

41. Martin G. Glaeser, "The Yardstick Once More," *Public Utilities Fortnightly,* Dec. 7, 1939, 733–39.

42. Franklin D. Roosevelt, "Campaign Address on Public Utilities and Development of Hydro-Electric Power," Portland, Oreg., Sept. 21, 1932, *The Public Papers and Addresses of Franklin D. Roosevelt: Volume I, The Genesis of the New Deal, 1928–1932* (New York: Random House, 1938), 739–40. Pritchett, *The Tennessee Valley Authority,* 100–101. McCraw, *TVA and the Power Fight,* 30–33.

43. Pritchett, *The Tennessee Valley Authority,* 100–104. McCraw, *Morgan vs. Lilienthal,* 109. McCraw, *TVA and the Power Fight,* 54–56.

44. NA: "The Power Policy," Aug. 24, 1933. Arthur E. Morgan, "Purposes and Methods of the Tennessee Valley Authority," *Annals of the American Academy of Social and Political Science,* Mar. 1934, 55. Arthur E. Morgan, "Selfish Interests Must Go," *Forum,* Mar. 1935, 131–32. Arthur E. Morgan, "Yardstick and What Else?" *Saturday Evening Post,* Aug. 7, 1937, 78.

45. Glaeser, "The Yardstick Once More," 737. MVC: Crawford interview with Morehouse, July 31, 1971, 17.

46. DEL: Chattanooga Rotary Club Speech, Sept. 28, 1933, 5; Memphis Rotary Club Speech, Oct. 17, 1933, 5–6; Nashville Rotary, Chamber of Commerce and Exchange Club Speech, Nov. 7, 1933, 4; Address of David E. Lilienthal before the League of Women Voters, Boston, Mass., Apr. 24, 1934, 2; Frankfurter to Lilienthal, Nov. 2, 1934. Lilienthal, "T.V.A. Seen Only As Spur," 687. FFHLS: Lilienthal to Frankfurter, Nov. 5, 1934. Lilienthal, "Business and Government in the Tennessee Valley," *Annals of the American Academy of Political and Social Sciences,* Mar. 1934 (speech given before academy on Jan. 5, 1934, in Philadelphia), 46. "TVA Head Attacks Holding Concerns," *New York Times,* Jan. 22, 1935, 20 (report on remarks given before Economic and Harvard Business School Clubs of New York, previous day).

47. DEL: Lilienthal, "Figures Show TVA's Electricity Plan Works," speech delivered to members of the American Society of Mechanical Engineers, and members of the Society for Promotion of Engineering Education, Norris, Tenn., June 22, 1935, 1; Lilienthal to Frankfurter, June 10, 1935. McCraw, *Morgan vs. Lilienthal,* 52.

48. DEL: David E. Lilienthal, "The Yardstick in Action," address to the annual meeting of the American Historical Association and the American Political Science Association, Chattanooga, Tenn., Dec. 29, 1935; same address delivered to a League of Women Voters meeting in St. Paul, Minn., Jan. 8, 1935.

49. Schlesinger, *The Politics of Upheaval,* 374.

50. "Tennessee Project Held Rate Yardstick," *New York Times,* Sept. 14, 1933,

financial sec., 35. DEL: Memphis Rotary Speech, Oct. 17, 1933, 9; Nashville
Rotary Speech, Nov. 7, 1933, 8. "T.V.A. Seen Only As Spur," 688.

51. Much of the analysis of the EHFA is derived from Gregory B. Fields's definitive
study, "'Electricity for All': The Electric Home and Farm Authority and the
Politics of Mass Consumption, 1932–1935," *Business History Review,* Spring
1990, 32–60. Franklin D. Roosevelt, "Authorization of the Electric Home and
Farm Authority. Executive Order No. 6514," Dec. 19, 1933, *The Public Papers
and Addresses of Franklin D. Roosevelt: Volume II, The Year of Crisis, 1933*
(New York: Random House, 1938), 526–30.

52. Fields, "Electricity for All," 43–44. "TVA Appliances," *Business Week,* Mar. 17,
1934, 10.

53. DEL: Frankfurter to Lilienthal, Jan. 10, 1933; Lilienthal, "The Electrification of
the American Home," CBS Broadcast, Jan. 20, 1934; League of Women Voters
speech, Boston, Apr. 24, 1934; Lilienthal to Frankfurter, Apr. 29, 1934. FDR: two
letters between Lilienthal and Eleanor Roosevelt, June 20, and July 14, 1934.
Lilienthal, "Business and Government." "Utility Investors Reassured by TVA,"
New York Times, May 18, 1934, financial sec., 37 (report of Lilienthal's speech
"The Tennessee Valley Authority and the Investor," to the National Association
of Mutual Savings Banks, in New York City, May 17, 1934). Considering the fact
that Lilienthal spent most of the first three months of 1934 recuperating from his
"nervous breakdown," it seems clear that he devoted much of his work time to
EHFA. Two major speeches in January and negotiations with the appliance
industry probably constituted a good portion of his business hours during this
period.

54. Fields, "Electricity for All," 48–52, 56. Ted Leitzell, "Uncle Sam, Peddler of
Electric Gadgets," *New Outlook,* Aug. 1934, 51–53.

55. Fields, "Electricity for All," 53, 58.

56. Lilienthal, *Journals* 1:59. *Investigation,* 3316, 3332, 4218, 6222–23.

57. Many scholars have analyzed these two cases. Two of the best include McCraw,
TVA and the Power Fight, 111–15, 117–20, and Pritchett, *The Tennessee Valley
Authority,* 60–65, 68; see also Richard Lowitt, *George W. Norris: The Triumph
of a Progressive, 1933–1944* (Urbana: Univ. of Illinois Press, 1978), 112–17.

58. Joseph Barnes, *Willkie: The Events He Was Part of, the Ideas He Fought for*
(New York: Simon & Schuster, 1952), 68–69, 104. Dillon, *Wendell Willkie,* 49.
Barnard, *Wendell Willkie,* 87, 107–8. DEL: "Lilienthal-Willkie Correspondence";
Lilienthal, "Preliminary Memorandum of Conference with Alexander Sachs,"
Mar. 26, 1936.

59. Pritchett, *The Tennessee Valley Authority,* 66–67. McCraw, *TVA and the Power
Fight,* 127–30.

60. McCraw, *Morgan vs. Lilienthal,* 67–80. McCraw, *TVA and the Power Fight,* 91–
107. Pritchett, *The Tennessee Valley Authority,* 70. Schwarz, *The New Dealers,*
228–31. DEL: correspondence between Lilienthal and Cooke, Oct. 9 and 29,
1936; Lilienthal, "Preliminary Memorandum of Conference with Alexander
Sachs," Mar. 26, 1936; U), Mar. 27, 1936. *Investigation,* 865. McCraw's account
of the power pool in both his books is the definitive tale of the pooling episode. I
have drawn extensively from them as well as from Louis B. Wehle's interpretation
in *Hidden Threads of History: Wilson through Roosevelt* (New York: Macmillan
Co., 1953), 161–77.

61. *Investigation,* 898–99. McCraw, *Morgan vs. Lilienthal,* 75–77. McCraw, *TVA
and the Power Fight,* 100–101. Willkie quotation in Wehle, *Hidden Threads of
History,* 164–70. FFHLS: Lilienthal's version of the Sept. 30 meeting and his
increasing reservations about pooling are reported in a long report to Norris,
Nov. 2, 1936.

62. Quotation from letter to La Follette in McCraw, *Morgan vs. Lilienthal,* 71. Willkie quotation in Wehle, *Hidden Threads of History,* 165–66.

63. Schlesinger, *The Politics of Upheaval,* 368. Morgan quotation in McCraw, *Morgan vs. Lilienthal,* 72–77. McCraw, *TVA and the Power Fight,* 98–99. Wehle, *Hidden Threads of History,* 170–71. FFHLS: correspondence between Arthur Morgan and Wehle, Oct. 24 and 26, 1936; Milton to Norris, Nov. 4, 1936. Lowitt, *George W. Norris,* 199.

64. Wehle, *Hidden Threads of History,* 166–67, 171–74. McCraw, *Morgan vs. Lilienthal,* 78–79. McCraw, *TVA and the Power Fight,* 102–7.

65. See Talbert, *F.D.R.'s Utopian,* and McCraw, *Morgan vs. Lilienthal,* passim., for superb discussions of Lilienthal's and Morgan's personalities, traits, and beliefs. For contemporary accounts see J. Charles Poe, "The Morgan-Lilienthal Feud," *The Nation,* Oct. 3, 1936, 385–86; and Willson Whitman, "Morgan and Morgan and Lilienthal: The Personalities in the TVA Wrangle," *Harper's Monthly Magazine,* Sept. 1938, 352–61.

66. MVC: Crawford interview with Louise Allen, July 13, 1970.

67. Lilienthal, *Journals* 1:66–67. Morgan quoted in Talbert, *FDR's Utopian,* 171.

68. McCraw, *Morgan,* 107. Wehle, *Hidden Threads of History,* 164.

69. Poe, "The Morgan-Lilienthal Feud," 386. Whitman, *David Lilienthal,* 35–38. Niehoff, *Floyd W. Reeves,* 215. Talbert, *FDR's Utopian,* 129. Lilienthal, *Journals* 1:66. Joe Swidler thought that part of Morgan's problem with Lilienthal was that he had never "been in a situation where lawyers were important before," and that he simply could not understand the lack of black and white alternatives when it came to matters of the law. MVC: Crawford interview with Joseph Swidler, Dec. 8, 1969.

70. Morgan, *The Making of TVA,* 9–17. Talbert, *FDR's Utopian,* 153–56. Niehoff, *Floyd W. Reeves,* 194. McCraw, *Morgan vs. Lilienthal,* 50–51. Lowitt, *George W. Norris,* 21, 41–42. DEL: Lilienthal to Frankfurter, June 10, 1935; Clapp to Lilienthal, Mar. 10, 1938 (Clapp's recollection of his warning to A. E. Morgan in this letter). Clapp's brother Norman recalled in an interview with the author that his brother, who believed in the merit principle as much as Morgan, was satisfied with Lilienthal's explanation of the so-called patronage hirings, Washington, D.C., July 28, 1987. It is interesting that many of the principals in this case either failed to capitalize on the charges or made little of them. Morgan did not bring up Clapp's findings in the 1938 hearings (allegedly to protect Clapp). There is no mention, either, of the issue in Richard Niehoff's biography of Floyd Reeves. Finally, in the 1938 hearings, Gordon Clapp denied that he knew of any "appointments made upon the basis of political tests or affiliations" at TVA. Perhaps Morgan's reticence can be explained by Clapp's finding that Morgan himself was not totally innocent of merit irregularities.

71. Talbert, *FDR's Utopian,* 158–59. McCraw, *Morgan vs. Lilienthal,* 50–52. Ickes, *The Secret Diary,* 566. Morgan, *The Making of TVA,* 83–84, 166–67. George Norris, *Fighting Liberal: The Autobiography of George W. Norris* (New York: Macmillan Co., 1945), 273. Lowitt, *George W. Norris,* 123.

72. DEL: Marguerite Owen to Lilienthal, May 18, 1936; Lilienthal to Norris, May 4, 1936; UJ, Aug. 17, 1936; GRC: Clapp, "Memorandum Concerning Incidents the Week of May 10–18, 1936, Related to the Pending Reappointment of Mr. David E. Lilienthal," Mar. 15, 1938. Roosevelt quotes from Lilienthal, *Journals* 1:61–62. Talbert, *FDR's Utopian,* 160–61. McCraw, *Morgan vs. Lilienthal,* 54–55. FDR: Roosevelt to Morgan, May 15, 1936.

73. McCraw, *Morgan vs. Lilienthal,* 90. *Investigation,* 120. 592.

74. McCraw, *Morgan vs. Lilienthal,* 60. DEL: Arthur Morgan to Lilienthal and Harcourt Morgan, June 4, 1936. *Investigation,* 449.

75. *Investigation,* 367–70. MVC: Crawford interview with Richard O. Niehoff, Mar. 5, 1970, 16–17. Speech quotations are taken from "A. E. Morgan Absent as TVA Begins Vital Budget Parleys," *Knoxville News-Sentinel,* July 14, 1936, 1, 10. McCraw, *Morgan vs. Lilienthal,* 60–61, 63–64.

76. *Investigation,* over a thousand pages of testimony on the Berry case were included in the official transcript. Talbert, *FDR's Utopian,* 177–78, 181. Owen, *The Tennessee Valley Authority,* 68–72. McCraw, *Morgan vs. Lilienthal,* 91–93. Pritchett, *The Tennessee Valley Authority,* 194–202.

77. "Dr. Morgan Pleads For 'Cooperation' With The Utilities," *New York Times,* Jan. 17, 1937, 1, 34–35. "Cheap Power and Fair Play," *New York Times,* Jan. 18, 1937, editorial sec., 16.

78. Roosevelt quotation in Lilienthal, *Journals* 1:65–66. DEL: Lilienthal to Szold, Feb. 9, 1937; Lilienthal to Norris, Feb. 24, 1937; Lilienthal to La Follette, Feb. 26, 1937; Lilienthal to Frankfurter, Mar. 25, 1937. FDR: Lilienthal and Harcourt Morgan to Roosevelt, Mar. 5, 1937. Quotation from Lilienthal's May 10, 1937, memorandum to the reorganization committee from Talbert, *FDR's Utopian,* 176.

79. Morgan, "Yardstick—And What Else?" 80. Morgan, "Public Ownership of Power," *Atlantic Monthly,* Sept. 1937, 344–46. Willkie, "Political Power," *Atlantic Monthly,* Aug. 1937. FFHLS: Lilienthal to Frankfurter, Sept. 23, 1937; unsigned and undated "Memorandum of Analysis of Articles by Dr. A. E. Morgan and Mr. Wendell Willkie, in *Atlantic Monthly,* Sept. 1937." The memorandum was written soon after Willkie's September article and before the Sept. 23 letter to Frankfurter. The analysis is Lilienthal's style all the way. DEL: Harcourt Morgan to Roosevelt, Aug. 31, 1937; Roosevelt to Arthur Morgan, Sept. 3, 1937.

80. Talbert, *FDR's Utopian,* 180–81. McCraw, *Morgan vs. Lilienthal,* 94–95. Fly and O'Brian's testimony about Morgan's behavior is in *Investigation,* 957–64, 1014–16. DEL: Harcourt Morgan and Lilienthal to Roosevelt, Nov. 19, 1937.

81. Talbert, *FDR's Utopian,* 181. "TVA Chief Scores Claims of Berry," *New York Times,* Dec. 21, 1937, 9. "Two TVA Directors Assail Dr. Morgan," *New York Times,* Dec. 23, 1937, 5.

82. Nichols letter in Freedman, *Roosevelt and Frankfurter,* 375–76. MVC: Crawford interview with Walter Kahoe, Apr. 26, 1971, 15, 28. Talbert, *FDR's Utopian,* 186.

Chapter 6. TVA: Vindication and Consolidation

1. "Two TVA Directors Assail Dr. Morgan," *New York Times,* Dec. 23, 1937, 5. Lilienthal, *Journals* 1:68. FDR: Harcourt Morgan and Lilienthal to the President, Jan. 18, 1938.

2. Barnard, *Wendell Willkie,* 119. Barnes, *Willkie,* 130. McCraw, *Morgan vs. Lilienthal* (Chicago: Loyola Univ. Press, 1970), 98–99. Talbert, *FDR's Utopian,* 183–84. DEL: exchange of letters between Lilienthal and Frankfurter, Jan. 26 and 28, Feb. 2, 1938. U.S Congress, Joint Committee on the Investigation of the Tennessee Valley Authority, *Investigation of the Tennessee Valley Authority* (Washington, D.C.: GPO, 1939), 229–34. "Dr. A. E. Morgan's Letter Assailing 'Intrigue' in TVA," *New York Times,* Mar. 7, 1938, 6.

3. Talbert, *FDR's Utopian,* 185–86. McCraw, *Morgan vs. Lilienthal,* 99–100. FDR: Rowe to James Roosevelt, Mar. 5, 1938. Turner Catledge, "Full Tennessee Valley Authority Inquiry Asked of Congress," *New York Times,* Mar. 3, 1938, reprinted

in *Investigation,* 263. Lilienthal, *Journals* 1:70–72. *Investigation,* 234–68. Dorothy Thompson, "L'Affaire Morgan," n.d., reprinted in *Investigation,* 266.

4. "Message from the President of the United States Transmitting Information Relative to the Removal of a Member of the Tennessee Valley Authority, the Opinion of the Attorney General, and the Transcript of the Hearings Held on Mar. 11, 18, and 21, 1938," Senate Document No. 155 (Washington, D.C.: GPO, 1938), 16–17. Lilienthal, *Journals* 1:73. Talbert, *FDR's Utopian,* 187. Morgan, *The Making of TVA,* 169–70.

5. Roosevelt quotation in Lilienthal, *Journals* 1:73–74.

6. Lief, *Democracy's Norris,* 513–14. Lilienthal, *Journals* 1:72–74. "Message from the President," 15, 21–26, 70–73.

7. "Message from the President," 73–96. Talbert, *FDR's Utopian,* 189–92.

8. "Message from the President," iii, 97–105. Talbert, *FDR's Utopian,* 192–93.

9. Lowitt, *George W. Norris,* 212–14. "Troubles of TVA," *Newsweek,* Mar. 28, 1938, 12. "The Tennessee Valley Authority Inquiry," *Christian Century,* Apr. 6, 1938, taken from *Investigation,* 255–56. "Hatfields and McCoys in the TVA," *New Republic,* Mar. 23, 1938, 192.

10. DEL: Lilienthal to Herb Marks, Mar. 26, 1938; exchange of telegrams between Arthur Morgan and Harcourt Morgan, May 13 and 16, 1938, Lilienthal to James Roosevelt, May 17, 1938. McCraw, *Morgan vs. Lilienthal,* 103. Lilienthal, *Journals* 1:74–75.

11. *Investigation,* passim. "Report of the Joint Committee on the Investigation of the Tennessee Valley Authority, Congress of the United States" (Washington, D.C.: GPO, Apr. 3, 1939), Report plus Appendix A, "Reports and Exhibits" and Appendix B, "Report of Chief Engineer." Pritchett, *The Tennessee Valley Authority,* 247–48. Lilienthal, *Journals* 1:74. Davidson, *The Tennessee* 2:319.

12. DEL: Lilienthal to Frankfurter, Aug. 10, 1938. Francis Biddle, *In Brief Authority* (Garden City, N.Y.: Doubleday, 1962), 54–55. Whitman, *David Lilienthal,* 44.

13. DEL: "Chronology of Undulant Illness," n.d., written sometime after Apr. 2, 1939; Lilienthal to Morgan, n.d., context suggests the date is between Nov. 15 and 25, 1938. Lilienthal, *Journals* 1:83–92, 103. Helen Lilienthal, *Family Chronicle,* 197. Lilienthal, *Journals* 7:778.

14. "TVA Fight Fizzle," *Newsweek,* June 6, 1938, 10. "Morgan, Morgan and Lilienthal," *Time,* June 6, 1938, 11–12. *Investigation,* 1–3, 35, 148–49, 222. Lilienthal, *Journals* 1:76. Whitman, *David Lilienthal,* 44.

15. Whitman, *David. Lilienthal,* 48. Jonathan Daniels, "Three Men in a Valley," *New Republic,* Aug. 17, 1938, 35.

16. *Investigation,* 663–64, 771–75, 897.

17. *Investigation,* 4227. Whitman, *God's Valley,* 271–73.

18. Lilienthal, *Journals* 1:103. Pritchett, *The Tennessee Valley Authority,* 248. *Report,* III. *Report, Appendix A,* Leonard White, "Survey of Personnel Department, Tennessee Valley Authority," 70; American Farm Bureau Federation, "Practical Results of Tennessee Valley Authority Fertilizer Program from the Farmers' Standpoint"; Leland Olds, "Economic Analysis of the Tennessee Valley Authority Power Yardstick."

19. *Report,* "Minority Views," 263–77, 351–57.

20. Lilienthal, *Journals* 1:101–3.

21. Barnes, *Willkie,* 142. Dillon, *Wendell Willkie,* 87. McCraw, *TVA and the Power Fight,* 128–31. DEL: UJ, Mar. 27, 1936.

22. William E. Leuchtenburg's account in *Franklin D. Roosevelt and the New Deal,* especially the chapter entitled "A Sea of Troubles" (231–51), details this crisis in dramatic fashion. Barnard, *Wendell Willkie,* 122. Dillon, *Wendell Willkie,* 87. "Truce in Power Field Aided by Negotiations," *New York Times,* May 15, 1938,

editorial sec., 1. TVA: Lilienthal to Morehouse, Feb. 22, 1939. Lilienthal, *Journals* 7:778.

23. Barnard, *Wendell Willkie,* 121–22. McCraw, *TVA and the Power Fight,* 136. Lilienthal, *Journals* 1:85. Helen Lilienthal, *Family Chronicle,* 195. Whitman, *David Lilienthal,* 70.

24. Barnard, *Wendell Willkie,* 122. T.R.B, *New Republic,* Feb. 22, 1939, 72. Lilienthal, *Journals* 1:88.

25. Lilienthal, *Journals* 1:92–98.

26. Roosevelt quotation in Lilienthal, *Journals* 1:109–16. Barnard, *Wendell Willkie,* 123. Lief, *Democracy's Norris,* 522. McCraw, *TVA and the Power Fight,* 137.

27. Lilienthal, *Journals* 1:109–16. Lowitt, *George W. Norris,* 278–82. Barnard, *Wendell Willkie,* 123.

28. Lilienthal, *Journals* 1:119–21. Barnard, *Wendell Willkie,* 123–24. Dillon, *Wendell Willkie,* 88–89. "Utilities: Appomattox Court House," *Time,* Aug. 28, 1939, 53–54.

29. McCraw, *TVA and the Power Fight,* 64. Willkie quotation on Lilienthal in Barnard, *Wendell Willkie,* 140. Barnes, *Willkie,* 142–43.

30. Biddle, *In Brief Authority,* 69. Barnes, *Willkie,* 69, 142–43. MVC: Crawford interview with Joseph Swidler, Oct. 29, 1969, 20. Richberg quotation in Lilienthal, *Journals* 1:175, 190. Jonathan Daniels, "A Native at Large," *The Nation,* Aug. 24, 1940, 155. First Willkie quotation in Owen, *The Tennessee Valley Authority,* 242. Wendell L. Willkie, "Political Power," *Atlantic Monthly,* Aug. 1937, 212.

31. Willkie and Lilienthal quotations in Barnard, *Wendell Willkie,* 90–91, 124. Barnes, *Willkie,* 75. Helen Lilienthal, *Family Chronicle,* 195. Lilienthal, *Journals* 1:655. Lilienthal, *Journals* 7:777.

32. Biddle, *In Brief Authority,* 55. FDR: Roosevelt to Lilienthal, Mar. 22, 1939 (the letter from Roosevelt to Lilienthal has not been found—Lilienthal's daughter informed the author that Lilienthal had not had a stamp collection since he was a young boy), Lilienthal to Eleanor Roosevelt, Sept. 22, 1939. Lilienthal, *Journals* 1:151.

33. Bits and pieces about TVA's early administrative development are scattered throughout a number of sources including Talbert, *FDR's Utopian,* McCraw's two volumes, and Owen. The most thorough coverage is in Pritchett's chapter on "Administrative Organization," 147–84, and Richard O. Niehoff, "The Tennessee Valley Authority," in *Floyd W. Reeves,* 83–219. The Reeves quotations are taken from Niehoff, *Floyd W. Reeves,* 193–94. GRC: Clapp to Lilienthal, Mar. 10, 1938.

34. Pritchett, *The Tennessee Valley Authority,* 164.

35. Lilienthal, *Journals* 1:93, 605. Owen, *The Tennessee Valley Authority,* 260. McCraw, *TVA and the Power Fight,* 145. authored works by TVA personnel: see earlier endnotes for Niehoff, Owen, and Pritchett citations. Harry L. Case, *Personnel Policy in a Public Agency: The TVA Experience* (New York: Harper & Brothers, 1955); Gordon R. Clapp, *TVA: An Approach to the Development of a Region* (Chicago: Univ. of Chicago Press, 1955); Norman Wengert, *Valley of Tomorrow: The TVA and Agriculture* (Knoxville: Bureau of Public Administration, Univ. of Tennessee, 1952). MVC: Crawford interview with Joseph Swidler, Oct. 29, 1969, 24.

36. Lilienthal, *Journals* 1:49–50, DEL: Lilienthal to Frankfurter, June 10, 1935.

37. DEL: "The Labor Policies of the Tennessee Valley Authority," Detroit, Sept. 2, 1935; "Talk to TVA Employees," Chickamauga Dam, July 5, 1937; also see "Labor and the Tennessee Valley Authority," Tampa, Nov. 17, 1936. The

progressive label fits Lilienthal clearly in every respect except race relations. See discussion, next section.

38. Lilienthal, *Journals* 1:50, 66, 150. Erwin C. Hargrove, "David Lilienthal and the Tennessee Valley Authority," in Jameson W. Doig and Erwin C. Hargrove, *Leadership and Innovation: A Biographical Perspective on Entrepreneurs in Government* (Baltimore: Johns Hopkins Univ. Press, 1987), 58. MVC: Crawford interviews with Swidler, Dec. 8, 1969; Harry Case, Mar. 6, 1970; Roland Kampmeier, July 2, 1970. See other interviews with Louis Eckl, June 16, 1979; John Ferris, Dec. 7, 1970; George Gant, Dec. 28, 1971. Interview with Mr. and Mrs. John Oliver, Aug. 4, 1987 in Chattanooga, Tenn. Oxnam, *Personalities in Social Reform,* 99.

39. Pritchett, *The Tennessee Valley Authority,* 166–67.

40. MVC: Crawford interview with George Gant, Dec. 29, 1971, 3–4; with Joseph Swidler, Dec. 8, 1969, 15. interviews with Mr. and Mrs. John Oliver, Aug. 4, 1987, Chattanooga, Tenn., and Roland Kampmeier, Aug. 4, 1987, Chattanooga, Tenn. Lilienthal, *Journals* 1:537–42.

41. Both of Clapp's quotations are from Pritchett, *The Tennessee Valley Authority,* 166–67. Biddle, 63. Maverick quoted in Schlesinger, *Politics of Upheaval,* 375.

42. TVA Employee Series Oral History Interviews. Mark Winters interview with George Gant, Sept. 7, 1983, 6–7.

43. Little has been written about Gordon Clapp or Marguerite Owen. Clapp died suddenly in 1963 before having a chance to get his papers in order, except for a small collection at the Harry S. Truman Presidential Library in Independence, Mo. The only biographical piece of significance is an article by his former colleague at TVA, Harry L. Case, "Gordon R. Clapp: The Role of Faith, Purposes and People in Administration, *Public Administration Review,* June 1964. Even less has been written about the extraordinary Marguerite Owen, a pioneer woman federal employee. Many hoped her 1972 book on TVA would include significant autobiographical references and inside stories not previously published. True to her modesty and sense of professionalism, her book consisted of straightforward reporting with no "stories," and not one reference in the entire volume to herself. The insights about Clapp, with one exception, are taken from interviews. Lilienthal, *Journals* 1:360. Author's interview with Roland Kampmeier, Aug. 4, 1987, Chattanooga. MVC: Crawford interviews with Paul Ager, Apr. 15, 1970; Louise Allen, July 13, 1970; Harry Case, Mar. 6, 1970; Louis Eckl, June 16, 1979; George Gant, Dec. 28, 1971; Howard Menhinick, June 24, 1970; Richard O. Niehoff, Mar. 5, 1970.

44. MVC: Crawford interviews with Case, Mar. 6, 1970; Niehoff, Mar. 5, 1970; Swidler, Oct. 29, 1969; Lilienthal, Feb. 7, 1970. DEL: Lilienthal to Aneurin Owen, Mar. 21, 1944. Morgan, *The Making of TVA,* 29–30.

45. Interviews with Roland Kampmeier, Aug. 4, 1987 and Mr. and Mrs. John Oliver, Aug. 4, 1987, Chattanooga, Tenn. MVC: Crawford interviews with Case, Mar. 6, 1970; Niehoff, Mar. 5, 1970. Lilienthal, *Journals* 1:150, 208, 383–88, 411. DEL: correspondence between Owen and Lilienthal, Sept. 19 and 28, 1942.

46. For a comprehensive overview of TVA race relations, see *Investigation,* 1550–51, 2347–70, 2382–83, 3231–40. Houston quotations from 2350 and 2360; Clapp quotation from 3236.

47. *Investigation,* 2397. Schlesinger, *Politics of Upheaval,* 372–73, 432. Niehoff, *Floyd W. Reeves,* 199–200. Lilienthal, *Journals* 1:516, 614–15, 618.

48. Lilienthal, "Fact–finding Basis for Control of Public Utilities," *United States Daily,* Feb. 26, 1932, 1. DEL: Lilienthal, "Contest of the corn-feds," n.d., probably sometime in 1934; Lilienthal to Frankfurter, Aug. 7, 1934; Lilienthal, "Talk to TVA Employees," July 5, 1937. Gregory B. Field, "'Electricity for All':

The Electric Home and Farm Authority and the Politics of Mass Consumption, 1932–1935," *Business History Review,* Spring 1990, 58–59.

49. Rexford G. Tugwell and Edward C. Banfield, "Grass Roots Democracy—Myth or Reality?" *Public Administration Review,* Winter 1950, 49. Davidson, *The Tennessee,* 220–21, 255. Victor C. Hobday, *Sparks at the Grass Roots: Municipal Distribution of TVA Electricity in Tennessee* (Knoxville: Univ. of Tennessee Press, 1969).

50. Hofstadter, *The Age of Reform,* 315–18.

51. Schlesinger, *The Politics of Upheaval,* 386–97 (quotation on 393–94).

52. R. G. Tugwell and E. C. Banfield, "Grass Roots Democracy—Myth or Reality?" *Public Administration Review,* Winter 1950, 47–55. Lilienthal, *Journals* 2:120. FDR: Cooke to Lilienthal, Nov. 7. 1939; Jean Christie, *Morris Llewellyn Cooke: Progressive Engineer* (New York: Garland Publishers, 1983), 226.

Chapter 7. Crafting a Vision

1. Lilienthal, *Journals* 1:142. DEL: Lilienthal, "The TVA: An Experiment in the 'Grass Roots' Administration of Federal Functions," address to the Southern Political Science Association, Knoxville, Tenn., Nov. 10, 1939. UJ, Mar. 27, 1936. Lilienthal, *TVA: Democracy on the March* (New York: Harper and Brothers, 1944). See also *TVA: Democracy on the March,* "Twentieth Anniversary Edition," published in 1953 by Harper & Row.

2. Lilienthal to Arvin, reprinted in Lilienthal, *Journals* 1:79–82, 106, 114–15, 118. "TVA: The Second Phase," *New York Times Magazine,* Aug. 20, 1939, 2, 19.

3. Ickes, *The Secret Diary,* 3:25. Lilienthal, *Journals* 1:77–78, 126, 128. Arthur Goldschmidt, "The Curmudgeon: Harold Ickes," in Katie Louchheim, ed., *The Making of the New Deal: The Insiders Speak* (Cambridge: Harvard Univ. Press, 1983), 250. MVC: Crawford interview with Joe Swidler, Oct. 29, 1969, 7.

4. Ickes, *The Secret Diary,* 2:632, 660, 683, 690.

5. Lilienthal, *Journals* 1:125. FDR: Harcourt A. Morgan to Roosevelt, Sept. 23, 1939.

6. Lilienthal, *Journals* 1:126–28. Ickes, *The Secret Diary,* 3:25–26.

7. Lilienthal, *Journals* 1:125–26. TVA: Blandford to TVA Board, Oct. 10, 1939; Harcourt Morgan to Blandford, Oct. 11, 1939. FDR: Roosevelt to Harcourt Morgan, Via The Director of the Budget and Louis Brownlow, Oct. 3, 1939.

8. Lilienthal, *Journals* 1:136–38. Ickes, *The Secret Diary,* 3:45–46.

9. Lilienthal, *Journals* 1:231–32, 254. DEL: Lilienthal speeches, "The Decentralized Administration of Centralized Authority," Town Hall of Los Angeles, Nov. 25, 1940; "The TVA: A Step Toward Decentralization," Univ. of California, Berkeley, Nov. 29, 1940; "TVA and Regional Development," Reed College, Portland Oreg., Dec. 3, 1940.

10. Graham White and John Maze, *Harold Ickes of the New Deal: His Private Life and Public Career* (Cambridge: Harvard Univ. Press, 1985), 208. Ickes, *The Secret Diary,* 3:391–92, 399–400. Lilienthal, *Journals* 1:240–46.

11. FDR: Lilienthal to Watson with proposed draft of memorandum Roosevelt to Lilienthal, Dec. 20, 1940; Roosevelt to Watson, Dec. 23, 1940. Elliott Roosevelt, ed., *F.D.R.: His Personal Letters,* vol. 4 (New York: Duell, Sloan, and Pearce, 1947), Roosevelt to Lilienthal, Dec. 28, 1940, 1091. Lilienthal, *Journals* 1:254–55, 266–70. Ickes, *The Secret Diary,* 3:416.

12. White and Maze, *Harold Ickes,* 211–12. Lilienthal, *Journals* 1:313, 315, 339–42, 360–63, 365–67. Ickes, *The Secret Diary,* 3:585–87. Lowitt, *George W. Norris,*

274. Bureau of Demobilization, Civilian Production Administration, *Industrial Mobilization for War: History of the War Production Board and Predecessor Agencies, 1940–1945, Program and Administration*, vol. 1 (Washington D.C.: U.S. Government Printing Office, 1947), 107. TVA: Baruch to Lilienthal, undated, probably sometime in May or June 1941; two letters, Lilienthal to Baruch, May 22, and June 23, 1941. FDR: Ickes to Roosevelt, June 11, 1941, Lilienthal to Berle, June 24, 1941.

13. Lilienthal, *Journals* 1:375. White and Maze, *Harold Ickes,* 211–12. FDR: Ickes to Roosevelt, Jan. 14, 1943. DEL: Lilienthal, "MVA and TVA," transcript of a radio talk on Station KSD in St. Louis, Dec. 11, 1944. David E. Lilienthal, "Shall We Have More TVA's?" *New York Times Magazine,* Jan. 7, 1945, 10–11, 40–42. Daniels, *White House Witness,* 256.

14. Goldschmidt, "The Curmudgeon," 251. Lowitt, *George W. Norris,* 400–401. Lilienthal, *Journals* 1:150.

15. Lilienthal, *Journals* 1:141–42, 155; DEL: Cooke to Lilienthal, Nov. 7, 1939; Chase to Lilienthal, Dec. 21, 1939; White to Lilienthal, Jan. 3, 1940; Ascoli to Lilienthal, Jan. 5, 1940; Lerner to Lilienthal, Jan. 17, 1940; Berle to Lilienthal, Jan. 20, 1940; note to Lilienthal from an unidentified source advising him that the Knoxville postmaster had ruled that sending 130 copies of the grass roots speech using the TVA frank was appropriate.

16. Lilienthal, "The TVA: An Experiment," 3–4, 9, 12, 13, 22, 29.

17. Lilienthal, *Journals* 1:159, 446. DEL: Lilienthal to Eleanor Roosevelt, Mar. 26, 1941; Lilienthal to Frankfurter, July 21, 1942; exchange between Lilienthal and Eric Fromm, Jan. 5 and 14, 1943.

18. Lilienthal, "Management—Responsible or Dominant?" *Public Administration Review,* 1941, 390–92. Marquis W. Childs, . . . *I Write from Washington* (New York: Harper & Brothers, 1942), 62–63.

19. Lilienthal, *Journals* 1:472–73.

20. Lowitt, *George W. Norris,* 285. Lilienthal, *Journals* 1:345–47; 462–66, 482, 592. DEL: "Politics and the Management of the Public's Business," address before the Knoxville Kiwanis Club, Knoxville, Tenn., July 9, 1942.

21. Lilienthal, *Journals* 1:371–73, 470–71, 528–31 (Wilson quotation on 471).

22. Lilienthal, *Journals* 1:435, 492–93, 554–55, 578–79, 599. Daniels, *White House Witness,* 88–89. FDR: Lilienthal to Roosevelt, Nov. 26, 1942. TVA: Lilienthal to Bryson, Jan. 25, 1943; WN: Lilienthal to Nichols, Jan. 26, 1943.

23. Lilienthal, *Journals* 1:311, 407, 559, 577, 595, 605–6, 609–10, 612–14. WN: correspondence between Lilienthal and Nichols, Jan. 26, Mar. 8 and 10, 1943.

24. Daniels, *White House Witness,* 200–201. Lilienthal, *Journals* 1:627–29, 640, 672. TVA: correspondence between Lilienthal and Oxnam, Jan. 6, and Jan. 17, 1944. FDR: correspondence between Lilienthal and Wallace, Jan. 10, and Apr. 10, 1944, Lilienthal to Roosevelt, Mar. 15, 1944. FF: Lilienthal to Frankfurter, Dec. 22, 1943. The author conducted a thorough review of 1944 *Publishers Weekly's* best-seller lists. Information about foreign editions was gathered from an examination of copies of translations in the DEL papers and from a OCLC library search. In addition to the 1945 translations, *Democracy on the March* was published in three Spanish editions in 1946 and 1956 (Mexico), and 1967 (Argentina); another Chinese edition in 1954 (Singapore); a second German edition in 1950; Italian in 1946; Japanese in 1949; Oriya in 1953 (India); Arabic in 1953 (Cairo); and Portuguese in 1956 (Brazil). There may be others, but these are the only ones the author has been able to authenticate. Whitman claims that by 1948, twenty translations had been carried out, see *David Lilienthal,* 96. The United States Information Agency (USIA) sponsored the 1956 Portuguese and Spanish editions. They may have sponsored others, but USIA archives are

incomplete; GN. correspondence between Lilienthal and Norris, June 20, 23, and 26, July 18 and 27, 1944.

25. Lilienthal, *Journals* 1:637, 643, 669–70. FDR: correspondence between Lilienthal and Roosevelt, Sept. 1 and 9, 1944; Lilienthal to Hassett, Dec. 22, 1944; Early to Lilienthal, Dec. 28, 1944; Field to Roosevelt, Jan. 2, 1945 (telegram); Patton to Roosevelt, Jan. 3, 1945; Early to Patton, Jan. 12, 1945. Lilienthal, *TVA: Democracy on the March* (New York: Pocket Books, 1945).

26. Pare Lorentz, dir., *The Plow That Broke the Plains,* U.S. Dept. of Agriculture (Farm Security Administration), 1936. Pare Lorentz, dir., *The River,* U.S. Dept. of Agriculture (Farm Security Administration), 1937. Virgil Thomson, music from the films *The Plow that Broke the Plains* and *The River,* compact disc (Los Angeles: EMI/Angel Records, 1986). Wendell Willkie, *One World* (New York: Simon & Schuster, 1943).

27. Lilienthal, *TVA: Democracy on the March,* 2, 3, 179, 207, 225.

28. Lilienthal, *TVA: Democracy on the March,* 1–2, 58, 217.

29. Lilienthal, *TVA: Democracy on the March,* xii–xiii. Erwin C. Hargrove, "Introduction," in Erwin C. Hargrove and Paul K. Conkin, eds., *TVA: Fifty Years of Grass-Roots Bureaucracy* (Urbana: Univ. of Illinois Press, 1983), xv. Dorothy F. Lucas, *Library Journal,* Feb. 15, 1944, 159. Goldman, *Rendezvous with Destiny,* 304–8.

30. Lilienthal, *TVA: Democracy on the March,* 17, 76–79, 106, 146, 189–90. Chapters 6–8 (46–75) offer an extensive explanation of the concepts of unity, both unified development and unified purpose, within the organization.

31. Lilienthal, *TVA: Democracy on the March,* xii, 2, 207–16, 217.

32. Henry A. Wallace, "The Way to Abundance," *New Republic,* Mar. 27, 1944, 414, 416. D. F. Fleming, "The History of the Tennessee Valley Authority," *New York Times Book Review,* Apr. 9, 1944, 4. "Song of the Valley," *Commonweal,* Apr. 14, 1944, 655–56. Jonathan Daniels, "Power for the Making of Tomorrow," *Saturday Review of Literature,* Apr. 15, 1949, 25. Paul Hutchinson, "Democracy Still Works," *Christian Century,* May 3, 1944, 559. V.T.B., "Regional Development," *Engineering News-Record,* June 15, 1944, 111–12. Charles S. Ascher, *American Political Science Review,* July 1944, 561–63. Katherine Jocher, *American Sociological Review,* v. 10, 1945, 99–100. Other reviews read but not cited include Carl F. Reuss, *Rural Sociology,* v. 9, 1944, 297. Harlan Trott, *Annals of the American Academy of Political and Social Science,* Sept. 1944, 156–57. Paul W. Wager, *Social Forces,* May 1945, 462–64.

33. Davidson, *The Tennessee,* vol. 2. Philip Selznick, *TVA and the Grass Roots: A Study in the Sociology of Formal Organization* (Berkeley: Univ. of California Press, 1949). R. G. Tugwell and E. C. Banfield, "Grass Roots Democracy—Myth or Reality?" *Public Administration Review,* Winter 1950, 47–55. Richard Lowitt, "The TVA, 1933–45," in Hargrove and Conkin, *TVA,* 57–58.

34. Davidson, *The Tennessee* 2:252, 255–59, 326–27, 333. Edward Shapiro, "The Southern Agrarians and the Tennessee Valley Authority," *American Quarterly,* Winter 1970, 802–5; William C. Havard Jr., "Images of TVA: The Clash over Values," in Hargrove and Conkin, *TVA,* 297–315.

35. Selznick, *TVA and the Grass Roots,* 4, 63, 113, 220, 262–63, 326–27. Chapters 4 and 5 offer a comprehensive critique of the agriculture programs and institutional relationships.

36. Tugwell and Banfield, "Grass Roots Democracy," 53–55.

37. Lilienthal, *Journals* 1:330–31, 469–70, 600.

38. Selznick, *TVA and the Grass Roots,* 47ff. Lowitt, "The TVA," 56–57.

39. Lilienthal, *Journals* 1:526, 574.

40. Lilienthal, *TVA: Democracy on the March,* 12, 77. Lilienthal, *Journals* 1:542, 684. Selznick, *TVA and the Grass Roots,* 220.
41. McCraw, *TVA and the Power Fight,* 144. Wallace Sayre, [book review of Selznick's *TVA and the Grass Roots*] *American Political Science Review,* Oct. 1949, 1032. Gilbert Banner, "Toward More Realistic Assumptions in Regional Economic Development," in John R. Moore, ed., *The Economic Impact of TVA* (Knoxville: Univ. of Tennessee Press, 1967), 125. Norman I. Wengert, "The Politics of Water Resource Development as Exemplified by TVA," in Moore, *Economic Impact of TVA,* 58–63. See also Wengert, "TVA—Symbol and Reality," *Journal of Politics,* May 1951, 369–92, and *Valley of Tomorrow: The TVA and Agriculture* (Knoxville: Bureau of Public Administration, Univ. of Tennessee, 1952), 1–19. Schlesinger, *Politics of Upheaval,* 371–73.
42. Wengert in Moore, *Economic Impact of TVA,* 70.
43. Lilienthal, *Journals* 1:605. Lilienthal, *TVA: Democracy on the March,* xii. Lilienthal was successful in convincing Knopf to publish the photographic journal, R. L. Duffus, text, *The Valley and Its People: A Portrait of TVA* (New York: Alfred A. Knopf, 1944).
44. Lilienthal, *Journals* 1:551–52, 651. Mark Twain and Charles Dudley Warner, *The Gilded Age: A Tale of Today* (New York: New American Library, 1969), 23.
45. In an interview in New York City on July 23, 1886, John Burnett, a former vice-president of Lilienthal's Development and Resources Corporation (see chapters 12–13) told the author that he had read *TVA: Democracy on the March* while in combat on Guadalcanal.
46. The best compilation of critical essays was Hargrove and Conkin's 1983 edited volume, *TVA: Fifty Years of Grass-Roots Bureaucracy.* Even in this book, however, one can sense a great sense of respect for the fifty-year-old institution. See also Steven M. Neuse, "TVA at Age Fifty—Reflections and Retrospect," *Public Administration Review,* Nov./Dec. 1983, 491–99, and William U. Chandler, *The Myth of TVA: Conservation and Development in the Tennessee Valley, 1933–1983* (Cambridge, Mass.: Ballinger Publishing Company, 1984), 53, 56.
47. Roscoe C. Martin, *TVA and International Technical Assistance* (Syracuse: TVA Consultant Report, 1970), 62.

Chapter 8. TVA: Wartime Administration and Expansion

1. Lilienthal, *Journals* 1:122, 181–83 (Nashville man's quotation on 182).
2. Lilienthal, *Journals* 1:448–49 (Chicago friend's quotation on 448), 576, 625–26 (Winchell quotation on 626).
3. Don McBride, *TVA and National Defense* (Knoxville: TVA, 1975), chap. 3, pp. 15, 27. R. L. Duffus, "Our River of Power Flowing to War," *New York Times Magazine,* Mar. 28, 1943, 23.
4. Lilienthal, *Journals* 1:159, 164, 219, 381. DEL: Lilienthal to Frankfurter, Sept. 17, 1941.
5. The history of war preparedness activities is documented in a number of works, including Bureau of the Budget, *The United States at War: Development and Administration of the War Program by the Federal Government* (Washington, D.C.: GPO, 1946), 5–103. Bureau of Demobilization, Civilian production Administration, *Industrial Mobilization for War: History of the War Production Board and Predecessor Agencies, 1940–1945, Program and Administration,* 1 (Washington, D.C.: U.S. Government Printing Office, 1947), 3–200. Luther

Gulick, *Administrative Reflections from World War II* (University, Ala.: University of Alabama Press, 1948), 1–73. J. Donald Kingsley, "Top-Level Coordination of Wartime Programs," in *What We Learned in Public Administration During the War* (Washington, D.C.: Graduate School, U.S. Dept. of Agriculture, 1949), 1–16. Bruce Catton, *The War Lords of Washington* (New York: Harcourt, Brace and Company, 1948), 1–66.

6. The quotation in this paragraph is an anonymous penciled marginal note in the TVA copy of McBride, *TVA and National Defense,* chap. 1, p. 24. Needless to say, it is an appropriate observation.

7. McBride, *TVA and National Defense,* chap. 1, pp. 17–19, 21–22; chap. 3, pp. 2–3. Quotations from this source.

8. McBride, *TVA and National Defense,* chap. 2, p. 31; chap. 1, p. 24.

9. McBride, *TVA and National Defense,* chap. 3, p. 6. Charles C. Carr, *Alcoa: An American Enterprise* (New York: Rinehart & Company, 1952), 94. George D. Smith, *From Monopoly to Competition: The Transformation of Alcoa, 1888–1986* (Cambridge: Cambridge Univ. Press, 1988), 216. Lilienthal, *Journals* 1:314, 357, 395, 411.

10. Lilienthal, *Journals* 1:165–69. Bureau of Demobilization, 110.

11. Lilienthal, *Journals* 1:174–78. Bureau of Demobilization, 7. Bureau of the Budget, 22.

12. McBride, *TVA and National Defense,* chap. 8, p. 9. Owen, *The Tennessee Valley Authority,* 83. Lilienthal, *Journals* 1:189–93.

13. McBride, *TVA and National Defense,* chap. 3, pp. 10–12. Lilienthal, *Journals* 1:333.

14. DEL: "Speeches by David E. Lilienthal, 1933—2/15/50"; "National Defense: The Role of the Southeast and the TVA," address by David E. Lilienthal in Nashville, June 20, 1940 and over the Columbia Broadcasting System.

15. DEL: "Let Us Celebrate America," speech by David Lilienthal at the University of Oregon, Dec. 2, 1940; "Speeches by David E. Lilienthal, 1933– 2/15/50.

16. DEL: "Analysis of Travel—1941."

17. Lowitt, *George W. Norris: The Triumph of a Progressive,* 116. Pritchett, *The Tennessee Valley Authority,* 75.

18. Pritchett, *The Tennessee Valley Authority,* 76, 189. McBride, *TVA and National Defense,* chap. 3, p. 11. Lilienthal, *Journals* 1:282, 314, 316–17.

19. Smith, *From Monopoly to Competition,* 217. Lilienthal, *Journals* 1:350–52.

20. Lilienthal, *Journals* 1:352–53. Carr, *Alcoa,* 97–98. McBride, *TVA and National Defense,* chap. 3, p. 16. Owen, *The Tennessee Valley Authority,* 263. Pritchett, *The Tennessee Valley Authority,* 39–40.

21. Smith, *From Monopoly to Competition,* 215–17. Carr, *Alcoa,* 201–36, 255. Lilienthal, *Journals* 1:305, 308, 323, 334, 503.

22. MCK: McKellar to Lilienthal, July 8, 1933, and Sept. 20, 1933; Lilienthal to McKellar, Sept. 25, 1933; McKellar to Roosevelt and McKellar to Lilienthal, both Apr. 23, 1934; Lilienthal to McKellar, Jan. 7, 1937; correspondence between McKellar and J. W. Cooper, Jan. 15 and 16, Dec. 21, 23, and 24, 1937. Notations in the journal would normally signal significant relationships, positive and negative, between Lilienthal and others. Since the first reference to McKellar in the volume 1 index is to an October 1941 entry, one can probably assume that until that time the senator was little or no bother to Lilienthal.

23. Pritchett, *The Tennessee Valley Authority,* 129, McKellar quotation on 283; DEL: "Our Idol Stung," *Johnson City Chronicle,* Oct. 7, 1933. MCK: correspondence between McKellar and Milton, June 29, July 2 and 3, 1935.

24. MCK: McKellar, "The True Story of the Origin and Development of the Tennessee Valley Authority," n.d. (from text one can determine that it was written

sometime after Eisenhower's election in 1956 and McKellar's death in 1957), mimeographed manuscript written in the first person.

25. Lilienthal, *Journals* 1:444. FDR: McKellar to Roosevelt, Feb. 8, 1943. Allen Drury, *A Senate Journal, 1943–1945* (New York: Da Capo Press, 1972), 114. MCK: J. W. Cooper to McKellar, Jan. 15, 1937.

26. McBride, *TVA and National Defense,* chap. 3, pp. 13–14. Norris quoted in Lowitt, *George W. Norris,* 395. TVA: correspondence between Lilienthal and McKellar, Sept. 30, and Oct. 2, 3, and 7, 1941. Lilienthal, *Journals* 1:384–85.

27. McBride, *TVA and National Defense,* chap. 3, pp. 14–16. Owen, *The Tennessee Valley Authority,* 87–88, 91. Lilienthal, *Journals* 1:392–93, 396–97, 402, 415, 438, 458.

28. Owen, *The Tennessee Valley Authority,* 88–89. Pritchett, *The Tennessee Valley Authority,* 236, 264. Lilienthal, *Journals* 1:453, 487. Norris quotation in Lowitt, *George W. Norris,* 396–97.

29. Lilienthal, *Journals* 1:458, 482, 485. DEL: Lilienthal, "Remarks of David E. Lilienthal," Chattanooga Rotary Club, May 21, 1942.

30. Lilienthal, *Journals* 1:607–9, 626–40 (McKellar quotation on 627). Drury, *A Senate Journal,* 116–17.

31. Herbert Corey, "The Federals are Coming," *Public Utilities Fortnightly,* June 4, 1942, 729, 734.

32. Owen, *The Tennessee Valley Authority,* 84, 262–63. McBride, *TVA and National Defense,* chap. 2, pp. 20, 7. Lilienthal, *Journals* 1:556–57.

33. DEL: Lilienthal, "The Press Goes to War," speech to the North Carolina Press Association, Asheville, N.C., July 24, 1942; Lilienthal, "To Men Who Get Things Done," remarks to mass meeting of Douglas Dam workers, Oct. 6, 1942.

34. Duffus, "Our River of Power," 7–8, 23. Duffus, "A Giant Goes to War," *New York Times,* July 27, 1941, 8, 19.

35. Lilienthal, *Journals* 1:540, 549, 557. McBride, *TVA and National Defense,* chap. 4, pp. 1–15. TVA: Lilienthal to Patterson, June 28, 1943.

36. DEL: "Speeches by David E. Lilienthal," 1933–2/15/50. McBride, *TVA and National Defense,* chap. 3, p. 18. Lilienthal, *Journals* 1:610, 627.

37. DEL: Lilienthal, "The Grand Job of Our Century," commencement address at College of the City of New York, June 17, 1944.

38. Lilienthal, *Journals* 1:635–36, 654–65, 668–69. DEL: Lilienthal, "MVA and TVA," transcription of radio talk over KSD in St. Louis, Dec. 11, 1944. Lilienthal, "Shall We Have More TVA's?" *New York Times Magazine,* Jan. 7, 1945, 10–11, 40–42. Roosevelt, "Message to the Congress on the Missouri River Development Plan," Sept. 21, 1944, in Samuel I. Rosenman, ed., *The Public Papers and Addresses of Franklin D. Roosevelt,* 13 vols. (New York: Random House, 1950), 13: 274–78. Roosevelt's September message was a less-than-rousing endorsement of the MVA concept. As much as anything, it was a politically expedient response to a resolution by eight of the nine Missouri Valley governors urging a unified development plan instead of conflicting piecemeal projects proposed by the U.S. Army Corps of Engineers and the Bureau of Land Reclamation. In any case Lilienthal probably realized that Roosevelt's concern with ending the war and planning for peace would leave little time for aggressively pushing a project he had endorsed in the past (see the extensive note following his message, this citation).

39. Lilienthal, *Journals* 1:563, 567–69, 572, 574–75. Lowitt, *George W. Norris,* 434–40. GN: Lilienthal to Roosevelt; Lilienthal to Norris; Lilienthal, "Memorandum Re Senator Norris"; all dated Dec. 22, 1942.

40. Lilienthal, *Journals* 1:589, 613, 678–81.

41. James F. Byrnes, *All In One Lifetime* (New York: Harper & Row, 1958), 241–42.

Daniels, *White House Witness,* 264–65. Jonathan Daniels, *The Man of Independence* (Philadelphia: J. B. Lippincott, 1950), 291–92. Jordan Schwarz, *The Speculator: Bernard M. Baruch in Washington, 1917–1965* (Chapel Hill: Univ. of North Carolina Press, 1981), 457–58. Schwarz wrote that Daniels and Sam Rosenman wanted Lilienthal to head the SPB, but that Baruch had pushed Assistant Secretary of Commerce Will Clayton. Lilienthal, *Journals* 1:602, 631, 659–66.

42. Daniels, *White House Witness,* 258–59, 264. FDR: correspondence between Kefauver and Roosevelt, Feb. 6, and Mar. 2, 1945. Lilienthal, *Journals* 1:662–63 (Roosevelt quotation on 663), 682, 688.

43. HST: McKellar to Truman, Apr. 26, and Stewart to Truman, Apr. 30, 1945. Lilienthal, *Journals* 1:690–95, 697–701 (first Truman quotation on 698), 705–6. Second Truman quotation in Daniels, *White House Witness,* 286–87.

44. Lilienthal, *Journals* 1:703–5; Barrett C. Shelton, "Lilienthal and the Valley," *The Nation,* May 12, 1945, 544–55. "Mr. Lilienthal Should be Appointed," *Christian Century,* May 9, 1945, 573; and "People in the Limelight: David Lilienthal," *New Republic,* May 14, 1945, 662. "TVA's Triumph, *Time,* May 28, 1945, 12.

45. McBride, *TVA and National Defense,* chap. 4, p. 16.

Chapter 9. The Atomic Trust: Bright Fires, Bright Hopes

1. Lilienthal, *Journals* 1:549. Lilienthal, *Journals* 2:1–2.

2. Lilienthal, "The Moral Responsibility of Research," speech delivered at the Conference on Research and Regional Welfare at the University of North Carolina, Chapel Hill, May 11, 1945. Quotations are from portions of this speech in "Research Has a Moral Responsibility," *Christian Century,* July 4, 1945, 786–87.

3. "Machines and the Human Spirit," commencement address at Radcliffe College, June 27, 1945. Quotations from Whitman, *David Lilienthal,* 110–11. Lilienthal, *Journals* 2:2.

4. Lilienthal, *Journals* 2:637–45. P. M. S. Blackett, *Fear, War, and the Bomb: Military and Political Consequences of Atomic Energy* (New York: Whittlesey House, 1949), 114–15.

5. DEL: "Lilienthal-President Correspondence, 1946–1933." Lilienthal, *Journals* 2:2–12, 22. Dean Acheson, *Present at the Creation* (New York: W. W. Norton, 1969), 151–52. Richard G. Hewlett and Oscar E. Anderson Jr., *A History of the United States Atomic Energy Commission: The New World, 1939/1946* (University Park: Pennsylvania State Univ. Press, 1962): 531–34. Joseph I. Lieberman, *The Scorpion and the Tarantula: The Struggle to Control Atomic Weapons* (Boston: Houghton Mifflin Co., 1970), 235–38. Hewlett and Anderson and Lieberman present thorough narratives of the evolution of the Acheson-Lilienthal Report, from its genesis through the conflict with Bernard Baruch over U.S. international policy. For a good account of the conflict between the Acheson-Lilienthal perspective and Baruch's plan for the international control of atomic energy, see Schwarz, *The Speculator,* 490–507. Since the rest of this section relies heavily on these three sources, subsequent notes will only acknowledge direct quotations from them. Hewlett and Anderson cover the Acheson-Lilienthal report development on pages 531–54 and the history of the Baruch Plan on pages 554–79. Lieberman's coverage of Acheson-Lilienthal is on pages 235–59, and of Baruch on pages 260–300. Schwarz's consideration of the Baruch Plan is on 490–507.

6. Lilienthal, *Journals* 2:11–12, 14.

7. Lilienthal, *Journals* 2:13–15. Lieberman, *The Scorpion and the Tarantula*, 240. Norman Cousins and Thomas K. Finletter, "A Beginning for Sanity: A Review of the Acheson-Lilienthal Report," *Bulletin of the Atomic Scientists*, July 1, 1946, 11.

8. Lilienthal, *Journals* 2:34–35. U.S. Congress, Senate Section of the Joint Committee on Atomic Energy, *Confirmation of the Atomic Energy Commission and the General Manager* (Washington, D.C.: GPO, 1947), 1947, 422, 432, 566, 594 (hereafter cited as *Confirmation*).

9. Lilienthal, *Journals* 2:13, 16. Quotation from Peter Michelmore, *The Swift Years: The Robert Oppenheimer Story* (New York: Dodd Mead & Co., 1969), 126. James W. Kunetka, *Oppenheimer: The Years of Risk* (Englewood Cliffs, N.J.: Prentice-Hall, 1982), 101–2.

10. Kunetka, *Oppenheimer*, 106. Michelmore, *The Swift Years*, 126. Philip M. Stern, *The Oppenheimer Case: Security on Trial* (New York: Harper & Row, 1969), 89.

11. Lieberman, *The Scorpion and the Tarantula*, 242.

12. Lilienthal, *Journals* 2:19–20, 23–24. Hewlett and Anderson, *History of the United States AEC, 1939/1946*, 539. Kunetka, *Oppenheimer*, 103–4.

13. Lilienthal, *Journals* 2:26.

14. Lilienthal quoted in Hewlett and Anderson, *History of the United States AEC, 1939/1946*, 540.

15. Lilienthal, *Journals* 2:27–29. Acheson, *Present at the Creation*, 152. Kunetka, *Oppenheimer*, 105.

16. Acheson quoted in Lieberman, *The Scorpion and the Tarantula*, 255–56.

17. Lilienthal, *Journals* 2:27–29. Kunetka, *Oppenheimer*, 105.

18. Lilienthal, *Journals* 2:29–30. Kunetka, *Oppenheimer*, 106. Acheson, *Present at the Creation*, 153. Acheson et al., *A Report on the International Control of Atomic Energy* (Washington, D.C.: Dept. of State, 1946).

19. U.S. Dept. of State, Office of Public Affairs, Report No. 6; U.S. Dept. of State, Division of Public Liaison, *Analysis of Public Comments on Acheson Committee Report*. Three of the many journals and magazines with summaries and/or reviews of the report include "Atom-Control Program: Monopoly in an International Agency as Basis Proposed by U.S. Board for Discussion," *U.S. News*, Apr. 5, 1946, 67–72. "Report on International Control of Energy," *Power*, June 1946, 391–92, 420c, 421a. Norman Cousins and Thomas K. Finletter, "A Beginning for Sanity," *Saturday Review of Literature*, June 15, 1946, 5–9, 38–40.

20. "Atom-Control Program," 67.

21. Blackett, *Fear, War, and the Bomb*, 121.

22. Lilienthal, *Journals* 2:30.

23. Lilienthal, *Journals* 2:31–32, 39–40, 42–43. Truman quoted in Hewlett and Anderson, *History of the United States AEC, 1939/1946*, 558, and in Lieberman, *The Scorpion and the Tarantula*, 268.

24. Schwarz, *The Speculator*, 492.

25. Lilienthal, *Journals* 2:49–52.

26. Lilienthal, *Journals* 2:52–53. DEL: Oppenheimer to Lilienthal, May 24, 1946.

27. Lilienthal, *Journals* 2:59–60.

28. Lieberman, *The Scorpion and the Tarantula*, 309, 328. Hewlett and Anderson, *History of the United States AEC, 1939/1946*, 582–90. Lilienthal, *Journals* 2:69–71.

29. Paul Boyer, "'Some Sort of Peace': President Truman, the American People, and the Atomic Bomb," in Michael J. Lacey, ed., *The Truman Presidency* (New York: Cambridge Univ. Press, 1989), 196.

30. Lieberman, *The Scorpion and the Tarantula*, 409–11. Schwarz, *The Speculator,*

490–91. Blackett, *Fear, War, and the Bomb,* 120, 122–24. Hewlett and Anderson, *History of the United States AEC, 1939/1946,* 619. There was one erroneous technical point that the board, and especially Oppenheimer, regretted in their report, that of the feasibility of denaturing fissionable material in order to render it harmless for weapons use but still utile for other purposes. The Lilienthal-inspired concept crept into the report and assumed far more importance than it should have. Enrico Fermi, on reading about it, took Oppenheimer to task, telling him that "the denaturing story was grossly misleading and falsely reassuring to the lay public." Oppenheimer agreed and later corrected the over-optimistic possibilities of such a process. See Michelmore, *The Swift Years,* 128–29.

31. Lieberman, *The Scorpion and the Tarantula,* 409–11. Blackett, *Fear, War, and the Bomb,* 209.

32. Kennan is quoted in Lieberman, *The Scorpion and the Tarantula,* 306–7; also see 407. Lilienthal, *Journals* 2:26.

33. HST: Ayers Diary, Feb. 14, 1946. Lilienthal, *Journals* 2:19.

34. DEL: "Speeches by David E. Lilienthal, 1933—2/15/50." Lilienthal, *Journals* 2:77–80, 85–88. Rev. Thomas E. O'Connell, quoted from testimony given in support of David E. Lilienthal in *Confirmation,* Feb. 17, 1947, 443.

35. Lilienthal, "Science and Man's Fate," *The Nation,* July 13, 1946, 39–41. DEL: "Science and the Human Spirit," speech delivered to the General Council of the Congregational Christian Churches, Grinnell, Iowa, June 24, 1946. Lilienthal, "Science and Stewardship," *Land,* Winter 1946–47, 411–14.

36. Hewlett and Anderson, *History of the United States AEC, 1939/1946,* chap. 14, "The Legislative Battle," 482–530, and Appendixes 1 and 2, 714–24, provide the most comprehensive account of the act itself and the value of the assets transferred to the civilian commission. James R. Newman and Byron S. Miller, *The Control of Atomic Energy: A Study of Its Social, Economic, and Political Implications* (New York: Whittlesey House, 1948), 3–4.

37. Hewlett and Anderson, *History of the United States AEC, 1939/1946,* 530, 622. Harry S. Truman, *Memoirs of Harry S. Truman,* vol. 1 (Garden City, N.Y.: Doubleday, 1955), 296. Lilienthal, *Journals* 2:74–76.

38. HST: Hogness to Truman, June 17, 1946; Byron S. Miller to John R. Steelman, July 8, 1946; Wallace to Truman, July 16, 1946; Albert Cahn to Truman, July 24, 1946; Gore to Truman, July 29, 1946; Sabath to Truman, July 30, 1946; Bush to Truman, July 31, 1946. Hewlett and Anderson, *History of the United States AEC, 1939/1946,* 620–21. Lilienthal, *Journals* 2:73.

39. James B. Conant, *My Several Lives: Memoirs of a Social Inventor* (New York: Harper & Row, 1970), 493–94. HST: Truman to Bush, Aug. 2, 1946. Hewlett and Anderson, *History of the United States AEC, 1939/1946,* 621. Lilienthal, *Journals* 2:81–82.

40. Lilienthal, *Journals* 2:84–85, 89–90.

41. Lilienthal, *Journals* 2:90–92.

42. Lilienthal, *Journals* 2:93. CC: David E. Lilienthal to the President, Sept. 26, 1946. GRC: Confidential memorandum (draft) to the president from David E. Lilienthal. Probably written by Marguerite Owen.

43. Lilienthal, *Journals* 2:96–100. Hewlett and Anderson, *History of the United States AEC, 1939/1946,* 623. LS: Excerpts of a telephone conversation between Oppenheimer in California and Lilienthal in Knoxville on Oct. 26, 1946 (probably a tap on Lilienthal's or Oppenheimer's telephone).

44. Lilienthal, *Journals* 2:102. Hewlett and Anderson, *History of the United States AEC, 1939/1946,* 638.

45. Lilienthal, *Journals* 2:101–5.

46. Hewlett and Anderson, *History of the United States AEC, 1939/1946,* 623, 638,

641. Lilienthal, *Journals* 2:105–6. LS: handwritten note, Strauss to Lilienthal, Nov. 13, 1946; Strauss to Clifford, Dec. 2, 1946.

47. Lilienthal, *Journals* 2:105–10. Hewlett and Anderson, *History of the United States AEC, 1939/1946*, 641–42.

48. LS: Strauss to Clifford, Dec. 2, 1946. Lilienthal, *Journals* 2:120.

49. Hewlett and Anderson, *History of the United States AEC, 1939/1946*, 648, 650. Lilienthal, *Journals* 2:111, 115–16, 124–25.

50. Hewlett and Anderson, *History of the United States AEC, 1939/1946*, 642–44. Lilienthal, *Journals* 2:115, 119–20.

51. Hewlett and Anderson, *History of the United States AEC, 1939/1946*, 643, 649–50. Lilienthal, *Journals* 2:121–22. Richard G. Hewlett and Francis Duncan, *A History of the United States Atomic Energy Commission: Atomic Shield, 1947/1952* (University Park: Pennsylvania State Univ. Press, 1969), 666.

52. Hewlett and Anderson, *History of the United States AEC, 1939/1946*, 651–55. Lilienthal, *Journals* 2:127.

53. Lilienthal, *Journals* 2:115, 117–18, 124.

54. Lilienthal, *Journals* 2:126.

55. Harold L. Ickes, "Man to Man: Lilienthal attempt to Dominate Atomic Commission Seen Certain," *Evening Star* (Washington D.C.), Nov. 13, 1946, 11. "Harold Ickes: A Curmudgeon," *The Nation*, Nov. 23, 1946, 572. Lilienthal, *Journals* 2:111–12.

56. Lilienthal, *Journals* 2:123. HST: (Official File) James W. Farmer to His Excellency, the President of the United States, Dec. 8, 1946. Truman's Official File contains about five hundred letters to the president about Lilienthal's appointment. About 80 percent are positive. Many of the negative letters are anti-Semitic in tone or content. FBI: G. D. King to Director, FBI, Jan. 15, 1947; D. M. Ladd to the Director, Dec. 31, 1946; Walter Millis, ed., *The Forrestal Diaries* (New York: Viking Press, 1951), 240.

57. The critics included four former TVA employees, including Arthur E. Morgan, a Nashville businessman, and two women, one representing the Women's Patriotic Conference on National Defense, and the other, her own sad anti-Semitic biases. Pro-Lilienthal testimony came from ten Tennessee Valley businessmen, publishers, and heads of chambers of commerce, three members of his consultant board, Conant, Compton, Secretary of War Patterson, Baruch's top aide Hancock, and Baruch. Positive correspondence exclusively mentioning Lilienthal included a 153-signature petition from Yale University and New Haven, and one with the signatures of 334 Los Alamos scientists. *Confirmation*, 1–834, plus appendixes, 835–951. "An Analysis of Evidence in the Lilienthal Confirmation Hearings," *Washington Post*, Mar. 3, 47, 6–7. BH: Losalam to Hickenlooper, Feb. 25, 1947. HST: (Official Files). George H. Gallup, *The Gallup Poll, 1935–48*, v. 1 (New York: Random House, 1972): 505–6. Lilienthal 2 (1945): 133.

58. Lilienthal, *Journals* 2:134.

59. HST: draft of article from McNaughton to David Hulburd, Feb. 14, 1947.

60. During the hearings, a Hickenlooper staffer (name deleted by FBI censor) asked the bureau if Lilienthal's sister was married to an ex-Communist. A cryptic FBI memo a few days later reported that Lilienthal had no sister, and in the next sentence, "Information in Bureau files on [name deleted] fails to substantiate that he was ever married to Lilienthal's sister." Another time the bureau advised Hickenlooper to check local publications during Lilienthal's college days. Sure enough, by mid-February Hickenlooper's staff had accumulated copious material from old Greencastle newspapers and the DePauw yearbook. Committee files also included a document, "Notes on Lilienthal," prepared by the staff director of the Republican policy committee with sections on "mind and character," "adminis-

trative methods, "communists in government and "views on the role of government." FBI: Nichols to Tolson, Apr. 1, 1947; name deleted to Ladd, Apr. 5, 1947;
Hoover to SAC, Little Rock, Apr. 7, 1947; name deleted to Ladd, Apr. 11, 1947
(the April 5 memorandum established that there was no sister, but the bureau
persisted in trying to find out if she was married to an ex-Communist until April
11—a clear sign that thoroughness and stupidity are not mutually exclusive);
Nichols to Tolson, Feb. 14, 1947; Intra-agency Memoranda on Lilienthal; Edw.
A. Tamm to the Director, Feb. 12, 1947 and SAC; Boston to Director, FBI, Feb.
15, 1947; "DAVID ELI LILIENTHAL," and accompanying memoranda, D. M. Ladd to
the Director, Feb. 11 and 12, 1947; FBI memoranda regarding communications
with other U.S. senators, John Edgar Hoover to Mr. Tolson, Mr. Tamm, and Mr.
Ladd, Feb. 10, 1947; L. B. Nichols to Mr. Tolson, Feb. 25, 1947; Hoover to
Tolson, Tamm, Ladd, and Nichols, Hoover to Tolson, Tamm, and Ladd, both
Apr. 2, 1947. BH: various documents, some dated Feb. 19, 1947, and others, n.d.,
with information on Lilienthal prepared by staff for Senator Hickenlooper and
committee; Smith (Staff Director, Majority Policy Committee) to Hickenlooper,
memorandum accompanied by "Notes on Lilienthal," n.d. HST: Hoover to
Vaughan, Feb. 15, 17, and 25, Mar. 29, 1947.

61. HST: McNaughton to Hulburd, Feb. 14, 1947.
62. Lilienthal, *Journals* 2:133–34. *Confirmation, 7–25.* Whitman, *David Lilienthal,*
    152–53.
63. *Confirmation,* 31–34.; Lilienthal, *Journals* 2:134–35, 138. Hewlett and Duncan,
    History of the United States AEC, 1947/1952, 3–4.
64. *Confirmation,* 20–21, 80–98, 134–41.
65. Lilienthal, *Journals* 2:136, 141. Alfred Friendly, "Democracy Is a Belief in Man's
    Dignity, Lilienthal Explains to Senator McKellar," *Washington Post,* Feb. 5, 1947,
    1. *Confirmation,* 14, 122–30. Jeffrey Dean Brand, "David E. Lilienthal and 'This
    I Do Believe': An Axiological Analysis of Speaker and Audience" (M.A. thesis,
    Miami Univ., Oxford, Ohio, 1984). Brand's thesis is a wonderful analysis of the
    context and meaning of Lilienthal's influential address.
66. Friendly, "Democracy Is a Belief," 1. Carl Levin, "Lilienthal Turns Upon
    McKellar, Gives His Credo of Americanism," *New York Herald-Tribune,* Feb. 5,
    1947, 1. *Confirmation,* 130–32.
67. Friendly, "Democracy Is a Belief," 1. Anthony Leviero, "Lilienthal Rejects Red
    Aims in a Moving Credo at Hearing," *New York Times,* Feb. 5, 1947, 1.
    Whitman, *David Lilienthal,* 165. Hewlett and Duncan, *History of the United
    States AEC, 1947/1952,* 8. *Confirmation,* 132–44; Lilienthal, *Journals* 2:139,
    142–43.
68. Clark Clifford with Richard Holbrooke, *Counsel to the President: A Memoir*
    (New York: Random House, 1991), 131–36. Clifford did not acknowledge
    Lilienthal's remarks in his memoir.
69. Brand, "David E. Lilienthal," 50–53. Lilienthal, *Journals* 2:139. Harlan B.
    Phillips, ed., *Felix Frankfurter Reminisces, Recorded in Talks with Harlan B.
    Phillips* (New York: Reynal, 1960), 176. Bernard Baruch, *Baruch, The Public
    Years* (New York: Holt, Rinehart and Winston, 1960), 665–66
70. Lilienthal, *Journals* 2:140, 145–46, 148, 152–53, 156–57, 165–66.
71. Alfred Friendly, "False Testimony on Lilienthal Revealed," *Washington Post,* Feb.
    24, 1947, 1, 4. "An Analysis of Evidence in the Lilienthal Confirmation Hear-
    ings," *Washington Post,* Mar. 3, 1947, 6–7; *Confirmation,* 106–10, 114–19, 223–
    78, 324–66, 423–32, 438–40, 632–36.
72. See chapter 4 of this volume for a discussion of this issue; BH: typed report
    regarding Leitzel testimony and background on issue, n.d. *Confirmation,* 588–93,
    637–38, 783, 805–34. Lilienthal, *Journals* 2:148–49.

73. See chapter 4, note 91, for examples of correspondence between Lilienthal and his Chicago staff; Harry Booth's disaffection is implied by two items from Harold Ickes's papers in the Library of Congress Manuscript Division. One is a letter dated Aug. 17, 1947, from W. C. Clark to Ickes. Clark reports that Booth suggested that there was much more to the Leitzell affair than the committee had explored. The second was the draft of a letter (it is not known if the letter was ever sent) from Ickes to Booth regarding the publication of a letter from Booth critical of Lilienthal. The author has been unable to determine the roots of Booth's disaffection toward Lilienthal, other than the sometimes harsh treatment meted out by Lilienthal during the Chicago days.

74. "Bridges Asks Lilienthal Be Rejected," *Washington Post,* Feb. 10, 1947, 7B. Lilienthal, *Journals* 2:144–45. Hewlett and Duncan, *History of the United States AEC, 1947/1952,* 9–11. *Confirmation,* 691–92. Mary Spargo, "Vandenberg, Taft Heading for Split on Lilienthal," *Washington Post,* 1.

75. William J. Miller, *Henry Cabot Lodge* (New York: Heineman, 1967), 189. "By Their Words," *Time,* Mar. 3, 1947, 20–21. "Argument Over Mr. Lilienthal For Atomic Post: Views of Press," *U.S. News,* Feb. 28, 1947, 34. Gould Lincoln, "Lilienthal Approval Seen in Committee Vote Tomorrow," *Washington Star,* Mar. 10, 1947, 1A, 4A. BH: B. B. Hickenlooper, "Statement on Confirmation of Lilienthal," Mar. 10, 1947. Mary Spargo, "Lilienthal Is Endorsed 8 to 1 by Senate Atom Committee," *Washington Post,* Mar. 11, 1947, 1.

76. Lilienthal, *Journals* 2:157–58, 168. Hewlett and Duncan, *History of the United States AEC, 1947/1952,* 13–14, 48–52. William F. Flythe, "Charge Lilienthal Hiring Radicals," *New York Journal American,* Mar. 11, 1947, 2. BH: "Transcript of Senator John J. Bricker's Remarks During Press Conference Re Appointment of David Lilienthal to Atomic Energy Commission," Mar. 10, 1947, 2. "Majority in Senate To Vote for Lilienthal Senate Check Shows," *Washington Star,* Mar. 21, 1947, 1. "Senators Insist Marshall Be Atom Czar," *Washington Times-Herald,* Mar. 28, 1947, 1. Alfred Friendly, "Bricker Asks FBI Probe of Lilienthal," *Washington Post,* Mar. 29, 1947, 1, 7. William Moore, "Bridges Offers 4 Substitutes for Lilienthal," *Washington Times-Herald,* Apr. 2, 1947, 1.

77. "Lilienthal Gaining in Hot Debate," *PM Daily,* Apr. 1, 1947, 5. "Lilienthal Supporters Expect Confirmation Vote This Week," *Washington Post,* Apr. 1, 1947, 9. "Hint, How to Swing a Vote," *Time,* Apr. 14, 1947, 22. Hewlett and Duncan, *History of the United States AEC, 1947/1952,* 52–53.

78. Lilienthal, *Journals* 2:168–69. "Lilienthal's Wife and Daughter Called Pro-Red," *New York Journal-American,* Apr. 16, 1947, 3.

79. "The Atomic Adventure," *Collier's,* May 3, 1947, 12, 82–85. "Atomic Energy Is Your Business," *Collier's,* Jan. 1, 1948, 4–5, 50–55. DEL: "Speeches by David E. Lilienthal," 1933–2/15/50. DELAEC: "Tabulation of Official Travel of David E. Lilienthal, Chairman United States Atomic Energy Commission, Jan. 1947–June 30, 1949."

80. DEL: "Remarks of David E. Lilienthal, Chairman of Atomic Energy Commission, Before the American Society of Newspaper Editors," Washington, D.C., Apr. 19, 1947. Edward T. Folliard, "Lilienthal Speaks: Atom Study Is Lagging, Editors Hear," *Washington Post,* Apr. 20, 1947, 1.

81. DEL: Lilienthal speeches; "Remarks . . . Before the American Society of Newspaper Editors"; "Remarks Before Inland Daily Press Association," Chicago, May 26, 1947; "The People, The Atom and the Press," Albany, Jan. 19, 1948; "Democracy and the Atom," Chicago, Nov. 28, 1947; "Atomic Energy and the Engineer," Atlantic City, Dec. 2, 1947.

82. DEL: Lilienthal speeches, "Atomic Energy Is Your Business," Crawfordsville, Indiana, Sept. 22, 1947; "Atomic Energy and the Engineer." "Atomic Energy

'People's' Business, Says Lilienthal, Hitting Hush Idea," *New York Times,* Sept. 23, 1947, 1.

83. Lilienthal, *Journals* 2:170–71, 252–53, 269, 274, 287, 290;

84. Lilienthal, *Journals* 2: 189–90.

85. Lilienthal, *Journals* 2:190.

86. Lilienthal, *Journals* 2:190–91. Hewlett and Duncan, *History of the United States AEC, 1947/1952,* 89–90.

87. Lilienthal, *Journals* 2:175. Hewlett and Duncan, *History of the United States AEC, 1947/1952,* 57, 64–65, 129–30. An exchange of correspondence between Lilienthal and T. A. Solberg, Rear Admiral and Acting Chair of the Military Liaison Committee (MLC) on Apr. 15 and 20, 1947, exemplifies the touchy relationship. Solberg penned a fairly abrupt letter to Lilienthal demanding that the MLC be more closely involved in the commission's security matters including being "informed in writing of all individuals who are permitted continued access to 'Restricted Data' in spite of existing derogatory information and reasons therefor." Lilienthal's answer clarified the relationship and promised that most of Solberg's demands would be or were already being met. He made it clear, however, that he did not approve of the "slightly preemptory tone" of Solberg's memorandum (letters in DELAEC).

88. Lilienthal, *Journals* 2:175. Hewlett and Duncan, *History of the United States AEC, 1947/1952,* 64–65, 130–31.

89. Hewlett and Duncan, *History of the United States AEC, 1947/1952,* 94, 131–32. Lilienthal, *Journals* 2:203, 217–18—the entry on 203 is misdated. It is labeled as June 15, but the events recorded took place July 15. Millis, *Forrestal Diaries,* 290.

90. DELAEC: Lilienthal to Wilson, Jan. 20, 1948. Lilienthal, *Journals* 2:231, 236, 247, 249–51. Hewlett and Duncan, *History of the United States AEC, 1947/1952,* 136–37, 139.

91. Hewlett and Duncan, *History of the United States AEC, 1947/1952,* 151–52, 157–58. Lilienthal, *Journals* 2:303.

92. Lilienthal, *Journals* 2:204–5, 227–28. Hewlett and Duncan, *History of the United States AEC, 1947/1952,* 94–95. CC: Lilienthal, "Memorandum to the Joint Committee on Atomic Energy." July 21, 1947.

93. Lilienthal, *Journals* 2:248, 312, 322–23, 334. BH: Fred B. Rhodes, Memorandum for the Record, Oct. 22, 1947. Millis, *Forrestal Diaries,* 379. DELAEC: Lilienthal to Hickenlooper, July 11, 1947. Hewlett and Duncan, *History of the United States AEC, 1947/1952,* 325–26, 330–31.

94. Lilienthal, *Journals* 2:176, 267, 282. Hewlett and Duncan, *History of the United States AEC, 1947/1952,* 109, 283–84, 324. Millis, *Forrestal Diaries,* 319.

95. Lilienthal, *Journals* 2:208–9, 264. Hewlett and Duncan, *History of the United States AEC, 1947/1952,* 123–24. DELAEC: Lilienthal to Waller, July 29, 1947. HST: In Truman's Official File, there are scores of documents that track the attempts of administration officials to find jobs or contract opportunities for petitioners. One details the efforts of General Vaughan to facilitate contacts with the AEC on behalf of H. B. Deal of St. Louis. Deal first contacted Washington on May 23, 1947. Nearly a year later, after several intervention attempts, Deal still wondered "why he does not get some of these contracts."

96. Lilienthal, *Journals* 2:233, 274–75, 315–18. In each of three interviews in 1986, 1987, and 1988, Helen Lilienthal recalled that the Atomic Energy Commission days were the toughest of all for her and David, simply because he could not share his business with her.

97. DELAEC: Oppenheimer to Bacher, Aug. 6, 1947. Hewlett and Duncan, *History of the United States AEC, 1947/1952,* 78, 85–86, 97–98, 117, 125–26.

98. Hewlett and Duncan, *History of the United States AEC, 1947/1952,* 316.

Lilienthal, *Journals* 2:277. Interview with Joseph Volpe, July 28, 1987, Washington, D.C.

99. Lilienthal, *Journals* 2:229, 276; Hewlett and Duncan, *History of the United States AEC, 1947/1952,* 99–101.

Chapter 10. The Atomic Trust: Reality

1. Eric Goldman, *The Crucial Decade—and After: America, 1945–1960* (New York: Vintage Books, 1960), 37, 60, 67–69, 77, 97. Richard B. Morris, ed., *Encyclopedia of American History* (New York: Harper & Brothers, 1953), 391–92, 395–96. Robert A. Pollard, "The National Security State Reconsidered: Truman and Economic Containment, 1945–1950," 205; John Lewis Gaddis, "The Insecurities of Victory: The United States and the Perception of the Soviet Threat After World War II," 259; Charles S. Maier, "Alliance and Autonomy: European Identity and U.S. Foreign Policy Objectives in the Truman Years," 281; all in Michael J. Lacey, *The Truman Presidency.*
2. Morris, *Encyclopedia of American History,* 399. Goldman, *The Crucial Decade,* 100–101.
3. Lilienthal, *Journals* 2:354. Boyer, "Some Sort of Peace," in Lacey, *The Truman Presidency,* 186–89. "Lilienthal Names Industry Advisers," *New York Times,* Oct. 7, 1947, 28.
4. Hewlett and Duncan, *History of the United States AEC, 1947/1952,* 336–37. HD: General Advisory Committee, "Minutes of Tenth Meeting," June 3–5, 1948, Washington, D.C.
5. Hewlett and Duncan, *History of the United States AEC, 1947/1952,* 338. Lilienthal, *Journals* 2:354.
6. Interview with Joseph A. Volpe, July 28, 1987, Washington, D.C. Lilienthal, *Journals* 2:355. RO: Oppenheimer to Lilienthal, June 18, 1948. Hewlett and Duncan, *History of the United States AEC, 1947/1952,* 338.
7. Hewlett and Duncan, *History of the United States AEC, 1947/1952,* 338. Lilienthal, *Journals* 2:367–68.
8. HD: AEC, (General Manager's Report) "Organization of the Washington Headquarters and Field Operations Offices, and the Appointment of Certain Key Personnel," (report by the General Manager) Aug. 31, 1948; AEC, "Minutes: 194th Meeting," Sept. 17, 1948; General Advisory Committee, "Minutes: Eleventh Meeting," Oct. 21–23, 1948. Hewlett and Duncan, *History of the United States AEC, 1947/1952,* 339–40.
9. Hewlett and Duncan, *History of the United States AEC, 1947/1952,* 342–43. Lilienthal, *Journals* 2:343.
10. Lilienthal, *Journals* 2:343–44.
11. CC: AEC, "Press Release," June 1, 1948, Washington, D.C.: DELAEC: AFL, "Minutes of Atomic Energy Meeting," June 3, 1948. Lilienthal, *Journals* 2:353–54. Hewlett and Duncan, *History of the United States AEC, 1947/1952,* 344–45. "Atomic Workers Oppose Lilienthal Vote for Strike," *Washington Post,* June 9, 1948, 1.
12. HST: Lilienthal to Paul M. Herzog, Charles E. Wilson (two letters), and Wiliam B. Harrell, all Sept. 27, 1948; AEC, "AEC Actions Affecting Collective Bargaining," Information for the Press, No. 132, Sept. 29, 1948; letters between Lilienthal and Albert J. Fitzgerald, Oct. 6, 22, and 26, 1948; Lilienthal to Philip Murray, Oct. 6, 1948; Lilienthal to Charles E. Wilson, Nov. 1, 1948. Lilienthal,

Journals 2:411–13, 503. Hewlett and Duncan, *History of the United States AEC, 1947/1952,* 345–47.

13. Hewlett and Duncan, *History of the United States AEC, 1947/1952,* 159–61, 166–69. Lilienthal, *Journals* 2:373–75.
14. Truman quotation in Lilienthal, *Journals* 2:388–90.
15. Hewlett and Duncan, *History of the United States AEC, 1947/1952,* 169–70. Lilienthal, *Journals* 2:390–91.
16. Richard Pfau, *No Sacrifice Too Great: The Life of Lewis L. Strauss* (Charlottesville: Univ. Press of Virginia, 1984), 11–84, quotation on 76.
17. LS: Strauss to Clifford, Dec. 2, 1946. Lilienthal, *Journals* 2:106, 123, 142, 145, 358. Hewlett and Duncan, *History of the United States AEC, 1947/1952,* 9, 11. Pfau, *No Sacrifice Too Great,* 94.
18. Lilienthal, *Journals* 2:105. Pfau, *No Sacrifice Too Great,* 92, 95.
19. Hewlett and Duncan, *History of the United States AEC, 1947/1952,* 101, 109–10. Lilienthal, *Journals* 2:234–35, 383. Pfau, *No Sacrifice Too Great,* 100.
20. Pfau, *No Sacrifice Too Great,* 100–101. Lilienthal, *Journals* 2:238–40.
21. Lilienthal, *Journals* 2:383.
22. Lilienthal, *Journals* 2:385, 387. BH: Rhodes to Hickenlooper, July 22, 1948. LS: Strauss to Dewey, Aug. 10, 1948.
23. LS: Strauss to Lilienthal, Aug. 18, 1948; Lilienthal, "Human Relations and the Atom," speech at the Golden Jubilee Exposition, New York City, Aug. 21, 1948; Strauss to Volpe, Aug. 30, 1948.
24. LS: Lilienthal to Commissioners and Staff, Dec. 27, 1948.
25. Pfau, *No Sacrifice Too Great,* 94. LS: Strauss, Memoranda for file, Dec. 14, 1948; Feb. 21, Mar. 3 and 10, May 19 and 25, 1949.
26. LS: Strauss to James Marshall, June 16, 1949; Strauss to Truman, June 14, 1949.
27. DEL: UJ, Feb. 9, 1949. Lilienthal, *Journals* 2:445, 453, 463, 541. The portion of the sentence eliminated from the published journal is in brackets. Again, I assume that the "slippery playmate" is Strauss. "And especially I've vowed not to let [any] provocation [from my slippery Playmate at 1900 Constitution] induce me to hate, or malice, or a sense of revenge, or other such sentiments."
28. DELAEC: "Tabulation of Official Travel of David E. Lilienthal, Chairman United States Atomic Energy Commission, Jan. 1947–June 30, 1949." DEL: "Speeches by David E. Lilienthal," 1933–2/15/50; "Articles by David E. Lilienthal," 1924–2/15/50. Lilienthal, *Journals* 2:524. BH: Library of Congress, Legislative Reference Service, "David E. Lilienthal: Selected List of References to Articles Appearing in Periodicals Since His Appointment to Chairmanship of U.S. Atomic Energy Commission," Jan. 13, 1949; "List . . . Supplementary to the One Prepared on January 13, 1949," June 20, 1949. It is virtually impossible to determine how many of (and how many times) the speeches were reprinted in magazines
29. Lilienthal, "The Citizen as Public Servant," *Vital Speeches of the Day,* July 15, 1948, 578–81. Lilienthal, *Journals* 2:358, 364.
30. DEL: Address before the American Association for the Advancement of Science, Sept. 16, 1948. N. S. Haseltine, "Lilienthal Sees Atomic Science Hurt by Probes," *Washington Post,* Sept. 17, 1948, 1. "AEC Head Upholds Scientist's Charge," and "A-Scientist Asked to Prove Charges," both in *Knoxville News-Sentinel,* Sept. 16, 1948, 1.
31. Lilienthal, "The Wellspring of America's Strength," excerpts from an address delivered at Michigan State College, June 5, 1949, published in *Reader's Digest,* Oct. 1949, 129–31.
32. Lilienthal, *Journals* 2:356, 363, 424–26. "Atom Man," *Newsweek,* Feb. 7, 1949, 50–52.

33. Interview with Joseph Volpe, July 28, 1987, Washington, D.C. MacLeish quoted from Oxnam, *Personalities in Social Reform,* 92.
34. Archibald MacLeish, "A Progress Report on Atomic Energy: A Dialogue with the Chairman of the Atomic Energy Commission," *Life,* Sept. 27, 1948, 114–18.
35. CC: W. S. Parsons to Lilienthal, Dec. 10, 1948; Parsons to John L. Sullivan, Dec. 12, 1948; Lilienthal to Clark Clifford, Dec. 14, 1948; George M. Elsey to Clifford, Dec. 16, 1948; Clifford to Harry S. Truman, Dec. 29, 1948; handwritten note on previous memorandum: "Approved—no publication." Harry Truman, Dec. 29, 1948.
36. Lilienthal, *Journals* 2:378–79, 424, 433–35.
37. Lilienthal, *Journals* 2:459–61, 470–75, 524–28. Hewlett and Duncan, *History of the United States AEC, 1947/1952,* 353.
38. Lilienthal, *Journals* 2:501, 533. HAM: Lilienthal to H. A. Morgan, May 2, 1949.
39. Lilienthal, *Journals* 2:397. DEL: Lilienthal to the Commissioners and General Manager, Jan. 1, 1949.
40. Lilienthal, *Journals* 2:395–405, 477–82, 485. DELAEC: Lilienthal Office Logs, 1947–49. Interview with Joseph Volpe, Washington, D.C., Aug. 18, 1986.
41. Lilienthal, *Journals* 2:488–90. Hewlett and Duncan, *History of the United States AEC, 1947/1952,* 353–54.
42. Lilienthal, *Journals* 2:423, 483–85, 522–23.
43. Lilienthal, *Journals* 2:360–61, 518–19, 521–23. Hewlett and Duncan, *History of the United States AEC, 1947/1952,* 340–42. DEL: Lilienthal to Allen Lilienthal, n.d., probably April or May 1949.
44. Hewlett and Duncan, *History of the United States AEC, 1947/1952,* 356–58. U.S. Congress, Joint Committee on Atomic Energy, Congress of the United States, *Investigation into the United States Atomic Energy Project* (Washington, D.C: GPO, 1949), 1122–26. The appendix to the Hearings has an extensive "Analysis of public opinion regarding the issues involved in the investigation into the policies and administration of the Atomic Energy Commission." Subsequent references to this portion of the Appendix will be cited as *Analysis.* "Lilienthal's About Face," and "Checkup by FBI Kept Brooklyn MD Out of Job," *New York Journal-American,* May 20, 1949, 1, both articles. Lilienthal, *Journals* 2:530–32. DEL: "Yardstick for Democracy," address before the American Booksellers Association, Washington, D.C., May 18, 1949.
45. Hewlett and Duncan, *History of the United States AEC, 1947/1952,* 357–58. Lilienthal, *Journals* 2:531. *Investigation,* 360–63.
46. Lilienthal, *Journals* 2:533. "Resignation of Lilienthal Demanded," *Washington Post,* May 23, 1949, 1–2.
47. Lilienthal, *Journals* 2:533–36. DELAEC: Lilienthal to McMahon, May 25, 1949.
48. *Investigation,* 2, 5–13.
49. *Investigation,* 14. Lilienthal, *Journals* 2:535.
50. Lilienthal, *Journals* 2:537. "The Atom: Things to Explain," *Newsweek,* May 30, 1949, 19. "Hickenlooper Used Calculated Fear Tactics, Lilienthal Says," *Washington Post,* May 31, 1949, 1, 6.
51. *Investigation,* 24, 136.
52. *Investigation,* 109, 116–18, 133.
53. *Investigation,* 90, 97–99, 140–42.
54. *Analysis,* 1122–50. Joseph Alsop, "Matter of Fact: The Irresponsibles," *New York Herald-Tribune,* June 3, 1949, 21. BH: The Headline Writers Assn of America to Republican State Committee—Des Moines, Iowa, June 1, 1949. Lilienthal, *Journals* 2:538–40.
55. *Analysis,* 1150–72. BH: Ring Binder Collection—Index of "Issues Involved" and questions to ask. Lilienthal, *Journals* 2:547.

56. *Investigation*, 766. WW: Waymack to Lilienthal, Oct. 22, 1949.

57. Lilienthal, *Journals* 2:539, 542. HAM: Lilienthal to Morgan, July 1, 1949.

58. *Investigation*," parts 5 and 6. Lilienthal, *Journals* 2:541. Hewlett and Duncan, *History of the United States AEC, 1947/1952*, 303–4.

59. *Report*, Majority, 7, 18, 60–66, 74, 77–81, 83; Minority, 2–3. Hewlett and Duncan, *History of the United States AEC, 1947/1952*, 360. Lilienthal, *Journals* 2:562–63.

60. Lilienthal, *Journals* 2:543, 546, 560–61, 565–69. HAM: Lilienthal to H. A. Morgan.

61. Hewlett and Duncan, *History of the United States AEC, 1947/1952*, 362–63. Lilienthal, *Journals* 2:569.

62. Lilienthal, *Journals* 2:570–72. Hewlett and Duncan, *History of the United States AEC, 1947/1952*, 366–67. DELAEC: Lilienthal Official Appointment Book-AEC, Sept. 18–20, 1949, entries.

63. Lilienthal, "Where Do We Go from Here?" *Bulletin of Atomic Scientists*. Nov. 1949, 294, 308 (Freedom House speech reprint).

64. "Majority Report," *New York Times*, Oct. 14, 1949, 26. DEL: Helen Lilienthal to William Waymack, Oct. 8, 1949; Lilienthal to Clifford, Oct. 12, 1949.

65. Hewlett and Duncan, *History of the United States AEC, 1947/1952*, 369–74. Strauss quotation from Pfau, *No Sacrifice Too Great*, 112–14.

66. Hewlett and Duncan, *History of the United States AEC, 1947/1952*, 375–77. Lilienthal, *Journals* 2:577. Roger M. Anders, ed., *Forging the Atomic Shield: Excerpts from the Office Diary of Gordon E. Dean* (Chapel Hill: Univ. of North Carolina Press, 1987), 42;

67. HD: Lilienthal's opening remarks before the GAC, Oct. 29, 1949. Lilienthal, *Journals* 2:581–83. Hewlett and Duncan, *History of the United States AEC, 1947/1952*, 381–84. Anders, *Forging the Atomic Shield*, 59. Pfau, *No Sacrifice Too Great*, 116.

68. Pfau, *No Sacrifice Too Great*, 117. Lilienthal, *Journals* 2:583, 587–91. Brackets in Lilienthal quotation on 591 are his. Anders, *Forging the Atomic Shield*, 59–60. Hewlett and Duncan, *History of the United States AEC, 1947/1952*, 386–89.

69. Hewlett and Duncan, *History of the United States AEC, 1947/1952*, 390–91. DELAEC: AEC, "Memorandum to the President," Nov. 10, 1949.

70. Hewlett and Duncan, *History of the United States AEC, 1947/1952*, 394–95, 406–8. Acheson, *Present at the Creation*, 348.

71. Acheson, *Present at the Creation*, 348. Lilienthal, *Journals* 2:595. Anders, *Forging the Atomic Shield*, 43–48, 51–55.

72. Lilienthal, *Journals* 2:591–94. HD: Manley Diary, Oct. 30, 1949.

73. Lilienthal, *Journals* 2:579, 585, 596–600 (Clifford quotation on 597). DELAEC: Lilienthal to Truman, Nov. 21, 1949. HST: Truman to Lilienthal, Nov. 23, 1949; Lilienthal to Truman Jan. 24, 1950. Eleanor Roosevelt, "I Congratulate Mr. Lillienthal [*sic*] on Unselfish Job," *Washington News*, Nov. 28, 1949, 41. DEL: Berle to Lilienthal, Nov. 29, 1949.

74. DEL: Helen Lilienthal to Nancy and David, Nov. 25, 1949. Lilienthal, *Journals* 2:605–9, 616.

75. Lilienthal, *This I Do Believe* (New York: Harper & Brothers, 1949). R. L. Duffus, "David Lilienthal's Deep Faith in American Democracy," *New York Times*, book review sec., Oct. 9, 1949, 3. H. M. Kallen, *Annals of the American Academy of Political and Social Science*, May 1950, 153–54. *Christian Century*, Jan. 11, 1950, 51. Henry Steele Commager, "Lilienthal on TVA, Atomic Energy and Democracy," *New York Herald Tribune Book Review*, Oct. 9, 1949, 1. Norman Cousins, "Conversions and Convictions," *Saturday Review of Literature*, Oct. 8, 1949, 24–25. *Review of Politics*, v. 12, 1950, 261–62.

76. "Book Notes," *Harvard Law Review,* June 1950, 1486–87. A. S., "Books," *Canadian Forum,* Jan. 1950, 234–35. "Christian Science Monitor," Oct. 20, 1949, 20.

77. Lilienthal, *Journals* 2:559.

78. Lilienthal, *Journals* 2:522–23. Lilienthal, *This I Do Believe,* 120. FFHLS: correspondence between Barnes and Frankfurter, Jan. 5 and 14, 1950.

79. Hewlett and Duncan, *History of the United States AEC, 1947/1952,* 399. Lilienthal, *Journals* 2:618–19.

80. Lilienthal, *Journals* 2:599, 611, 633.

81. Anders, *Forging the Atomic Shield,* 62–63. Lilienthal, *Journals* 2:613–14. Acheson, *Present at the Creation,* 348. Hewlett and Duncan, *History of the United States AEC, 1947/1952,* 398.

82. Hewlett and Duncan, *History of the United States AEC, 1947/1952,* 399–409. Acheson quotation in Acheson, *Present at the Creation,* 348–49. Anders, *Forging the Atomic Shield,* 62–64. Lilienthal, *Journals* 2:623–34.

83. Lilienthal, *Journals* 2:635–36.

84. Harsch, "Lilienthal," 6.

85. Oxnam, *Personalities in Social Reform,* 90. Jameson W. Doig and Erwin C. Hargrove, "'Leadership' and Political Analysis," in Doig and Hargrove, *Leadership and Innovation,* 15–17. Erwin C. Hargrove, "David Lilienthal and the Tennessee Valley Authority," in Doig and Hargrove, *Leadership and Innovation,* 27.

86. Interview with Joseph Volpe, July 28, 1987, Washington, D.C.

87. Lilienthal, *Journals* 2:142. Lilienthal crossed swords with J. Edgar Hoover frequently during AEC days regarding security matters. Unclassified correspondence with Hoover, some quite strong, can be found in DELAEC: quoted in Archibald MacLeish, "Progress Report on Atomic Energy," *Reader's Digest,* Dec. 1948, 7.

88. Arthur Hendrick, ed., *The Private Papers of Senator Vandenberg* (Boston: Houghton Mifflin, 1952), 356. Interview with Robert Goheen, July 8, 1986, Princeton University.

89. Lilienthal, *Journals* 2:469–70, 506. Lilienthal, "Machines With and Without Freedom," *Saturday Review of Literature,* Aug. 6, 1949, 60.

90. Lilienthal, *Journals* 2:635. HST: handwritten note from HST to unknown person in response to correspondence with Lilienthal, about Jan. 15, 1955.

91. "Lilienthal Scores 'World End' Talk," *New York Times,* Mar. 2, 1950, 11. HD: Atomic Energy Commission, Press Digest, mimeographed, Mar. 31, 1950—report of Lilienthal speech in Atlanta. Lilienthal, "Can the Atomic-Bomb Beat Communism?" 14. Lilienthal, "When and Where," 30, 63.

92. "Lilienthal Scores 'World End' Talk," *New York Times,* Mar. 2, 1950, 11. Freda Kirchwey, "Death or Diplomacy," *The Nation,* Mar. 11, 1950, 216. "The Lilienthal Lullaby," *Christian Century,* Mar. 22, 1950, 358. HD: Atomic Energy Commission, Press Digest, mimeographed Oct. 16, 1950—report of Lilienthal speech in Cleveland. Szilard letter reprinted in Helen S. Hawkins, G. Allen Greb, and Gertrud Weiss Szilard, *Toward a Livable World: Leo Szilard and the Crusade for Nuclear Arms Control* (Cambridge: MIT Press, 1987), 90–91.

93. DEL: Lilienthal, "Private Industry and the Public Atom," address before the New England Council, Boston, Nov. 19, 1948, 14–15. Lilienthal, "Free the Atom," 13–15, 54–58. Lilienthal, "Toward the Industrial Atomic Future," 14–15, 68–70.

94. Lilienthal, "Free the Atom," 13, 15, 58. Lilienthal, "Toward the Industrial Atomic Future," 14, 69.

95. Lilienthal, *Journals* 3:26, 31. WW: Lilienthal to Waymack, July 23, 1950. DEL: "Meet the Press," July 1, 1951, mimeographed transcription, 3–5. LS: Dean to Strauss, July 31, 1951.

96. "Meet the Press," 8–10.
97. Lilienthal, *Journals* 3:357, 380, 390–91, 406. DEL: UJ, May 2, 1953. James Reston, "Dean Quits as Atom Chief; Action to Assure Ore Urged," *New York Times,* Feb. 11, 1953, 1. Paul Kennedy, "Strauss Will Get Atom Post as Liaison for the President," *New York Times,* Mar. 8, 1953, 1. Richard G. Hewlett and Jack M. Holl, *Atoms for Peace and War, 1953–1961: Eisenhower and the Atomic Energy Commission* (Berkeley: Univ. of California Press, 1989), 20, 47. "The Hidden Struggle for the H-Bomb," *Fortune,* May 1953, 109–10, 230.
98. DEL: UJ, Aug. 2, 1953.
99. "The Atom: A Matter of Energy," *Time,* Sept. 21, 1953, 25–27.
100. Lilienthal, *Journals* 3:423–25. LS: Dean to Strauss, Sept. 21, 1953; Strauss to Adler, Oct. 2, 1953; Strauss to Sulzberger, Oct. 5, 1953; Strauss to Commissioners, Oct. 5, 1953 (the last three documents are in draft form). Lilienthal, "The Case for Candor," 13, 60, 62–63.
101. Hewlett and Holl, *Atoms for Peace and War,* 71–72, 80. Lilienthal, "A Courageous Effort," 1. "Lilienthal Asks Start on Atom Pool Without Waiting for Russia to Join," *New York Times,* Dec. 27, 1953, 1, 12. "Mr. Lilienthal's Atomic Plan," *New York Times,* Dec. 28, 1953, 20. Lilienthal, *Journals* 3:457–58. Philip M. Stern, *The Oppenheimer Case: Security on Trial* (New York: Harper & Row, 1969), 233.
102. Stern, *The Oppenheimer Case,* 101–2, 114, Oppenheimer quotation on 129. See chapter 1 for details on Oppenheimer before 1942. Hewlett and Holl, *Atoms for Peace and War,* 36, 42, 46, 49–51.
103. Hewlett and Holl, *Atoms for Peace and War,* 51–57, 67–68, 71–72. Spencer R. Weart, *Nuclear Fear: A History of Images* (Cambridge: Harvard Univ. Press, 1988), 157. Stern, *The Oppenheimer Case,* 1–6.
104. Lilienthal, *Journals* 3:453, 467–68, 502–3. DEL: Lilienthal, "In the Matter of the Atomic Energy Commission's Letter of Dec. 23, 1953 to Dr. J. Robert Oppenheimer and the Proceedings Incident Thereto," mimeographed affidavit, Feb. 11, 1954. Stern, *The Oppenheimer Case,* 300.
105. Stern, *The Oppenheimer Case,* 299, 305. Hewlett and Holl, *Atoms for Peace and War,* 83–91. Lilienthal, *Journals* 3:505. United States Atomic Energy Commission, (USAEC) "In the Matter of J. Robert Oppenheimer: Transcript of Hearing before Personnel Security Board" (Washington, D.C.: GPO, 1954), Lilienthal testimony on 372–82, 398–425.
106. USAEC, "In the Matter of J. Robert Oppenheimer," 372–82, 398–407, 409, 415–17, 419. Stern, 305–9, 368ff. Lilienthal, *Journals* 3:505. Hewlett and Holl, *Atoms for Peace and War,* 94, 98, 106. LS: In a letter to Paul Mazur which was never mailed, Strauss denied that any documents had been withheld from the file examined by Lilienthal and, in fact, charged that "the only document 'removed' from the files had been removed by Lilienthal himself some months before, and he was provided with a photostat of that document before he testified."
107. Lilienthal, *Journals* 3:520–21, 555–56. DEL: UJ, June 20, 1954.
108. Lilienthal, *Journals* 3:562. James R. Shepley and Clay Blair, *The Hydrogen Bomb: The Men, The Menace, The Mechanism* (New York: David McKay Co., Inc., 1954). HST: Lilienthal to Truman, Nov. 18, 1954. Lilienthal (letter to editor), "Character of A.E.C.," *New York Times,* Nov. 10, 1954, 32.
109. Lilienthal, *Journals* 4:117, 256, 259, 306–8. Lilienthal, *Journals* 5:155–56, 198, 236–37, 274–75, 301, 424. Weart, *Nuclear Fear,* 293–94.
110. Lilienthal, *Journals* 5:424, 430. "The Mythology of the Atom," *Bulletin of the Atomic Scientists,* Oct. 1963, 21–24.
111. "Mythology of the Atom," 21–24. Lilienthal, *Journals* 5:437–44.
112. Lilienthal, "Whatever Happened to the Peaceful Atom?" third lecture of the

Stafford Little Lecture series, Princeton Univ., Feb. 19, 1963, reprinted in U.S. Congress, Joint Committee on Atomic Energy (JCAE), *Development, Growth, and State of the Atomic Energy Industry* (Washington, D.C.: GPO, 1963), 705–14.

113. Lilienthal, *Journals* 5:445–55, 460–61.

114. JCAE, *Development, Growth,* 527, 578, 609, 700–701. Lilienthal, *Journals* 5:460–61.

115. JCAE, *Development, Growth,* 703, 717–25, 729–31, 742.

116. JCAE, *Development, Growth,* iii–iv, 741. Lilienthal, *Journals* 5:461–62. Lilienthal, *The Journals of David E. Lilienthal,* vol. 6, *Creativity and Conflict, 1964–1967* (New York: Harper & Row, 1976), 2.

117. Lilienthal, *Journals* 5:468, 478–79. Richard Hudson, *Saturday Review,* Nov. 30, 1963, 29. Rory McCormick, *America,* Jan. 18, 1964, 116–18. J. David Singer, *American Journal of Sociology,* Sept. 1964, 249–50. David W. Tarr, *American Political Science Review,* June 1964, 475–76. Adolf A. Berle, "The Search for Universal Solutions Leads into Blind Alleys," *New York Times Book Review,* Nov. 10, 1963, 3.

118. Robert C. Cowen, "Lilienthal and the Atom," Christian Science Monitor, Oct. 23, 1963, 9. Singer, review of *Change, Hope, and the Bomb,* 249–50. Donald A. Strickland and Kathleen Archibald, "The Polemics of Science and Policy: A Review," *Journal of Conflict Resolution,* no. 2, 1965, 254–56. Tarr, review of *Change, Hope, and the Bomb,* 476.

119. Lilienthal, *Change, Hope, and the Bomb,* 3, 5, 17, 59–91.

120. "Atoms for Peace," *The Economist,* Dec. 21, 1963, 1270–71. Singer, review of *Change, Hope, and the Bomb,* 250.

121. Lilienthal, *Journals* 5:521–22. Mary Hornaday, "A-Experts Launch Attack on Lilienthal," *Christian Science Monitor,* Nov. 21, 1963, 6.

122. His last hurrah was a small book published in 1980, (*Atomic Energy: A New Start* [New York: Harper & Row, 1980]) shortly before his death. But the story of that book was really more one of love and reconciliation between father and the son who helped him write it. As such, it will be considered in the context of his last years. Lilienthal, *Journals* 7:216, 523, 544, 576. Weart, *Nuclear Fear,* 346. Henry Raymont, "Lilienthal Finds Source of Hope—Housewives," *New York Times,* June 23, 1971, 50; DEL: *Today Show,* "Interview with David Lilienthal," transcript, June 29, 1971. Lilienthal, "If This Continues, the Cockroach Will Inherit the Earth," *New York Times,* June 20, 1975, 35.

Chapter 11. Midcentury Passage

1. The two phrases in quotations are subtitles of volumes 3, 4, and 5 of the journals. DEL: "Foreign Travel by DEL," approximate date, Jan. 1961. FBI: FBI Office Memoranda; CENSORED to Belmont, Apr. 25, 1950; CENSORED to Belmont, May 8, 1950; CENSORED to Belmont, July 14, 1950; Nichols to Ladd, Nov. 17, 1950; Nichols to Tolson, Oct. 19, 1951; No Author, "Investigation Report on David Eli Lilienthal," Nov. 19, 1956.

2. Lilienthal's major publications during the period covered in chapter include the following:
    Books: *Big Business: A New Era* (New York: Pocket Books, 1956); *TVA: Democracy on the March,* Twentieth Anniversary Edition (Harper & Row: New York, 1953); *Change, Hope, and the Bomb* (Princeton: Princeton Univ. Press: 1963).
    Articles in *Collier's:* "Free the Atom," June 17, 1950; "Toward the Industrial Atomic Future," July 15, 1950; "Can the Atomic-Bomb Beat Communism?"

Mar. 3, 1951; "When and Where Do We Use the Atomic-Bomb?" Mar. 10, 1951; "Are We Losing India?" June 23, 1951; "Another Korea in the Making?" Aug. 4, 1951; "Big Business for a Big Country," five-part serialization: "Our Anti-Trust Laws Are Crippling America," May 31, 1952; "The New Competition," June 7, 1952; "The Kind of Nation We Want," June 14, 1952; "The Hazards of Bigness," June 21, 1952; "Toward a New Policy of Bigness," June 28, 1952.

Other articles: "The Case for Candor on Security," *New York Times Magazine,* Oct. 4, 1953; "'A Courageous Effort' Toward Mutual Faith," *Washington Post,* sec. 2, Dec. 13, 1953; Helen M. Lilienthal, "Climbing the Family Tree," *Atlantic Monthly,* Sept. 1, 1952, 81–82.

3. Lilienthal, *Journals* 3:361, 382, 392–93, 468. "Liberals Bar City Coalition; Halley Seen as Their Choice," *New York Times,* Apr. 27, 1953, 1. DEL: Fowler to Lilienthal, May 6, 1953.

4. DEL: UJ, Aug. 24 and 31, 1955, Jan. 1, 1958. Lilienthal, *Journals* 4:295–96.

5. DEL: Family financial records, including federal income tax returns—1950–55.

6. Lilienthal, *Journals* 3:3–5, 9, 344. DEL: W. Colston Leigh, publicity flyer on David E. Lilienthal.

7. Lilienthal, *Journals* 3:4–6, 23–24, 196.

8. Lilienthal, *Journals* 3:27, 269. Interview with Joseph Volpe, Washington, D.C., July 28, 1987. "Meeting Halfway," *New Yorker,* Dec. 8, 1951, 34–35.

9. "Meeting Halfway," 35. Lilienthal, *Journals* 3:350.

10. LS: Memorandum for Files, Jan. 11, 1951. Lilienthal, *Journals* 3:27, 149, 159, 261, 264–65.

11. "Meeting Halfway," 35. "Author! Author! Where's the Author?" Apr. 19, 1952; "Profiles: A Second Sort of Life," Apr. 29, 1961, all in the *New Yorker;* Lilienthal, "Needed: A New Credo for Foreign Aid," June 24, 1960; "Why Nigeria Is Different," June 11, 1961; and "Foreign Aid—For the Teeming City," Sept. 9, 1962, all in the *New York Times Magazine.*

12. Lilienthal, *Journals* 3:146, 180, 193, 221, 269, 277, 310. GRC: Lilienthal to Clapp, Dec. 17, 1951.

13. Lilienthal, *Journals* 3:353–54.

14. Lilienthal, *Journals* 3:31, 223, 261.

15. Lilienthal, *Journals* 3:55–57, 207, 221, 229, 231–32, 294, 296. John S. Porter, editor in chief, *Moody's Manual of Investment: American and Foreign Industrial Securities* (New York: Moody's Investor Services, 1933), 1716. "Profiles," 49. DEL: Lilienthal to James S. Adams, June 7, 1951; Lilienthal to Meyer, Aug. 8, 1951; Press Release, MSNA, Aug. 1, 1952.

16. Lilienthal, *Journals* 3:300, 339, 346 349–50, 357, 366, 376, 381, 384, 429–31. DEL: Minerals Separation North American Corporation, "Minutes of Special Meeting of Board of Directors," Nov. 22, 1952; MSNA Corporation to Lilienthal, Nov. 22, 1952 (two documents). John S. Porter, editor in chief, *Moody's Industrial Manual: American and Foreign,* 1954, 1158–59.

17. Lilienthal, *Journals* 3:436, 521. *Moody's Industrial Manual: American and Foreign,* 1968, 1480.

18. Lilienthal, *Journals* 3:460, 503, 521, 573–75, 579, 590. Lilienthal, *Journals* 5:346, 368, 387. DEL: Attapulgus Minerals and Chemicals Corporation to Lilienthal, Dec. 1953. *Moody's Industrial Manual: American and Foreign,* 1955, 2244; *Moody's Industrial Manual,* 1957, 1299; *Moody's Industrial Manual,* 1961, 1471.

19. *Moody's Industrial Manual,* 1967, 1358. Interview with David Morse, New York City, July 28, 1986. Lilienthal interview with Newman on "Speaking Freely," Mar. 16, 1969, 6. Interview with Joseph Volpe, Washington, D.C, July 28, 1987. "Profiles," 55.

20. Lilienthal, *Journals* 3:210–11, 294–95. Lilienthal, "We're Only at the Beginning," *Collier's*, Mar. 28, 1953, 82.

21. John Kenneth Galbraith, *American Capitalism: The Concept of Countervailing Power* (Boston: Houghton Mifflin, 1952). Lilienthal, *Journals* 3:298, 302, 310.

22. Lilienthal, "Our Antitrust Laws," 15. See note 2 for full titles of all five articles.

23. Lilienthal, *Journals* 3:313. Hearings before a Subcommittee of the Select Committee on Small Business, United States Senate, on the Impact of Monopoly and Cartel Practices on Small Business, 82d Cong., 2d sess. (1952), 66–67. HH: Hoover to Anthony, May 14, 1952. WW: correspondence between Waymack and Lilienthal, July 18 and 29, 1952. MC: Cooke to Hamilton, June 17, 1952; Cooke to Lilienthal, June 17, 1952; Cooke to Estes, July 1, 1952; Lilienthal to Cooke, July 10, 1952. Lilienthal, "We're Only at the Beginning," 82.

24. Lilienthal, *Big Business*, xiii, xv, 13, 17–19, 23–25, 145, 180–81.

25. Lilienthal, *Big Business*, 3, 5, 182, 186–88, 371. Galbraith, *American Capitalism*, 118–19.

26. The most favorable reviews include Louis M. Hacker, "The Heart of the Matter," *New York Times Book Review*, Feb. 22, 1953, 10; Philip Hampson, "David Lilienthal Extols Benefits of Big Business, *Chicago Tribune*, book sec. 6; Harry C. Kenney, "The Advantages of Bigness," *Christian Science Monitor*, Feb. 20, 1953, 13; Richard H. Rovere, *New Yorker*, Mar. 21, 1953, 132; Sumner H. Slichter, "Scheme of a Conversion," *Saturday Review*, May 9, 1953, 33. More critical voices included T. K. Quinn, "Too Big," *The Nation*, Mar. 7, 1953, 211; Samuel Lubell, "The Case for Socially Responsible 'Big Business' in Our Society," *New York Herald Tribune Book Review*, Feb. 22, 1953, 1; *American Mercury*, May 1953, 78; Peter Drucker, "The Liberal Discovers Big Business," *Yale Review*, June 1953, 232; James O'Gara, "Plea for Bigness," *Commonweal*, May 1, 1953, 105.

27. Lilienthal, *Journals* 3:298. Lilienthal, *Big Business*, 52, 71. Richard Lester, "A Giant to Live With," *New Republic*, Mar. 2, 1953, 21. Frank H. Towsley, *Columbia Law Review*, June 1953, 895; Drucker, "The Liberal Discovers Big Business," 529–30, 536.

28. Paul T. Homan, "Economic Systems; Planning and Reform; Co-operation," *American Economic Review*, June 1952, 432. Theodore Kreps, "Countervailing Power," *New Republic*, Mar. 24, 1952, 19. Keith Hutchison, "Economic Power," *The Nation*, Feb. 23, 1952, 185; Samuel Lubell, "New Light on the Nature of Capitalism," *New York Herald Tribune Book Review*, June 29, 1952, 3; Michael Hoffman, "The Weight in the Balance," *New York Times Book Review*, Feb. 24, 1952, 3.

29. Lilienthal, *Big Business*, 25–29, 71–84.

30. Hofstadter, *Age of Reform*, 323. Schlesinger, *The Politics of Upheaval*, 391–93. Schwarz, *The New Dealers*, 235.

31. HAM: Lilienthal to Morgan, July 26, 1950. John N. Popham, "T.V.A. Detractors Scored by Lilienthal," *New York Times*, Apr. 13, 1955, 1.

32. Lilienthal, *Journals* 3:159, 194, 202, 216 (Lilienthal's paraphrase of Clapp's letter).

33. Lilienthal, *Journals* 3:393, 403–6, 560–62 (Woods quotation on 562), 598–607. Lilienthal, *Journals* 5:12, 293. Richard A. Couto, "New Seeds at the Grass Roots: The Politics of the TVA Power Program since World War II," in Hargrove and Conkin, *TVA: Fifty Years*, 232–36.

34. Interview with Adolfo Orive de Alba, Mexico City, Aug. 1981. Lilienthal, *Journals* 2:48, 475, 578, 593, 622. Lilienthal, *Journals* 3:10–11, 13–14, 16–18 (Atlee quotation on 18), 20. HAM: Lilienthal to H. A. Morgan, July 7, 1950. DEL: Lilienthal to Roosevelt, Nov. 21, 1942, and Jan. 25, 1943.

35. Lilienthal, *Journals* 3:54–73; McGhee quotation on 63.

36. DEL: "Foreign Travel by DEL," approximate date, Jan. 1961. Lilienthal, *Journals* 3:81–82, 86–88, 91–92, 105–6, 109–11, 113.
37. Nehru quotation in Lilienthal, *Journals* 3:94–104.
38. Lilienthal, "Are We Losing India?" 13–15, 42, 44, 46.
39. Lilienthal, "Another Korea in the Making?" 22–23, 56–58. "Engineering Study of Indus River May End India-Pakistan Feud," *New York Times,* May 30, 1953, 2. Lilienthal, *Journals* 3:199, 218, 230–31, 234–35, 323, 375, 448–49, 462, 464, 470–71. Lilienthal, *Journals* 5:115–16.
40. Lilienthal, *TVA: Democracy on the March,* 205.
41. Lilienthal, *Journals* 3:204, 250–53, 301, 316–17, 374.
42. Lilienthal, *TVA: Democracy on the March,* 210–11, 216–17, 256–57. The few reviews of the Twentieth Anniversary Edition were generally favorable. The most substantial include Saville R. Davis, "TVA—Ambassador at Large," *Christian Science Monitor,* May 21, 1953, 9; Lee S. Greene, *Annals of the American Academy of Political and Social Science,* vol. 290, Nov. 1953, 147–48; Charles M. Hardin, *American Journal of Sociology,* vol. 59, Nov. 1953, 295–96; Lilienthal, *Journals* 3:430.
43. International Bank for Reconstruction and Development, *The Basis of a Development Program for Colombia* (Washington, D.C.: International Bank for Reconstruction and Development, 1950). International Bank for Reconstruction and Development, *The Autonomous Regional Corporation of the Cauca and the Development of the Upper Cauca Valley* (Washington, D.C.: International Bank for Reconstruction and Development, 1955). Lawrence S. Graham, "Regional Development Policy in Brazil, Mexico, and Colombia: A Comparative Analysis," *Ibero-Americana, Nordic Journal of Latin American Studies* 1 (1968):23–39. Gayle Pendleton W. Jackson, "Making Policy in a Latin American Bureaucracy: The Cauca Valley Corporation of Colombia," Ph.D. dissertation, Washington Univ., 1972, 84–86, 96–97, 100; Antonio J. Posada and Jeanne de Posada, *The CVC: Challenge to Underdevelopment and Traditionalism* (Bogota: Ediciones Tercer Mundo: 1966), 18, 40.
44. Lilienthal, *Journals* 3:419, 448, 466, 468, 472–90.
45. DEL: Lilienthal, "Recommendation on the Establishment of Regional Development Authorities by the Republic of Colombia," an informal report submitted, upon invitation of the President of the Republic, His Excellency, General Gustavo Rojas Pinilla, (New York: mimeographed, 1954), passim.
46. Jackson, "Making Policy," 101–3, 145–46. Lilienthal, *Journals* 4:10–13, 99–115, 173. DEL: translations of Colombian newspaper reports regarding Lilienthal and the CVC, 1956; Clapp to Bernardo Garces, Oct. 16, 1956.
47. Roscoe C. Martin, "TVA and International Technical Assistance: A report to the board of Directors and the General Manager" (Syracuse: Tennessee Valley Authority, 1970), 74–75. Lilienthal, *Journals* 5:283. Lilienthal, *Journals* 6:531. AP: Pampanini to Lilienthal, June 25, 1973.
48. Lilienthal, *Journals* 3:514, 620–33. DEL: Lilienthal to Fred Newton, Aug. 13, 1955.

Chapter 12. Lilienthal and the World

1. Eric Goldman, *The Crucial Decade and After: America 1945–1960* (New York: Vintage Books, 1960), chap. 4, and 181–82. Robert A. Packenham, *Liberal America and the Third World* (Princeton: Princeton Univ. Press, 1973), 24–49. See also Joseph Marion Jones, *The Fifteen Weeks: February 21–June 5, 1947* (New York: Harcourt, Brace & World, 1955).
2. Lilienthal, *Journals* 3:631. Lilienthal, *Journals* 4:1–2; AA: "Certificate of Incorpo-

ration of Development and Resources Corporation," June 6, 1955. DEL: Lilienthal to Meyer, Oct. 15, 1956; John Oliver to Carl Marcy, Apr. 6, 1962; UJ, May 4, 1956. Later, at Lilienthal's request, half of his stock was allocated to Clapp.

3. Lilienthal, *Journals* 4:22. "New Dealers Become Free Enterprisers," *Fortune*, Oct. 1955, 36. AA: D&R Board of Director minutes, Sept. 28, and Nov. 22, 1955; Sept. 11, 1956. DEL: Lilienthal to Meyer, Jan. 1, 1956 (draft copy); "Contract between Plan Organization, Tehran, Iran and Development and Resources Corporation, New York, N.Y., U.S.A.," Mar. 29, 1956.

4. DEL: Clapp to Meyer, June 27, 1957; D&R, "Staff of Development and Resources Corporation, Apr. 1, 1958; Oliver to Lilienthal, July 7, 1958; UJ, Apr. 8, 1965, July 19–20, 1969, Oct. 14 and 26, and Nov. 18, 1965. AA: D&R Board Minutes, Feb. 8, and Apr. 30, 1956, Oct. 14, 1965. Lilienthal, *Journals* 4:80, 205. The D&R records are not complete. Please refer to the Bibliographic Essay in this volume.

5. Lilienthal, *Journals* 5:127–28. DEL: UJ, Nov. 6, 1960; Clapp to Meyer, Nov. 7, 1960.

6. Most of the insights about the Lilienthal-Clapp relationship are from interviews with John Burnett (July 23, 1986), Norman Clapp (July 28, 1987), Joseph Volpe (July 28, 1987), and Mr. and Mrs. John Oliver (Aug. 4, 1987). Information about Lilienthal's foreign travel over the years has been pieced together from personal travel logs for the years 1950–61 and 1963–70 and from published and unpublished journal entries and other documents. The logs, other documents, and unpublished journal entries are in DEL. Subsequent references to this travel will be noted as "Travel Documentation."

7. Lilienthal, *Journals* 4:349; 5:15, 315, 365, 386, 469. DEL: UJ, Sept. 7, 1957, Feb. 11, 1959, Jan. 23, 1962, Oct. 23, 1964, Apr. 15, 1965.

8. The number of trips to Iran was derived from "Travel Documentation" (in DEL). The number of visits with the Shah, at home and abroad, has also been calculated from the journal.

9. Mark J. Gasiorowski, *U.S. Foreign Policy and the Shah: Building a Client State in Iran* (Ithaca: Cornell Univ. Press, 1991), 59–80, 102–4. James A. Bill, *The Eagle and the Lion: The Tragedy of American-Iranian Relations* (New Haven: Yale Univ. Press, 1988), 125. Frances Bostock and Geoffrey Jones, *Planning and Power in Iran: Ebtehaj and Economic Development under the Shah* (London: Frank Cass, 1989), chaps. 5 and 6. The Bostock and Jones book is a biography of Abol Hassan Ebtehaj. It is thorough and perhaps the most insightful of all interpretations of Lilienthal's relationship with Ebtehaj.

10. Bostock and Jones, *Planning and Power in Iran,* 115–17, 120–21, 135–36. Bill, *The Eagle and the Lion,* 121. Lilienthal, *Journals* 4:26, Abol Hassan Ebtehaj, letter to Helen Lilienthal, July 29, 1987, in Abol Hassan Ebtehaj, *Khatirat-i Abu al-Hasan Ibtihaj* [memoirs of Abol Hassan Ebtehaj] (Tehran: Ilmi, 1992), 793.

11. Bostock and Jones, *Planning and Power in Iran,* 133–37. WB: Prud'homme to Black, Jan. 8, 1956. Lilienthal, *Journals* 4:77–81. DRC: Lilienthal to Eleanor Roosevelt, Mar. 15, 1956. DEL: Lilienthal and Clapp, Mar. 5, 1956. Ebtehaj, *Khatirat-i Abu al-Hasan Ibtihaj,* 793.

12. DEL: Lilienthal and Clapp to Meyer, Mar. 2, 1956. DRC: Lilienthal and Clapp to Ebtehaj, June 15, 1956; Clapp to Ebtehaj, June 16, 1956. Gordon R. Clapp, "Iran: A TVA for the Khuzestan Region," *The Middle East Journal* 11, 1957, 2–6. Bostock and Jones, *Planning and Power in Iran,* 123.

13. DRC: Clapp and Lilienthal to Ebtehaj, June 15, 1956; Clapp to Ebtehaj, June 16, 1956; Lilienthal to Clapp, May 7, 1958. Bostock and Jones, *Planning and Power in Iran,* 137. Lilienthal, *Journals* 4:178. DEL: Clapp to Meyer, June 27, 1957.

14. Bostock and Jones, *Planning and Power in Iran,* 129. DRC: Oliver, memorandum to file Mar. 28, 1957. Lilienthal, *Journals* 4:180. WB: G. W. Keep to files June 27, 1957.

15. WB: DeWildes to Rucinski, Aug. 19, 1957; Rucinski to Dorr, Aug. 23, 1957. DEL: transcript of telephone conversation between Clapp and Rucinski, Aug. 23, 1957. Lilienthal, *Journals* 4:214–19. "Big Dam Planned in Iran Project," *New York Times,* Oct. 8, 1957, 6.

16. WB: Dorr to Rucinski, Sept. 12, 1957; Keep, memorandum to files, May 1, 1958. Lilienthal, *Journals* 4:228, 261–63, 273–75, 347. DRC: Clapp to Oliver, Nov. 8, 1957; Clapp, memorandum to files, May 2, 1958. DEL: Lilienthal to Black, Sept. 3, 1958; Clapp, memorandum to files, Oct. 6, 1958.

17. DEL: Clapp to Meyer, Apr. 24, 1958. Lilienthal, *Journals* 4:273–75, 316–20, 340, 342. WB: Prud'homme to Knapp, Mar. 18, 1959. Development and Resources Corp. (D&R), *A Report to Plan Organization, Government of Iran: The Unified Development of the Natural Resources of the Khuzestan region,* unpublished report, Mar. 1959.

18. Lilienthal, *Journals* 4:347–48. DEL: UJ, June 2, 1959; Heydayat to Clapp, July 25, 1959. Bostock and Jones, *Planning and Power in Iran,* 129–30. WB: Prud'homme to Knapp, May 27, 1959; Knapp to Black, June 5, 1959; Prud'homme to Ebtehaj, June 19, 1959.

19. DEL: Seymour, memorandum to files, July 23, 1959; Clapp to Heydayat, July 23, 1959; Clapp to Meyer, Feb. 24, 1960. WB: IBRD Staff Minutes, vol. 16, July 30, 1959. Lilienthal, *Journals* 5:4. DRC: Voorduin, "Rough Transcript of Hand-Written Notes by WLV on World Bank Meetings Held in Teheran, Aug. 29, 1959," Sept. 17, 1959.

20. Bill, *The Eagle and the Lion,* 125–26. Lilienthal, *Journals* 4:278, 290; 5:8.

21. DRC: Pincus to Clapp, Dec. 12, 1958; Haldore Hanson, Transcript of Interview with Kenneth Hansen on Financial Situation in Iran, Feb. 8, 1960. Bostock and Jones, *Planning and Power in Iran,* 127, 143. WB: Pollen to files, Jan. 15, 1959; Prud'homme to Knapp, Mar. 18, 1959.

22. Lilienthal, *Journals* 4:212–13, 242, 261–63. Bostock and Jones, *Planning and Power in Iran,* 124.

23. Bostock and Jones, *Planning and Power in Iran,* 141, 147–58. Nikki R. Keddie, *Roots of Revolution: An Interpretive History of Modern Iran* (New Haven: Yale Univ. Press, 1981) 148. Amin Saikal, *The Rise and Fall of The Shah* (Princeton: Princeton Univ. Press, 1980), 61. George B. Baldwin, *Planning and Development in Iran* (Baltimore: John Hopkins Univ. Press, 1967), 113–14. Ebtehaj, *Khatirat-i Abu al-Hasan Ibtihaj,* 469–71.

24. Bill, *The Eagle and the Lion,* 122. Lilienthal, *Journals* 5:276.

25. Peter Gabriel, *The International Transfer of Corporate Skills: Management Contracts in Less Developed Countries* (Boston: Harvard Univ., Graduate School of Business Administration, Division of Research, 1967), 117, 128, 156. Thomas Mead, compiler, *Development and Resources Corporation Archives: The Khuzestan Development Program* , July 23 1955 through Jan. 21, 1975 (Princeton: Princeton Univ. Library, n.d. [around 1975–1976]), 26–27, 76 (hereafter cited as *D&R Archives*). David and Helen Lilienthal paid for the compilation of this catalogue, which includes narrative and extensive annotated listing of correspondence and documents related to the Khuzistan project; Lilienthal, *Journals* 5:212, 447.

26. *D&R Archives,* 45. DEL: Clapp to Heydayat, Sept. 21, 1959. Lilienthal, *Journals* 5:14, 25. There are literally hundreds of references over the years which detail D&R's agonizing effort to make Iran live up to their financial obligations. The following citations are representative, not exhaustive: Lilienthal, *Journals* 5:169, 380, 387; 6:293. DRC: Anderson to Oliver, June 7, 1960; Oliver to Asfia/Ansari,

May 30, 1961. DEL: Clapp to Lilienthal, Mar. 9, 1961, UJ, Aug. 22, 1962, and Sept. 25, 1966, Jan. 1 and 17, 1967. *D&R Archives,* 66, 68, 90–91, 115–16.

27. Lilienthal, *Journals* 5:312–13, 316–17, 329–30. *D&R Archives,* 65, 99. Aramesh quoted in Bill, *The Eagle and the Lion,* 122. DEL: UJ, Apr. 1, 1962, Apr. 5, and Aug. 9, 1965; Clapp to J. W. Fulbright, Sept. 26, 1961, and Jan. 26, 1962. DRC: Oliver to Lilienthal Feb. 12, 1964. Lilienthal, *Journals* 6:141, 272. Questions about D&R's financial affairs in Iran had been increasing since the publication of "Is There a Foreign Aid Racket?" in the *American Mercury* in Feb. 1958, 107–10. In mid-1961, the Senate Foreign Relations Committee asked Clapp for information on D&R's financial activities in Iran. In early 1962, inspired in large measure by Lilienthal's old nemesis Bourke Hickenlooper, arrangements were made by committee chair J. W. Fulbright for Lilienthal to testify before his committee in March.

28. Bill, *The Eagle and the Lion,* 121. Lilienthal, *Journals* 5:67, 173, 339; 6:42, 484.

29. Lilienthal, "Enterprise in Iran: An Experiment in Economic Development," *Foreign Affairs,* Oct. 1959, 132–33. DEL: "The Road to Change," Development and Resources Corporation, 1964, an adaptation from the 1964 Hillman Lecture at Columbia University, 8–12; UJ, Dec. 20, 1969. DRC: Lilienthal, "The Brass Tacks of Agribusiness," speech before the National Industrial Conference Board, Sept. 11, 1967. Keddie, *Roots of Revolution,* 160–68.

30. DEL: UJ, Aug. 19, 1966. Lilienthal, *Journals* 4:247, 278; 5:173, 339; 6:484–87. DRC: "Remarks by Mr. David E. Lilienthal . . . to KDS Staff Members on March 8, 1960." Lady Bird Johnson, *A White House Diary* (New York: Holt, Rinehart & Winston, 1970), 562–63.

31. DEL: T. H. Baker interview with Lilienthal for LBJ Presidential Library Oral History Collection, June 18, 1969, 1–8. Lilienthal, *Journals* 5:101–2.

32. Lilienthal, *Journals* 5:162–63, 188, 199, 208, 214, 222; 6:40, 48 (Johnson quotation). DEL: UJ, Feb. 7, 1961, May 25, 1964.

33. Eric F. Goldman, *The Tragedy of Lyndon Johnson* (New York: Knopf, 1969), 387–88, 409, 443. Albert P. Williams Jr., "South Viet-Nam's Development in a Postwar Era: A Commentary on the Thuc-Lilienthal Report," *Asian Survey,* Apr. 1971, 352–53. Lilienthal, *Journals* 6:280, 283–84, 287, 318; 7:498. DEL: UJ, Sept. 2 and 9, 1966. Drew Middleton, "Lilienthal Gets a Vietnam Role," *New York Times,* Dec. 17, 1966, 1, 3. "Mr. Lilienthal to Head U. S. Team Studying Vietnamese Development," *Department of State Bulletin,* Jan. 9, 1967, 69. Joint Development Group, *The Postwar Development of the Republic of Vietnam* (New York: Praeger Publishers, 1970), viii.

34. DEL: Interview of Lilienthal by Bill Ryan, Mar. 24, 1967, transcript of tape for NBC "Viet Nam Review." Lilienthal, *Journals* 6:445–47. LBJ: Interview of Lilienthal by Helen Meyner, Apr. 4, 1967, transcript of tape of Helen Meyner Program, Channel 47, Newark, N.J. "Selling Self-help—at a Profit," *Business Week,* Aug. 12, 1967. "Lilienthal Maps Postwar Vietnam, *New York Times,* Oct. 29, 1967, 10. Lilienthal, "Postwar Development in Viet Nam," *Foreign Affairs,* Jan. 1969. "South Vietnam after the War: How It Could be Rebuilt," *U.S. News & World Report,* Apr. 21, 1969, 34–35. AP: Interview of Lilienthal by Edwin Newman, Mar. 16, 1969, transcript of tape for WNBC Television program, "Speaking Freely."

35. Lilienthal, *Journals* 6:350–56. LBJ: Richard Moorsteen, Memorandum of Conversation between Lilienthal, Oliver, and Komer, Jan. 11, 1967.

36. Lilienthal, *Journals* 6:365–98. LBJ: anonymous *"PARAGRAPH ON LILIENTHAL,"* Feb. 24, 1967, probably by Komer for the president.

37. "Economic Situation in Viet-Nam," *Department of State Bulletin,* Mar. 20, 1967, 467–69. Ryan interview. Meyner interview.

38. Lilienthal, *Journals* 6:506–22. "Mr. Lilienthal Discusses Viet-Nam's Economic Development Program," *Department of State Bulletin,* Dec. 25, 1967, 864.

39. Lilienthal, *Journals* 6:526–29. "Mr. Lilienthal Discusses Viet-Nam," 864–67.

40. LBJ: Leonhart to Johnson, Apr. 10, 24, and 29, 1969. Lilienthal, *Journals* 6:37–38, 42, 45. DEL: UJ, May 8 and 10, 1968; Mead to Lilienthal, May 22 and 28, 1968.

41. Lilienthal, *Journals* 7:57. DEL: correspondence between Lilienthal and Mead, June 7 and 8, July 20 and 30, 1968; UJ, 16, 21–22, 24, 26–27, July 1968.

42. Lilienthal, *Journals* 7:8–9, 20–21, 28–29, 36–38, 83, 88. DEL: UJ, Sept. 13, Oct. 6 and 23, 1968 (Lilienthal quotation in last entry).

43. Lilienthal, *Journals* 7:119, 121–22, 124 (Nixon quotation), 143–44. DEL: correspondence between Lilienthal and Mead, Oct. 3, and Nov. 30, 1969; Development and Resources Corporation, "Final Report, Contract AID/fe-291," July 1970, 12, 14; UJ, Jan. 8, 22, 27, and Apr. 29, May 13 and 14, Sept. 17, Oct. 3 and 8, 1969, Jan. 11, 1970.

44. Lilienthal, "Postwar Development," 325, 330, 332. "The Long View," *Newsweek,* May 12, 1969, 56–57. AP: Newman interview, 13–16; interview with Charles Collingwood, CBS News, Jan. 24, 1973. Lilienthal, "Reconstruction Days," *New York Times,* Jan. 31, 1973, 41.

45. Joint Development Group, *Postwar Development of Vietnam,* v.

46. Williams, "South Viet-Nam's Development," 355, 358.

47. Joint Development Group, *Postwar Development of Vietnam,* 344–45. Williams, "South Viet-Nam's Development," 354, 356, 361–64.

48. DEL: UJ, Aug. 19, 1966.

49. Packenham, *Liberal America and the Third World,* xxi, 4. Carl N. Degler, "The American Past: An Unsuspected Obstacle in Foreign Affairs," *American Scholar,* Spring 1963, 192–209. Hartz, *The Liberal Tradition in America,* 5–16, 270–86.

50. Packenham, *Liberal America and the Third World,* 20, 112–51.

51. Lilienthal, *Journals* 4:261–63; 6:378–79, 415. Marshall Windmiller, "Agents of the New Empire," *The Nation,* May 10, 1971, 593.

52. Lilienthal, *Journals* 5:75. Grace Goodell, *The Elementary Structures of Political Life: Rural Development in Pahlavi Iran* (New York: Oxford Univ. Press, 1986), 10. DEL: David E. Lilienthal Jr. to Lilienthal, Mar. 24, 1967; Lilienthal, "The Road to Change," 2; Lilienthal, "An American Renaissance," the 1965 Stephen S. Wise Memorial Lecture, Brandeis Univ., Feb. 18, 1965, 5–6.

53. DEL: Lilienthal, "Decade of Decision: 1960–1970, The Prospects for the Under-developed Countries in the Decade of the Sixties," Newton D. Baker Memorial Lecture, Cleveland Council on World Affairs, Jan. 14, 1960, 14, 17.

54. Lilienthal, "Reconstruction Days," 41. AP: Collingwood interview. DEL: Lilienthal, "The Road to Change," 3.

55. DEL: Lilienthal, "The Road to Change," 7–8.

56. DEL: correspondence between Lilienthal and Newton, Jan. 4, and Nov. 9, 1960; Lilienthal to Alfred Fisher, Nov. 9, 1960; UJ, Dec. 26, 1960. "2 Smith Teachers Held in Vice Case," *New York Times,* Sept. 4, 1960, 16.

57. Lilienthal, *Journals* 5:467; 6:68, 93, 123. DEL: UJ, Feb. 23, 1965.

58. Lilienthal, *Journals* 5:467. DEL: Lilienthal to Ebtehaj, June 3, 1963; Lilienthal to Don L. Bowen, Aug. 6, 1963. Lilienthal did write a short introduction to Harry L. Case, "Gordon R. Clapp: The Role of Faith, Purposes and People in Administration," *Public Administration Review,* June 1964, 86–91. Interviews with Helen Lilienthal, July 25, 1987; Norman Clapp, July 28, 1987; and Mr. and Mrs. John Oliver, Aug. 4, 1987.

59. Lilienthal, *Journals* 4:111; 5:358, 466. DEL: UJ, May 9, 1959, Aug. 21, 1961, Jan. 12, and Apr. 11, 1962, May 10, 1963, Aug. 4, 1968. Between 1960 and 1967 there are scores of entries in the unpublished journals of the intense family

conflict. Although the view is Lilienthal's, and often highly emotional, there are striking moments of introspection and candid reflection which offer what I perceive to be an overall fair picture of the positions of all of the principals. Entries in the 1960s also reflect an increasingly troubled personality, punctuated by painful moments of depression, escalating insomnia, and increasing bitterness toward people and events of the day.

60. DEL: UJ, May 2, July 5 and 30, Aug. 18, Sept. 4, and Oct. 7–8, 1964.
61. DEL: David Lilienthal Jr., quotation in UJ, Dec. 16, 1966. Interview with David E. Lilienthal Jr., July 25, 1986.
62. David Ely, *The Tour* (New York: Delacorte Press, 1967). Lilienthal, *Journals* 6:401. DEL: Helen Lilienthal quotation in UJ, Feb. 26–27, 1967; Lilienthal to Dee Szold, May 29, 1967.
63. DEL: UJ, Jan. 31, and Mar. 25, 1967 (Peggy Lilienthal quotation from second UJ entry).
64. DEL: David Lilienthal Jr. to Lilienthal, Mar. 24, 1967.
65. DEL: undated letter from Helen Lilienthal to her son David and accompanying note by Lilienthal indicating that the letter was never sent; UJ, Mar. 28, Apr. 5 and 12, May 23 and 28, and June 15, 1967 (David Lilienthal Jr. quotation from last UJ entry); Lilienthal to David Jr., Jan. 23, 1977.
66. Lilienthal, *Journals* 5:298.
67. Representative journal entries reporting his "low" periods include: Lilienthal, *Journals* 5:438; 6:147. DEL: UJ, July 10, 1961; Jan. 21, Feb. 19, and Nov. 21, 1962; Feb. 17, and July 18, 1963; July 14, 1965; July 10, 1966.
68. I have benefited from Peter D. Kramer's discussion of rapid cycling and stress in his book *Listening to Prozac* (New York: Viking Press, 1993), chap. 5. See also Robert M. Post and James C. Ballenger, eds. *Neurobiology of Mood Disorders* (Baltimore: Williams & Wilkins, 1984).
69. DEL: "Staff of Development and Resources Corporation," Oliver to Clapp, June 29, 1956; Clapp to Meyer, Apr. 24, 1958; G. N. DeMare to Lilienthal et al.; "Balance Sheet as of June 30, 1959," July 24, 1959; June 28, and Aug. 10, 1966. AP: D&R, "Contracts Active in Current Fiscal year Ending June 30, 1970," Apr. 30, 1970. D&R, Comparative Statement of Revenues, Expenses and Net Income, Fiscal Years Ending June 30," June 30, 1970. AP: Andrea Pampanini to Lilienthal, "Historical Summary of D&R's Financial Results," Feb. 22, 1974. Lilienthal, *Journals* 5:27–30, 127, 434–35; 6:149.
70. AP: Andrea Pampanini to Lilienthal, "Historical Summary of D&R's Financial Results," Feb. 22, 1974. The net loss this year was $28,051. DEL: UJ, Jan. 14, May 18, June 30, Nov. 7, and Dec. 3 and 6, 1969, Mar. 24, June 26, and Sept. 17, 1970.
71. DEL: UJ, Jan. 14 and 15, Mar. 2, 1969; Levin to Lilienthal and Oliver, Feb. 24, 1969. AA: D&R Board Minutes, Mar. 19, 1969.
72. DEL: Wood Tate to Levin, May 27, 1969; Levin to Lilienthal, June 5, 1969; Lilienthal to Mead, Nov. 30, 1969; Lilienthal to Meyer, "A Statement Concerning Development and Resources Corporation (D&R)," Jan. 7, 1970; UJ, Jan. 15, July 31, Oct. 17, and Nov. 30, 1969; Jan. 15, and Mar. 19, 1970. AP: Newman interview. Lilienthal, *Journals* 7:143, 169.

Chapter 13. Life at a "High Trot"

Unfinished Business is the subtitle of Lilienthal's seventh and last journal volume, published two years after his death under Helen Lilienthal's editorship. I have used this as the subtitle for this chapter in honor of Mrs. Lilienthal's dedication to

the journal, which she edited after David Jr. relinquished that responsibility in
1969. I use it to acknowledge that David Lilienthal's business was *never*
finished—he lived life at a "high trot" until the day of his death.

1. DEL: UJ, May 7, 1980. At this time Lilienthal estimated that his and Helen's
holdings were worth more than $2.25 million.
2. DEL: UJ, July 1 and 10, Dec. 11, 1969, Feb. 12, and Mar. 27, 1970; Lilienthal,
"Personal memorandum of telephone conversation with Sol M. Linowitz," Feb.
19, 1970.
3. Lilienthal, *Journals* 7:172. Interview with Rodman Rockefeller, July 22, 1986,
New York City. Interview with Roland Pampanini, July 13, 1988, New York
City. DEL: Lilienthal to Rockefeller, Apr. 22, 1970.
4. DEL: the unsettling events of that summer season were recorded in great detail in
the unpublished journal. See especially May 19, 20, and 30, June 26, July 8 and
9, Sept. 2, 4, 17, and 20, 1970; DEL to Joseph Flom [Lilienthal's personal
attorney], Sept. 7, 1970.
5. DEL: UJ, Sept. 22, 23, and 27, Oct. 3 and 8, 1970; Lilienthal memorandum to
files regarding telephone conversation with Todd Parsons of IBEC, Oct. 1, 70;
Lilienthal to Pritchard, Oct. 14, 1970; Donald Meads, IBEC to Lilienthal and
Walton Seymour, D&R, "Confirmation of agreement between Development &
Resources Corporation ('D&R'), its principal stockholders, and International
Basic Economy Corporation ('IBEC')," Oct. 28, 1970. "Companies Announce
Merger Actions," *New York Times,* Oct. 30, 1970, 65.
6. Interview with Pampanini, July 13, 1988, New York City.
7. DEL: UJ, Nov. 11, 16, 26, 28, and 30, 1970, Jan. 14 and 16, 1971. Lilienthal,
Journals 7:202.
8. AP: Meads and Rockefeller to IBEC Officers, Mar. 3, 1971. AA: IBEC, *Annual
Report, 1977,* New York, N.Y., Mar. 31, 1978.
9. Lilienthal, *Journals* 6:294; 7:135. Interview with Pampanini, July 13, 1988. DEL:
UJ, Feb. 7, 1961.
10. Lilienthal, *Journals* 5:310–11; 6:133.
11. DEL: UJ, Dec. 28 and 29, 1964, Feb. 23, 1965, July 19 and 20, 1964. Lilienthal,
Journals 6:73–75, 150.
12. Lilienthal, *Journals* 7:198. DEL: Levin to SERETE, Nov. 20, 1970; Lilienthal to
"my fellow workers in D&R," Feb. 1, 1972.
13. AP: Pampanini to Lilienthal, May 19, 1972. Lilienthal, *Journals* 7:299–300, 315.
DEL: Seymour to Files, June 28, 1972; Pampanini to Seymour, June 30, 1972; UJ,
July 1 and 2, Sept. 21, 1972; Seymour to files, July 21, 1972; "Contract Between
D&R and Brazil for San Francisco Valley Project," Sept. 19, 1972; D&R press
release regarding contract, Sept. 19, 1972; Pampanini to Staff, Nov. 6, 1972.
14. Lilienthal, *Journals* 7:348. DEL: "Sao Francisco Valley Summary," Mar. 3, 1973.
15. Lilienthal, *Journals* 7:363–66, 388–89, 426. DEL: UJ, May 29, and July 18,
1973; Lilienthal to Rockefeller, Mar. 15, 1974.
16. Lilienthal, *Journals* 7:438, 440, 476. DEL: Rocha to Lilienthal, June 1, 1973;
Pampanini to Rocha, June 11, 1973; Lilienthal to Rocha, June 13, 1973;
Pampanini to Lilienthal, June 22, 1973; Pampanini to Frederiksen, May 6, 1974;
Frederiksen to Lilienthal, May 15, 1975 (these letters chronicle the rise and fall of
the D&R–DeS relationship). AA: D&R Board Minutes, June 27, 1974. Graham,
"Regional Development Policy," 23–39.
17. DEL: Seymour, memorandum to files, July 21, 1972; Robock quotation in UJ,
Feb. 14, 1973.
18. Peter Kihss, "Two City Officials Clash on Need for Power Plant," *New York
Times,* Aug. 5, 1970, 39. Bundy quotation in Lilienthal, *Journals* 7:206. DEL:
Lilienthal to Bundy, Feb. 11, 1970; Lilienthal to files, Feb. 18, 1970; UJ, Feb. 13,

17, 18, and 21, 1970; Lilienthal to Ray, July 28, 1973; F. A. Spencer to D&R files, Aug. 10, 1973; Pampanini to Frederiksen, Aug. 22, and Sept. 5, 1973; Pampanini to Lilienthal, Sept. 12, 1973.

19. Lilienthal, *Journals* 7:216, 543–45. Lilienthal, "If This Continues, the Cockroach Will Inherit the Earth," *New York Times,* June 20, 1975, 35.

20. Lilienthal, *Journals* 7:576–78. "Atomic Engineers Resign over Safety," *Facts on File World News Digest,* Feb. 14, 1976, 115 A1. "Why the Dream Gets Dimmer by the Day," *U.S. News & World Report,* Feb. 16, 1976, 49. Samuel H. Day Jr., "Lilienthal's Warning," *Bulletin of the Atomic Scientists,* Mar. 1976, 7.

21. Lilienthal, *Journals* 7:497–98, 501, 514–15, 519, 566, 589–90. "Notes on People," *New York Times,* Dec. 13, 1975, 23.

22. Lilienthal, *Journals* 7:589–90, 601. Lilienthal, "New Opportunities for 'Underdeveloped' America to Seize," *Smithsonian,* July 1976. DEL: Lilienthal to Macy, May 6, 1976; Seymour to Lilienthal, May 21, 1976; John Cunniff, "Lilienthal Sounded Energy Warning 24 Years Ago," "Negativism Stunting America," "Diversity Key to Future, Lilienthal Says," June 1976. These articles are from Lilienthal's clipping file. They appeared in many papers across the country.

23. Lilienthal, "Energy from Waters," *New York Times,* Dec. 28, 1976, 27. Lilienthal, *Journals* 7:624, 645, 652, 660–61, 669. AA: D&R Board Minutes, Nov. 17, 1976 and June 29, 1977. DEL: Lilienthal to files, Dec. 21, 1976; Macy to Lilienthal, Jan. 18, 1977; Lilienthal to Rockefeller, Jan. 27, 1977; Lilienthal to files, May 17, 1977.

24. Freeman quotation in Lilienthal, *Journals* 7:659–61. DEL: Macy, memorandum for the record, Mar. 15, 1977.

25. Lilienthal, *Journals* 7:674, 679, 682–83 (Fri quotation on 682). DEL: Lilienthal to File, May 17, 1977.

26. Lilienthal, *Journals* 7:665, 698–99, 716. DEL, UJ, Oct. 3 and 4, 1977; Garner to Files, Dec. 29, 1977; Lilienthal to Macy, Jan. 12, 1978.

27. DEL: Clapp to Lilienthal, Macy, and John Silveira, Mar. 24, 1978. AA: "Corporate Development Project Summary," Mar. 23, 1978; "Corporate Development Summary," Nov. 30, 1978.

28. "Small-hydro power starting comeback," *Business Week,* Mar. 20, 1978, 146L. "Championing the Cause of Small Hydroelectric Units," *National Journal,* Apr. 29, 1978, 674. AA: William H. Gill to Silveira, "Summary of Corporate Development Activities, June 1978, June 23, 1978. DEL: Garner to Files, "Allis-Chalmers," July 19, 1978; Clapp, Memorandum for Record, "Telephone conversation with Thomas L. Dineen," Aug. 18, 1978; Clarence E. Korhonen, "D&R Small Hydro Program Strategy," Sept. 19, 1978; Lilienthal to Macy, Sept. 22, 1978; "D&R Contractual Commitments, Feb. 8, 1979.

29. Interview with Norman Clapp, July 28, 1987.

30. Interview with Norman Clapp, July 28, 1987. Interview with David Morse, July 28, 1986. DEL: UJ, June 15, 1976; correspondence between Lilienthal and Macy, Apr. 26, and May 19, 1976, Sept. 22, 1978.

31. AA: Pampanini to Helander, "D&R Operations Reports to IBEC," Dec. 29, 1972; Pampanini to Lilienthal, Seymour, Frederiksen, Silveira, and Wimmer, "New Business development, CY 1972," Feb. 12, 1973; D&R, "Table of Current Programs and Schedules," Feb. 1977. DEL: Lilienthal to the Shah, Apr. 11, 1973; Lilienthal to Assadollah Alam, minister of the Imperial Court, June 2, 1971; UJ, Apr. 14, 19, and 20, May 13, June 2 and 8, July 6, and Oct. 18, 19, and 21, 1971. Lilienthal, *Journals* 7:391.

32. Lilienthal, *Journals* 7:448. DEL: UJ, July 16, and Nov. 4, 1974. AP: Pampanini to Lilienthal, Nov. 8, and Nov. 18, 1974.

33. AP: Pampanini to Lilienthal, "Iran Public Sector Management Preliminary

Mission Report," Dec. 17, 1974; Pampanini to Macy, "Project Budget and Staffing Schedule," Jan. 23, 1975.

34. DEL: UJ, Apr. 14, and May 13, 1971, Aug. 10 and 19, Sept. 7, 1974.

35. Shah quotation in Lilienthal, *Journals* 7:488. DEL: UJ, May 21, Aug. 10 and 19, Sept. 7, 1974

36. DEL: UJ, Aug. 13, Oct. 29, 1974, Jan. 9, 1975. AA: D&R Board Minutes, Dec. 6, 1974.

37. DEL: UJ, Nov. 21, 1970, Apr. 19, 1971 (Shahgholi quotation from first UJ entry). Macy to Lilienthal, Apr. 26, 1976. DRC: Lilienthal to Samii, July 6, 1971. AP: Pampanini to Shahgholl, Feb. 29, 1972; Pampanini to Senior Staff, Dec. 12, 1972; Pampanini to Lilienthal, Aug. 14, 1973.

38. Lilienthal, *Journals* 7:321, 399, 401, 439, 556. DEL: Farmanfarmaian quotation in UJ, Apr. 19, 1971. Ebtehaj, *Khatirat-i Abu al-Hasan Ibtihaj,* 791.

39. Keddie, *Roots of Revolution,* 231. Bill, *The Eagle and the Lion,* 181–82, 202–3. Amin Saikal, *The Rise and Fall of the Shah* (Princeton: Princeton Univ. Press, 1980), 182ff.

40. DEL: Lilienthal, "The Brass Tacks of Agribusiness: The Case of Persia's Khuzestan Region," speech to the National Industrial Conference Board, Sept. 11, 1967; Lilienthal to Pritchard, Jan. 21, 1971; UJ, Sept. 22, Nov. 1, 11, and 13, 1969, Dec. 21, 1970, Nov. 12, 1974, May 4, 1975 (Ebtehaj quotation in last UJ entry). Grace E. Goodell, *Elementary Structures of Political Life,* 168–69. Keddie, *Roots of Revolution,* 165–67. Robert E. Looney, *Economic Origins of the Iranian Revolution* (New York: Pergamon Press, 1982), 53. Cheryl Payer, *The World Bank: A Critical Analysis* (New York: Monthly Review Press, 1982), 274–76.

41. AP: Pampanini to Macy, Oct. 29, 1975, Jan. 3, and Feb. 6, 1977. DEL: UJ, Oct. 24, 1976, and May 31, 1977; Macy to Lilienthal, Jan. 29, and Apr. 28, 1976, Feb. 1, Feb. 13, May 11, and Sept. 9, 1977, Apr. 27, 1978.

42. DEL: Lilienthal to Macy, May 6, 1976; UJ, May 23, and June 6, 1976.

43. AP: Pampanini to Macy Feb. 6, 1977. AA: D&R Board Minutes, June 28, 1978. DEL: Macy to Lilienthal, Feb. 13, 1977; D&R, "Iran Public Sector Management Project Report of Phase II, June 1, 1978.

44. AP: Pampanini to Macy, Jan. 24, and Feb. 8, 1975. DEL: Macy, Memorandum for Record, Feb. 5, 1976.

45. Lilienthal, *Journals* 7:728. DEL: Macy to Lilienthal, Apr. 27, 1978; UJ, June 20, 1978.

46. Lilienthal, *Journals* 7:730–41. DEL: Macy to Lilienthal, Oct. 2, 1978; Macy for the record, Nov. 2, 1978.

47. Lilienthal, *Journals* 7:739–43. DEL: Macy to Rockefeller/Lilienthal, Jan. 17 and 23, 1979; UJ, Jan. 7 and 15, 1979; "D&R Contractual Commitments," Feb. 8, 1979; D&R, "Press Release," Mar. 1, 1979. Bradley Graham, "Turmoil in Iran to Kill Off Firm," *Washington Post,* Mar. 1, 1979, D12. AA: D&R Board Minutes, Feb. 7, 1979; D&R, "Summary of Assets in Iran as of April 15, 1979," Apr. 14, 1979.

48. Correspondence between David Lilienthal Jr. and Lilienthal, Feb. 5 and 19, 1979. Helen Lilienthal, "Editor's Note," in Lilienthal, *Journals* 7:xiii.

49. DEL: UJ, Oct. 24, and Dec. 6, 1971, Nov. 19, 1977; Macy—Memorandum for Record, Nov. 9, 1977. Lilienthal, "The New Iran," *Asia,* May 1974, 3. Lilienthal, "My Turn: Rebirth of a Nation," *Newsweek,* July 15, 1974, 9. Lilienthal, *Journals* 7:585.

50. DEL: Macy to files, Nov. 9, 1977; UJ, Nov. 19, 1977.

51. DEL: A series of four letters, two each by father and son are attached to unpublished journal entries, Feb. 21, and Mar. 15, 1977.

52. Lilienthal, *Journals* 7:739, 742, 762. DEL: Macy, "What Influence did Adminis-

trative Reform, Particularly as Assisted by American Professionals, Have Upon the Counter Revolutionary Forces in Iran?" mimeographed paper, Mar. 31, 1979.

53. Lilienthal, *Journals* 7:762. Ebtehaj, *Khatirat-i Abu al-Hasan Ibtihaj,* 791–93.

54. Goodell, *Elementary Structures of Political Life,* 25–26, 29, 30–31, 175–76, 185, 200, 232, 343–44. Keddie, *Roots of Revolution,* 147–48.

55. See Bill's excellent discussion of American supporters of Iran in *The Eagle and the Lion,* especially 180–81, 203, 320–21, 428–29.

56. Goodell, *Elementary Structures of Political Life,* 31. Harald Mehner, "Development and Planning in Iran after World War II," in George Lenczowski, *Iran Under the Pahlavis* (Stanford: Hoover Institution Press, 1978), 195. Lilienthal, *Journals* 7:627–28. DEL: UJ, Apr. 14, 1971, Jan. 20, and June 20, 1978.

57. AP: Pampanini to Lilienthal, Feb. 12, 1974. Lilienthal, *Journals* 7:448, 541. DEL: UJ, Feb. 21, 1977. This entry includes a copy of Lilienthal's response to David Jr.'s Jan. 31 letter.

58. Lilienthal, *Journals* 7:567, 604, 606. DEL: UJ, Oct. 4, 1971, Dec. 20, 1973, Oct. 5, 1976. AP: Frederiksen, "notes on October 5, 1976 meeting with Lilienthal," Oct. 22, 1976. Several letters in the AP file after the publication of the last journal volume, deny that Frederiksen acted improperly when he formed his own company in 1975. Frederiksen to Morse, Dec. 23, 1983, Ferrel H. Ensign to Frederiksen, Mar. 5, 1984, Francis E. Brocalli to Frederiksen, Mar. 19, 1984, Jack Buckley to Frederiksen, Apr. 27, 1984. Ensign, Brocalli, and Buckley had all worked for D&R in California before signing on with Frederiksen's new company.

59. AP: Pampanini to Lilienthal, Sept. 16, 1974.; interview with Norman Clapp, July 28, 1987. DEL: UJ, Mar. 11, 1975.

60. Interview with Rodman Rockefeller, New York City, July 22, 1986. Interview with David Morse, New York City, July 28, 1986.

61. Lilienthal, *Journals* 7:588–89, 642. DEL: UJ, Aug. 14, and Nov. 28, 1971, Dec. 18, 1976 and Jan. 8, 1977; Lilienthal to Pampanini, May 6, 1974. AP: Lilienthal, "Development And Resources Corporation Chairman's Report to the Board of Directors: Associations with Princeton Univ.," Mar. 1976. "Shorter Reviews," *New York Times Book Reviews,* Jan. 30, 1972, 33. There were only a few other reviews of volume 5, two of them by Arthur Schlesinger Jr. and James MacGregor Burns. Schlesinger recognized Lilienthal's underlying currents of ego and insecurity when he noted that "the need to assuage some inner insecurity is suggested by the pleasure he evidently feels when he can record testimony about how much influence he has, especially among the young. . . . David Lilienthal really does not need to tell us—and should not have to tell himself—how good he is." "On a Worldwide Mission to Make Things Work Better," *Bookworld,* May 30, 1971, 4. In 1976 there were only two short reviews of volume 6, both in trade journals *Booklist* and *Publishers Weekly.*

62. DEL: "A Testament of Faith in America," an address by David E. Lilienthal at commencement exercises, DePauw Univ., Greencastle, Ind., May 24, 1970, "The Rebirth of a Nation," discourse by David E. Lilienthal before the Annual Meeting of the American Philosophical Society, Philadelphia, Apr. 24, 1976; Lilienthal, "The American Ethical Revolution," Gordon R. Clapp Lecture at Lawrence Univ., Appleton, Wis., Sept. 29, 1976. See also Lilienthal, "The Coming Renaissance of the United States, address before the VII Pan American Management Conference, Cali, Colombia, Sept. 8–10, 1971; Lilienthal, "Economic Growth: A Humanist View," address before the American International Club of Geneva Switzerland, Oct. 13, 1972; Lilienthal, "America: The Greatest Underdeveloped Country," address to the American Institute of Planners and the American Society of Planning Officials, Washington, D.C., Mar. 22, 1976. The same sentiments are

voiced in his editorial in *Newsweek,* July 15, 1974, and the article in *Smithsonian,* July 1976.

63. Lilienthal, *Journals* 7:470, 760–62. Lilienthal, *Atomic Energy: A New Start* (New York: Harper & Row, 1980). DEL: "Summary List of Atom Book Reviews," Sept. 19, 1980. Richard Brookhiser, "Books in Brief," *National Review,* Aug. 8, 1980, 979. David Quammen, "Reactor Race: Did We Back a Loser?" *Christian Science Monitor,* Aug. 11, 1980, B3. *New Yorker,* Aug. 25, 1980, 102–3. T. C. Holyoke, *Antioch Review,* Winter 1981, 129. "Notable Books of 1980," *Christian Science Monitor,* Jan. 12, 1981, B6.

64. Lilienthal, *Journals* 7:743–45, 757–59, 762–83.

65. Lilienthal, *Journals* 7:788–89, 791. DEL: David Lilienthal Jr. to Lilienthal, Sept. 22, 1980; Lilienthal to Dilworth, Oct. 23, 1980; Lilienthal to David Lilienthal Jr., Dec. 20, 1980; UJ, May 15 and 29, 1980.

66. Helen M. Lilienthal, "Epilogue," in Lilienthal, *Journals* 7:795–96. DEL: Order of Service, "Service of Remembrance for David E. Lilienthal"; Eulogy texts of John W. Macy Jr., J. Richardson Dilworth, and Donald Straus.

Chapter 14. Assessment

1. The unpublished documents in this section are drawn from three major sources: the office of Representative Edward J. Markey (D-Mass.), the U.S. Dept. of Energy (DOE) information center in Las Vegas, Nev.; and the Advisory Committee on Human Radiation Experiments (via Joseph Volpe). All the DOE documents, including those from Markey and the Advisory Committee, are available from the information center, and thus are marked DOE. When available, a document or accession number is included. The total figures on human radiation experiments were derived from the following documents: U.S. Congress, Subcommittee on Energy Conservation and power of the Committee on Energy and Commerce, U.S. House of Representatives, *American Nuclear Guinea Pigs: Three Decades of Radiation Experiments on U.S. Citizens* (Washington, D.C.: GPO, 1986). Task Force on Human Subject Research, *A Report on the Use of Radioactive Materials in Human Subject Research that Involved Residents of State-Operated Facilities within the Commonwealth of Massachusetts from 1943–1973* (Boston: Dept. of Mental Retardation, Apr. 1994), 15. "Statement of Representative Edward J. Markey before the Presidential Advisory Committee on Human Radiation Experiments" (Washington, D.C.: transcript from Markey office, Apr. 21, 1994).

2. Joseph Volpe Jr. to Steven M. Neuse, Sept. 6, 1994. Telephone interview with Joseph Volpe, Jan. 17, 1995. It can be inferred that Lilienthal knew about the polonium studies because a 1950 volume with an essay about those experiments includes a foreword by him: David E. Lilienthal, "Foreword," in Robert M. Fink, ed., *Biological Studies with Polonium, Radium, and Plutonium* (New York: McGraw-Hill, 1950), v.

3. DOE: U.S. Atomic Energy Commission, Interim Medical Committee, "Report" (mimeographed, Jan. 23–24, 1947) (140375); Carroll L. Wilson to Stafford L. Warren, Feb. 6, 1947 (700017); John L. Burling to Edwin E. Huddleston Jr., Mar. 7, 1947; and Huddleston to Wilson, Mar. 10, 1947 (both 702114); Wilson to Warren, Apr. 30, 1947. Staff to Congressman Edward J. Markey, Memorandum: The Plutonium Papers, Mar. 20, 1994, 9–10;

4. U.S. Atomic Energy Commission, *Third Semiannual Report* (Washington, D.C.: GPO, 1948), 16. DOE: U.S. Atomic Energy Commission, Medical Board of

Review, "Report," (mimeographed, June 20, 1947), 11 (79430); Lilienthal to
G. W. Beadle, Aug. 6, 1947 (708789); Wilson to Robert Stone, Nov. 5, 1947,
quoted from letter Shields Warren to Leslie M. Redman, Mar. 5, 1951 (702133).

5. Volpe interview, Jan. 17, 1995. By June 30, 1947, the Manhattan Project and
AEC had distributed 407 shipments of radioactive isotopes for medical therapy
and 945 for research to institutions throughout the nation; U.S. Atomic Energy
Commission, *Seventh Semiannual Report* (Washington, D.C.: GPO, 1950), 200.
Telephone interview with Martha DeMare, DOE Information Center, Las Vegas,
Sept. 28, 1994. Telephone interview with Robert Schlinker, Argonne Laborato-
ries, Chicago, Aug. 25, 1994. The latter two DOE officials have both been
involved with the release of human subjects materials over the past year. A. C. Ivy,
"The History and Ethics of the Use of Human Subjects in Medical Experiments,"
Science, July 2, 1948, 3.

6. Energy Research and Development Administration, "Fact Sheet on Manhattan
Engineer District (MED) Plutonium Excretion Studies," Feb. 1976. DOE: "Cal4
Records (Americium)" (0700298); "Summary Factsheet Human Experimenta-
tion-SFS1.003" (704271); "Factsheet Human Experimentation—SFS1.003"
(704168); "Human Use Experiments with Polonium" (700140). *American
Nuclear Guinea Pigs,* 26. John Abbotts to Neuse, Oct. 5, 1994.

7. S. Allan Lough to Clemens E. Benda, Nov. 3, 1949. *Seventh Semiannual Report,*
200.

8. Kurt Vonnegut, *Wampeters, Foma & Granfalloons (Opinions)* (New York:
Laurel Edition, 1989), 98–99. DEL: UJ, June 12, 1976. Telephone interview with
John Abbotts, Oct. 4, 1994.

9. See U.S. Dept. of Energy, *Human Radiation Experiments: The Department of
Energy Roadmap to the Story and the Records* (Washington, D.C.: DOE, Feb.
1995), for the first published compendium on this issue. DEL: Lilienthal, "The
Multinational Corporation," a paper prepared for a symposium "Management
and Corporations, 1985," Graduate School of Industrial Administration of the
Carnegie Institute of Technology, Apr. 21–22, 1960 (New York: Development &
Resources Corporation, 1960), 17, 24, 27. Also reprinted in Melvin Anshen and
Leland Back, eds., *Management and Corporations, 1985* (New York: McGraw-
Hill, 1960), 119–58.

10. Glendon A Schubert Jr., "'The Public Interest' in Administrative Decision-
Making," in Robert T. Golembiewski, Frank Gibson, Geoffrey Y. Cornog, *Public
Administration: Readings in Institutions, Processes, Behavior* (Chicago: Rand
McNally & Company, 1966), 393. Schubert's essay, originally published in the
American Political Science Review (June 1957), 346–68, is a masterful attempt to
come to grips with the elusive notion of "the public interest." Schubert artfully
develops the notion of the administrative Platonist, drawing from the works of
Merle Fainsod, Emmette Redford, and Paul Appleby, three of America's most
distinguished political scientists.

11. Interview with Gerald Levin, July 28, 1986, New York City. Interview with
Joseph A. Volpe, July 28, 1987. DEL: Levin to Lilienthal, Nov. 30, 1971.

12. Interviews with Rodman Rockefeller, July 22, 1986, New York City, and Edward
Falck, July 21, 1987, in Washington, D.C.; DEL: incomplete manuscript by Fred
Arvin, sent to Lilienthal after the former's death in Mar. 1963, 52–55, 58.
Lilienthal, *Journals* 1:147. *The Mirage of 1918* (Anderson, Ind.: Herald Publish-
ing Company, 1918), 145. Oxnam, *Personalities in Social Reform,* 92, 102–3.
DEL: "Speeches by David E. Lilienthal, 1933–2/15/50," and "Articles by David
E. Lilienthal, 1924–2/15/50." Lilienthal gave no speeches before "sacred"
audiences before 1942. Between then and 1950, however, he made two Chapel
addresses at DePauw College, spoke to a national conference on science, philoso-

phy, and religion in New York City, a Roman Catholic gathering, two Protestant meetings, and a Rochester synagogue. Many of his speeches were covered extensively in *Christian Century* and reprinted in ecclesiastical publications, including *Zion's Herald, The Churchman,* and *The Methodist Layman.* DEL: UJ, Oct. 1, 1965. Schwarz, *The New Dealers,* 198.

13. DEL: Lilienthal to Bea, May 29, and Aug. 2, 1968, June 5, 1969, Jan. 11, 1973; Lilienthal to Allen, May 29, 1968, Apr. 21, 1967; UJ, Nov. 24, and Dec. 18, 1976; Lilienthal to Dee Szold, Jan. 13, 1981. Lilienthal, *Journals* 7:470. Quotation from Murrow note in Lilienthal, *Journals* 6:60. DEL: Lilienthal to Moses, Jan. 14, 1981 (Lilienthal must have misdated this note. He died sometime during the night of Jan. 13–14).

14. First quotation from Lilienthal, "My Turn," 9. DEL: Lilienthal, "A Testament of Faith in America," a commencement address at DePauw Univ., Greencastle, Ind., May 24, 1970. Virtually all his addresses and writings in the 1970s include this sense of optimism and hope.

15. Richard Sennett, *The Fall of Public Man* (New York: Vintage Books, 1978), 87. "Fires Blast at Critics," *Chattanooga Daily Times,* Sept. 29, 1933, 1.

16. George Will, "Listen to the Bridges," *Newsweek,* Apr. 25, 1988, 70.

17. DEL: Arthur M. Schlesinger Jr. to Helen Lilienthal, Jan. 16, 1981.

Bibliographical Essay

The most thorough collection of papers pertaining to David E. Lilienthal is in the Seeley G. Mudd Manuscript Library at Princeton University. In addition to Lilienthal's extensive papers, which cover every period of his life except the very earliest, the Mudd Library holds many Development and Resources Corporation (D&R) files on Iran in another collection, a large number of uncatalogued items on D&R, and some unopened files Lilienthal feared might be detrimental to Iranian citizens who worked for D&R. It is fortunate that Lilienthal and his wife Helen, at his insistence, kept almost everything he wrote. The family deeded virtually everything, including documents that flatter and many that do not, to Princeton, along with generous monetary contributions to catalogue the collection.

Much Lilienthal material can be found in four presidential libraries, the Herbert Hoover Library in West Branch, Iowa; the Franklin D. Roosevelt Library in Hyde Park, New York; the Harry S. Truman Library in Independence, Missouri; and the Lyndon Baines Johnson Library in Austin, Texas. The Hoover library possesses Lewis L. Strauss's and Bourke B. Hickenlooper's papers, two of Lilienthal's strongest atomic energy opponents. In addition to the FDR papers, the Roosevelt Library holds key papers of Morris Cooke and Adolf Berle. The Truman Library has official presidential papers, as well as those of Clark Clifford and Gordon R. Clapp. The Johnson Library details Lilienthal's involvement in Vietnam during the late 1960s.

The Library of Congress Manuscript Division holds other relevant archives, those of Felix Frankfurter, Harold Ickes, William I. Nichols, George Norris, and J. Robert Oppenheimer. Other useful collections include additional Frankfurter papers at Harvard Law School; H. A. Morgan at the University of Tennessee, Knoxville; Kenneth D. McKellar, Memphis Public Library; and William Waymack, Iowa Historical Society, Iowa City. Two private collections proved helpful in understanding the D&R years. Andrea Pampanini of New York City shared his extensive D&R file with me. There is also a substantial accumulation of D&R papers at the Rockefeller family Arbor Acres Corporation, Glastonbury, Connecticut, which Rodman Rockefeller allowed me to use. Finally, I received invaluable assistance in gathering information about Lilienthal's early life from local historians, historical societies, and public and school librarians in Morton, Illinois; Valparaiso and Michigan City, Indiana; and the DePauw University Library Archives in Greencastle, Indiana.

It seems appropriate, considering Lilienthal's consistent opposition to excess security measures and limiting public debate on atomic energy policies, to comment on government sources of information on Lilienthal other than libraries: The National Archives, Department of Energy (DOE), Federal Bureau of Investigation (FBI), and Tennessee Valley Authority (TVA). In several instances, gaining access to and using documents at some agencies were painful reminders of the legacy of secretiveness that Lilienthal resisted so strongly. It took more than two years and repeated prodding before the FBI honored my Freedom of Information Act request for Lilienthal's file and his correspondence with J. Edgar Hoover. The file that finally appeared was voluminous, but disappointing. There was no Lilienthal-Hoover correspondence, and many of the records were either so heavily censored or poorly copied that they were virtually useless—indeed, I had, in the meantime, located in other archives uncensored documents that had been thoroughly blacked out by the bureau. The file was most useful in revealing the FBI as a high-powered clipping service and frenetic gossip mill. The bulk of what I received consisted of hundreds of newspaper articles from the late 1940s on the AEC and many memoranda on rumors and allegations about Lilienthal's alleged left-wing ties. Trying to use the Department of Energy's (DOE) History Division holdings at Germantown, Maryland, was also frustrating. DOE historians were helpful in locating a few items, but the vast majority of documents, some more than thirty years old, remained classified—including most of minutes from the nearly four hundred AEC meetings while Lilienthal was chairman.

The TVA Corporate Library in Knoxville has an excellent collection of oral history employee interviews, as well as many important official files. Some years ago, TVA microfilmed an extensive Lilienthal official file, one copy of which is in the Mudd Library and the other in the National Archives' Atlanta Branch. Unfortunately, the file is difficult to use because it is often poorly reproduced and inadequately indexed. Access at the National Archives in Washington, D.C., to material relating to the 1938 TVA congressional investigation and to Lilienthal's AEC Office files was superb. The DOE, particularly the staff at the agency's national clearinghouse in Las Vegas, provided excellent service in retrieving information on human radiation experiments in the 1940s. Congressman Edward Markey's (D-Mass.) office also contributed substantial documentation regarding early human radiation experiments.

The International Bank for Regional Development (World Bank) Archives in Washington, D.C., is an indispensable source of information on the D&R–Bank relationship regarding Iran. Unfortunately, after one useful session in their archives, I was discouraged from returning because of the sensitivity of the Iranian material. I was reminded in courteous, but firm, fashion that the World Bank was as an international organization and thus not subject to U.S. freedom-of-information laws.

Other widely available government publications are also important. Those covering the TVA years include the multivolume U.S. Congress, Joint Committee on the Investigation of the Tennessee Valley Authority, *Investigation of the Tennessee Valley Authority* (Washington, D.C.: GPO, 1939) and "Message from the President of the United States Transmitting Information Relative to the Removal of a Member of the Tennessee Valley Authority, the Opinion of the Attorney General, and the Transcript of the Hearings held on March, 11, 18, & 21, 1938," Senate Document No. 155 (Washington, D.C.: GPO, 1938). U.S. Congress, Senate Section of the Joint Committee on Atomic Energy, *Confirmation of the Atomic Energy Commission and the General Manager* (Washington, D.C.: GPO, 1947) and U.S. Congress, Joint Committee on Atomic Energy, *Investigation into the United States Atomic Energy Project* (Washington, D.C.: GPO, 1949) are crucial for understanding the conflicts during Lilienthal's tenure as AEC chairman. His later involvement in atomic energy matters is covered in United States Atomic Energy Commission, "In the Matter of J. Robert Oppenheimer: Transcript of Hearing before Personnel Security Board" (Washington, D.C.: GPO, 1963) and U.S. Congress, Joint Committee on Atomic Energy, *Development, Growth, and State of the Atomic Energy Industry* (Washington, D.C.: GPO, 1963).

Two oral history interview collections were especially useful. In addition to the TVA Corporate Library collection, I utilized Charles W. Crawford's magnificent set of TVA employee interviews, reposited in the Mississippi Valley Collection, John Willard Brister Library, Memphis University.

Specific studies of Lilienthal are limited in number. The earliest and most sympathetic is a short biography by Willson Whitman, *David E. Lilienthal: Public Servant in a Power Age* (New York: Henry Holt & Company, 1948). Two years later G. Bromley Oxnam, in *Personalities in Social Reform* (New York: Abingdon-Cokesbury Press, 1950), featured Lilienthal as one of his leading "personalities." More recently, there is another positive essay, J. W. Macy Jr., "David E. Lilienthal: The Manager as Humanist," in Robert Haught, ed., *Giants in Management* (Washington, D.C.: National Academy of Public Administration, 1983), and two fine critical studies of Lilienthal and TVA: Erwin C. Hargrove, "David Lilienthal and the Tennessee Valley Authority," in Jameson W. Doig and Erwin C. Hargrove, eds., *Leadership and Innovation: A Biographical Perspective on Entrepreneurs in Government* (Baltimore: Johns Hopkins Univ. Press, 1987), and a chapter on Lilienthal in Jordan A. Schwarz, *The New Dealers: Power Politics in the Age of Roosevelt* (New York: Alfred A. Knopf, 1993). A final essay that examines Lilienthal's public role is my "David Lilienthal: Exemplar of Public Purpose," *International Journal of Public Administration,* vol. 5, 1991.

The relevant secondary literature is vast and varied. Some studies concentrate more narrowly on particular topics such as TVA. Other works are more panoramic. Sometimes Lilienthal is barely mentioned, and other times he plays a major role in the author's narrative. Richard Hofstadter, *The Age of Reform: From Bryan to F.D.R.* (New York: Alfred A. Knopf, 1981); Eric Goldman, *Rendezvous with Destiny: A History of Modern American Reform* (New York: Vintage Books, 1958); and Louis Hartz, *The Liberal Tradition in America* (New York: Harcourt, Brace & World, 1955) are important studies of American Progressivism and liberalism. While Hofstadter uses Lilienthal as a major example, Goldman mentions him once, and Hartz not at all. Two works set forth thoughtful explanations for the failure of American liberalism abroad: Carl N. Degler, "The American Past: An Unsuspected Obstacle in Foreign Affairs," *American Scholar,* Spring 1963; and Robert A. Packenham, *Liberal America and the Third World* (Princeton: Princeton Univ. Press, 1973).

One of the best general treatments of the 1920s is Arthur M. Schlesinger Jr., *The Crisis of the Old Order, 1919–1933* (Boston: Houghton Mifflin Company, 1957). Irving Bernstein, *The Lean Years* (Boston: Houghton Mifflin Company, 1960), is a thorough analysis of the labor movement in the same era, and Thomas E. Vadney, *The Wayward Liberal: A Political Biography of Donald Richberg* (Lexington: Univ. of Kentucky Press, 1970), contributes an incisive portrait of Richberg and his relationship with Lilienthal. The battle over public utilities is dealt with in almost any issue of *Public Utilities Fortnightly* between 1925 and 1935. The scholarly, yet readable, William E. Mosher and Finla G. Crawford, *Public Utility Regulation* (New York: Harper & Row, 1932), is a good technical primer on the utility controversies of the times. Forrest McDonald, *Let There Be Light: The Electric Utility Industry in Wisconsin, 1881–1955* (Madison, Wis.: American History Research Center, 1957), is an excellent background study of the conflict over public utility regulation in Wisconsin. The Philip La Follette era is covered in John E. Miller, *Governor Philip F. La Follette, The Wisconsin Progressives and the New Deal* (Columbia: Univ. of Missouri Press, 1982), and in Donald Young, ed., *Adventures in Politics: The Memoirs of Philip La Follette* (New York: Holt, Rinehart & Winston, 1970). Eli Winston Clemens, "Public Utility Regulation in Wisconsin since the Reorganization of the Commission in 1931" (Ph.D. dissertation, Univ. of Wisconsin, 1940), focuses better than any other work on the Wisconsin Public Service Commission and offers a thoughtful criticism of Lilienthal as commissioner.

For general background on the Roosevelt era I relied on William E. Leuchtenberg, *Franklin Delano Roosevelt and the New Deal: 1932–1940* (New York: Harper & Row, 1963), and Schlesinger's two studies, *The Coming of the New Deal* and *The Politics of Upheaval* (Boston: Houghlin Mifflin Company, 1959 and 1960, respectively). Schlesinger's works also include considerable commentary on TVA. Other primary material with observations on Lilienthal can be found in Jonathan Daniels, *White House Witness: 1942–1945* (Garden City, N.Y.: Doubleday & Co., 1975): and the first three volumes of Harold Ickes, *The Secret Diary of Harold L. Ickes* (New York: Simon & Schuster, 1954 [all three volumes]). Richard Lowitt, *George W. Norris: The Triumph of a Progressive, 1933–1944* (Urbana: Univ. of Illinois Press, 1978), and Jordan A. Schwarz, *Liberal: Adolf A. Berle and the Vision of an American Era* (New York: The Free Press, 1987), are also rich with insights on the New Deal and Lilienthal.

More has been written about TVA than perhaps any other modern federal agency. The first book-length study was Willson Whitman, *God's Valley: People and Power along the Tennessee River* (New York: The Viking Press, 1939), a journalistic effort as laudatory as her biography. It was soon followed by another sympathetic but well-done scholarly effort, Herman Pritchett, *The Tennessee Valley Authority: A Study in Public Administration* (Chapel Hill: Univ. of North Carolina Press, 1943). Marguerite Owen, *The Tennessee Valley Authority* (New York: Praeger Publishers, 1973), is a thorough historical review by the former Washington office director. Many old-timers were disappointed with this work because it had nothing of the "insider's" touch. Some thought her strong sense of loyalty to TVA kept her from revealing much beyond the bare facts. Others were sure that she allowed top TVA officials to review and revise the manuscript before publication. Any study of TVA would be incomplete without Arthur E. Morgan, *The Making of TVA* (Buffalo: Prometheus Books, 1974). While much of Morgan's analysis is flawed by unreliable memory and his own biases, it is an invaluable commentary on TVA and its internal conflicts from a very different perspective.

The best works on TVA and Lilienthal are Thomas K. McCraw, *Morgan vs. Lilienthal: The Feud within the TVA* (Chicago: Loyola Univ. Press, 1970); Thomas K. McCraw, *TVA and the Power Fight: 1933–1939* (Philadelphia: J. B. Lippincott Company, 1971); and Roy Talbert Jr., *FDR's Utopian: Arthur Morgan of the TVA* (Jackson: Univ. Press of Mississippi, 1987). All three studies rely heavily on archives, and each contributes a thoughtful analysis of Lilienthal. Gregory B. Field, "'Electricity for All': The Electric Home and Farm Authority and the Politics of Mass Consumption, 1932–1935," *Business History Review*, Spring 1990, is the definitive study of TVA's efforts to increase consumption through the sale of home and farm appliances, and Don McBride, *TVA and National Defense* (Knoxville: TVA, 1975), provides a valuable interpretation from a former board member of TVA's role in the prewar buildup and World War II. Louis B. Wehle, *Hidden Threads of History: Wilson through Roosevelt* (New York: Macmillan Co., 1953), offers a firsthand account of the 1936 power-pooling negotiations. Ellsworth Barnard, *Wendell Willkie: Fighter for Freedom* (Marquette, Mich.: Northern Michigan Univ. Press, 1966), and Joseph Barnes, *Willkie: The Events He Was Part of, The Ideas He Fought For* (New York: Simon & Schuster, 1952), both fill in the details of the Lilienthal-Willkie relationship. Victor Hobday, *Sparks at the Grass Roots: Municipal Distribution of TVA Electricity in Tennessee* (Knoxville: Univ. of Tennessee Press, 1969), analyzes the development of TVA's linkages with local governments in the Tennessee Valley. Finally, Roscoe Martin, *TVA and International Technical Assistance* (Syracuse: TVA Consultant Report, 1970), is a comprehensive account of the international TVA vision that Lilienthal tried so hard to bring to the rest of the world.

While TVA was often criticized in the press and by industry groups, academic criticism did not surface until the late 1940s. Donald Davidson, *The Tennessee: The New River, Civil War to TVA*, vol. 2 (New York: Rinehart & Company, 1948), makes a scathing attack on TVA and Lilienthal from a Southern Agrarian viewpoint. Philip Selznick, *TVA and the Grass Roots: A Study in the Sociology of Formal Organization* (Berkeley: Univ. of California Press, 1949), and R. G. Tugwell and E. C. Banfield, "Grass Roots Democracy—Myth or Reality?" *Public Administration Review*, Winter 1950, are important critiques of Lilienthal's much-vaunted notion of grass roots administration and democracy.

The next series of critical analysis did not surface until around TVA's golden anniversary. North Callahan, *TVA: Bridge over Troubled Waters* (South Brunswick, New Jersey: A. S. Barnes, 1980) a highly controversial volume, was followed by a marvelous compilation of critical essays, Erwin C. Hargrove & Paul K. Conkin, eds., *TVA: Fifty Years of Grass-Roots Bureaucracy* (Urbana: Univ. of Illinois Press, 1983). Even in this volume, one senses great respect for the venerable Authority. Another TVA analysis in the fiftieth year is my "TVA at Age Fifty—Reflections and Retrospect," *Public Administration Review,* Nov.–Dec. 1983. Finally, William U. Chandler, *The Myth of TVA: Conservation and Development in the Tennessee Valley, 1933–1983* (Cambridge, Mass.: Ballinger Publishing Co., 1984) sets forth a strong and persuasive critique of TVA's much-touted positive economic impact on the Tennessee Valley.

Five studies with important background on the Truman administration include Joseph Marion Jones, *The Fifteen Weeks: February 21–June 5, 1947* (New York: Harcourt, Brace & World, 1955); Eric Goldman, *The Crucial Decade—and After: America, 1945–1960* (New York: Vintage Books, 1960); and Robert A. Pollard, "The National Security State Reconsidered: Truman and Economic Containment, 1945–1950"; John Lewis Gaddis, "The Insecurities of Victory: The United States and the Perception of the Soviet Threat After World War II"; and Charles S. Maier, "Alliance and Autonomy: European Identity and U.S. Foreign Policy Objectives in the Truman Years," all in Michael J. Lacey, ed., *The Truman Presidency* (New York: Cambridge Univ. Press, 1989). Jonathan Daniel's already-cited book has a good account of Lilienthal's reaction to the Roosevelt-Truman transition and to Truman's reappointment of Lilienthal. Dean Acheson, *Present at the Creation: My Years in the State Department* (New York: W. W. Norton & Co., 1969); Clark Clifford with Richard Holbrooke, *Counsel to the President: A Memoir* (New York: Random House, 1991); and Jonathan Daniels, *The Man of Independence* (Philadelphia: J. B. Lippincott Co., 1950) are important firsthand accounts of the Truman years. Acheson also contributes his own interpretation of Lilienthal's role in the debates over international atomic energy policy and the 1949–50 decision about the hydrogen bomb.

Without a doubt, the most comprehensive works relating to atomic energy are the first three volumes of the history of the AEC under the direction of former AEC-DOE historian, Richard G. Hewlett. Hewlett and Francis Duncan, *A History of the United States Atomic Energy Commission: Atomic Shield, 1947/1952* (University Park: Pennsylvania State Univ. Press, 1969), is an invaluable analysis of AEC and Lilienthal's role in the development of atomic energy policy. Hewlett and Oscar E. Anderson Jr., *A History of the United States Atomic Energy Commission: The New World, 1939/1946* (University Park: Pennsylvania State Univ. Press, 1962), and Hewlett and Jack M. Holl, *Atoms for Peace and War, 1953–1961: Eisenhower and the Atomic Energy Commission* (Berkeley: Univ. of California Press, 1989), yield additional perspectives on atomic energy issues before and after Lilienthal's tenure as AEC chairman. In spite of their length and attention to technical detail, these studies are compelling and readable. P. M. S. Blackett, *Fear, War, and the Bomb: Military and Political Consequences of Atomic Energy* (New York: Whittlesey House, 1949), and a more recent interpretation, Joseph I. Lieberman, *The Scorpion and the Tarantula: The Struggle to Control Atomic Weapons* (Boston: Houghton Mifflin Co., 1970) both shed light on the evolution of U.S. international atomic energy policy.

Several biographies provide pertinent insights on this period, including Jordan Schwarz, *The Speculator: Bernard M. Baruch in Washington, 1917–1965* (Chapel Hill: Univ. of North Carolina Press, 1981); Richard Pfau, *No Sacrifice Too Great: The Life of Lewis L. Strauss* (Charlottesville: Univ. Press of Virginia, 1984); Peter Michelmore, *The Swift Years: The Robert Oppenheimer Story* (New York: Dodd Mead & Co., 1969); James W. Kunetka, *Oppenheimer: The Years of Risk* (Englewood Cliffs, N.J.: Prentice Hall, 1982); and Philip M. Stern, *The Oppenheimer Case: Security on Trial* (New York: Harper & Row, 1969). The Baruch and Strauss biographies both develop critical perspectives on Lilienthal: Schwarz concentrates on the early conflict over control of U.S. international atomic policy and Pfau on debate within the AEC. The first two Oppenheimer biographies have detailed sketches of the Lilienthal-Oppenheimer relationship. Stern's book is about the 1963 Oppenheimer hearings. Two diaries contain unique outlooks on the postwar years: Walter Millis, ed., *The Forrestal Diaries* (New York: Viking Press, 1951) is an insider's viewpoint on the military-civilian struggle for control of the atom and Lilienthal's role in that process. Roger M. Anders, ed., *Forging the Atomic Shield: Excerpts from the Office Diary of Gordon E. Dean* (Chapel Hill: Univ. of North Carolina Press, 1987), adds critical insights about Lilienthal's last year at AEC.

Finally, Archibald MacLeish, "A Progress Report on Atomic energy: A Dialogue with the Chairman of the Atomic Energy Commission," *Life,* Sept. 27, 1948, and Joseph C. Harsch, "Lilienthal: A Whole Span of History," *Christian Science Monitor,* Nov. 25, 1949, offer telling commentaries on Lilienthal's public years. MacLeish's exquisite interview is a revealing account of Lilienthal's personal uneasiness over the atom and his ambivalent feelings toward the inordinate attention given the martial atom. Harsch's column is perhaps the best interpretation anywhere of Lilienthal's significance in the great transformation of American political life in the 1930s and 1940s.

There are relatively few published accounts of Lilienthal's work in international development. The Cauca Valley Corporation project is considered in some detail in Gayle Pendleton W. Jackson, "Making Policy in a Latin American Bureaucracy: The Cauca Valley Corporation of Colombia" (Ph.D. Dissertation, Washington Univ., 1972), and in Antonio J. Posada and Jeanne de Posada, *The CVC: Challenge to Underdevelopment and Traditionalism* (Bogota: Ediciones Tercer Mundo, 1966). My essay "The TVA Dream: David Lilienthal in Latin America," *International Journal of Public Administration,* vol. 6, 1992, is a broad analysis of D&R's Latin American projects through its twenty-five years. Peter Gabriel, *The International Transfer of Corporate Skills: Management Contracts in Less Developed Countries* (Boston: Harvard Univ. Graduate School of Business Administration, 1967) compares D&R's Iranian contract with similar contracts held by three other international consulting firms. Gabriel's work is less useful for this study because it is an abstract organizational analysis, and each of the companies and quoted individuals is treated anonymously. More useful, in some respects, is Thomas Mead, comp., *Development and Resources Corporation Archives: The Khuzestan Development Program,* July 23, 1955, through January 21, 1976 (Princeton: Princeton Univ. Library, n.d. [probably 1976 or 1977]). This volume has a comprehensive citation of company documents relating to the Khuzistan program and useful short historical summaries of D&R activities in Iran.

As one might expect, there are many sources on Iran. Nikki R. Keddie, *Roots of Revolution: An Interpretive History of Modern Iran* (New Haven: Yale Univ. Press, 1981), provides excellent background on Iran after 1950. Other important accounts of Iran during Lilienthal's time there can be found in James A. Bill, *The Eagle and the Lion: The Tragedy of American-Iranian Relations* (New Haven: Yale Univ. Press, 1988); Grace E. Goodell, *The Elementary Structures of Political Life: Rural Development in Pahlavi Iran* (New York: Oxford Univ. Press, 1986); Frances Bostock and Geoffrey Jones, *Planning and Power in Iran: Ebtehaj and Economic Development under the Shah* (London: Frank Cass, 1989); and Abol Hassan Ebtehaj, *Khatirat-i Abu al-Hasan Ibtihaj* [Memoirs of Abol Hassan Ebtehaj] (Tehran: Ilmi, 1992). Bill's study is a groundbreaking review of U.S.-Iranian relationships after World War II until the fall of the Shah. He also includes fascinating insights regarding the role Lilienthal and other American elites played in defending the Pahlavi regime. Goodell, a social anthropologist, interprets the failure of Khuzistan policies in terms of misguided top-down development and D&R's cultural insensitivity and political naiveté in its role as an international consultant and contractor. Bostock and Jones's biography of Ebtehaj details the rise and fall of Ebtehaj and his relationship with

Lilienthal. Ebtehaj's Farsi memoirs, with several English-language appendixes, offers a highly personal view of Lilienthal's role in Iran.

The single most important source for this study has been Lilienthal's *The Journals of David E. Lilienthal*. Seven volumes were published between 1964 and 1983 by Harper & Row. Hundreds, if not thousands, of additional entries remain unpublished in the Mudd archives. That they were flawed, there is no doubt—they represent his story, and his chance to vent his frustrations or preen in private. The published journals written after his decision to publish them are arguably more questionable in terms of reliability. Nevertheless, the large number of scholars who have quoted from the published journals without any caveat or caution is testimony to Lilienthal's reputation. I cannot begin to describe the frustration of turning from a book index rife with Lilienthal citations to find that virtually every reference was from one or another volume of the journals.

In addition to the journals Lilienthal published six other books, scores of articles, and gave several hundred speeches, many of which are available in one print form or another. Two bibliographies of speeches and articles include "Speeches by David E. Lilienthal," 1933–2/15/50, and "Articles by David E. Lilienthal," 1924–2/15/50, both at Princeton. In many, if not most instances, Lilienthal's speeches formed the basis for his writings. Indeed, his speeches were often reprinted verbatim in popular journals. Other than the journals, five of his six other books were spinoffs or extensions of earlier writings or speeches. Without a doubt, other than the journals, *TVA: Democracy on the March* (New York: Harper & Brothers, 1944) (see also "Twentieth Anniversary Edition" [New York: Harper & Row, 1953]) is Lilienthal's most important book. It provided a protective ideology for the authority for more than three decades and inspired Lilienthal to begin thinking about TVA as a model for the rest of the world to follow. The 1953 edition adds a new chapter on the TVA vision abroad and an extensive appendix detailing TVA-like projects in the rest of the world. It remains a marvelous example of American political rhetoric.

None of his other books came close to matching his paean to TVA. *Big Business: A New Era* (Pocket Books: New York, 1956), an expansion of a five-part serialization in *Collier's* in 1952, is another tribute to Lilienthal's rhetorical skills and is important for understanding his transformation from champion of big government to big business. *Change, Hope, and the Bomb* (Princeton: Princeton Univ. Press, 1963) reveals his changing views on atomic energy in the post-AEC decades and his chronic aversion to the abstractions of academic discourse. Next to *TVA: Democracy on the March*, this may have been his only other volume (other than the journals) that had a meaningful impact on public discourse. *Atomic Energy: A New Start* (New York: Harper & Row, 1980), his last book, with his son as collaborator, was a small, readable volume that despite the title, is more an argument for incremental changes in post-1980 atomic policies than for a "new start." *This I Do Believe* (New York: Harper & Brothers, 1949) is an edited volume of his speeches woven together in thematic fashion by Helen Lilienthal. If one has no other source for Lilienthal's addresses, it is a helpful volume. *Management: A Humanist Art* (New York: Carnegie Institute of Technology, distributed by Columbia Univ. Press, 1967) is a thin volume of lectures delivered at the Carnegie Institute of Technology in the mid-1960s. The familiar themes are all present: action over contemplation, suspicion of academic theorizing, and increasing the capacity of ordinary citizens in order to spur progress in the third world.

No study of Lilienthal's shorter communications would be complete without examining "The Mission of the Jew" (1917—printed copy at Princeton) and "The Amateur Accepts the Challenge," *Theatre Magazine*, June 1920, his first article. Already, in these first works, the reader senses his mastery of language and power of persuasion. "Labor and the Courts," the *New Republic*, May 16, 1923, his first article in that journal, is representative in style and substance of the many essays he published during the rest of that decade and later in prominent liberal journals—brash, bumptious, and full of self-confidence.

"The Regulation of Public Utility Holding Companies," *Columbia Law Review,* April 1929, and "Recent Developments in the Law of Public Utility Holding Companies," *Columbia Law Review,* February 1931, were two of his best law review efforts and important contributions to the holding company debate of the time. "The TVA: An Experiment in the 'Grass Roots' Administration of Federal Functions" (Knoxville: TVA Reprint, November 1939), was perhaps the most important speech of his career. It formed the basis for his spirited defense of TVA against Ickes's and others' efforts to restrict TVA's autonomy, and became the inspiration for *TVA: Democracy on the March.* The second address that catapulted Lilienthal to national attention was his short but eloquent reply to Senator Kenneth McKellar's badgering at the AEC confirmation hearings in February 1947. Those words were immediately reported in full in newspapers across the country, including in Alfred Friendly, "Democracy Is a Belief in Man's Dignity, Lilienthal Explains to Senator McKellar," the *Washington Post,* Feb. 5, 1947.

Lilienthal's vision of international development and the role of the international consultant is best captured in "Enterprise in Iran: An Experiment in Economic Development," *Foreign Affairs,* October 1959; "Postwar Development in Viet Nam," *Foreign Affairs,* January 1969; "The Multinational Corporation," in Melvin Anshen and Leland Back, eds., *Management and Corporations, 1985* (New York: McGraw-Hill, 1960); and "The Road to Change," Development and Resources Corporation, 1964, an adaptation from his 1964 Hillman Lecture at Columbia University (copies at Princeton). The first two are revealing testimonies of his commitment to those ultimately tragic projects. The other two, both speeches adapted to print, reflect more generally the American liberal philosophy that (mis)informed most of his overseas ventures.

Finally, there is "Learning to 'Think Small' about Dams Could Nearly Double the Hydropower Capacity of The United States," *Smithsonian,* September 1977. It is symbolically significant because it was Lilienthal's last article. It is substantively significant because it demonstrates his irrepressible optimism and spirit. Faced with declining business abroad, failing health, and uncertain prospects at home, he argued persuasively for his last domestic vision, the development of small hydroelectric projects on the thousands of yet-untapped American streams and rivers. Even near the end, this grand old man of American liberalism never gave up.

Index